It is a privilege and a blessing to be in a mission partnership with Samuel Cueva – and a little bit scary too! Because, as this book shows, here is a clear and informed mind married to a passion for mission, in a man who wants us to create new and more biblical patterns to reach and change our world. I find the church-to-church paradigm Samuel explores to be powerful and persuasive, and my prayer is that other churches will find the blessing in partnership we have come to know.

Chris Green
Vicar, St James, Muswell Hill, London

This book is a helpful tool for missiological studies as it explores the concept of partnership in Christian missionary practice and missiological reflection. Its valuable bibliography not only gives an idea about the amount of research carried on by its author, but it is also most helpful for those interested in continuing an exploration of an important chapter of mission studies. Samuel Cueva's proposal of new partnerships in creative tension is an expression of the missionary dynamism that has developed in the Majority World.

Samuel Escobar
Founding member of the Latin American Theological Fellowship,
Professor of Mission at the Facultad Protestante de Teología UEBE, Madrid, Spain.

Samuel Cueva has set out in detail important aspects of a renewed understanding of what partnership in mission between Western mission agencies and the churches of the global South should entail. He writes with conviction, enthusiasm and a good deal of personal experience of the need for new patterns of mission engagement. He advocates a reciprocal relationship between Christians on different continents in which all forms of dependency have been eliminated, and sending and receiving churches in both directions acknowledge their equal, mutual responsibility to global mission and their need to learn from one another. Although written with Latin America in mind, the arguments and conclusions are applicable across all global links. I thoroughly commend this new addition to creative thinking about the theory and practice of mission partnerships in a world of increasing international collaboration in the task of making known the good news about Jesus Christ.

Andrew Kirk, PhD
Mission theologian, Educator and Author

This masterful work by Samuel Cueva is a scholarly, in-depth treatment on the topic of global mission partnerships that continues to be of great importance and relevance the more the world globalizes and the church evangelizes. Of particular value is chapter 4 where Cueva details six current areas that need full consideration when forging international partnerships. I suggest that this section alone is a must-read for global mission leaders no matter what part of the world they represent.

Marvin J. Newell, Dr Miss
Senior Vice President, MISSIO NEXUS

Dr Samuel Cueva takes a robust approach to questions relating to the so-called 'older' and 'younger' churches in their relationship to each other in mission, and genuine global South-North partnerships. There is a great need to explore strategies that avoid the too-common paternalism, dependency and neo-colonialism that has plagued the church and its mission to the world in the last century and seriously distorted relationships. Writing from his personal experience as a Peruvian evangelical missionary in Britain for many years, Cueva makes practical suggestions on how to overcome the historical inequalities, and his rich study combines theory and praxis in a fresh and insightful way.

Allan H. Anderson, DTh
Professor of Mission and Pentecostal Studies, University of Birmingham

Living in a world of endless domination, Sam Cueva has opened a needed conversation for a renewed sense of partnership in mission today. His journey as a missionary and church planter has enriched his thinking and reflection on the complex issue of working together in mission. More than robust insights of missiological nature, Sam invites the reader to look deeply at God's relational interaction within the Trinity where mutuality and interdependence illuminates our conflicted human endeavors in mission. It is on the basis of this argument that he sketches and provides historical, theological and practical suggestions towards a more viable partnership in *missio Dei* for the twenty-first century. As a writer from the Majority World, Sam brings a fresh look at the issue of partnership with new lenses. This is a resource worth reading and sharing with mission leaders and organizations. Its reading is a must!

Wilmer Villacorta, PhD
Faculty member at Fuller Theological Seminary, School of Intercultural Studies, Pasadena, California

Samuel Cueva is a thinker, an astute student of culture, and observer of missiological models. It's easy to see the influence of other great thinkers to whom he has been exposed, from the likes of John Stott to Samuel Escobar to his own father, John, one of the early missiological pioneers in his native Peru. Now, as a Latin American living in Western Europe, Samuel Cueva is in a unique position to offer valuable insights in his new book *Mission Partnership in Creative Tension*. I love the phrase "creative tension"! We need this.

Jeff Adams, PhD
Senior Pastor of Graceway Church, Kansas City, USA

Mission Partnership in Creative Tension

An Analysis of the Relationships in Mission within the Evangelical Movement with Special Reference to Peru and Britain between 1987 and 2006

Samuel Cueva

MONOGRAPHS

© 2015 by Samuel Cueva

Published 2015 by Langham Monographs
An imprint of Langham Publishing
www.langhampublishing.org

Langham Publishing and its imprints are a ministry of Langham Partnership

Langham Partnership
PO Box 296, Carlisle, Cumbria, CA3 9WZ, UK
www.langham.org

ISBNs:
978-1-783689-31-6 Print
978-1-783689-29-3 Mobi
978-1-783689-30-9 ePub
978-1-783680-61-0 PDF

Samuel Cueva has asserted his right under the Copyright, Designs and Patents Act, 1988 to be identified as the Author of this work.

All rights reserved. No part of this publication may be reproduced, stored in a retrieval system or transmitted, in any form or by any means, electronic, mechanical, photocopying, recording or otherwise, without the prior written permission of the publisher or the Copyright Licensing Agency.

Unless otherwise stated, Scripture quotations are taken from the Holy Bible, New International Version®, NIV®. Copyright ©1973, 1978, 1984, 2011 by Biblica, Inc.™ Used by permission of Zondervan.

British Library Cataloguing in Publication Data

Cueva, Samuel, author.
  Partnership in mission in creative tension : an analysis of the relationships in mission within the evangelical movement with special reference to Peru and Britain 1987-2006.
  1. Missions--Theory. 2. Missions--Theory--History--20th century. 3. Missions--Theory--History--21st century.
  4. Evangelicalism--History--20th century.
  5. Evangelicalism--History--21st century. 6. Missions--Peru. 7. Missions--Great Britain.
  I. Title
  266'.001-dc23

ISBN-13: 9781783689316

Cover & Book Design: projectluz.com

Langham Partnership actively supports theological dialogue and a scholar's right to publish but does not necessarily endorse the views and opinions set forth, and works referenced within this publication or guarantee its technical and grammatical correctness. Langham Partnership does not accept any responsibility or liability to persons or property as a consequence of the reading, use or interpretation of its published content.

Contents

Acknowledgements xiii
Abbreviations xv
Abstract xvii
Introduction 1
    Justification for the research topic 4
    The research problem 5
    Research question 5
    Hypothesis 6
    Secondary questions 6
    Field of study 8
    Scope 8
    Limitations 9
    Methodology 9
    Sources 10
        Primary sources 10
        Secondary sources 10
    Structure of the study 11

Chapter 1 17
    Partnership in Historical Perspective
    The meaning of perspective in mission partnership 17
    Historical, theological and missiological origins and roots of the
        evangelical movement in Latin America 18
    An ecumenical understanding of partnership:
        Edinburgh 1910 to Whitby 1947 32
            Edinburgh 1910 32
            Jerusalem 1928 34
            Tambaran 1938 35
            Whitby 1947 37
    An evangelical understanding of mission partnership:
        from Lausanne 1974 to Amsterdam 2000 39
            Lausanne 1974 39
            Pattaya 1980 44
            Manila 1989 45
            The Grand Rapids Report 1982 46

    Amsterdam 2000 50
  A Latin American understanding of partnership –
    CLADE I 1970–IV 2000 51
      Integral Mission...57
  Towards a definition of partnership in mission..................................61
  A new definition: reciprocal contextual collaboration in
    Christian mission 67

Chapter 2 71
Partnership in Mission and its Theology
  Introduction 71
  Partnership and the *missio Dei*..72
  Partnership and God's kingdom 82
  Partnership and God's church 88
  A Trinitarian theology of partnership 91
  A christological theology of partnership 100
  A missiological understanding of partnership in Paul's theology 102
      Preparing servant leadership for mission partnership................102
      Helping one another in mission partnership 103
      Participation of the church in mission partnership...................107
      God's glory and mission partnership 108
  Partnership as a tool of establishing the *basileia*..............................109
  Conclusion 111

Chapter 3 113
Current Models of Partnership in Mission: an Analysis of their Main Characteristics, Policies and Impact on the Evangelical Movement
  Introduction 113
  The traditional model 114
      Historical, theological and missiological characteristics 114
      Policies of the traditional model...126
      Impact of the traditional model 127
      New trends in the traditional model 133
  The innovative networking model 135
      Historical, theological and missiological characteristics 135
      Policies of the networking model 142
      Impact of the networking model..142
  The emergent model 153
      Historical, theological and missiological characteristics 153
      Policies of the emergent model 158
      Impact of the emergent model 160

Conclusion 166

Chapter 4 171
Current Issues of Partnership in Mission
    Introduction 171
    Theological issues of contextual partnership 171
        First presupposition 172
        Second presupposition 176
    Missiological issues of contemporary partnership 180
        Third presupposition 190
    Ecclesiological issues in partnership..191
    Sociological and cultural issues of partnership................................195
    Economic issues in partnership 200
        Fourth presupposition 201
    Relational issues in partnership 211
        Fifth presupposition...211
    Conclusion 217

Chapter 5 221
Case Studies of Three Models of Partnership
    Introduction 221
    Latin link case study 222
        Historical origins 222
        The mission context 225
        Analysis of mission development.......................................226
        Conclusion with an evaluation of positive and
            negative tensions 241
    COMIBAM case study 244
        Historical origins 244
        The mission context 249
        Analysis of mission development.......................................252
        Conclusion with an evaluation of positive and
            negative tensions 271
    St James Church, Muswell Hill, London case study 275
        The historical origin...275
        The mission context 277
        Analysis of mission development.......................................282
        Conclusion with an evaluation of positive and
            negative tensions 296

Chapter 6 307
A Novel Innovative Model Related to Reciprocal Contextual Collaboration in Creative Tension
    Introduction 307
    Mission theology of reciprocal contextual collaboration 308
    Biblical approach to reciprocal contextual collaboration 318
    Foundational reciprocal contextual collaboration 321
    The glory of God in reciprocal contextual collaboration 330
    The spiral mission theology 333
        Key components of reciprocal contextual collaboration 339
        Key organic values for healthy reciprocal contextual
            collaboration 340
        Key biblical assumptions regarding reciprocal contextual
            collaboration 341
        Key motives of reciprocal contextual collaboration 342
    Mission tensions in reciprocal contextual collaboration 343
    Innovative models relating to reciprocal contextual collaboration 346
        The Synergy Model 352
        The Spontaneous Model 357
        The Integrated Model 367
        The Contextual Model 375
    Conclusion 384

Chapter 7 389
Conclusion and Challenges for Reciprocal Contextual Collaboration in the Evangelical Movement for the 21st Century
    Introduction 389
    Reciprocal contextual collaboration as the new definition
        of partnership 390
    The recovery of a mission theology of reciprocal contextual
        collaboration 391
    Reciprocal contextual collaboration within current models 392
    The global context of reciprocal contextual collaboration for
        the 21st century 394
    Reciprocal contextual collaboration within the
        Latin American church 396
    The relevance of mission models in reciprocal multipolar
        contextual engagement 402
    Reciprocal contextual collaboration and the global church
        mission in context 407

  Reciprocal contextual collaboration mission and cross-mission pollination 408
  Challenges for reciprocal contextual collaboration in the 21ˢᵗ century mission 412
  Challenges for a dynamic missiology of North-South mission collaboration 419

Bibliography 427
 Primary Sources 427
  Mission archives, letters, bulletins, CDs, conversations and electronic information 427
  Interviews and questionnaires 430
  Unpublished material, manuscripts and documents 431
  Pamphlets and newspapers 439
 Secondary Sources 440
  Books 440
  Journals, articles, bulletins and magazines 454
  General information on internet 459
  Dictionaries 463
  Bible 464

Appendix 1 465
Three Basic Models of Mission

Appendix 2 467
Latin Link Roots and History

Appendix 3 471
The Place of COMIBAM in the Protestant Historical Global Mission

Appendix 4 475
Analysis of the Short Term Mission Trips to Peru

Appendix 5 479
Ten Influential Models of Mission in Latin America

Acknowledgements

This doctoral research is a sacrificial effort to make a contribution to academic reflection on, and to the church's practice of, mission. The reason I undertook this effort is due to the fact that in recent years there has been little by way of doctoral investigation related to partnership in mission in creative tension, which implies a reciprocal contextual collaboration for God's kingdom. I decided to conduct this research with special reference to the relationships between Peru and Britain and to limit my study to the years 1987 to 2006.

I owe a word of thanks to my supervisor Professor David P. Davies, who gave me all his wisdom without reservation during the process of the research. He spent hours reading and commenting on my work. Professor Dr Bettina Schmidt was very supportive in revising parts of the final manuscript. My sincere appreciation goes to the University of Wales – Trinity Saint David, whose staff have been very supportive to me. Librarians in Britain and Peru have been most kind, providing books, journals and articles. The internal examiner Dr Noel Davies and the external examiner Dr Andrew Kirk gave me great insights for revising some parts of the research after the 'Viva'.

I am grateful to all my friends from different contexts. Through their knowledge and experience I have received advice, information and clarification regarding different aspects of the study. In particular, I wish to thank Carlos Scott, Jesus Londoño, David Ruiz, Federico Bertuzzi, Alex Araujo and Bertil Ekstrom for providing me substantial information in relation to COMIBAM.

I also wish to thank the leadership and staff members of Latin Link, including Alan Tower, Simon Baker, and former director Donald Ford, for helping me by answering questionnaires, and to Charlotte Barker for sending me specific information regarding that organization. In this regard, I wish to acknowledge the invaluable support of the staff of St James Church, who gave me their time for interviews, questionnaires, and access to the mission archives. In particular, my gratitude goes to the Reverend Will Hunter-Smart, church wardens Jonathan Thorton and Julian Slater, Jimmy Peppiatt, who passed away in 2013; to Ann Twisleton, Isobel Lee and Richard and Cathy Dormandy, short-term mission members to Peru. A huge thanks to the Rev Alex Ross for providing me key elements of the life at St James. Special thanks to the Iglesia Misionera Evangélica in Peru for the research they allowed me to do.

The encouragement of former missionaries from Scotland, Stewart McIntosh and Stuart Harrison, who allowed me to interview them and to examine the archives of Latin Link in Edinburgh, has been invaluable. I am particularly grateful to Dr Steve Griffin, who read my drafts and commented wisely, and for the input of Jason Barrington in some chapters.

My wife Noemi and my two daughters Noemi Delia and Claudia have been a constant support, looking forward enthusiastically to the completion of the thesis. With her wisdom Noemi helped me to clarify my illustration of the spiral mission theology, and Claudia was keen on drawing diagrams of mission models which I made in draft papers. I express my deepest thanks for your love and great encouragement during my studies.

Abbreviations

CMA	The Christian and Missionary Alliance
CMS	Church Mission Society
COMIBAM	Congreso Misionero Iberoamericano
EUSA	The Evangelical Missionary Union of South America
GAFCON	Global Anglican Future Conference
GC	Global Connections
IEP	Iglesia Evangélica Peruana
IME	Iglesia Misionera Evangelica
IMTN	The International Missionary Training Network
MEMCA	Member Care/Global Member Care Resources
OCMS	Oxford Centre for Mission Studies
OMF	Overseas Missionary Fellowship
OM	Operation Mobilization
PCC	Parochial Council Church
RCC	Reciprocal contextual collaboration
RMBU	The Regions Beyond Missionary Union
SAMS	The South American Mission Society
SEALINK	South East Asia Network
STM	Short Term Mission
WEA	World Evangelical Alliance
WEC	Worldwide Evangelization for Christ
WMG	World Mission Group St James' Church-Muswell Hill
WEA-MC	World Evangelical Alliance-Mission Commission

Abstract

This study explores new models for partnership in mission in a creative tension for the twenty-first century within the evangelical movement. Radical changes in the theology of mission, decision making and the control of power are necessary. Our approach to the study is based on the assumption that new models of partnering may be found through a theological reinterpretation of cooperation based on a fresh understanding of biblical relationships related to the theology of the *missio Dei*, God's kingdom, God's church, a Trinitarian theology of partnership, christological theology of partnership under the influence of a spiral mission theology.

The thesis focuses on the need to replace the old concept of partnership with what we shall call reciprocal contextual collaboration and we shall examine the historical, theological and missiological context of the development and impact of partnership within the evangelical constituency. It is a thesis devoted to a missiological understanding of current mission models – traditional, networking and emergent – in order to contribute to Majority World Missiology.

Chapter 1 examines the development and characteristics of partnership in mission and how these have impacted the evangelical movement. Chapter 2 reviews partnership in mission and its theology by considering the historical framework that influenced evangelical theologians in particular. Chapter 3 undertakes an examination of three models of partnership in mission, by analyzing their main characteristics, historical, theological and missiological, as well as their policies and impact; these are the traditional, networking and the emergent models. Chapter 4 provides specific current issues regarding partnership in mission and chapter 5 examines three case studies: Latin Link, COMIBAM and St James Church. Chapter 6 develops the synergy, the spontaneous (a novel model), the integrated and the contextual models and chapter 7 presents conclusions and challenges for reciprocal contextual collaboration in the evangelical movement for the twenty-first century.

Introduction

The Protestant Latin American church has grown in the last twenty years, and in consequence, its participation in decision making, interdependence and mature relationship for partnership in mission, seems to be a dilemma for the twenty-first-century mission enterprise. How? One of the issues is to deal with the interpretation of cooperation, the other is related to what equality-inequality means, and the third issue is related to control of power and the political theology of partnership behind the current mission task. Is the actual partnership in mission growing or is it declining? Are the poor churches in a condition to develop a new partnership paradigm that can replace the existing partnership paradigms? Two partners will be the focal point of this study: the British church that has been running its different varieties of traditional partnerships and the emergent Protestant Latin American church that wants to be accepted as a partner, while avoiding paternalism and colonialism, and allow this new force of mission to develop a contextual and indigenous partnership. This work is not confined to the mission enterprise of the Roman Catholic Church.

In this introduction, I will outline the background, the motivation, the scope and the purpose of this study. The background relates to my interest of finding new appropriate models for mission for the twenty-first century that will help to produce a healthy reciprocal contextual collaboration within the Christian church. One of the problems is that the Protestant Latin American church still lacks clear policies of mission partnership; there is a need for critical evaluation of the results, impact and influences of partnership. Sometimes this can give a picture of conformism or indifference for partnering between the North and the South partners. In this way, a contextual missiology seems to call for a new partnership paradigm that needs to be studied in depth.

This study is motivated by the interest I have had for a very long period of time in thinking of the mission enterprise in relation to the theme of partnership. I arrived at the conclusion that there is a huge need for exploration and there are many questions regarding what is the best way to find appropriate partnership models for the twenty-first century. I would like to show that there are some elements that are hindering the present mission partnership between North and South. On the other hand, it will be helpful to understand what have been the missionary tensions in developing a Christian partnership between Great Britain and Peru.

These points will be developed through an analysis of the Christian mission enterprise during the period 1987–2006. I have selected this period of time because in 1987 a big change started for the Latin American missionary movement, when many people in the Latin church understood that they were no longer a mission field and declared that they were now a mission force to send missionaries to other parts of the world. And 2006 was another important time for the Latin movement due to the Congress of COMIBAM in Granada, Spain, where they evaluated what they had achieved during twenty years of a new Christian partnership from a Latin American perspective.

The scope of this study includes a historical, theological and missiological analysis in order to understand the thought processes and the insights of the missiological reflection that has taken place in the evangelical movement from 1987 to 2006. This will be done in parallel with critical deductive reading to understand the negative and positive tensions of mission partnership. I will also develop three case studies, different in origin and context, but perhaps similar in their understanding of how to accomplish the *missio Dei*.

In all three case studies I will use the same pattern of analysis, taking account of the historical, theological, and missiological factors. The first will be the mission Latin Link, a British mission society founded in 1991 that is still working in Peru. The second case study will be related to the Latin American mission movement COMIBAM, which started officially in 1987; and the third will be related to St James Church in London, a local church with 700 members that has sent short-term mission teams to Peru since 1999.

I accept that different models of have partnership developed between 1987 and 2006. However, my research question is related to whether there are possibilities of finding more appropriate partnership models for the twenty-first century. My research will be directed to identifying what is lacking at present and what elements need deeper analysis in order to discover a new model of healthy partnership to strengthen the mission task for the twenty-first century.

I will concentrate mainly on specific models of mission developed both by Western evangelical Christian mission agencies in Latin America and evangelical partnership mission models from Latin America that have been created to work with evangelical churches in Europe, especially in Great Britain. A historical analysis will be developed in order to show key aspects of partnership that need to be either re-orientated or, in some cases, changed radically.

This research is related to the discussion within the evangelical constituency around partnership models, especially in the context of the relationship between Latin America and Western Europe.

We want to concentrate on three specific models of mission developed by the British evangelical Christian mission in Latin America as well as the evangelical partnership paradigm from Latin America developed to influence the Western evangelical church, especially in Great Britain.

For the purpose of this study, I have chosen the topic of partnership in mission, in order to contribute to Majority World Missiology. I want to contribute to ongoing studies of partnership from a Latin American perspective. This research matters because there is a gap that needs to be bridged in relation to partnership in mission in order to discover appropriate partnership models for the twenty-first century. Leaders of the Christian church, such as theologians, missiologists and pastors, and mission structures such as mission societies or traditional mission models, networking mission models and the emergent mission models working in the twenty-first-century mission will obtain benefit from this study.

It is necessary to discover the process through which partnership has developed to analyse the elements that have been hindering a healthy partnership. Therefore, the nature of partnership has been established and also we answer to what extent good practice has been achieved. This has entailed evaluated the mission history of some mission organizations.

In this study I will redefine the concept of partnership as reciprocal contextual collaboration, which highlights the difference from the old concept of partnership in a new way. I will consider the importance of reciprocal relationship of harmonious freedom in creative tension to accomplish the *missio Dei*.

Within the study, we approach the biblical text in order to study those interchangeable words that are applicable within reciprocal contextual collaboration for the mission activity of the church: labourer as worker (*ergatēs*); joint-worker, a worker together with (*sunergos*); and fellow worker, as in holding with (*metochē*). These words are applicable within reciprocal contextual collaboration for the mission activity of the church. It is a mission relation of two-way traffic where individuality and autonomy do not end but rather work within the freedom of reciprocal agreement. There is a double tension of privilege and responsibility when one is chosen by Christ to take on active co-participation in his redemptive mission. Hence, we develop four biblical aspects of reciprocal collaboration: mission relations between co-labourers, diversity with multiple ministries, skills distribution, and spiritual gifts.

Justification for the research topic

Since being involved in ministry I have realized that an adequate partnership between Latin American and Western churches is lacking. Despite the efforts that have been made in the past, the present and the future do not look bright. There is apparently something hindering the present partnership effort. We need, therefore, to research the possibilities that may exist for discovering more appropriate partnership models that can empower mission for the twenty-first century.

The research problem

Following the inauguration of the Latin American movement COMIBAM in 1987 that was held in São Paulo, Brazil 3,000 delegates attended its first Congress; the pivotal point was to move "from a missionary field to a sending field". I had the privilege of attending and it seems to me that an appropriate partnership paradigm between the emerging Latin American evangelical mission movement and the Western Christian church is still lacking. This mission partnership in creative tension was undoubtedly a great achievement in relation to the extension of the gospel. However, the development, characteristics, and motives for why this mission partnership was made have generated a kind of incredulity, non-conformism and question marks behind the Latin American churches.

Despite the massive theoretical influence of the Western academy, both theologians and missiologists who have been studying different issues in relation to the Latin American churches have been struggling to find new partnership paradigms. The actual development of these requires a study of their historical, theological and missiological roots.

I am aware that the evangelical partners struggle over such matters as the control of power, the use of finances, and especially the acceptance of new ways of partnering together that enable decision making to operate equally for both sides. In this way, it is necessary to thoroughly research the theology, policy, motives, dependency, etc., of partnership paradigms, which have been developed principally in three particular ways: traditional partnership through mission societies; a 'post-modern' networking partnership related especially to building up contacts that strengthen aims strategically; and an 'emergent partnership' which is a partnership that encourages projects that were previously ignored by established partnerships around the world, but which now have space for creating their own partnership with others.

Research question

What are the possibilities of bringing about appropriate partnership models for the evangelical movement during the twenty-first century?

Hypothesis

For the consistency and the complexity of the research we have provided three hypotheses, which are as follows:

If the development and characteristics of partnership in mission caused a lack of freedom in the relationship, dependence and sharing of the control of power, then these factors have affected the possibility of finding appropriate partnership paradigms.

The instability and dependence of the Latin American partnership can be overcome through more holistic biblical teaching that can lead to a more mature participative church in mission.

Latin American partnership in mission has become a tool in the development of the evangelical movement despite its limitations in the political, economic and sociological context.

Secondary questions

For the purpose of solid research we had to set up a number of theological and missiological questions that would help us to concentrate our effort in specific particularities rather than the general view of finding issues. Hence, we intentionally established the following questions:

Why has the evangelical movement not found appropriate paradigms for developing an indigenous partnership?

Why has the evangelical movement not found appropriate partnership models for developing new forms of interdependence and mature relationship?

Why has the Latin American evangelical church not sought more biblical foundations of partnership in mission?

Why it is necessary and urgent to discover appropriate partnership models for the twenty-first century?

Why it is still difficult to create positive tensions to overcome the paternalistic approach of partnership in the Latin American evangelical church?

Why do we need to make changes to the partnership which has developed?

Why has the partnership between South and North been weak?

Why must the mission context be evaluated?

What are the big issues in the relationship between North and South?

What is the nature of partnership in mission?

What about the policies of partnership in mission?

What has been achieved? (Results, impact, effects, etc.)

What has been hindering appropriate partnership paradigms?

What are the most important challenges for a new theology of partnership?

What could be the role of new structures of mission?

Who were those who brought new insight to some of the partnership paradigms?

Who are the partners?

How has mission in partnership come together?

How can we support the new forces in mission of the Latin American church?

Which are the main issues that have been hindering an effective theology of partnership between the North and the South during this last 20 years?

Where was the main focus of partnering together?

Is it possible to discover appropriate partnership models to overcome the new forms of dependence and a lack of reciprocal freedom in partnering with the Latin American church?

Is the actual partnership in mission acceptable to the Latin American church?

Field of study

I will concentrate on historical, theological, and missiological studies in relation to mission partnership models in the evangelical movement with special reference to the beginning with the founding of COMIBAM in 1987 and ending in 2006 where, from 13 to 17 November, this Iberoamerican missionary movement held its third missionary congress in Granada, Spain when 2,000 delegates attended the congress.

Scope

I will concentrate mainly on specific models of mission developed both by Western evangelical Christian mission agencies in Latin America and evangelical partnership mission models from Latin America that have been created to work with evangelical churches in Europe, especially in Great Britain. A historical analysis will be developed in order to show key aspects of partnership that need to be either re-orientated or, in some cases, changed radically.

This research is related to the discussion within the evangelical constituency around partnership models, especially in the context of the relationship between Latin America and Western Europe.

We want to concentrate on three specific models of mission developed by the British evangelical Christian mission in Latin America as well as the evangelical partnership paradigm from Latin America developed to influence the Western evangelical church, especially in Great Britain.

Limitations

The limitations of this research relate to the evangelical discussion around partnership models, especially in the context of the relationship between Latin America and Britain. This missiological analysis seeks to understand the effects, implications, issues and achievements in the development and efforts of Christian partnership in the evangelical movement starting from the period of COMIBAM in 1987 until 2006. Consideration has been limited to two case studies which have a history of being in partnership, especially in Peru, and the third one COMIBAM with its development in Latin America.

Methodology

Qualitative methodology will be employed to undertake an analytical investigation into the relationship in partnership in mission. A historical analysis will be developed in order to find some key issues that are hindering actual partnership in mission. A critical study will be used for identifying responsibilities between partners to investigate new perspectives of a contextual partnership in mission. Literature review and oral history will be used with the intention of sketching the development of partnership in mission. I will use books to compare between some specific Western and Latin American missiologists that have been influencing the development of partnership in mission.

An inductive and diagnostic methodology will be used for some chapters. In this way I will approach the research question through discovering the best theoretical standards in the relevant literature for Christian partnership in mission. Also I intend to work on discovering relevant biblical principles to evaluate good and bad practice of mission partnership.

Second, I want to devote one chapter to three case studies that are different in their origins and theological influence, but at the same time valid and significant. The three case studies to be undertaken will follow a uniform methodology. To begin with, there will be the historical origins, followed by an analysis of the main characteristics which the mission partnership developed, including the context where the mission was developed, the kind of mission structure it adopted, its influence, and concluding with an evaluation of the positive and critical aspects. In the analysis, I will draw attention to the missiological tension, the implication of this creative tension and its significance for twenty-first century missiology. Primary sources like documents, bulletins and personal interviews will be used to analyse these different models of mission.

I will also use the participant-observer method, since I have been involved in the mission task with different theological, missiological thinkers as well as practitioners of the mission enterprise since 1985.

Sources

Primary sources

I will collect primary data through the leaders of those churches, institutions, and structures of mission that allow me to do research on their organizations. Also I will depend on text and context, especially for the first three chapters. Both documentary sources and oral sources will be used for the case studies of the Latin American regional network of COMIBAM and the Western mission, Latin Link, working in Latin America. Material from different mission conferences, congresses and consultations in which I had the privilege of participating will also be used; and talks with colleagues of the mission enterprise will help me in finding new experiences that I shall apply to partnership in mission.

I have had access to mission archives for Latin Link, St James Church (London), and the IME Church (Peru). I have primary documents produced by COMIBAM for its first Congress held at São Paulo, Brazil in November 1987, documents of their second Missionary Congress held in Acapulco, Mexico in 1997 and documents of the recently held Congress in Granada, Spain in 2006, which I attended.

Secondary sources

We will use general literature, online essays, overviews, the writing of key Latin American and Western thinkers, and special attention will be given to the work of the German Lothar Bauerochse, the American missiologist Phill Butler, David Bosch a South African missiologist, Samuel Escobar a Peruvian missiologist, René Padilla an Ecuadorian theologian, and the British theologian Andrew Kirk.

Structure of the study

The thesis is divided into the following chapters:

In **chapter 1** the historical perspective of partnership in mission will be set up, before coming to a discussion and analysis of some current partnership models. Our historical discussion will be undertaken in dialogue with the roots of the evangelical movement in Latin America. We will see the development and characteristics of the ecumenical, the evangelical and the Latin American understanding of mission partnership, using key words like partnership, reciprocal contextual collaboration, cooperation, co-participation, integration, fellowship, synergy, strategic alliances, and unity. I will accept what I consider to be the best theoretical standards in the relevant literature. Then I will attempt to suggest a new definition of mission partnership as reciprocal contextual collaboration, which will be part of my argument.

Chapter 2 will then give a synthetic analysis of partnership in mission and its theology in the way that practitioners and theologians have understood this together with their understanding of positive and negative tensions. We will try to understand why theology has an important role to play in developing a mission partnership. According to this perspective we will study the *missio Dei*, God's kingdom, God's church, a christological mission partnership and Paul's understanding of mission partnership theology.

After these first two chapters, the historical analysis of partnership in mission and partnership in mission and its theology, **chapter 3** will present the current models of mission partnership. Consequently, this chapter will address and analyse the main characteristics, policies, impact, influences and effects of traditional, networking and emergent partnerships, all of them in relation to what has been hindering a positive developing partnership in creative tension for the last twenty years and why. Strengths and weaknesses will be discussed.

As we know, mission partnership raises a variety of different kinds of issues, thus **chapter 4** will discuss those current issues of partnership in mission with relevant themes that can shed light on the complexity and the simplicity of partnering with others. I will concentrate on current issues, (i.e. theological, missiological, the economic, sociological, and relational issues). These can help us understand why each mission partnership model has its own missiological tension with negative and positive influences and effects.

After these first four chapters, I will then work through three case studies with the purpose of probing my hypothesis that will lead me to general conclusions. This will be **chapter 5.** Through the analysis of the three case studies, possible conclusions of the research will suggest the hypothesis that mission for the twenty-first century is taking place with some weaknesses and some strengths, but empowered by the Spirit and a clear decision on the part of the evangelical movement to accomplish the christological double mandate. I will try to determine if this kind of partnership has been dependent on the power of God or on the power of money, internal or external factors. By external factors I mean those factors related to economic, social and political factors that have been influencing these case studies, and by internal factors I mean those related to the activity of the institutions under examination themselves.

In **chapter 6** I will propose a novel element of '**reciprocal contextual collaboration**', and endeavour to emphasize that mission reciprocity is mainly a reciprocal relationship in freedom, trust, reciprocity, and respect. I try not to over emphasize such terms as 'sending and receiving', or 'young and mature' with respect to missiology. It is more a team-working collaboration where we avoid dividing the relationships into unities, which may function differently but which work as one body united through a strong relationship. This is working together in the same purpose, and existing to improve contextual approaches to the *missio Dei*, God's kingdom and God's church, and the decisive and wider participation of the Majority World in the mission enterprise of the twenty-first century. This same chapter will be a chapter that invites the reader to rethink the dimensional tension of the Trinity, the political tension of the church, the dynamic tension of the kingdom, and the relational tension of partners which brings imaginative and creative tensions of reciprocal contextual collaboration in the *missio Dei*. I provide in this chapter four models of mission collaboration: the synergy model, the spontaneous model (a novel model that stresses a more relational emphasis empowered by the Spirit, enjoys dialogical and spontaneous work, is less interested in the control of power, is driven by migration, and is influenced by external factors), the integrated model and the contextual model. All four models are included within what we have called reciprocal multipolar contextual engagement.

In chapter 7 I will provide conclusions and some challenges related to reciprocal contextual collaboration. I shall arrive at conclusions of the study by pointing out the relevance of mission models of cooperation. I will consider seriously the spirit of Latin American mission collaboration, the political and social context of mission collaboration for the twenty-first century and the recovery of an inclusive mission theology as a tool for strengthening the mission enterprise. This mission reciprocity will lead us to some challenges like the need for missiological improvement, new mature relationships, new goals within relationships, new structures of mission, and a new global mission collaboration theology for twenty-first-century mission. The influence of the mission reciprocity through these last two decades is considered.

PART I

Development and Characteristics of Partnership in Mission

CHAPTER 1

Partnership in Historical Perspective

The meaning of perspective in mission partnership

The British evangelical Anglican theologian, Max Warren (Yates 1994, 138), at the Annual Conference of the Evangelical Fellowship for Theological Literature in 1962, took up an important theme relating to the concept of power when he developed this topic under the concept of perspective in mission. He explains (Warren 1964, ix, x) 'perspective' as "some ability to discern the proportion of events and their relation to one another". This implies that a historical perspective of partnership in mission is an account of the historical, theological, missiological, cultural, political and economic discernment to understand the relationships between partners in the mission enterprise for this twenty-first century. Andrew Kirk brings a complementary interpretation of perspectives when he explains that freedom has at least seven perceptions, which have been given a wide range of interpretation and application for the modern period of European history (Kirk 1998, 59). These perspectives of freedom are a negative view, a positive view, the liberal tradition, the socialist tradition, the perspective of existentialism, spiritual freedom and aesthetic freedom (Kirk 1998, 59). This assumption shows that the meaning of perspective helps to set up a theological, missiological and historical framework to analyse or to describe internal or external aspects of partnership in mission study.

Different projects have been undertaken through many kinds of mission activities, which have brought about huge development in the Christian mission enterprise. In this way it is vital to discern what the development has been in order to understand its main characteristics in the historical context of partnership in mission. Perspectives in mission partnership are also related to an evaluation of particular situations and facts, including personal points of view. It is also a measured assessment of a situation that our study includes the history, theology and missiology of mission partnership, which results in different tensions because of the dynamic activity of the mission enterprise that has been developed with both strengths and weaknesses.

It is clear that our personal perspective influences our understanding of partnership in Christian mission and, in consequence, our perspectives bring practices that need to be evaluated continually in order to find new ways of understanding different perspectives to accomplish the *missio Dei*. This is why it is vital to understand different approaches of partnership that have been developed by the Christian mission enterprise through different decades.

Historical, theological and missiological origins and roots of the evangelical movement in Latin America

Latin America is a continent that, historically speaking, is a suffering continent, where the Incan and Mayan Empires flourished for many centuries. These empires were totally destroyed with the invasion of the Spanish led by Christopher Columbus in 1492. Columbus entered into partnership with the Catholic Spanish king and queen, Ferdinand and Isabel. It was an agreement whereby all lands conquered had to belong not only to the Spanish empire, but also to the Catholic Church. As Mackay points out, 'Ferdinand and Isabel, the conquerors of Granada, willed that the united Spain should be only for Christ and Christians' (2001, 23); in the same way the conquered lands of Latin America should be for the Catholic Church and Spain. As a consequence, Spanish Catholicism is a 'religious system' (Mackay 2001, 93) that has influenced the cultural behaviour of Latin America for more than five hundred years.

We need to understand that the development and characteristics for controlling the new land of the Americas were under the direction of papal policy through a special bull, with both temporal and spiritual powers over the church. Mackay (2001, 42–43, 50, 53) describes what I would call a political and religious cooperation between Spain and Rome, a summary of which is as follows: first, the Spanish king had the right to nominate bishops in each land. (A similar policy was developed by the king of Portugal for all the new Portuguese dominions.) Second, "by another bull in 1501, the tithes of the Indies were ceded to the Spanish kings in perpetual right for the expenses incurred. The kings in their turn bound the building of churches and equipment for the inhabitants in every region occupied" (2001, 42). Third, "the propagation of the religion was a function of the state" (43). Fourth, one of the methods of controlling religious policy was the institution of the inquisition that operated from 1569 until 1813 with its headquarters in Lima. This was only abolished by the liberating forces of General San Martin in 1821 (50).

In this context, religious festivals were brought from Spain to Latin America and the images of the saints were carried in procession. Christ and the Virgin became regionalized. On the one hand, churches, schools and hospitals were founded by different Catholic orders such as the Jesuits, Augustinians, Franciscans, etc. On the other hand, cemeteries and weddings were controlled by Catholic power through the policies of the so called 'Concordato', whereby all education and public affairs would be organized in accordance with the dogmas and morals of the Catholic religion (Mackay 2001, 71). The time arrived when, under the influence of the French Revolution, liberation from colonialism started in 1810 in Venezuela and Argentina and went on until 1831 when the Pope recognized the new republics (Mackay 2001, 60). It was a long process of political change, despite the religious environment remaining under the influence of Roman Catholicism. There follows a very brief summary of how Protestantism arrived in Latin America, starting at the beginning of the nineteenth century with the presence of James Thompson.

According to the Argentinian theologian, Miguez Bonino (1997), the development process for Latin American Protestantism includes three 'faces' which are as follows: the Liberal face, the Evangelical face, and the

Pentecostal face, but he deliberately adds a fourth one, the Ethnic face. Here, I want to draw attention to historical discussion in connection with the development process of the evangelical church. For Miguez Bonino, there is no difference between the terms Protestant and evangelical, in the sense that evangelicals have their roots in the Lutheran and Calvinist reformation (1997, ix), but in this study I will use the term evangelical with reference to particular theological, missiological, sociological and cultural features. This clarifies the contextual background of the evangelical mentality, especially for the Pentecostal movement, because the term 'Protestant' seems to arouse suspicions for evangelicalism. However, I agree with Miguez Bonino that evangelical roots come from the Reformation period, but on the other side I am aware that he, as a liberation theologian with an interest in treating the issue of ecclesiology and ecumenism (Davies 2006, 2, 114–115), prefers to use the term Protestant for the evangelical movement in Latin America.

For Orlando Costas (1976, 41, 43–329), a Puerto Rican missiologist, the Latin American Protestant church has chosen to call themselves evangelicals to be clearly disassociated from the ritualistic Christian faith of the established Roman Catholic Church. In Costas' view it is essential to differentiate evangelical Protestantism which is defined under Anglo-Saxon influence as having the following characteristics: insistence on the authority of the Bible, conversion as a distinct experience of faith in Christ as Lord and Saviour, and the practice of evangelization as the fundamental dimension of the mission of the Christian faith. In this perspective, one of the basic characteristics of evangelicalism is the recognition of the authority of the Bible as the Word of God.[1] In fact, the declaration of the First Latin American Congress on Evangelization (CLADE I) affirms the "truths of the Bible, as the Word of God" (43). Equally the Latin American Theological Fraternity, started in 1970, affirms that "the Bible derives its authority from its link with that revelation of God that culminates in Jesus Christ" (44). Analysing those factors proposed by Costas, we should add a fourth factor in relation to the Pentecostal movement, which is the charismatic manifestation of the Spirit.

---

1. For the term evangelical see further Sharon Heaney (2008, 43–48).

The Peruvian missiologist, Samuel Escobar (2002, 41, 155), and Miguez Bonino (1997, 28), point out similarly that the post-reformed period of the Protestant mission came with Moravian Pietism from Germany in the mid-eighteenth century. In fact, this movement developed its partnership with discipline, evangelical piety, worldwide vision, and rigorous training (Escobar 2002, 155) and made a missiological impact on the spiritual awakening of the eighteenth century in England and North America (155). Somehow, this spiritual influence took in the evangelical student movement in the nineteenth century. As a result of this long missiological process, new mission traffic was established to propagate the gospel in Latin America. We need to bear in mind that during this process the Catholic Church was the 'owner of Latin America' from the conquest period in 1492 until the emancipation period in 1831.

With reference to theology, Bosch (1991, 325) explains that overemphasis on premillennialism, postmillennialism and amillennialism during the nineteenth century influenced and diluted evangelicalism in the direction of a more worldly liberalism and the social gospel and Western missionaries brought with the gospel new ideas of the enlightenment like rationalism, evolutionism, pragmatism, secularism and optimism. So this was exported overseas by the mission enterprise of Western mission societies. As a result, these were the revolutionary influences of liberalism on the beginning of evangelical fundamentalism (1991, 297).

A predominant tendency appeared in the later nineteenth century for evangelicalism, with different doctrinal convictions mainly in North America. One of these tendencies was premillennialism,[2] which claimed

---

[2]. Regarding the time of the second coming of Christ, Ralph Allan Smith explains that "Premillennialism teaches that Christ returns *before* the end of history to inaugurate an earthly kingdom of a thousand years. Amillennialism denies an earthly kingdom age and says the coming of Christ is the end of history. Postmillennialism agrees with amillennialism that the coming of Christ ends history. It also agrees with premillennialism that there will be a kingdom of God on earth and in time. However, the postmillennialist believes that Christ will bring in his kingdom through the work of the Holy Spirit in the church and then return to this world at the end of history when God's kingdom purposes have been fully realized". Ralph A. Smith, Berit. Org, Essays, *The Covenantal Kingdom*, chapter 1: 'The Biblical and Theological Issues', http://www.berith.org/essays/esch/esch04.html (Accessed 16 August 2010 at 17:20). Charles Hodge also cited Brown's work as an important response to premillennialism. See Charles Hodge, *Systematic Theology*, Vol. III (Grand Rapids: William B. Eerdmans Publishing Company, 1979), 863–64.

that the present age was to come to a close with the Second Advent, thus the millennium would be after. Therefore, its strong teaching was that Christ would come literally to the earth. This produced an imminent hope, but with a pessimistic worldview, that the world is becoming worse (Bebbington 2005, 190–192). Consequently, mission was related to the imminent coming of Christ, and the urgency of evangelization was demanded of all believers; literal interpretation was the hermeneutical horizon of premillennialists (Kuzmic 2009, 141). Another tendency was postmillennialism,[3] which was more optimist about the course of the events, believing that God was ruling over human affairs to establish his kingdom on earth (Bebbington, 141), so it put more emphasis on present concern with the gradual improvement and redemption of the world, similar to the social gospel movement in America.[4] This view was held and promoted by Jonathan Edwards, and John and Charles Wesley in the eighteenth century revival (Kuzmic 2009, 138). Kuzmic (138–139) shows clearly that postmillennial theology believes in gradual improvement and redemption of the world, in a golden age of prosperity, justice and peace as the rule of Christ extended on this earth prior to his second coming, greater emphasis on the demand of the Bible and those commands of Christ that require social justice, the elimination of poverty, exploitation and disease. Clothing of the naked and feeding of the hungry are taken as part of the

---

3. Kim Riddlebarger says: "An important distinctive of American postmillennialism, at least in the forms of it influenced directly by Whitby, is the concept that the millennial age is not co-extensive with the entire period of time between the first and second advent, nor that the millennial age has already commenced but has yet to reach its zenith, but that the millennial age lies yet entirely ahead in the future. There is certainly a natural tendency to justify one's commitment to a 'golden age' – a Christianizing of the nations – in the face of contrary evidence in the form of empirical evil all around us, by assigning this 'golden age' to some distant point in the future. It is perhaps this distinctive that gives postmillennialism its reputation for militant optimism about the great triumph of the gospel". See Kim Riddlebarger 1996 "Princeton and the Millennium: A Study of American Postmillennialism", The Mountain Retreat, http://www.mountainretreatorg.net/eschatology/princetonmill.html).

4. The social gospel movement started with the need to apply Christian questions to economic questions between 1850 and 1870, and relates to the participation of the church in social improvement and political economic affairs, which focused on applying moral principles to the improvement of industrialized society through application of the biblical principle of justice, and particularly to reforms such as the abolition of child labour, a shorter work week, and factory regulation. See further Bebbington (2005, 246–251).

church's mission, which is to share the compassion of Christ for suffering humanity, and the conversion of all nations is anticipated along with the advance of civilization.

By 1820, the mission enterprise had become the most important target of the American churches, and the return of Christ was a common theme of premillennialist circles (316). There was an intimate correlation between mission and millennial expectation (314). Until the nineteenth century, there was a spirit of cooperation among denominations (315), and no clear division between pre- and postmillennialists. However, after 1830 the united evangelical front disintegrated because differences rather than similarities were emphasized between pre- and postmillennialists (315), and differences became apparent in interpreting eschatology, soteriology and humanization. A common theme in pre- and postmillennialist circles was the return of Christ; however, postmillennialists tended to put more emphasis on present concerns, individualism rather than the body of Christ was also emphasized (317), and preaching stressed personal rather than structural sins (318). It is a historically observable fact that premillennialist doctrine in North America included a belief in an imminent second coming of Christ to earth before his millennial reign. Such eschatology went hand in hand with a dispensational theology and an emphasis on the holy life – the former relating to the rapture of the church, and the latter to sanctification (Bebbington 2005, 190,199, 200–204).[5] In contrast, postmillennialism emphasized a social concern, which implied participation in politics and in efforts to overcome oppression, crime, corruption, and famine (Bebbington, 139–140). Postmillennialism thus assumed a view of human progress and a social dimension to personal faith.[6]

---

5. According to Peter Kuzmic, the Princeton School influenced the postmillennial reading of Scripture. He surveys the history and trends of three traditional views of the millennial reign, namely, postmillennialism, millennialism and premillennialism. See Kuzmic, in Vinay, Samuel and Chris Sugden, eds. (2009, 134–147). In 1909, Cyrus Ingerson Scofield produced a premillennialist Scofield Reference Bible, which influenced the teaching of fundamentalists in America (142).

6. One example of this theological influence was the school for teaching modern knowledge in English in India, set up by Alexander Duff, in which medical care was included in the mission activity (Bebbington, 142, 144); as such, "the gospel and culture were in remarkable degree of harmony" (147).

The main characteristics of North American evangelicalism might be summarized as follows: (1) Its origins are to be found in the context of socio-political changes brought about by the Civil War in North America that took place in the middle of the nineteenth century, the French revolution, and the emergence of nonconformism (Bosch 1991, 280, 281, 284; Marsden 1985, 13).[7] (2) It was rooted in the theological context of the Great Awakening (1720–1740s) (Marsden 1980, 11; Bosch 1991, 278, 282).[8] (3) Theologically, it stressed the need for evangelism, conversion, and personal holiness,[9] and, through the postmillennialism of virtually every Protestant denomination, sounded an optimistic mood with its understanding of a supernatural kingdom of God and of sin as structural in addition to being personal (Bosch 1991, 282, 284). It was to this context that during the late-nineteenth to the mid-twentieth century, premillennialism brought to American evangelicalism a theological variety, introducing dispensationalist and fundamentalist theologies (Marsden 1980, 49–51; Bosch 1991, 284).

Movements such as the World Student Christian Federation (WSCF), the Student Volunteer Movement (SVM), and the International Missionary Council (IMC), embraced both social gospellers and premillennialists, keeping alive the holistic understanding of the Christian faith until the split of Christians under the influence of rationalism (324). Bosch explains that the social gospel has been the great contribution of the American mission enterprise (327), and nearly 13,000 missionaries sailed through the SVM after it was formed in 1886 (323). These theological and missiological influences have also permeated evangelicalism in Latin America.

---

7. Bosch (1991, 281) explains that "it is important to note that evangelicals – whether in the United States, Britain, or the continent, and whether Anglicans, Lutherans, or members of non-established churches – were nonconformists in the true sense of the word". 'Nonconformist' relates to people interested in the social change of the world.

8. The Great Awakening was influenced by John Wesley and George Whitfield. Similarly, Charles Finney became the most prominent leader of the Second Awakening (1790–1825), while the American revivalist, postmillennialist and founder of Princeton University, Jonathan Edwards, became its most important theologian (Marsden 1980, 11, 49; Bosch 1991, 278).

9. McGrath (1995, 29) indicates that most 19th century forms of American evangelicalism were culturally centrist, committed to transforming culture through the gospel.

Historically, the liberal face of evangelicalism in Latin America "starts with the historical, liberal, modernizing systems of political sectors, the beginning of both the North American influence and Protestantism" (Miguez Bonino 1997, 2). The Protestant gospel was brought to Latin America by James Thompson, a Baptist minister, who went to Argentina in 1818 and founded schools based on the Lancastrian (also called 'Lancasterian') system and distributed the Bible in other countries such as Chile, Peru and Colombia (Kessler 1967, 19–22; Davies 2006, 15). Thompson was a great contextual partner collaborator with governments and worked closely with the Catholic Church. Why does his social influence seem to go further than promoting an educational programme? He wanted to start a mission society to send missionaries from Britain to Latin America; this was delayed until 1854, when he founded the first Bible mission society in Colombia. We have thus examined the beginnings of the Protestant movement in Latin America that was initiated by the British church, especially through Scottish missionaries like Thompson.

Miguez Bonino's first face of Latin-American Protestantism represents the development of the evangelical movement in Latin America from the Panama Congress held in 1916. This Congress was controlled by the historic liberal-progressive denominations of North America. He comments:

> Methodists, Presbyterians, Disciples of Christ, the American Baptist Convention (of the North), and even more the liberal missionary sectors of these denominations *controlled with their theological and missiological influence.* There was no decisive presence of British missions or of the Southern Baptist Convention, the Christian Missionary Alliance, the Church of the Nazarene, or Plymouth Brethren, who already were present in Latin America (Miguez Bonino 1997, 6, italics mine).

In other words, it seems that American missions made an impact in Latin America, despite the presence of British missions there for many years before the Americans arrived in this new missionary territory for evangelicals.

This first 'face' of Latin-American Protestantism has the following characteristics (Miguez Bonino 1997, 7–24), which emerged under the influence of the Panama Congress 1916:

1. It has connections with the liberal development of the political and economical expansion of the United States, which started in 1820, when the trading relationship with Great Britain lost ground. As a consequence, the trade model was replaced by the production model, "incorporating a new force into the economic system which meant the stimulation of immigration and the education of the people" (1997, 7).
2. In the 1900s there were tensions between liberal trends and the Catholic Church, which in the end recovered control of the Latin American church.
3. A kind of 'Panamericanism', which was opposed to armed interventions and the unity of the emergent countries, came to light under the influence of Simon Bolivar, but the American government exercised political control.
4. The United States promoted a 'Panamericanism' at missionary, educational, social and economic levels, which made an impact on Latin America.
5. Two contradictions appeared as a result of Panamericanism: the theological contradiction which was the result of the academic formation and the spiritual orientation of spiritual groups, with progressive ideologies and individualistic and subjective soteriology; and the political contradiction related to the new ideas of democracy as protective, a capitalist model ruled by the market and society and democracy as development democracy, a model where the human being wants to achieve greater freedom and equality, and this through distribution of resources, the creation of cooperatives and of political parties, with a distinction between state and community and education.
6. There was an emphasis on education as a development of integral growth.
7. There was a lack of theological self-understanding of the new political Panamericanism influenced by the United States.

8. An economic crisis of world capitalism emerged in the 1930s and made an impact on the social, political and economic life of Latin America. Unemployment, poverty and social protest opened the doors to socialist movements.
9. From the 1930s to the 1950s, the first ideas of partnership between churches appeared in most countries of the continent. Councils of churches were formed with the aim of cooperation in literature publication, representation before public authorities, defence of religious liberty, cooperation in evangelization and Christian education. Interdenominational and denominational seminaries were founded.
10. The first Latin American Evangelical Conference emerged in 1949 (CELA I).

The second face that Miguez Bonino (1997, 27–28) proposes is the evangelical face. This refers to the missionary work of the British and American mission enterprise that developed from the 1840s, which made an impact through its theology of pietism and of the Great Awakening of the eighteenth century, associated with the influence of Wesley and Whitfield in Great Britain and with Jonathan Edwards in the United States. I agree with Miguez Bonino that this influence permeated most Anglo-Saxon Protestantism and its missionary activity. This is the theological background of the mission to Latin America with its origins in the second half of the nineteenth century. Some of the principal characteristics of the second 'face' are as follows (1997, 29–50):

1. The second awakening, associated with D. L. Moody, Charles Finney and Jonathan Edwards, responded to the growth of urban populations.
2. There was theological conflict between the Calvinists and the Arminians over the notion of free will and growing in holiness.
3. The 1850s are seen as the moral improvement of society, with the abolition of slavery and the struggle against poverty.
4. Polemics against Catholicism made new converts acknowledge arguments against the corruption, obscurantism and authoritarianism of the Roman Catholic Church. In consequence there was

great emphasis on study of the Bible and of the basic doctrines of Protestantism.

5. Evangelical piety was the result of the holiness movement where Wesleyan sanctification and the experience of the 'second blessings' gave rise to divisions. In consequence, new movements came to light like the Salvation Army in England 1880, the Church of God in Indiana 1880, the Christian and Missionary Alliance 1887, the Church of the Nazarenes 1908 and the Pilgrim Holiness Church 1897. All of these churches entered Latin America creating a new evangelical influence with a diversified theology, especially with the growth of premillennialism and later dispensationalism led by the Scot, John Nelson Darby, with its great emphasis on personal salvation, the separation of Christians from the 'world' and eschatological interpretation of the 'rapture'.

6. The Bible had to be read literally – plenary and verbal inspiration, literal and inerrant interpretation, were features of fundamentalism. This theological interpretation resulted in diversification within the evangelical movement in Latin America.

One of the separatists in the evangelical movement was the International Evangelical Council of Carl McIntyre, who accused evangelicals of being modernist at the Latin American Evangelical Conference (CELA I) in Buenos Aires in 1949, and after that year, as Miguez Bonino points out, new organizations were formed in Latin America (1977, 44–45) clearly defined, as he explains, as 'right' or 'left', evangelicals or liberationist (1977, 45): Movimiento Estudiantil Cristiano (MEC), Iglesia y Sociedad en America Latina (ISAL), Consejo Ecumenico de Educación Cristiana (CELADEC). These organizations were influenced by international ecumenism. However, later in the 1960s, after CELA II in 1961 and CELA III in 1965 there was a split among evangelicals with the formation of 'Confraternidad Evangelica Latinoamericana' (CONELA) and the ecumenical 'Consejo Latinoamericano de Iglesias' (CLAI). Consequently, these two interpretations had an impact on all Protestant mission developed thereafter and this tension permeated the Latin American church.

A third face is the 'Pentecostal face', which, according to Miguez Bonino, does not include the charismatic movement due to sociological differences. I agree with this assumption because Pentecostalism started from marginal sectors, whereas charismatics made an impact among the middle classes emerging from the traditional churches. Pentecostalism is an evangelical movement which started in 1909 in Valparaiso, Chile, with the American revivalist Willis Hoover, a Methodist missionary, and in São Paulo, Brazil with the Waldensian Italian, Luigi Francescon, in 1910 (Allan Anderson in *An Introduction to Pentecostalism,* 2004, 64, 70; Miguez Bonino 1997, 56). According to Miguez Bonino, the main characteristics of Pentecostals in Latin America are as follows (1977, 53–73):

1. Personal experience is central to conversion and the baptism of the Holy Spirit which is interpreted as a 'second experience', with the evidence of speaking in tongues.
2. Divine healing is part of Pentecostal theology and their eschatology is apocalyptic and premillennial.
3. The fourfold pattern, "Christ the Saviour, Sanctifier, Healer and coming King" expresses the common tradition of Pentecostals.
4. Pentecostalism in Latin America has connections with the awakening in the United States.
5. Social conscience in relation to the most needy people and ethical reflection with reference to society were developed after 1988 (66). However, not all Pentecostals share this new conscience for political and social activity.

In analysing the Pentecostal movement we need to bear in mind that they have permeated the whole evangelical movement in Latin America and one of their contributions is promoting the participation of women in church leadership. Works on Pentecostalism have been published by scholars like the Swiss historian, Walter Hollenweger, with his important work *The Pentecostals* (1972), Allan Anderson with his expertise at Birmingham University on Global Pentecostalism and his book entitled *Pentecostals after a Century* (Anderson and Hollenweger 1999, 20–21), and the American theologian Harvey Cox with his work *Fire from Heaven* (1999, 8–12). The Pentecostal Chilean pastor Juan Sepulveda (1999, 16), the Peruvian Bernardo Campos (Miguez Bonino 1977, 64), and the

Swiss sociologist, Christian Lalive d'Epinay (1977, 58) with his studies on Chilean and Brazilian Pentecostalism and Robert Beckford[10] as an expert on Black Pentecostal Theology (Beckford 2000) are some of those who are very involved in developing a deeper study of Latin American and world Pentecostalism.

Hollenweger offers a wider academic discussion of the growth and characteristics of Pentecostalism around the world and his central thesis is that Pentecostals have failed to understand themselves (Anderson 1999, 20–21). Anderson interprets the study of Hollenweger by saying that Pentecostalism in the Third World is at a crossroads where the way forward is to reconsider its roots and its spirituality and also to understand that Pentecostalism should not be described in western categories because of its roots in the spirituality of nineteenth-century African American slave religion (23). Juan Sepulveda, in his doctoral research, gives an analysis of the indigenous Pentecostalism in the Chilean experience (111–134); he wants to highlight a different perspective with the attempt to understand Pentecostal growth in Latin America as an indigenous Christianity, an idea suggested by Eugene Nida in 1961 (112). Sepulveda agrees with Hollenweger that the American Willis Hoover is the founder of Pentecostalism in Chile, started in 1909 but not connected to Azusa Street in Los Angeles 1906 (113).

Here, I would like to refine what Miguez Bonino has described so far, and this in relation to the development of the roots of evangelicalism in Latin America, by positing three periods as part of this evangelical process: the first period is the emergent evangelicalism started in 1818 with the presence of the Baptist pastor James Thompson in the context of the independence of the Spanish colonies; the second period is the transitional evangelicalism started with the Panama Congress in 1916 under the influence of American Panamericanism, the expansion and influence of different missions, founding different denominations; and the third period is the contextual evangelicalism which starts with the formation of the Latin

---

10. Robert Beckford draws, in his book *Dread and Pentecostal,* an analysis of the relationship between the black church in Britain and its political theology. He explains the importance of the black diaspora for a political theology, where African Caribbean Christianity arrived in post-war Britain from the West Indies and they have developed not because of racialized oppression, but by the consciousness of a universal mission (2000, 16).

American Theological Fraternity (FTL) in 1970, in the context of the start of the Theology of Liberation in the 1960s, the political influence of the 'Alliance for Progress', launched in 1961 by President Kennedy, the activities of the guerrilla movement under Fidel Castro and Che Guevara in the 1960s (Yates 1994, 178–179), and economic oppression by the International Monetary Fund (IMF). By contrast, the interest in developing the double mandate in parallel, in words and in deeds and participation in reflection of the political, economic and social reality of Latin America was the theological aim of the FTL. We have also to add a fourth period, which is Pentecostal evangelicalism resulting in considerable growth in the 1980s, with 37 million Pentecostals (Miguez Bonino 1997, 35).

After my analysis of what Miguez Bonino (1997, 108–112) has defined as three faces of the Latin American Protestantism, I observe that he proposes that the future of the Protestant churches in Latin America will include the following characteristics: (1) a continuing growing church with an average at present of 80 million members;[11] (2) the Protestant presence is no longer a peripheral or accidental phenomenon, and will replace the Roman Catholic Church as a social and cultural influence; and (3) Protestants' responsibility will be measured by faithful witness to the gospel. The origins and roots of the Latin American evangelicalism was permeated by the western mentality under the political influence of the Civil War of the United States in 1860s, the war of liberation from the Spanish empire started in 1810 with General San Martin and Simon Bolivar, the First World War 1914–1918, and the Second World War 1939–1944. Latin America has no prospect of avoiding these external factors that have hindered the possibility of developing stable countries with a macro-economy and their own technology to create a new industrial era and more jobs for workers. This is the context where partnership in mission has been developed for many years in the evangelical arena and produced different models of relationships between evangelical partners.

---

11. Allan Anderson (2004, 63) in *An Introduction to Pentecostalism* provides statistics borrowed from Barrett and Johnson which estimate 141 million Latin American Pentecostals/Charismatics/Neo-Pentecostals in 2000; a higher number than in any other continent; Brazil has a half of that numbers cited by Anderson.

An ecumenical understanding of partnership: Edinburgh 1910 to Whitby 1947

I would like to start my discussion by clarifying that I will limit my historical analysis to four major mission conferences: Edinburgh 1910, Jerusalem 1928, Tambaram 1938 and Whitby 1947. This is because these conferences define the beginnings of mission partnership from the Protestant perspective, and secondly because they are the main focus for different scholars, both Western and from the Majority World. I am trying to define an ecumenical approach, which includes all participants from the wider spectrum of the Protestant movement after the period of the Reformation, including Lutherans, Calvinists, Baptists, Anglicans and Methodists. Catholics were also present at Edinburgh 1910. However, we need to bear in mind that Edinburgh 1910 was preceded by the New York conference 1900 under the influence of the Student Volunteer Movement (SVM), the Young Men's Christian Association (YMCA) and the World Student Christian Federation (WSCF), whose leaders influenced the Protestant missionary movement of the early twentieth century (Yates 1994, 11).

Terms such as 'extension and expansion' (1994, 11) were the missiological insight of this missionary development, and we understand that this missiology also made an impact on subsequent congresses, especially Edinburgh 1910. Politically, influence was the nineteenth-century idea of progress, which was part of the American development. Partnership in mission was developed in this context. Theologically, Puritan theology of the seventeenth century on the sovereignty of God and the kingdom of God was emphasized in terms of social progress and the action of man. This tendency emphasized by Jonathan Edwards made an impact on Protestant missionary movements of the nineteenth century (10). Here again we see the idea of expansion and extension.

Edinburgh 1910

'Edinburgh 1910' was held in Scotland under the leadership of the American, John Mott, with his famous watchword "the evangelization of the world in this generation", and the Scot, J. H. Oldham (Yates 1994, 21–24). This Congress can be defined as the beginning of the new age of post-colonial mission, where the idea of partnership was addressed in relation to the principle of relationships between mission societies and the so-called 'young churches'. The profile of a partnership theology in this Congress was weak due to the unwillingness of Western missiology to accept the new churches they founded as brothers and sisters in Christ; there was lack of equality in the practice of policies for mission at that time.

For Lother Bauerochse (1996, 4–10), a missiological tension of Edinburgh 1910 was identified as the need for independence on the side of the new churches founded by Western mission societies, and she makes a succinct statement about the need to clearly establish who was responsible for the work, who made the decisions especially on the use of finances, and how far the mission societies would permit an indigenous theology to develop with an indigenous spirituality and a contextual liturgy. On the other hand, the Anglican scholar, Timothy Yates (1994, 7) provides a historical perspective on the development of Christian mission and points out that, after Edinburgh 1910, mission as expansion was considered a dominant understanding, including the Anglo Saxon world. For Yates, the motives of partnering in mission were fear of the growth of Islam and the need to promote unity between churches and mission societies (1994, 28). Equally, it is interesting to note that the Catholic Church was included in this first 1910 predominantly Protestant congress, but Latin America was excluded from this Protestant mission enterprise (1994, 29). The reason for this exclusion is explained in Escobar's words:

> When Protestant missions from Europe and North America began to send missionaries to Latin America in the mid-nineteenth century, the Catholic Church rejected their presence, claiming that the region was Christian and was already evangelized. The organizers were bound by the position that Latin America was not a mission field, and hence they did not invite any of the Protestant missions that were then working in the region or any of the Protestant churches that were established at that time (2004, 24).

Some historical facts behind Edinburgh 1910 were nationalistic political change with the success of Japan in the war with Russia in 1905, a growing racial antagonism in India and the idea of world conquest inside the mission societies (Yates, 30–31). It seems that mission partnership perspective is defined in Edinburgh as going together to conquer the world for God's kingdom. Timothy Yates (1994, 31) points out clearly that such militaristic metaphor were commonly used by the organizers of Edinburgh 1910 like Mott, Warneck, Bashford, Horton and others. Was this a good goal for the *missio Dei*? Or was it just an expansive and imperialistic missiology as developed in the nineteenth century with the conquest of new territories for the colonial empires? I notice that Edinburgh 1910 tried to reinforce the unity of the church with the goal of extending and expanding God's kingdom.

Jerusalem 1928

'Jerusalem 1928', organized by the IMC, which was formed in 1921 after Edinburgh 1910 (Bosch 1991, 356), may be defined as the new era of equality in mission. A committee was established with John Mott as chairman and J. H. Holman as secretary (Bevans and Schroeder 2004, 255). In this conference real partnership was demanded between missions and local churches. The concept of partnership is understood as more than cooperation, because church partners demanded a new relationship with mission societies, with mutual understanding and trust of one another. Cooperation was understood as giving financial aid, but the 'younger' churches demanded a new spiritual fraternal relationship beyond that cooperation (Bauerochse 1996, 15–18). The theological concept of partnership started in this conference (1996, 26), and mission partners were linked to the relationship between mission societies and churches. James H. Franklin from the American Baptist Mission demanded a change in the relationship to pass from paternalism to partnership relationship (1996, 15). As a result, local churches demanded independence and liberation from Western missions in order to collaborate as co-workers for the mission mandate. This process shows that paternalism was part of the mission theology, which was understood in terms of providing resources for the new established churches with no discernment as to what spiritual maturity meant. In the same way, paternalism included the control of power with no sharing of decision making. In consequence we understand that Jerusalem 1928 was an emergent discussion of partnership with more weaknesses than strengths.

Tambaran 1938

'Tambaran 1938' was held in Madras, India, at the beginning of the Second World War (1939) where political tensions had started with Adolph Hitler in Germany in 1939 after the invasion of Poland. This Congress, organized by the IMC, also had the political context of war between Japan and China, which included the bombing of Shanghai in 1937 (Yates 1994, 86). However, participants from both countries were present at Tambaran. At the same time Europe had experienced the civil war in Spain. I would like to define this conference as the beginning of a new ecclesiology for mission enterprise, but why? Because the mission spirit on this occasion was to strengthen the founding churches by giving them the recognition that they were part of the worldwide church and that they were ready to be allowed to make their own structures. On the other hand, the question of the nature of the church was related to the indigenization missiology and the need for cooperation and unity demanded by the transplanted churches (Bauerochse 20–24). In relation to theology, the Dutch theologian Hendrick Kraemer was the architect in developing an emphasis on Christology at Tambaran, and this was the framework for mission partnership theology (Yates 1994, 109). As noted by Yates, Kraemer brought a powerful Christ-centric missionary vision (119). However, this perspective appears not to have had enough influence to overcome the effects of mission expansion delivered at Edinburgh 1910. In fact, this is a pattern that was hindering mission relationships at that time, and Kraemer tried to develop a christological emphasis for mission partnership.

In analysing Edinburgh, Jerusalem and Tambaran, the German missiologist and radio journalist, Lother Bauerochse, who has written on partnership in Christian mission from an ecumenical perspective, presents her understanding as follows: Edinburgh is directed to the church in the mission field, Jerusalem points out the relationships between churches, and Tambaram emphasizes the worldwide mission of the churches. She adds that Jerusalem stressed equality as a relationship of confidence and fellowship, while Tambaram pointed out effective cooperation (Bauerochse 1996, 25). On the other hand, David Bosch, in relation to Protestant thinking of mission, explains that in Edinburgh "a major concern was the absence of missionary enthusiasm in the West" (Bosch 1991, 369), Jerusalem touched 'the relationships between 'older' and 'younger' churches as a prominent issue' (369), and Tambaran analysed in a more theological manner 'the relationships between founded churches and mission societies' (369). I agree with Bauerochse in the way that she offers a useful clarification of the relationships between churches and mission societies, but perhaps she should go more deeply into analysis of the motives and the goals of these mission conferences to find the weaknesses and strengths of the thirty years of mission partnership from Edinburgh 1910 to Tambaran 1938. On the other side, Bosch (1991, 368) is trying to identify the shifts in Protestant thinking, which according to him have developed through missionary conferences.

What is not clear is whether or not Bosch regards mission partnership as an important element treated at the mission conferences since he avoids for one reason or another explicitly discussing partnership in mission. However, it seems that he does give a view of implicit partnership in his chapter "Elements of an Emerging Ecumenical Missionary Paradigm" (369) where he considers the relationship between church and mission as a kind of partnership between the church and others. I would say that here he refers to the role of the churches and mission societies in the mission enterprise which is related to the mission mandate. Both Bauerochse and Bosch appeal to these three major conferences to strengthen their arguments and the historical analysis of the ecumenical understanding of relationships. The Western church has now, from these perspectives, a mission partnership for the 'Christopagans', as Bosch proposes, due to the historical context which he describes as follows:

> In a Europe traumatized by the First World War and challenged by the rise of totalitarian ideologies like National Socialism, Fascism and Marxism, the anthropocentric theology of liberal Protestantism, epitomized in the views of Adolf Harnack and Ernst Troeltsch, was found wanting (1991, 370).

On the one side, it seems to me that partnership here is understood as a partnership for a strong ecclesiology to complete the task. Also it was an appeal to the planted churches to help the Western churches by sending to them a mission of witness and fellowship. Partnership was intended to give the churches of the South the right to a greater say and more participation in the planning, by combining their personal and financial sources of help. On the other side, the mission partnership task looks as if it is centred on the local church – a weakness in interpreting the christological mission mandate.

As we have seen before, this historical perspective of partnership in Christian mission had the theological justification of sending missionaries to the mission field and this was fundamentally in partnership with mission societies and missionaries; local churches from the sending countries were outside the Christian partnership; everything was carried out through the mission societies that were totally outside the control of the sending churches. This was the mission model that had its own missionary tensions in developing a partnership mission theology, and the impact of the following decades has had great repercussions in bringing about the continuity of the "traditional partnership model". It is clear that the context of this missiological development of partnership was the influence of pre- and post-war Europe, but the *missio Dei* reminds us that the double mandate compels the church to accomplish the redemptive mission despite the weaknesses of the relationships between North and South or the political and sociological tension of our circumstances.

Whitby 1947

'Whitby 1947' was held in the town near Toronto in Canada. I would define this mission conference as the turning point of post-Second World War missiology. The political arena of the 1940s and 1950s was dark and suspicious because of the tension between America and the Soviet Union by dividing Germany into 'two countries'. The world economy was devastated in Europe; the basic infrastructure of factories had to be reoriented; inflation and lack of work were two of the issues to be sorted out. Churches lacked strength to accomplish the evangelistic target, but mission partnership in this conference revitalized the missionary spirit of Edinburgh 1910.

As Neil comments in the same year: "the years of war from 1939 to 1945 were inevitably in some ways a time of suspended activity for the worldwide church" (1952, 8).

'Partnership in Obedience' developed at Whitby (Bosch 1991, 379; Neil 1952, 27), clarifies the need for a new relationship between churches and mission societies with a recognition that divided forces cannot go anywhere; it was a call to genuine partnership, to recognize the threats from outside; Christ's command to preach the gospel to every creature, a call to the church to unite all their powers, to understand that time was pressing and the situation extremely urgent to accomplish the mission mandate were its characteristics (Bauerochse 1996, 31). In her dialogue with interchurch partnership as ecumenical communities of learning, Lothar Bauerochse (1996, 32) reflects the state of partnership in mission for the Whitby declaration by mentioning four areas in conflict: staff cooperation, financial aid, responsibility for decision making, and administration.

Therefore, the issues of divided forces, the need of a genuine partnership and the urgency to accomplish the mission mandate mentioned above at 'Whitby 1947' brought an agreement for: a) priority training for church leaders, b) independence on financial matters to be dealt with from a biblical perspective, c) mission loses its traditional geographical emphasis, and d) a call to work closely together in the planning task (1996, 32–33). It seems to me that the Whitby declaration made an effort to develop a good mission theology of partnership, but the reality is that this missiological agreement had tensions in interpretation on both sides and generated a lack of validity of this declaration when partners came to put it into practice. We can add that 'Whitby 1947' was a kind of romantic missiology where two parties had a similar perspective on mission partnership theology, but with a failure in practical application for the benefit of both sides, North and South. Missionary tensions such as the control of money and interdependence were some issues that were not resolved at that time. However, the positive thing is that mission partners made a great effort to be more effective in their missiological perspective on a biblical Christian theology of partnership. Accordingly, 'Whitby 1947' was without any doubt an effort to improve the relationship between mission partners.

An evangelical understanding of mission partnership: from Lausanne 1974 to Amsterdam 2000

This historical analysis is now developed by taking account of four major mission congresses in the evangelical movement: Lausanne 1974, The Consultation of Pattaya 1980, The Manila Consultation 1989 and Amsterdam 2000.

Lausanne 1974

The Lausanne Congress 1974 was conceived as a result of the theological and missiological tensions between the WCC and the emergent evangelicalism of the 1960s and 1970s. After Edinburgh 1910, in the middle of the political, economical and social aftermath of the Second World War, the WCC, formed on 23 August 1948 in Amsterdam, totally absorbed the IMC in 1961 with complete integration (Bosch 1991, 370; Neill 1952, 65, 75). The WCC laid emphasis on the social dimension of mission, which brought about tension in the interpretation of the missionary mandate by emphasizing the social mandate over and above the spiritual mandate. In consequence, the evangelical movement split from the WCC as was prophesied by Max Warren in 1947 (Yates 1994, 193), who supported cooperation but opposed integration between IMC and the WCC (Bevans and Schroeder 2004, 259).

It is quite remarkable to indicate as a matter of historical fact that the IMC and the WCC integration took place in New Delhi in 1961, and the conciliar ecumenical movement practitioner and theoretician, Lesslie Newbigin, as General Secretary of the IMC in 1956 guided its integration into the WCC (The New Delhi Report 1962, 3–7, 56–60).[12] The effect of this development in the context of social and political tensions of the Cold War, and the perspective of Johannes Hoekendijk in 1960, are the

---

12. See further *The New Delhi Report: The Third Assembly of the World Council of Churches 1961* (Willen A. Visser 't Hooft Editor 1962), held in New Delhi, 18 November–5 December 1961 (1962, 329). See also *New Delhi Speaks: The Message of the Third Assembly New Delhi, with the Reports of the Assembly's Section on Christian Witness, Service and Unity and an Appeal to All Governments and Peoples* (1962). Bevans and Schroeder (2004, 259), and Bosch (1991, 370), takes an account of this process.

background of the Berlin Congress on Evangelism and the Wheaton Congress on the Christian World Mission, both in 1966. The Indonesian-born Dutch missionary Hoekendijk, known as an ecumenical theologian, made proposals with a secularizing focus in the 1960s, that is, he opposed ecclesiocentrism or 'church-ism' (Hoekendijk 1966, 52), which means centring our view of God's mission in the world through the church. Instead he proposed that we should focus on the secular world as the place of God's action and God's intention.[13] In this line, Wilhelm Richebacher (2003, 591–592; Bosch 1991, 326)[14] points out that Hoekendijk's insistence was to desacralize the church-centred mission in the context of the new ideas of the *missio Dei* started by Barth in 1932 and strengthened during the 1952 Willingen conference of the WCC. His definition of mission was no longer confined to the activities of the church, as had often been the case over the centuries, but he found himself in danger of going in the opposite direction, by giving too much attention to the world instead of the church. Therefore, it seems that he went so far with a Trinitarian overemphasis, thus, his trend clearly reflects the critical moment of the mission activity at that time.[15] Regarding Hoekendijk's ecclesiology, some issues are briefly surveyed here. He points out that the missionary existence of the church now expresses only one of many forms of God's mission and in consequence it is the world that sets the agenda for mission, not the church that is the sign and instrument of God's presence (Hoedemaker 1995, 167); he criticizes the church for missing the opportunity to learn from society and insists that the church is a function of the apostolate (Hoekendijk 1966, 41; Bevans and Schroeder 2004, 251, 290); he exposes self-sufficiency in

---

13. Hoekendijk develops his view by calling the church to adopt a shift in focus from the church to the world in need of shalom (Moreau 2000, 447). However, Hoekendijk did not suggest that the church was unimportant, but rather that it was an instrument of God instead of the focus of God's intention (2000, 447).

14. See Wilhelm Richebacher "Missio Dei: The Basis of Mission Theology or a Wrong Path?" (*International Review of Mission*, Vol. XCII No. 367 October 2003, 591–592).

15. See Bert Hoedemaker, "The Legacy of J. C. Hoekendijk", *International Bulletin of Missionary Research*, Issue 19:4, October 1995: 166–170.

the institution of the church; however, he argues that there is no room for an 'ecclesiology' (Hoekendijk 1966, 38, 84–85).[16]

In his book *The Church Inside Out* (1966), Hoekendijk proposes an ecclesiology based on the belief that the church is a Christian community, which has become a partaker of shalom, that means that the church is a company of strangers and pilgrims in the world.[17] Thus, salvation in Hoekendijk's theology (1966, 19)[18] is considered the action of God in history in bringing shalom, which is much more than personal salvation – 'it is at once peace, integrity, community, harmony and justice'; thus, he suggests that shalom is a more important concept than salvation. His humanistic view maintains that "the church is at best, only a pointer to the way God acts in respect of the world, and mission is viewed as a contribution toward the humanization of society – a process in which the church may perhaps be involved in the role of consciousness-raiser" (Hoedemaker in Bosch 1991, 381).[19] Therefore, his theological thinking insisted on revolutionary ferment as a legitimate form of missionary theology, which implies taking the secular world seriously as the arena where *kerigma*, *koinonia*, and *diakonia* appear as reference to the coming kingdom (Hoekendijk 1966, 23–29; Anderson 1998, 297; Hoedemaker 1995, 167). Consequently, Hoekendijk's interpretation of the *missio Dei* as the historical work of God in the world mainly gained strength as a result of the contribution made by the strong American delegation at Willingen (2003, 592). It appears

---

16. Hoekendijk (1966, 6, 64) states that "the congregation is the bearer of the apostolate, and she will have to make the Word and thus also the apostolate credible through her existence and life, through word and deed". The apostolate refers to the messengers of the end time, announcers of the approaching day of the Lord who proclaim the fulfilment of the Messianic promises – it also refers to the eschatological and redemptive-historical dealing of God".

17. It is in fact the 'messianic community' that is to live in self-emptying service and solidarity with the people; and he challenges class structures in the church by arguing for a return to the secret of the church-of-the-poor (Hoekendijk 1960, 27, 69, 180).

18. See also the explanation of Bosch (1991, 396).

19. This can be achieved through the life of the Christian community expressing the solidarity of Christ with the world, nurturing their hope as a better society for humankind (Hoekendijk 62, 83). Put differently, he emphasized flexible ecclesial structures for mission, the laity as the primary agent of mission, and an everyday life presence in society. See further chapter V "The life of the Christian Community" (Hoekendijk 1966). Also Bosch's analysis of Hoekendijk's thinking in relation the apostolate of the laity (1991, 472).

to me that Hoekendijk's theological interpretation of ecclesiology and the integration of the IMC into the WCC are the historical context, which produced a reaction that led to Lausanne 1974, which was sponsored by the Billy Graham Evangelistic Association, with a high degree of evangelical identity and solidarity in mission and evangelism (2004, 261).

Stephen Neill (1952, 75–88) explains that from the beginning, the WCC experienced mission tensions in four respects: (1) christological tension, with three interpretations – the Orthodox church demanding a more explicitly Trinitarian view, conservatives demanding sincerity, and the liberals demanding inclusive Christology; (2) theological tension again with the Orthodox view representing the Eastern church, then the extreme conservatives (classified under the American term as fundamentalist), and third the liberals who were mainly not interested in ecclesiastical issues; (3) political tension, in the context of the Second World War, anti-communist hysteria and the promotion of capitalism by the Americans, the accusation that the WCC aspired to political power, the atomic crisis, the takeover of China by the communists, the Korean War, and a lack of Christian freedom to give a point of view on conflict ideologies; (4) the tension which has connection with four perspectives – the Orthodox churches claiming that they had the monopoly of the sacraments; the Anglicans believing that they were the orthodox, catholic and apostolic Church of England with the validity of Anglican ordinations and consecrations in their churches; the Free churches recognizing the ministries of sacraments of all Christian fellowships which maintained historic faith, and finally Congregationalists and Baptists that are organized on the basis of the autonomy of the local church. This brief historical, theological and missiological context explains why Lausanne occurred in 1974, 26 years after the WCC was formed. These tensions had an impact on the relationships between liberals called ecumenicals and conservatives called evangelicals, in the way that it was a declining relationship which reflected structural and political tension rather than a sense of relational one as at the beginning at Edinburgh 1910.

How has the idea of partnership developed in evangelicalism through the Lausanne movement? Timothy Yates clarifies:

> The tendency towards Gnostic and dualistic separation of the spiritual from the bodily, message from deed, conversion as purely vertical experience related to God rather than one which also related the Christian to the neighbour was clear enough to the philosophically minded Francis Schaeffer, leader of the evangelical community, L'Abri, in Switzerland: as a participant at Lausanne, he drew attention to what he called the Platonic element of evangelicalism, so damaging and so deadly (Yates 1994, 202).

In consequence the need for recovering a social emphasis in the evangelistic message by evangelicals was highlighted in Lausanne, which produced the 'Lausanne Covenant'; in section 5 on Christian Social Responsibility it clearly states:

> Although reconciliation with man is not reconciliation with God nor is social action evangelism, nor is political liberation salvation, nevertheless we affirm that evangelism and socio-political involvement are both part of our Christian duty. For both are necessary expressions of our doctrines of God and man, our love for our neighbour and our obedience to Jesus Christ. The message of salvation implies also a message of judgment upon every form of alienation, oppression and discrimination, and we should not be afraid to denounce evil and injustice wherever they exist.[20]

In my view the double mandate includes the spiritual and the social dimension of the gospel, which must be understood as a mission unity.[21] This in-

---

20. See 'The Lausanne Covenant', section 5 on Christian Social Responsibility in The Lausanne Movement (ttp://www.lausanne.org/covenant). See also The Lausanne Covenant in *Making Christ Known: Historic Mission Documents from the Lausanne Movement 1974–1989* (Stott, Editor 1996, 24).
21. Latin American theologian René Padilla and missiologist Samuel Escobar pointed out at Lausanne the need for social responsibility in mission (Yates 1994, 203; Bevans and Schroeder 2004, 261). Equally, David Bosch identified at Lausanne the lack of a proper understanding of what he calls 'the double mandate' (1994, 202–208).

terpretation affects all Christian mission partnerships and should permeate the church's mission for the twenty-first century. Escobar (2003, 21, 164) clearly highlights that within Lausanne 1974, evangelical missiologists reached a consensus to reflect in light of God's word, theological truth and new missionary challenges to envision new models of missionary obedience. In this regard, Padilla (1985, vii) who presented a paper in Lausanne 1974 entitled "Evangelism and the World" points out the impact the Congress has produced around the world. Apart from the social responsibility in section 5, the Lausanne Covenant (see the whole document in Claydon 2005),[22] with its fifteen sections, has brought to the light other crucial issues relating to mission such as the nature of evangelism (section 4), Christian cooperation and evangelism (section 7), churches in evangelistic partnership (section 8), gospel, evangelism and culture (section 10).

The horizontal aspect of mission – the social gospel rather than salvation – was the theological and missiological emphasis at the 1968 WCC Assembly in Uppsala (Bosch 1991, 383). At that time evangelicals were anxious and Donald McGavran from the evangelical side asked for serious consideration. However, fragmentation was the consequence and distrust by evangelicals for the WCC, which started in 1957, climaxed at Uppsala in 1968. What was the result? Billy Graham sponsored Lausanne in 1974 (Bevans and Schroeder 2004, 261). As a result LCWE was formed and McGavran's assumptions formed the theoretical basis for this new evangelical movement. Equally, Ralph Winter with 'unreached people' and Wycliffe Bible Translators became part of the new evangelical movement started in Lausanne 1974, which held consultations at Pattaya 1980 and Manila 1989 (2004, 262).

Pattaya 1980

In comparison with Pattaya in Thailand 1980, Lausanne 1974 had a wider impact in the sense that interpretations on theological reflection of the double mandate were emphasized. However, Pattaya was more concentrated on a consultation on world evangelization under the title "How shall

---

22. The whole document of the 'Lausanne Covenant' is registered in Stott (1996, 7–55), and Claydon (2005, 711–728).

they hear?" (Stott 1996, 156) with an emphasis on "Cooperation in World Evangelization" (1996, 61). 800 delegates attended this consultation and produced a handbook on church and para-church relationships entitled "Co-operating in World Evangelization", which identified five hindrances to cooperation, as follows (1996, 164): dogmatism about non-essentials, the threat of conflicting authorities, strained relationships, rivalry between ministries, and suspicion about finances. The spirit of Pattaya was understood as a deep concern to strengthen evangelical cooperation in global evangelization and they recognized that no single agency could accomplish the *missio Dei* (1996, 161).

Cooperation for Pattaya is understood in these six terms: (1) the churches are bound together with one another, (2) true unity in Christ is not necessarily incompatible with organizational diversity, (3) competitive programmes and needless duplication of effort waste resources and call into question our profession to be one in Christ, (4) it is imperative that they work together to fulfil the task of world evangelization, (5) cooperation must never be sought at the expense of basic biblical teaching, and (6) cooperation reflects either social, political, geographical and cultural circumstances or ecclesiastical traditions. These conclusions at Pattaya show that the evangelical movement understood that something was hindering mission evangelization, and terms like 'together', 'unity', and 'cooperation' were contrasted with 'duplication', 'incompatible', and 'competitive'. This analysis shows that the influence of Edinburgh 1910, with its missiological emphasis of extension and expansion, is still behind the mentality of evangelicalism and needs to be changed by a reoriented holistic mission theology.

Manila 1989

The Manila Consultation 1989 produced *The Manila Manifesto*, printed in the book *A New Vision, a New Heart, a New Call* (Claydon Volume I, 718). This has twenty-one affirmations, and one of them relating to partnership is expressed in the following way: "We affirm the urgent need for churches, mission agencies and other Christian organizations to cooperate in evangelism and social action, repudiating competition and avoiding duplication." This suggests that, since the first Lausanne Congress of 1974, there is a change in the evangelical mentality because gathered at Manila in 1989 they made new affirmations which are more inclusive of the double mandate: evangelism and social action. The seventeenth affirmation of the Manila Manifesto also proposes a new relationship between the different structures of mission that is in relation to partnership and for that affirmation this manifesto uses the word 'cooperation'.

In respect of cooperation, the *Manila Manifesto* defines this concept as "finding unity in diversity. It involves people of different temperaments, gifts, calling and cultures, national churches and mission agencies, all ages and both sexes working together" (Claydon I, 725). My understanding is that partnership in mission has been developed by promoting the idea of working together, but without any clear appropriated information given to the donors of what the *Manila Manifesto* has been proposing to the mission enterprise in terms of clear fellowship and policies for partnering together between North and South. One reason for this weakness is the failure to permeate the worldwide church with this 'partnership affirmation' which has been ignored by the evangelical mentality, especially among those local church donors in the North and the Majority World in the South. According to the Catholic theologians Bevans and Schroeder in their book, *Constants in Contexts,* the so-called Lausanne II-Manila 1989 has the following insights: reaffirmation that mission was an urgent task but to look on present efforts of interreligious dialogue (40), strong concern for the poor and a more holistic approach (262, 373), the centrality of Christ in world evangelism (326), and witness as the common engagement of world evangelization (356).

The Grand Rapids Report 1982

It is remarkable to mention that 'The Grand Rapids Report on Evangelism and Social Responsibility 1982',[23] pointed out that the oppression of others

---

23. "The Grand Rapids Report on Evangelism and Social Responsibility: an evangelical commitment" (The International Consultation on the Relationship between Evangelism and Social Responsibility, Grand Rapids, Michigan, 19–25 June 1982). See the whole report in Stott, ed. (1996, 165–213). See also "The Grand Rapids Report" in "Evangelism and Social responsibility: An Evangelical Commitment" (http://www.arabvision.org/docs/Evangelism%20and%20Social%20Responsibility%20%28Grand%20Rapids%20Consultat.doc, Accessed 23 August 2010 at 12:34).

is political, so the church needs to make a radical response of compassion. Accordingly, two forms of social responsibility are provided: social service (relieving human need, philanthropic activity, seeking to minister to individuals and families, and works of mercy); and social action (removing the causes of human need, political and economic activity, seeking to transform structures of human society, and the quest of justice). This report gives evidence that evangelicalism went forward towards an integral mission.

There are three possible relationships between evangelism and social responsibility outlined in the Grand Rapids Report; briefly summarized these are (Stott 1996, 181–182): (1) Social responsibility is a consequence of evangelism. This implies that evangelism is the means by which God brings new birth, and their new life manifests itself in the service of others. (2) Social responsibility can be a bridge to evangelism. It can break down prejudice, open doors, and gain a hearing for the gospel; and (3) social activity not only follows evangelism as its consequence, and precedes it as its bridge, but also accompanies it as its partner. This relationship is seen in the public ministry of Jesus who served by preaching the gospel and by feeding the hungry and healing the sick. Thus, evangelism and social responsibility, while distinct from one another, are integrally supported by each other, and are both in obedience to the gospel.

Some images or metaphors used for these relationships are (182): social responsibility as "bridges of love to the world"; the partnership between evangelism and social responsibility is "in reality a marriage"; and evangelism and social responsibility are like "the two blades of a pair of scissors or the two wings of a bird".

For Stephan Bevans (2004, 262), Manila reaffirms the primacy of proclamation, but also concern for the poor and a more holistic approach. Timothy Yates' opinion is similar to Bevans, but he adds that the basic dichotomy approach was still present (1994, 222). According to this analysis, it seems that the spirit of Lausanne 1974 was still hindering the theological interpretation of evangelism, which always has a double mandate. To explain this, Bosch (1991, 405) argues that Lausanne recognized evangelism plus social responsibility as two separate components, a theological dichotomy which demonstrates that it is possible to have evangelism without social responsibility or social responsibility without evangelism.

Bosch's analysis maintains that the dichotomy was upheld as the official evangelical position by stating that evangelism is primary (406). It seems that despite Lausanne recognizing the need for more emphasis on social responsibility, the response of the church had only just begun to digest a new mission theology of the double mandate as holistic mission, thus, we can see that there was a mission process of implementing a new mission theology of holistic mission.[24] However, Bosch's view concludes that the understanding was too weak in that the evangelistic mandate was still the primary emphasis among evangelicals (404–407). It seems that Bosch went too far in criticizing radically the spirit of Lausanne due to the fact that the awareness for social responsibility within evangelicalism was, it seems to me, at its beginning. In contrast of Bosch's view, the Brazilian theologian Valdir Steuernagel (1995, 53),[25] indicates that despite Lausanne becoming one of the most representative expression of evangelicalism, the movement paid a high price for overcoming the dichotomy between evangelization and social responsibility. Steuernagel explains that Lausanne promoted undertaking the task of evangelization in the context of the modern world by including in its covenant recognition of social concern and social justice (53). However, in the final analysis, Steuernagel (54) concludes that social concern was primarily the contribution of third world evangelicalism and states:

> *Social concern* primarily reflected the contribution of third world evangelicalism that was reading the Bible in context of dependency, poverty, injustice and oppression. This evangelicalism, in its search for a missionary obedience, was prepared to revaluate the evangelicalism imported from the North and to face the challenge of becoming more contextual (italics mine).

---

24. See further *How Evangelicals Endorsed Social Responsibility* (Padilla and Sugden, eds. 1985).

25. See Valdir Steuernagel's article "Social Concern and Evangelization: The Journey of the Lausanne Movement" (*International Bulletin of Missionary Research* 1991 Vol. 15, No. 2 April, 53–56).

This is indeed the way Lausanne has often been viewed by many of the Latin-American thinkers such as Escobar and Padilla who presented two major papers at Lausanne;[26] Steuernagel (54) clearly points out that this was a kingdom-oriented evangelicalism, with the Latin American Theological Fraternity as one of the interpreters of Lausanne covenant. In fact, Escobar and Padilla brought to the debate of Lausanne the theology of *misión integral* – holistic mission – which provided room to accomplish the evangelistic and social responsibility of the Lausanne Covenant. Put differently, Stott has clarified that the distinction between evangelism and social action is often artificial; however, this theological issue was unresolved at the Lausanne Congress 1974 (Padilla and Sugden 1985, 12). As for the Lausanne Covenant, René Padilla (1976, 11–12) explains that, in a remarkable way, corrections to the Covenant eliminated the dichotomy between evangelism and social responsibility. In fact, he adds that "no one would claim that socio-political concern was a new discovery for evangelicals at Lausanne". He states:

> The fact remains, however, that Christian social responsibility (as grounded in the doctrine of God, the doctrine of man, the doctrine of salvation and the doctrine of the kingdom and therefore, inextricably connected with evangelism), is given in the Covenant a place of prominence that can hardly be regarded as characteristic of evangelical statements. In fact, a cursory look at the differences between the third draft and the final statement on social responsibility was considerably strengthened by (a) the replacement of the expression 'social action' with 'socio-political involvement', (b) the addition of direct reference to alienation, oppression and discrimination and to the denunciation of evil and injustice.

To conclude, Padilla's view is distinct from Bosch and Yates in that he provides three dichotomies eliminated within the Lausanne Covenant

---

26. Padilla presented a major paper at Lausanne entitled "Evangelism and the World" and Escobar presented a paper on "Evangelism and Man's Search for Freedom, Justice and Fulfilment" (Padilla and Sugden 1985: No. 59 p. 10).

after corrections of the document: elimination of the dichotomy between evangelism and social responsibility, elimination of the dichotomy between evangelism and Christian discipleship, and elimination of the dichotomy between evangelism and church renewal (Padilla and Sugden 1985, 11–13). The positive side is that the process of painful theological understanding within Lausanne 1974, in relation to evangelism and social responsibility, has continued, and can be summarized in the following documents:[27] The Thailand Statement 1980, The Grand Rapids Report 1982 on Evangelism and Social Responsibility, and The Manila Manifest 1989, all of which we have discussed very briefly already.[28] To conclude, the fact is that since the 1990s more mission societies are becoming involved in integral mission.

Amsterdam 2000

As for Amsterdam 2000, I had the privilege of attending this Evangelical Congress where 10,500 delegates from 200 different countries were present. The purpose was to make a new impact and to be renewed by a new evangelistic spirit to accomplish the mission mandate. The discovery of how the evangelical church worldwide can further the kingdom of God by the proclamation of the gospel was pointed out clearly (*The Mission of an Evangelist,* edited by the Billy Graham Evangelistic Association 2001, 13). In this Congress, in 'Partnership Strategy for Evangelism', Luis Palau called for building partnerships with other evangelists, and urged that we need each other all the time and that we need to invest in other evangelists (2001, 234). On the same lines, his son Kevin Palau calls for a cooperative evangelism because this theological understanding helps churches in working together and this reaches more people than a local church and provides a clear expression of unity in the church (2001, 319). In contrast, the Latin American Congress "Los Angeles 88" (1988: Congreso Internacional para la Evangelización del Mundo Latino, July 25–29), organized by the Argentinian evangelist Alberto Mottesi, which I also attended, had the

---

27. The full reports edited by John Stott are found in *Making Christ Know: Historic Mission Documents from the Lausanne Movement 1974–1989* (1996).

28. See further Stott, John, 1995 "Twenty Years After Lausanne: Some Personal Reflections", International Bulletin of Missionary Research 1995 Vol. 19, No. 2 April, 50–55.

emphasis of reaching the Latin American people and making an impact through new strategies of partnership in mission, but narrowed for a saving souls theology. In both cases mission partnership was emphasized for evangelism and winning souls, but a lack of biblical theology and missiological analysis of Trinitarian theology was one of their weaknesses. Strengths were found in the biblical call of 2 Timothy 4:5 "do the work of an evangelist".

A Latin American understanding of partnership – CLADE I 1970–IV 2000

From the Latin American perspective the study of partnership in mission is so recent a phenomenon that there seems to be no work on deeper analysis and this seems to me another reason for trying to make a contribution in this field. Latin American scholars have been developing more contextual theology, with an emphasis on integrated mission. Examples of this development include scholars like the Ecuadorian, René Padilla; missiological reflections on the history of mission by the Peruvian, Samuel Escobar (2002); theological reflection by Puerto Rican, Orlando Costas (1976); the Argentinian, José Miguez Bonino (1997); recently the Brazilian, Valdir Steuernagel; anthropological analysis from the Peruvian, Tito Paredes (2000);[29] the Argentinian, Pablo Deiros;[30] the Cuban, Justo González[31] taking account of the history in Latin American church; the

---

29. Paredes in his book *El Evangelio: Un Tesoro en Vasijas de Barro* develops anthropological and missiological perspectives between the gospel and culture.

30. Pablo Deiros and Carlos Mraida (1994) have written *Latinoamerica en Llamas: Historia y Creencias del Movimiento Religioso mas Impresionante de Todos los Tiempos*. Deiros and Mraida are evangelical Baptist ministers at the Iglesia Evangelica Bautista del Centro, a renewed church in Buenos Aires.

31. González has strongly specialized in church history. Some of his important works are: *The Story of Christianity, Volume 1: The Early Church to the Dawn of the Reformation* (1984); *The Story of Christianity, Volume 2: The Reformation to the Present Day* (1985); *A History of Christian Thought, Volume 1: From the Beginning of the Council of Chalcedon* (1993 New Edition); *A History of Christian Thought, Volume 2: From Augustine to the Eve of the Reformation* (1986); *A History of Christian Thought, Volume 3: From the Protestant Reformation to the Twentieth Century* (1987); *Church History: An Essential Guide* (1996).

Argentinian, Norberto Saracco;[32] the Peruvian, Bernardo Campos and the Chilean, Juan Sepulveda[33] (Miguez Bonino 1997, 64) with their expertise in Pentecostalism and many others. All of them have developed a critical analysis of the Latin American church, but none of them has given special and extended attention to the relationships of partnership in mission from a Latin American perspective. However, some contributions have been made implicitly through their important contributions to Latin American mission development, through what I can call partnership history or partnership as history. One of those contributions comes from *The Fullness of Mission* of René Padilla (1985, 129–141).[34] In this essay he included a brief account of the challenge of partnership and unity (Padilla 1985, ix, 133). Also Samuel Escobar gives very brief attention to new partnerships for mission in his book *The New Global Mission*[35] (2003, 164–167).

The Fraternidad Teológica Latinoamericana (FTL) was founded in 1970. Before that Escobar, Arana and Padilla in the context of the student work of IFES had been exploring the development of a theology of evangelization that would be at the same time evangelical and contextual. In that effort they had interacted critically with the movement ISAL (Church and Society in Latin America, WCC related) during the 1960s. The critical approach to liberation theology came later on; it was not the main motivation. After 1970 FTL theological work was carried on in a critical dialogue with liberation theologies on the left and church growth missiology on the right.[36] Thus the FTL was founded in 1970 in Cochabamba, Bolivia

---

32. Saracco's most important contribution to Latin American mission theology is *Argentinian Pentecostalism: Its History and Theology*, PhD thesis, University of Birmingham (1989). He also has written many articles, one of them, Charismatic Renewal and Social Change: A Historical Analysis from a Third-world Perspective. See his article in *Transformation* 1988 (Vol. 5, No. 4, October–December).

33. Sepúlveda has written "Indigenous Pentecostalism and the Chilean Experience", one of the chapters in *Pentecostals After a Century: Global Perspectives on a Movement in Transition* (1999).

34. For Padilla, partnership is no more than a myth if the West missiology maintains a one-way relationship with a younger church, which may or may not be regarded as independent (1985, 134).

35. Escobar's opinion is that global partnership of churches will be indispensable for mission in the twenty-first century and he challenges the missiological school of 'managerial missiology' (2003).

36. Information provided by Samuel Escobar to the author, 3 February 2011.

(Escobar 2002, 120; Heaney 2008, 60) as a result of a new theological understanding of mission theology after the First Latin American Congress of Evangelism held in Bogotá, Colombia in November 1969 (CLADE I). The main concern of the FTL was the development of a contextual theology of evangelization in dialogue with evangelical theologians in other parts of the world (Escobar 2002, 120). The FTL began on the margins of the dominant cultural establishments of Latin America, but at the centre of the missionary action of the churches. They reflected for the benefit of evangelical activists rather than for academics; it was acknowledged, however, that in those theologies the self-criticism, the return to biblical sources and the emphasis on relating theology and praxis were promising signs.[37] When the FTL was founded in 1970, they were part of a growing number of evangelical pastors, missionaries and theologians searching for answers to questions that came from evangelistic and missionary commitment within a context of social change in Latin America (Escobar 2002, 112). Escobar (1995, 2) points out that there was a commitment to the doing of theology that emerged from churches that were relatively young, working on the margins of the dominant cultural establishments of Latin America; it was a context of communities that saw the world as a territory to be "conquered for Christ",[38] and the gospel as a transforming message that was going to bring a new spiritual, social and political change.

Escobar provides some remarkable insights into the FTL.[39] First, during the 1970s, evangelical reflection about political responsibility in Latin America was set within the theological frame of the kingdom of God; in 1983 the issues of political power were addressed. The approach to the

---

37. See Escobar (1995, 2), "Faith and Hope for the Future: Toward a Vital Evangelical Theology for the 21st Century", presented first at the WEF 1995, and later appeared in the *Evangelical Review of Theology* (1996, October). In relation to liberation theologies, the most extensive organic works for the critical task within the FTL come from Andrew Kirk, Emilio A. Nunez and Samuel Escobar, and for developing a constructive task within the FTL, René Padilla produced *Mission Between the Times* (1985) and Orlando Costas *Christ Outside the Gate*. See further Escobar (2002, 114–15).

38. Escobar, "Faith and Hope for the Future"; see also Samuel Escobar, "Mañana: Discerning the Spirit in Latin America" *Evangelical Review of Theology* 20, no. 4 (1996): 312–326.

39. See further Escobar "Faith and Hope for the Future" and chapter X "From Mission to Theology" in Samuel Escobar, *Changing Tides: Latin America and World Mission Today* (New York: Orbis Books, 2002), 11–130.

issues of 'justice' and 'power' was basically christological in the work of Padilla and developed from the eschatological dimension of his Christology. Second, in the 1990s, two theological themes were related to intentional reflection on justice and power, and themes related to questions of 'poverty' and 'terrorism'. These are not theoretical questions for Latin American evangelicals; that reflection was focused on experiences as politicians and lawyers working in human rights issues, and pastors in areas of insurgency and counter-insurgency. And third, in the development of the FTL, one of the most important aspects of the Christian situation in Latin America was the change in the perception of history. In the academic atmosphere of Latin America, the concept of utopia had a powerful influence during this second half of the twentieth century. In fact one of the distinctive notes of Liberation Theologies was their use of Marxist categories for social analysis, historical criticism and the formulation of a political project. The most extensive study on the FTL is Sharon Heaney's *Contextual Theology for Latin America* (2008), where she presents systematically the historical background and primary themes of this significant theological movement in Latin America. Heaney's study contains the first overview of the Latin-American evangelical theology such as contextual hermeneutics, contextual theology, Christology, ecclesiology and missiology.

Other factors that influenced the theological agenda of the FTL sprang from the new presence of liberation theology as a result of post-conciliar Latin American Catholicism, the new challenges of communism to overcome poverty and corruption and the need for an evangelical ecclesiology that would respond to the demands of the radical Catholic theologians.[40] In brief, liberation theology emerges within the context of socio-political and economic conflicts in Latin America in answer to two very radical social documents produced by the Roman Catholic Church – *Populorum Progressio* (1967),[41] and the *Medellin Documents of the Latin American*

---

40. See further Heaney 2008, 13, 184–186.
41. Phillip Berryman (1987, 20), an ex-Catholic priest points out that one of the key documents was Pope Paul V's 1967 encyclical *Populorum Progressio* (On the Progress of Peoples), focusing on Third World development issues.

Episcopal Conference (CELAM, 1968).[42] Kirk (1980, 114–115) indicates that equally, the sense of guilt and mission, and the protest against the Latin American Roman Catholic Church were factors in the origins of the liberation theology. An attempt to define liberation theology is made by Kirk (1980, 117) when he affirms that "it is a revolutionary theory in the service of action, which seeks to change situations and systems of exploitation". Kirk (1980, 115–116) states that the liberation theology was born out of a protest against the prevailing social and political conditions of Latin America.[43] Liberation theology came to light in 1965 following the theological reflection of Vatican II about the need for a 'revolutionary theology' (Kirk 1979, 23).[44] Gutierrez (1973, 8–10) explains that the function of theology as critical reflection has been influenced by the presence of the following factors: the participation of Christians in important social movements of their time; the importance of human action as the point of departure for all reflection; the influence of Marxist thought focusing on praxis as a fruitful confrontation with theology; and the rediscovery of the eschatological dimension as the full and definitive encounter with the Lord and with the other men. The most exponential thinkers of liberation theology at its beginning were the Peruvian theologian, Gustavo Gutierrez

---

42. Gutierrez points out that these documents are intimately related to two themes: transformation of the Latin American reality and the search for new forms of the church's presence on the contemporary scene Gutierrez (1973, 108). See further Gustavo Gutierrez, A *Theology of Liberation* (1973, 107, 141). See also chapter 2 "The Immediate Origins" in *Liberation Theology: An Evangelical View from the Third World* (Kirk 1979, 16, 21, 27), and Muskus (2002, 8, 148, 153–160).

43. Kirk (1980, 115–116) insists that liberation theology arose as a sharp protest against the kind of theology being taught and studied in the academic centres of Western Europe and North America; second, he explains that liberation theology accepted the current explanation of the causes of under-development being put forward by a new generation of Latin American economists working with Marxists categories of analysis, and third, it is also pointed out that they believed that, in the light of increasing poverty and economic exploitation, Christian faith needed to adopt a particular ideological framework to give fresh impetus to its commitment (Kirk 1980, 127).

44. Certain political events such as the Cuban revolution, military coups in Brazil 1964, and the guerrilla insurgence in Colombia, which the priest Camilo Torres joined (Berryman 1987, 17–18), began to raise institutional questions. This historical context also includes the use of Marxist categories to explain the reasons for poverty in Latin America, the rejection of categories such as under-development elaborated in the United States and the rejection of the categories of development by economists and thinkers due to its liberal influence (Gutierrez 1973, 24–36; Kirk 1979, 23–24). Muskus (2002, 54) adds the influence of the Peruvian socialist thinker Jose Carlos Mariategui.

(born 1928),⁴⁵ the Uruguayan Jesuit, Juan Luis Segundo (1925–1996), the Brazilian theologians, Hugo Assmann (1933–2008)⁴⁶ and Leonardo Boff (born 1938),⁴⁷ the Catalan Jesuit, Jon Sobrino (1938) who worked in El Salvador, and the Protestant Brazilian, Rubem Alves (1933).⁴⁸

Kirk summarizes the main liberation theology's characteristics as follows (Kirk 1980, 116–118):

1. The development of the 'action-reflection' concept, where truth is grasped in experience only as the subject of liberating action.⁴⁹
2. The deliberate use of ideologies as part of theology's task and the church's mission.⁵⁰
3. The awareness of tendencies of harassment within the church, domestication of the language of liberation, and an oversimplification of theological questions by its main exponents (Segundo in Kirk 1980, 18).⁵¹

---

45. Gustavo Gutierrez is known as the father of the liberation theology; Gutierrez (born 8 June 1928 in Lima) is a Peruvian theologian and Dominican priest regarded as one of the principal founders of liberation theology in Latin America (Muskus 2002, 3–5) In *The Origins and Early Development of Liberation Theology in Latin America*, the Venezuelan Eddy Muskus (2002) provides a well-documented account of Gutierrez's Liberation theology and its origins.

46. The Brazilian Catholic pioneer of liberation theology Hugo Assmann, accused the Latin-American Catholic Church of isolating itself from the poor. In 1971 Gutierrez and Hugo Assmann, published full length books on liberation theology that mapped the terrain of the emerging questions; while Gutierrez' frame-work was that of Scripture and modern theology, Assmann emphasized a new method of theology; similarly the Argentinean Enrique Dussel suggested a new way of reading Latin American church history by proposing philosophical categories in relation to a situation of oppression (Berryman 1987, 24).

47. For a synthesis of liberation theology see *Introducing Liberation Theology* (Boff 1987).

48. One of Alves' important works is *Protestantism and Repression*. See Alves (1970).

49. Gutierrez states that to reflect on the basis of the historical praxis of liberation is to reflect in the light of the future, which is believed in and hoped for (Gutierrez 1973, 15).

50. Kirk (1979, 162) suggests that "perhaps one of the most important contributions of Marxist theory to biblical hermeneutics is its emphasis on the structural dimension of liberation, which implies discerning the fundamental play of economic forces as one aspect of man's present alienation". See further Kirk's analysis on Marxist interpretation within liberation theology (1979, *Liberation Theology*, chapter XVI).

51. Berryman (1987, 25) points out that liberation theologians began to consciously take Latin America as their context for raising questions, and adds: "As they realized that their theology was emerging out of a particular context, they began to see that the same thing was true of any theology – including the theology they had learned in Europe – so they began to see a theology of the North Atlantic as a theology of the rich world" (25).

4. A new hermeneutical process using the methodology of the hermeneutical circle for interpreting the Bible.[52] Juan Luis Segundo has a prominent place among the liberation theologians who argue for the *hermeneutic circle* as the central methodological tool.[53]

Integral Mission

The concept of integral mission has been a process of theological reflection. As Escobar explains, "several members of the FTL were engaged in evangelistic work, especially among students and professional people with the effort to communicate the basics of the Christian faith to people who had rejected any connection with churches and were sometimes adopting Marxism as a worldview" (2002, 119). In consequence, John A Mackay's christological agenda (119), the influences of Marxism in Latin America and the challenges of liberation theology and political changes became the basis for a new theological interpretation and debate inside an emerging group of Latin-American evangelical thinkers. In addition, as many of the missionaries working in Latin America came with a dispensationalist theological framework; another theological ingredient in the formation of the FTL was in relation to its critique to a kind of otherworldly pietistic

---

52. Kirk provided a brief description of the principal characteristics of a theological method within the liberation theology that differs from the old methods that has been elaborated over the centuries. See further Kirk (1979, 72–92).

53. Juan Luis Segundo, one of the founders of Latin American liberation theology, in his primary work *The Liberation of Theology* (1976), stands in line with Gutierrez when he says of the necessity of challenging the theological methodology in the sense that "it may be time to get down to analysing not so much the content of Latin American theology, but rather its methodological approach and its connection with liberation" (1976, 5). Thus Segundo's theology is to link the past with the present, therefore, the hermeneutic circle is needed, and consequently, he rejects the naïve belief that the word of God is applied to human realities inside some antiseptic laboratory that is totally immune to the ideological tendencies and struggle of the present day (1976, 7). That is why Segundo's own approach is summed up in the concept of the *hermeneutic circle*. Segundo defines the *hermeneutic circle* as "the continuing change in our interpretation of the Bible which is dictated by the continuing changes in our present-day reality, both individual and societal" (1976, 8). In Segundo's view, two preconditions are necessary for accomplishing the hermeneutic circle in theology: the first precondition is profound and enriching questions about our cultural and social reality; the second precondition is a new interpretation of the Bible to answer the new questions that arise from present reality (1976, 9). The term hermeneutical circle is usually referred back to Hans G. Gadamer who described it in his book *Truth and Method* (1982).

evangelicalism that had been brought to the Latin American soil (2002, 101). Dispensationalist views emphasize the 'dispensations' in which they divide biblical history into successive ages, the last of which will see Christ on the throne of a restored nation of Israel, in which the church has no part at all (Dann 2004, 411, Martin 1990, 48), and pietistic evangelicalism implies to be immersed in the spiritual life without consciousness of participation in the need of society (Bosch 1991, 252–253).[54] It has the characteristics, as Escobar explains, of a pragmatic view of Christian life and a personal experience on conversion in individual obedience to the divine commandments (2002, 101). Padilla (1985, 9) emphasizes that the concept of the church as an entity 'separated' from the world lends itself to all kind of false interpretation. Consequently, the FTL began to try to recover for the Latin American churches the fullness of evangelical Biblical theology, which has been defined as 'misión integral' or holistic mission.[55] This new missiological reflection on biblical Christology was a contribution at the Lausanne Congress in 1974 by Samuel Escobar and René Padilla.[56] In 2006, Padilla clarified again that they were concerned with holistic mission.[57] Therefore, integral mission proposes the inseparability of evangelism and social responsibility; it is the double mission mandate the church has to fulfill in the power of the Holy Spirit.

---

54. Bosch says: "In pietism the formally correct, cold, and cerebral faith of orthodoxy gave way to a warm and devout union with Christ. Concepts such as repentance, conversion, the new birth, and sanctification received new meaning. A disciplined life rather than sound doctrine, subjective experience of the individual rather than ecclesiastical authority, practice rather than theory – these were the hallmarks of the new movement", therefore, Bosch concludes that "the separation between the 'secular' and the 'religious' was particularly striking in the case of Pietism" (1991, 252–253, 276).

55. For Martin (1990, 131), the FTL aimed to be distinctively Latin American as well as distinctively evangelical. For him, this implies that "they wanted to peruse social issues without abandoning evangelism, deal with oppressive structures without endorsing violence, and bring left- and right-wing Protestants back together again" (131).

56. This theological influence made an impact that still has a strong influence on evangelical circles around the world.

57. For Yates, Padilla criticized the confusion between the worldly hope proclaimed by Marxism and Christian hope (Yates 1994, 202). Padilla mentioned in September 2006 at the Global Connections Forum held in London that they were not influenced by Marxism, this was not the case because they were concerned with holistic mission. (Personal data written at the Latin American Forum, Global Connections, London 24 September 2006). See also Sharon Heaney in *Contextual Theology for Latin America* (2008, 238–242).

The FTL has developed a consistent theological and missiological reflection through the different congresses organized since its foundation. CLADE I marks the formation of the FTL, and theological reflection on the kingdom of God was the framework in the 1970s (Escobar 2002, 145). CLADE II 1979 in Lima, and CLADE III 1992 in Quito, had 1008 participants with the slogan, "The whole gospel, for all peoples from Latin America" (2002, 164). As a consequence, mission from Latin America became part of the agenda which included a self-critical evaluation (165) and CLADE IV in Quito 2000, which I attended, had more that 1300 participants and the agenda was "The Evangelical Testimony towards the New Millennium: The Word, Spirit and Mission". Here pneumatological issues and the consequences of mission were addressed, and all the debates offered insights of biblical principles. The main concerns were spiritual warfare, faces of Latin American Protestantism, and stewards of creation. Six biblical plenary sessions were held with a clear emphasis on the third person of the Trinity: The Holy Spirit. (*Documento de Trabajo* CLADE IV, September 2000).[58]

Samuel Escobar, one of the founders of the Latin American Fraternity (FTL), offers some insight of partnership in his critical analysis of the mission enterprise, but he concentrates more on the historical interpretation of mission history with an application to the present church and the consequences for the Latin American church. Missionary cooperation in Escobar's view should be understood in the context of a dichotomy theology between evangelism and social responsibility developed through American missionaries working in Latin America (2002, 119). We agree with Escobar in the sense that there was both a lack of understanding of the social context and a lack of incarnate mission in the middle of Latin American history. However, one of the main issues was the lack of biblical teaching to develop a cooperating role between mission societies and the emergent Latin American church at the beginning of the twentieth century. For Escobar, the new ways of partnerships should include the reality of the new missionary era where "missionaries should flow ever more freely from and to all six continents in a spirit of humble service" (2003, 164).

---

58. For more details of CLADE I, II, III and IV see Heaney (2008, 62–68).

René Padilla (1985, 129–132) brings his perspective on partnership and points out that there is no room for the traditional distinction between sending churches and receiving churches and presents a challenge to fullness in mission by avoiding the emphasis on quantitative church growth, while proclaiming the gospel everywhere. In that context Padilla has challenged the church by saying that "Christian mission lies in the hands of Western strategists and specialists" (1985, 134), where they maintain a one-way relationship with a younger church. As a consequence he concludes that "as long as this situation endures, partnership is no more than a myth" (134). It seems to me that 'one way relationship' is another myth created by Western missiology that has been hindering mission partnership. In this respect, I agree with Padilla when he affirms that "partnership in mission is not merely a question of practical convenience but the necessary consequence of God's purpose for the church and for the whole of humanity revealed in Jesus Christ" (1985, 136).[59]

Padilla proposes a "radical restructuring of the economic relationships among Christians everywhere, to take seriously 'evangelical poverty' to develop a reciprocal giving between churches, avoiding paternalism and dependence with a more interdependent relationship" and to put in practice the nature of unity[60] (134–136), which for Andrew Kirk is the "essence of the church" (Kirk 1999, 186). Similarly Kirk makes some assumptions on partnership when he affirms that "partnership in Christian mission expresses a relationship between churches based on trust, mutual recognition and reciprocal interchange" (Kirk 1999, 184). For Kirk the nearest equivalent of partnership is *koinonia,* which means, "partaking together in a group which has a common identity, goals and responsibilities" (188). From this assumption, he develops a theology of partnership based on the New Testament which is as follows: sharing in a common project, sharing of gifts, sharing of material resources, and sharing in suffering. In analysing

---

59. Padilla argues that partnership in mission from the West is developed from a position of political and economic power and with the assumption of superiority in matters of culture and race (1985,134) and that most traditional mission agencies can no longer avoid the issue of partnership in mission (135).

60. Kirk states that all churches, theologically speaking, belong to one another as God, according to 1 Corinthians 1:9, has called each into the fellowship *(Koinonia)* of his Son Jesus Christ our Lord (1999, 187).

Padilla and Kirk's thinking we see that mission partnership as the need to find new perspectives of interpretation and to recognize the historical, theological and missiological implications, which affect the relationship of all Christian partnership. It seems that Padilla is more radical than Kirk in the way that Padilla argues clearly against the Western mission partnership.

Towards a definition of partnership in mission

A brief reference to some definitions of mission partnership will show the main historical and theological emphasis, and the missiological approach that has been given to this concept. Words like cooperation, collaboration, networking, synergism, and strategic alliance have been used in the evangelical arena at various times.

According to Lothar Baurochse (1996, 89–92), the term 'partnership' came to the fore in 1905 at the beginning of the twentieth century and before the First World War (1914–1918), and was related to the British colonial empire, where the discussion was about self-determination for the so-called colonial countries. This term was used to regulate policies between the colonial and the British governments, and this influence affected the use of this term in theological debate. White colonies like Canada, Australia and New Zealand had 'relative independence' (90), but not Africa and India. In this way, complaints about self-determination from colonial countries are related to partnership, and after 1919, 'trusteeship' was coined as a term to allow colonies self-responsibility, but with the retention of some British governmental power and a protective function towards the colonies. Then 'indirect rule' was established to give more governmental power to the British colonies.

It was after 1942 that the British government defined a new policy towards its colonies with the term partnership as a new relationship between the United Kingdom and the colonies. However, during the process of decolonization in the 1960s, one of the concepts of partnership was understood in the political arena as "demands for equal rights of the white minorities in the colonies" (92). My analysis is that the British government believed that overseas partners were not mature enough to rule themselves and made the process of self-government and handover of power too slow for the colonized countries. As Baurochse points out, the British empire "did not want to give up their power and influence entirely to the Asian or African partners, because overseas partners were not yet mature enough, without education, capabilities or personnel with leadership qualities" (93). In consequence, a kind of political, economic and social protest came to light in the colonial countries due to bad relationships cultivated from the political and economic empires and decolonization came to an end in the 1960s and 1970s. Our hypothesis is that this political spirit permeated the term partnership and its use in mission conferences from the beginning in 1905.

It is clear that control of power was the motive to rule those countries overseas dominated by the British Empire. In this context the term partnership was used after the Second World War "to consolidate the greater unity of the ecumenical mission enterprise" (1996, 93). It was a borrowed concept with a political, economic and social consequence for the mission enterprise. Why? Because this term permeates the mission theology's perspectives in contrast to what I want to call a reciprocal contextual collaboration in Christian mission. We need to bear in mind that partnership is used in the evangelical movement as a concept of unity and good relationships between those who are involved in mission partnership. This is one explanation for why evangelicals still use this term for the theological and missiological debate of the relationships in the *missio Dei*. 'Partnership' was theologically coined after Whitby 1947 to define mission relationships between North and South in obedience to God's mandate.

We have the insights of the Anglican Bishop Stephen Neil, who developed an important role in the mission enterprise with his theological understanding of partnership between the 1940s and the 1960s. Neil explains that partnership in mission "starts with the recognition that the source of fellowship is in a common obedience to the living Word of God, given once for all in Jesus Christ, yet given anew through the Holy Spirit in every generation" (Neil 1952, 21). He then applies this assumption to the 'Whitby declaration' within an ecclesiological perspective by saying that partnership has consequences for personnel, finance, policy and administration (1952, 21).

In his book *Christian Partnership*, Stephen Neill (1952, 11) draws attention to the analysis of the Whitby mission conference organized by the Committee of the International Missionary Council in June 1947; this conference was held after the Second World War and partnership and relationships were thoroughly discussed. It was recognized at that time problems of the church in a worldwide sense, giving their partners an absolute spiritual equality, control of power to frame their own policies, and to bear their own distinctive witness in the world (Neill 1952, 14). What is very interesting for the present church is that at the conference, South and North mission leaders discussed partnership separately, but amazingly the conclusions were very similar. In consequence, this was one reason why the document of the Whitby Conference is cited in different books and articles of mission, and it brings different emphases and perspectives when we challenge our minds about the complexities of Christian partnership. We conclude that, while our points of view can be similar, the practical application, which is related to missiology, tends to be different, and this reflects the difference in the Western and the Latin American mentality.

Historically speaking, Neill explains that the Christian church in the West has myths to develop their mission agenda and the idea of going out to non-Christian people was one of those myths which motivated people to mission. Robert Beckford goes beyond Neil and affirms, "I do not believe that theology is neutral or objective. Such myths in white Christianity in Britain have acted as smoke screens which maintain white male elitism" (Beckford 2000, 27). What was the main issue? Identifying the evangelistic task with Western culture. It is therefore imperative to analyse the danger of new mythologies from the Majority World that will bring their own mission mythologies for developing a mission theology of partnership. As noted by Lee Hong Jun, the mythology of Korean Pentecostalism has made a religio-social myth of miraculous growth with a syncretistic combination of capitalism, shamanism and religious fundamentalism (Anderson 1999, 138). Equally this phenomenon would be a risk in Africa, Asia and Latin America, bringing syncretistic consequences for partnership in mission. In contrast to the Western mission mythology, partnership for Neil must include a clear relation to policy-making; administrative issues should be treated as part of life, avoiding defective theology, seeing the church's mission as witness as the very nerve centre, prayer as intercession and sharing the gospel with understanding of the mystery of the cross (Neil 1952, 36–38).

In the consultation of the World Evangelical Fellowship held in Manila in June 1992, 95 mission leaders from 35 nations discussed "Towards Interdependence Partnerships", from the perspective of indigenous, national movements, regional and international groups (Taylor 1994, 1). In this consultation, Luis Bush[61] (Taylor 1994, 4) defines partnership as an association of two or more autonomous bodies that have formed a trusting relationship and fulfil agreed upon expectations by sharing complementary strengths and resources to reach their mutual goal. Lothar Baurochse has made a deeper analysis of partnership from the ecumenical perspective, starting from Edinburgh 1910 until the assembly of the World Council of Churches in Canberra in 1991. She deliberately goes further, asking for what she calls inter-church relationship between churches and church districts in Germany. For Baurochse "partnership is formed usually because of personal relations or contacts. The idea of seeking a partnership relationship with Christians overseas, in the case in African countries, stems almost always from the fact that members of the congregation have some personal connection to the partner country or partner's church" (1996, 97).

The evangelical American, Phill Butler (2006, 5), started to develop his ideas of partnership from 1986. Actually he uses the phrase 'strategic alliances' for partnership, which implies a concept under the influence of the American desire to achieve goals strategically. This definition comes from a global contextual perspective of mission and makes a contribution due to its wider impact on the mission mandate. For Butler, partnership means "two or more people or ministries who agree to work together to accomplish a common vision" (2006, 2). He goes further and refers to strategic partnership in this way: "strategic partnership is looking at the whole challenge; identifying all the needed resources; then engaging those varied elements in a single lasting collaboration. Realizing a challenging goal that

---

61. In the middle of the growing evangelical mood for practical cooperation in mission, Bush presented his definition of partnership at the Working Consultation on partnership at Wheaton, Illinois, held 9–11 May 1991. See more in his article "In Pursuit of True Christian Partnership: A Biblical Basis from Philippians" (Kraakevik and Welliver 1991).

may be simple to state but complex to achieve" (2006, 6). Finally, he arrives at his conclusion by saying that partnership is "any group of individuals or organizations, sharing a common interest, who regularly communicate, plan, and work together to achieve a common vision beyond the capacity of any one of the individual partners" (2006, 34–35).

Daniel Rickett,[62] an American mission researcher, and the Argentinian missiologist, Omar Gava, who works for COMIBAM (2005, 12–14), published a book in Spanish called *Alianzas Estrategicas [Strategic Alliances]* where they defined partnership in terms of self-development which avoids falling into paternalism. For them self-development includes growth in learning, growing to make appropriate changes. Above all, they define alliances for development in Christian ministry as "a relation of cooperation between two autonomous bodies in order to train one another to make possible a growth in their abilities to initiate and to accomplish things for the gospel" (2005, 15).

The former leading South African missiologist, David Bosch,[63] does not mention mission partnership explicitly, but we understand that he develops mission partnership inclusively in his "elements of an emerging ecumenical missionary paradigm" (Bosch 1991, 368), because he points out that there is a mission with a creative tension (381) and that the universal and the local church are part of this missionary tension, which includes participation in any social, political and economical project (387). He points out that "Christian mission gives expression to the dynamic relationship between God and the world, portrayed first in the story of the covenant people of Israel, and then, supremely, in the birth, life, death, resurrection, and exaltation of Christ" (Bosch 1991, 9). In analysing this, mission partnership in Bosch's perspective conveys a historical, theological and missiological

---

62. In his book *Making your Partnership Work* Rickett adds that partnership is not a technology that can be engineered although one has all the right parts. For him, principles and practices for mission partnership should come from experience including without substitution the careful and prayerful reflection on the Word of God for divine guidance (2002, XV).

63. David Bosch was born in South Africa in 1929 on 13 December and died in a car accident on 15 April 1992 in South Africa at the age of 62; just one year after *Transforming Mission* was published (Kritzinger "Klippies" JNJ and Willem Saayman Editors 1996, 1; Bosch 1991, xiii).

approach to the relations between God and church, church and missions, and mission and missions. He mentions that "a spirit of cooperation between denominations in America[64] was until the early nineteenth century without a clear dividing line between pre-and post-millennialists until the new era of controversy" (1991, 315). This is explained in relation to eschatological concern for the church, which is part of the mission theology frame that has hindered partnership in mission due to the different eschatological emphases by denominations and mission societies.

In summary, we arrive at the conclusion that, while Baurochse emphasizes the historical perspective of mission partnership, Butler suggests more a strategic partnership in terms of strategic alliances. In this way, Daniel Rickett and Omar Gava define partnership in terms of self-development which avoids falling into paternalism. All of these definitions contrast with Bosch in the way that Bosch's concern is the whole mission enterprise relating to God, church, mission and the world. It seems to me that Bosch has no intention to show that mission partnership is joining together to do something for God's glory, but to understand the dynamic relationship between God and the world, and God and the church.

In their book *Promise of Partnership*, James Whitehead and his wife Evelyn argue that "partnership, both in the gospel and in contemporary life, is an experience of shared power" (1991, 8). They make a contribution by saying that using equality as a criterion for partnership is tricky. They explain this in the following way:

> Equality stresses sameness, while partnership delights in diversity. Partners recognize that their differences often expand and enrich their relationships. Equality, as a quantitative image, hints that we should be keeping score. But measuring our respective contribution more often defeats than strengthens partnership. More than on strict equality, partnership

---

64. However, after 1830, competition started between denominations due to the theological interpretation of pre- and postmillennialists, a term that was coined in the 1840s. See more Bosch (1991, 315). It seems to be that the era of controversy emphasized differences rather than similarities.

depends on mutuality. The giving and the receiving go both ways (1991, 8).

According to this concept, for Whitehead the giving and the receiving should be two-way traffic where partners share what they have in their hands. This partnership should be developed with the ingredient of a mutual relationship, recognizing the value of each partner, and with respect, which helps to develop a mutual exchange of gifts. Letty Russell, talking about the theology of partnership in *The Future of Partnership,* gives clues and insights into the nature of partnership in the following way: "Partnership may be described as a new focus of relationship in which there is the continuing commitment and common struggle in interaction with a wider community context – such a partnership of Christians could be described as a new focus of relationship in common history of Jesus Christ that sets persons free for others" (1979, 18–19). Both Whitehead and Russell agree that mission partnership has to be orientated towards relationships. While Whitehead emphasizes a missiological point of view, the practice; Russell stresses partnership mission theology, the theory.

A new definition: reciprocal contextual collaboration in Christian mission

Evangelicals adopted 'partnership' after Whitby 1947 for the theological and missiological debate of the relationships in the *missio Dei*. However, Whitby 1947 had a weak impact on relationships of mission; one reason was the myths[65] of the Western church to develop their mission agenda. Therefore, I agree with the view that 'partnership in obedience' was not achieved properly by Whitby 1947.

Butler (2006) develops partnership from 1986, through 'strategic alliances'. Manila 1992 discussed 'partnerships', from the perspective of

---

65. Neill (1952) mentions the myth that the Christian church in the West had to develop their mission agenda with the idea of going out to non-Christian people, which motivated people to mission. Beckford (2000) adds that myths in white Christianity in Britain are identified with the evangelistic task with Western culture.

indigenous, national movements, regional and international groups. In this consultation, Bush (Taylor 1994) emphasizes partnership as an association of two or more autonomous bodies to reach their mutual goal. Baurochse (1996) asks for inter-church relationship, concentrated in a chronological perspective on the relationship, and Rickett and Gava (2005) define partnership as self-development, which avoids paternalism. Bosch (1991) does not mention mission partnership explicitly but inclusively in this process of partnership concept.[66]

Here, I attempt to give a definition of what I call 'reciprocal contextual collaboration', which highlights the difference from the old concept of partnership in a new way. Reciprocal contextual collaboration can be defined as a reciprocal relationship of harmonious freedom in creative tension, which exists between two or more of Christ's disciples as they seek to accomplish the *missio Dei* through the christological double mandate, which includes commitment to the cosmos and people for the glory and benefits of God's kingdom. The christological mandate implies a historical, theological, political, economic, social and cultural dimension of the redemptive mission.

By reciprocal contextual collaboration we mean:
- 'Reciprocal' implies that we are the body of Christ with diverse and multiple ministries, with gifts and resources to help one another reciprocally.
- 'Contextual' implies the incarnational attitude of Christian mission that includes conscious acknowledgement of the reality of the social, political, religious, cultural and economical context.
- 'Collaboration' implies that we acknowledge that the *missio Dei* belongs to God and we are just collaborators in God's kingdom in freedom of prophetic imagination.[67]

---

66. It seems to me as if the Protestant mission had made a political and religio-social myth of partnership growth with a syncretistic combination of capitalism and managerial missiology, there is mission theology space for a more and new appropriate definition related to partnership in Christian mission. One example of this assumption is the idea of going out to non-Christian people, which motivated people to mission (Neill 1952).

67. Prophetic imagination means the innovative ways to develop the mission task for the fulfilment of the *missio Dei*. Also related to this are the new ways of non-Western traditional views of doing mission, which includes missiological imagination.

This definition, which will be developed in the following chapters, will be used as part of my analysis of relationships in mission partnership. At the outset, three points should be clarified: first, reciprocal collaboration is not primarily quantitative, but instead is qualitative, because reciprocity is strongly related to the pneumatogical work of the Spirit who empowers the work of each partner in mission within a relational relationship; second, reciprocity relates more to relationships between people rather than to structural or managerial missiology, which emphasizes the organization since reciprocity is rooted in the spiritual, moral, and supra-cultural biblical values of unity, truth, trust, humility, patience, harmony, thankfulness, relational commitment, flexibility (flexible policy), co-responsibility, accountability, local decision making, respect for personal identity and interdependence; third, reciprocal collaboration implies the rejection of any sense of superiority or inferiority, as reflected in attitudes of paternalism, colonialism, imperialism, individualism and independentism. We have been created in the image of a relational God, who challenges us to prioritize partnership in mission according to the pattern of biblical relationships, which is linked to the intentional action of partnering with others. The joy of true relational partnership of Christian commitment to Christ in love, peace and harmony has a pivotal link with the glory of God the Father, Son and the Holy Spirit. Therefore, the nature of reciprocal contextual collaboration is rooted in the essence of biblical relationships.

It is within such a definition of reciprocal contextual collaboration, as Bosch implies, that there lies a rediscovery of the concept of the body of Christ and the missiological insight of the Christian mission as the church which shares a common destiny (1991, 362). I have sought to avoid the psychology of separatism (the cultural attitude) in order to reconstruct a definition with reference to an epistemology of participation in unity, but with reciprocity; of participation in love, while bearing in mind the context in which the mission task is developed; and of participation in hope, coupled with mature collaborative spirit in mission. "Reciprocal contextual collaboration" has been defined with the following presuppositions in mind:

- A historical perspective: The Enlightenment,[68] which prepared the way for modern liberalism, brought about the idea that every person was free to pursue their own happiness. This philosophy led to an exaggerated self-confidence, an excess of autonomy, deep autonomy, a misunderstanding of freedom, and the refusal to risk interdependence (Bosch 1991, 362). We have to bear in mind that reciprocal contextual collaboration arose out of a world of globalized interdependence.
- Theological perspective: The biblical teaching on Trinitarian theology which originates the 'helping one another', provides the fundamental basis for reciprocal collaboration in the body of Christ.
- Missiological perspective: Contextualization in mission helps us to define the real understanding and implicitness of mission activity within different cultures and assures us that the gospel is translatable.

---

68. A philosophical movement of the 18th century stressing the importance of reason and individualism instead of tradition and established doctrines, which brought about many humanitarian reforms; it is often considered as the starting point of the modern era.

CHAPTER 2

Partnership in Mission and its Theology

Introduction

Despite a much more mature theology of mission, which includes a Trinitarian theology (Migliore[1] 1991; Grenz[2] 2004) developed by Western

---

1. Daniel Migliore (1991) in *Faith Seeking Understanding* states the need for a critical reflection on God's power and presence in Trinitarian terms. He points that God must be seen "not as an all-controlling heavenly monarch but as the triune God who lives and acts in mutual self-giving and community-forming love" (xv). Stanley J. Grenz, who studied under the supervision of Wolfhart Pannenberg, in his book *Rediscovering the Triune God,* introduces a chapter on the 'Trinitarian Theological Story', and states that wherever the story of the doctrine of the Trinity is told in the last hundred years, specially following the First World War, the rediscovery of the doctrine of the Trinity must be given centre stage. The rebirth of Trinitarian theology has to be presented as the far-reaching theological development of the century. See further reading (2004, 1–5). Jurgen Moltmann (born in 1926), Wolfhart Pannenberg (born in 1928), and Robert Jason (born in 1930) develop a Trinitarian theology by the working of the three Trinitarian persons in history. In their estimation, the triune God emerges as the God of history (73). Grenz also presents the Trinitarian theology of Karl Barth, Karl Rahner, Leonardo Boff and others in making a critical analysis in their works. See (Grenz 2004).

2. Grenz notes that, according to the two church historians, John P. Whalen and Joraslav Pelikan, the formulation of the doctrine of the Trinity became the most important theological achievement of the first five centuries of the church. It is noted that a deplorable amnesia forms a central characteristic of the modern church. In consequence a renaissance was necessary in the very Trinitarian theology of the church, initiated by Friedrich Schleiermacher (1768–1834) with his monumental work *The Christian Faith*; George W. F. Hegel (1770–1831), who became the most important example of nineteenth-century intellectual history (bear in mind that philosophers, and not theologians, played the prominent role in keeping alive the idea of the Trinity during the Enlightenment); the Protestant theologian Karl Barth who proposes that the only true analogy to the Word of God is the doctrine of the Trinity of God; the Catholic theologian Karl Rahner with his 'Rahner's Rule' (known for this approach since 1980s) states: "The 'economic' Trinity is the 'immanent' Trinity and the 'immanent' Trinity is the

academics after the First and Second World Wars, there is a danger that aspects of partnering look as though both the North and the South churches give glory to one of the partners rather than to God. For this reason, I want to analyse some key elements that may help us to understand what the biblical basis for a good theology of partnership is.

In this chapter, I will therefore give a synthetic analysis of partnership in mission and its theology and the way practitioners and theologians have understood this partnership in mission, explaining both positive and negative tensions. We will analyse why theology has an important role in developing a mission partnership. From this perspective we will study very briefly the *missio Dei*, God's kingdom, God's church, christological mission partnership and Paul's understanding of mission partnership theology.

Partnership and the *missio Dei*

The question we will attempt to answer here is this: What is the nature of partnership in mission? Are partners giving themselves glory rather than God? This chapter will focus on an analysis between the *missio Dei* concept and its influence through the Trinitarian view of the Christian movement. The *missio Dei* concept and its understanding in historical perspective are always in connection with the kingdom of God and the church. In this sense, it seems that the term *missio Dei* related to the doctrine of the Trinity goes back to Augustine and the thirteenth-century scholastics like Thomas Aquinas (Bevans and Schroeder 2004, 289; Moreau 2000, 632); but it was at the Tambaran IMC Conference 1938 and during Willingen IMC Conference 1952 that the term undergirded the theological discussion in conciliar Protestantism, but not through the term as such, but in calling for

---

'economic' Trinity"; Jurgen Moltmann, one of the best known Reformed theologians in the twentieth century, states that the genesis of Trinitarian theology lies in history, above all in the history of Jesus Christ, and also in the history of God viewed as the history of the communal relationship of the three divine persons; Wolfhart Pannenberg, with his expertise in the relationship between theology and science, has offered a systematic and philosophical orientated development of the idea that the Trinity is the fullness of the historical process (2004, 17, 25, 38, 57, 73, 75, 88–89). See further reading in Grenz (2004).

a Trinitarian understanding of mission rather than an ecclesio-centric one (Davies 2006, 143). Also it was after the Willingen Conference of 1952 that the German missiologist Karl Hartenstein[3] coined the phrase *missio Dei* with the emphasis on the sending of the Son, with an inclusive aim of restoration of the whole creation (Engelsviken 2003; Davies 2006, 143; Bevans and Schroeder 2004, 288).

The Evangelical Dictionary of World Missions (Moreau 2000, 631, 638) defines the *missio Dei* as,

> The missio Dei (lit. 'sending of God' in Latin) is everything God does for the communication of salvation and, in a narrow sense, everything the church itself is sent to do. The missio Dei *is therefore* the mediate purpose of the Triune God in the sending of the Son and giving the church the task of world evangelization. Recently many have acknowledged *the holistic nature of the task, such that it includes* social responsibility (Italics mine).

I understand that *missio Dei* is not the same topic as Trinitarian theology. *Missio Dei* on the one hand, speaks specifically of God's plan and purposes for humanity in terms of creation, the fall, salvation and the consummation of God's sovereign reign over all things. Missio Dei came into theological and missiological thinking in the 1950s as a way of expressing the relationship between God's redeemed people and the redemption (or restoration) of the created order. It put the question of the *missio ecclesiae* into its proper perspective. Trinitarian theology, on the other hand, is designed to clarify,

---

3. John A. McIntosh, in his definition of the *missio Dei*, mentions that this was first used in a missionary sense by Hartenstein in 1934, motivated by Karl Barth's emphasis on the *actio Dei* – the action of God, over against the human-centred focus of liberal theology at that time. Later, the Dutch missiologist Johannes C. Hoekendijik, in 1960, at the world conference of the World Student Christian Federation in Strasbourg urged the need to develop an understanding of the *missio Dei* "as the world for human affairs and the human condition, instead of the church" and to push the realization for 'shalom'. These ideas appear to dominate the subsequent WCC reports after the 1960s, and the new missionary pattern was expressed in 'God–world–church' meaning that the church should act in partnership with the sending God, not by world evangelization but by promoting political and economic welfare. See more in *The Evangelical Dictionary of World Missions* (2000, 632).

as far as is possible when speaking about God, the relations between the three persons of the Godhead (technically in terms of begotteness and procession), and to define in what sense God can be both a unity and a trinity, both singular and plural. In the second place, Trinitarian theology seeks to understand the way in which the Trinitarian God relates to the created universe as Father, Son and Holy Spirit, Creator, Redeemer and Sanctifier. Of course, the *missio Dei* is really the *missio Trinitatis*.

Kirk (1999, 25) defines the *missio Dei* as the purposes and activities of God in and for the whole universe, and Pachuau[4] (Corrie 2007, 232–234) emphasizes the mission activity of the triune God, which has important theological implications for the unity of the church's mission, and can be seen in two approaches: the church as the principal vehicle of God's mission, and God's activity in the world over and beyond the church. Therefore, I assume that the *missio Dei*[5] is grounded in a Trinitarian theology which derives from the very nature of God himself and from this assumption emerges the nature of partnership in mission, where the existence and church's purpose are inseparable from God's mission rooted in the undivided being and act of God (Flett 2009, 8; Guder, 64).

In Bosch's view it was after the First World War in 1932, at the Brandenburg Missionary Conference, that Karl Barth became the first scholar to introduce mission as an activity of God himself (Bosch 2001, 389; Davies[6] 2006, 143). As a result this offered a new theological paradigm, and at the IMC Conference of Willingen in 1952[7] it was presented

---

4. Lalsangkima Pachuau is Associate Professor of History and Theology of Mission at Asbury Theological Seminary, Wilmore USA.

5. According to these definitions, the *missio Dei* is primarily an action which starts from God and is delegated to the church for the accomplishment of God's mission. Van Engen (1996, 27, 37, 42) in *Mission on the Way* in the context of discussing the question of constructing theologies in specific contexts, emphasizes that mission is the *missio Dei*, and yet the *missio Dei* happens in specific places and times in our context, and its content, validity and meaning are derived from Scripture; its action, significance, and transforming power work today. See also Philip L Wickeri's article *Mission from the Margins* (2004), and Chris Wright's book *The Mission of God* (2006).

6. For Davies (2006, 142) it was Barth who re-established the emphasis on a Trinitarian missiology, recovering God's self-revelation through the message of God's saving and redeeming activity in Jesus Christ and the Holy Spirit.

7. The WCC celebrated in 2002 the 50th anniversary of the Willingen conference and made an evaluation of what was said at the IMC conference in 1952. Jacques Matthey

with three main emphases (Bosch, 390): (1) mission was understood as being derived from the very nature of God, (2) mission was put in the context of the doctrine of the Trinity, not ecclesiology or soteriology, and (3) mission was emphasized as the Trinitarian theology of the Father, the Son and the Spirit sending the church into the world. In consequence, we need to bear in mind that a positive mission tension at Willingen was the starting point for understanding the participation of the church in the sending of God, the mission of God being linked to the doctrine of Trinity. I agree with Bosch when he affirms that the innovation shows that the *missio Dei* concept proclaims not primarily an activity of the church, but an attribute of God (2001, 390). As a result a new understanding of *missio Dei* was adopted by the conciliar Protestant church, then the Eastern Orthodox church, Catholic theology and later by many evangelicals (2001, 391).

Since the days of the German missiologist George F. Vicedom's *Mission of God*,[8] in the 1960s,[9] the phrase *missio Dei* was adopted into Protestant missionary circles starting at the Willingen Conference of the IMC (Pomerville 1985, 138). For Vicedom, *missio Dei* had a Trinitarian content, theology and terminology (138). Accepting this assumption, the Pentecostal scholar Paul Pomerville (137) in his book *The Third Force in*

---

brings an interesting evaluation and points out that this conference was held in a time of major missiological crisis to define what mission was in a time of uncertainty. He adds that today there is an analogy with our present situation due to the fact that after September 11th there is a new political and economic context in the majority churches which seem to move toward minority status or, in my perspective, less power and influence. For Matthey, Willingen did not come to a satisfactory approval of missiological priorities but Willingen brought a Trinitarian basis for mission which was related to the *missio Dei* concept, with God as the main actor in mission, and he concludes by saying that Willingen could have become the starting point for an enlarged ecumenism, leading to much closer cooperation and relationship with Pentecostals but because of the contextual interpretation of *missio Dei*, it contributed to aggravating the already existing split with Protestant mission organizations which led to the formation of two competing movements as from 1974 (Matthey 2007, 1–9).

8. For an overview of the implication of mission theology and the *missio Dei* described by Vicedom, see Van Engen (2000, 151).

9. The missiological interpretation of the 1960s is explained in three major influences as follows: (1) the structural influence with the integration of the IMC into the WCC; (2) the birth of the Trinitarian concept of the *missio Dei* which derives from the Trinitarian being and action of God; and (3) the influence of ecumenical missiology with a series of study groups examining the missionary structure of the congregation. See Van Engen (2000, 150–152).

Missions analyses the concept of *missio Dei* and explains that a redefinition of mission lies behind this concept, which is not new but was used by conciliar missiologists[10] and Roman Catholic missiology. He points out that the *missio Dei* concept arose in connection with a discussion of the Trinitarian view of mission with the principle of delegated mission and the roles of the Son and the Spirit in commissioning the church in mission (1985, 137). At the same time, Pomerville (1985, 138–143) takes account of H. H. Rosin's theological explanation of the *missio Dei* concept, which can be summarized as follows:

1. The *missio Dei* concept originally refers to the Trinitarian view of mission. This was used by conciliar missiologists to support a new way of understanding mission.
2. The *missio Dei* in the Trinitarian sense refers to God as the protagonist of mission (He sends), but also the one who is sent. The Son is sent (Gal 4:4–6); the Holy Spirit is sent (John 14:16); and the disciples are sent (John 17:18).
3. One of the *missio Dei* issues is how to differentiate between God's immediate activity and God's mediate activity in the world. Also there should be a clear distinction between God's providential activity and God's redeeming activity.
4. Finally, for Pomerville, there is a hermeneutical error in the *missio Dei* concept that would compromise the heart of God's mission, which is the Great Commission mission, because encompassing both the evangelistic and cultural mandate is problematic, and the praxis nature of mission strategy brings the theological issue of biblical authority into the arena for the twenty-first century mission enterprise. The reason for this interpretation, in Pomerville's view (1985, 140–141), is that the *missio Dei* began to put too much emphasis on the world's mission agenda

---

10. Pomerville argues that the change emphasized more the world than the church, instead of the view God-Church-world, conciliar missiologists moved to God-world-church. See more in Van Engen (2000, 145–156) *Mission on the Way*, especially chapter 8 "Conciliar Mission Theology 1930s–1990s", with a wider explanation of the *missio Dei* context.

rather than on the mission of the church.[11] The ecclesio-centric view of mission (the missionary activity of the church) moved to God's action in history (God's redemptive action in the world). Therefore, for Pomerville the authority of the Great Commission (the evangelistic mandate) seems to be diluted and replaced by the needs of the world's mission agenda.[12] In contrast with Pomerville's view, a proper understanding of the *missio Dei* relates, as we mentioned before, to God's mission activity in the world within history.

This summary seems to create a negative tension in that Pomerville is arguing for the limitless use of the *missio Dei* concept due to the emphasis of contextualization theology, an effort to make theology relevant to a new context of needs, bringing a more holistic view of mission, but with the danger of diluting the evangelistic mandate and promoting the absence of biblical authority. In terms of these assumptions, two points are clearly important for partnership in the twenty-first century: first, to revitalize the church's mission activity with the emphasis on the *missio Dei* theology and, second, to clarify the emphasis of distorted understanding of God's mission simply as an individualist tendency of salvation, lacking interest in the recovery of the creation for God's kingdom, which negatively affects a biblical theology of partnership. The *missio Dei* implies the undivided being and act of God, hence, there is no first and second step in the *missio Dei* as was stated in the past by emphasizing the sending God (Guder 2009, 63).

In regard to *missio Dei* theology, Miguez Bonino emphasizes that, 'it is God's person and not only God's action that originates impulse for

---

11. For Richebacher, "the church no longer had a part in God's mission, by bringing people into the body of Christ. The church simply became a visible sign of God's eschatological activity without being a goal in itself". See further Wilhelm Richebacher, "Missio Dei: The Basis of Mission Theology or a Wrong Path?" (*International Review of Mission*, Vol. XCII, No. 367 October 2003, p. 593).

12. This is a negative tension needs to be dealt with as a great concern for evangelicals. Richebacher points out that due to this theological polarization, the opposing interpretations of the *missio Dei* concept have produced a split between the evangelical churches and the ecumenical movement. See Richebacher, (*International Review of Mission*, Vol. XCII, No. 367 October 2003, p. 593).

Christianity' (Davies 2006, 141).[13] This is due to the fact that the church has both a missionary dimension[14] and a missionary intention (Newbigin 1958, 21; Bosch 2001, 373). A Catholic approach offered by Bevans and Schroeder[15] considers the *missio Dei* as mission in the participation of the triune God (2004, 286). This perspective[16] on Trinitarian theology starts with the interpretation of mission as "the continual self-giving and self-revelation of God within the history of creation; Trinitarian processions are understood not only as movements within the mystery of God, as such, but as God moving in saving love within the world" (287). With that assumption Bevans and Schroeder arrive at the conclusion that the church is the chosen people of God as agent and co-operator in God's mission plan to the whole of creation and not just a saving divine community (287).

In other words, the *missio Dei* is really the *missio Trinitatis*[17] (Kirk 1999, 27) at work since the creation (Genesis chapter 1, also see Moltmann 1981,

---

13. Paul Davies interprets Miguez Bonino's *missio Dei* theology as the *Opera Dei Personalia* which express the work of the inner life of the Trinity; for Miguez Bonino it is not only the action of God but also the triune being of God, the very life of God and he brings an understanding of the relationships between the members of the Trinity. See more in Davies (2006, 141ss).

14. In Bosch's perspective the missionary dimension relates to a local church's life mission expressed in its worship, welcome to outsiders, members equipped for serving God in society, etc., and the missionary intention directs involvement in society where the church works in such a way for evangelism, justice and peace (Bosch 2001, 373). Just teaching the double mandate will not be enough to accomplish God's mission intention which is part of the *missio Dei* concept equally as the emphasis of God's mission dimension and, secondly, involvement in society will be vital to strengthening evangelical missiology.

15. This understanding comes from two documents of mission: The Vatican Council II, *Ad Gentes – Decree on the Church's Mission Activities,* and The Vatican Council II, *Lumen Gentium – Dogmatic Constitution on the Church* (Bevans and Schroeder 2004, xxi–xxii, 286–304).

16. In comparison, the theological approach of the *missio Dei* theology in Catholic and evangelical theology shows differences but we need to bear in mind the historical fact that it was the Protestant movement that influenced the Trinitarian Catholic theology of the Vatican Council II, *Ad Gentes, Decree on the Church's Missionary Activity.* This is the influence of Protestant mission theology, started by Karl Barth in 1932 and then Karl Hartenstein, who in 1934 coined the term *missio Dei* to distinguish it from the term *missio ecclesiae*, and Lesslie Newbigin in 1952. See more in Bevans and Schroeder (2004, 290).

17. For example, the scholar Tormod Engelsviken, professor of missiology at the Norwegian Lutheran School of Theology, Oslo, in celebrating the 50th anniversary of Willingen 1952, develops this in an interesting lecture entitled: *Missio Dei: The understanding and misunderstanding of a theological concept in European churches and*

113) and, as Johannine theology says, 'until now' (John 5:17), with the purpose of making everything for his glory. This is also the purpose of partnership in mission, wherever, whenever and by whomsoever Christian partnership is developed. This argument is related to my proposal of what I have called in my previous chapter reciprocal contextual collaboration. On the other hand, this analysis helps us to understand what Moltmann (1981, 105) explains in his book, *The Trinity and the Kingdom of God*, when he affirms that "the free nature of the act of creation and its character as a pure act of grace ascribes to God absolute liberty in the sense of unlimited power of disposal." In fact, this affirmation is foundational in Christian partnership.[18] Therefore, the Trinity is really the ownership of church's mission.

The development and characteristics of the *missio Dei* theology have practical implications for the mission enterprise in the sense that the *missio Dei* theology needs to empower the church's mission. In this sense, one of my understandings is in fact that partnership in mission also belongs to the *missio Dei* concept and this is the nature of partnership in mission. Why? Because God is the originator of every partnership for the sake of his double mission mandate (Matt 28:19–20 and Luke 4:18–19) and again, as I have said in my previous chapter, mission partnership is joining together to do something for God's glory and understanding the dynamic relationship between God and the World, and God and the church. In fact, reciprocal contextual collaboration is rooted in the biblical meaning that the *missio Dei* theology shapes its theology in the sense that we see God as creator (Gen 1:1); God as sender (John 3:16); God as servant (Mark 10:45); God as saviour (2 Cor 4:6); and the church as co-operator of God (1 Cor 15:28; 1 Tim 2:1–4). From these biblical facts, we conclude that the Trinitarian God empowers the *missio Dei*. "God's very nature, therefore, is missionary" (288), and partnership is rooted in this mission theology.

---

missiology. See *International Review of Mission*, Vol XCII No. 367 October (2003, 481–497).

18. One positive need is to recapture the biblical notion that God need not have created the world but he did so because of God's free will and God's essential nature of love and his good pleasure under the relationship of love and mutual friendship with his creation (Moltmann 1981, 105–106), and these foundations are the nature of every Christian and mature partnership in mission.

As Timothy Stagich, speaking of how to develop collaborative leaders and high synergy organizations in his book *Collaborative Leadership and Global Transformation* (2001, 258), states, there is a synergy principle that creates order from disorder. In missiological application this helps us to be aware of the different issues that missiology brings to the reality of the missionary tension that comes from different perspectives of interpreting the *missio Dei* theology, both for missiological order and for missiological disorder. In consequence, I agree with the missiological order of Andrew Kirk when he defines the *missio Dei* as "God's plan and purposes for humanity in terms of creation, the fall, salvation and the consummation of God's sovereign reign over all things."[19] This implies that the *missio Dei* theology speaks about the undivided being of a sending God and the acting God, who has a mission plan and purpose of salvation and redemption for humanity and the whole creation according to his sovereign rule and reign.[20]

In summary, the fact is that not all of the interpretations given to the *missio Dei* theology are mutually distinct; some in fact are relatively compatible with others. While Bevans and Schroeder emphasize a Catholic perspective of the *missio Dei* concept, the Protestant Miguez Bonino's interpretation suggests that it is God's person and not only God's action that creates the beginning of Christianity because the church has both a missionary dimension and a missionary intention. Kirk defines the *missio Dei* as the *missio Trinitatis*. In this sense, the importance of this understanding is that the mission activity has a Trinitarian base (Kirk 1999, 27); the *missio Dei* is God's activity, which embraces both the church and the world, and in which the church may be privileged to participate (Bosch 1991, 391). This indicates that God's concern is for the entire world, so this affects humankind in all its activities and life, and mission is understood as God's care in creation, redemption and consummation. Consequently, the *missio Dei* participates in ordinary human history without any exclusiveness

---

19. Personal dialogue with Andrew Kirk by email, relating to the *missio Dei* concept and Trinitarian theology, London, 25 October 2007.

20. For further discussion on the *missio Dei* theology see the different articles by John Flett, Ross Wagner, Scott Sunquist, Karin Heller (a Catholic theologian), Darrell Guder and Mark Laing in *Missiology*, Volume XXXVII Number 1 January (2009, 5–73, 89–98). Fundamentally, the argument of those articles is based on the theological assumption that God is a missionary God without dichotomy of his being from acting.

on the part of the church (391). In analysing Kirk and Bosch, we arrive at the conclusion that the *missio Dei* provides a new theological approach by stating that neither the church not the human being can be considered the author of mission. In supporting this, we say that mission is, primarily and ultimately, the work of the triune God, Creator, Redeemer and Sanctifier, in which the church is privileged to participate, and God's mission is rooted in God's amazing love (Bosch 1991, 392). For Bosch, Bevans and Schroeder, and Davies and Pomerville,[21] it is Willingen 1952 that introduced a new way of interpreting Trinitarian theology by emphasizing God's mission and the world (with an emphasis on the world's mission agenda by including justice, poverty and social concern – it is God's missionary activity in history) instead of God's mission and the church (with an emphasis on the evangelistic mandate – the church becomes the tool of God's missionary work).[22] This created a new missiological environment for partnership in mission with two new influences: first, theologically, the

---

21. The evangelical Paul Pomerville, from a Pentecostal perspective, seems more radical than Bevans and Schroeder, and Bosch and Miguez Bonino, in that Pomerville's opinion supports the 'distortion interpretation' of the *missio Dei* by saying that this theology has diluted the effort of the evangelistic mandate to promote the absence of biblical authority (this is due to the excessive impact of the context of mission rather than on the content of mission theology. For Pomerville, Scripture was not the starting point for theologizing) and also fails to articulate the role of the Holy Spirit (1985, 142). While Pomerville makes an effort in bringing the need to recover a christological and pneumatological theology, Bevans and Schroeder (2004, 291) point to the new orthodoxy under the influence of Karl Barth and Karl Rahner by emphasizing the activity of God in the world. Pomerville refers to the 'distortion interpretation' as the static intellectual-orientated expression of Christianity of the West, and the excessive impact of Western culture on the Christian faith, which contrasts with the experiential dimension of the Christian faith empowered by the dynamic and evidential experience of the Holy Spirit (1985, 63). However, Pomerville fails to take account of the fact that the *missio Dei* concept "is grounded in an intra-Trinitarian movement of God himself, and that it expresses the power of God over history", where obedience is a key element for all human mission as participants of the divine sending (Wright 2006, 62–63). Therefore, it is not the *missio Dei* concept that is at fault, but its interpretation and the applications of it.

22. In celebrating the 50th anniversary of Willingen 1952, the Norwegian, Tormod Engelsviken, provides some distinctions related to the *missio Dei* concept by stating that from the 1960s, a more anthropocentric understanding of mission to a more theocentric mission was emphasized, and a more ecclesio-centric perspective to a more cosmocentric missiology was emphasized (the world, both in its socio-political and religious dimension, becomes the centre of attention). See further "Missio Dei: The understanding and misunderstanding of a theological concept in European churches and missiology" *International Review of Mission*, Vol. XCII No. 367 October 2003, 481–497.

classical doctrine of the *missio Dei* as God the Father sending the Son, and God the Son sending the Spirit was expanded by adding God the Father, Son and Spirit, sending the church into the world (Bosch 2001, 390); second, missiologically, mission was understood primarily as an attribute of God and not as an activity of the church due to the assumption that the *missio Dei* is God's activity, embracing both the church and the world. In this way the church becomes an instrument to accomplish God's mission plan of creation, redemption, restoration and fulfilment of the new order, which is related to missionary eschatology.

Partnership and God's kingdom

In 'The Gospel of the Kingdom' article, Ladd defines the meaning of kingdom as the authority to rule, or the sovereignty of the king, and the synonyms for kingdom are power, might and glory; all are expressions of authority which identify the kingdom as the rule given by God to the King, Jesus[23] (Winter 1981, A66; Kirk 1999, 29). In consequence, the kingdom of God is his kingship, his rule, his authority; it is neither a realm nor a people but God's reign, and the church's destiny is to seek first his kingdom (*basileia*) and his righteousness (Matt 6:33). From this biblical perspective, the Synoptic Gospels offer a mission theology of Jesus' proclamation, which affirms that his teaching was centred in the good news of the

---

23. Ladd suggests a christological biblical introduction to understand the procession between the *missio Dei* theology that helps us to relate with God's kingdom theology announced and developed by the incarnate Christ to the world's need of salvation, restoration and redemption. This christological approach will be amplified later, but now we want to concentrate on the kingdom of God which christologically is the kingdom of Christ. For Moltmann, from an eschatological point of view, the kingdom of God is the kingship of Christ "at first not over the natural world around man, but leadership towards the land of promise, and thus a historic lordship which shows itself in unique, unrepeatable, startlingly new, purposeful events" (1965, 216). Thus, the kingdom of God relates to the resurrection of Christ and his new creation; this is the hope of God's kingdom, which is present as promise and hope for the church (223). Therefore, I agree when Moltmann states; "the *pro missio* of the kingdom is the ground of the *missio* of love to the world" (224).

kingdom of God.[24] Mark 1:15 says, "the time is fulfilled; the kingdom of God is at hand; repent and believe the good news"; Matthew 4:23 states, "Jesus went to Galilee, teaching in their synagogues, preaching the good news of the kingdom" (see also Matt 6:33, 5:19, Luke 6:20, 9:62, 10:9; John 3:3, 18:36).

In referring to the church's global mission, Gordon Fee suggests that the kingdom of God is rooted in Jesus' proclamation of the kingdom of heaven, which is already present in his own mission and message, and that constitutes good news of the kingdom, especially for the poor (Dempster, Klaus and Petersen 1999, 7). Following Fee's argument, the kingdom of God is an eschatological term which belongs to the category of 'time' rather than 'space'. Thus, Fee states that our interpretation of God's kingdom should be understood in relation to the time of the future, the *eschaton*, meaning the end when God will finally rule over the whole of his created order (1999, 8). From a different perspective George Eldon Ladd[25] (Winter and Hawthorne 1981, A–64), who was Professor Emeritus of New Testament at Fuller Theological Seminary, explains that the Hebrew-Christian faith[26] expresses its hopes in terms of the kingdom of God which is related to the presence and mission of Jesus who came to announce "repentance because the kingdom of heaven is at hand" (Matt 4:17). This biblical reality of

---

24. The kingdom is a radically forward movement with a new radical ethic based on the Sermon of the Mount. This can be understood as the most radical and immediate transformation for the history of creation. See further Young (2004, 271).

25. A wider explanation of the kingdom of God theology is developed in the book, *A Theology of the New Testament*, that brings different interpretations of God's kingdom. See further Ladd (1974, 57–70). For Ladd the kingdom as a present gift brings three gifts: the gift of salvation, the gift of forgiveness and the gift of righteousness (72–80). "The presence of the kingdom should be understood from the nature of God's present activity and the future is the redemptive manifestation of his kingly rule at the end of the age" (81).

26. This is against the ancient perspectives of the Greek poets and seers who longed for an ideal society like Plato, due to the fact that the Bible reveals confidence in God through Jesus Christ. Ladd points out, "the kingdom of God is grounded in the confidence that there is one eternal, living God who has revealed himself to men and who has a purpose for the human race which he has chosen to accomplish through Israel. The biblical hope is therefore a *real* hope; it is an essential element in the revealed will and the redemptive work of the living God" (1981, A 64, italics mine).

the kingdom of God is rooted in the Old Testament with its purpose for humankind.[27]

A third view comes from the Latin American theologian, Miguez Bonino, who defines the kingdom of God as "the sovereign action of God over the world, natural and historical in its totality and there are no two histories, a secular and a spiritual" (Davies 2006, 106). Following this third view, for a positive partnership theology, I agree with Davies (2006, 107), who concludes that Miguez Bonino's concept of the kingdom is that God's kingdom is God's action in the history of Israel and of Jesus Christ who is the pivotal centre of the prophetic and apostolic testimony of the self-revelation of God and its purpose (2006, 88), and that is a dynamic missionary theology of the kingdom of God; neither church nor world is definitive in the establishment of the kingdom and, finally, there are both theological and practical dangers of the one history which leads to a dialectical tension (2006, 107).

Ladd clarifies the meaning of the term *basileia*-kingship (in Hebrew 'malkuth') (1974, 63) by saying that many scholars have defined the 'eschaton' as the final eschatological order, but he argues that it is difficult to see how the 'eschaton' can be both future and present.[28] Ladd is right in affirming that the *basileia* concept speaks of three points: the glory of the kingdom which is an everlasting kingdom whose dominion endures through all generations; the kingdom of God which means God's rule or sovereignty; and "God is now the King and must be also become King" (1974, 63). Equally, for the Mennonite, Wilbert Shenk (1983, 207), the *basileia* theology includes terms such as kingship, reign, rule, kingdom, and becomes personified in Jesus Christ who came to do the will of the Father. Applying the *basileia* theology to our missiological analysis of relationships for

---

27. With a foundational mission theology Ladd shows what the nature of "the kingdom is God's kingdom, not man's: *basileia tou theou*. The emphasis falls on the third word, not the first; it is the kingdom of God" (1974, 81), and from this assumption Ladd makes his argument to demonstrate that "the presence of the kingdom is to be understood from the nature of God's present activity; and the future of the kingdom is the redemptive manifestation of his kingly rule at the end of the age" (81).

28. The solution Ladd presents is that in the Old Testament and in rabbinic Judaism, God's kingdom, that is, his reign, can have more than one meaning; God is now the King, but he must also become King. For Ladd (1974, 63), this is the key to the solution of the problem of the gospels.

partnership in mission, it seems that this theological principle is sometimes diluted by the influence of 'commercial partnership' as it is practiced in the secular world. Thus the already/not yet double-tension of God's kingdom is resolved in favour of the former.[29] 'Commercial partnership' relates to an organization and attitude that is influenced by the criteria of productivity and profit, thus, the main objective is economic success. By adopting the 'commercial partnership' as a model, some missionary organizations adopt the criteria of productivity and profit as a method to carry out mission and a way of evaluating it.[30] The main objective becomes missionary success, even to the point of reaching the status of a transnational corporation with economic power and influence.[31] This has been well argued by Escobar (2003, 57) within what he calls 'managerial missiology', whereby mission is reduced to a method aimed at producing a certain number of churches or conversions within a given time frame.[32] In practice, 'commercial partnership' fosters a spirit of duplication, competition or even imposition. Missions are tempted to use money or power for quick 'success' instead of going through the difficult process of developing true partnership with their non-Western partners. The challenge to reaffirm a commitment to living in humble service to Christ becomes paramount, in particular if it is not successful by commercial standards. The 'already' of God's kingdom

---

29. The tension between 'present-already fulfilled' and 'future-not yet completed' contains the key to understanding the entire New Testament. Cullmann emphasizes the 'salvation history' and the 'already/not yet' eschatology. See further *Christ and Time: The Primitive Christian Conception of Time and History* (Cullmann 1951, 199). The tension between a realized and future kingdom is standard comment in most scholarly NT theology

30. Kirk (1999, 199) points out that "undoubtedly, members of the church have sometimes unnecessarily succumbed to the entrepreneurial spirit of the age, initiating projects, and founding institutions and organizations which have been detrimental to mission rather than furthering it".

31. In this line, Max Weber (2003, 138) states that "from an economic point of view, a loan of capital in return for the payment of fixed interest was constructed in the form of partnership". For further reference see *The History of Commercial Partnership in the Middle Ages* (Weber 2003). See also *The Bible and the Flag: Protestant Missions and British Imperialism in the Nineteenth and Twentieth Century* (Stanley, 1990, 70–74). In relation to Christian mission, Padilla corroborates Warren who states that "partnership is an idea whose time has not yet fully come" (1985, 139).

32. A great concern is pointed out by Padilla (1985, 17) in the same line as Escobar, when he deals with the same issue in 'cultural Christianity'. He states that it reduces the gospel to a formula for success and equates the triumph of Christ with obtaining the highest number of conversions; it turns the gospel into a product.

implies that the church's mission becomes service under Christ's rule while the 'not yet' as the full manifestation of God's kingdom is still to come.

The 'already' of God's kingdom needs to be understood as the presence of Jesus who has already come to inaugurate his reign, and the 'not yet' of the kingdom becomes the fullness of God's kingdom through Jesus' sovereign reign over all its creation and people at the 'eschaton'.[33] This is why I also agree with Ladd when he concludes that "God is now the King, but he must also become King" (1975, 63). Equally, righteousness implies a right relationship with God and to seek the kingdom means to seek God's righteousness; it is a gift from God (78).

My theological point of view is similar to Ladd's interpretation in the sense that Jesus saw his ministry as a fulfilment of the Old Testament promise in history, short of the apocalyptic consummation (for example, when Jesus cited Isaiah 61:1–2 to confirm in Luke 4:21 the fulfilment of his presence, and then he cited Isaiah 35:5–6 in response to John the Baptist in Matthew 11:2–6 to explain that he is the Coming One). On the same lines, another theological foundation for a proper theology of partnership is that the victory of God's kingdom is a victory of God's triumph over Satan (1 Cor 15:25) and this biblical affirmation lies in the fact that Jesus as king of the *basileia* is the king over the whole creation and humankind, at present in his church and in everything at the 'eschaton'. On this assumption, we suggest that the church should recover a more positive partnership

---

33. Because the kingdom of God is already here, believers in the kingdom theology expect to see God actively working, sometimes even miraculously, in the present day. Because the kingdom of God is not yet here in its full expression, the works of this present evil age continue though not as unlimited as it would without the presence of the kingdom of God. The phrase 'Already/Not Yet' as a description of our understanding of the kingdom of God in its present and future state has become very familiar. See Trevin Wax, "Kingdom Now and Not Yet", Kingdom People, 7 April 2009 (http://trevinwax.com/2009/04/07/kingdom-now-and and the coming of the kingdom in glorious power, it was God's purpose that the powers of that eschatological kingdom should -not-yet/). As with many others who follow the teachings of George Ladd, dominion theology believes that we are in the kingdom age, but the kingdom in another sense is yet to come. We are in the kingdom, and have kingdom authority, but on the other hand, we are ushering in the kingdom through our efforts. 'The kingdom is now, but not yet,' is popular with dominion theology. See further Biblical Discernment Ministries 1997 'Dominion Theology' /Kingdom Now/ Reconstructionism, http://www.rapidnet.com/~jbeard/bdm/Psychology/cor/dominion.htm ((Accessed on 25 August 2010 at 22:02). See also 'the fulfilment of Jesus' and 'the fulfilment without consummation' (Ladd 1964, 106–117),

theology with the understanding that the church's mission belongs to Jesus' kingdom; it is not ours, and this is due to the fact that we are collaborators of God's kingdom. In consequence a negative tension between partners would be reduced in the church's mission if missiologically we applied radically the biblical fact that God's kingdom belongs to the *missio Dei* and Jesus is the King for whom the church works.

We arrive at the conclusion that, while Fee and Shenk (1983, 208) agree that the kingdom of God is to be understood eschatologically, Ladd and Miguez Bonino suggest that the tension of establishing God's kingdom is a reality at present, but it will be established fully at the 'eschaton', and at present there is a tension between the 'already' and the 'not yet' of God's kingdom. The question is how this kingdom theology brings a positive insight to the theology of partnership, or what I call reciprocal contextual collaboration? It affects it positively in that if we intentionally teach God's kingdom theology which includes the *basileia* and the righteousness concept, then these will reduce distortion in the interpretation of God's mission since in evangelicalism there seems to be a lack of understanding of the *basileia* theology in their policies of mission and relationship between partners. It seems that partnership in mission demands a theology where the intentional thinking of the *basileia* theology matters, permeating the whole Christian leadership and, secondly, the finding that God's kingdom theology is translatable to every context, no matter North or South. Missiology is developed with a Trinitarian approach, as Moltmann (1981, 212) points out because the Trinitarian doctrine of the kingdom is the work for the Trinity in creation, liberation and glorification. My agreement with Moltmann[34] (212) is that the kingdom of glory is the goal for all God's works and ways in history; this theology leads us to work for partnership under the kingdom of freedom in Christ.[35]

---

34. In his book, *The Trinity and the Kingdom of God,* Moltmann (1981, 191–219) develops a historical and theological approach in relation to the kingdom of freedom and the Trinitarian doctrine of freedom. For him the Trinity has implications for practical social and political life where relationships between the Father, the Son and the Sprit work in unity.

35. Moltmann's opinion (1981, 203) is that the theological doctrine of freedom is connected with the lordship and kingdom of God, and Davies (2000, 145) suggests that freedom is unrestricted participation in the eternal life of the triune God.

Partnership and God's church

Following the discussion of the *missio Dei* and God's kingdom theology, here I make a brief analysis of partnership in God's church. Andrew Kirk (1999, 30–31; Volf 1998, 128) states that the church is by nature missionary, therefore the church has been called, with a sense of identity, to share and live out the good news of Christ in the world in response to the *missio Dei*. For Volf (1998, 128)[36] and Zizioulas,[37] the church is an image of the triune God, and John Smith points out that the church is the "visible communion of the saints" (quoted in Volf, 135). We define the church as the elect people of God, with a privilege and responsibility of service. We see the church as witnessing to the kingdom, serving as an instrument of the kingdom and as representing the kingdom. In other words, as the elect people of God, the church waits for the eschatological consummation, but, while this is yet to come, participates in God's kingdom by proclaiming the good news in word and in deed, all for God's glory. In consequence, the elect people of God bring an impact of partnership theology as 'light and salt' (Matt 5:13–14) in the world due to its missionary nature, but in partnership with the Trinity.[38] From this theological understanding we derive two principles for a biblical theology of partnership which are as follows: first, the church is the *ekklesia*[39] determined as the congregation or assem-

---

36. In his book, *After Our Likeness,* the Yugoslavian theologian Miroslav Volf argues against individualism in the church, and he engages in a critical and ecumenical dialogue with both the Catholic ecclesiology of Joseph Ratzinger and the Orthodox ecclesiology of John Zizioulas. Volf states that the church comes to participation in the communion of the triune God, through faith in Jesus Christ. He also brings a definition of the church with an emphasis on its eschatological character that begins with God's new creation in its relationship with God's people (1998, 128).

37. John Zizioulas from an Orthodox perspective makes a contribution to Trinitarian theology with an emphasis on Christology and ecclesiology, clarifying that the church is the image of the triune God, which works in free communion as love (1985, 48–49). For him the Trinity is a primordial ontological concept (1985, 17). See Zizioulas (1985).

38. Barth (1949, 141), in *Dogmatics in Outline*, defines the church (*ekklesia*) as the congregation, a coming together, which meets at the call of the messenger or 'the sound of the herald trumpet'. A congregation is 'the coming together' of those who belong to Jesus Christ through the Holy Spirit.

39. According to Bevans, the church is understood as the people of God to be an agent and co-operator in God's outreach to the whole creation; it has an apostolic spirit. Second, in relation to Trinitarian theology, God is a community of Father, Son and Spirit,

bly of Yahweh (Matt 16:18–19), and this *ekklesia* belongs in a peculiar way to Jesus; and second, the kingdom is not identified with its subjects – they are the people of God's rule who enter it, live under it, and are governed by it (109, 111). A summary of Ladd's interpretation of the kingdom and the church is therefore foundational for a positive theology of partnership. First, the church is not the kingdom and the first missionaries preached the kingdom of God, not the church. Second, the kingdom creates the church because the church is the result of the coming of God's kingdom into the world by the mission of Jesus, thus entrance into the kingdom means participation in the church. Third, it is the church's mission to witness to the kingdom – the church cannot build the kingdom or become the kingdom since the church witnesses to the kingdom, to God's redeeming acts in Christ both past and future, and illustrations of this include the commission of the twelve (Matt 10) and of the seventy (Luke 10). Fourth, the church is the instrument of the kingdom to proclaim the good news with a delegated power (Matt 10:8; 16:18; Luke 10:17). Fifth, the church is the custodian of the kingdom (Matt 10:40; Mark 9:37).

The implications of a political theology of partnership are related then to ecclesiology in the way that every church, as Rufus Anderson and Henry Venn say, is self-supporting,[40] self-governing and self-propagating to accomplish its mission task (see Van Engen 1996, 134; Bosch 2001, 307, 331, 450; Shenk 1983, 133; Taber 2003, 174–179). But in an innovative way the Yugoslavian theologian, Miroslav Volf,[41] speaks of the church as

---

constantly involved in the world; salvation, human wholeness. Third, christologically speaking, God is involved in history through Jesus Christ of Nazareth as both truly divine and truly human, working in a true incarnation, as a servant. And fourth, the Holy Spirit, "gives the entire church unity in fellowship and in service and from a community in mission that would overflow in a Trinitarian life" (2004, 287).

40. In relation to the 'three selfs', Taber (2003, 174–179) emphasizes the relation between indigenization, inculturation and contextualization; Saayman in Shenk's book points out the historical fact (1983, 133), and Van Engen (1996, 134) clarifies the fact that evangelicalism took seriously the 'three self formula' from Berlin 1966 under the influence of Melvin Hodge thinking of indigenization as a legitimate goal of missions, and Bosch (2001, 307) brings the perspective of using the 'three self' as a western idea within the new missionary force of evangelicalism.

41. Volf tries to develop a non-hierarchical and communal ecclesiology based on a non-hierarchical doctrine of the Trinity (1998, 4). He is interested in the transmission of the faith (1) with a constructive theology with both a culturally sensitive and a critical social embodiment of the gospel (5). Volf believes that the Free Churches, to which in

the image of the Trinity and the genesis of the concrete church (1998, 175) including a critique of ecclesial individualism as false autonomy (1998, 3). On the other hand, political theology of partnership implies the role of the local churches and the participation of the leadership closely linked to the double mandate for the church, that is, the evangelistic and the social mandate. In both cases the church is alive and empowered by the Spirit to bring the good news in word and in deed to make possible the accomplishment of the *missio Dei* according to their missionary role given by the *missio trinitatis*. This possibility is understood from the fact that mission partnership has its origin in the Trinity. David Bosch (2001, 391) clarifies that for the *missio ekklesiae*, which is related to the missionary activity of the church, the *missio Dei* brings important consequences. However, it is worth reflecting properly on the tension of church-centred and kingdom-orientated theology.[42] Here, I suggest three points for an appropriate theology of partnership: first, the church represents God's kingdom presence

---

my perspective he refers as the 'Third Church', is a new movement from the 'Two-Thirds World' (11), which need to be studied by theologians of the West, with the purpose of understanding their implicit and explicit ecclesiology and theologies. There is a moving from the traditional hierarchical model to participative models of church configuration, and participation and flexibility are characteristics of the growing Protestants, especially Pentecostals and charismatics (12). On the other hand, for Volf, the genesis of the church rests on the Spirit of God who acts through the word of God and the sacraments ('from above'); it is the Spirit who constitutes the church, therefore it is not primarily an accommodation to social circumstances, but a matter of theological identity of the church. Thus, every local church is God's work, where members are initiated into a twofold communion, communion with God and a concrete communion with Christians both by the sacrament of baptism, which is preceded by faith, and the will of each of person (176–177). It seems that for Volf, the vision of the triune God provides the foundations for the formal relations between person and community.

42. However, we have to reflect properly on the tension of church-centred theology with the 'three self' formulas given by Henry Venn and Rufus Anderson, which came after pietism and earlier individualistic mission theories of personal conversion of the latter half of the nineteenth century and the first half of the twentieth century; and similarly, there is a tension in the kingdom-orientated theology with an emphasis on the world. Church-centred concept was related to the practical goal of the so-called foreign missions focused on personal conversion to a new focus of church centred on the 'three self', thus, by 1910 foreign mission work was understood as church extension overseas (1999, 83). For Scherer, the kingdom-orientated theology shows that it is impossible to speak of the church's mission apart from the mission of the triune God – *missio Dei* – or apart from a fully Trinitarian theological standpoint (85). See James Scherer in Van Engen (1999, 82–88).

but neither in a triumphalistic[43] sense nor in a moralistic sense; second, the church is the place where God's power is manifested in a community of sinners and, according to John 12:32, is the place where the promise of Jesus is fulfilled; and third, the mission is not ours and belongs to God, but he is pleased to share the *missio trinitatis* with the church. In consequence, political theology of partnership calls the church to participate in at least four kinds of sharing: common projects, gifts, material resources and in suffering (Kirk 1999, 188–191). Thus, church's mission develops a double identity, by worshipping God and by witnessing and serving the world. The first express a mark of holiness because the church belongs to God and the second refers to the apostolic work in the sense that the church is sent out on its mission (Stott 1992, 242).

A Trinitarian theology of partnership

The question that I want to pose is this: what are the principles of a Trinitarian theology[44] that make an impact on mission partnership theology? I will

---

43. For Newbigin the church represents the presence of the reign of God in the life of the world, neither in the triumphalistic sense as the successful cause, nor in the moralistic sense as the righteous cause. But in the sense that it is the mystery of the kingdom present in the dying and rising of Jesus, that all people, righteous and unrighteous are enabled to taste and share the love of God. The church is the place where the glory of God is revealed in Christ and is available to sin-burdened men and women (John 17, 22–23); it is also the place where the power of God is manifested in a community of sinners, and it is the place where the reign of God is present and love. See *The Open Secret* (1995, 54).

44. The starting point of Trinitarian language begins with the bishop of Lyon, St. Irenaeus (ca. 125–202 AC). Confronting speculations of the Gnostics, he persuades them of the eternal essence of the Trinity and used the term economy to stress on the salvific dimension of the Trinity, with especial reference to the Son, who pre-exists and has true communion with the Father and the Holy Spirit (Boff 1986, 50–52). Sometimes he suggests modalism or subordinationism. Origen, who taught in Alexandria, saw the Trinity as an eternal dynamism of communication, and was first to use the term *hypostasis* (individual-*person*, italics mine). For him, the Father is the origin of the Son (Logos), and Father and Logos the origin of the Holy Spirit (52). He saw three distinct persons but falls into modalism and subordinationism like Irenaeus. Tertullian (160–225 AD AC) was the creator of the language of Trinitarian orthodoxy by coining the term '*Trinitas*' and the formula which came to express true faith in the triune God – 'one substance, three persons'. "Substance is what embodies the unity of the divine Three, and person denotes what distinguishes them. In God, therefore, there exists the unity of equal substance in the Father, Son and Holy Spirit, and the diversity of persons of the Father, Son and Holy

deal very briefly with two aspects – theology and missiology. What are the implications of the immanent[45] and the economic[46] Trinity? The immanent

---

Spirit, which derives from the same substance" (53). The Cappadocian Fathers of Asia Minor, St Basil the Great (330–379 AD), his brother Gregory of Nyssa (d. 394) and their friend Gregory Nazianzen (329–390 AD) emphasize not the unity of the divine nature but the three divine Persons. The major contribution was to clarify that the Holy Spirit is truly God and one of the divine persons of the Trinity (54). St Augustine developed a systematic exposition of the mystery of the Trinity in his book *De Trinitate* with a big influence on all Latin theologians after him. In contrast with the Eastern theologians who define that God is the Father, Augustine puts the emphasis on the Trinity as the Father, Son and Holy Spirit. The three persons of the Trinity are consubstantial, and unity belongs to the divine substance-essence or nature. He develops two analogies to explain unity in Trinity and Trinity in unity; he speaks of mind, knowledge and love (*mens, notitia, amor*), or memory, intelligence and will (*memoria, intelligentia, voluntas*); "the three Persons are respective subjects, that is, they are concerned with one another and related to one another" (56). Thomas Aquinas (1224–1274 ADAC) emphasized both the study of the consubstantial character of the three Persons, and the 'procession', the different ways in which one proceeds from the other to analyse the real relation between them, defining the divine Persons as subsistent relationships. (57).

45. The immanent Trinity emphasizes the being of God as he is in himself, who seeks to draw humanity into his eternal glory. The focus is on the transcendent unity of the Trinity, with a tendency towards a monarchical approach, Christology from above, and bringing people into a personal relationship with God. See Corrie (2007, 397). With a different emphasis, for Migliore (1991, 69), responsible Trinitarian thinking begins with the economic Trinity – the one yet threefold agency of Father, Son, and Spirit in the economy of salvation; and the immanent Trinity is the eternal distinction of persons within the being of God. For Boff, the immanent Trinity is the internal relationship between the three Persons, the eternal mystery of Trinitarian procession and the Trinity understood in itself (1988, 96).

46. Economy emphasizes the history of God's revelation in the world. It focuses on the distinctive role of the Trinity, tends towards an incarnational view of God who reveals his historical identity through Christ; Christology is from below which offers personal and social transformation. See Corrie (2007, 397). Moltmann explains the relation between the immanent and economic Trinity in the following way (1981, 151–152): (1) "The economic Trinity designates the triune God in his dispensation of salvation, in which he is revealed. The economic Trinity is therefore also called the revelatory Trinity"; (2) the distinction between an immanent Trinity and an economic Trinity secures God's liberty and his grace which is the correct presupposition for the appropriate understanding of God's saving revelation (151); (3) distinguishing between the immanent and economic Trinity is found in doxology, which implies that the assertion of the immanent Trinity about eternal life and the eternal relationship of the triune God in himself have their *Sitz im Leben* (the situation of life), in the praise and worship of the church; (4) the early church distinguished between the doxological knowledge of God and the doctrine of salvation, the *oeconomia Dei*; (5) the economic Trinity is the object of *kerygmatic* and practical theology; the immanent Trinity is the content of doxological theology. Boff states that the economic Trinity "designates the presence of the Trinity or the persons of the Trinity within the history of salvation. This history was seen by the early church as an *oeconomia* that is, as series of phases of a divine plan being progressively both realized

Trinity[47] is sometimes called the ontological,[48] or essential Trinity, all three terms referring to God's own self and helping us to claim that God is an eternal Trinity of love (Jewett 1991, 305; Bevan and Schroeder[49] 2004, 291). To distinguish the ontological or immanent[50] Trinity theologians speak of the 'economic'[51] Trinity, which refers to the order or realm of creation and of redemption. As Jewett explains, "both creation and redemption

---

and revealed. The Trinity revealed in this historical-salvific process is called the economic Trinity" (Boff 188, 95).

47. With history as the centre of his theological approach (Grenz 2004, 73), Moltmann (1981:151) explains that, "the immanent Trinity is the name given to the triune God as he is in himself. The immanent Trinity is also called the substantial Trinity". For Moltmann, Karl Rahner developed his doctrine of the Trinity similarly to Karl Barth. He challenges their tendency to speak in terms of 'modes of being' rather than 'persons' to refer to the three Trinitarian beings: "a single divine subject in three called 'distinct modes of subsistence *or modes of being*' (italics mine)" instead of the orthodox concept of *una substantia-tres personae* (139, 144). This new Trinitarian thesis of "modes of beings", for Moltmann, leads to a profound alteration in the substance of the Christian doctrine of the Trinity with a danger of approaching an idealistic modalism, as it sometimes seems to appear in the tendency of Rahner, Schleiermacher and Barth (144). Idealistic modalism, or Sabellian modalism, defines the Trinity as the three manifestations or modes of appearance of the One God, which leads to the conclusion that God is incommunicable and hence unknowable (136). What dominates in modalism is the basic idea of One God, manifested in three modes of being, "as the Father, as the Son and as the Spirit", and of the universal monarchy, which can be exercised only by one subject (1981, 134,136, 139).

48. See also the ontological emphasis of *The Theology of Hope* (Moltmann 1965).

49. Bevans and Schroeder (2004, 288) summarize Trinitarian theology, "God's *exitus* in sending the Son and Spirit results in a *reditus* in which the church cooperates with God in making as 1 Corinthians 15:28 says: 'all in all'", and "the church is in mission because it has been graciously caught up in the *missio Dei*, the very mission of God in creation, redemption and continual sanctification" (288). On the other hand, for Bevans, the Orthodox Church places the centre for a Trinitarian theology in the last quarter of the twentieth century by stating that Trinitarian theology points to the radical communal nature of God as such, that is, there is an involvement with history, inviting humanity and creation to draw near to God.

50. A theology of immanence is the legacy of Kant, Schleiermacher and Hegel for modern theology. See Gunton (1993, 36).

51. Colin Gunton (1993, 161), former Professor of Christian Doctrine at King's College, London, clarifies that the concept has limits of time, space and reality. On the other hand, the idea of an economy of divine generosity through Jesus Christ with his suffering and death is expressed by the apostle Paul as an explicit financial metaphor to overcome human conceptions of economy (2 Cor 8:9). In other words, Christology is the heart of the matter. See Gunton (1993, 157–162). For Moltmann, the economic Trinity is the object of kerygmatic and practical theology; the immanent Trinity is the context of doxological theology (Grenz 2004, 87). Also see Kevin Daugherty in "Missio dei: The Trinity and Christian Mission" (*Evangelical Review of Theology*, Volume 31 No. 2 April 2007, 151–168).

concern the world" (1991, 305) and he adds: "economic Trinity refers to the Trinitarian way in which God relates to the world, the way he, who is eternally a Trinity, has revealed himself as our Maker and Redeemer" (305). This economic Trinity is sometimes called the 'revelational' or 'functional' Trinity. Here, I will follow Jewett's principal interpretation, first of the immanent Trinity and then of the economic Trinity.

Paul K. Jewett,[52] from a perspective of a neo-evangelical theology, points out that there is a Trinitarian consciousness through the Old and New Testament which is the biblical basis of the doctrine that compels the church to confess that there is one God who is a Trinity of persons – Father, Son and Holy Spirit (1991, 268–272). From this assumption we understand that Trinitarian theology speaks about God and the relations between the three persons of the Godhead – a term that denotes deity-divinity that theologically includes the begottenness[53] and procession.[54] The Christian

---

52. For Jewett, to be a Trinitarian is not just to reject a Unitarian view of the Father, the Arian view of the Son, and a Pelagian view of the Spirit, it is also not to understand that God is our creator, as in natural theology; nor is Jesus simply the supreme instance of God consciousness as in liberal theologians' approach; nor is the Spirit the potential of the human spirit to achieve the good, as in ethical idealism. Rather, salvation is wholly God's work, the God who adopts us as his children in Christ, through the Spirit, who enables us to cry 'Abba Father', according to Romans chapter 8. See further Jewett (1991, 264).

53. The Son as begotten of the Father implies that there is an eternal difference between them, a distinction of the Father and the Son in the one God. As Paul Jewett clearly says: "The one is God, the other is also God; yet the other is not just God, but the God who is 'out of' God, the God who is distinct from God – not distinct as God, for there are not two distinct Gods – but distinct as God the Son from God the Father" (1991, 288), and Jewett concludes that 'begotten' describes the mysterious relationship where God is the Father and God is the Son (288). With this theological interpretation was denied the Arian doctrine that denies the full deity of the Son. 'Begotten', in the Trinitarian theology, refers to the idea that Jesus was uncreated and 'eternally begotten' of the Father. Sinclair B. Ferguson's *The Holy Spirit* discusses the revelation of the Spirit with pneumatological emphasis: 'procession' as *paraclete* and *perichoresis* (1996, 72–78, 186–188).

54. The theological term procession is recognized as the best term to describe the relation between the Spirit and the other members of the Godhead. In this way, the eternal procession of the Spirit is the incommunicable property. The term 'procession' is taken from John 15:26 which speaks of the *paraclete*. Jewett (1991, 293–294) explains that the one who will be sent by the Son as the other *paraclete* is identified as the Spirit who proceeds from the Father. For Jewett the procession of the Spirit in Western churches affirms that this comes from both the Father and the Son, and the Spirit comes to the church as revelation in revelation as Spirit of Christ because he is eternally the Spirit who proceeds not only from the Father, but also from the Son. Bevans and Schroeder's Trinitarian procession includes movements within the mystery of God and also God moving in saving love within the world (2004, 287).

God is the Father, the Son and the Spirit; they too subsist eternally as distinct persons in the Godhead.[55] In consequence, the Godhead is both a unity[56] and a trinity,[57] both singular and plural, and this Trinitarian theology is foundational to the mission enterprise of the third millennium. The fact is that a Trinitarian partnership theology through its understanding of how the Trinitarian God relates to the created universe as Father, Son and Holy Spirit, Creator, Redeemer and Sanctifier becomes essential for the development of a more appropriated and positive impact for the *missio ecclesiae*. Gunton in his book *The One, the Three and the Many* explains, like Jewett (1993, 158), but he adds the element of fall and eschatology. For him the persons of the Trinity are distinct, but not separate, and they interrelate with each other. The Brazilian liberation theologian Leonardo Boff speaks of the Trinity from a sociological[58] point of view when he explores

---

55. Ray L. Hart, in *Theology in Global Context,* has a chapter developing the meaning of Godhead from a philosophical perspective of religion. He points out that Godhead and God are to be distinguish technically and analytically; they are distinct although inseparables in act. See further Young and Peter G. Heltzel (2004, 244–263). The Godhead refers to the abstract and essential divine nature of God. The divinity of the Trinity is sometimes referred to as the Godhead. The Free Dictionary states that in Christianity, the Godhead is a term denoting deity or divinity. It expresses a unity of God the Father, God the Son, and God the Sprit. It is used interchangeably with the concept of the Trinity but it is an error to use it as a synonym of the English word Trinity. http://encyclopedia.thefreedictionary.com/Godhead+(Christianity) Accessed 7 December 2007 at 10:15 am).

56. Christianity believes that Trinitarian theology express a divine unity, but it is a unity in diversity. Evangelicals do not believe that God is one as Allah is one because Christians are not monotheists in a Unitarian sense (Jewett 1991, 296). Christians are monotheists in a Trinitarian sense.

57. "God is who is 'One in Three' and 'Three in One', a fellowship of holy love". This helps us to understand that Trinitarian theology has two aspects, the essential unity of God and the personal distinction in God (Jewett 1991, 297). Both are integral to the Christian understanding of God and this theology is essential to the integrity of the Christian message and to the nature of the church's mission. This Trinity express the Oneness of God (1 Cor 8:4–6), that is, one God in his essential being yet three in the personal mode of his being, Father, Son and Holy Spirit, are consubstantial, that is, of one and the same essence. See Jewett (294–296). See also Gunton (1993).

58. For Grenz (2004, 85), Moltmann tends to link Trinitarian theology and social anthropology. This is seen in his political theology, which has been appropriated by liberation theologians such Boff. Moltmann also develops a social Trinitarianism, which has elevated the three persons to the detriment of the divine unity and therefore it borders on tritheism, emphasizing three distinct subjects or centres of activity.

the Trinity in theological imagery[59] (1988, 107–108), and the communion of the Trinity as a basis for social and integral transformation[60] (123–154).

Second, the economic Trinitarian theology is described in Jewett's words, "in creation the *Father* becomes the One-who-is-for-others-outside-himself, namely, his creatures. In redemption, the *Son* becomes the One-who-is-for-sinful-others, namely, his people whom he restores to fellowship with himself. Thus the eternal fellowship of the divine, Trinitarian life grounds God's fellowship with us to whom he gives himself in love as our Maker and Redeemer" (1991, 299–300, 308–315, italics mine). Jewett (1991, 312) states:

> The Holy Spirit becomes the One who is our sanctifier and gives us a new past (in our effectual calling) and a new future (in our glorification), but also a new present (in our

---

59. Building on Moltmann's concept of *perichoresis*, Boff suggests the connection between the community of the three persons of the Trinity and the ideal human community for insight into the ultimate mystery of God (Grenz 2004, 119). Boff points out that human society interacts with three basic structures, economic (production and reproduction), politics (organization of social relationships), and symbolic (ideas, philosophies, religion, etc.), which no human organization can survive without these three basic structures (1986, 107). Stanley J. Grenz, in his book *Rediscovering the Triune God,* explains that the Brazilian Roman Catholic lay theologian and former Franciscan, Leonardo Boff, provides a historical approach that tended to focus on the work of Moltmann, Pannenberg, and Jeson. Boff, who emerged in the 1970s, develops an explicit implication of the Trinity in human society – the contemporary social context of Latin America seen characterized by oppression and a desire of liberation. See further (Grenz 2004, 118–120).

60. Also Boff proposes that consideration of the communion of the three persons of the Trinity produces a critical attitude to personhood, community, society and the church. In the light of the Trinity, being a person in the image and likeness of the divine Persons means acting as a permanently active web or network of relationship. Therefore, personalization through communion must not lead to a personalism alienated from the conflict and processes of social change, but must seek to establish a more participative and humanizing relationship (1986, 149). "In the Trinity there is no domination by one side, but convergence of the Three in mutual acceptance and giving. They are different but none is greater or lesser, before or after" (151). Therefore, biblical partnership rooted in Trinitarian communion cannot tolerate class differences, or dominions based on economic, political or cultural power. I agree with Boff when he states that the Trinitarian model of communion should be an inspiration of fellowship, equality of opportunity, and generosity for the society, which can be well applied to the mission enterprise, which needs to empower a positive Christian society in mission with no competence at all. A Trinitarian model leads to social relationships that are not characterized by their power or possessions. See further Boff (1986, 150–152).

sanctification), being the seal of the promise and the guarantee of our inheritance (Eph 1:13–14).

In fact, one missiological consequence of this Trinitarian principle shows that the unity of the Godhead speaks of the relationship that members of the Trinity have with one another as the one God (298). As Lesslie Newbigin (1995, 29) points out in *The Open Secret,* God has revealed himself as proclaiming the kingdom of the Father, as sharing the life of his Son, and bearing the witness of the Spirit; this is the Trinitarian mission that empowers God's church. Daniel L. Migliore,[61] a reformed American Protestant theologian of Princeton, presents a chapter on the triune God with a similar perspective to Jewett, but adding that God is described in the Bible most frequently in personal imagery and also in impersonal metaphors such as rock, fire and water. Nevertheless, God is someone rather than something (1991, 60–66).

Missiologically speaking, for a healthy partnership theology, following Nicholas Lash (1992), who in his *Three Ways in One God* analyses the importance and impact of the Apostle's Creed on the church's mission, I wish to suggest that God's church needs to formulate a creedal statement regarding reciprocal contextual collaboration due to the fact that creeds are acts of fellowship, and of covenant and public commitment. However, we need to bear in mind that Trinitarian relationships cannot be reduced to a formula (West 1999, xv; Lash 1992, 8). We are not speaking of a creed without spirit, since it has life; it is the gospel revealed in Christ that the church has received, which makes it possible for God's people to live with joy and peace in the power of the Holy Spirit.[62] From this argument we propose

---

61. Migliore and Jewett develop the 'type C' theology given by Bevans and Schroeder which is related to Karl Barth's theology, called the new orthodoxy. For Migliore, "the logic of Trinitarian theology moves from the differentiated love *and roles* (italics mine) of the Father, Son, and Holy Spirit in the economy of salvation – the economic Trinity, to the ultimate ground of this threefold love in the depths of the divine being – the immanent Trinity" (1991, 62). In consequence, the glory of the triune God will be culminated when creation is set free from all bondage (71). Migliore (1991, 61–69) develops a wider explanation in his book, *Faith Seeking Understanding: An Introduction to Christian Theology.*

62. In this sense, in speaking of the gospel, Charles West (199, xv) points out that a Trinitarian relationship implies the long history of God's covenant love, justice, and

to develop a contextual prophetic imagination that offers tools for new ways of partnering between North and South churches. Thus, a Trinitarian theology reminds us that partnership theology has one goal: God's glory to God the Father, the Son and the Holy Spirit. As the creed is to perform an act with one objective, which is right worship of the mystery of God, so too partnership theology has to be rooted in biblical foundations, as the church has defined the foundations for a right Trinitarian theology for God's glory.

What follows is an attempt to formulate a credo for a Trinitarian reciprocal missiology:[63]

> I believe *firmly* that God is the creator of everything and the owner of his mission and that his church works for God's kingdom.
>
> I believe ***radically*** in practising a Trinitarian missiology within the love of God the Father, the grace of God the Son, and the power of God the Holy Spirit, acting in the church through different models of mission.
>
> I believe *joyfully* that God has given a call and that the church has been chosen, equipped and empowered by the Holy Spirit to fulfil its mission for holistic evangelization of the gospel.
>
> I believe ***absolutely*** in the missionary endeavour of Christ's body, which is both united and diverse, with multiple ministries, gifts and resources to help one another reciprocally.
>
> I believe ***insistently*** that an integrating work between the missionary forces of all nations is possible as long as every endeavour is submitted to a christological relationship.

---

faithfulness towards a rebellious and self-centred people.
63. See further Samuel Cueva "Misión, misioneros y la evangelización de Europa: Hacia una misiología integradora" (Malaga, Torremolinos, Spain, 14 May 2009).

I believe ***fully*** that Christ's church is capable of serving in reciprocal harmony for God's glory through both the horizontal and vertical dimensions of a reciprocal relationship with responsibility before God and others.

I believe ***consciously*** that the church's creativity expresses the confidence that God has sovereign power to sustain his church in reciprocal relational unity.

Therefore, the success of the church's mission is rooted in the oneness and Trinity of God the Father, Son and Holy Spirit, where an immanent[64] and economic Trinity is fundamental in making a positive impact in the relationships of each mission partnership. In what way? In the way that no relationship of the Trinity has a negative impact. Seng-Kong Tan describes four models of the Trinity,[65] which relate to each other in eternal harmony

---

64. For the Pentecostal Seng-Kong Tan, economic and immanent Trinity have an inseparable link. See his article: "A Trinitarian Ontology of Mission", in *International Review of Mission* Volume 93, 2004 p. 280.

65. Seng-Kong Tan develops four paradigms of the Trinity: the processional, the revelational, the dispositional, and the social paradigm. The fourth one is a counterpoint of the previous three, focusing on the fundamental unity and interrelatedness between the nature and work of the Trinity; it is related to the eternal communion of the Father, Son and Holy Spirit – the *perichoresis* – the 'divine dance' (280, 291). The preponderance of contemporary Trinitarian theology which attempts to replace the "monarchical, hierarchical and patriarchal psychological model by emphasizing the ontological equality of the Father, Son and Holy Spirit tends to devaluate the doctrine of God's sovereignty (28). Essentially, the perichoretic-social nature of the ontological Trinity is expressed by the interdependent and unified economy of the Father". See further Seng-Kong Tan (2004, 279–296). The first model describes God the Father as the unifying principle within the Godhead, and the primordial source of the Son and the Holy Spirit. The Father is one who comes but is not sent (John 14:23), and citing Ephesians 1:4–9, Tan concludes that, although the whole Trinity is the Creator and Redeemer, the design of creation and recreation is appropriate to God the Father (280). The second model describes how the incarnation of Jesus Christ is not only a revelatory event; it is the revelation of God as triune, and from this view we can speak of the triple office of Jesus Christ (285); and the third one is the dispositional model which is specific to the Holy Spirit's role in effecting an interpersonal communion of love between humanity and God and is the gratuitous nature of the Holy Spirit's proper, personal indwelling in the believer. The unitive nature and function of the Holy Spirit brings us into a vertical oneness with God, and into a horizontal communion with other believers. (290) With this understanding, a mutual responsibility and interdependence among Christians is foundational for a proper partnership mission theology.

and with a positive impact. An appropriate partnership in mission and its theology invites us to rethink our missionary role avoiding a pathological activism, not to missionize merely from command, but with an identity as God-related, Christ-like and Spirit-filled (Seng-Kong Tan 2004, 292).

A christological theology of partnership

Seeking a christological theology of partnership brings to the arena some aspects of the relationship between the Father and the Son in the light of the gospel and its influence on disciple partners with Jesus as Servant, who came to give freedom to humankind, with special attention to the poor and the weak (Luke 4:18–21). We start with the clarification that Jesus as servant is the Christ, the Son of the living God (Matt 16:17), a gift from the Father; this is the work of the Spirit of God himself (1 Cor 12:1–13). Interpreting this biblical argument, Jesus is the fulfilment of Isaiah 61, which is quoted by Jesus in the synagogue of Nazareth (Luke 4:21). But what was the purpose of this reading? As Newbigin (1995, 42; 1963, 18) affirms, it is to confirm the fulfilment of the promise to forgive the sin of God's people and to believe and affirm the final authority of Jesus Christ. This compels the *missio ecclesiae* to accept the fact that the reality of God's reign is "effectively present in Jesus in its double character of blessing and judgment" (32). In a complementary explanation Newbigin (44–48) sees five insights in Jesus' ministry: (1) Jesus saw the final consummation of God's purposes of blessing and judgment as an imminent, pressing and immediate reality. (2) The New Testament shows a church that understands itself as having Jesus Christ as its foundation (1 Cor 3:11) with the practice of baptism "into the death of Jesus" (Rom 6:3) and the regularly shared meals (1 Cor 10:16), as participation in the body and blood of Christ. (3) Jesus' vision of the immediacy of the end rests upon salvation and judgment as the central point of the Christian view of the 'the last things'. (4) Jesus' intention after his resurrection is to remind his disciples in the last supper that they are to be Jesus' partners afterwards and this double sharing for the 'bread', and the 'cup' will be a continually renewed act of participation in his dying and his victory. And (5) from a biblical understanding, the fourth gospel gives us an account of the launching of the church upon its mission (John 20:19–23; 17:18; 20:21; 20:22; 20:23).

Bevans and Schroeder sum up that the "reflection of Jesus' person which no doubt involves one in Trinitarian theology" (2004, 38). Following this view, they launched a search, under the guidance of the Cuban theologian Justo González, to produce an interesting study of three different paradigms of theology, Protestant Orthodoxy as A, Liberal Protestantism as B, and radical theology which I call *the new orthodoxy* as C (2004, 35–72, italics mine). In analysing this study, we see how Christology[66] is central when we speak about the *missio Dei* because there is no *Deus* without Christ as there is no *Deus* without Spirit; it is a Trinitarian work expressed through the love of God through his only begotten Son. A similar view is developed from an ecumenical perspective by Lesslie Newbigin[67] (1995, 30–65) clarifying the relevance of the Trinitarian doctrine (1963, 31–34). By contrast, George Eldon Ladd[68] presents an emphatic evangelical Christology (1974, 237–253).

Turning back to the theme of christological partnership, it is worth summarizing our mission theology, which offers an introduction to the christological public ministry of Jesus as the one who is acknowledged as the Son of God and is anointed by the Spirit of God. According to Mark 1:1–15 this summary is as follows (Newbigin 1995, 21–23): first, Jesus' ministry is to announce the reign of God; second, Jesus is acknowledged as the Son of God as is well described in the fourth gospel (John 1:14); and

---

66. Each of these types or paradigms that are models has been considered to be an orthodox expression of Christian faith and can be traced back to the earliest centuries of Christianity and has survived through the ages (Bevans 2004, 35).

67. From a Trinitarian perspective in his book *The Open Secret,* Newbigin reminds us that the mission of the triune God has three actions: Proclaiming the kingdom of the Father-mission as faith in action, sharing the life of the Son-Mission as love in action, and bearing the witness of the Spirit-mission as hope in action. Similar to Newbigin, at the celebration of the 50th anniversary of the IMC Willingen 1952, the German Lutheran Bishop Martin Hein gave a meditation based on John 3:17 stating three biblical foundations: the origin of mission is God, the horizon of God's mission is the world, and the aim of God's mission is salvation. See further *International Review of Mission*, Vol XCII, No 367, October 2003, 478–480.

68. Ladd, in his book *A Theology of the New Testament,* presents Jesus as the Logos, Messiah, the Son of Man, the Son of God, the divine Son and then he emphasizes the humanity of Jesus, which in partnership mission theology is fundamental to understanding the development of a positive relationships. See Ladd (1974, 237–252).

third, Jesus is anointed by the Spirit (Luke 4:18–19), which took place at his baptism. This biblical theology helps the church to answer the question, "who is Jesus?", a question that is foundational for a christological partnership mission theology. In other words, the evidence is that there is no appropriate partnership mission theology without the presence of the incarnated Jesus Christ; he is the pivotal centre of the *missio Dei*, God's kingdom, God's church and missiological thinking; the Spirit is the agent. We conclude that there is no appropriate partnership theology without Christology[69] due to the fact that Christ is the pivotal centre of the *missio Dei* and from this theology emerge the principles of reciprocal contextual collaboration.

A missiological understanding of partnership in Paul's theology

As scholars have shown at different periods, Paul's mission theology is deep and vast. For this reason I will limit my discussion by concentrating on four specific principles that are applicable to every mission partnership context. These are as follows:

Preparing servant leadership for mission partnership

In Paul's thinking, the righteousness of God, according to Romans 3:21–31, is to be interpreted as a gift to the community rather than to the individual. This is clearly developed in his two letters to the Corinthians (Bosch 2001,

---

69. Moltmann has written five books with an emphasis on Trinitarian Christology. His first major work, *Theology of Hope*, develops a perspective on the relationship of the triune God to history; his second book, *The Crucified God*, relates to an exposition of the cross as a Trinitarian event; the third work, *The Church in the Power of the Spirit*, engages with aspects of Trinitarian theology. *The Trinity and the Kingdom*, is the most complete explication of his doctrine of the Trinity in which "he clarifies that the complete divine unity belongs to the eschatological future". Moltmann bases his breaks with Barth and the patristic writers on the Trinitarian character of the history of Jesus who is manifested as the Son. He points out that "the history of Christ is already related in Trinitarian terms in the New Testament itself" (Grenz 2004, 75, 77, 79). In *Experiences of Theology*, Moltmann proposes that the nature of God's creating act is closely connected to the divine *perichoresis*. His view is that the eternal dance of the three persons is not only a movement of each in the others but also each offering others space for movement (83).

166). This implies that individualism is prohibited in a biblical mission partnership since Paul develops a theology of Christ's body, which is the *ekklesia*. In consequence, leadership for partnership in Christian mission implies the following four aspects. First, mission is to be conducted according to what the leaders are in Christ, which is manifested in reciprocal relationship and in admonishing those who threaten harmony in the *ekklesia* (166). Second, unity among believers has its basis in the fact that through baptism (1 Cor 12:13) they are incorporated into Christ (Rom 6:3–11, Gal 3:26, Col 3:10). Baptism consciously brings about a change in social relationship and self-understanding, since faith in Christ makes fellowship possible. Third, the celebration of the Lord's Supper (1 Cor 10–11) offers a sustained argument in support of a greater social integration between rich and poor. Thus the Lord's Supper should become a sign of missiological encounter[70] between partners in mission. Reconciliation with God is in jeopardy if Christians are not reconciled to each other. Likewise, segregation in the *ekklesia* on grounds of race, ethnicity, gender or social status is not acceptable because God in Christ has accepted believers unconditionally. Fourth, partnership in mission is not undertaken in order to resolve differences or establish agreements, but rather to develop a transformed human relationship by Christ's work of reconciliation (168).

Helping one another in mission partnership

The Pauline theology of partnership is based on the *koinonia* concept (Phil 1:5), which is related to a relationship of common goals, but also to a common understanding of reciprocity between those partners in God's mission. Paul uses the word *koinonia* four times in Philippians (1:5, 2:1, 3:10, 4:14) to speak of a full relationship of participation in the proclamation of God's kingdom which avoids a unilateral approach and dichotomy while seeking a functional servanthood and functional cooperation which means serving with a useful purpose. *Koinonia* implies fellowship, association, community, communion, joint participation, partnership, contribution, sharing of friendship, practical sharing and partnership in the work of Christ (Peters

---

70. According to Galatians 2:9 it is interesting to note that James, Peter and John, leaders of the early church, shook hands with Barnabas and Paul as a sign of partnership. See Whitehead (1991, 7).

1972, 233–234). Equally, partner, partaker and *koinonoi* are linked to the concept of *koinonia*. For this reason, the word partnership has been chosen as the more appropriate equivalent.

A complementary concept to *koinonia* relates to solidarity, which is defined as active participation and collaboration and unanimity; it is related neither to human relationships nor to the world as such, but rather to communion with Christ and with those who have come to the gospel. This implies a reciprocal recognition of belonging to Christ (1 Cor 1:9; 2 Cor 13:13; Phil 1:5, 3:10).[71] It seems to me that this clarification should lead to an intentional situation of free sharing of resources, natural reciprocity, permanent reciprocity, and of a relationship grounded in fellowship in and through a christological understanding of mission.[72]

In connection with this, for the Irish Catholic theologian James Whitehead (1991, 7) *koinonia* describes the relationship of determined adults struggling to resolve their conflict. Alec Motyer (1984, 47) defines partnership as joint-ownership or participation in a common purpose. For Whitehead, "partnership, both in the gospel and in contemporary life is an experience of shared power" (1991, 8). With this in mind, we see that this shared power has to be based firmly on the rejection of domination on both sides, while the word equality needs careful clarification due to the fact that the term can mean sameness, and suggests an image of quantity, while partnership stresses diversity in which partners enrich their relationship. Consequently, I agree with Whitehead when he points out, "More than on strict equality, partnership depends on *reciprocity*. The giving and the receiving go both ways; in a *reciprocal* relationship each *autonomous body* brings something of value" (1991, 8 italics mine). *Koinonia*,[73] which also implies spirituality, goes beyond the local church, making a contribution to the need of the saints (Rom 12:13). The church participates in God's

---

[71]. See further Coenen, Beyreuther and Bietenhard, *Diccionario Teológico del Nuevo Testamento* Vol. IV (1980, 226–233).

[72]. See further George W. Peters in *A Biblical Theology of Mission* (1972, 233–236).

[73]. Partnership invites us to bring something of value, receive something of worth, recognize each other and respect one another with a wide variety of gifts. These characteristics bring the reality of practical *koinonia* between partners, which is always developed in a missiological tension. Displaying a practical concern for the material needs of fellow members expresses maturity.

kingdom[74] as its members are sensitive to the needs and circumstances of others.[75]

Karl Barth (1962, 15–16) defines *koinonia* as participation in the gospel which leads Paul to joyful prayer.[76] This is an expression of solidarity and hence supplication, prayer and intercession, giving thanks to God that the Philippians stand with the apostle in his mission. This participation in the gospel implies, consequently, financial support received (Phil 4:10–12). However, the main point has to be concentrated in the proclamation of the gospel. It was a participation of active collaboration of the Philippians in spreading the gospel "from the first day until now". It means that it is not just financial support to someone who is sent in mission. Rather, according to verse seven, it accompanies Paul's mission according to God's grace and *synkoinonia* (co-partnership).[77] This implies a relationship of people who believe in the gospel and who have made a radical commitment to the good news, but with joy (Rom 5:2). There are no existential gaps in this kind of relationship between Paul and the Philippians, since they are eager and right to maintain and strengthen that *missio* relationship in biblical reciprocity.

For Gordon Fee (1999, 12), Philippians is a letter of friendship with instructions that are personal on the one hand and related to business on the other. Fee analyses the cultural context of friendship in the Greco-Roman World, which establishes a friendship between equals (and also between those not considered equals, such as women and men, gentiles and Jews) whose relationship implies goodwill, loyalty, trust, and enjoyment of the same thing.[78] A philosophical discussion of friendship is mainly based

---

74. This argument shows that this is why "it appears that mission partnership theology seems weak and negative when we develop a missiology divorced from Christology and eschatology" (Baker quoted in Bosch 2001, 169).

75. There is no dualism between the human soul and the external world; there is a profound solidarity and interdependence between the church and the world because the church is the *ekklesia* to create new relationships among themselves and in society.

76. For F. F. Bruce, the clause "because of your partnership" is literary rendered to "because of your participation"; it was a cooperation with Paul in the gospel since first he visited their city. See further F. F. Bruce in *New International Biblical Commentary, Philippians* (1989, 31–33).

77. See further Karl Barth, *The Epistle to the Philippians* (1962, 15–16).

78. See further Gordon D. Fee, *Philippians* (1999, 15–16).

on loyalty (fidelity), affection as reciprocal goodwill, and social reciprocity (27) that implies a giving and receiving of benefits, including the form of gratitude (Fee, 15). This interpretation leads us to reflect on the biblical understanding of Paul's missional relationship to the Philippians. The reciprocity of friendship includes moral exhortation and humility within relationships (Phil 2:3). As Fee points out clearly, it is participation or partnership in the gospel (1:5). In other words, it is a reciprocal contextual collaboration of all participants that empowers the *missio Dei*. Philippians 1:4–5 anticipates the theme of increasing recognition of care and loving relationship with gifts (4:10–20), which is preceded by the exhortation regarding sharing the defence of the gospel (1: 27–2:18).

A reciprocal contextual collaboration is intimately linked with the proclamation of the gospel, which implies salvation and integral transformation from sin to a new creation in Christ. This is the reason why there is a reciprocal sharing in suffering (4:17–21), reciprocal sharing of joy (4: 1–9), and reciprocal sharing of gifts (4:10–20). The basis for thanksgiving in Paul's theology relates to the *missio* collaboration (*koinonia*) in the furtherance of the gospel. But *koinonia* refers primarily to participation in something (the gospel) rather than sharing something (gifts) in common with others (Fee, 47). It is the gospel that makes possible a long-term reciprocal contextual collaboration in which both mission participants (*koinonoi*) are complementary and reciprocal co-participation in the proclamation of the gospel and the sharing of practical resources are developed naturally. Kirk (1999, 19, 201) defines partnership as the essence of the church in mission and, by way of complementing Barth and Fee, he identifies some obstacles to partnership, like the effect of non-cooperation, and the concept of power within all relationships (194–198) that have to be challenged in any reciprocal missiology.

A christological mission reciprocity implies that there are observable facts that are evidence of a true relationship of God's people, which is based not only in institutional relations but in the essence of the gospel. Alec Motyer (984, 46–47) in *The Message of Philippians* states six evidences of a *koinonia* gospel: unanimity in the truth / partnership in the gospel (v. 5), the defence and confirmation of the gospel (v. 7), the confirmation of the gospel (establishing believers), perseverance, endurance and identification.

The Philippians produced an effective and active work for the gospel sacrificially identified with Paul's mission. The origin of this reciprocal *koinonia* is that the church in Philippi is partnering with Paul by grace, and that reciprocal contextual collaboration in the gospel has made them mature partakers of salvation that has a trans-temporal eternal glory.[79] In this line, the Australian Alan Tippett (1987, ix, 40–45), from an anthropological view, provide seven elements of key values of a group in biblical *koinonia*, which are as follows: spiritual experience of the *koinonoi*, focused in worship, a rigorous commitment to the Lord, a high moral life (as essential for the *koinonoi*), fellowship in suffering, fellowship in service, and an obligation for world mission.[80]

Participation of the church in mission partnership

The church is called to be a community of those who glorify God, manifesting the reconciliation and redemption found through Christ (1 Cor 5:18). Herein is found the positive creative tension between being exclusive and practising solidarity with others. The uniqueness of the church reflects the uniqueness of Christ in the sense that both are unique in their mission role: Christ gave his life for the world, while the church shares this news of reconciliation in Christ. Ekklesia's primary mission in the world is to be the new creation whose motive is God's glory. Paul emphasizes not ethical passivity but active participation in God's redemptive will; he does not permit an illusory escape from suffering for the church, since suffering is a mode of missionary involvement. On the one hand, Paul's theology of the church has a bifocal vision: God's work in Christ is both past and future, and through the ethical order which is a moral order (Bosch 2001, 176). In fact, one of the internal aspects of partnership is that missionary unity does not mean working in the same place or with a local or specific missionary vision, but rather, as Bosch (168) says, to be united in mutual love, biblical conduct and a radical joy.[81]

---

79. See further Alec Motyer, *The Message of Philippians* (1984, 446–447).

80. Tippett deals with missiological theory, anthropological and historical dimension of missiology. See further Alan Tippett, *Introduction to Missiology* (1987, 41–43).

81. These elements are part of the very nature of the ekklesia, which provides the basis for a positive theology of reciprocal contextual collaboration. For Pauline mission theology,

Hugh Palmer, Rector of All Souls Church, Langham Place, London, elucidates this dimension of partnership when he points out that, according to 1 Corinthians 12:1–11, believers are the body of Christ because they are baptized by the same Spirit. Thus, the church is collectively the body of Christ. This implies that Christians are individuals, but not individualists; in Christ's body there is no room for individualism. However, because Christians are different, they can contribute in different ways because each member is distinct, indispensable and different. I agree with Palmer in the sense that in any reciprocal contextual collaboration each member has a role, which must be undertaken with joyful humility, serving one another reciprocally.[82] Reciprocal contextual collaboration does not happen automatically; Christians are not clones but they are still united, it is a Christian unity in diversity, it is all about differences but empowered by the same Spirit. The church is not divided by its members' gifts; on the contrary these unite the church, since particular gifts of service are determined by God's Spirit. Consequently, spiritual gifts are not for each individual's glory; they are manifested for the common good of God's kingdom.[83]

God's glory and mission partnership

For Paul, partnership is a tool for establishing the *basileia*. In this respect, Bosch, in contrast to Roland Allen's *Missionary Methods: St Paul's or Ours?* (1983), develops Paul's mission theology using Paul's letters as primary sources.[84] Following his methodology we might summarize this biblical theology as follows: historically,[85] Paul and early Christians were motivated by the eschatological glory of God (Pocock 2005, 163). Theologically, Paul's motivation is God's glory. In their book *The Changing Face of World*

---

the church is now the eschatological people of God, and is the Christ-body on earth.

82. See further Hugh Palmer (2009 "How to be gifted and godly" (1), 1 Corinthians 12:1–11, All Souls Church, Langham Place, London, C149/01-CD).

83. See further Heewoo Han (2009 "How to be gifted and godly" (2), 1 Corinthians 12:12–31, All Souls Church, Langham Place, London, C149/01-CD).

84. In applying this methodology, Bosch uses seven of them: Romans, 1 and 2 Corinthians, Galatians, Philippians, Thessalonians and Philemon; Acts remains as a secondary source

85. However, we should not idealize the early Christian period. Why? Because the Pauline and Johannine writings reflect mixed motives. Some preach Christ for envy, but others for goodwill (Phil 1:15). See Pocock (2005, 164).

Missions, Michael Pocock, Gailyn Van Rheenen and Douglas McConnell (2005, 173) include a chapter on the theology of God's glory, and they state:

> Christians are called to taste the glory of God, enabling them to reflect God's glory to the world. This desire for God – to be with him, to reflect his glory, and to perceive life beyond these human bounds – is the core of Christian motivation. Glory is a quality belonging to God and Christians, therefore, must first perceive God's glory and then participate in it

Missiologically, Paul's motivation for mission is shaped not only by Spirit-guided responses to God's revelation, but also by cultural and historical perspectives.

Partnership as a tool of establishing the *basileia*

In his first chapter of *Transforming Mission,* Bosch (1991, 31) introduces a brief analysis of the basileia concept in relation to both Jesus' entire ministry and his own redemptive mission. He explains that it is not easy to define Jesus' view of the basileia because Jesus speaks of it mainly in parables. Bosch suggests that God's reign in Jesus (*basileia tou Theou*) is eminently political, a subversive activity[86] not to be tolerated by the establishment of

---

86. For example, the evangelical theologian Andrew Kirk (1980, 42–56) presents in *Theology Encounters Revolution,* an overview of Walter Rauschenbusch (1861–1918), Reinhold Niebuhr (1892–1964), Karl Barth (1886–1968) and Dietrich Bonhoeffer (1906–1945). Revolutionary theology started in the post-war period as a result of bad conscience and with a transforming mission in mind, challenging modern theology to social questions. Thus, revolutionary theology was born when Christian thinkers realized the political and economic reality of the Third World (42–43). The German jurist Arnold Ehrhardt (Bosch 1991, 47) provides elements of the subversive nature of the early Christian faith. He was able to identify many early Christian sayings and seditious attitudes on the part of early Christians at the time of the Roman and Greek empires. This applies to the Jesus' movement in Palestine around AD 30, and that of Paul, Luke and other New Testament writers. For Bosch (1991, 47–48), the Christian movement of the first century was a radically revolutionary movement but not to be evaluated in terms of terror. It was a revolution against all gods and had the following three characteristics: A rejection of all gods to demolish the metaphysical foundations of prevailing political theories. Christians confessed Jesus as the Lord of all lords, which was the most

his epoch.[87] Therefore, for partnership in mission, I agree with Bosch when he states that we may legitimately extrapolate from Jesus' model of mission, according to which partners may apply Jesus' words and ministry by just deducing principles of his teaching out of the mission context in today's world. It is necessary for all partners in mission to contextualize Jesus' basileia teaching properly. In fact, I suggest that the nature of all reciprocal contextual collaboration in mission becomes a mission tool for establishing the *basileia tou Theou*. Consequently, the right motive to partner with others includes a reciprocal desire to live according to the missionary nature of the church, which has a Trinitarian *missio* mandate. One negative tension, which hinders Christian partnership, arises when the church tends to forget that basileia implies that God's reign is at one and the same time a future as well as present reality. Therefore, eschatological reality should be included in all mission partnership theology as a clear understanding that partnership is a collaboration tool in the *missio Dei*. On the other hand, a positive tension emerges from the biblical understanding of Jesus' basileia teaching, mentioned in Mark eighteen times, and in Matthew fifty times, both of which contain a double dimension, the "good news of the gospel" and the "gospel of the basileia". The second refers to Jesus himself, and the first refers to preaching the gospel of the kingdom (70–71). Equally, reciprocal contextual collaboration in mission should be understood as a tool to collaborate with this double mission dimension: the gospel as the good news, and Christ himself as the *basileia gospel*. In parallel with the *basileia* concept, the *dikaiosyne*[88] concept works together and is inseparable from an appropriate mission theology of partnership.

---

revolutionary political demonstration in the Roman Empire. And the idea of religion as a positive affair, since divorcing the spiritual from the physical was unthinkable for every Christian of the first century.

87. For Bosch "To declare lepers, tax collectors, sinners and the poor to be 'Children of God's kingdom' is a decidedly political statement", especially over against the Jewish establishment at that time (1991, 34).

88. For Bosch the translation of *dikaiosyne* is problematic and it may refer to justification or to righteousness. See the fourth beatitude (Matt 5:6, 6:33). The solution he proposes it to translate it 'justice-righteousness' (1991, 72), in an attempt to hold both dimensions. *Dikaiosyne* is translated variously as 'justice', 'holiness', 'piety', and 'godliness'. Bosch follows Michael Crosby' analysis stating that righteousness has a double dimension: first, the constitutive dimension – "God justifying us, making us righteous and holy in his sight. Once constituted in God's justice, God uses us to make justice and praise spring up

Conclusion

We have developed partnership in mission and its theology with three current theological emphases: the *missio Dei*, God's kingdom and God's church. We have also considered mission partnership in a christological and Pauline perspective. Conscious of the problems which arise as we seek to relate the complexity of the organized church to its missionary task, we have suggested a theological emphasis on the *missio Trinitatis* to adequately develop the inclusiveness of reciprocal contextual collaboration in twenty-first-century mission. We have approached the question bearing in mind the variety of different theologies that influence mission partnership. To conclude, given that the church is by nature missionary, it has the important privilege of participating in the *missio Dei,* which has a Trinitarian mission plan, since it is the *missio Trinitatis* that empowers the whole mission activity of the church in the world. In this sense, it seems that the challenge which lies before us is to foster a synergy partnership, with a reciprocal contextual collaboration in God's church, within all different mission structures and partnership models, and so to develop a more contextual and reciprocal partnership influenced by the example of the *missio Trinitatis*. This is one reason why competition between local churches and mission societies, and between missionaries and different ministries, must be recognized as sin that seeks a horizontal glory between partners rather than the vertical, that is, to the *missio Trinitatis* to whom eternally belongs all the glory[89] of all *missio partnership* activity. Therefore, it is time to rethink our mission partnership theology in the light of the *missio Dei*

---

before all the nations" (Isa 61:11); and second, the normative dimension – "God raising up people who become ministers to others of the same justice they have experienced from God" (72). Therefore, *dikaiosyne* is 'faith in action' (72) and this perspective is crucial to apply in the church's mission for the sake of an appropriate healthy mission theology of partnership.

89. The emphasis on God's glory becomes a key element in all Christian reciprocal contextual collaboration; in the way that God's kingdom belongs to Christ, not to us; and the church needs to be aware that in Christ we become collaborators of his kingdom. Therefore, we are not allowed to act either as owners of the *missio Dei* or of the *missio partnership*, but yes, we are allowed, encouraged and commanded in biblical, theological and ecclesiological perspective to partner as co-participants, heralds, ambassadors, and athletes that belong to and work for God's kingdom in reciprocal contextual collaboration with the *missio Trinitatis*. This mission view is reinforced by the emphasis on the *missio*

with a Trinitarian theology, but in parallel with a conscious theological and missiological determination within God's kingdom. On the other side, the basileia concept helps us to understand the glory of the kingdom, which is an everlasting kingdom, as God's rule or sovereignty, since it is Christ the King who is coming to reign above all mission partners. Therefore, all true reciprocal contextual collaboration in mission, informed by biblical and right theological interpretation, has to offer models which are rooted in the *missio Dei*, and in the *missio kingdom* theology with a Trinitarian emphasis. Otherwise, there is a danger of multiplying damaged relationships between mission partners in the twenty-first-century mission.

Trinitatis, which helps the church not to reduce the eternal and infinite mission work of God the Father the Son and the Holy Spirit.

CHAPTER 3

Current Models of Partnership in Mission: an Analysis of their Main Characteristics, Policies and Impact on the Evangelical Movement

Introduction

In this chapter we will try to discover what has been hindering a positive developing partnership in the last twenty years or so within the evangelical movement. Obviously there could be many different models of partnership in mission, but I have chosen three models that are influencing the mission evangelical enterprise. They are as follows: Traditional Partnership (***Traditional Model***) between mission societies and churches, Innovative Networking Partnership (***Networking Model***) between mission societies in a non-territorial way, and Emergent Partnership (***Emergent Model***) between local churches and indigenous mission societies. This chapter will analyse their main characteristics – historical, theological and missiological; policies in respect of personnel and finances; and the impact – sociological, cultural, ecclesiological, economic and global.

The traditional model

Historical, theological and missiological characteristics

Traditional Partnership (The Traditional Model) has been promoted during the last two hundred years, and the nineteenth century, called by Latourette 'the Great Century' of World Missions (1800–1914), is thus the first century in which Protestantism was heavily involved in missions. Winter (1981, B54) states that this century was also the lowest point of Catholic mission energy.[1] Klaus Fiedler[2] (1994, 9–20–21) defines Traditional Partnership as 'classical missions' by which he refers to denominational and interdenominational missions working independently of the control of any church, but related to some churches of the same type. My assumption is that the Traditional Partnership model has its origins in the Protestant movement, with the beginning of the Baptist Society for Propagating the Gospel, known also as the Baptist Missionary Society (BMS) founded in 1792 by William Carey.[3] The impact of this first mission society on the Protestant movement led to the London Missionary Society (LMS) in 1795 as an interdenominational mission (Bosch 2001, 330). Later the Anglican Church Missionary Society (CMS) appeared in 1799; most of its missionaries were German Lutherans at the beginning.

In contrast with the classical missions we have the post-classical mission known as 'faith missions', with less concern for the theological view

---

1. The origin of mission societies goes back to the formation of the Catholic order during the fourth century, but in the Protestant movement this model started with what Klaus Fiedler calls pre-classical mission, initiated by the Society for the Propagation for the Gospel (SPG), 1701, and the Moravian Mission (1732). See Fiedler (1994).

2. The German scholar Fiedler who works at the University of Malawi, in his book *The Story of Faith Missions*, describes three main divisions for the origin of the mission societies: pre-classical which refers to the Society for the Propagation of the Gospel – 1701, the Danish Hallesche Mission – 1706, and the Moravian Mission – 1732. All of them have their origin in the first great revival after the Reformation; second, the classical missions, which refers to mission societies organized independently of any church with the concept of the church as corporate body. This classical mission includes the interdenominational missions which worked indirectly for churches. And thirdly, the post-classical missions with the practice of faith support and non-denominational structure. See further Fiedler (1994, 11–25).

3. William Carey is known as "the father of the modern missions" for "the modern era". See further Gerald H. Anderson, Robert T, Coote, Norman A. Horner and James M. Phillips (1994, 245).

of doctrine, becoming more widely interdenominational and with a concept of direct and individual responsibility to God, and of faith support. This model starts with Hudson Taylor who founded the China Inland Mission (CIM) in 1865 (Fiedler 1994, 12), called the Overseas Missionary Fellowship (OMF) from 1975.[4] Thus the resulting CIM/OMF made a missiological impact on the following missions (11–19; Winter and Hawthorne 1981, B–54): Livingstone Inland Mission (LIM), 1878; Regions Beyond Missionary Union (RMBU), 1881; Christian and Missionary Alliance (CMA) 1887; South Africa General Mission (SAGM), 1889; Sudan Interior Mission, now SIM International (SIM), 1900; Sudan United Mission (SUM), 1904; Worldwide Evangelization Crusade (WEC),1913; Neukirchen, 1882; and the Pentecostal faith mission – Assemblies of God Mission, 1908. William Booth will not be considered here because he established the Salvation Army as a denomination (Benge 2002). It is important to understand that British missionaries worked in British colonies and it seems that missionaries became pioneers of Western imperialism during the high imperial era of 1880–1920 (Bosch 2001, 304). In consequence, from these classical and post-classical missions mentioned emerge the contribution of traditional partnership models with the influence of Carey's characteristics and policies,[5] leading to networking and the emergent partnership.

Here, I attempt to define the Traditional Model (Traditional Partnership): It is the mission activity of the church, related to the formation of mission societies or mission agencies that structurally work independently[6] of local churches as autonomous bodies, but in partnership with them to accomplish the double mandate of the Great Commission. Consequently, Escobar (2002, 47) gives five pivotal characteristics of the

---

4. See more: http://www.omf.org/omf/uk/about_omf/omf_cim_history

5. Bosch (1991, 330) explains that Carey took his analogy in the formation of his mission structure from the contemporary commercial world, from the organization of an overseas trading company. There was something businesslike to work as an instrumental society with the purpose of evangelizing distant people. This kind of mission structure was established for both denominational and non-denominational missions.

6. My missiological assumption is that Traditional Partnership was expanded in the Protestant movement through the influence of mission societies' structures, working independently of the local churches as non-ecclesiastical initiatives but with the influence of mission-minded leaders that belonged to a local church.

Moravian movement,[7] which I relate to Traditional Partnership; however, I identify ten key characteristics and policies:
1. Commitment to the Lordship of Jesus Christ and the fulfilment of His Great Commission.
2. Commitment to the unity of the Body of Christ to work in partnership with others from diverse backgrounds culturally and ecclesiastically.
3. Commitment to evangelization, in a broad sense of incarnational and transformational ministry, with the inclusion of a non-territorial mission.
4. Salaried position for missionaries as employees.
5. Finances are provided by the gifts of individuals, and contribution of churches.
6. Membership fees, insurance for health and prompt return, periodical visiting to the sending country generally after four years, etc.
7. Missionaries cannot leave the sending country before raising their budget for the mission field, and accountability is essential.
8. Every mission has a budget for single persons, married couples and couples with children.
9. In most cases, missionaries consider a percentage of their income as being for the administration of the mission society.
10. Churches channel their financial support to missionaries through the mission society.[8]

Some key elements of Traditional Partnership, which are the basic pattern for those mission societies which appeared after 1792, are seen in Carey's characteristics and policy (Anderson et al. 1994, 246–249):
1. Integrated mission enterprise participating in private enterprise and intellectual activity.

---

[7]. These characteristics are as follows: (1) church and school go together, (2) the Bible must be available to people in their own language, (3) preaching of the gospel must be understandable to the people, (4) the goal of mission must be conversion, and (5) as soon as possible there must be a native church with its own national pastor (2002, 47–48).

[8]. Missionaries belong to the mission society, not to the local churches because they make an agreement as employees of the mission society who provide the logistic tools including care, channelling donations, supervision for the mission task for missionaries, etc.

2. To convert India's people and those who were part of the European occupation.[9]
3. The creation of team work, with the known 'Serampore Trio'.[10]
4. Mission management and practice of the civil service.[11]
5. Developing a task to earn money by making contracts with the government for the Serampore Mission Press, making Carey and the mission financially independent of the BMS.
6. Practice of a long-term mission commitment, making an impact by becoming a mission catalyst rather than a mission strategist.
7. Encouraging Western Christian denominations to cooperate voluntarily for the propagation of the gospel.
8. Mission policies by establishing printing and publishing press, public relations, developing a mission strategy, opening boarding schools and day schools, orphans, philology, orientalism, literacy, social reform, botany, evangelization and mission promotion, to bring young British Baptist missionaries to help Carey's mission.[12]

By analyzing Carey's traditional partnership, we find that this model was developed in two ways: as a 'primitive model', which is related to financial independence, and as a 'professional model', linked to the BMS as a practical

---

[9]. Carey appears to be quite radical, holistic and ingenious.

[10]. It was a solitary mission until the arrival of William Ward and Joshua Marshman, the two volunteers who provided the skills needed for the creation of a team in 1799, known as 'the Serampore Trio' and defined by Christopher Smith (Anderson et al.1994, 246) as Carey's partners.

[11]. Carey worked in Bible translation, as a tutor and professor with the Indian government.

[12]. Bosch (1991, 296) explains that William Carey and William Wilberforce (who spent three decades campaigning for the abolition of the slavery in the British Empire) worked similarly together for both civilization and the spread of the gospel. Therefore, I understand that Carey practised a holistic mission due to the fact that he was very involved in knowing the needs of the world and bringing practical solutions for contributing to the development of the society. Carey practised an integrated mission enterprise due to the fact that pragmatic enlightenment values operated within evangelicalism at that time (Anderson et al. 1994, 248). He published *An Enquiry into the Obligation of Christians, to Use Mean for the Conversion of the Heathens* (1792), accepted work as a manager of an indigo plantation in Bengal, was a professor of Bengali and Sanskrit at Fort William College, Calcutta, worked in partnership with other veteran colleagues and Indian people in the areas of philology, Bible translation, Orientalism, literacy, education by founding the Serampore College in 1818. See further Anderson Gerald (1998, 115).

expression of solidarity from the sending country with an informal, cordial and intimate relationship until the mission became institutionalized (250). Hence, I agree with the analysis of Christopher Smith (Smith in Anderson et al. 1994, 250), whose experience with non-Western Christianity and cross-cultural Christian partnership has led him to advocate a missiological realism (understood as a realistic assessment of the cost of mission service) with respect to achievements in the mission task. Evidently, Smith is eager to relate these achievements to the kind of missiological realism the Bible demands of those who are involved in mission activity. This would also imply a practical understanding of the mission context, which avoids idealized demands.[13] Why? As has already been observed, the fact is that there was no appropriate training, and no financial assistance, from the BMS before sending Carey to the field. These two factors appear to hinder[14] the impact in spreading the gospel among India's people, with the consequence that Carey had to find ways to manage these two key issues. In fact, protection for the family was very weak, as Guthrie (2000, 33) explains; Carey's wife paid the price with mental illness. However, the strength of this traditional partnership is that Carey's[15] mission structure established the pattern for the coming of many young missionaries,[16] which is still a model for many mission societies.

Historically, traditional partnership is linked to the formation of mission societies starting with Catholic societies (Beaver in Winter and Hawthorne

---

13. In my understanding, some lessons of Carey's achievements also suggest ways in which one might apply a biblical mission theology to a practical understanding of the mission context, and thereby avoid an idealized or romantic view that insists on getting great results without taking into consideration the tensions of gospel and culture. For example, the mission of the twenty-first century might avoid an overemphasis on Carey's achievements, given that he and his team, while 'expecting great things' and accomplishing 'great things' through radical self-denial, in fact experienced unnecessary suffering and a lack of balance with respect to cross-cultural missiology (Anderson et al. 1995, 249–250). Thus, a realistic understanding of mission, regardless of one's mission model, will depend in part on the proper consideration of the context.

14. On the other side, it seems that Carey focused on incarnating the gospel directly in the midst of India's rural population; he tried to protect the institutionalization of the mission, its maintenance and also spent time in linguistics and translation (251).

15. I consider Carey to be the major influence on modern Protestant mission societies.

16. There was a lack of indigenous followers with the consequence of the collapse of the Serampore Mission after Marshman died in 1837.

1981, B58–B72) and then Protestant societies like the Moravians 1732 (Grant, B73–73; Howard, B78). Later the classical and post-classical missions we mentioned before appear. Thus, the worth of traditional Protestant partnership begins with the experience of the British missionary William Carey,[17] a non-conformist and self-educated tradesman, known as the pioneer of the modern mission era 1761–1834, who went to India, with his family (Guthrie[18] 2000), sent by the BMS (Anderson et al. 1994, 247–248).

It appears that in Traditional Partnership, the local church becomes just a moral and financial support but does not have any part in making decisions for allocating missionaries in mission; this is the duty of each traditional mission agency. In Winter's analysis[19] we find that he makes a clear difference between mission agency structure called 'sodality', and mission by the local church called 'modality' (1981, B-45–56), thus, the Lausanne movement defines[20] mission agencies as "the religious order whose purpose is to plant, strengthen and partner with churches around the world" (2005, 135).

---

17. Carey, with a Calvinist theology, contributed to the running of the 'Serampore Mission', which functioned independently of the Baptist Missionary Society that was founded after his call to preach the gospel throughout the world. This mission structure was set up by twelve Baptists as a voluntary society. According to the policy of the BMS, Carey became a missionary to Bengala, India, which was an unprepared mission for a family with six children. At that time, pragmatic enlightenment values operated within the framework of evangelical Calvinism in the era of Britain's industrial and agriculture revolutions. See further Anderson et al. (1994, 247–248).

18. Stan Guthrie, associate editor of *Christianity Today*, in his book *Missions in the Third Millennium: 21 Key Trends for the 21st Century*, speaking of missionary care, describes the painful experience of Carey's wife Dorothy. See further Guthrie (2000, 32–34).

19. For Winter, there are two mission structures of God's redemptive mission: the New Testament church like a Christian synagogue (modality), and the pre-Pauline Jewish proselytizers work following the same model as Paul's team, as a missionary endeavour of experienced workers affiliated as a second decision beyond membership in the first structure (sodality). See further Winter (B-45–B-56). But the question is whether Winter seeks a dynamic equivalent and not just formal replication of the historical structures. The analysis offered by this scholar helps to clarify that traditional partnership is the functional equivalent of the effective mission structure developed by Paul's missionary model. But I challenge the overemphasis Winter gives to the concept of 'sodality'. However, we are aware that the monastic tradition followed this second model.

20. This definition was given by the issue group on the Two-Thirds World Church after the 2004 Forum for World Evangelization in Pattaya, Thailand. They try to amplify the definition by attempting to answer what is the function of a mission agency but they do not use a critical analysis of the nature of a mission agency. See further Claydon (2005).

With regard to theology, traditional partnership has rooted its development in a biblical understanding, taking for granted key texts of both the Old and the New Testaments, but I will limit myself to emphasizing the evangelistic mandate, given in a christological remark, which is as follows: Matthew 28:19-20, known as 'the Great Commission',[21] with a Trinitarian emphasis – "in the name of the Father and of the Son and of the Holy Spirit"; Mark 16:15 with a universal mission emphasis – "preach the gospel to every creature"; Luke 24:47 with a christological historical emphasis – "it was necessary for the Christ to suffer"; John 20:21 with a missiological emphasis – "As the Father has sent me, I also send you"; and Acts 1:8 with a pneumatological mission emphasis says – "You shall receive power when the Holy Spirit comes upon you". Yet, the most powerful mobilization and the direct challenge to empower the mission enterprise can be measured in the evangelical movement through the Great Commission mandate. Therefore, scholars have contributed to mission theology in connection with the evangelistic mandate. John Charles Ryle, the Anglican bishop of Liverpool, emphasized the cooperation of the Trinity to create mankind and to save them[22] (McGrath and Packer 1993, 295). Escobar gives a missiological emphasis on the propagation of the gospel (2003, 11). Padilla disapproves of the lack of theological understanding of an integral evangelistic mandate [23](1985, 37), and Mortimer Arias[24] (1976, 87), in interpreting one of the 27 theses on *Evangelism in Latin America Today*, states that

---

21. For Bosch (1991, 340), the appeal to the 'Great Commission' has always been important in Protestant missions, especially for the evangelical Anglo-Saxon sphere. In the United States it was the main focus for missions after 1810, and Robert Morrison (1792–1834), and Adoniram Judson (1788–1850) went to the mission field in obedience to Christ's command. Bosch also clarifies that it was the Dutch theologian Adrian Saravia (1531–1613) who published a tract in favour of the 'Great Commission' before Carey. Equally did the Dutchman J. Heurnius in 1648 and the Lutheran nobleman Justinian von Welz in 1664. See further Bosch (1991, 247, 529).

22. In fact, God's salvation is completed through Christ's suffering, death and resurrection; this is the good news that all Christian partnership has to bear in mind as part of its mission theology.

23. See further Padilla's essay: *Evangelism and the World* included in his book *Mission Between the Times* (1985). He defines the Great Commission of Luke 24:47 by repentance and forgiveness of sins (1985, 37).

24. Mortimer Arias was a former bishop of the Methodist church in Bolivia; with an ecumenical approach he defines the Great Commission as a permanent task where no situation absolves us from proclaiming the great work of Jesus. See further (1976, 87–88).

the Great Commission makes evangelism an essential task for the church. For an innovative perspective, Andrew Walls[25] argues that there is not only one Great Commission, "there are in fact several Great Commissions in the New Testament. The most familiar is Matthew 28 but John 20:21 is another Great Commission". Minoru Okuyama,[26] at the ALCOE V 2002, uses 'commandments' for some key mission texts.

The British scholar Michael Green (1998, 316–320) emphasizes that the pivotal point of world mission started with the resurrection of Christ since the resurrection of Christ is the heart of the good news, the proof of his sonship, the springboard for mission, which shows that his power and his presence are available, and are the key to eternal life and the new community. The German theologian Jurgen Moltmann[27] (Grenz 2004, 75) and Stanley Samartha[28] (Anderson and Stransky 1976, 235), from an Indian perspective, agree with Green in believing that the cross is central for Christianity. Therefore, I agree that the commandment of the risen Christ is given to the church that they must go and make disciples of all nations. As a result of this theological interpretation, I assume that from this perspective all three models, traditional, networking and emergent partnership have taken account in their mission activity of what Green explains

---

25. The whole of Walls' work in relation to the Great Commission and the celebration of Edinburgh's conference 1910 in 2010 can be seen at http://www.towards2010.org.uk/downloads/t2010paper01walls.pdf. Like Walls, in innovative theological reflection, the Asian theologian Choan-Seng Song, from the WCC, in his article *From Israel to Asia: a theological leap,* relates mission to God's redemption, presented as God's revolution (Anderson and Stransky 1976, 214).

26. The Japanese leader Minoru Okuyama, at The Fifth Asia Church Leaders Conference on Evangelism ALCOE V "Partnership in the Gospel" held at Seoul in 2002, in his paper "The Answer is Mt. 10:23" uses the word commandments instead of 'Great Commission' for the key mission texts of Matt 28:19; Mark 16:15, and Acts 1:8. See (ALCOE V Partnership in the Gospel 2002, 173–175).

27. Moltmann especially focuses in his first major works on the cross and resurrection, the two events within a wider context which for him imply the entire history of God, considering the church's context from the perspective of the triune God acting in the world (Grenz 2004, 75).

28. Samartha, who worked with the World Council of Churches, delivered *Mission and Movements of Innovation* at the 1974 meeting of the International Association for Mission Studies in Frankfurt, Germany stating that we need certain criteria both for discernment and for cooperation, but the central criterion is Jesus Christ. See more in *Mission Trends* No. 3 (1976).

in relation to the resurrection event.[29] Contrary to Green, Moltmann and Samartha, the American scholar of philosophy, religion and theology at Boston University, Robert Cummings Neville points out that the blood and cross symbols need to be replaced but without losing the concept of sacrificial assumptions of the Bible (Mark Heim in Young and Heltzel 2004, 292).

The question that I want to pose in relation to current partnership models is this: Who inspired the mission partnership in the way traditional, networking and emergent models have been developed? Bosch's analysis (2001, 56–57) describes how it was in the twentieth century that scholars like Harnack, Michel, Lohmeyer, Lange, Hubbard, and Meier paid attention to the Great Commission and scholars agree that Matthew 28:16–20 is a pericope of climax for the mission enterprise and that the entire gospel points to these final verses. However, Bosch argues that the way the Great Commission has traditionally been utilized has to be modified, due to the fact that interpretations have been offered with no reference to the entire book and the context in which it first appeared. While agreeing with Bosch's proposal that it is a great responsibility for the *missio ecclesiae* to avoid mere slogans from this passage, I would argue that traditional understanding of the Great Commission is something that has been hindering those partnership models that we mentioned before, but in what sense? In the sense that the Great Commission has had a reductionist, individualistic and spiritualized interpretation, trying to get souls for heaven with no consideration of the double mandate of the Great Commission, which in Padilla's mission theology firmly also has a social mandate[30] (1985, 192).

---

29. Additionally, Green adds six insights which I call contemplations of the Great Commission for the mission enterprise, and those involved in mission partnership seem to have understood as principles for their missiology, as follows: first, the Great Commission implies considering the unevangelized nations, *ta ethne;* second, it is the response to meeting the risen Christ; third, it is the counterpart of the great commandment to love God and one's neighbour; fourth, it is a matter of obedience; fifth, it includes the baptism and careful discipling of new believers; and sixth, the great commission is always directed outwards to the unreached (1988, 321–323).

30. The Latin American theologian René Padilla argues that Christians receive a paradox given by Christ to be in the world but not to be of the world. He encourages maintaining a missionary understanding of an integral mission, which is also known as a holistic mission. See his article *Evangelism and the World* in *Mission Between the Times* (1985).

In consequence, our assumption is that Matthew's pericope does not allow us to use it as a battle-charger, not as a pretext for what we have decided to do with either conscious or unconscious priority to protect mission structures. The Great Commission is a matter of recovering the emphasis on the Trinitarian view for the recreation of everything.

By referring to missiology for Traditional Partnership, the Enlightenment[31] put the West at an advantage in relation to the rest of the world with the influence of scientific and technological advances, bringing about confusion between the gospel and cultural superiority (Bosch 2001, 291). Thus, missionaries confused views about morality, individualism, order, efficiency, etc., which produced a lack of ability to appreciate the culture they went to evangelize, developing their mission according to Western standards and cultural values. Bosch points out that the discussion in the middle of the nineteenth century about "self governing, self expanding and self supporting missiology" was perhaps without effect on the national churches, due to the fact that they were treated as children in need of care, control and guidance, and the Edinburgh Mission Conference 1910 was the high point of the influence of those mission societies working at that time (295). Categorically Bosch (295) observes that finances were behind the controlling spirit of mission societies, which I understand as a mission reality hindering the effectiveness of the mission enterprise.

In Bosch's view (298) the idea of 'Manifest Destiny' is a product of nationalism, linked with the belief of Western culture that God, in his

---

31. In his book *The World is too Much with Us* the American missiologist Charles Taber highlights three factors of the Enlightenment: scepticism in relation to faith, discovering of facts about the universe and human beings, and diversifying contact with the non-Western world. These three factors created an intellectual and social climate for human autonomy with the following ideas: emphasis on the natural law for sciences; autonomy of the human mind with an emphasis on rationalism; autonomy of human institutions, especially the state; issues of freedom and determinism; idealism as an emphasis in philosophy and materialism with an emphasis on material reality in Marx's ideas; universal history with ideas of homogeneity; and the idea of evolutionism, with the long-term future of the human being, which implies total autonomy from God. See further Taber (2003, 24–26). For Wilbert Shenk, the Enlightenment is the most important development in the eighteenth century with fresh ideas that affected the political arena with the formation of the United States of America and the French revolution of 1789, based on liberal, democratic and nationalistic ideals. Religion was challenged by the new ideas of rationalism. See further the introduction in Taber's book.

providence, had chosen the Western nations, the 'Christian civilization',[32] to save the world from a pagan and depraved life. However, as Bosch (298) explains, it was the catalytic event of the French Revolution that made an impact on the idea of self-determination as the basis for a new political order. In consequence the mission enterprise of Western mission societies absorbed the ideology of 'manifest destiny' into their mission spirit and Germans, French, Russians, Britons, Dutch, and Americans developed their missionary vocation under this philosophical influence, but this was not the case for the missionaries of the eighteenth and early nineteenth century (299). As a result, the missiological impact of the American missionary force increased from 2,716 in 1890 to, to 4,159 in 1900, to 7,219 in 1910, and to over 9,000 in 1915; and The Student Volunteer Movement formed in 1886 had a particular influence recruiting 3,000 volunteers, and in this context it is worth remembering that modern missions originated in the context of modern Western colonialism (Anderson quoted by Bosch 301–303).

Orlando Costas' analysis (1974, 13; Jenkins 2002, 40) observes that Traditional Partnership could be called the imperialistic philosophy and practices of a mission model, distorting the gospel sometimes and setting up ideological and cultural roadblocks to the understanding of God's mission. In a radical missiological characterization, Escobar (2003, 87; Phillips and Coote 1993, 133) states that these 'roadblocks' for Christian mission in Latin America are related to the imperialistic nature of managerial missiology, which stresses verbal proclamation and numerical growth as the main components of Christian mission. At the *Iguassu Dialogue 1999* organized by the WEF, Escobar (Taylor 2000, 109–112) argued against managerial missiology.[33] Both authors, Costas and Escobar, concur in the opinion that

---

32. Non-westerners were thought to be barbarians with a need for the civilizing western mentality and this view justified conquest, colonization, and slavery. These ideas made an impact on the missionary movement as they tended to see it as bringing civilization to the mission field (Taber 2003, 24). For Newbigin, the concept of Christian civilization is not viable because Europe has lost its confidence that inspired Edinburgh 1910 due to the fact of two World Wars and the division into two ideological camps. In consequence the relationship between Christianity and the Enlightenment is no longer valid. See further *Toward the 21st Century in Christian Mission* (Phillips 1993, 3–4).

33. Escobar develops a critical analysis of managerial missiology by pointing out that this influence comes from the Church Growth School in Pasadena California, and movements

'roadblocks' affect the effectiveness of Traditional Partnership, which in my understanding includes sophisticated techniques of technology for the success of evangelism, quantification of work, promotional fund raising, statistics, the influence of social science, etc. One example is the use of the 'Pattaya Scale'[34] implemented to reach out to every child in the world (Claydon 2005, 332). The Argentinian missiologist Federico Bertuzzi[35] equally argues against these 'roadblocks' when he clarifies the need for a mutual relationship in a proper interdependence partnership (1994, 94). On the same lines, Padilla[36] argues against "the cultural Christianity" and the technological mentality of American Christianity (1985, 17). Historical, theological and missiological roadblocks of Traditional Partnership relate to denouncing the excess of paternalism, colonialism[37] and imperialism (Jenkins 2002, 55–56; Sanneh in Phillips 1993, 85–86; Escobar[38] 2002, 45–48, 83; Bosch 1991, 226–227, 295–296).

---

such as the AD2000 and Beyond Movement. Characteristics of managerial missiology in Escobar's view are as follows: quantitative approach, the pragmatic orientation of mission, and the strong influence of American functionalist social sciences. See further Taylor (2000).

34. 'The Pattaya Scale' has two components: the process of evangelization by defining ten levels of intentional progression for the church's mission to children, and the partnership for evangelization by providing and identifying resources to make the intentional progression more effective globally. See further Claydon 2005, 332–336).

35. At the WEF Missions Commission Consultation Manila 1992, *Towards Interdependence Partnership* (Taylor 1994, 93), Bertuzzi rejected terms used like first world, second and third world, and the concept of 'developed world' and 'developing world' for the reason that this is one of the roadblocks for mature relationships with the Western church and its mission theology.

36. For Padilla (1985, 17), the cultural Christianity of our day has at its disposal the most sophisticated technological resources to propagate its message of success in the world, while the technological mentality is related to efficiency, which seeks the systematization in human life of methods and resources to obtain pre-established results. It relates to a civilization of technology obsessed by the best way to achieve things with less human effort.

37. Jenkins (2002, 59) points out that, alongside Nelson Mandela, Archbishop Desmond Tutu became a symbol of South African Liberation and the process of autonomous growth is illustrated by the church in Uganda with more than 7,000 parishes and Nigeria with 20 million baptized Anglicans.

38. Escobar explains the social impact of mission starting from the Constantinian period until the arrival of Protestant missions, and its effect on the social transformation of Latin America. Also he explains paternalism, as a sociological factor of Latin American Protestantism, creating dependency by the older and more established churches.

We arrive at the conclusion that traditional partnership is characteristic of traditional Protestant countries like Great Britain, Germany, the Netherlands, Switzerland, the Scandinavian countries and the United States (Bosch 2001, 327), with the following characteristics: (1) in the course of the nineteenth century, evangelicalism became a respected power (307), (2) the new missionary force did not have enough missionaries available for the task, (3) the 'three self formulas' were simply forgotten by the young churches, (4) mission agencies and missionaries were very patriotic until colonialism was withdrawn (312), and (5) in the 1880s, a second wave of missionary societies came to the fore in traditional Protestant countries. At World War II, another wave of new mission societies appeared. Actually, in America 81 societies were founded before 1900, 83 between 1940–1949, 113 during 1950–1959, and 150 new societies between 1960–1969 (Wilson and Siewert quoted in Bosch 327). As Taber explains: "the industrial revolution, the abolition movement, and the colonial enterprise, with their interconnections and their multidimensional consequences, profoundly affected the fourth current process, the missionary enterprise, and also the intellectual baggage which missionaries carried with them" (2003, 36). However, Traditional Partnership remains alive and is still influencing Networking and Emergent Partnership.

Policies of the traditional model

In the book *Toward the 21st Century in Christian Mission*, the Peruvian missiologist Samuel Escobar (Phillips 1993, 128) observes that during the 1990s there were 12,000 Protestant foreign missionaries working in Latin America.[39] This implies the work of different mission societies with a variety of mission policies like long-term commitment; missionaries are sent when the budget is fully financed; missionaries work under the umbrella of mission societies; investment in mission promotion; strong links with churches and individual donors; hierarchical structure; and mono-cultural teams. Moreover, the Iguassu Consultation seems to promote the distribution of the territorial field to avoid duplication (Taylor 2000, 554). But

---

39. Because this missionary force emerges from the missiological transformation of European and American influence, we understand that this mission force was sent by the traditional partnership and traditional policies we have mentioned.

today when we speak about policies for finances, it seems to give rise to a negative tension to support personnel and missionaries, especially for those involved with Traditional Partnership model, which as Guthrie[40] (2000, 21–24) points out are lacking in donors in a way never experienced before. This is why this model is trying to invest more and more in publicity and communication in order to survive the competition with bigger mission societies and also to cope with the impact of the Networking and Emergent Partnerships which are both less bureaucratic and more flexible in their policies on personnel. The Scottish missiologist Steward McIntosh[41] suggests that the increasing of personnel administration fees for mission societies generated a big pressure which led some small mission societies to be merged during the 1970s and 1980s.

Impact of the traditional model

Carey's Traditional Partnership characteristics and policies have made an influential impact among the new wave of mission societies in different periods of the modern Protestant Christian movement. Many mission agencies originated both in Great Britain and other countries under the image of Traditional Partnership. However, during the last three decades, the effect is still there, but with less effectiveness.[42] Sociologically, Traditional Partnership is an inspiration for other missions to launch an era of more structured evangelical mission overseas, but Stanley Davies points out that today most traditional mission agencies that cannot reshape both their mission and structure are in danger of disappearing (Taylor 1994, 45). Culturally, Traditional Partnership, with a heavy individualistic Western culture, affects relationships within missions, and the possibility of partnership with non-Western agencies is hindered by this individualistic tendency

---

40. Guthrie gives statistics of US missionaries serving oversees, which show the decreasing number of candidates from 50,500 in 1988 to 44,386 in 2001. He presents four key issues of the negative tension for raising finances: God and mammon, indifference, misperceptions and self-centredness (2000, 22–27).

41. Steward McIntosh is a former missionary in Peru. Information provided by McIntosh on 20 March 2008.

42. This is one reason why there is a significant opportunity for a new reciprocal contextual collaboration between mission societies and local churches, since Traditional Partnership has to reshape its structures and policies with a more appropriate understanding of God's kingdom theology.

(44). The ecclesiological impact shows that there is a declining participation of denominations and individual local churches,[43] and in consequence economic affluence has been substantially reduced. In terms of global impact we see that many Western mission agencies are trying to be part of the Innovative Networking Partnership and become an internationalized mission, in order to survive the changing times of the declining church in the Northern hemisphere. In consequence, I agree with Guthrie when he suggests that Traditional Partnership will require reengineering[44] in terms of their mission role (Guthrie 2000, 17). In global mission, Traditional Partnership has caused repercussions in British and American Protestant circles to initiate new mission societies, and the repercussions have equally permeated the 'Third Church'.

One of my findings is that, in one or another sense, the effectiveness of Traditional Partnership is seen in many denominational and non-denominational missions that have taken for granted Carey's model for their mission structures. The influence has caused repercussions in the case of the former Evangelical Union of South America (EUSA), now Latin Link in Britain, a traditional mission agency renamed in 1991 in London, which will be one of our case studies later. In respect of the 'Third church',[45] the Korean missiologist David Tai Woong Lee, in the *Dictionary of Mission Theology* (2007, 406), explains that by the early 1980s Ralph Winter estimated a "Third World Missionary" force of 8,000, and David Barrett

---

43. Today, there is a new tendency for mission to be developed by local churches, working independently with a new leadership of mission-minded pastors.

44. My missiological analysis of Western civilization shows me that it is not a matter of discussion that Traditional Partnership has to be reengineering, it is a matter of why, when and where Traditional Partnership has to be reengineered. In this sense I propose three questions for further analysis: The question, 'why?' relates to partnership's purpose, which in turn is related the vision partnership; 'when?' relates to partnership time, which means God's kairos partnership, and 'where?' relates to the partnership space, which implies the partnership context. Reengineering does not mean that everything is wrong; it means that some pieces have to be changed because they are not working properly or are damaged due to various internal or external factors.

45. The Korean missiologist David Tai Woong Lee uses the term 'Third Church', which includes the missionary force of churches in Africa, Asia and Latin America as the Third World Missionary Movement. This term was coined during the 1970s by the Catholic theologian Walbert Buhlmann in his book *The Coming of the Third Church*. He worked as a missionary in Tanganyika, belonging to the Capuchin order. See further Buhlmann (1976).

and Patrick Johnstone listed 95,428 non-Western missionaries by 2002, compared with Western missionaries. The *World Christian Encyclopedia* (2001) estimates that there are 336,070. It is said that COMIBAM has more than 8000 missionaries, but I observed in Granada 2006 that they targeted 12,000 missionaries for the following years.[46]

To describe the impact of Traditional Partnership, the book *Kingdom Partnerships for Synergy in Mission* (1994, 187–235) provides seven models of partnership with different perspectives. However, I will limit myself to mentioning two of them, but adding SAMS from a different source, as they originated in Great Britain and are related to Traditional Partnership:

1. **Partnership in mission by Overseas Missionary Fellowship (OMF).** This faith mission, formerly known as the China Inland Mission (CIM) through its 127 years, worked with different models of partnership in mission, first in China and then in East Asia. This mission develops different models of partnership in the following ways: (1) Associate missions. Under Hudson Taylor's leadership OMF made at least 15 partnerships with agencies with China Inland Mission. (2) Western missions. This refers to joint work between Western missions for the task of evangelism, church planting and theological education. (3) Mission Partnership with the Asian Churches, which refers to partnership with the national churches planted by OMF. (4) Mission Partnership with Asian and Western organizations, which refers to an international and cross-cultural combination of partners. (5) Mission Partnership with Asian parachurch organizations; this refers to OMF partnership with national mission agencies of other countries. It seems that reciprocal contextual collaboration can develop to strengthen the goals and strategy for evangelizing

---

46. I had the privilege to attend São Paulo 1987 and Granada 2006, taking the information in situ. Federico Bertuzzi, Rudy Girón and others are some of the initiators of this movement. The new target of a missionary force was mentioned during one of the last evenings in Granada, Spain, in November 2006. Perhaps most of the missionaries will go on belonging to mission agencies; this movement will be another of our cases studies. Tai Woong Lee notes that COMIBAM began in 1984 holding three major congresses: São Paulo 1987, Acapulco 1997 and recently Granada 2006, all of them to mobilize the Ibero-American church. See Corrie (2007, 406).

China and the Asian countries. Its impact is expressed by the internationalization of the mission, by a new policy of personnel showing that in 1965 Asian partners were accepted as full members with the same duties. OMF Partnership's missiological principles are as follows: Partnership is dynamic, not static; requires integrity, long-term thinking and clarity of purpose (189–191). OMF has 1,300 missionaries from 30 different countries.[47]

2. **Partnership in mission by WEC.** Towards interdependent partnership by the Worldwide Evangelization for Christ[48] (WEC). Dietrich Kuhl from WEC International, which is cooperating in multiple partnerships with about 250 partners between churches, missions and associations, provides insights into dependent partnership. He clarifies that the most important ingredients for cooperation seem to be flexibility, teachability, humility, patience, and mutual trust (Taylor 1994, 217–222). WEC practises four models of partnership: first, mission/mission partnership related to WEC and other mission agencies; second, mission/church partnership that includes more participation of local congregations in sending their missionaries; third, cooperation with associations of national missionary movements, and fourth, mission with non-Western countries which implies reciprocal contextual collaboration with non-Western missionaries. In a complementary observation, the International Service Fellowship called Interserve (131–141) uses a new terminology for its mission policy – for example, partner instead of missionary, and partner rather than member. Financially, as Interserve is not a funding organization, in 1989 it made a policy of 'Common Commitment of Partners', to define financial relationships with all partners. Interserve encourages the development of indigenous missions to

---

47. See OMF History (further http://www.omf.org/omf/uk/about_omf/omf_cim_history).
48. WEC is an international and interdenominational faith mission founded in 1913 by the Charles Thomas Studd who worked with Hudson Taylor's China Inland Mission – CIM and today OMF. Today WEC has 1,500 missionaries from 41 nationalities serving in 57 countries on all continents and 140 missionaries come from the 'Third Church' (Kuhl in Taylor 1994, 217).

establish links with international organizations, and practises four different model of partnering: (1) agency sends money, nationals do the job; (2) missionaries work under national structures; (3) united mission efforts, which refers to when agency representation takes place at board level and personnel become full members of the united mission; and (4) networking with other organizations, which is used for creative access to countries where Interserve has self-supporting partners. These models, Interserve and WEC, seem to have developed to become a non-traditional mission agency and to mix their traditional identity with a new reciprocal contextual collaboration.

3. **Partnership in mission by SAMS.** Partnership in mission by South American Mission Society. SAMS was founded in 1864 by the British military commander Allen Gardiner (Mackay 2001, 237–238).[49] In the process of growing, SAMS has extended to other countries and merged with CMS in 2010.[50] This mission is

---

49. Gardiner born in Basildon, Berkshire, entered Portsmouth naval college, but decided to commit his life to mission and, accompanied by his family, undertook extensive travel in search of suitable locations, for instance, in South Africa. However, he was repeatedly thwarted in his efforts by political indifference and the previous establishment of Catholic missions. In 1841 Gardiner decided to visit the Falkland Islands in order to explore the possibility of establishing missions in nearby Patagonia and Tierra del Fuego and founded the Patagonian Mission Society (PMS); this was renamed in 1864 the South American Missionary Society. Gardiner's original plan for the Society was threefold: to supply the spiritual wants of his own countrymen, of Roman Catholics, and of the unreached in South America. With these aims in mind, the Secretary of the PMS, the Rev George Despard, determined to persevere with the work initiated by Gardiner. In 1860, Allen Gardiner's son, Allen Gardiner Jr, was sent by the Society to the Mapuche people of southern Chile. To further this work, Gardiner Jr became a chaplain to the British residents of Lota; due to Spanish and Portuguese legislation, furtherance of Protestant causes in most South American republics was extremely difficult at the time. Thus, rather than establishing actual mission stations, the South American Missionary Society concentrated on establishing chaplaincies, and working with seamen, during the latter half of the 19th century (http://www.mundus.ac.uk/cats/61/1054.htm).

50. Today SAMS Great Britain, SAMS Canada, SAMS Ireland and SAMS USA carry on the legacy and work of the early SAMS missionaries. Founded in 1976 SAMS USA partners with the Episcopal/Anglican Church in Latin America and Spain to spread the Good News of Jesus Christ through both word and deed (http://www.samsusa.org/about_history.html). See also "CMS and SAMS have integrated" (http://www.cms-uk.org/Whoweare /CMSandSAMS/tabid/485/language/en-GB/Default.aspx).

linked to the Anglican church[51] and operates in many countries of Latin America. SAMS has had 71 missionaries,[52] and from the 1990s has developed multi-way mission traffic.[53] It appears that SAMS practice a traditional policy for personnel and finances that includes:[54] (1) an agreement on the monthly salary budget for candidates, (2) candidates for mission are sought by high promotion, and (3) children are included in the budgeting process each year. The fact is that SAMS has found candidates through a long process of selection with none of them going into the mission field before covering their budget (a key policy of the traditional model process for both selection and finances).[55] In contrast, the Church 'Casa de Oracion' in Chulucanas, Peru, has sent missionaries to Brazil and France with only a symbolic financial support, hence without a monthly salary and without financial support for children, but with spiritual and moral

---

51. SAMS is one of the 11 Anglican agencies which make up the Partnership for World Mission (PWM) www.pwm-web.org.uk. It has sought to plant and partner with Anglican churches in South America, the Iglesia Episcopal Reformada Española (IERE) in Spain and the Lusitanian Church in Portugal – these are both extra-provincial dioceses of the Anglican Communion. (Data provided by Robert Lunt 2008).

52. In 2008, SAMS has had 44 expatriate mission partners, consisting of 17 married couples and 10 single people. However, 7 of the married women and one married man are Latin American. SAMS also has 29 Latin Partners, consisting of 28 couples and one single person. These are church leaders recommended by their own dioceses and supported by SAMS on a diminishing scale each year. Most work in their own countries, but some work in another Latin American country or in Spain (Lunt 2008).

53. Multi-way mission is firmly on SAMS' agenda, with support for a Portuguese worker in Jersey and two Chilean evangelists in Spain, plus schemes involving Brazilian, Argentine and Bolivian evangelists. In 1994 to mark the 150th anniversary SAMS' vision for the future was unveiled in 'The Challenge for Change': "We seek to be an agent of multi-way international mission; to represent the church of South America to the church in the UK; to shift our focus away from sending missionaries to supporting national mission; to take appropriate initiatives in partnership with other mission agencies." See further in Robert Lunt: *Significant Dates Relating to SAMS* (SAMS 'Mission Education' med@samsgb.org, received on 13 April 2008 at 13:10).

54. Jo Hazelton suggests that both SAMS and CMS are considered traditional mission societies because they are quite old; they are linked to the Church of England which in and of itself is considered a traditional institution, and they have both had many years of working on the mission field (CMS around 210 years and SAMS around 170 years). Electronic information sent to the author by Jo Hazelton on 13 August 2010.

55. For the traditional policy of SAMS (Electronic information sent to the author by Jo Hazelton on 18 August 2010).

support through prayer and blessing.[56] They have to find their own support as there is no policy to cover their budget before going to the mission field.

Other traditional partnership mission agencies are: Global Mapping International (GMI), to provide maps and other search tools to like-minded agencies around the world; Interdev, which focuses on strategic evangelism today with a less formal basis, with an influence over 300 million people; Partners International, considered by Guthrie as the most respected and trusted Western agency, promoting joint ministries with non-Western agencies, today supporting more than 3,800 missionaries (Guthrie 2000, 121–122).

New trends in the traditional model

A new trend for traditional partnership was established in the first consultation, *Supporting of Indigenous Ministries*, held at the Billy Graham Center, Wheaton in 1996. Daniel Rickett and Dotsey Wellivern note that more than 52 American agencies attended[57] to discuss issues on partnership in mission to support indigenous initiatives,[58] which Charles Taber addressed in *'Structures and strategies for interdependence in world mission'*. Taber emphasizes the main characteristics of an interdependent partnership and identifies fours aspects: mutual trust, local decision making,

---

56. The Pentecostal church 'Casa de Oracion' was founded in Chulucanas, Peru in 1974 by the Swedish missionary Carlos Olson. At present they have 80 'daughter churches' and 90 missionaries. In the case of the mission activity for planting churches within the Peruvian territory, the following policy is provided for missionaries: (1) Missionaries pray, fast and preach the gospel, until they have a family converted to Christ and then they start in their house a new branch of the mother church. (2) Financially, support is distributed from the general funds that come from the income of each church. They do not include any support for children. Most of the missionaries have a secular work to cover the difference of their budget because financial aid does not provide a proper salary. (3) Missionaries are accountable to the mother church, which define the place of the mission field. Missionaries have a monthly meeting to inform about the need and mission activity. (4) Some financial support comes from friend churches in France to help children of those who have less income than others. (5) A missionary believes in God's provision and never claims financial aid. (6) The structure of the mother church is used for sending people to mission. (Information sent to the author by Carlos Olsson, the founder of the Church 'Casa de Oracion' in Chulucanas, Peru, on 3 October 2011, from Lund, Sweden).

57. Data provided in the preface of the book *Supporting Indigenous Ministries*. See further Rickett and Welliver (1997).

58. Indigenous initiatives are related to what I call 'emergent partnership'.

encouraging local initiative, and giving without strings (Rickett and Welliver 1997, 77–80). It seems to me that Kuhl from WEC emphasizes interdependent characteristics in term of personality, while Taber gives two characteristics for personality with two concentrated on structural missiology. However, both agree in mutual trust that is a pivotal characteristic of a Trinitarian partnership and a key element of every reciprocal contextual collaboration between traditional, networking and emergent partnership models. In contrast to the positive benefit of interdependence, Charles Van Engen reminds us that paternalism[59] is an ever-present danger in mission and ministry, but should not deter us from seeking ways to share globally the church's resources for mission (1997, ix). In the same vein as Van Engen, Guthrie (2000, 123) provides a summary of Rickett's seven common mistakes partners often make: assuming you think alike, promising more than you can deliver, taking to the road without a map, underestimating cultural differences, taking shortcuts, forgetting to develop self reliance, and running a race with no end. From my perspective, these common mistakes cause mission partners to neglect and hinder the *missio Dei* and God's kingdom. Moreover, the idea of supporting indigenous mission is not new; this was Rolland Allen's missiology in proposing new ways for the Western mission. Supporting indigenous missions includes the reality that there is no partnership with just positive tensions; there are no romantic partnerships, which according to history are a fallacy. The following diagram portrays the Traditional model.

---

59. In the foreword to *Supporting Indigenous Ministries*, Van Engen, born in Mexico of missionary parents and a missionary with the Reformed Church in America in Mexico, clarifies that paternalism is not only a matter of money; it includes more than material resources. It deals with relational and faith issues, and appears mostly when we hold to some position or idea, or take some action regardless of the circumstances, opinions, wisdom, or feelings of the people we are called to serve. In this way, personal relationships are a key principle for addressing issues of paternalism and Van Engen suggests awareness of what I call reciprocal contextual collaboration of the church as one Spirit, one Body and one hope and calling. See further Rickett and Welliver (1997).

The Traditional Model

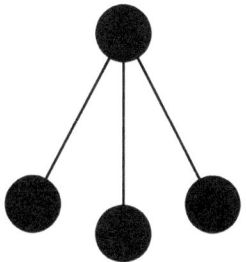

Structured, uni-directional, specialized

The innovative networking model

Historical, theological and missiological characteristics

In the years following World War II, political, economic, cultural, social and religious changes were experienced, which had an impact on the new context of the *missio Dei*, especially between the 1970s and 2000. One symptom is that missions started both consciously or unconsciously to use the new innovative networking model, in applying more technology in their mission activity. The American writers and consultants on organizational networks, Jessica Lipnack and Jeffrey Stamp, suggest that networking is a recent phenomenon started in the 1990s[60] with the growth of technological communication. My assumption is that with this global change of communication systems, the innovative networking model permeates all kinds of mission structures of Christian partnership today. Why? There is

---

60. Jessica Lipnack and Jeffrey Stamps, cofounders of The Networking Institute, have written three books from the secular business perspective which are worth reading. *The TeamNet Factor*, discusses the network as a form of organization, from the small, to alliances, and to nations. The second is entitled *The Age of the Network*, where they provide an overview of the impact of networks and their strategic importance. The third is *Virtual teams*, where they implement the idea of small groups of people working, supported by the new computer and communications technology known by a select group of people in the 1990s. Virtual teams are non-traditional face-to-face teams which use the web, email and sky technology (1997, xviii).

rapid growth in the use of computers, Internet, voice mail, mobile phones and emails, which brings a new situation of less face-to-face work.

From a Protestant perspective, the book *Kingdom Partnership for Synergy in Missions* contends that networking partnership[61] takes place when "similar individuals or groups pool resources for the greater advancement of the common objective, sharing information, ideas, and resources" (Taylor 1994, 244). In Taylor's analysis (1994), the networking model has the following four characteristics between partners: it is a means of connecting people with one another, it is a means of creating and exchanging knowledge, it has an informal and formal basis, and it becomes strong when people acknowledge its presence, engender its activity and actively respond to others in the network. Thus, networks are formed by independent institutions that have the same or similar purpose to accomplish one mission task. In consequence, they seek each other to share resources and skills, but they do not lose their individual identity as a mission structure, local church or mission network. COMIBAM, one of our case studies, is neither a mission society nor an independent movement, but it is an evangelical regional mission network with an increasing influence in Latin America. Another networking partnership is Global Connections,[62] the British network influencing 190 agency members and about 100 church members (Lee 2008).

Here, I attempt to define Networking Model (Networking Partnership)[63] as the new mission tool for global Christianity and global evangelism. The

---

61. In secular understanding, network can be defined also in four ways: "as an intricately connected system of things or people, as a communication system consisting of a group of broadcasting stations that all transmit the same programme simultaneously, as an interconnected or intersecting configuration or system of components, and also implies a communication with and within a group" (The Web Dictionary 2008).

62. In respect to the impact of Global Connections, Stanley Davies, a former General Secretary, has pointed out that the UK no longer thinks it has all the answers to this world's need and he recognizes that Europe has a great need of new forms of partnership to re-evangelize this continent (Taylor 1994, 47).

63. Lise Rosendal Østergaard, and Joel Nielsen who work in Copenhagen V, Denmark in their article "To Network or not to Network: NGO Experiences with Technical Networks" discuss the factors that make networks useful and attractive to NGOs. It suggested a useful definition of a network which is provided by Church et al (University of London 2002, 12) who state that "A network can be called a network when the relationships between those in the network are voluntarily entered into, the autonomy of participants remains intact and there are mutual or joint activities". This definition builds on the fact that 'true' networks are voluntary rather than imposed, they facilitate some

aim is to provide contributions in the relationships of mission agencies, local churches, denominations, missionaries, and all kind of Christian institutions and people who want to share resources for the fulfilment of the *missio Dei*, without diluting their own identity and taking advantage of new technologies. This definition seeks to avoid competition and to promote God's kingdom with a global missiology. In a novel approach, Tolly Bradford's article[64] "Networking: Global Perspective on Nineteenth Century British Mission" (2002, 375) suggests that networking goes back to the practice of the nineteenth-century British mission movement.

In this part, I will follow Phill Butler's book, *Well Connected*, by providing some principles of the differences between partnership and network. From this analysis, we will then give a synthetic summary of networking effectiveness. For Butler (2005, 34), network is "any group of individuals or organizations, sharing common interests, who regularly communicate with each other to enhance their individual purposes". Key phrases are: common interest, regular communication and individual purpose. In Butler's opinion, the study and understanding of human networks has actually become a new specialism in the fields of sociology and communications. From this perspective, he points out that networks can be simple or complex, weak or strong. Weak or informal networks are less active or intense in their relationships, often only sharing information or interests, and are frequently 'on demand,' or fellowship-oriented, while a strong network is a more structured network, which is often task, project, or issue-orientated, has well-defined structures, responsibilities and objectives, and requires substantial time commitments. From an Asian perspective, the

---

form of collaborative action, the organisational autonomy of the member organisations remains intact and they have a common objective. Church et al. (2002) also make a useful distinction between networks and networking, namely, that networks are a structure or architecture whereas networking connotes the active participation in activities together with other network members. Therefore 'joining a network' is not necessarily the same as 'networking', though these terms are often wrongly conflated. See (http://www.intrac.org/docs/To%20network%20or%20not%20to%20network.doc).

64. The author argues that the system of global network is not new, but has links with the work of the traditional partnership of the nineteenth century. His article examines this approach through examples from the CMS mission in UK. See more Bradford (2002, 375–380).

Indonesian Iman Santoso[65] at the Fifth Asia Church Leaders Conference on Evangelism (ALCOE V) develops the concept of network and the Great Commission from a historical, biblical and missiological insight. He also provides three dangers of networking: building up an empire in the name of unity, swallowing particularly smaller organizations, and confusing people with networks and becoming partners suspicious in the mission enterprise.

One of the principal assumptions of network in Butler's perspective is that this is generally designed to facilitate on-going communication and information sharing, helping members of the network do their own individual work more effectively. He concludes that the only real points of connection may be a common area of concern and regular communication. Therefore a network may be for pastors, building contractors, doctors, mission agencies, or neighbours. The effectiveness of networking is seen in two ways – structured, with membership, regular meetings, newsletter, website, etc, or it may be informal, with an agreement to meet on certain occasions to share information and encouragement.

On the one side, Butler's partnership definition implies any group of individuals or organization, sharing a common interest, who regularly communicate a plan, and work together to achieve a common vision beyond the capacity of any one of the individual partners (2005, 34). For Butler, partnership goes beyond networking because the first goes into

---

65. Santoso (2002, 169–171) suggests in his presentation "Network and the Great Commission" that the kingdom of heaven is like a net, based on the text of Matthew 13:47. He also provides a definition of network: "A network is any set of individuals or organizations who, on a voluntary basis, exchange information or undertake joint activities and who organize themselves in such a way that their individual autonomy remains intact" (quoting from Paul Starkey). In this definition, intact individual autonomy is the pivotal concept for developing network with others. Santoso provides four points to summarize the historical struggle in mission: the unfinished task, the growing of complexities in mission, lack of collaboration and the need of ecumenicity for mission. Then he presents two issues for networking: first, the danger of building up empires, where one organization becomes the centre, and second, the danger of 'kingdom', where one organization dominates the whole vision of a network. The function of a network is connecting, bringing, facilitating and empowering. In this sense, for Santoso, every organization is a 'node', with its own need, its own circle of influence and its special gifts. He points out that "through the interaction of these nodes-new combinations, new breakthroughs could happen. A net is empowering its nodes in efficiency, capability, capacity (wider horizons), and empowerment for difficult projects (e.g. research)" See further, The Fifth Asia Church Leaders Conference on Evangelism, ALCOE V 2002 Partnership in the Gospel: The Lausanne Movement in the 21st Century Asia.

coordinated action around a common concern and the second is closer to seeking good communication and fellowship. Consequently, partnership takes many forms for different purposes, from simple to complex, informal or well structured, for either a short-term or a long-term period of time. The key elements of partnership are: common interest, regular communication, working together to achieve a common vision, and going beyond the capacity of any one of the individual partners (35).

Butler suggests four characteristics of networking partnership, which make the following impact: encouragement, information/education, access to each other's strengths, and potential help in times of emergency (Butler 2005, 35–36). On the other hand, traditional partnership or classical partnership is characterized more by a commitment component, which provides all the elements of network mentioned above like shared information, encouragement, and education, but goes beyond the network partnership due to the fact that this partnership has four key elements (38–40): the diversity of the partners (bilateral; multilateral, large and small); the duration of the partnership (short term, medium, and long term partnership); the structure of the partnership (simple as possible); and the context of the partnership (the place). Butler[66] suggests that there can be a mutual and complementary influence between networking and what I call traditional partnership. However, it seems that Butler's missiology has the risk of producing managerial thinking, generating inevitable roadblocks for the new missiological gravity centre. The reason is that he tries to make too easy the nature of partnering, when the reality shows that all kinds of partnerships produce both positive and negative tension, which is not recognized in his perspective.

Networking partnership's key characteristics have similarities with the traditional model, but the first has a pivotal difference in the sense of a

---

66. In contrast to networking characteristics, Butler (2005, 36) gives four elements that create more effectiveness in partnership: (1) providing opportunity to look at the 'big picture' and dream dreams beyond the capacity of any of the individual partners, (2) providing through several working groups within the partnership action plans that turn the specific initiatives from dreams to reality, (3) providing a greater kingdom impact in the region in becoming real, tangible with benefits for each of the participating partners, and (4) building on the best of each partner's capacity to accomplish something bigger, making possible mission plans that alone will be impossible to achieve.

non-territorial outlook; globalization is the main influence; partnership is developed in terms of strategic alliances and this model uses all kind of communicating technologies. Other characteristics include:

1. Historically, in the evangelical arena, the networking model has a connection with what Phill Butler (2005, 34) calls strategic alliances, which differ from the partnership concept. The second refers to a coordinated action, and the first to a fellowship and communication. For the British missiologist Bryan Knell (2001), there is an influence of cultural impact between the 'Builders and the Boomers', born before 1964, and 'Generation X and Y' born after 1964. The second one seeks relationships and the first one seeks structure. My finding is that networking partnership is, in part, an effect of this generational tension. Why? In the sense that networking partnership avoids diluting personal identity and a rigid policy of relationships, like written agreements. For example, it may be structured with membership or it may be informal, with some meetings from time to time.

2. Theologically. As we mentioned in chapter 2, Trinitarian theology and kingdom theology are the basis for the networking model, and the pivotal point of the networking model theology rests on the analysis of relationships.[67] McConnell's[68] opinion confirms this perspective. For Butler, networking has a biblical foundation in the sense that God himself dwells in community outside time in eternity.[69] Therefore, effective networking partnership states that there is no possible personal relationship with God unless

---

67. There is a tendency towards belonging in everyone but without diluting our personal identity. Hence, this tendency makes networking partnership hard work and easy-going. Hard working in relation to producing a long-term relationship and easy-going in relation to a non-dependent work to produce more appropriate results for missions. The consequences depend on how the partner uses the tools they obtain from the network to which they belong.

68. McConnell's analysis suggests that networking is a focus on relationships rather than the more traditional views of location and kinship (kinship means a relationship between any entities that share a genealogical origin, through biological, cultural or historical descent). See more in *Working Together: Beyond the Individual Effort to Networks of Collaboration* (2005, 257).

69. Butler observes that wide ranging sections of Genesis, Job, Daniel and Ephesians speak of God as dwelling in a community of personalities or beings. It is not surprising then that

we have an open relationship with colleagues (Matt 5:21, 18:17; 2 Cor 2:5–11; and 1 Pet 3:7). Restoration and reconciliation is a key theology for healthy relationships in mission (Col 3:2–17; 2 Cor 5:18–19). The Great Commission is part of its theology as it is of traditional partnership.

3. Missiologically. The networking model develops a more collaborative style of leadership. This model tries to avoid the term 'equality' and prefers to use 'diversity'; they recognize that their differences create a synergy partnership to overcome hindering relationship between members of the network (Whitehead 1991, 8). Therefore, it is not the network, which makes the partners strong; it is the partners who make the network strong and useful. Butler's networking partnership goes in two ways: vertical and horizontal (Taylor 1997, 13–14). While vertical network represents a conscious effort to get all the key elements needed to reach something in common, each partner plays a unique role but all linked in a conscious commitment to a common objective; horizontal network implies a specialized working group and is related to an specialized agency, like Bible translation in Wycliffe's work. Douglas McConnell (Pocock, Rheenen and McConnell 2005, 249) in the book *The Changing Face of World Mission* provides three major elements shaping the trend of networks: social network, team effort, and companies and collaboration, all making a frame for the trend of moving from the individual effort of missionaries to a network of collaboration in global mission. On the other hand, McConnell proposes three types of networks: local network initiatives, specialized network initiatives, and global network initiatives[70] (258–260). Alan

---

God made man to dwell in relationship first, with himself and then with others, but sadly this relationship was damaged in Eden (1994, 15).

70. On the other hand, McConnell observes that building on the structural element of the local and specialized network initiatives, the third type of network is characterized by a global focus intrinsic to its purpose. Global network brings together churches, agencies, and individuals with a broad vision to affect the entire world through alliances and partnerships. Global network initiates often operate with a selection of delegates to participate on broad invitations (2005, 261).

Hirsch (2006, 201), in *The Forgotten Ways*, also suggests three types of networks: the ***chain network*** (it moves along a line of separated contacts and communications travels through the intermediate nodes), the ***star network*** (where the agents are tied to a central – but not hierarchichal – node and communication flows from and to a central node; and the ***all-channel network*** (everybody is independent but connected to everybody else).

Policies of the networking model

In respect to policies, personnel who partner under this model work on both a full-time and part-time basis; they are specialized people with specific skills that can be interchanged with members of the network. Financially people work in two ways: with a salaried position or as a volunteer. Those with a salaried position have a professional or technical skill in theology, administration, business, planning, etc., and volunteers are workers for specific projects and events. As part of the Innovative Networking Partnership, Scott Moreau's[71] article *Missions Fund Raising* (2002, 236–240) provides advice for those who want to raise support through the Internet.

Impact of the networking model

What is the impact that networking partnership is achieving? Sociologically, as a recent phenomenon, it works under the influence of the new era of globalization; isolation or globalization is the new mission fashion;[72] culturally, there are multicultural teams, but English is still the main language for communication. For ecclesiology, negatively, Shenk (2007, 123) points out that in the 1980s a new movement began with the concern that Christianity in Europe, North America and Australasia was in deep difficulty.[73] From

---

71. See further Moreau (2002). Also Scott Morton has produced four video series "Raising Personal Support", and more than 70 mission agencies worldwide have used this material to train missionaries. It can be found also as a book, *Funding your Ministry* (2007).

72. Guthrie (2000, 88) presents some needs of networking, like team models popular for evangelistic and social work. An urban network called 'Urban Street Ministries' was formed in 1991 to partner with local Christians, equipping them to do work alongside the missionaries.

73. In fact, Lesslie Newbigin was a key leader with a prophetic proposal of a radical change in the declining ecclesiology of those countries. As Shenk notes, Newbigin became

a positive perspective, there is a sense of church involvement as the body of Christ, where the territorial tendencies of traditional partnership have been overcome. Economic impact is made by the influence of mass media and the use of the Internet and electronic information. Global technology means that there are no frontier mission statements, which become a barrier for uniting efforts in mission.

Now, to see the practical impact of the networking model we give three models that in one or another sense, directly or indirectly, are working with the 'Third Church':

1. **The World Evangelical Alliance (WEA).** The World Evangelical Alliance started in 1846[74] and was officially established as the World Evangelical Fellowship in 1956,[75] and changed its name to World Evangelical Alliance in 2003, actually has five key

---

the driving force in *The Gospel and our Culture Program,* a six-year national initiative with the aim to enlist Christians in politics, the economy, the sciences, the humanities, and the arts, along with church leaders, in fostering renewal at all levels of church life. See editorial of *Missiology, International Review* (2007).

74. In 1846, Christians from ten countries met in London to establish a definite organization for the expression of unity among Christian individuals belonging to different churches. This vision was fulfilled in 1951 when believers from 21 countries officially formed the World Evangelical Fellowship. Data from: http://www.worldevangelicals.org/wea/.

75. At present, "World Evangelical Alliance is a global ministry working with local churches around the world to join in common concern to live and proclaim the good news of Jesus in their communities. WEA is a network of churches in 128 nations that have each formed an evangelical alliance and over 100 international organizations joining together to give a worldwide identity, voice and platform to more than 420 million evangelical Christians. Seeking holiness, justice and renewal at every level of society – individual, family, community and culture, God is glorified and the nations of the earth are forever transformed". Data from: http://www.worldevangelicals.org/wea/.

characteristics[76] and six commissions.[77] The WEA includes in its policy three types of members: Regional and National Alliances, global partners and associate members.[78] The World Evangelical Alliance Mission Commission[79] (WEF-MC) started in 1977,[80] and is defined by William Taylor[81] (1994, xiii–xviii) as a global

---

76. First, a doctrinal confession guides it – grounding it in historic evangelical affirmations. Second, it has constitutionality – governed by bylaws and general assembly delegates, which guarantee historical continuity. Third, it is a church-based movement – listening to its constituency as its core authority. Thus, it is not an organization established and maintained by individuals. Fourth, its constituency is global – rooted in 128 national and seven regional alliances, 104 associate members, six affiliated specialized ministries and six commissions, and fifth, it functions as a network while providing the services of an alliance – through its resources, departments and commissions. WEA looks like the broadest organizational and global manifestation of the evangelical movement. William Taylor has prepared a very good synthesis of the history, mission and theology of the WEA. See the whole document in: http://www.worldevangelicals.org/wea/history.htm.

77. The six commissions are: Mission Commission, Religious Liberty Commission, Theological Commission, Women's Commission, Youth Commission and Information Technology Commission.

78. There are three types of membership, each with its distinct qualifications and responsibilities: Regional and National Alliances include regional evangelical fellowships and their national fellowships/alliances. There are nine Global Partners at the present time. These are independently incorporated organizations which work in harmony with WEA structures and serve the WEA constituency. Associate Members are independently incorporated organizations with their own specific ministries and accountability, an international scope of ministry, and the capacity and authority to serve in and beyond the WEA community". Data from: http://www.worldevangelicals.org/members/define.htm

79. In connection with the WEA-MC missiology, a network generally refers to a group of individuals or agencies with similar interests or concerns, interacting and remaining in informal contact to share ideas and information. Some networks are organic components of the WEA-MC and are included in the MC budget such as MEMCA (Member Care/Global Member Care Resources) and IMTN (The International Missionary Trining Network). Other networks are linked or docked with the WEA-MC but are autonomous in their governance and funding, such as Mission Mobilization Network – OM, TIE (Tentmakers International Exchange), Interdev Partners Associates, SEALINK/Ethne06 (South East Asia Network). Networks are expected to contribute a minimal annual financial investment in the MC that goes to cover space in each issue of *Connections* for their report (Ekstrom Bertil and William D. Taylor, http://www.worldevangelicals.org/commissions/mc/purpose.htm).

80. The Missions Commission was launched in Korea, 1975, under the Korean woman missiologist Chun Chae Ok as its first Executive Secretary and later the Indian Theodore Williams. The MC emerged as a player in the global missions scene with its early focus on "Two-Thirds World emerging missions" (Taylor: 1994, xiv).

81. Taylor (1994, 8), a son of missionaries, born in Costa Rica, has developed ministry at the Central American Theological Seminary in Guatemala. He was a missions professor at Trinity Evangelical Divinity School.

network of national missions leaders, with many of its members fulfilling wider international roles. Its main characteristics related to the core values are to serve as an international partnering/networking team, sharing ideas, information, and resources to empower the global missions movement; its goal is to work worldwide with evangelical churches, in particular the mission of the WEA-MC, in order to carry out the Great Commission; its vision is to bring closure to Christ's Great Commission through a dynamic, unified, global missions movement focused on effectively training and sending missionaries. The policy of the membership currently includes general members[82] and consultants. Regarding its missiological impact, they have formed an international missionary training, publication programme and both a task force on tent-making, and a task force on Muslim ministries. Another network similar to WEA-MC was the Great Commission Global Roundtable, started in 1999[83] (Guthrie 2000, 121), but at present this network is no longer working.[84]

In a similar way to WEA, the Interdenominational Foreign Mission Association (IFMA), now CrossGlobal Link[85] was

---

82. The Mission Commission draws its membership primarily from the World Evangelical Fellowship member association and they are executive officers of regional missions associated to WEF. They also invite to their membership specialists in mission to work as consultants. See further Taylor (1994).

83. Stan Guthrie states that in 1999, the WEA, the Lausanne Committee for World Evangelization, and the AD2000 and Beyond Movement, agreed to form a global evangelization network called Great Commission Global Roundtable, to hear, serve and connect diverse segments of the body of Christ in the hope of achieving closer coordination and cooperation in sharing the Gospel (121).

84. Electronic information provided by William Taylor (April 2008).

85. Marvin Newell explains the change of name of the Interdenominational Foreign Mission Association of North America (IFMA), now known as CrossGlobal Link. Association leaders accentuated their focus on 'internal networking' among current mission agency members with a deliberate new effort to link with North American churches, especially churches bypassing agencies as they do mission directly. IFMA has its headquarters at Wheaton, Illinois. Full-time directors were: John O. Percy (1956–62); Jack Frizen (1963–90); John Orme (1991–2006), and now Marv Newell, who defines the nature of this network: "The purpose of this association is to establish standards of accountability and integrity; to foster networking and strategic alliances for world mission; to stimulate fellowship, mutuality, and prayer among members; to provide specialized mission training and leadership development; to maintain a unified testimony

founded by seven faith mission agencies at the First Presbyterian Church of Princeton, NJ, during the First World War in 1917. CrossGlobal Link is a North American-wide association of mission agencies and churches[86] that together field over 15,500 missionaries around the globe.[87]

2. **Global Connections** (Web 2008, 1–2; 1–3).[88] An innovative networking model of evangelical agencies and churches has the

---

and establish a united voice in our mutual commitment to the Word of God and the overarching responsibility for global evangelization". (http://www.crossgloballink.org/Our_Story).

86. CrossGlobal Link mission policy includes: announcing Jesus Christ globally as highest priority; standards of integrity are a key element of the network, and member missions benefit from connecting together in mission. The nature of CrossGlobal Link is summarized in three statements: mission is to advance the effectiveness of the membership in global mission; vision to see members thrive in their God-given mission; passion is to glorify God together by reaching people everywhere with the gospel of Jesus Christ. The policy of benefits for its members includes: (1) stimulating fellowship, mutuality, prayer and commitment to the Word of God; (2) fostering networking and strategic alliances; (3) providing specialized mission training; (4) sponsoring leadership development; (5) keeping members current with relevant mission information; (6) promoting a unified testimony and united voice for mission in both the domestic and global arenas; (7) representing faith missions globally; and (8) setting and maintaining standards of accountability and integrity. (http://www.crossgloballink.org/About_Membership).

87. My finding is that this changing fashion of names shows the desperate spirit of old mission structures to survive the growing influence of the emergent partnership. It seems that the identity of traditional partnership has been diluted profoundly. The fact of the matter shows that this North American mission association has changed its name, trying to reinforce its identity, to reflect a more global perspective missiology. (http://www.highbeam.com/doc/1G1-173923117.html).

88. This UK evangelical network formerly known as the UK Evangelical Missionary Alliance (EMA) was founded in 1958 but its background goes back to the International Missionary Fellowship (IMF) formed in 1941 for consultation and prayer fellowship between only interdenominational missions and leaders due to the war. In 1946 during the post-war era and the end of the colonial era, the name was changed to the Fellowship of Interdenominational Missionary Societies (FIMS). Nevertheless, this network lacked the authority for appropriated recommendations and guidance for the British mission movement. In consequence the EMA was founded to provide closer relationship with the fast-growing Evangelical Alliance, membership was defined to be open to denominational and interdenominational mission agencies, and a central office with part-time staff was established. However by 2000 the name was changed to Global Connections, in recognition of the continuing change of the mission world. Its main characteristics are: contributing to the development of the non-Western church; fixing the distortion of false dichotomy between 'here and there' by promoting mission for everywhere to everywhere; recognizing that the UK is becoming a mission field with mission partners coming from other latitudes; a new attitude toward its ethnic diversity; the involvement of local churches directly in mission; and the developing understanding of mission and its variety

aim of helping God's people in the UK to be active and effective in global mission. Global Connections as an innovative network 'is the sum of all its members and contacts, rather than an organization in the traditional sense'. GC provide services in the following way: networking for members; helping the churches to be more involved in global issues, including world mission; raising standards through multidirectional learning; exploring the future of mission; supporting members through advice, services and information; and representing the UK mission community to government and media, and internationally. Regarding its policy this network can link to others who work in similar areas to give help on practical, legal or missiological issues, and promotes forums for cooperative action. Membership policy at GC covers the following types: (a) Agency: includes sending missions, funding organizations as well as agencies involved in relief and development; (b) College: mission training colleges, academic institutions with a mission focus, mission courses; (c) Church: individual churches of all denominations that are passionate about mission; (d) Church stream: church groupings and denominations; and (e) Support agency-providers of services to the missions community including charities and non-charities.

In 1996 a new corporate image and literature along with website development was carried out by Richard Tiplady.[89] A second key point was achieved in 1997 by setting up a church relations section to develop initiatives with UK churches to be more active and effective in world mission. My finding is that it was in 2000 that the UK Evangelical Missionary Alliance became an innovative networking model in recognition of the continuing

---

of expression. The first president was Gilbert Kirby (1958), then Ernest Oliver (1966), Stanley Davies (1983) and Martin Lee from 2004. See further in Global Connection http://www.globalconnections.co.uk/aboutus/visionandstrategy.htm (Accessed 17 February 2008 at 22:20).

89. From a missiological perspective, Tiplady is one of the ideological thinkers to make GC a more contextual model, moving from Traditional Partnership to a more Networking model. He is former Director of the European Christian Mission UK. See further Tipaldy (2003b, 151–153).

change of the mission world, which it reflected by changing its name to Global Connections. From my missiological perspective I notice three factors in this model: (1) There was an introductory relationship with local churches started from 1997, but it seems to be weak due to the fact that local churches are developing their own mission model 'church to church', and 'church to agencies' rather than 'agencies to church', which has the influence of traditional partnership. (2) It seems that there is lacking appropriate promotion between non-Western mission movements, as this is a recent phenomenon especially when we speak in relation to Latin America. For example, of 290 associates of GC, only 11 have links with the church in Peru.[90] And (3) it seems that there is a wider sense of reciprocal contextual collaboration under the new leadership of Martin Lee[91] in the way that he is trying to understand the theological, missiological, sociological and cultural background of the Latin American movement in order to improve the Latin American Forum, which GC develops for new ways of partnership in mission in creative tension. In fact, we can see Lee's (2008) missiological thinking in relation to GC as follows:[92] (1) Members at GC: GC has 190 agency members and about 100 church members. (2) The policies of membership. Agencies have to agree to the statement of faith, basis of fellowship and basis of management. They need two referees known to the network. (3) Supported: GC is funded by 60% fees, 15% donations, 20% grants/sponsorship and 5% other. (4) The impact of GC in Britain: This is a difficult one! It is **very** hard to see where GC has had impact. GC has some influence though:

---

90. Missions that have some link with the church in Peru are as follows: Guildford Baptist Church, Medical Service Ministries, WorldShare, Tearfund, Links International, Scripture Union, Bible Society, Latin Link, BMS World Mission, South American Society (SAMS), and Echoes of Service. See more: http://www.globalconnections.co.uk/OneStopCMS/Core/ (Accessed Wednesday 27 February 2008 at 14:30).

91. Personal dialogue with Martin Lee, during my trip to the conference "In the Eye of the Storm" at The Hayes Conference Centre, Swanwick, UK, 28 to 30 November 2007. (28 November 2007).

92. Questionnaire answered by Martin Lee. Electronic information provided on 13 March 2008, 09:22.

(a) Sociologically – uncertain; even the membership is still very white and middle class in staff terms. The network has few links with Black majority or other migrant groups, or even those who have been in the UK a long time. So it is uncertain if GC has had any impact here yet. (b) Ecclesiologically – GC vision is to see mission at the heart of what the church is in the UK. GC would hope that things are changing and some of that is due to the effort of mission leaders. However, most churches have a poor ecclesiology when it comes to mission. They see the role of the church as caring for their own flock **firs**t. This is changing and Lee hopes that the GC message is getting through, or at least causing debate, but he recognizes that their reach into the church in the UK is small. Most outreach comes through individual members and he is not sure they take the core messages to the church – 'intentionally missional church', 'mission at the heart of church, the church at the heart of mission'. (c) Missiologically – Lee hopes that they have had more impact here. Yet many missions are still in the old paradigm of taking people from churches to send them out under their umbrella. GC has done a lot of work on business and mission, the role of migrants in mission, and missional lifestyle. (d) Theologically – GC is promoting the concept of *missio Dei*, the missional heart of God, having the right understanding of the Trinity, etc. There is some useful material available and in the mission training colleges. Lee concludes that he is very happy with the theology being taught and how the network helps them learn from each other. However, he is less sure about general theological training colleges.

Additionally, the effectiveness of the networking impact is seen in the mission activity between poor children that should be mentioned: The Viva Network practises the networking partnership model. It was founded by Patrick McDonald, as an Oxford-based international partnership movement to provide help to poor children. It is estimated that 1.8 billion children are at risk around the world; 110,000 full-time workers and 20,000 ministries work with children worldwide (Guthrie 2000, 117).

3. **Partnership for World Mission** (PWM), founded in 1978, is a partnership between the General Synod of the Church of England and its World Mission Agencies. It is governed by the PWM Committee drawing its members from General Synod and from the 11 agencies such as SAMS. Its main tasks are concerned with the Church of England's role in furthering partnership in mission within the Anglican Communion; supporting the work of Diocesan Companion Links; and coordinating the policies and selected tasks of the Church of England's World Mission agencies (*Church of England Yearbook* 2004, 26). PWM includes in its network the following missions, which cause an effective mission transformation in partnership with different ministries around the world: Church Army, the largest evangelistic UK agency with 350 evangelists, focus on evangelism, church planting, children and young people, older people and the homeless; The Church's Ministry Among Jewish People (CMJ), to encourage people to come to faith in Christ; Church Mission Society (CMS), one of the largest mission agencies in Britain supported by over 4,000 churches; Church Pastoral Aid Society (CPAS), which seeks to enable evangelism and encourage leaders in the churches of the UK and Ireland; Crosslinks, which seeks to make the Christ of the Scriptures fully known; Intercontinental Church Society (ICS), partner with 65 international churches, ministers to holidaymakers in over 20 resorts, principally in Europe and Mediterranean; The Mission to Seafarers, which serves seafarers of all races and creeds in 300 ports worldwide; The Mothers' Union (international work), promoting the wellbeing of families worldwide with over one million members in 70 countries, with a policy of prayer, spiritual growth of families, taking practical action to improve conditions for the families; South American Missionary Society (SAMS), with strategic mission in South America, Spain and Portugal linking partners and projects, and short term missions; The Society for Promoting Christian Knowledge (SPCK), the oldest Anglican mission agency founded in 1698, supports literature and education through

publishing, bookselling and grant-making to equip Christians for mission and ministry; and the United Society for the Propagation of the Gospel (USPG), founded in 1701, known as the biggest Anglican mission society in Britain, working with the Anglican and United Churches in more than 50 countries worldwide, with the policy to exchange people, resources and training for mission (http://www.pwm-web.org.uk/partners.shtml. See also Fiedler 1994, 12, 16).[93]

In relation to the innovative approach of partnership,[94] in the article *What do the Mission Agencies do?* Canon Mark Oxbrow former international leader of CMS,[95] speaking of the PWM network points out:

> Do we primarily think of the church as being defined by its local manifestation? Or is the primary focus its structures – a Council or Synod? What about the religious orders? Where does my home fellowship group fit? Is the Anglican Communion a 'church'? Once we have begun to get a clearer idea of the identity of 'church' then we can ask how we understand the relationship of the mission agency to 'church'?

Then he gives a response to this missiological question in this way:

> I would like to suggest that all these can be understood as manifestations of 'church' and that within the Anglican Communion mission is a task which requires co-operation

---

93. SPCK and SPG (now USPG) both were founded by Rev Dr Thomas Bray as individual initiative and sponsored by the state support and contributions of people. These missions are defined as pre-classical (forerunners) the seminal model of mission societies, which were related to a denomination or to a group of related denominations. See Fiedler (1994, 17, 20).

94. In February 2008, a consultation was held at High Leigh, Hertfordshire UK, exploring the kind of relationships the Church of England might have in the future within the Anglican Communion. At the consultation were representatives from the variety of organizations, agencies and networks that are channels for these relationships. In this consultation the Rev Canon Mark Oxbrow, former International Mission Director of CMS, presented papers of the role of the Mission Agencies within the Anglican Communion.

95. See the whole article at http://www.pwm-web.org.uk/features/article1.shtml

between the church local, national church bodies and the specialist mission agencies. In thinking about the role of the mission agencies within the Anglican Communion, we are therefore thinking about one aspect of the life of the 'church', not 'para-church' activity.

Hence, it seems that from the reality of WEA-MC, GC and PWM, there is a conscious attitude in Western thinking to recognize that relationships between agencies and local churches are very important for reinforcing partnership for the mission task. Andrew Walls suggests that a change in motive and method will help agencies that "have never wavered from its Anglican or its evangelical allegiance" (2004, 110). The following diagram portrays the networking model.

The Networking Model

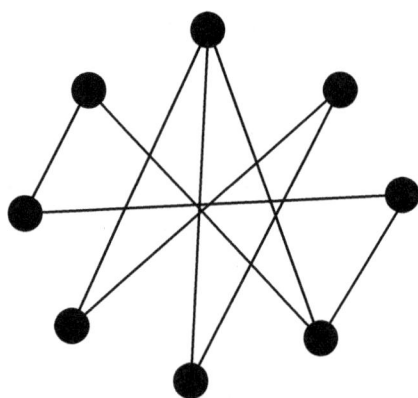

Orientational multidirectional, relational

The emergent model

Historical, theological and missiological characteristics

In his book, *A Time for Mission*, Samuel Escobar points out that "for the old traditional denominations, partnership with the new immigrant[96] churches brings the need for serious self-appraisal" (2003, 18; Taylor 2000, 34). This interpretation provides a view of missiological renewal in that traditional partnership has to be less institutionalized, which in Escobar's view is difficult for middle-class evangelical churches, for whom it is not easy to accept the emergence of the Third Church. In analyzing Escobar's view I find four characteristics of the emergent model that he defines as mission from below (2003, 17–18), or what the Scottish missiologist Stewart McIntosh[97] has defined as '*mision al ras de suelo*': they do not come from people in positions of power or privilege; they are those who have little material, financial or technical support; they are open to the power of the Spirit; and churches of ethnic minorities and immigrant churches are mainly involved.

Furthermore, the emergent model comes to the light from the influence of southern Christianity (Jenkins 2002, 3), with grassroots churches (Berg and Pretiz 1996), popular Protestantism (Escobar 2002, 85), mission from the periphery (128), or indigenous churches (Rickett and Welliver 1997), also known as independent churches (Anderson 2001). Therefore, I define the emergent model as the missionary movement of the Third Church,[98]

---

96. Speaking about 'the migration model', Escobar explains that this model has functioned through the centuries, and today some denominational mission societies and faith missions are trying to set up connections with the migration movement of people from poor countries moving in search of economic survival, carrying the gospel and missionary initiative with them. See more in Taylor (2000, 34).

97. For McIntosh, a missionary in Peru for 30 years '*misión al ras de suelo*' implies the use of new structures of mission that emerge from the periphery of the church, from poor countries with an indigenous missiology. See his books *Una Introducción a la Misiología Latinoamericana* (1986) and *Siete ensayos de la realidad Misiológica* (1993).

98. The term 'Third Church' was coined around the 1970s by the Catholic theologian Walbert Buhlmann, on the analogy of the 'Third World' (Jenkins 2002, 3). Before the 1990s the new non-Western missionary movement was called 'Two-Thirds World Missionaries' or 'Missionaries from the Third World' but now there is a missiological change and they are called: 'Non-Western Missionaries', 'The Majority World', 'The South', 'The Southern Hemispheres'. All of these new titles refer more to the spiritual change than the political, social, territorial or geographical one. Some explanation of the Two-Thirds World Church is given by Makito Yashimoto (Claydon 2005, 143–145).

which includes Africa, Asia and Latin America that emerges from the new missiological context,[99] where the Holy Spirit is taking churches from those regions for a new reciprocal contextual collaboration[100] with the aim of empowering the double mission mandate Christ has given to the church. The emergent model depends on the pivotal policy of the Spirit, who is calling thousands of missionaries and mobilizing them to mission, even though many of them are without any kind of influential power from Western traditional mission structure due to the fact that this movement includes tent makers, immigrants,[101] asylum seekers, and missionaries sent by their local churches, denominations or indigenous mission agencies.

This recent emergent partnership phenomenon model related to the fast-growing churches and the sending of missionaries from the South to the North has the following characteristics: in a negative way, weak mission structures, few proper written policies like Western missions has, missionaries are not properly cross-culturally trained, weak financial support, etc. The positive impact is that there is strong commitment to the Great Commission mandate, powerful enthusiasm to infect others, faith in God's provision, ability to survive with little money, ability to pray constantly, natural evangelism, practising of business as mission, influence of 'faith mission' model, etc. My assumption is that this new mission force is using the emergent partnership model; as a result traditional partnership has

---

99. Jenkins calls this new phenomenon of emergent partnership the 'The Mission Churches' (2002, 57–60).

100. In the book, *Making your Partnership Work*, the author analyses the need for collaboration between North and South churches. He states that over the past three decades the 'Third Church' has altered the mission landscape and this change is forging new alliances in mission. See further Rickett (2002, 19).

101. The work *Immigration and Entrepreneurship,* edited by Ivan Ligth and Parminder Bhachu, provides an interesting study of immigration in relation to the reality of California and the USA in comparison with places like Paris, Berlin, Israel, Canada, Korea, Japan, and Armenians in Moscow; it was developed by the International Studies and Overseas Programs and Institute of Social Science Research at the University of California, Los Angeles. In the case of Latin America the data shows that in 1989 there were 120,000 Latino immigrant workers in California, most of them from Mexico, and 81 percent were undocumented (1993, 63). In 1986, the federal government approved the Immigration Reform, which included sanctions upon employers who employ undocumented workers. This new law granted amnesty to undocumented immigrants who have been stable residents in the United States since 1981. As many Latinos were eligible for that amnesty, this made an economic impact on contracts and employers as many Latinos worked in this activity (66).

become old-fashioned with a lack of effectiveness in sending missionaries, channelling the mission task with local churches as it was in the past, and weaknesses when applied to the contextual situation of the Majority World. Thus, my finding is that the emergent partnership reality seems to be more recognized in the work of theologians and missiologists of both the Third Church and the Western World (Padilla 1985, 129–141; Berg and Pretiz 1996; Guthrie 2000; Escobar 2002, 18–119; Pocock, Reheenen and McConnell 2005; Kirk 2006). The reason is that emergent partnership is fundamentally related to what Escobar calls mission from below (2003, 17), or what the Scottish missiologist Andrew Walls (2004, 41), speaking of the Christian cross-cultural diffusion, calls the new centre of gravity from the West to the South. In the same line, Makito Yoshimoto (in Claydon 2005) presents a useful perspective of the 'Two-Thirds World Churches', when he makes an analysis of mission in the twenty-first century.

The emergent model reflects the influence of grass-roots churches (Berg and Pretiz 1996, 11), which are independent of the traditional mission structures and denominations, with characteristics of a marginal economy, diluted social power and economic dependence of poor people. These independent churches have the indigenous nature of a grass-roots movement with a cultural orientation of worship, church ministries, community orientation, outreach of the ordinary members, spirituality, a message of submission to God, a message of hope in desperate and oppressive situations where the reality of warfare is taken seriously, mobilization of the laity which produces spontaneous growth with a powerful effect on the life of the church and its mission (7–9). Charles Taber's analysis (2003, 21) is that this political, cultural, economic and sociological environment goes back to the first large-scale encounter of Iberian expansion (1450–1750) with the non-Western world. I argue that from this context three things influenced the mission activity of the Western world, which had a negative social impact because of the mission policy: self-conscious superiority to an inferior culture, radical replacement of indigenous culture by the 'Christian' model, and mission allied with secular power, the state (Taber 2003, 21).

Historically, Philip Jenkins (2002, 55) describes how "the Bandung conference 1955, the starting point of organized decolonization, became a symbol of the emergence of the Third World within the British imperial era, this with the community of new nations that aspired to be independent of both capitalist West and communist East".[102] My assumption is that emergent partnership began to grow after the Second World War, due to the political, economic, and cultural context of liberation from imperialism and colonialism, because a movement of independence between many countries who belonged to a colonial power took place. In fact, Jenkins' analysis helps to clarify that this emergent Third World started with the collapse of the imperial era, which began with the independence of India and Pakistan in 1947 from the British empire, and culminated in the collapse of The Soviet Union in 1991 (55). This political phenomenon is seen in a similar way between the influence of traditional partnership mission and the emergence of independent movements, in the way that the third model – emergent partnership – appears to be more contextual for the indigenous missionary movement of the Majority World, less bureaucratic and more flexible in its mission policy.

Theologically, the emergent model seems to rest on God's provision, and the fulfilment of the Great Commission. Why? The pivotal reason is that this model emerges from the periphery of marginal economy, social and political instability, where Western cultural influence, economic dependence and a lack of self-governing decisions has produced a negative impact on the natural development of the Third Church. As Valdir Steuernagel (Taylor 2000, 130) points out, commitment to relationship rather than hierarchical submission and administration becomes essential for emergent partnership. Somehow, these elements show why missionaries from this context promote a policy of spirituality, which emphasizes

---

102. This is the Asian-African conference that was held in Bandung, Indonesia from 18–24 April 1955. The countries of Indonesia, Burma, Ceylon (Srilanka), India and Pakistan, met together to promote the 'Bandung Conference', with the aim of discussing political, economic and cultural issues of national sovereignty, racism, colonialism, world peace, and economic and cultural cooperation among the participating countries, as the natural interest of the Asian-African countries. 29 countries attended this conference, which was held at a time when the post-war movement for national liberation in Asia, Africa and Latin America was strongly emerging, when imperialism and colonialism clashed by going in different directions of political influence. This was the first international conference held by Asian and African countries with no participation of any colonial western power. The Portuguese empire did not disintegrated until 1975 and the Russian empire lasted as the great vestige of European colonialism until its collapse in 1991 (2002, 55).

prayer, trusting God, faith in God, and confidence in God. This model also seems to rest on the nature of God's kingdom and the fulfilment of the Great Commission, with the weakness of an overemphasis on saving souls. The Anglican Liberian, Burges Carr, in *Mission Trends No 3* argues in an article "The Relation of Union to Mission" that emergent partnership definitely emerges from these newly emergent nations "euphemistically called the Third World, but nevertheless are the proud owners of the primary resources that produce wealth and power" (Carr in Anderson 1976, 165). For Escobar, two characteristics of the evangelical churches in the Third World is their evangelistic and missionary dynamism, but he argues that it is necessary to distinguish between the gospel and the ideologies of the West with a multinational corporation approach (Taylor 2000, 112). Consequently, it seems to me that Escobar[103] (2003), Costas (1974) and Padilla (1985), offer pivotal elements for the emergent model theology[104] in relation to mission and social transformation. The emergent model develops a theology of a missionary God who has a *missio Trinitatis*.

Missiologically, this emergent movement has influenced more than 50 million (65 million according to Padilla[105]) Latin Americans (Jenkins 2002, 57; Pocock 2005, 142), especially in the Pentecostal and charismatic movements, which bring to the missiological arena the reality of a new era for mission, with thousands of non-traditional missionaries that cannot be counted according to the western statistical methods due to the fact that many of them, perhaps the majority, are not working for a formal or conventional mission structure, but their work can be seen in the growth of the Third Church. However, there is a minority of 'formal' or conventional

---

103. A summary of Escobar's mission theology is as follows: God wants to be known and does not remain hidden, God has revealed himself in and through historical events and ultimately in Christ, God both chooses and sends (Luke 4:18; John 20:5, 20:21), and the Bible warns us against triumphalistic attitudes that will give glory to the human agent (2003).

104. For Escobar, two pivotal elements have been produced by Costas and Padilla for a missiological approach of evangelicals from the Third World, which can be applied for emergent partnership theology; these are the criticism of existing patterns of mission and the proposal of a missiology that corresponds to the missionary challenges of the present (Taylor 2000, 112).

105. Data provided by René Padilla at the Global Connections Mission Consultation. Personal notes, London 2006.

missionaries that are the ones generally counted by western statistics who are partnering with some mission societies and local churches, though the majority are working with local churches without the formal title of a 'missionary', but with the same purpose of extending God's kingdom; this I call a natural mission expansion of God's kingdom. This is thanks to external factors of migration, poverty and political change in the world economy, and due to internal factors of the Holy Spirit in the church, moving the centre of gravity of global Christianity from the Northern to the Southern hemisphere, which obeys the sovereign rule of God's will (Rickett 2002, 18; Walls 1996). Consequently, I agree with Luis Bush[106] (Rickett and Welliver 1997, 13) in following the transformational approach rather than the transactional one. The second refers to a managerial missiology and the first to an interactive relationship between donors and emergent partnerships. On the other side, emergent partnership empowers local initiatives, as Steuernagel (Taylor 2000, 131) says, "to replace centralized activities with partnership and more relational participation of the donors".

Policies of the emergent model

Regarding the question of personnel, the emergent model enjoys a policy that is very flexible with respect to contracts with candidates. The reason is that many of the emergent formal missionaries (i.e. those registered in a mission society or in a local church) working under this model are influenced less and less by the traditional model, and more and more by the networking model, while the emergent model and the 'Faith Mission' philosophy mentioned before are common. At the same time, many emergent missionaries (i.e. those who are sent apart from mission structures) have been sent by the 'wind of the Spirit'[107] to various mission fields through

---

106. In his article "Greater Glory Yet to Come: Trends Regarding Indigenous Ministries", Bush's analysis, gives a perspective of the new possibilities for the Third Church with less emphasis on accountability, policies and procedures, which is the transactional view, and proposes that the transformational approach would make an impact of God's breakthrough and the vitalization of a people in one culture to another culture. He suggests that the West should learn from what the Spirit of God is doing in the non-Western world (Rickett and Welliver 1997, 13).

107. I refer to 'wind of the Spirit', in the context of John 3:8 and Acts 16:6–10. It is the authority of the Spirit who moves people to mission in different ways to different cultures

external factors, including economic (migration as a result of poverty), political (motivated by the need for asylum) and cultural (as with students). This phenomenon has been studied by Garcia and Escobar[108] in the context of the Spanish reality (2003, 57–76; 129–152), and by Jenkins in the context of what he calls *The Future Demographic of Religion*[109] (2002, 89–105). Financially some mission agencies of the emergent model try to raise some basic budget for their candidates like the church 'Las Flores' in Lima, Peru, who sent Angela Docto to work in Great Britain with Latin Partners;[110] others cover the total budget, especially those who belong to a mega-church movement like the Christian and Missionary Alliance of Lince in Lima Peru with 5,000 members, who in 2005 sent the Peruvian missionary Juan Zuñiga to plant a church in Madrid. The effectiveness of the emergent model is shown in the sending of thousands of missionaries from the Third Church, estimated in 400 mission agencies sending 13,000 missionaries in 1980 (Winter 1981, B43), and Larry Pate (Dempster, Klaus and Petersen1991, 245) estimated the sending of 162,360 by 2000. In the case of the American movement, in his book *Mission in the Third Millennium,* Stan Guthrie (2000, 6) gives an analysis of the issue of raising money for candidates. He clarifies that today this is an obstacle for traditional independent agencies where the process can last between 18 to 24 months in visiting many churches to cover the budget. He argues that American missionaries have to target huge financial support of at least $50,000–$75,000 to cover travel ministry expenses, pension fund, insurance, school for the children, salaries, etc., in comparison with the service of a native missionary from missions like Gospel for Asia who receives between $60 to $120 dollars a month. Equally Guthrie (109) points out the

---

and in different circumstances. The work of the Spirit is not possible to measure through the western academic model; the Spirit blows wherever he pleases.

108. See the articles about migration in the book *Las Iglesias y la Migracion* (2003)

109. Jenkins suggests that immigration is due to poverty and environmental catastrophe. Europe has between 10 million and 20 million illegal immigrants from Africa and Asia (2003, 97). By 2000 the United States had 30 million immigrants. Today there is an estimated 30 million Latinos in America alone, apart from other countries. Jenkins estimates that by mid-century, 100 million Americans will claim Hispanic origin, which will then constitute one of the world's largest Latino societies (100).

110. Latin Partner is a branch of Latin Link mission with the aim of introducing Latin missionaries in Britain.

tendency for sending more short-term mission teams in America, which was launched after the World War II by Operation Mobilization and Youth with a Mission; it is estimated that there was a mobilization of 450,000 laypeople in 1998. The emergent model provides a policy relating to the overflowing of missionaries freely going from and to all six continents under God's initiative, developing a missionary theology of reciprocal contextual collaboration.

Impact of the emergent model

This model is growing through the southern hemisphere churches, which include Asia, Africa and Latin America. With regard to social impact, in the middle of resistance to Western culture, the emergent model provides a positive repercussion, bringing the gospel with a wider receptivity in non-Western countries than Western culture. However, as Guthrie argues "the non-Western missions movement is much better known for sending people out than for keeping them on the field" (2000, 35). Guthrie quotes the figure mentioned at the Brazilian National Mission Congress 1993, that of 5,400 Brazilian missionaries sent out in previous years, the vast majority returned within a year and about 90 percent of the returnees did not return back (35).

What about the cultural impact of the emergent model? Barry R. Taylor's analysis clarifies the impact of contemporary culture through mass media, which has experienced important shifts since 1985. From this analysis, my assumption is that modernity influenced the traditional model, but today post-modernity has made a cultural impact on the networking and the emergent partnership. Let me explain. Culturally, there is a change from structural emphasis on policies and strategies to relationships by all types of communication, which is part of a reciprocal contextual collaboration paradigm. Culturally, the Third Church has a sense of personal identity for going into mission. The ecclesiological impact of the emergent model has its roots within the Pentecostal movement, which starts from the poor and marginalized people (Escobar 2003, 17), from the emergence of new independent churches (Anderson 2001), from mission minded churches[111] (Guthrie 2000, 4) and from the new Christian centre of gravity (Walls 2004, 41). One sign of the emergent model is seen through London's Kingsway International Christian Centre (KICC), with 5,000 members, founded in 1992 by Pastor Matthew Ashimolowo, a missionary from Nigeria (Jenkins 2002, 98); or by the largest Latin American church, with 2,000 members in London, founded in 1987 by the Peruvian missionary Edmundo Ravelo.

Economic impact: As this model emerges from the periphery of marginal people it is worth acknowledging that the emergent model is developed from what I call a 'mission faith statement',[112] where candidates accept that they have to find their own support through friends, churches, or by what Patrick Lai (2005) in his book *Tentmaking* calls tent-maker missionaries.[113] In contrast to those mentioned before is the immigrant-self-support model,[114] called a migratory model by Escobar (2002, 163). This is the financial formula that emerges from the majority of this partnership model due to the fact that it is rooted under the pneumatic and theological influence of the mission mandate, not from the structural and rationalistic one as with the traditional model, which considers the priority of planning, budgeting, predictions and possible results of the mission enterprise.

---

111. Guthrie refers to those churches in USA that are developing their own mission project mobilized by the entrepreneurial spirit of their business members, short-term mission, and creating awareness of the multicultural change. These churches have the following characteristics: an outward focus, 30 percent of the budget going to mission, a training programme for candidates, missions education through the church's plan, sending its own people, concern and prayer for the lost, a pastor who leads in mission, assistance to other churches in mission, and strong local evangelism. This is a summary of Guthrie, which comes from Tom Telford book *Mission in the Twenty-First Century: getting your church into the game.* See Guthrie (2000, 4).

112. This influence comes from the post-classical missions started by Hudson Taylor.

113. Lai (2005, 11) defines tentmaking as a biblical term because tentmakers are on God's assignment; it communicates a vocation of serving God. This is the basic reason why tentmakers are missionaries. Another related missiological term is the term bi-vocational worker, emphasizing two roles: business people and career missionaries. Lai clarifies that it is wrongly perceived that all tentmakers have to be fully self-supported. The apostle Paul received some support from churches (2 Cor 11:8; and Phil 4:15).

114. This model is related to the informal missionary effort that cannot be counted by managerial statistics due to the fact that external factors, political, economic, religious, social, etc., are behind the 'third mission force' movement. I define them also as informal missionaries because they are not registered in any mission society but they evangelize wherever they go.

In thinking of the emergent model globally, I agree with Guthrie (2000, 13) when he affirms that "the growth of the movement supporting non-Western Christians is a post-World War II phenomenon", in the sense that from that time there were political, ideological and economic changes in the world, and that reality made an impact on the Protestant missionary movement. In this way, there are important contributions to the understanding of the emergent model. In the work *Supporting Indigenous Ministries* edited by Daniel Rickett and Dotsey Welliver (1997), their approach coincides with the development of a new and more flexible approach in the interpretation of the history of the traditional model, seeking new effectiveness with the cooperation of supporting indigenous ministries in the non-Western world. In my understanding Guthrie and these works edited by Rickett and Welliver are aware of the new centre of Christian missionary gravity, where a new supply of mission energy for Christian mission has emerged for the twenty-first century. Since 1996[115] more that 52 agencies, gathered at the Billy Graham Center in Wheaton, Illinois, formed a network to help emergent partnership by discussing issues like accountability by indigenous missionaries, church and denominational relations, dependency and interdependency, fundraising, future planning, links with traditional mission agencies, mutual accountability, standards of practice, and vision sharing with the whole church (1997, xii).

Global impact: The new global order has brought to the mission enterprise the presence of the Third Church, which has grown rapidly in recent decades. Ethnic immigrants, diaspora churches from the South, are crossing the political, cultural, economic and religious boundaries of the North to preach the gospel in the power of the Spirit. Michael Pocock (2005, 143) summarizes the global impact of the Latin American church as follows: liberation theology, theological education by extension, Pentecostalism, Latin American evangelists, and Latin Americans in mission. This reality demands a new challenge to partnership in mission that the western

---

115. Rickett (1997) shows that more that 113 US mission agencies were concerned in supporting independent missionary movements in the non-Western world before the consultation with missions. Key leaders like Chuck Bennett of Partners International, Jim Kraakevik of Billy Graham Center and Bernie May of Wycliffe Bible Translators initiated this network.

mentality in mission has to understand as a new way of Christian partnership for the twenty-first century. The emergent model is not a matter of reinventing the wheel; it is a matter of making a contribution to the Great Commission which has not yet been fulfilled as was predicted by Peter Wagner in 1993 (Guthrie 2000, 76). Nor is it a matter of finding scapegoats; it is a matter of why the emergent model is a new tool to fix what has been neglected before; in this sense reciprocal contextual collaboration is linked to the emergent model. The following diagram portrays the emergent model.

The Emergent Model

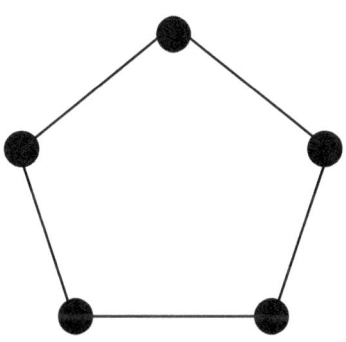

Flexible, bipolar, autonomous

To show the missiological impact of the emergent model here, I offer five models of what it is as follows:

1. **The Christian and Missionary Alliance in Lima, Peru.** A local church with 5000 members. Under the leadership of a mission-minded senior pastor, Wilson Chavez,[116] it has sent out 27 Peruvian missionaries both in Lima, the capital, and overseas. Seven missionaries are working in Peru and twenty outside Peru, three in Japan, one in India, two in Spain, one in France, one

---

116. Questionnaire answered by Wilson Chavez, April 2007.

in England, one in Norway, one in Mexico, eight in the USA and two in Cuba. Support seems to be total, partial/in part, and symbolic. The majority went out during Wilson Chavez's pastorate.[117] In 2005 Juan Zuñiga with his wife and three children went out as missionaries to Spain. The church gave €1550 euros per month for four years towards his support, and the American CMA mission gave €450.[118] The support Zuñiga received from the Christian and Missionary Alliance of Lince covered 40% of his budget, 10% was covered by the American CMA mission, while 50% came from the congregation he raised up. In this model, some projects are shared and supported by other churches and partner missions. We can observe a relational interdependency tendency in this situation between the missionary and sending church with monthly reports. In the case of the Lince church, the kind of support can be total (100% of the budget), partial (up to 50% of the budget), or symbolic (10% of the budget), and shared when they are in partnership with other churches or missions. The total budget means that only one church absorbs the support, while 'total shared' means that the missionary is completely supported, but in a shared way – which is the case for Juan Zuñiga in Spain. Partial/shared is used to refer to a missionary who is supported in partnership with other churches and missions.

2. **Iglesia Misionera Evangélica**. An indigenous missional church established in Huancayo, Peru in 1985 (Cueva 1991). Enrique Nickl (interview), pastor of this church, supports different mission projects in Europe, developing partnership with the Anglican church, St James in London, Iglesia del Monte in Malaga-Spain, and the Swedish Pentecostal church, Smyrna, in Gothenburg-Sweden.

---

117. Telephone information from Lima sent to the author by Rosa Espinoza, 17–22 May 2007, 7:00 pm.
118. Information sent to the author by Juan Zuñiga, 17 May 2007, 10:29 pm.

3. **PM International**. Founded by the Mexican missionary, Pablo Carrillo, with more that 100 non-Western missionaries working in poor countries. They are linked to more that 100 churches for supporting their missionaries currently working in more that 30 countries (PM 2006, 1–11).
4. **Latin churches in Spain.** From 1995 to 2010, there were six million Latin Americans[119] living in Spain with a population of 45 million. This country has the highest number of immigrants in Europe. The Spanish bishop, Carlos Lopez, of the Iglesia Evangélica Reformada (IERE) in Madrid has set up a congregation of 400 Latin people under the mission model of practical support to the immigrants, called 'The Latin American Mission'.[120]
5. **Latin churches in London.** There are 400,000 Latin Americans and 50,000 Spaniards. In this context nearly 20 Spanish-speaking evangelical churches[121] have been initiated: the first church founded by Claudio Sheperd in 1961 is the 'Congregación de Evangélicos en Londres',[122] and since 1987 new independent churches[123] have emerged, the majority with a Pentecostal background.

---

119. This is an estimation provided by Bishop Carlos Lopez. However, other evangelical pastors from Spain estimate between three and four million Latinos living in Spain.

120. This project has been implemented since 1996 and 50% of their churches work in partnership through this project. It is said that in 2006 more that 35,000 people benefitted from the 'Misión Anglicana Solidaridad' (*Share*, 10, Issue 1, winter 2008). Also the First Baptist Church of Madrid is working with immigrants and it is estimated that at least 30% of the congregation (300 members) comes from Latin America. Data provided by Tony Vazquez on my visit to Madrid on 6 May 2008.

121. In my survey I have found at least 20 evangelical congregations in London, none of them with their own building but using rented or rent free British churches. See more Cueva (2005).

122. Claudio Shepherd, telephone interview held in London on 1 December 2009.

123. The main characteristic of these churches is that they have been planted by immigrant Christians without participation of any traditional or networking partnership model. Most of them started their work at the level of cell groups. The largest congregation founded in 1987 is the 'Comunidad Cristiana de Londres' with 1,300 attendants.

Conclusion

We have developed three current partnership models, conscious of the complexity of the organized church. We have approached understanding the legitimacy of different models of mission partnership, and the necessity from all mission structure models not only to exist, but to work together harmoniously for God's kingdom and suggested developing the inclusiveness of reciprocal contextual collaboration in the twenty-first-century mission. We conclude that while the traditional model is more related to sending missionaries overseas with less direct intervention of churches, the networking model relates to churches and missions sharing resources without losing their own identity, overcoming the concept of territorial mission. The emergent model is about sending, sharing and creating new mission structures with less or even no participation of mission agencies.

Traditional partnership looks more effective in long-term mission work, while the networking model is more effective in sharing resources and relationships, and the emergent model becomes more effective in creating new ways of reciprocal contextual collaboration. It is right to mention that there are some missions that are surviving the new challenges of a global mission by reinventing themselves; for example, in the case of an evangelical networking, the Pentecostal World Fellowship reiterated its commitment to participating in the work of the WEA and strengthening relations.[124] That is also the case within the ecumenical movement with models such as the *Council for World Mission* (CWM) with 32 members, and the *Communaute*

---

124. During the PWF Congress held in Stockholm 2010, Dr Geoff Tunnicliffe from the WEA thanked the Pentecostal leaders of the PWF for their great contribution to the life and growth of the church around the world by being active participants and leaders in most of the WEA's 128 national Evangelical Alliances worldwide. The outgoing chairman of the PWF, Bishop James Leggett, publicly announced a new partnership between the PWF and the WEA through a deepening collaboration between the two bodies. Both networks have shared fruitful discussions regarding the work of Christ in recent year. Reiterated commitment to participating in the work of the WEA and strengthening relations was emphasized. The PWF is a fellowship of Pentecostal believers from around the globe, meeting triennially in different parts of the world for the purpose of mutual edification. See World Evangelical Alliance, CEO addresses Pentecostal World Fellowship (Electronic information sent to the author on 30 August 2010)

Evangelique d' Action Apostolique (CEVAA)[125] with 47 member churches and the *United Evangelical Mission* (UEM) with 32 members; these mission structures reinvented themselves in 1971, 1977 and 1996 by sharing their resources (people, money and ideas) and have become much acclaimed models within ecumenical partnership.[126] However, it seems to me that the traditional model within evangelicalism, born in Europe, suffers some fatigue with a sense of declining effectiveness in its role as a catalyst of mission efforts to achieve God's mission plan for the church.[127] By contrast, the emergent model seems to grow more and more, working as a new tool to cooperate with the global mission within evangelicalism in the Third Church and the rest of the world. It is neither a warning for the traditional partnership or for networking, nor a revolution to overcome old models; it is a new contribution for God's kingdom and it should be understood as such, otherwise global evangelicalism is in danger of producing more clashes than ever before. For this reason, I agree with Graham Duncan (2007, vi) in pointing out that authentic partnership in mission includes

---

125. During the World Council of Churches Assembly at Harare 1998, the three leaders of CWM, CEVAA and the *United Evangelical Mission* (UEM) decided to share evaluations of each organization's current mission engagement with an aim to (1) learn from and challenge each other, (2) give fresh impulses to the ecumenical movement, and (3) to identify areas for co-operation. See further 'Report of the CEVAA, CWM, UEM Joint Consultation, CWM's Network of Theological Enquire' (http://www.cwmnote.org/uem.php). The article entitled "Towards A New Missionary Consciousness" by Jean-Paul Gabus announced the creation of the Communauté Evangelique d'Action Apostolique (CEVAA). On 30 October 1971, the Paris Missionary Society had restructured itself into 'the Evangelical Community of Apostolic Action'. This model seems to derive from similar experience to the London Missionary Society, which became the Council for World Mission (CWM) in 1977. See further William J. Nottingham, 2001 "Getting to Know CEVAA", *International Review of Mission* vol. 90 October, 455–461. See further the website of CEVAA (www.cevaa.org); CWM (www.cwmission. Org) and UEM (www.vmission.org).

126. These mission initiatives that emerged since the 1960s with an optimistic approach of partnership as cooperation in evangelism seek to find new structures of mission that may help them to survive or to reinforce their participation in mission by using more dynamic structures according to the changing time within a global mission environment. See further Kai Michael Funkschmidt (Partnership Between Unequals – Mission Impossible?: Mission Structures revisited, *International Review of Mission* 2002, 395–412).

127. Nevertheless, Carey's characteristics and policies have made an influential impact among the new wave of mission societies of different periods of the Christian movement. The evidence is that many mission agencies have originated both in Great Britain and other countries under the image of traditional partnership. The effect is still there, but as Stanley Davies warns, with less effectiveness during the last three decades

"horizontal relations and management of the gifts of God for the people of God".

Part II

Rediscovering our Missionary Consciousness

CHAPTER 4

Current Issues of Partnership in Mission

Introduction

Mission partnership involves a variety of different kinds of issues, thus chapter 4 will discuss current issues of partnership in mission with relevant themes that can shed light on the complexity and the simplicity of partnering with others. I will concentrate on current issues (i.e. theological, missiological, economical, cultural and relational). These may help us understand why each mission partnership model has its own missiological tension with both a negative and a positive impact.

Theological issues of contextual partnership

I shall attempt to answer the following question: Is it possible to discover appropriate partnership models which might help to overcome the new forms of dependence and a lack of reciprocal freedom? The African theologian Kwame Bediako says: "theological freedom is the freedom of the Gospel" (1992, 252).[1] However, the reality and complexity of different perspectives on freedom has had a great influence on all models of partnership in Christian mission. The fatal political, economic, cultural and social

---

1. Kwame Bediako (1992, 252) tries to link the impact of culture in the Christian thought of the second century and in modern Africa. He assumes that theological freedom was not generally facilitated by the Western missionary movement for African theology. See further Bediako (1992).

experiences of 11 September 2001 (USA), 11 March 2004 (Madrid), and 7 July 7 2005 (London), are signs of opportunities for a new theological interpretation of freedom, power, justice, etc., in dialogue with contemporary global issues and partnership in mission.[2] Thus, here I will limit myself to providing a brief discussion by focusing on five theological presuppositions for Christian partnership: (1) there is no appropriate Christian reciprocal contextual collaboration (partnership) without biblical freedom; (2) there is no appropriate Christian reciprocal contextual collaboration (partnership) without consideration of contextual theologies; (3) there is no appropriate Christian reciprocal contextual collaboration (partnership) without consciousness of the influence of external factors in mission (I will deal with this under missiological issues); (4) there is no appropriate Christian relationship without sharing the control of power and decision making (addressed under economic issues); and (5) there is no appropriate Christian reciprocal contextual collaboration (partnership) without reciprocal christological relationship. This fifth one will be treated under relational issues on partnership.

First presupposition

My first presupposition is that there is no appropriate Christian reciprocal contextual collaboration (partnership) without biblical freedom. Under this presupposition, it is imperative to discuss the meaning of freedom in Christian partnership. Charles K. Barrett (1978, 345–346) defines Biblical freedom (eleutheria) as Christian liberation from sin; being made free is a synonym of salvation.[3] This freedom flows in harmony with the Father's will, thus to be freed by the Son (John 8:36) is to be freed by God himself

---

2. President George Bush addressed the theme of freedom at the USA Congress on 20 September 2001. In his speech: "We Are a Country Awakened to Danger and Called to Defend Freedom," he said: "Freedom and fear are at war. The advance of human freedom, the great achievement of time and the great hope of every time, now depends on us". (http://www.september11news.com/PresidentBushSpeech.htm). News by senior investigative producer Robert Windrem. He reported that terrorists killed 191 people and wounded more than 1,500 at two Madrid train stations. NBC News, msnbc (2005), http://www.msnbc.msn.com/id/7158191/. On Thursday 7 July, terrorists killed 52 people and injured more than 770 in central London (http://news.bbc.co.uk/1/shared/spl/hi/uk/05/london_blasts/what_happened/html/default.stm).

3. Eleutheria in Greek, from the Analytical Concordance to the Holy Bible (1977, 373).

who allows us to share the only true freedom with others. Therefore, in reciprocal contextual collaboration each partner has his own freedom, understood as a self determination within the limits of a harmonious autonomy, which brings a relationship of synergistic interdependence, avoiding any interference from the other without diluting unity and the sharing of reciprocal gifts. It is an interdependent freedom that provides openness to joyful missionary relationships and hope for appropriate models in the church's mission.

One way to address a harmonious autonomy is to develop a biblical mission theology of both personal sin and structural sin (political, social and economic), and the recovery of a new lifestyle under christological truth, which provides a positive dimension of reciprocal contextual collaboration.[4] Freedom from sin and reconciliation with God originated in the triune God and this is manifested in God's kingdom theology as a pivotal foundation for mission. This is developed in Christ's mission manifesto from the beginning, and it is expanded to the church.[5]

Given that biblical freedom based on Trinitarian truth is an incarnated truth manifested in Jesus Christ (John 14:6), truth is the instrument of freedom. Through freedom in Christ, the Holy Spirit gives a new lifestyle (Rom 8:2), and leads to a new covenant relationship with God.[6] Therefore,

---

4. James Danaher's article "Our Journey into the Truth, Beauty and Holiness of the Gospel" develops a Christian perspective on what is truth. See further *Evangelical Review of Theology* (2008, 57–58).

5. The great manifesto: "The Spirit of the Lord is on me, because he has anointed me to preach good news to the poor. He has sent me to proclaim freedom for the prisoners and recovery of sight for the blind, to release the oppressed, to proclaim the year of the Lord's favour" (NIV Luke 4:18–19). This passage comes from Isaiah 61:1. Wright (2006, 301) links this with jubilee theology and calls it the 'Nazareth manifesto'. Bevans and Schroeder (2005, 308) explain that The World Council of Churches in its mission conference at Melbourne, Australia, 1980, developed the centrality of the reign of God by stating that the origins of the church's mission is in Jesus, so the church's understanding of its own vocation to proclaim the reign of God is one that commits it to a gospel of liberation and justice. Then it is quoted from the Melbourne Conference: "mission that is conscious of the kingdom will be concerned of liberation, not oppression; justice, not exploitation; fullness, not deprivation; freedom, not slavery; health, not disease; life, not death" Quoted in Bevans and Schroeder (2005, 308). It seems that freedom is intended to overcome all social sinful dimensions of mission. Freedom also should be interpreted within a holistic dimension in relation to all things that oppress people, spiritual, political, economic, social and cultural.

6. Yet the whole creation will be set free of corruption (Rom 8:21).

the presence of the Holy Spirit provides an everlasting freedom: "where the Spirit of the Lord is, there is freedom" (2 Cor 3:17), freedom in God's love linked to truth and justice. This biblical freedom is foundational for any healthy reciprocal contextual collaboration, bringing partners in mission to a fellowship with God and then to a fellowship of unity with others. For this reason, denominationalism and competition, which are mainly expressed in disunity, must be addressed too.

The fact is that internal factors like the pre-packaged doctrinal confessions of denominations and the inflexibility of Western missiology that accompany the political, economic, and social systems, brought dependence and anti-reciprocal freedom to the 'new emergent church'. This finding leads us to discuss the following issue: Why did the Latin American evangelical church not seek more biblical foundations of partnership in mission? I see at least two reasons: the impact of theological denominationalism and the lack of biblical freedom to interpret the text of missionary theology, including both the missionary's hermeneutical horizon and the unfamiliar notion of holistic mission.[7] It seems that Western missiology was much less aware of teaching that sooner or later mission has to involve multidirectional mission traffic. Therefore, the domesticated and provincial understanding of freedom theology of the past, which stressed personal sin within the saving souls theology of Western mission, which Wright (2006, 287; Thomas 1995, 162–163) refers to as spiritual evangelism, needs to be reconsidered in order to empower at the same time social responsibility.[8]

---

7. From the 1960s, non-Western Christians have come to learn how to read the Bible through their own eyes, asking questions addressed by the daily life of their churches, considering the transforming power of Christ, especially on the lives of the poor (Escobar 2003, 148). Escobar explains how evangelicals rediscovered holistic mission in the 1960s when evangelistic mission took place in a painful process of social transformation. This rediscovery was initiated through congresses organized by Billy Graham in Berlin (1966) and Minneapolis (1968), which clarified that evangelism was impossible without confronting issues of social justice and structural sin; the Latin American Congress on Evangelism in Bogota (1969) concluded that "true evangelism could not take place without adequate reference to the social and political context within which it is done". In that Congress they approved that evangelism goes together with social action; God is equally interested in our service and in our evangelistic task (Escobar 2003, 146–147). Holistic mission can be interchanged with the concept of social transformation too. See also the holistic understanding in Wright's theology (2006, 39–61).

8. Norman Thomas in *Reading in World Mission* agrees with Wright in pointing out the negative view of individualistic evangelism by clarifying that true evangelism implies a

Subsequently to this, one reason why Gutierrez's Liberation Theology (Kirk 1980, 114–130; Bevans and Schreiter 2004, 312) based on Israel's liberation and the poor's liberation emerges in the 1970s to promote freedom from the oppressive political, social, and economic situation in Latin America is to the devastated economy and social struggles, a reality which seems to be ignored by the missionary endeavour of Protestant missions before the 1970s, given the absence of a theology of poverty, economic and contextual theology.[9] From an evangelical perspective, René Padilla's thesis proposes a change to a more holistic mission in the evangelical arena with an emphasis on spiritual and social change in parallel due to the fact that they are inseparable. A similar approach is pointed out in the mission theology of Escobar and Costas, which has been analyzed and reflected on seriously in the Latin American Theological Fraternity since its foundation

---

holistic evangelism. See further Thomas (1995).

9. From an evangelical and historic-theological perspective Kirk (1980, 114–130) explains some insights of Liberation Theology and reminds us of its Catholic background. Bevans and Schroeder (2005, 310–322) provide a summary of Liberation Theology in relation to 'Theologians and missiologists' and "The reign of God and the six constants of mission". See also Schreiter in *Constructing Local Theologies* (1985, 2–3). Gustavo Gutierrez (1973, 6) uses for this contextual theology the methodology of critical reflection on praxis, which means that critical reflection considers going beyond the visible boundaries of the church and the presence and action of Christians in the world with openness to the world; and praxis, which interprets historical events with the intention of revealing and proclaiming their profound meaning but in the light of the future to transform the present (15). For Gutierrez the term 'liberation' has three approaches to the process of liberation: it expresses the aspiration of oppressed people and social classes emphasizing the conflict aspect of the economic, social and political process between wealthy nations and oppressive classes; 'liberation' can be applied to an understanding of history and to use 'liberation' is more useful than 'development' because of the biblical source (37). See further A *Theology of Liberation* (1973, 155–159). Liberation theologians emphasize three liberations of the poor: the experience of the poor and the need for liberating them from any kind of oppression, liberation from their own participation in the drama of history, and liberation from the personal and structural bonds of sin (the structural reality of sin) (Bevans and Schroeder 2005, 312–313). A theology of poverty is presented by Gutierrez in clarifying the ambiguities of this term. The term designates a material poverty, as the lack of economic goods necessary for human life; poverty is seen as the condition of certain fatalism of marginalized people. For Gutierrez, a biblical meaning of poverty is: "a central theme both in the Old and New Testaments. It is treated both briefly and profoundly; it describes social situations and expresses spiritual experiences communicated only with difficulty; it defines personal attitudes, a whole people's attitudes before God, and the relationship of people with each other" (1973, 291). See further chapter 13: 'Poverty: Solidarity and Protest' (Gutierrez 1973). For an evangelical view see *Justice, Mercy and Humility* (Chester 2002).

in 1970.[10] Thus, I agree with the mission theology of Padilla, Escobar and Costas, in the sense that partnership in mission is not just a matter of philosophical ideology and historical analysis of dominance from the West; it implies a fundamental *christological freedom* originated in a Trinitarian theology, in which holistic mission has its origin.[11] This christological freedom has a missionary dimension in being free from personal and structural sin, experienced in rejection of injustice and unbalanced dominion of political and economic power by all kinds of spiritual, structural and evil forces. Christological freedom comes from God's grace; it is a gift of grace (Kirk 2006, 23).

Second presupposition

My second presupposition is that there is no appropriate Christian reciprocal contextual collaboration without consideration of contextual theologies. To revitalize mission theological dialogue between mission partners,

---

10. In *Mission Between the Times,* Padilla concludes that evangelism and social responsibility are inseparable. For Padilla, the gospel is the good news about God's kingdom and good works are signs of the kingdom and we must hold both together in the church's mission (1985, 197). The kingdom of God is a new reality of dynamic power working in history, which affects human life spiritually, morally, physically and psychologically, materially and socially; this has been inaugurated in the person and work of Christ (1985, 189). For a penetrating analysis of holistic mission see Wright (2006, 303–323). See also Tizon (2008, 92–97) for similarities between 'holistic mission' and 'mission as transformation' promoted by Oxford Center for Mission Studies (OCMS).

11. One of the issues is that the 'third emergent church' will no longer accept Christianity because of its association with the political, economic and cultural power of the West; this kind of association will generate another 'roadblock', as we mentioned in chapter 3. In consequence, for Padilla (1985, 136), the Christian mission today has to be carried out from a position of weakness, which means a new possibility to present the christological gospel rather than as the ideology of the West. In his book, *A Time for Mission,* chapter 10 'A New Way of Looking at the World' in analyzing the Lausanne Covenant 1974, Escobar discusses the issue of the need for a global partnership in mission between churches. He states that at Lausanne, evangelicals agreed that global Christian mission is not a privilege of the Western church, and they recognized that the dominant role of Western mission was fast disappearing, "and missionaries should flow ever more freely from and to all six continents in a spirit of humble service"; in my analysis Lausanne recognized the need of what I call a christological freedom but they lacked permeating their covenant in the evangelical movement. See further Escobar (2003, 165). Costas (1974, 11) develops in, *The Church and its Mission: A Shattering Critique from the Third World*, a critical analysis on issues of evangelism and social action in the North Atlantic hemisphere in relation to world evangelism. He clearly states that a commitment to a holistic mission is urgent, and challenges the North-Atlantic church to be more integral in her view of mission. See further Costas (1974).

Robert Schreiter (1985, 6–20), in *Constructing Local Theologies*, provides three approaches for analyzing local theologies, which implies what Hiebert (1999, 99–101) calls theology in context and Wright defines as multicultural hermeneutic (2006, 38): the translation model, the adaptation model and the contextual model, all with an intentional contextual theology.[12] In a positive interaction Bevans (2007, 31–33) provides six models of contextual theologies: the translation model, the anthropological model, the praxis model, the synthetic model, the transcendental model and the countercultural model; all of which include experiences of the present and the past (context), human experiences (personal and communal), culture (secular and religious), social location, social change and Scripture tradition. Schreiter (2004, 28–45) complements this by giving clues of intercultural hermeneutics (2004). According to these models, my assumption is that a new theology of partnership will be firmly reconstructed by giving parallel priority attention to the gospel, church and culture – issues working hand in hand with christological freedom theology, but avoiding the reductionist ethnographic approach of liberation theology, which seems to overemphasize the social context.[13] As we want to avoid a peripheral missiology,

---

12. The first, the translation model prefers to be used for immediate adaptation to local circumstances; it has a positivist understanding of culture. The second, the adaptation model tries to take the local culture more seriously. And the third, the contextual model is more concentrated in the cultural context. From this theological approach, my assumption is, as was mentioned previously in this chapter, that both domesticated and dislocated Western-North Atlantic mission theology was brought to the non-Western churches due to the fact that contextual local theology was not considered at all. Local theology refers to the complex process of dynamic interaction between gospel, church and culture, where the gospel is always incarnate both in the reality of those who bring the gospel and in the reality of those who receive the gospel. "Therefore, there is no local theology without the universal church, and without church there is no integral incarnation of the gospel." See further Schreiter (1985, 20–21). In my perspective, local theology is the incarnation of the gospel in the reality of every culture working in dynamic interaction with gospel, church and culture without diluting the reality of the universal church.

13. Ethnographic approach is concerned with what is called cultural identity, which is concerned with identity and dignity that have been denied; it addresses issues of oppression, social illness, and the need for social change. Two factors are important: social change expressed in urbanization and youth population; and social change expressed in oppression, poverty and hunger. Both affect cultural identity. See further Schreiter (1985, 14–15). However, the ethnographic approach has at least three dangers, one of cultural romanticism "unable to see the sin in its own personal experience"; second of popular religiosity (the adaptation of symbols indiscriminately), and third, the danger to eclipse traditional culture by the reality of social change (Bevans 2007, 25–26). Local theologies

christological freedom theology in partnership is foundational. In this sense, external and internal factors need to be dealt with properly.[14]

Contextual theology, which includes the issues of poverty, justice and freedom, is not a fashion theology that has to be forgotten; it also includes political, economic, cultural and social dimensions that emerge from the suffering continents of Africa, Asia and Latin America, and struggling with more appropriate models of reciprocal contextual collaboration.[15] Again, I argue that freedom theology relates to love, justice, compassion and the biblical spiritual attitude of proper distribution of wealth and economy.[16] Hence, a biblical, theological and missiological prophetic imagination is necessary to maintain this mature ability to distribute resources properly in creative collaboration. 1 John 3:16–17 gives a biblical paradigm for new creative partnership models, which relate to sharing our possessions with those in need. This is also seen in the models of the early church (Acts 6:1–7) where just distribution was demanded between Christian Jews and Gentiles, or in the church in Corinth (2 Cor 8), where poor Christian people decided why, where and how to invest their limited resources in

---

are developed through the missiological process of contextualization, described equally as enculturation, indigenization or incarnation of the gospel.

14. External factors include: (1) general dissatisfaction, (2) the oppressive nature of older approaches, (3) the demanding development of contextual theologies and (4) the understanding of culture provided by social science. Internal factors include: (1) the incarnational nature of Christianity, (2) the sacramental nature of reality (God is revealed in concrete reality), (3) the nature of divine revelation as being an internal factor determining the contextual nature of theology, (4) the catholicity of the church, and (5) the doctrine of the Trinity. See further Bevans (2007, 12–15). See also Tienou in "Forming Indigenous Theologies" (Phillips and Coote 1993).

15. Why is cross-mission collaboration occurring more in recent years? James E. Austin (2000, 7–8) in his book The Collaboration Challenge: How nonprofits and business succeed through strategic alliances, gives some clues of the collaboration imperative mentioning that the macro-level which includes society where different factors are creating an environment of great collaboration, and at the micro-level which refers to institutions, there is a positive partnership achievement. The macro-level forces include political forces, economic forces and social forces, and the micro-level forces include the size, capital, personnel, etc. See also the 99 statements of "Commonalities, Divergence and Cross-fertilization among the Third World Theologies", a document based on the Seventh International Conference of the Ecumenical Association of Third World Theologies, Oaxtepec, Mexico, 7–14 December 1986 (Abraham 1990, 195–213).

16. For example the Evangelical Alliance discussed 'Hope for the Economy' as one of the 66 biblical propositions given at 'Hope for Europe' Budapest Consultation 2002. For further discussion see Schirrmacher (2002, 70–71).

the mission enterprise. Thus, my finding is that the church in Corinth has a threefold pattern of theology, missiology and ecclesiology, which is grounded in a pivotal christological *missio freedom*. The first refers to the understanding of the *missio Dei*, the second relates to the dynamic practice of mission, and the third rests on the organizational mission activity of the church. Moreover, local theologies have to deal with the message and the messenger, such that the content of the gospel message is preserved, that is, the essential message for all partners in mission relates to the supracultural (Bevans 2007, 40) gospel message, which is presented through the messengers, whether these are professional missionaries or lay missionaries.

It is essential, therefore, that the following theological and missiological issues be met with critical analysis in order to reinforce a creative partnership within evangelicalism: religious resurgence and globalization, which relates to the need for more information about religious differences (Beattie in Tiplady 2003, 220–222); globalization and the implications of economics for mission (Valerio, 13–30); terror culture (George, 55–69); multiculturalism with the aim of making culture heterogeneous (Lundy, 71); healthcare and mission, which relate to clean water, sanitation, food, rural economy and urban migration, energy crisis, etc., (Fouch,123–132); the challenge of secular feminism and women in global mission (Dowsett, 151–153); theological education, cultural identity (Campbell 2008, 15–25); intercultural theology (Cartledge 2008, 92–100), global engagement trips; overcoming the old concept of the traditional missionary; theology of migration (Grooody and Campese 2008); global theology (Hiebert 1999, 112–114), etc.[17]

---

17. For example, Campbell argues that Pauline transformation in Christ does not mean the creation of a new group without ethnic identity; all Christians can retain their own ethnic identity. See further Campbell (2008). This issue becomes a key element when multicultural teams are formed in mission partnership. In the same vein Campbell extends his perspective in *Paul and the Creation of Christian Identity* (2006). Global engagement trips refer to traditional short-term mission teams (personal dialogue with Kim Swithinbank, vicar of St James Church, Muswell Hill, London).

Missiological issues of contemporary partnership

One of the issues for creative partnership is the geographical myth that mission has to do only with distant countries (Bosch 1995, 31). This interpretation threatens the reality that mission by its very nature belongs to the church and remains, as Bosch says, 'a contingent activity' (31).[18] This theological approach produces a peripheral missiology, which is seen in Western European mission agencies making efforts in sending people overseas to remote lands. One way for the new emergent church to avoid this peripheral missiology is to develop a *missio theology*, or what Paul Davies (2006) calls a missionary theology.[19] The second emphasizes the praxis, the church working in partnership with God, while the first, *missio theology*, emphasizes the origin of the action, God working with his church. It is more closely related to the *missio Dei*.[20] A second issue of diluted mission partnership is that it leads to an intentional recovery of a *unity mission theology*, which will permeate mission societies and local churches.[21] For example, the African theologian Kwame Bediako (Engelsviken et al. 2008, 215) stated in 1995 that "the church in Africa is set to play a crucial role in the future of mission", and the Norwegian Roar Fotland (215–229) interprets this statement in a such a way as to open up a way of new reciprocal collaboration, meaning that the South has something to teach the North. Similarly, I agree with John Moldovan (Bonk 2003, 147–162) in the sense that the church in Africa, called 'the third opportunity' (Bediako 1992, 225), has something to contribute in mission partnership as they belong to the new emergent church.[22]

---

18. By mission as 'contingent activity', Bosch suggests that the church goes only to those territories where the gospel is not yet firmly established, and it remains peripheral, just as missiology remained peripheral in Western institutions (Bosch 1995, 31).

19. Other mission theologians call this mission theology or theology of mission.

20. For Miguez Bonino, the mission of the church comes first; theological reflection is a second act; a clear liberation theology interpretation (Davies 2006, 48). As we noted in chapter 2, Trinitarian and God's kingdom theology are pivotal elements of a proper *missio theology*.

21. For more analysis see the article of Bruce K. Camp 'A Survey of the Local Church's Involvement in Global/Local Outreach' (Bonk 2003).

22. Bediako, in his book *Theology and Identity* (1992), states that the emergence of African theological literature, with its intellectual convictions and its own agenda, has contributed

Now, I want to address the issue of dependence, independence and interdependence partnership. The reality of the growing Latin American church in mission leads us to the question, Why does the evangelical movement struggle to find appropriate partnership models to develop new forms of interdependence and mature relationships? Some of the obstacles in mission partnership relate to the following issues: denominationalism, lack of missiological unity, imperial motives (impure motives), paternalistic mission, guilt for the past, anti-christological relationship, a narrow mission hermeneutic, individualism, confusion between unity and diversity, diluted Trinitarian theology, spirit of competence and duplication, economic disparity, misuse of autonomy, and global suspicion of Western missiology. These factors are not incidental and irreversible; they correspond to missiological thinking and world issues that cannot be separated from it. These issues have fostered mission in Latin America's twenty-four countries, making conditions that hinder the development of new forms of mature and interdependence relationship.[23]

---

to the shape of the emergent African theological consciousness. However, he adds that the history of Western Christian missions in Africa belongs to, and is a direct response to, a longer history of African contact with European people that is largely melancholy one. He concludes that: "The forces which operated in the earlier formative period *of the African church*, had become determining factors for the missionary programme of the important 'third opportunity'" (1992, 250 italics mine). For Bediako, the 'third opportunity' represents the mission activity of the 19th and early 20th centuries developed in Africa; the first was in apostolic times, which ended with the Muslim invasion of North Africa in the 7th century, and the second began with the Portuguese explorations in the 15th century but finished soon in the 16th century (252). This interpretation seems to be more historical than futuristic as it is after my interpretation of the 'Third Church' in the sense that this 'Third Church' has just emerged recently as a new Christian phenomenon and its influence has to be known, analyzed and studied properly sooner or later by Western scholars. Bediako passed away on 13 June 2008; he was general secretary of the African Theological Fraternity and founder of ACROFI-CHRISTALLER the Institute for theology, mission and culture in Ghana ('Revista Digital INTEGRALIDAD del CEMAA' <integralidad@cemaa.org, 4º Edición 2008). See the whole article of Roar G. Fotland 'The Southern Phase of Christianity: The Contribution of the Global South to the Church in the Global North' (Engelsviken et al. 2008). The Romanian, John Moldovan, takes an account of the African-American Community context. See the whole article 'Changing the Face of World Missions in the Twenty-first Century: A Fervent Appeal to the African-American Community for Effective Partnership in World Missions', Bonk (2003).

23. This number is based on the following countries: Argentina, Belize, Bolivia, Brazil, Chile, Colombia, Costa Rica, Cuba, Dominican Republic, Ecuador, El Salvador, French Guayana, Guatemala, Guayana, Honduras, Mexico, Nicaragua, Panama, Paraguay, Peru, Puerto Rico, Suriname, Uruguay, Venezuela. Global Ministries considers 23 countries

The presence of Latin America in mission collaboration means that there is a fragmented political, economic, social and cultural society, which is seen in many forms in the development of the evangelical mission due to the lack of stable democracy, economic affluence, increasing poverty and lack of employment, which makes Latin America a vulnerable continent that struggles to overcome unemployment, terrorism, violence, drugs-production, street-children, state-corruption, etc. From this political, sociological, economic and cultural context emerges the divine miracle of a growing evangelical church that lives within this dialectic and dynamic mission tension, which either consciously or unconsciously affects its partnership in the mission enterprise. By contrast, the North Atlantic partners have the influence of a more rationalistic approach, a worldview of economic affluence, unilateral forms of decision making, a sense of superior power and lacking in a theology of poverty, and a polarized missiology of a socialized gospel as opposed to the saving of souls. These are some of the factors that complicated the development of new forms of interdependence and mature relationships for appropriate reciprocal contextual collaboration.

In a new missionary tension, a third issue is the demand for new mission fertilization, which is necessary as we have had the contributions of mission renewal like that of the British Rolland Allen (1868–1947) with *Missionary Methods: St Paul's or Ours?* (First published 1912, reprint in 1962), which gives an analysis of missionary principles for strategic discipleship and organization of the church within a moral and social context to extend the gospel;[24] Max Warren (1904–1977) in *Social History and Christian Science* (1967), from a historical perspective in interaction with political, social, economic and religious factors in mission of traditional partnership, taking

---

(http://www.globalministries.org/lac/countries/), and Latin American Information Centre (Lanic) provides data of 21 countries (http://lanic.utexas.edu/subject/countries/).

24. Rolland Allen was a British missionary sent by the Society for the Propagation of the Gospel (SPG) to China in 1895; trained at St John's College Oxford. One of his major prophetic imaginations was to argue against the paternalistic missionary work lacking dependence on the Holy Spirit to guide the new church in its interdependence missionary activity (Anderson 1998, 12). In a complementary work he wrote *Educational Principles and Missionary Methods* (1919) with a radical critique to the Western mission church and paternalistic approach to indigenous churches, and *The Spontaneous Expansion of the Church and the Causes which Hinder It* (1927), voicing the secret of an expansion with characteristics of the apostolic churches.

into account the African and Asian context;[25] Lesslie Newbigin (1909–1998) in *Foolishness to the Greeks* (1986), which displays a prophetic imagination of missionary encounter between the gospel and culture by people of Europe and North America;[26] Stephen Neill (1900–1984) in *Partnership in Mission* (1947) taking the African context analysis;[27] the American Eugene Nida (1914–2011) in *Religion Across Cultures* (1968), taking account of the psychological and dynamic factors in communication;[28] Bishop Azariah, from an Indian perspective calling for real friendship in mission;[29] Helmut Richard Niebuhr (1894–1962) in *The Social Sources of Denominationalism* (1928), from a sociological perspective, calling for an understanding of the social problem of denominationalism and offering a more significant approach to the question of unity.[30] All of these contributions have made an impact within their mission context, which still has valuable perspectives for mission today.

It seems that these prophetic imaginative thinkers raised their voices against inappropriate Western partnership as signs of a lack of

---

25. Max Warren, trained at Cambridge in history, and general secretary of the Church Mission Society, with a prophetic imagination in history, "stressed God's involvement in history and God's action on people outside of the covenant", published a CMS newsletter with 14,000 worldwide circulation (Anderson 1998, 719).

26. Lesslie Edward James Newbigin was a British missionary bishop in India. Ordained by the Church of Scotland to work as a missionary with the Church of South India; became general secretary of the International Missionary Council in 1959 and guided integration with the World Council of Churches in 1961, a theologian with passion for unity of the church and engagement of Christian faith in society (Anderson 1998, 491).

27. British bishop Stephen Neill was a scholar, theologian and missionary to India, published more than 50 books, one of them *History of Christianity in India*. He studied at Trinity College, Cambridge (Anderson 1994, 445–451).

28. The American, Eugene Nida, was a PhD linguistics scholar on linguistics and anthropology, a Baptist minister of the Northern Baptist Convention and worked with the American Bible Society in 85 countries and 200 languages, studying linguistic, cultural and translation issues (Anderson 1998, 494–495).

29. Samuel Vedanayagam Azariah (1874–1945), the first Indian bishop of the Anglican Church, was a YMCA secretary, and established the Indian Missionary Society (IMS) in 1903. He made his call prophetic imagination for better relationships between missionaries and national Christians at the Edinburgh 1910 Conference; he played a key partnership role in the formation of the Church of the South India (Anderson 1998, 35).

30. Helmut Richard Niebuhr was an American Protestant theologian; a PhD scholar educated at Yale University, he had a prophetic imagination voice of Christian ethics, social analysis of religious history and American denominationalism (http://www.hds.harvard.edu/library/bms/bms00630.html).

multi-interdependence solutions to discover a healthy missionary consciousness in the development of Western mission in the areas of leadership, finances, structures, culture, relationships, etc. By contrast, the Latin American prophetic *missio imagination* through the Latin American Theological Fraternity (1969) with Padilla, Escobar, Costas, etc., develops a strong motivation in practising interdependent reciprocal contextual collaboration with a holistic missiology.[31] In this sense, Padilla (1985, 137) states that paternalism can be corrected not by independence but by interdependence, which comes with both deeper understanding of the nature of the unity in Christ and the living situation of other members of Christ's church. This implies that reciprocal contextual collaboration demands a new force of mission theologians addressing mission issues with prophetic *missio imagination* for a new 'multipolar world' (Schreiter 2004, 5).[32]

The socio economic issue of how and why the theory of 'dependence' affects partnership in mission is a fourth concern that brings the following insights (Kirk 1980, 115): First, it was recognized in the non-developed world and the capitalist world due to the excessive nature of economic exploitation-relations. And second, income is influenced by internal factors: the repatriation of dividends on capital investments; high interest in loans from the IMF, the World Bank, government and business consortiums and tariff protection against imports; and the fluctuation in prices of raw materials. These factors lead to the origin of the economic theory of dependence. Regarding the dependence issue, Escobar (2003, 148–149) recognizes that economic development, poverty and oppression in the Third World require a change of mind and lifestyle, a will to change the world, and a hope to persist in spite of opposition or failure. He suggests that projects of economic development have a better chance of success due to the fact that the spiritual infrastructure of Christian transformation has more safeguards against paternalism by applying biblical principles of reciprocity and solidarity.[33]

---

31. The initial view of holistic mission at the Lausanne Congress (1974) was a controversial development.

32. Schreiter (2004) contrasts a bipolar world (democratic and capitalist versus socialist and communist systems) with a multipolar world (the rich and the poor, neo-liberal capitalism and the collapse of the distribution of power between two poles).

33. Escobar (2003, 148) adds that, "development projects that connect with peoples and movements among whom spiritual revival is taking place have more chance of long-term

Spiritual transformation becomes conversion to Christ with the benefit to a whole community; it is the other side of economic development activities, which are an expression of faith in action. Transformation and development are the recognition of a deep and inseparable connection between the practical and spiritual aspects of Christian life. My finding, following the dependence economy theory, is that the Western mission enterprise did not succeed in avoiding economic dependence in the development of national churches they established, for either consciously or unconsciously they did not want to lose control of economic power by making decisions which avoided the risk of forming a multicultural leadership. These issues remain to be solved, but promoting holistic co-participation creates hope for a healthy reciprocal contextual collaboration.

A fifth issue relates to political change in the world. Colonial independence started after the Second World War when missionaries started to leave the field; a sense of nationalism came to light and national churches started their period of expansion. In 1971 the African, John Gatu, called for a moratorium of missionaries and mission activity in Africa, producing a sense of independence from Western mission activity, and started to ask what had been done wrong.[34] Some analysis began, but primarily with pragmatic as opposed to biblical questions (Busch and Lutz 1990, 36–37). Allen (1962, 123, 125) pointed to the "doctrine of mutual responsibility" and "corporate responsibility" in mission partnership as crucial, arguing that "dependence does not train for independence, as slavery does not educate men for freedom". His criticism is that Western mission was "everywhere dependent" (141).

In my observation of Yates's doctoral thesis on Venn's mission policies, Yates (1978, 16–19) states that Venn pursued a policy of accommodation during the period 1841–1872; this was implemented in the context of the British promotion of trading interests with their colonies; Sierra Leona and Niger were the setting for Venn's experiment of an indigenous missiology

---

success. Also, when foreign catalysts and resources have departed, these projects have more chance of becoming indigenous projects that will last".

34. As Sanneh mentions, this was a call for the All African Council Churches in the 1970s, which led to a defensive attitude of European and North American churches with a 'noninterference policy of mission' (2003, 17).

of the three-self formulas in 1861.³⁵ Venn's main strategy was the planting of indigenous churches that were to be self-supporting, self-governing and self-extending, with the aim of ending the foreign intervention of European and missionary presence in order to bring independent indigenous churches into being. This policy gave rise to the phrase 'euthanasia of mission', which meant that mission should withdraw to allow national churches' self-development. As Yates (16) suggests, Venn was confronted with a context of widely differing settings for missionary activity of colonial rather than imperial influence, and the main difficulty in the implementation of his mission strategy for Venn, Yates (136) explains, arose from cultural and sociological factors.

Promotion of the 'three self-mission theory, self-support, self-government, and self-propagation', began with Henry Venn, General Secretary of CMS, and Rufus Anderson for the American Board, the two largest Protestant mission societies in the mid-nineteenth century (Bosch 1991, 331). They elaborated 'the three self-formulas' to help the advance of mission through autonomy for 'young' churches from foreign mission societies. Some remarkable characteristics of indigenization in Venn's policy include: the 'three self-formulas' as the aim of mission, the planting of indigenous churches, and allowing national churches to stand on and develop their own national character with an indigenous leadership (Yates 1978, 17; Bosch 1991, 302, 331).³⁶ Kirk (1999, 89) adds that indigenization was intended to create as rapidly as possible local churches without dependency on foreign assistance; thus, church independence was the emphasis at that time.

---

35. See further Timothy Yates (1978) *Venn and Victorian Bishops Abroad: The Missionary Policies of Henry Venn and their Repercussions upon the Anglican Episcopate of the Colonial Period 1841–1872*. Bishops of the Episcopal Church of Scotland and American bishops of the Protestant Episcopal Church, were excluded from his strategy vision (Yates 1978, 18).

36. By implementing his mission policy, Venn could be seen to be expanding the ecclesiastical framework of the Anglican Communion; his indigenizing policy includes the following characteristics (Yates 1978, 17, 18, 134): (1) the appointment of 'missionary bishops' to help the implementation of self-governing within indigenous churches, (2) the accommodation of the CMS as voluntary society to the wider structure of the church to support the self-expanding policy, and 3.self support implementation within the new churches.

In thinking of the monumental debate on contextualization at an earlier time, people spoke about 'accommodation' of the gospel to culture, but then within Protestant circles developed the use of 'indigenization' and, as Kirk (1999, 89) states, "the most famous expression of indigenization has been the 'three-selfs'– self-support, self-government and self-propagation – invented by Henry Venn and Rufus Anderson and developed by Roland Allen". In connection with 'accommodation' and 'indigenization', 'enculturation' was coined to express the transformation of a culture by the gospel, and contextualization appeared to emphasize "the reciprocal influence of culture and socio-economic life" (Kirk 1999, 91). Roland Allen (2006, 26) explains that Bishop Tucker of Uganda popularized Venn's 'three-self formulas' of self-extending, self-supporting and self-governing churches as summing up the object of its mission, therefore, for the establishment of indigenous churches. This was the main missiological emphasis. Allen (26–27) argues that 'the three-self formulas' was misunderstood in the sense that it was used as if they were distinct and separate things; he explains that self-supporting was considered as a mere matter of finance, but for him any true self-support is more than financial. Allen claims that the ministry is the key for self-government and authority, and self-extension is bound up with self-support and self-government, thus, "the three are intimately united", says Allen (27).

From this understanding, Luis Busch (1990, 37–40) identifies four issues of partnership that in my observation appear in process of radical adjustment in a changing multipolar world: (1) Western missions developed ethnocentric mission with the belief that 'the West is best', (2) Western mission developed a donor mentality by providing money and personnel for the national churches, (3) the 'two-thirds world' became a prisoner of history due to the fact that control and resources of power of the West had weakened *the emergent churches* (italics mine), (4) the 'three-self' mission theory hindered the development of partnership as there was a polarization between indigenization and interdependence missiology.

The three-self mission theory hindered the development of partnership due, first, to a radical process to create independent national churches, producing a misunderstanding of the theory's interpretation; second, mission organization instituted radical reductions on funding for national churches, misunderstanding the biblical principle to help those in need and one another; and third, widely differing cultural and sociological factors affected the process of indigenization. The consequence is a polarization between indigenization and interdependence missiology.[37] But the concept of the three-self formula has in itself a revolutionary theoretical missiology which can be contextualized.

In contrast to Bush's view, *Supporting Indigenous Ministries* (Rickett and Welliver 1997) presents a positive advance in mission relationships between Western and indigenous missions since 1996.[38] Therefore, these two views offer clarification to identify that the mission activity has its own tensions between theory and practice.

For the interdependence issue, following Glenn Fritz's analysis in 'Towards Interdependence Ministry Partnership' (2002, 212–218), I provide a three-fold pattern to interpret the process of partnership relationship for reciprocal contextual collaboration. While dependent partnership (infancy model) includes passivity and poor creativity, as well as working under the control of others, independent partnership (adolescent model) has people who appeal to the self-sustaining, self-governing and self-propagating missionary paradigm of the past, practising a weak team working and accountability. By contrast, interdependent partnership (adulthood model) involves joint responsibility and mutual accountability with a good mission structure. It is collegially driven, decision making is given direction through open discussion, and its leadership style involves cooperative effort with the outcome of a satisfying partnership. It must focus on the internal building blocks of ministry before it begins to focus on the external needs (215).[39] Three key elements are pivotal for interdependent

---

37. In my view, it is also right to say that the three-self-mission theory has the purpose to help transitional change in the new configuration of mission's leadership to national leadership; therefore, we acknowledge that this process within the mission activity has its own tensions between theory and practice.

38. Data provided show that 113 missions in USA are identified as being primarily concerned with supporting independent missionary movements in the non-Western world. See further Rickett and Welliver (1997, xi).

39. Fritz develops an interdependent ministry partnership as Canadian director for International Needs Network with a pastoring role. He defines interdependent partnership as "the collaboration of two or more partners who, in full recognition of one another's unique gifts and capabilities, have deliberately yet voluntarily agreed to submit their

reciprocal contextual collaboration: autonomy-capable and the ability to make one's decisions; compatibility, in which there are common beliefs and values; and complementary participation that implies that each must bring something of value to share (quoted from Rickett 1998, 439). I agree with Fritz that these characteristics help in solving issues of reciprocal communication, team working, cooperation, and mutual accountability. As such, interdependent partnership is based on five key elements:. the interdependent nature of the body of Christ, the universal gift of the Holy Spirit, that leadership is something to give away as soon as possible, the sharing of financial resources in keeping with the New Testament practice of generosity, and that all have a responsibility to give and promote the dignity of the person. Interdependence partnership involves a tremendous complexity, in which a consideration of dynamic analysis will be necessary from time to time. In this way, Moldovan (Bonk 2003, 148) attempts to identify three development stages: consultative partnership, consensus partnership, and constitutional partnership. Moreover, interdependent partnership has to deal with historical, socio-political, theological, structural and cultural issues (Costas 1974, 153–174).

The question remains: why and how is the interdependence tension to be resolved? Bishop David Evans (Cueva 2004, 59) argues that Christianity has more than 28,000 denominations with more than 1,590 missionary plans for world evangelization. In this global Christian complexity, I see two perspectives: the negative, with the increase of multiple denominations and independent churches, with the risk of imposing their own agendas and strategic plans and building up little kingdoms; the positive, in which there can be opportunities for practising a Trinitarian unity in diversity, which includes the *missio Dei*, the *missio ecclesiae* and the *missio context*. There will be a need for more mature relationships, both vertical and horizontal, nurtured for both biblical and holistic mission.

---

ministry goals and aspirations to one another's scrutiny and activity so that their common aims might be most fully achieved" (2002, 214).

Third presupposition

My third presupposition is that there is no appropriate Christian reciprocal contextual collaboration without consciousness of the influence of external factors in mission. In a new changing order of a multipolar world, partnership in mission has to be aware of the future global environment in which reciprocal contextual collaboration will take place in the following decades. I refer to the new 'Pacific era' that implies the new economic gravity centre of the Asian Pacific (including India), which is the recent success of economic development and technological modernization. To confirm this, during 1994, the ten largest economies in Asia accounted for 40 percent of the world's total economy, becoming since the 1990s the largest source of investment capital (Castells 1998, 206).[40] The truth of the matter that we have to acknowledge in our theological and missiological thinking is that the old concepts as North, South, and Third are going to disappear due the fact that the new giants, China and India, the 'tiger zone', and 'the Pacific era' will dominate the new global mission with their increasing population, geo-politic situation, and socio-economic impact.

This implies that the old centres produced by the 'American dream' and the European empire will become forgotten centres as happened with Rome, Spain, Portugal and Russia; old empires will decline. In consequence, I agree with Manuel Castells (1998, 206–207) who points out:

> The Asian Pacific has become the main centre of capital accumulation in the planet, the largest manufacturing producer, the most competitive trading region, one of the two leading centres of information technology innovation and production, and the fastest growing market. The rise of the Pacific has undoubtedly changed the geo-economics and geopolitics *new atmosphere for reciprocal contextual collaboration in mission in this new millennium* (italics mine).

---

40. These are the following countries: China, Indonesia, Japan, Korea, Malaysia, Philippines, Singapore, Thailand, Taiwan, and Hong Kong (Castells 1998, 211).

Therefore, in the new global mission of reciprocal contextual collaboration, there will be economic activity and geopolitical conflicts especially with the Russian Pacific as one of the suppliers for energy and natural resources to the Asian Pacific. However, as Castells (309) says, "the Pacific rise is the multicultural foundation of the new global economy". Contrary to the 'Pacific force' there will be the presence of the so-called G8 and the G20 trying to maintain economic and geopolitical control, but with less social global acceptance.[41]

Ecclesiological issues in partnership

The task of discovering appropriate partnership models for the twenty-first century is aimed at strengthening the church's missionary responsibility in

---

41. G8 is formed by these countries: France, Germany, Italy, Japan, United States of America, Canada, the United Kingdom (they are the G7) and Russia (with membership since 1998 as part of the G8). The G7 has its origin in 1975, with the aim to prevent any bureaucratization of the institution. The objectives were also limited to fostering global financial stability by providing a forum for building cooperation in macro-economic policy (http://www.utoronto.ca/cis/skeltonlecture_ostry2002.doc). G8 discussed at Japan 2008 issues such as improvement of energy efficiency, greater use of clean energy, adaptation, technology, finance, market-based mechanisms and tariff reduction. On renewables, sustainable biofuel production; on nuclear, more interest in nuclear power programmes as a means of addressing climate change and energy security concerns; on adaptation, continuing and enhancing cooperation with developing countries in their efforts to adapt to climate change; on technology, establishing international initiatives by developing roadmaps for innovative technologies and investing in the next years over US $10 billion annually; on finance the establishment of the Climate Investment Funds including the Clean Technology Fund (CTF) and the Strategic Climate Fund (SCF) with US $6 billion budget; on market mechanisms, emissions-trading within and between countries, tax incentives, performance-based regulation, fees or taxes and consumer labeling, negotiations to eliminate tariffs and non-tariff barriers to environmental goods and services were agreed; on finances, progress on multilateral development banks with the ambition to mobilize public and private investments of over US$ 100 billion. See further 'G8 Summits, Hokkaido, Japan, Official Documents' (9 July 2008).

The G20 forum of finance ministers and central bank governors created in 1999 has the aim to "promote discussion and study and review policy issues among industrialized countries and emerging markets with a view to promoting international financial stability." Members consisted, in addition to the G7, of Argentina, Australia, Brazil, China, India, Mexico, Russia, Saudi Arabia, South Africa, South Korea, and Turkey. The G20 was created as a deliberative rather than decisional body, but one designed to encourage "the formation of 'consensus' on international issues". See further Kirton (http://www.g8.utoronto.ca/g20/g20whatisit.html).

a multipolar world, and at revitalizing and empowering its missionary dimension and its missionary intention. In Costas' theology this aim has six pivotal approaches: mission as proclamation, mission as disciple-making, mission as mobilization, mission as integral growth, mission as liberation and mission as celebration (1979).[42] From this assumption, here I identify some weaknesses and strengths of the Latin American church that will help us to understand why it is difficult to work in long term projects of mission partnership. Some weaknesses are: (1) a triumphalistic approach to mission, (2) a lack of cross-culturally trained missionaries, (3) a lack of appropriate economic participation of local churches, (4) weak mission structures to support the fast growing sending of missionaries, and (5) a need for appropriate interdependence mission theology. The fact is that mature leadership and weak finances are key issues, due to the fact that mission is growing faster than the provision of the kind of resources we have mentioned. On the other side some strengths are: (1) a dynamic process of fast new emergent church growth, (2) the sending of thousands of missionaries from the new emergent church to the global hemisphere, (3) the increase of more mission theologians, (4) the recognition and acceptance of the imperative mission mandate as holistic, and (5) the increasing participation of indigenous mission agencies and local churches in the mission activity such as was never seen before. The Lausanne Consultation 2004 (Claydon 2005, 159–160, Vol. II) provides a wider synthesis, identifying hindrances and effectiveness.

For the Western church, which lives in a no longer bipolar world, we observe a decline in its membership and a need of urgent spiritual strength (Walls 1996, 237). This affects its participation in mission partnership as follows: finances are diluting more and more; there are difficulties in finding new mission candidates; there is reluctance to engage in long term mission projects; and denominationalism and disunity hinder cooperation. On the positive side, there is a more participative presence of mission-minded leaders like Kenneth Hemphill, who seeks to involve local churches in the sending of missionaries with the Southern Baptist Convention, and from the British church models, Ichthus, Mission Frontiers, and Pioneers

---

42. See further *The Integrity of Mission* (1979).

by planting churches (Kay 2008, 36), or the mission network 'Faith in the Local Church' in promoting missionary theology.[43] In our analysis we discover that the local church has diluted its missionary dimension and struggled to permeate a non-church Christian society. For this reason, as the Lausanne Covenant, clause 6 says (Stott 1996, 28; Padilla 1976, 103):

> *It is essential for each local church that evangelization implies that* "the church is at the very centre of God's cosmic purpose", the church is the community of God's people rather

---

43. Hemphill's missional church summary focuses on four tasks: (1) Praying. A mission passion is nurtured when a strategic plan for praying is developed among the members of the church. (2) Going. The first impulse of the first disciples was to go, and the first impulse of the kingdom-centred church will be to go. This implies mobilizing church members in mission teams participating in all four quadrants of the Acts 1:8 challenge. (3) Sending. Every church would have the privilege of sending 'one of their own' to the ends of the earth. This begins with appropriate mission education for every age group. Pastors should regularly invite people to respond to the call to the 'ends of the earth'. And (4) Giving. This implies sending missionaries with commitment. The church must demonstrate good stewardship by adopting a church lifestyle that will enable it to allocate a minimum of 20 percent of its budget for the Acts 1:8 task. (http://www.bpnews.net/BPFirstPerson.asp?ID=25657).

For Hemphill, the International Mission Board has identified four stages through which churches progress in their mission involvement: (1) The supporting church engages in mission by supplying the needs of missionaries through the denomination and mission agencies. (2) The exploring church has begun to ask the Spirit to reveal to it where it might actually join him in mission activity. (3) The engaging church has developed partnerships that allow it to participate with mission partners on the field. (4) The multiplying church is already involved in mission and is actively seeking opportunities to assist other churches in becoming involved. His warning is that the kingdom-centred church does not simply focus on church growth; it desires to be engaged in kingdom expansion to the ends of the earth, which requires that it partner with other like-minded kingdom entities. ((http://www.bpnews.net/BPFirstPerson.asp?ID=25657). 'Faith in the Local Church' is an ecclesiological Anglican model that runs once a year in London with the following core values: (1) a biblical, evangelical view of the gospel; (2) a commitment to every member ministry; (3) a recognition that all kind of new, emerging and mission-shaped churches and Christian organizations have their part to play, but a belief that local church continues to be a primary means to proclaim the gospel and incorporate believers into the church of Christ; (4) a desire to reach the varied people groups, reflecting the heterogeneity of the local community; (5) a cooperation among us to strengthen other local churches in their ministry; and (6) a hope that evangelical churches traditionally strong in city centres, seaside towns and suburban population may also gain strength and viability in many other places. Partners of this network are the following churches: Grace Church (Muswell Hill), St James (Clerkenwell), St James (Muswell Hill), St John's (Downshire Hill Hampstead), St Luke's (West Hampstead), St Paul's (Headley Wood) and St Thomas' (Oakwood). (Pamphlet for the Faith in the Local Church's conference entitled 'For Joy' 5–7 June 2008).

than an institution and must not be identified with any particular culture, social or political system or human ideology (italics mine).

It is, therefore, a call to rediscover a missionary consciousness for the local church in its understanding of its missionary nature. In this sense the Lausanne Consultation 2004 provides some tools for what it means to be a missional congregation (Claydon 2005, 568–586, Vol. I). But the issue is that this theoretical frame seems not to have been successful in fertilizing mission in the local churches.

On the other side, massive Christian denominations in a globalized world, partners of traditional, independent churches and the powerful influence of the Pentecostal and charismatic movement have to work hand-in-hand under the mission theology of God's kingdom, otherwise they are in danger of diluting mission partnership. As Niebuhr (1929, 135) explains, this was an issue for American denominationalism.[44] Therefore, with the same determination, a danger of provincial partnership, which implies doing mission with no consideration for the rest of the church, must be avoided for the followings reasons (Stott 1996, 102–103): each church is part of the universal church, each church worships the living God of cultural diversity, and each church should enter into a partnership of giving and receiving (Phil 4:15). One consequence of provincial partnership is the loss of a comprehensive mission theology that John Stott (1996, 30) notes, as was recognized at Lausanne 1974, that theologically, the "church's visible unity in truth is God's purpose" and 'cooperation in evangelism' (a missiological unity), which implies diversity and flexibility. It is inconceivable, therefore, that sinful individualism and duplication persist within models of evangelical partnership. Stott (31) clearly complains

---

44. Historically, Niebuhr (1929, 135) explains that the primary social sources of American denominationalism are seen in the European history of immigrant churches, "with more than two hundred varieties and with the issues of separated individuality, sectionalism, the heterogeneity of an immigrant population and the presence of two distinct races are primary important". Thus, this reality shows that it is necessary to overcome a provincial concept of a narrow ecclesiology if we want to find more appropriate mission partnership models for twenty-first-century mission.

that evangelicalism appears to build a little empire rather than cooperate for common action for the common good.

In consequence, the church has different models to work within its ecclesiology but the pivotal point is to recognize that the evangelistic mandate has not been fulfilled and the church must seek revitalized and more appropriate mission partnership models not just for sending more missionaries but to live as the body of Christ, united not only by pragmatic mission partnership models, but by the *missio* Spirit of the Lord to whom belongs the *missio* kingdom. The fact is that mission societies, being a non-ecclesial movement, require a reorientation in the theology of unity to overcome the dichotomy between local churches and mission agencies. At the same time, contextual theologies for mission policy remind us that societies are no longer the 'sacred mission cow',[45] but a mission structure permitted by God's permissive will. Thus, sodalities and modalities must function interactively, overcoming a dichotomous work paradigm, meaning individualism from each other (Costas 1974, 169), due to the biblical fact that competitive spirit is inconceivable in reciprocal contextual collaboration's mission, as it is essential to strengthen an 'evangelical catholicity'.[46]

Sociological and cultural issues of partnership

To begin with, Kirk (1998, 44) points out that religious identity was dependent on the territory into which one was born in Europe.[47] Such a mission

---

45. The German theologian, Walter Kunneth (Henry and Mooneyham 1967, 176), at the World Congress on Evangelism, Berlin, 1966, pointed out clearly in 'Hindrance to Evangelism in the Church' that the structure of the church in itself is never 'sacred' but determined only on the basis of suitability for the proclamation of the gospel.

46. Evangelical catholicity implies the unity of the church by the spirit of reconciliation, universal gospel, presence in society and missionary consciousness. The Lutheran Norwegian, Ola Tjorhom (2004, 22–27), gives the historical and theological roots of this term, linked to the Reformation period. See also Schreiter (2004, 123).

47. This implies that the Protestant Reformation made an impact on social, political, economic and cultural life through three key elements: the emphasis on an unmediated relationship between individuals and God, the authority of the church through making the Bible accessible to everyone, and the Reformation doctrine of the priesthood of all believers where monastic vocation was no longer considered superior. As a result, the Counter-Reformation brought to the arena "intolerant and brutal repression with

model, which cannot be ignored, was translated to Latin America, creating mission tensions in the expansion of Protestantism within a Catholic context, since according to the Argentinian Saracco (Taylor 2000, 357) almost 85 percent of the population is Roman Catholic. Consequently, that evangelical mission partnership has to consider political, economic, social and cultural issues as part of its mission activity. Seven general issues can be identified in evangelical missionary circles with respect to mission partnership. These are as follows:

1. A perceived cultural and racial superiority of the Western and the North Atlantic mission enterprise affects the relationship between mission partners.[48] As the Gambian theologian, Lamin Sanneh, explains in *Whose Religion is Christianity?*, the major concern in the past was the "Christian discovery of indigenous societies rather than indigenous discovery of Christianity". This view translated into a lack of contextual theologies (2003, 4, 10). This is one reason why missiology speaks today of a 'Christian resurgence', the new mission gravity centre or what I call the 'new emergent church'.[49]

2. Failure to translate a more contextualized gospel was noticed earlier by Nida and Niebuhr in the context of the American church. The second challenged the ethical failure of the divided church and the nationalism of the church; the first author analyses the

---

persecution" (Kirk 1998, 46). For the Protestant Reformation, accountability to God through the offer of free grace in Jesus Christ (the doctrine of justification) was primarily emphasized. See further Kirk (1998, 46–47).

48. See the work of Manickam (Corrie 2007, 326–328).

49. "The Christian discovery of indigenous societies describes the process of missionaries from the West coming to Africa or Asia, converting people, often with political incentives and material inducements. The indigenous discovery of Christianity, by contrast, describes local peoples encountering religion through mother tongue discernment and in the light of people's own need and experiences". For Sanneh, the first stresses external transmission with the influence of cultural values and the second internal appropriation with the open way of local consequences for both indigenous agency and leadership (Sanneh 2003, 55). Lamin Sanneh (2003, 3) points out that worldwide Christian resurgence seems to proceed without Western organizational structures, including academic recognition, in the middle of political instability and the collapse of public institutions. I agree with Sanneh in the sense that this is a mission – time to speak of post-Western Christianity in parallel with the contributions of the new forces in mission with emergent partnership models.

communication of the Christian faith (1968, 81–92).[50] This reality hinders mission partnership in the sense that culture is underestimated by missionaries and mission structures due to the fact that they still unconsciously associate the gospel with the political, economic and cultural power of the West. As Padilla (1985, 136) argues, "Jesus was presented as the ideology of the West", and Krallmann (1992, 174) warns of practising cultural dissonance in cross-cultural evangelism.[51]

3. The recent infiltration of Western lands. *Supporting Indigenous Ministries* (Rickett and Welliver 1997) suggests that emergent partnership has recently infiltrated Western lands, making an impact on their mission mentality. In fact, the 'new emergent church' grows with transatlantic influence by crossing political, cultural, economic, religious and social borders in North America and Europe. The crucial question that emerges is: Are the global evangelical rich churches welcoming the 'new emergent mission force'?

4. A new *perestroika* of mission collaboration. Thousands of Latin American people have arrived in Europe especially since the fall of the Berlin Wall and the Soviet Union in 1991, following Gorbachev's perestroika (restructuring) reform which, as sociologist Manuel Castells (1998, 5–8) points out, tried to engage radically with the changing world. However, a new anti-immigration law has been issued by the European Union recently and this will affect the new emergent mission force.[52] As this happened with

---

50. Nida presents the differences of worldview between Christian faith and non-Christian faith. He says: "to understand certain essential features of religion communication, it is important to contrast several basic elements of Christian and non-Christian communication" (1968, 81).

51. The German, Gunter Krallmann (1992, 174), in *Mentoring for Mission* defines cultural dissonance as the danger of missing the dynamic equivalence (appropriated meaning) when the Bible is translated into another language.

52. The process of Gorbachev's perestroika began in 1983 with the pressure of a nearly disintegrated state. It was in 1986 at the 27th Congress of the Communist Party (CPSU) he addressed his new policies for the Soviet Union that remain in history as Gorbachev's perestroika (Castell 1998, 47–47). Disintegration of the Soviet Union began in the spring of 1989 with the independence of Estonia, Lithuania and the Baltic Republics; in 1991 Boris Yeltsin became the first Russian president of state to be democratically elected

Russian *perestroika,* so it could happen with the changes of the whole spectrum of partnership in mission if creative tension is not refined appropriately by 'giving voice to the voiceless'.⁵³ My assumption is that the *perestroika mission* collaboration of the twenty-first century will not have an appropriate improvement if political, economic, cultural and social mission collaboration issues are not addressed radically under a Trinitarian mission theology and *christological missio freedom*.⁵⁴

5. Becoming a mission laboratory. To avoid forgetting the context applied to the Latin American scenario, Michael Reid (2007, 4) in *The Forgotten Continent* provides tools to understand the political, economic, sociological and cultural reality in which the Latin American church is situated.⁵⁵ This analysis helps us to un-

---

and on December 1991, Yeltsin convinced the Ukrainian and Byelorussian Communist leaders to dissolve the Soviet State and to create a Commonwealth of Independent States as a mechanism to distribute the legacy of the Soviet Union among the new sovereign republics (Castells, 60–62). The Spanish sociologist Manuel Castells provides in *End of Millennium, The Information Age: Economy, society and culture,* three issues which hindered the process of changing the critical situation of the Soviet Union during the 1980s: the structural inability of statism, the Soviet variant of industrialism and the transition towards the information society. See further Castells (1998). The Bolivian president Evo Morales argued against the implicitness of the anti-immigrant law on 16 June before the European Union made its decision. See the whole document 'Carta del Presidente Boliviano Evo Morales', 'MINKA NEWS' minkanews@btconnect.com This anti-immigration law was approved on 18 June 2008 ('MINKA NEWS' ntermediatv@btconnect.com).

53. Donal Dorr, from the context of the Irish Missionary Union, suggests multicultural forums rather than rational discussion (2000, 164).

54. In finding the main issues of a weak partnership, this will lead to a perestroika change but avoiding collapsing experience as the Soviet Union failed. Thus, I will attempt to bring some issues that help to bring a wider discussion for possibilities of restructuring traditional, networking and emergent partnership models through the transition of the new informational paradigm of reciprocal contextual collaboration.

55. Reid, who is based in Lime, Peru, traveled widely in Latin America from 1982 to 1990 working for the *Guardian,* the BBC, and as the editor of the American section of *The Economist.* He points out that the 'old model' of protectionist state-led development was still working in the 1980s. For Reid, the context is seen as follows: dictatorship departing and the emergence of *Mercosur* (Chile); hyperinflation; the terrorist insurgence of *Sendero Luminoso* (Peru); economy reform (Bolivia); drug traffickers, guerrillas and paramilitaries (Colombia); modernizing authoritarian political system (Mexico); low oil prices (Venezuela); the orphanity (Cuba); and the forming of the *Southern Cone* (Brasil). On the one hand, Reid concentrated on large countries avoiding work on the issue of environment and natural resources and on business and finances – Central American wars

derstand the implications of mission collaboration with and from the Latin American context. Reid states that since the 'Miami Summit' 1994, Latin America has become a laboratory for the viability of democratic capitalism as a global project.[56]

6. Understanding cultural values for mission in reciprocal contextual collaboration. From a biblical view, there is a dynamic process of cultural diversity and cultural change; however, in a world of diversification and multicultural change, ethnocentrism is not acceptable at all.[57] As the Willowbank Report (Stott 1996, 89) states, partnership in mission needs "humble messengers of the gospel", with a missionary humility and an incarnational model. The post-industrial society, with issues of individualism, uncertainty values and beliefs, cultural diversity, and the fragmentation of society, demands a theology of culture (Tiplady in Taylor 2000, 464).

7. Disparities in economy. The Western missionary endeavour for the past two hundred years has a massive economic superiority, and 78 percent of North American missionaries enjoy incredible economic and material superiority in the social context of their mission activity (Bonk 1991, 4–5). Therefore, reciprocal contextual collaboration in mission has to be confronted with disparities in the economy, sociological facts and cultural identity, which are seen in the current difficulties of multiculturalism

---

or transitional justice (the issue of holding past dictatorships to account of their crimes). On the other hand, the book focuses on the history, experience, problems and possibilities of democracy and of economic reform and development in Latin America (2007, xiii-xv).

56. The 'Miami Summit' 1994 was a conference organized by President Bill Clinton with the perspective of new collaboration in the middle of the historic transformation for Latin America (Reir 2007, 5).

57. 'The Willowbank Report on Gospel and Culture' in Bermuda (1978) explains the origin of the human culture, that God created mankind with human faculties, rational, moral, social, creative and spiritual with the free will to procreate to fill the earth and to subdue it (Gen 1:26–28). But none of our culture is perfect in truth, beauty or goodness – because of the fall it is disfigured by selfishness. But at the same time there is a positive human dignity and human cultural achievement through social organization, art and science, agriculture and technology, which reflects God's image. See further Stott (1996, 78). For a complementary reference see the work of Pachua (Corrie 2007, 112–114).

and religion in Western culture.[58] Equally, in the Latin American context this is seen in current changes of massive migration to rich countries, e.g. 41 million in the United States (Reid 2007, 3) and the increasing poverty for 205 million in Latin America.[59] In this sense, Jonathan Bonk points out that economic disparity would produce envy wherever Western missionaries work (1991, 49, 56).

Economic issues in partnership

The intense debate regarding economic freedom (Kirk 1998, 10–11; 2006, 15–17) implies the recognition of autonomous existence (free will), the recognition of human rights, the recognition of free access to information, equality of opportunity, self-determination (identity), and the language of freedom.[60] From the mid-eighteenth century, freedom impacted economic development in Europe starting with the industrial revolution, which strengthened the beginning of modern capitalism, and generated manufacturing processes, mercantilism, protectionism, the granting of monopoly

---

58. Economic disparities have grown and incomes are lower in about 100 countries. See Fouch (Tiplady 2003, 125). For example see Valerio's data: 1.3 billion people have to live on less than $1 a day and in 1997 Switzerland was 50 times richer than Mozambique (Tiplady, 21). Sociological facts refer to a group of individuals' role not to individuals; it refers to a collection of normative expectations for patterns or behaviour that a group of society agree to behave in a specific manner (http://www.csudh.edu/dearhabermas/read09.htm#samantha01). In the case of Britain this is seen in consumerism, humanism and in relation to mission – there is a sense of guilt for mistakes in the past; this is seen in resistance to building up new ways of partnering in mission with others.

59. Michael Reid (2007, 4, 322) argues that Latin America has a less attractive distinction with the most unequal distribution of income. Almost 205 million people live below the country's national poverty line, which according to the World Bank is an income below $2 dollars per day (this is the international measurer of poverty). Bolivia, Haiti, Honduras and Nicaragua are poor countries according to this economic measure.

60. Kirk argues that one reason for the development of the modern world has been the desacralization of structures where personal change is part of the civil society, granted that the institution is no longer considered completely immobile and irremovable (15). There is a philosophical freedom from the Greek philosophers, political freedom in relation to the state, and an interpretation of freedom by Augustine in *the City of God*. See also, 'The Question of Economics' in *Mission under Scrutiny*, (Kirk 2006, 15–17).

rights, free trade competition, and super-plus capital investment in rural development (36). Thus, I agree with Kirk when he concludes that:

> The Christian concern for freedom is expressed in searching for and discovering the right balance between liberty from arbitrary authority and liberty for non-oppressive structures. The authenticity of such structures is measured by their ability to enable people to become what God, as revealed in Jesus Christ, created them to be (1998, 221).[61]

Fourth presupposition

From the socio-economic assumption, we draw the fourth presupposition: there is no appropriate Christian relationship without sharing the control of power and decision making. Another obstacle for partnership in mission is inflexibility in sharing the control of power in all aspects. Kirk in *Theology Encounters Revolution* (1980, 11) argues that Western theology dictates the way in which Scripture is to be understood, and implies doctrinal confessions historically and culturally conditioned to Western missiology.[62] Therefore, this leads to a model of inflexibility lacking spiritual maturity and reciprocal partnership of God's kingdom theology in danger of provoking the presence of relational violence, which in mission partnership is seen in the distribution of money, power and making decisions between partners. From the beginning of creation Adam and Eve misused their harmonious freedom (Gen 3), and they failed by disobeying God's commands, thus, they started to practise a weak, limited and imposed

---

61. In *The Meaning of Freedom,* Kirk (1998, 4) argues for a concentrated study of the dynamic tension between freedom and social personal relationships in the context of secular views and great religions. He states that freedom is not a static reality; it has tensions of belief systems, intellectual process, historical movements, political, cultural changes, etc. (36). Kirk points out that "freedom is the ability to engage with meanings, values and purposes that we set for ourselves after intelligent reflection according to an orderly set of criteria" (230).

62. Kirk (1980, 11) concludes that for churches and missions "loyalty to a particular confession, formulation or tradition has become a serious substitute for creative study and application of the Scriptures". My argument is that this theological approach leads towards a model of lacking a more biblical approach for an appropriate reciprocal contextual collaboration in the *missio Dei.* See also Tienou (Phillips and Coote 1993, 249).

reciprocal freedom. From this understanding, my finding is that an anti-reciprocal freedom was originated for all Christian partnerships. This is seen in relationships of economic disparity, dependence, independence, disunity, and the little empires in which some mission societies, denominations and missionaries expand mission corporations instead of God's kingdom. As Newbigin suggests (1986, 146), there is a need to restore the church with more coherent and credible Christian witness.

Economic issues, which belong to the practical dimension of mission partnership, always become a sensitive matter for Christian mission, especially the Western mission. To consider briefly an approach, the Mennonite, Jonathan Bonk, in *Mission and Money* provides an analysis of six issues regarding missionary affluence, of which I mention two: missionary insulation, meaning made into an island because of Western affluence and unimaginable prosperity in comparison with the vast majority of the people Western missionaries serve; and missionary isolation, whereby independent private life is protected. Isolation is a lack of contact, genuine communication or interaction between persons or groups within society (1991, 45–47).[63] Bonk claims that both insulation and isolation have an adverse effect within the Western missionary affluence and concludes that the Western church has to deal with "the sociology and psychology of economic disparity or disappear as a Christian force" (57).[64] In line with

---

63. Here is a summary of the other four issues given by Bonk: (1) Affluence and an unbridgeable social gulf, with a lack of ability to establish friendship with the poor that produces an obstacle to 'fraternal social reciprocity'. (2) Social disparity and the illusion of superiority, which inevitably is accompanied with wealth. Superiority is shown in economic and social ascendancy. (3) Affluence and relationship of mistrust, implies mutual misunderstanding between missionaries and nationals due to the economic gulf in salaries. (4) Affluence, envy and hostile relationships. This implies that "with affluence comes social advantage; with social advantage comes personal security and power – power over those with less, power over one's own destiny, the power of choice". Envy frequently is an effect of economic and social disparity, and Western missionaries, points out Bonk, produce envy wherever they go. Thus financial disparity perpetuates bad interpersonal relationships (Bonk 1991, 45–58).

64. In this sense, Andrew Walls (1996, 230), in 'The American Dimension of the Missionary Movement' of the nineteenth and early twentieth century, explains that the transformation of the nation's economy shaped its mission activity. This was a similar process in Europe, but in Britain and in most of Europe the industrial process accompanied Christian decline. Today, we see Walls' prophecy of an unprecedented Christian expansion of the South and unprecedented recession of the North (1996, 237). In this chapter, Walls states that mission agencies were set up in society rather

Bonk's claims, I agree with Padilla (1985, 137) when he argues that "the possibility of reciprocal giving between churches is a basic premise" for a healthy relationship between rich and poor churches.

The question is, why develop a biblical ethic to improve a holistic mission of reciprocal contextual collaboration with this new emergent church? The reason seems to me to be that all kinds of resources for mission require good administration and biblical stewardship on the part of the donor and the receiver; these are a fundamental matter in mission too. In this sense, the Filipino-American, Al Tizon (2008, 78), in *Transforming after Lausanne* provides views of transformational economics addressed since the Wheaton Consultation (1983) by catalyzing transformational thinking and then empowered by OCMS (88–90) through Oxford I (1987), a conference which examined relevant issues in economics from a Christian perspective; Oxford II (1990), where "theologians affirmed free market strategies and conservative market economists demanded a special focus on justice for the poor";[65] Oxford III (1995) held at Agra, India, focused on the effect of the market economy on the poor. This theological and missiological process implies that the evangelical movement has taken seriously the double mission mandate raised specially for the so called radical evangelicals by emphasizing holistic mission or what Tizon calls 'mission as transformation'(3).[66]

---

that ecclesiastically, which allowed laymen to have a major role in shaping of activities. Separation of church and state has distinguished American Christianity from the European model (1996, 230, 232).

65. The Oxford II conference concluded with the 'Oxford Declaration on Christian Faith and Economics', a document organized in four parts: creation and stewardship; work and leisure; poverty and justice; and freedom, government and economics. This calls attention to the deep interest in economic matters when it is remembered that "both freedom rights and sustenance rights are important, not grounded in social authorization but in God's creation of persons in the divine image" (Tizon 2008, 89).

66. Tizon (2008, 3) calls radical evangelicals those with an Anabaptist, Anglican, Wesleyan and Reformed background, developing a theology of radical orientation to faith and society, questioning injustice and social and economic disorder. His analysis is based on the work of Gabriel Fackre (3) who identifies five types of evangelicals: fundamentalists, traditional, Neo, Charismatic and Pentecostal, and justice and peace, so called radical evangelicals. See further Tizon (2008). Holistic mission and mission as transformation are interchangeable terms; both emphasize the double mandate, spiritual and social responsibility. Tizon summarizes eight key elements of mission as transformation given by Vinay Samuel and Chris Sugden, some being an integral relationship between evangelism

As we have mentioned before, christological *missio freedom* for reciprocal contextual collaboration is an indispensable missionary theology to overcome dependence and independence in mission partnership. Consequently, a negative point is that wealth and its distribution, and a lack of sharing the control of power is strongly connected with what Buhlmann (Bonk 1991, xii) calls 'transnational religious corporation', and has to be reoriented for a healthy reciprocal contextual collaboration in mission.[67] The positive side is that an economic reorientation for mission funding within giving and receiving has been proposed by the Lausanne Consultation 2004 (Claydon 2005, 142–144, Vol III). It is called 'the mutual commitment' (horizontal model), with five key concepts: stewardship, relationship, accountability, interdependence and the role of intermediaries. It is contrary to the 'vertical model', which operates one way, creating dependency, which is unsustainable, and with limited results. However, at least two issues demand urgent attention:

1. Generosity as sacrificial giving. From a Catholic perspective, Gustavo Gutierrez (1983, 8) states that our relationship with God is expressed in our relationship with the poor, thus the reciprocal relationship between God and the poor person is at the very heart of biblical faith.[68] In a wider sense, the evangelical Craig Blomberg (1999, 142) in *Neither Poverty nor Riches,* provides a biblical theology of material possessions, pointing out that generosity towards the poor is the regular mandate in both the Old and New Testament. In the same line as Blomberg, the Evangelical Alliance in Britain states that, "giving to the poor is absolutely basic in the Bible"

---

and social change, freedom and power for the poor, mission in context, etc. See further Tizon (2008, 5).

67. Walbert Buhlmann (Bonk 1991:xii) argues that money is important but open to so many abuses that need careful attention and has the danger to corrupt the message, the messenger and reception of the gospel.

68. Andrew Kirk (1980, 114) points out that liberation theology was born as a movement of protest within the Latin American Roman Catholic Church in the 1970s. For Michael Reid, liberation theology began in the 1960s, at the 1968 Medellin Conference where Catholic bishops declared Latin America a region of structural sin and institutionalized violence, heavily influenced by dependence theory. It worked with base communities but liberation theology fails, concludes Reid, for not creating a mass popular church (2007, 228).

(1993, 13; *Banking on the Poor* 1988, 28; Bonk in Phillips and Coote 1993).[69]

In dialogue with these assumptions, my biblical missional hermeneutic is that both the rich and the poor, the multipolar world, are in condition to participate in mission partnership. The widow, explains Jesus, (Luke 21:1–3; Mark 12:41–43) gave all she had, and the rich man (Luke 18:18–23) was advised by Jesus to "go and sell all you have and give to the poor". This implies that sacrificial giving in reciprocal contextual collaboration is a matter of generous giving, never reducible to the cultural or economical context. Generosity originates in a Trinitarian theology; therefore, guilt of non-sacrificial giving can be overcome with a generous heart rooted in a holistic mission theology containing an ethical emphasis on love, justice and compassion for the poor that I call the option for emergent people, which implies mission from a context of poverty. Therefore, I agree with Blomberg (145–146) that material possessions can then be freed to give more generously in a self-denying sacrifice, and with Padilla (1985, 170–185) when he argues for a simple lifestyle by Western Christians.[70]

2. Sharing the control of power. Why the link between the economic issue and power? In Acts 2 we find the early Christians sharing their goods and possessions, thus expressing a vital experience of power, joy and faith (Tippet 1987, 58). Hence, it seems to be that among the early Christians there were activities in which power was shared in reciprocal harmony. In relation to the concept of power, James Whitehead (1991, 166) gives two basic concepts of power: power-activities and power-structures. The second refers to roles and rule-setting by a group to achieve its aims, while the first refers to the way people initiate actions and influence one another. In

---

69. Sadly, *Money for God's Sake* (1993) produced by the Evangelical Alliance does not provide any mission theology of generous sacrificial giving. Bonk gives three approaches to overcome unbalanced economic power: the incarnation approach – great renunciation; the cross approach – self denial; and the weakness approach – self humility. See Phillip and Coote (1993, 302–305).

70. In this way, within missiological insights, Tom Sine in his article 'Setting the Scene for 2020: Shifting Missions into the Future Tense' provides an analysis for the future of the global poor linked to the 'Mc World' economy. See further Corwin & Mulholland (2000, 45–49).

Mission from the Third World, James Wong and Peter Larson (1973, 61–63, 67, 76–80) provide data on the power-activities and power-structures operating in Africa since the 1970s, in Asia with the formation of many indigenous missions and Latin American power-mission activity structures similar to those of Africa.[71]

Power can be defined (West 1999, 101) as the insatiable appetite of individuals and societies such that no one can be content with moderate power. To protect their power, states West (101), people acquire more and more power and by ambition or fear they try to expand their power with no limits. Reinhold Niebuhr (1947, 15) states that society will probably never be sufficiently intelligent to bring all power under control. Therefore, the will to live becomes the will to power, which in consequence brings instruments of multiple forms of aggression. By way of complementing West's and Niebuhr's insights, Kirk (1999, 194) clarifies that a "truly mutual relationship cannot exist between two parties who possess unequal power". However, biblical Christian mission is grounded in the Lord of relationships who is a Trinitarian God revealed in Christ who brings hope, trust, justice and freedom, and guides his church into its mission destiny.[72] Therefore, as West (1999, 103) points out, God's power is not abstract omnipotence, it is self-limited by God's own character. Barth clarifies (West, 103) that God is free in word and deed because he is the source and measure of all freedom. Hence, the power of God to reign, to judge, to save,

---

71. First, in Africa, with the formation of denominational churches, affiliated to the World Council of Churches; second, new denominations and the independent missionary boards; third, national churches with their own mission boards; and fourth, the independent and indigenous church movements. Asia initiated in 1971 eleven indigenous missions in Japan, organized themselves into the Japan Overseas Missionary Association to promote more cooperation, and in 1968 David Cho founded the Korean International Mission Inc. to promote inter-missionary activities. For Latin America, the survey shows the power-activity and power-structure through traditional denominations, interdenominational groups and immigrant churches (receiving for example Japanese missionaries in Brazil), or the Asociación Misionera Evangélica Nacional (AMEN) in Peru mentioned as one of the pioneer indigenous missions. See further Wong and Larson (1973).

72. For a wider perspective on biblical power see the trilogy work of the Methodist, Walter Wink, who specialized in biblical interpretation. *Naming the Powers: Language of Power in the New Testament* (1984); *Unmasking the Powers: The Invisible Forces That Determine Human Existence* (1986); and *Engaging the Powers: Discernment and Resistance in a World of Domination* (1993).

and to fulfil is covenantal (104). This implies, in my view, that mission reciprocity means that all participants in God's kingdom have authority and power to fulfil God's covenantal missionary plan. Thus, the fundamental reason to sustain and to exercise power in all reciprocal mission collaboration relates to God's kingdom. Principally, power is the freedom and ability to make choices and act. It is not for producing inequalities, since it is the transparent use of freedom which makes possible a controlled exercise of power in all reciprocal mission (Kirk 1999, 194, 197).[73]

We live in a time of increasing secularization and in a pluralistic society which assumes the reality of a culture network. This reality challenges us to clarify the concept of power in mission, to which West (1999, xxi), from the perspective of Christian witness to the economy of God between nations, rulers and powers, provides the following clues:

> The power of God is covenantal. It is expressed in the relationship of justice and mercy, of promise and forgiveness, that God establishes with believers. Christians are stewards of this power, witnesses to the plan of God to fulfil all things in Christ. They are called to deal responsibly with such a human power and authority as is given them in the light of this divine work, to make it serve God's covenant in all the varieties of its forms.

In that sense, I agree with West (108-109), who insightfully provides some key characteristics of how the power of God acts, as follows: (1) The power of God is the power to destroy the consequences of all human sin, to justify and sanctify the sinner, and to make a human being new in Christ. (2) There are supernatural powers, power in human activity and institutions (e.g. government), the power of economic activity, ideological power, the power of law or social customs, etc. (3) All powers are created by God and have their authority, their value, and their meaning in God's plan (Col 1:16). (4) Power seeks to follow its own direction and its own sufficiency

---

73. Kirk (1999, 198) concludes that the worst form of power is the disguised and manipulative sharing whose aim is control of opinion and decision making; against that he suggests transparency.

apart from, and at times in rebellion against, God (Eph 6:12). (5) Christ in creation was the origin and meaning of the powers (Eph 1:10; 2 Cor 15:24; Col 2:15). (6) Human beings are caught up in this conflict between God and rebellious power, because they are themselves the battleground, trying to grasp power from self or world to form their own centre of power apart from the relationship with God given in Christ.

Consequently, West (113) is right in discerning that the scientific, technological and economic structures created by humanistic and rationalistic influences are the principal powers at work in our global society; human power struggles against the system and against all the social and political institutions. What is clear from our study is that the struggle for power becomes a matter of competition. It is a fact that domination and lack of sharing of power in all varieties and forms hinders the process of the Christian mission enterprise.

Bearing in mind what has been summarized above, a study of power provides elements for understanding the ways in which reciprocal contextual collaboration in mission is nurtured within a tension between the church as an agent of salvation and all powers at work in the world. The dangers lie in failing to understand the use of 'powers' between mission co-laborers, or in falling into internal confusion regarding what Christian mission is for. In this sense I agree with Charles West when he argues that Western society is in trouble, due to the fact that a market economy and the social order face humanistic powers related to global investment, finances and industrial production with which ideology cannot deal. In this regard he concludes that (1999, 123):

> The ideologies of human power, both individualist and collectivist, both liberal and revolutionary, are in crisis. Global investment, finance, and production operate by laws that create enormous wealth for few but pay little attention to the welfare of noninvestors, workers, and the poor. Basically economic progress is limited to certain nations and certain classes.

This suggests that the liberal, revolutionary, individualistic or collectivist ideologies are no longer able to deal with powers of global investment, finance and production. No power, political or economic, can control forces of exploitation of natural resources and of a global economy. Applied to society it means that power cannot satisfy the human hope or address the moral problems of an unjust society (124). Nonetheless, in one way or another, power influences relationships in mission because the church and its mission activity are carried on within a world where power in its different manifestations is out of control. Those involved in mission practice and study must be aware of this fact and alert against its consequences. For this reason, it becomes necessary to clarify the church's role in relation to the control of power. In this sense, as the church is witness to and steward of the gospel, and since this implies relationships with others, I agree with the following suggestions offered by West (124–127):

1. The church is not primarily an agent of human power, whether managerial, revolutionary or even sacerdotal; the church is a witness to the judging and transforming power of God in Christ.
2. Christians are stewards of the mysteries of the power that has been given to the church, which has a call to deal with this in repentance and with responsibility. The church is called to struggle with unjust power, with human depredation, the power of money, the power of information through media, etc.
3. The church bears witness to the fact that power is not only the self-expression of a subject, human or divine, not only a form of control over things, but an ingredient in a relationship that also contains other elements. When services, which are intended to benefit others themselves, become powers over our lives, their character changes.

For instance, it is quite remarkable that reciprocal relationships between power, freedom, justice and compassion – all theological and missiological foundations – may hinder or provide healthy mission fertilization for all models of the mission enterprise. They are neither arbitrary nor relative; on the contrary, these factors are radically important in God's kingdom and the church's mission. Justice,[74] freedom, compassion and integrity are key

---

74. For a wider study on justice, see the work of the Brazilian, Valdir Raul Steuernagel, in 'To Seek to Transform Unjust Structures of Society' (Walls and Ross 2008, 62–76).

elements in all relationships and are linked to the use of the power that has been given to the church. Thus it is possible to rediscover our missionary consciousness by recognizing that cooperation is not enough for healthy relationships in mission; mission structures are compelled to face the question of unity to discuss issues regarding the control of power.[75]

Regarding what was mentioned before, I want to pose this question: What are the issues which hinder economic power for the 'new emergent mission'? Some difficulties are due to economic factors of external debt, increasing poverty and reduced employment, which make it difficult to improve salaries and lead consequently to low income for churches in mission activity. *Banking on the Poor* analysis (1988, 5) explains that between 1982 and 1987 the total foreign debt of developing countries almost doubled from $650 billon to $1,190 billon. From an angle other than that of debt, Peter Heslam (2002, 9) argues that private capital flow to low-income countries was six times greater in 2001 than in 1990 with a significant improvement; a similar argument is given by Michael Reid for Latin America.[76] However, we argue that the issue of appropriate technology, capital investment, right prices for primary materials, free export from developed countries, high rate interest to repay loans, etc., make it difficult to overcome a macro-structural dependent economy, which is a consequence of the external factors of the economic and political policy of the World Bank and the International Monetary Fund (IMF), both founded after the Second World War 1944 for a rapid and harmonious growth in the post-war period (2002, 6).[77] Obviously, there are other internal factors like: (1) the frequent tendency of Western mission agencies to bypass their indigenous partners, (2) expensive Western models of mission societies, (3) gross inequalities which make partnership impossible, (4) traditional

---

75. See further Lesslie Newbigin in *One Body, One Gospel, One World: The Christian Mission Today* (1958, 53–55).

76. Reid (2007, 7) mentions that according to the World Bank, 62 billion export trades has been the result for the year 2006 for Latin America.

77. The IMF controls the world economy with the following policy: (1) exchange controls and import controls are either abolished or significantly liberalized. This policy allows free market policy; (2) the local currency is devalued; and (3) an anti-inflationary programme is introduced, which reduces the amount of credit available, making borrowing more expensive by increasing interest rates, etc. (Christian Aid 1988, 9).

mission practice which reflects a very weak concept of the church (Escobar in Taylor 2000, 44–45), and (5) a lack of teaching economic mission theology and external factors that affect the economy like corruption, political instability, national health, disasters, etc. But sharing the control of power relates also to what Vinay Samuel (Phillip 1994, 320) says:

> Much of contemporary Christian enterprise is still part of the Western universalizing enterprise. Christian theology, research, communication and mission are still mostly created in the Western church and consumed by the *new emergent church*; who dares to unmask the situation is immediately seen as a threat, 'the other'; we need to go beyond these games to being in Christ, yet all one in him. (italics mine)

Relational issues in partnership

Fifth presupposition

As we noted at the beginning, my fifth presupposition is that there is no appropriate Christian reciprocal contextual collaboration without reciprocal christological relationship (Luke 9:1–6; 10:1–12, 17–20). In discussing relational partnership, I want to pose three questions: first, why do we need to reconstruct a new relational theology of partnership? My assumption is that culture and mission policies often produce a gulf between personal and interpersonal relationship between partners. This is due to different factors like economic, social, theological, worldview, etc. Al Tizon (2008, 147) provides three key components to improve kingdom relational partnership: integration, incarnation, and commitment to the poor; all to help engage appropriately with the world.[78] However, two key elements must be included; sharing leadership power and decision making; but sharing of power with threefold insights rooted in a *metanoia* relationship. These are: kingdom *missio* relationship, christological *missio* relationship and *holistic*

---

78. Integration refers to unifying missionary practice, incarnation unifies humanity and the world, and commitment to the poor refers to solidarity with the marginalized and the powerless. See further (Tizon 2008, 153–156).

missio relationship, which are contrary to just personal relationship, which at times seems polite, superficial or cultural conditioned to the context.[79]

It seems to me that *metanoia* can be applied to the inner mission relationship due to its double dimension of relationship, with God and with others, which has to be applied with joyful freedom (Luke 15:6–7). In my theological understanding, *metanoia relationships* overcome the 'old relationship' from sin and are rooted in the 'new relationship' through conversion (*metanoia*), producing a transformational relationship with both God and man. Hence, reconciliation with God is the starting point to initiate a reciprocal contextual collaboration in mission. Jan Henzel (2007, 13–17) examines the vertical and horizontal dimension of reconciliation and Max Turner (2007, 37–45) develops the process by which Paul takes reconciliation as reestablishing appropriate interpersonal relationship in a total harmonious unity, which is already inaugurated in Christ (Col 1:15–20; Eph 1:9–10), and concludes that human reconciliation, theologically speaking, is not just about fixing bad relationships, but about re-integrating people under the image of a Trinitarian personhood. In my view, this implies the biblical, supracultural, doctrinal teaching Jesus gave to his disciples, and involves practical policy instruction, which confronts negative tensions, but empowering positive relationships in mission. Christological *missio relationship* implies to me: First, that Jesus calls and gives his partners kingdom-teaching on making commitment with him in love, compassion, self-denial and spiritual power. This was not an imposed mission because there was a reciprocal agreement. Second, that he helps partners in making a commitment to kingdom mission. Third, that he trains and equips mission partners in holistic mission. And fourth, that Jesus makes a reciprocal agreement (Luke 9:1–6) in sending them as co-laborers of his kingdom. Thus, christological *missio relationship* is grounded in God's kingdom mission relationship, which implies that reciprocal contextual collaboration in mission demands a Trinitarian relationship with a double dimension,

---

79. For further reading see the Czech, Jan Henzel's article, 'From Discord to Concord' in *European Journal of Theology* (2008, 13–17). For further discussion see also Max Turner's article 'Human Reconciliation in the New Testament with Special Reference to Philemon, Colossians and Ephesians' in *European Journal of Theology* (2007, 37–45). Kimball develops what I call a mission apostolic relationship. See further (1987, 57).

a private dimension and a public dimension. Moreover, it is necessary to understand the nature of the global-local relationship, which in Tizon's view includes international institutions, multinational corporations, states, non-governmental organizations and expresses the new order relationship of what Paul Freston calls 'globalization from below' (211).[80]

Second, why has partnership between South and North been weak? Since the beginning of the Protestant mission partnership after the Panama Congress in 1916, evangelical North-Atlantic partnership has produced a sense of mission-superiority and disincarnated mission, lacking awareness of the influence of external systems operating from the side of the Western church, which since the 1970s has generated a mission-protest from the new emergent mission theologians in different ways (i.e. historical, theological, missiological, social, economic, and cultural, etc.) This is also seen in the context of recent Asian and African mission-theologians like Kwame Bediako (Tizon 2008, 5) and David Gitari (Africa), Melba Maggay and David Lim (Asia). This *Protest demonstration* mission theology emerged not to destroy the cultural identity of the West or North-Atlantic side but to empower the dynamic work of the 'new emergent mission' in humble and missionary consciousness neither with triumphalism nor with revenge, still less with a justified euphoria. It is a mission-reverse traffic of what I call the construction of a two-way missionary bridge for the fulfilment of the *missio Dei*.

In my theological understanding, *missio freedom* means both the Christian liberation from sin, personal and social, and freedom to serve God's kingdom in free interdependence, thus, being made free is a synonym of salvation. In this sense, Christ becomes the pivotal centre of liberation from sin. Therefore, freedom from sin and reconciliation with God become the essential foundation for mission where every Christian has the duty to participate in God's Trinitarian plan of salvation. By christological *missio* relationship, I mean that in Christ it is possible to develop harmonious relationships with one another in the power of the Holy Spirit. Thus, when Christ makes people free from sin, he also makes his people free to

---

80. Globalization from below refers to the 'New emergent Church', and implies a lay people driven nature as well as social nature, especially referring to the Pentecostals.

develop reciprocal relationship, which is self-denial, in compassion and in reciprocal interdependence with others; this christological *missio* relationship is both vertical and horizontal, with God and with all people for the benefit of God's kingdom.

Missio freedom is a component of Christology (John 8:31–32), which gives the church a vision to serve in harmonious reciprocity; however, there is a tension between the finished work of Christ that delivers from sin and the actual experience of individuals and the Christian community that sin is still very much with us – hence we confess our sins in every worship service.[81] In this sense, from my observation over the last twenty years, I identify twelve characteristics for the development of mission partnership between the 'old mission' and the 'new emergent mission'. These will contribute to a penetrating analysis for a biblical dimension of christological *missio relationships* in which Christ becomes the model of relationships as we see them in the narratives of the four Gospels. Thus we develop an inclusive missionary theology of the threefold work's nature: instrumental, relational and ontological (Cosden 2004, 10–17):[82]

Lack of reciprocal control of power between partners.

Lack of christological *missio* relationship theology.

Lack of christological *missio freedom* by setting up the mission agendas.

Lack of training mission-minded leadership.

Lack of strengthening local theologies to understand culture.

---

81. Jesus then said to the Jews who had believed in him, "If you continue in my word, you are truly my disciples, and you will know the truth, and the truth will make you free." (John 8:31–32). Here, Jesus was speaking about spiritual freedom from having to commit sins. The individual who is truly free is one who is free spiritually from sins that are bound to overcome. We are free from transgression against the will of God, but tendencies are behind the individual that eventually control his free will with a propensity to continue to behave in the fashion of sinful nature.

82. Instrumental refers to a work as useful for some end in the maturing spiritual life; it is contrary to secular economic growth; relational work implies an appropriated social relationship (the way human organizations work) and to some form of existential realization by producing and making contribution to the world; and ontological work relates to the understanding that work's essential nature is God's creation; therefore a person is a worker not as an accident of nature. Work transcends and is more than a functional essence, therefore, "theologically, the Sabbath is the crown of God's creation", consequently work is permeated with the ethos of the Sabbath and transformational work aims at the realization of the Sabbath (184). See further Cosden (2004).

Lack of preparing transitional leadership for the new global mission.[83]
Lack of overcoming dependence and independence.
A weakness in forming multicultural teams.
A weakness in collaboration, bearing in mind the *missio context.*
A weakness of reciprocal freedom in mission structures.
A weakness of consciousness of the presence of evil forces *operandi.*
A weakness of understanding that global economy influences mission collabaoration.[84]

Third, what are the big issues in the relationship between North and South? On the one side, the Iguassu Consultation 1999 (Taylor 2000, 478–488) addresses issues of important relevance for understanding reciprocal contextual collaboration of global missiology for the twenty-first century like unnecessary competition, the urgency to find guidance for emerging movements, etc.[85]

---

83. The work of the Norwegian, Dag Hakon Eriksen, on 'Transition of Leadership' gives key elements for renewing leadership from the founder to the next leaders. Today, mission organizations experiment with giving more participation to the non-Western leaders in the mission board, for example. All Christian mission organizations have both an eschatological transcendent (God is the one who ultimately is building its church) and a socio-historical dimension. See further Engelsviken (et al. 2008, 354–371).

84. The statement of the Council for World Mission's Missiology Consultation gathered in Singapore 2007 provides a view of issues on global economy: "We live in a world that is driven by the interests of empire and neo-liberal globalization, with extremes of excessive wealth on the one hand and object poverty on the other; a world facing the impact of injustice, climate change, HIV and AIDS, religious and ethnic tension; a world in which the voices of people are being silenced by violence, force and coercion, and a world in which there is diminishing confidence in global institutions to provide security, coherence and peace". See 'Partners in Mission: The Practice and the Promise' *Council for World Mission* (7 January 2008).

85. This is my summary that will help further analyses: (1) Church centredness, which is essential to twenty-first-century missiology and holistic ministry is a necessary concern of the church but still they are inadequate. (2) Unnecessary competition and redundancy are facts which require urgent attention; avoiding the 'Adam Syndrome' (history starts with us) by training pastors in the process of missiological thinking and fostering partnership. (3) Regarding national missionary movements it is urgent to find guidance for emerging movements through the process of discerning their own unique context. (4) Missionary training is essential both for a person and for a mission team; this includes the participation of the church and the national missionary movements, as well as dialogue and partnership among educational institutions. (5) Partnership is hindered by two competing models, the business model and the family model. The second views people as stockholders, and control is maintained with money. The emphasis is on activities and contributions are seen as competitive, while the first sees them as members and it is relationships that keep control, and value fellowships; these contributions are

On the other side, in the Bible a missiological analysis of 'reciprocal relationship' is shown when Jesus calls the Father, 'Abba' (Mark 14:36; Rom 8:15; Gal 4:6). This word 'Abba' expresses love and fellowship in reciprocity as we read through the missionary consciousness of Jesus' sacerdotal prayer in John 17. From this biblical angle, the American strategist, Kenneth Hemphill (2007; Tippet 1987), offers five undeniable truths for nurturing biblical fellowship, which are as follows: (1) fellowship is not optional to biblical Christianity, (2) fellowship with other believers is essential to personal spiritual growth, (3) fellowship is essential to ministry since the unified body is the platform for the proper functioning of the spiritual gifts, (4) authentic fellowship – 'koinonia' – can only be found in Christ, and (5) fellowship is essential to kingdom expansion.[86] But the fact is that reciprocal christological relationship is probably one of the biggest issues in contemporary mission of the twenty-first century. In what sense? First, it is due to the forgotten biblical approach that where the body of Christ is, there are spiritual gifts and material resources to share with other Christians in the world; in consequence, disunity is expressed in an anti-mission spirit. Second, the control and retention of power in making decisions generates roadblocks for biblical reciprocity. Third, disparity of economy and a weak understanding of cultural values is seen when partners try to form multicultural teams. Fourth, there are four common fears in relationships:

---

seen as complementary, and both models pursue accountability. (6) Diverging agendas, insufficient emphasis on relationships and the indiscriminate use of old sponsorship methods hinder the achievement of true partnership (2000, 483). (7) Tent-making (bi-vocational ministry) requires attention, as it is suggested that this model will not produce the same results as traditional missionary effort. (8) An uncritical use of media and technology treats missions and missionaries, which in my view implies depersonalization of relationship, for example. (9) The issue of remaining in the field demands the ongoing care of both agencies and churches. (10) There is a concern to clarify a Trinitarian-based missiology with an inclusive perspective of gender (the role of women in mission) and generational sensitivity (the world's young). For full detail see Taylor (2000) *Global Missiology for the 21st Century: The Iguassu Dialogue*.

86. Kenneth Hemphill is national EKG (Empowering Kingdom Growth) strategist for the Southern Baptist Convention – USA (http://www.bpnews.net/BPFirstPerson.asp?ID=25657). See also Tippet, chapter 5 'The Florescence of the Fellowship: Missiological Ecclesiology', which provides seven elements of Christian relationship: spiritual experience, focus in worship, vigorous commitment, high moral life, fellowship in suffering, fellowship in service and obligation for world mission (1987, 40-43). See also Scopes 'A Journey Towards Partnership' (2008).

manipulation, failure, rejection and pain (Kimbal 1987, 64–88).[87] Fifth, denominationalism hinders unity, expressing proud individualism lacking an understanding of God's kingdom theology.

Conclusion

To conclude this chapter, we have sought to situate a dynamic reciprocal relationship of reciprocal contextual collaboration within a matrix of economic, cultural and sociological issues informed by macro-economic theory, which establishes that international economic laws influence every system, even the mission enterprise. As we have seen before, reciprocal relations in Christian partnership tend to be diluted by external factors like economic forces of globalization, the World Bank, the IMF, the policy of mission agencies, or by internal factors such as the lack of mission-minded leaders with reciprocal mission relations, pastoral care and ethical behaviour, disparity in economy, cultural understanding, inadequate mission theology assumptions, etc.; these complex issues remain to be dealt with in creative positive tensions by rediscovering our missionary consciousness of mission-church coexistence as an indissoluble relationship. Thus, chapter 5 will focus on the analysis of three case studies to clarify how the issues mentioned in this chapter have been developed in partnerships in mission.

---

87. In this sense, my assumption is that fellowship in the early church was not an option but a necessity due to the fact that they trusted together that Jesus was the Messiah and this was the root of a deep level of fellowship. Thus, it is shown in the gospel that *christological relationships* nurtured the relationship of the disciples. According to this biblical interpretation, Hemphill's opinion is that Acts 1:14 provides our first hint of the depth of first-century fellowship (2007). Therefore, *christological fellowship* is a key theological element of reciprocal contextual collaboration because collaboration implies that we are not owners of the *missio Dei* but privileged helpers, responsible stewards, humble heralds, and bold mission disciples. Christ the pivotal centre of the *missio Dei* allows all Christian to co-participate in his mission fellowship.

Part III

Seeking the Missiological Reality in Practice

CHAPTER 5

Case Studies of Three Models of Partnership

Introduction

The Latin American movement COMIBAM started in 1987, in São Paulo, Brazil with 3,000 delegates attending its first Congress. The pivotal point has been 'from missionary field to sending field'. Since the Panama Congress in 1916 there has been no major missionary event, apart from the CLADES, that has made a greater difference for strengthening the Latin American missionary movement than COMIBAM. For this reason, in this chapter, three missionary efforts will be analysed based on the period of time cited above and they are as follows: (1) Latin Link from the United Kingdom. This mission society started its mission work in 1991, as a result of the merging of two mission societies that worked in Peru and other parts of Latin America, the Evangelical Missionary Union of South America (EUSA) and the Regions Beyond Missionary Union (RMBU). (2) COMIBAM from Latin America, is the first Latin American mission network, started as a result of many previous mission consultations on how to empower the mission task of Latin American churches. (3) St James Church from London and the Iglesia Misionera Evangelica from Peru, two local churches that have been partnering since 1997 and which offer a mission partnership model of reciprocal contextual collaboration with a missiological and theological influence emphasizing the participation of the local church in Britain.

Though the analysis may suggest that mission for the twenty-first century is taking place with some inappropriate models of mission, there is a clear decision by the evangelical movement to accomplish the mission double mandate. I will therefore try to clarify if this kind of partnership has been dependent on the power of God or on the power of money, internal or external factors.[1]

These cases are different in their origins and theological influence; however, I will follow a uniform methodology. To begin with there will be a review of historical origins followed by an analysis of the mission, including the context within which it was developed, the structure, a summary of its mission policy and the perspective from which this mission is developed, concluding with an evaluation on the basis of weaknesses and strengths, which will help us to establish if models are appropriate. In the analysis, special attention will be given to the missiological understanding of each case study, the implications of this understanding for mission partnership and their significance for the new reciprocal contextual collaboration in the evangelical movement.

Latin link case study

Historical origins

Latin Link is a British mission founded on 5 June 1991 in London (International Handbook 2006, 11) as a phenomenon of merged mission structure between two missions (EUSA and RMBU) with the aim of developing mission in both Europe and Latin America. Actually, this mission works within eleven Latin American and three European countries with more than one hundred twenty long-term and forty-four short-term missionaries, a staff of twenty-one people and ten volunteers.[2] As a surviving

---

[1]. By external factors I mean those factors related to economic, social and political factors that have been influencing these case studies, and by internal factors I mean those related to the activity of the institutions in the study themselves.

[2]. Latin Link Staff Britain and Ireland: 15 full-time staff. Then there are 4 part-time staff (of these 4 part-time staff, 1 person works 4 days a week, 3 people work 2 or 3 days a week). They also have 1 freelance writer (approx 1 day a week), Andrew Johnson,

mission Latin Link's origin goes back to the early twentieth-century mission, with the name of The Evangelical Union of South America (EUSA), initiated in London in 1911. EUSA initiated its mission activity as a direct result of the Edinburgh 1910 conference, which did not consider Latin America as a continent to be evangelized.[3] As 'The Twenty-Fifth Milestone' (1936, 17) mentions, British missionary leaders made a decision to unite three small mission societies, the Region Beyond Missionary Union (RBMU) founded in 1894, the South American Evangelical Mission (SAEM) founded in 1895 and the Help from Brazil Mission founded in 1892, which joined EUSA two years later.[4] In the 1970s the UK Andes Evangelical Mission (AEM) became part of EUSA, but the North American section joined with Sudan Interior Mission. At the time of EUSA's existence, Donald Ford became General Secretary from April 1979 until February 1991, handing over the international role to John Chapman.[5]

One of the external factors that has an influence in the work of Latin Link is related to the RBMU mission, founded when the East London Training Institute for Home and Foreign Missions was opened by Henry Grattan Guinness (1835–1910) in Stepney Green, Clapton, London. RBMU initiated its work in Peru and Argentina in the early 1890s, concentrating their efforts on Lima and Cuzco. In 1897 Henry Grattan Guinness visited South America with the aim to support work in Bolivia and Chile. Missionaries from RBMU in Argentina were largely self-supporting and

---

who works for Latin Link International. (Data provided by Charlotte Barker, 14 October 2008c).

3. See further 'The Twenty-Fifth Milestone' (1936, 1). See also Hans Jurgen Prien (1978, 626–636).

4. Mundus, Gateway to Missionary Collections in the UK (http://www.mundus.ac.uk/cats/3/1229.htm). Historically, all the missions that formed Latin Link later were interdenominational, thus, the work done in the past by these missions included church planting, medical and educational work, and Bible and Christian literature distribution.

5. Ford comments that both mission agencies agreed that it would only be fair to appoint someone from outside to take on the role of CEO of the new agency – hence John Chapman's appointment. Dennis Smith was the UK Secretary and remained in this role for a couple of years more. He and I and the EUSA International Council (with representatives from Brazil, Argentina, Bolivia and Peru, as well as the UK board) negotiated the merger with the RBMU's Peru field. Geoff Larcombe was the UK Secretary of RBMU and we discussed many aspects of the new agency with him. As both RBMU and EUSA were partners in Whitefield House (where the EA now has its base) this was an added bonus for communication (data provided by Donald Ford 2008).

achieved a certain amount of success especially through their schoolwork. In Peru, however, the workers faced a difficult battle against persecutions, illness and indifference. Despite attempts to establish themselves through teaching, industrial schemes at Cuzco, a farm for the training of Quechua Indians, and building a network of support in North America, the mission always struggled and there were disagreements between missionaries and the London base as to how it should be organized. These internal factors and financial problems at home persuaded Guinness to hand over the work in 1911 to the Evangelical Union of South America, which consequently was founded on 9 May 1911, launched at Westminster Chapel, London, under the leadership of Campbell Morgan, Stuart Holden, George Grubb and Harry Guinness.

The Peru Inland Mission (PIM) started their work with the nurse Annie Sopper, supported through Canadian and North American friends, in the region of Moyobamaba, San Martin, by establishing a hospital. In 1929 they moved to Lamas where they opened hospitals, orphanages and, later, a Bible institute and where the Peruvian Inland Mission (later Peru Inland Mission) was born, but RBMU took responsibility for the PIM in 1948, with the retention of its autonomy. Later, theological differences caused some friction and from 1971 RBMU workers from the UK and from North America worked in different areas until the separation of RBMU UK and RBMU International in 1979. During the 1970s and 1980s there was a policy of slow withdrawal from church building, particularly in urban areas, and co-operation with other missions such as EUSA. As Caroline Brown indicates (2001), the RBMU UK was finally dissolved in 1990 and on 5 June 1991 the Peruvian section joined with EUSA to form Latin Link,[6] the Scot, John Chapman, became the first international director.[7]

The mission context

Latin America is the context in which Latin Link develops its partnership in mission with the Latin American church. This began in the countries of Peru and Argentina and later Bolivia, Ecuador and Colombia. In the case of Peru, which is our focus, the political, social and economic context of the 1910s was related to the starting point of a post-colonial republic. Fredrick Pike (1973, 107–114, 159–161) points out that the reformist, President Manuel Gonzales Prada (1890), developed his government under the influence of socialism, and during the 1920s Jose Carlos Mariategui promoted an unorthodox communism. The first political power of militarism emerged with Augusto B. Leguía, who became a dictator president from 1919 to 1930.[8] The Alianza Popular Revolucionaria Americana (APRA) came to light in 1924 leading a new movement under Victor Raul Haya de la Torre and a new government was installed in 1930 under General Luis M. Sanchez Cerro, elected president in 1931 but assassinated in 1933; General Oscar Benavides then led the government until 1939. This pattern of militarism is seen in nearly every decade of the Peruvian republic.[9]

---

6. Caroline Brown (2001), Adam Matthew Publications, Imaginative Publishers of Research Collections. See also the brief history of Latin Link (International Handbook 2006, 11). According to McIntosh, the reasons to merge EUSA and RBMU were the economic instability of the two missions whose home bases were non-viable with a small number of missionaries and the separation of the North American, Canadian and Australian fields due to the charismatic polarization left the few RBMU Britons isolated in Peru. But there was an underlying reason that neither RBMU nor EUSA had any clearly defined way forward in missiological terms due to the fact that their commitment to the IEP and the Asociación de Iglesias Evangelicas del Nor-Oriente Peruano (AIENOP) disallowed them to do church planting in or for other areas nor had they a clear vision of how/if to integrate in the mission of the IEP/AIENOP. Also, several of the older couples in both missions had retired or left for other reasons, e.g. Ford, Davies, Turner, McIntosh and Scotts or were pursuing other goals. It may also have been that the executive secretaries Ford and Larcombe were tired of it all as well. (McIntosh Questionnaire 2008:3).

7. John Chapman (2008) Questionnaire.

8. This was under the influence of the USA government but with no support of the middle class and the intellectuals

9. After political battles, the civilian Manuel Prado was elected president from 1939 to 1945, but again another military dictatorship Manuel A. Odría ran the government

Between 1985 and 2005, the presidents of Peru were Alan Garcia from APRA (1985–1990 and re-elected from 2006 until 2011), the originator of the devastating hyperinflation and unemployment; Alberto Fujimori from 'Cambio90' (1990–1995 and again until 2000), a controversial figure; and Alejandro Toledo from 'Peru Posible' (2001–2006), the ideologist of a neo-liberal economy.[10]

Between 1940 and 1961 Peru had a population of 11 million. Sadly, since that time there has been political, economic and social instability due to the lack of employment and technology for developing industrial agriculture. 2005 statistics show that Peru has a population of 27.2 million people, with 7.8 million living in Lima, the majority with a Catholic background and recently with at least 15 percent evangelical presence, of whom the majority are Pentecostals.[11]

Analysis of mission development

Type of mission structure

Latin Link is a traditional mission structure due to the fact that their mission policy involves very formal candidates and missionaries for mission with a clear long process for selecting candidates, a structured budget for financial support before going to the mission field and a policy of careful prevention to avoid future problems in partnering with the candidate. In consequence, this is not a faith mission model due to the fact that this mission structure rests on a financial budget covered by the mission candidate

---

from 1948 to 1956. However, Manuel Prado was elected again, but another military intervention stopped his final year of government after a year of military intervention.

10. In 1985 Alan Garcia from the APRA party become president but failed with a severe economic crisis. Between the 1980s and 1990s there were increased guerrilla activities and violation of human rights by both guerrillas and Peruvian military. The controversial Alberto Fujimori was elected president in 1990 and re-elected in 1995; he has been credited by many with restoring macroeconomic stability to Peru after the turbulent presidency of Alan Garcia Perez (1985–1990) and bringing peace to the country after many years of political violence. However, he has been criticized for adopting an authoritarian leadership style particularly after dissolving the Peruvian Congress. President Alejandro Toledo (2000–2005), from a neo-liberal wing, made a contribution to stabilize the economic growth of Peruvian exports; his party lost the re-election and Alan Garcia has become the new president from 2006 to 2011.

11. Instituto Nacional de Estadistica (http://www1.inei.gob.pe/inicio.htm).

before going to the mission field and from which it derives part of the income for the staff to support the expenses of the mission administration. As the International Team Leader Marcel Durst states, this is a mission to help people raise funds rather than pay them (2008, 5).[12]

The financial model of the old traditional structure (EUSA, later Latin Link) relates to the principle that people gave money to the mission, and the structure gave a salary to all missionaries. The new model structure relates to the principle that people give money to missionaries and Latin Link becomes a fund-raising structure.[13]

It appears that the changing structure in Latin Link maintains most of the values of the 1991 policy (totally different before the 1990s when they operated as EUSA mission), like the three key emphases of partnership (as the old structure), networking (as a more relational traditional structure), and local churches (as a traditional link representing and receiving resource from the local church).[14] For the networking emphasis, Latin Link seems to be strengthening its power to make its structure more solid by employing the philosophy of global networking thinking.[15] However, the recent International Handbook provides a reoriented strategy in line with the new Strategy Commitment (StraCom), which has been implemented since 2006 by Marcel Durst, a former ideologist for Latin Link expansion.[16] This new strategy is focused on three missiological perspectives: its emphasis (where they focus), its target group (whom they serve) and its activity

---

12. Data provided by Marcel Durst (Questionnaire 2008).
13. Stuart Harrison, interview by the author, held in Edinburgh on 5 March 2009a.
14. See the International Handbook (2006, 15). Three emphases seem to be based on the traditional mission policy. Youth and children have been excluded as a key emphasis.
15. It seems that Latin Link wants to become a more interconnected mission, overcoming its origins of a regional mission concentrated in Latin America. The code-named 'global' (multiple centres) seems to have replaced the era of the word-concept 'international' (the British industrial pre-eminence) and the word-concept of 'multinational' (the American era). See further Michael Borrus and John Zysman in *Enlarging Europe: The Industrial Foundations of a New Political Reality* (Zysman and Schwartz 1998, 28–30).
16. Ideology is defined not as mere schematic conception of any reality that helps social groups to develop actions according to their interest. Moreover, an ideology is a theoretical conceptualization related to a strategy and a programme of action to be actualized in a concrete historical situation, which has an independent/autonomous character (Costas 1976, 34).

(what they do or enable others to do).[17] The new strategy implies that all Latin Link members have to identify with, be resourced by and meet with colleagues in one of the strategy commitments as being the main focus of their work, which includes five areas: proclamation of the gospel, preparation of people, social action, communication resources, and business as mission.[18]

A new basic structure of Latin Link (International Handbook 2006, 19–20) appears practising a circular model that implies decentralized control of power (different from the hierarchical model), which has been implemented since 2006.[19] However, we cannot assume that Latin Link structure is a bottom-up (from below) model because the control of power and decision making comes from the office in Reading, UK (top-down model). Its intention of practising a decentralized control of power looks seminal or it has a transitional phase. In a top-down model (centralized), an overview of the system is first designed, which is one of the characteristics of Latin Link mission structure, where mission policies originated in the UK are transferred to each national team leader in each country. Thus, a top down model of power and decision making is applied to the policy of sending long-term missionaries and executing principles of the Handbook Mission by the Latin Link office in UK. Consequently, Latin Link seems still to be a centralized traditional mission structure; it is not a mission network model.

It appears that decentralized decision making for Latin Link refers to the relationships between team leaders of each country, who after being appointed have autonomy for making decisions in relation to the country where they lead a team, but according to Latin Link mission policy. For

---

17. International Handbook (2006, 16).
18. Here is a summary of the five strategy commitments: (1) Proclamation of the gospel seeks to enable and facilitates the working out of the global concern of the Latin American churches. (2) Preparation of the people seeks to assist in the development of leaders at every level of the Christian community. (3) Social action seeks to work with Latin American Christians in social projects. (4) Communication resources seeks to develop literature and other resources with the aim of helping people lead a transformed life. And (5) business as mission seeks to develop with Latin American Christians sustainable business for job and income generation and to fund mission. See further International Handbook (2006, 117–18).
19. Circular structure tries to distribute the control of power and the hierarchical retains decision-making at the top with a few people.

example, Latin Link UK cannot interfere by introducing a missionary in a country without the approval of the team leader of the country.

The organization is based on the International Assembly (decides policy and general direction), the International Leadership Forum (implements Assembly decisions, agrees appropriate structures), International Team Leader (leads Latin Link and implements decisions of International Leadership Forum), Regional Team leadership (leads regional teams and implements decisions of the International Leadership Forum) and Latin Link members (select delegates for the Assembly).[20]

Moreover, Latin Link mission expansion includes the intentional approach of traditional mission merged with the networking model, producing what I call the 'traditional mission network',[21] but under the emphasis of the traditional philosophy of partnership. This phenomenon can be seen in its links with the following missions:[22] Latin Partners in the UK (to facilitate mission from Latin America to Europe); Apoyo in Germany (to facilitate the mission of Latin America and transfer of funds to further this); and since June 2008 Latin Link has made an agreement with Cuba Para Cristo in the UK (to help mission in Cuba).[23] One of the dangers of this kind of partnership is the risk of absorbing small missions with the temptation to deny theological freedom in making decisions. We should not forget that behind this intentional desire to become a non-rigid traditional mission, or a 'traditional mission network', there are issues relating to control of power and affluence. Another disturbing consequence of partnership from this angle is the fact that any traditional mission can become a promoter of

---

20. The old model differs in that Latin Link members are paramount in the old model but in the new model the International Assembly represents the power of decision making and the International Leadership Forum replaces the International Executive, which in one sense has the same authority to implement the Assembly decisions. The strength of this new structure seems to be that it has circular power in decision making, unlike the hierarchical model which has vertical power in decision making.
21. Traditional mission network means that the structure remains traditional with formal contacts like autonomous bodies, written agreements, etc., but adding some ingredients of the innovative networking philosophy such as personal relationship, links for sharing human resources, legal advice, etc.
22. These traditional networking partnerships with Latin Partner and Apoyo include the policy of fixed budgets for mission candidates. It is neither innovative networking nor reciprocal.
23. Personal data, June 2008 London.

imperial expansion, or just a transnational corporation.[24] Hence, we need to try to adhere more closely to the New Testament models of mission and allow the Spirit 'to blow where he wills'. We need a greater consciousness of the Sprit of God as the director of mission. Of course, missionaries do need some kind of mission structure to function well, and in this case, Latin Link is a mission corporation, but with the aim of glorifying God and fulfilling the *missio Dei*. Therefore, it seems that the principles which Latin Link states as evidence of desire of genuine reciprocal contextual collaboration are the entry of people in God's service, the catalyst emphasis, and the interdependence recognition in reciprocal collaboration.[25]

Main characteristics

Latin Link's Mission Statement 1998 declares its vision, calling and nature.[26] Its vision is to work in partnership with Latin American Christians for the advance of the mission of Christ. Their call has three key elements: to love God and neighbour by proclaiming the good news of Christ, in whom alone there is salvation, liberation and hope; the training of the people of Christ, forming leaders, who will be Christ-like in character and behaviour as well as in word; and the sharing of the compassion of Christ, in co-operation with the church to provide resources to the poor and marginalized in society. The nature of Latin Link is defined through six concepts: (1) unity, by commitment to demonstrating the interdependence of the worldwide church; (2) diversity, by accepting a diverse group in personality, gifts, church background and culture, united in open and caring fellowship for the furtherance of the mission of Christ; (3) creativity, in allowing for the development and use of gifts and talents; (4) accountability, by developing a structure which is flexible and encourages as much decentralized decision

---

24. René Padilla defines 'imperial expansion' as the influence of transnational corporations. Data provided at the mission conference organized by the London Institute of Contemporary Christianity, London 2007. The same suggestion has been made by Padilla at the Global Connection Consultation with the theme 'Global Challenges that the Church Faces Today', held in Oxford at the Church Mission Society (CMS) office on 8 October 2008.
25. See further the International Handbook (2006, 16).
26. The whole declaration starts with the Latin Link fellowship statement (International Handbook 2006, 7–8).

making as possible; (5) humility, to be facilitators in the work of God in and from Latin America, through service in genuine partnership; and (6) integrity, aiming for lifestyle and witness which are biblical, evangelical and in harmony with their statement of faith..[27] This policy has been applied to the different countries where they have missionaries working in different areas like recruitment, training and people care in Argentina or the church's music ministry or Sunday School teaching materials in Peru.[28]

Mission theology

In a complementary mission theology to the vision, call and nature, Latin Link's basis of faith is committed to the fundamental truths of historic, biblical Christianity, which are in agreement with the Lausanne covenant 1974 and the CLADE III Declaration 2000. The basis of faith includes theological definitions of God, the Bible, the human race, the Lord Jesus Christ, salvation, the Holy Spirit, the church and the future.[29] It appears that, in agreement with its Basis of Faith, Latin Link structure defines its spirituality and values through three theological assumptions of fellowship (International Handbook 2006, 9):[30] (1) fellowship of living worship by grace, goodness, integrity, and unity and peace; (2) fellowship of vision through clear purpose, servant leadership, networking, openness and wholeness; and (3) fellowship of relationships marked by commitment of people, commitment to justice, repentance, respect, humility, a value of history and lastly freedom. Thus, it seems that this three-fold theological fellowship is the ground for their relationship with the church, stating that, for them, the church is commissioned by Christ to make disciples of all nations, believing that the church's primary mission is to present Christ by

---

27. Latin Link's mission statement (http://www.latinlink.org/missionState.asp).
28. See the Latin Link Prayer Calendar 2008 (2–29).
29. Latin Link's basis of faith (http://www.latinlink.org/basis_of_faith.asp).
30. These values have a theological background. For grace they use words like generosity, trust, mercy and forgiveness, integrity, love. These word concepts seem to convey the principle of providing security and value between Latin Link memberships. For goodness they propose learning and development in humility, and for freedom, they seek truth with intellectual discipline, exploring ideas without fear of judgment (see further International Handbook 2006, 9).

the power of the Holy Spirit (2006, 12).[31] From this missionary theology assumption of the church, Latin Link develops a relationship with sending churches, serving[32] churches and with inter-church relationships (they believe in the interdependence of the worldwide church).

Mission policy

In relation to the mission policy for candidates, this includes at least three types of membership: (1) Steps (Handbook 2006, 53), which provides the opportunity to partner with Latin American people. It works generally in response to requests by national churches, groups or projects.[33] They offer shorter programmes from 4 to 7 weeks and longer programmes for 6 months; members are aged over 17 years old. (2) Strides (2006, 54), which implies a team or an individual placement with the aim of service, witness and discipleship. Members are expected to attend Latin Link conferences, to be accountable, and they are responsible for raising their own finances.[34] (3) Placements, which are from 6 months to 2 years.[35] Long-term member missionaries (2006, 28) are single missionaries, couples and couples with children. Long-term candidates require interviews, fund raising and signing

---

31. As an essential part of the Latin Link mission theology they define the meaning of the church, the relationship with churches, varieties of church practice and pastoral concern and sending church issues. See further the International Handbook (2006, 12–113).

32. Step teams work on a basic building project alongside a Latin American church community. Teams also help churches with evangelism, working with young people, music, drama, etc. Destinations include Argentina, Brazil, Bolivia, Cuba, Ecuador, Mexico and Peru, as well as our newest and nearest – Spain and Portugal. See Latin Link, Step Teams (http://www.stepteams.org/apply.php#01).

33. International Handbook (2006, 53). The clear concept of social mission has been changed in the new International Handbook for a more general view. They use "the nature of the work involved is often building with other practical aspects", instead of the old concept of "providing the opportunity to partner with Latin American people by helping in building orphanages, classrooms for local schools and church community centres, drama, evangelism and university Christian Unions". (International Handbook 1998 H3: 1).

34. Placements for Strides can start any time after the main orientation programme in September or a shortened course in January. The deadline for applications is 30 April for a September departure, or 1 August for a January departure. The main selection days are held at the Reading office. For applicants in Scotland and Ireland, interviews can be held with local area Latin Link coordinators. See Latin Link, Strides (http://www.latinlink.org/stride.asp).

35. For the Step and Stride programmes accepted applicants are required to obtain a disclosure from the Criminal Records Bureau before the appointment is confirmed.

a contract to respect the ethos and policy of Latin Link (2006, 28–43). However, my finding is that decisions on receiving candidates and sending missionaries are finally made under the administration of the Reading office in the UK where the political power lies to apply its mission policy for candidates, that in my view, have to be analysed if it is to be reconstructed in such a way as to empower the receiving of Latin American candidates. Latin Link seeks candidates according to their ethos of true partnership, which involves transparency and loyalty, flexibility, adaptability, and commitment to Christ. The fact is that these kinds of Latin Link candidates differ widely from the Latin American missionaries, which the Peruvian missiologist, Miguel Angel Palomino (1999, 7), classifies as itinerant missionaries (simple believers who left their country for a better economy), informal missionaries (they do not get any support from their home churches) and conventional missionaries (with some theological training but no experience in learning the new culture and language).

Statistics worked on at the end of 2007 show the numbers of (Britain and Ireland based) Latin Link members who did short-term mission before becoming long-termers. Number of people who have ever done Stride: 326 (since 1987); number of people who have ever done Step: 2,384 (since 1987); total number of Step teams: 327. In terms of numbers in 2008, they have had: Summer Step: 104; Spring Step: 48; Stride: 44; current long-term members: approximately 120, which include all Britain and Ireland members as well as the international team members and the Latin partners.[36]

At the time John Chapman became the first International Director of Latin Link in 1991, they had 64 missionaries in the field and there were no candidates; moreover, there were no Latin male members.[37] His theological and missiological vision was to see a mission that truly worked in partnership with both Europeans and Latins (not North Americans because they had a partnership with LAM) in leadership as well as membership and it was also to be thoroughly interdenominational. Therefore, Chapman provides three key elements of Latin Link partnership in the following way:

---
36. Data provided by Charlotte Backer on 19 September 2008b.
37. Data obtained from my questionnaire to John Chapman (2008).

1. Healthy partnership in Latin Link has been hindered often by an expectation of finance that Latin Link just did not have but once that was understood they began to have partnership as truly accompanying each other in the gospel.[38]
2. In respect of the issue of independence, Latin Link has been exemplary in that it does not allow its members to operate independently of national leadership. There is no case in his experience where this was so and in fact in two cases they suggested that people leave because they were unwilling to do this.[39]
3. For the control of power, the policy has been to share power with Latins in senior leadership as well as Dutch, Germans, Swiss and others.

With reference to the development and characteristics of partnership in mission which caused a lack of freedom in the relationship, dependence and sharing the control of power, Chapman is not content since for him this is an issue of individuals on both sides and there are those from both continents who find partnership difficult, often due to self-identity, but there are also those from both sides who live it.[40] However, the partnership tension is not clearly explained by Chapman; he cites the fact that the misunderstanding in the church according to Acts 6 was between cultures – something that will always be with us, but with love and grace and humility we can truly serve as sisters and brothers in Christ.[41] Since 1991 Latin Link adopted a new mission policy for making decisions. This is due to the new missiological understanding to create team leaders in each mission base, allowing the responsibility of a missionary team in one country, and the development of relationships with the national church so that the international leader cannot interfere with decisions made in each country.

To confirm the new missiological approach of freedom theology, the Britain and Ireland Latin Link team leader, Alan Tower, describes two

---

38. John Chapman (2008) Questionnaire: question 4.
39. Ibid., question 9.
40. Ibid., question 6. With a different view McIntosh points out that he believes there was probably freedom in the relationship but the process was irrelevant to the growth and development of world mission. Mission was occurring elsewhere! (Questionnaire 2008, 6).
41. Ibid., question 10.

negative and two positive achievements of this mission in the following way: Latin Link needs to work on the balance between individual calling to ministry and a community feel as a mission agency and, second, they do not always show a coherent direction overall due to lack of resources at the international level and as a flip side to celebrating diversity and local initiative. On the positive side he states that Latin Link celebrates relationships of partnership and service with national and regional Latin American ministries and, second, they are flexible and prepared to experiment with a prophetic edge and humility.[42] In clarifying why Latin Link should be a traditional, networking or an emergent mission structure, Tower explains:[43]

> Latin Link is an agency serving the Latin Church through placing personnel with partner ministries. This has traditional elements in the care we offer personnel and decision-making structures. It is a networking approach in putting people in touch with ministries and then expecting the key relationship to be at the local level, but also expecting Latin Link to act as an umbrella to broker issues, so not totally a networking approach. We are emergent in that we are prepared to work with new groups and challenge established ways of working but not in the sense of doing new things without reference to national partners.

Finances

In relation to the economic disparities between British missionaries and Latin American missionaries working with Latin Link, Tower says:[44]

> There are disparities between British (and other European) missionaries – depending on the sending churches and other factors such as communication. There are different situations between our Latin missionaries, depending on the economic

---
42. Alan Tower (2008) Questionnaire: question 8.
43. Ibid., question 9.
44. Alan Tower (2008) Questionnaire: question 10.

situation they come from and how well their churches support. Also, depending on the ministry situation in Britain, Ireland or elsewhere in Europe, and if they are married to someone with strong supporting church links. So, differences between Latins and Europeans can also be seen between Europeans and between Latins, but overall, as the economic situations vary there are differences between Latins and Europeans. Latin Link helps under-supported members raise support but does not provide central finance for them so inequalities do exist.

In connection with Tower's perspective, Simon Baker (2008, 4), a former Latin Link doctor missionary in Peru, points out that the issue of dependence or economic independence to avoid paternalism with the church in Peru will not entirely avoid paternalism, but relationships which are genuine; interdependence, working together and love and mutual respect will help.[45]

According to Tower's explanation, it seems that the theory of economic dynamism (Winters 1985, 43) is behind Latin Link mission philosophy in the sense that they use the technological approach to discover what causes innovation and then they apply this technology to develop partnership in mission. This is why they have a department of human resources and it is possible to see this perspective when Tower tries to explain that they are part traditional, part networking and part emergent model. But the fact is that it is a traditional model, with a rigid western structure for sending missionaries with a fixed financial budget before going to the mission field, which has a similar approach to other Western missions in Britain, in promoting their mission policy overseas.

Financial support is developed through a network of friends and local churches in Britain and Ireland, through which they channel economic help under the administration of Latin Link's mission policy. It seems that missionaries are not allowed to go overseas before completing their minimal budget for the mission field. For short-term mission in the summer, the STEP programme cost is £2,150 for seven weeks, a four weeks

---

45. Data provided by Simon Baker (Questionnaire 2008: answer 4).

project £1,850, and STEP Spain is £750.[46] The Stride programme cost has two levels: Classical Stride cost is £1,700–£2,000 and Stride Electives one £1,200–£1,400. This does not include the £450 monthly budget for living expenses[47] A candidate selected by a committe is set up in a specific city or village before going to the field, and a contract must be signed in a reciprocal agreement with the mission policy and core values of Latin Link.[48]

According to the support levels 2008–2009, Latin Link Britain and Ireland offers two financial schemes for long-term members, which are Shared Supporters[49] and Self Funded.[50] The first model has to contribute 15 percent of the missionary budget to cover administration; for self-supporters this contribution is 12.5 percent of the annual missionary budget. Both financial models in the case of Peru are for a single missionary £13,665 and for couples £24,850, adding £4,350 for each child. This policy teaches us the lesson that traditional mission structures are centred in the logistics of the organization, prevention of future financial issues by making a careful budget which includes allowance, accommodation, team (national office), ministry and training, work travel, visas and permits, bank charges, international contribution (to Latin Link office), national insurance, pension,

---

46. Step programmes lasts 4 weeks to six months. See Latin Link, Step Teams (http://www.stepteams.org/apply.php#01)

47. The Stride programme is from six months to two years. All placements are self-funded. To cover the necessary start up costs for going to Latin America, each Strider needs to raise approximately £1,700. In addition, a maximum budget of £450 monthly is necessary to budget for on-going living expenses such as food, accommodation, etc. Additionally, any language training needed is offered at an additional cost. Advice is provided for funding and raising support. See Latin Link, Stride (http://www.latinlink.org/stride.asp).

48. See the policy of contract and termination of service in the International Handbook (2006, 32, 37).

49. For shared support members, the figure allocated for sending costs (to cover pastoral, communications and finance work) is set at 15% of the support level. For shared support, members who raise amounts exceeding their support level, and expenses for the year where this varies, 50 percent of the excess will be shared with colleagues who do not meet the target level. The other 50 percent can be nominated for a ministry account, given to other ministries or colleagues' support, or put towards next year's support (Latin Link, Support Levels 2008–2009).

50. For self funded members 12.5 percent will be charged on support raised (representing pastoral, communications, and a less involved finance work). Out of this the international membership will be paid on your behalf. A minimum overall membership contribution per year of 12.5 percent of the adult single or married support level in your country of service applies as appropriate (Latin Link, Support Levels 2008–2009).

health insurance, leave allowance, leave rent, leave medical, leave study, leave travel, (Britain and Ireland office).[51] In contrast, Stewart McIntosh (interview 30 September 2008), a former 1970s RBMU missionary in Peru, explains that they had a salary for their work and all funds to the mission structure were to be administrated as a general fund and then to be distributed to missionaries in equal part.[52] Under the mission policy described above, for 2008, Latin Link is working in 14 countries: Argentina, Bolivia, Brazil, Chile, Colombia, Costa Rica, Cuba, Ecuador, Guatemala, Nicaragua, Peru, Spain, Switzerland, Britain and Ireland. This data shows that today Europe is included as part of its target.[53]

Stuart Harrison, former Latin Link missionary who worked in Peru, points out that in the 1960s, they had to find 100 supporters before going to the mission field, but they received a salary from the mission where all the money raised came to the mission; they never knew how much they received from supporters because people gave money to the mission, not to the missionary, but this has changed since the 1990s.[54] Regarding the policy of children, Harrison clarifies that the old structure had a policy to cover financial support for four children, and in the case of a fifth child, this had to be covered by the salary of the missionary. Every four years, missionaries had a home leave.[55]

---

51. Ibid., Support Levels 2008–2009.
52. McIntosh worked with RBMU in Peru for nearly 20 years with a missiological contribution in theological education. Steward and wife Juanita McIntosh applied to RBMU in October 1964 at the London office Thurleigh Rd., Balham, and were accepted in January 1965 to sail for Peru in May of that year. The executive secretary of the Mission was Ernest Oliver. The focus of the mission at that time was its motto 'to preach the Gospel in the Regions Beyond' 2 Cor. Their commitment was to the Quechua world. They had one child and therefore could be accepted by RBMU and not by EUSA who only accepted single or engaged people at that time. The Document of the Congo Balolo Mission (Later RBMU Congo) gives the idea of the ethos of RBMU as late as 1964. They resigned from RBMU in 1986 as the mission structure did not provide for the ministry that God had given them within the church in Latin America. (Questionnaire 2008: question 1).
53. See Latin Link Prayer Calendar 2008.
54. Stuart Harrison, interview held in Edinburgh on 6 March 2009b.
55. Stuart Harrison, interview by the author, held in Edinburgh on 5 March 2009a.

A new missiological insight

The new missiological insight of Latin Link seems to be that a new focus will emphasize global involvement through the 'house model'.[56] The fact is that Marcel Durst has given the basis for internationalizing the mission, moving from a regional mission to a global mission. In the case of Latin Link Switzerland, Durst was the sole personnel in 1994, but by 2008 they had an office, six people working with them and had also sent over 60 people for short-term mission and 18 long-term missionaries. Durst favours supporting Latin American missionaries because the church in Europe is well able to finance missionaries. However, the churches and Latin Link should be aware of this role. For him Latin America has the people and the first world the money, thus, the old model (traditional) will be replaced by short-term mission teams, language students and especially the migration movement. "Latin Link is not a grant-making entity but a human resource organization, specializing in people to help them in raising funds rather than pay them."[57]

The 'Latin Link Tunnel'

Here, I want to describe the 'Latin Link Tunnel' by defining the process of how they recruit new members for long-term mission.[58] This includes the process of short-term mission through Step and Stride candidates where they go with a fixed budget to different countries in Latin America. In the last twenty years nearly 3,000 Step and Striders have been mobilized for Latin America (Lesson 2008). The weaknesses of this process stem from the rigidity in accepting candidates according to the budget specified and the strengths are based on the promotion in local churches and their database of more than 10,000 contacts. A negative view is that the number of long-term candidates seems to be small in terms of the investment in mobilizing

---

56. The house model is developed by Ernie Addicott, a former International Director of Interdev and actually serving as the International Director of the European Christian Mission International (ECMI). The house model has three basic levels: exploration (initiatives to find partners), formation (partners agree to work together) and operation (the work to be done in partnership, serving the purpose of the groups they deal with specific issues, seeking a functional partnership). See further Addicott (2005, 60–87).
57. Marcel Durst (2008) Questionnaire: questions 4–5.
58. The title for missionary has been changed to the title of member.

short-term people, but the positive is that they have doubled the long-term missionaries from 64 to 120. The challenge is how to involve more candidates in less time with less operational cost.

The Latin Link Tunnel: statistics of mobilizing people from 1987 to 2008[59]

Step since 1987	Stride since 1987	Step 2008	Spring Step 2008	Stride Step 2008	Long-term Missionaries 2008
2,384	326	104	48	44	120

Mission relations

The fact is that from the beginning Latin Link developed a selective partnership to work with the Iglesia Evangelica Peruana (IEP).[60] This is due to the historic relationship developed with the IEP since EUSA arrived in Peru in 1911. In the past (Kessler 1967, chapter XIII–XIV), mission relationships with the Peruvian church were through the formation of new churches, establishing schools, farmers, bookstores, printing works and the training of national leadership. However, after the 1990s Latin Link seems to have changed this policy by working also with the Christian and Missionary Alliance and helping Peruvian initiatives instead of setting for them a mission agenda.[61] Reciprocal relationship has grown in that Latin Link missionaries are working in a more horizontal, more bottom-up relationship with the Peruvian church, which was not the case in the past from the 1910s to 1980s, in the phase of paternalism, a time lacking in reciprocal mission policy with national leadership and the traditional distribution of territories by the mission societies. Thus, the 1980s to the 1990s can be

---

59. Data provided by Charlotte Barker (11 September 2008a).
60. Kessler describes in detail the relationship at the beginning of EUSA in Peru. See Kessler (1967, 167, 173–184).
61. Latin Link has a relationship with the Christian and Missionary Alliance of Peru with missionaries working in strategic projects and by helping Peruvian missionaries from the CMA to come to Britain through Latin Partners, a branch of Latin Link trying to practise reciprocal contextual collaboration with Latin missionaries.

seen as the transition phase of power sharing with the Peruvian leadership.[62] It appears that after the 1990s Latin Link and the Peruvian church started to practise a reciprocal contextual collaboration with a more participative leadership in decision making for allocating missionaries.[63] This phenomenon was seen with different mission societies in Peru and elsewhere, showing a concern to practise a reciprocal freedom and the process of interdependence mission theology, but it was at the level of seminal thinking.[64] In this sense, Latin Link must be open to other Peruvian initiatives apart from the IEP and the CMA if they want to remain an interdenominational mission.

Conclusion with an evaluation of positive and negative tensions

It seems to me that one of the new and recent strengths of Latin Link after the 1990s rests on pre-field decision making between churches in Latin America and Latin Link missionaries. Thus, in referring to the control of power between partners Baker (2008, 15) clarifies that Latin American churches have the power to say no to Latin Link if they do not want someone to come. Latin Link does not have the power to require a missionary to work in a particular situation. Even in the late 1990s there was considerable dialogue. Churches in Peru often asked for a missionary to do this or that. If Latin Link agreed to the request they would put it in the list of needs for the country, but were always dependent on who applied; in that sense a wants list, whether from a church or mission team, is very limited.[65]

Latin Link is undoubtedly one of the Western British missions that have made an impact in Latin America. However, it seems that an appropriate partnership paradigm between the emerging Latin American evangelical

---

62. EUSA missionaries at that time started to reduce their hierarchical leadership within the IEP church.
63. Latin Link missionaries come to help, not to lead the Peruvian church.
64. Butler, at the WEF Missions Commission in Manila 1992, presented 'Kingdom Partnership in the 90s: Is there a New Way Forward?', a paper that dealt with the changing time of mission. See Taylor (1994, 9–30).
65. For Baker (Questionnaire 2008, 15) Latin Link can be seen as the agency having a relationship with Latin American denominations. Many UK churches would see things very differently and rather look at local church relationships with local churches.

mission and the Western church is still lacking. In relation to this assumption, John Chapman's opinion is that this is due to the fact that both partners need humility and he suggests that pride and imperialism is to the fore both in the Western and in the Latin church.[66] He gives the advice that we need to manifest God's grace together and that there also needs to be an understanding of different histories in the two continents that affects how both see decision making and structural organization. Therefore, one of the weaknesses in Latin Link is that an image of unconscious pride and imperialistic expansion could negatively be affecting all kinds of relationships with the Latin church. This makes for a negative tension to develop a healthy reciprocal contextual collaboration, which is possible both for the Western and the Latin American church. In addition to this, humility is essential in any reciprocal contextual collaboration, because this is a sign to reveal God's grace in partnering with others from a different culture, language, theology, social and political and economic context, which brings consequences when partners are part of decision making within structural organizations like Latin Link.

A critical aspect seems to me that with a budget of £24, 850 for a couple of Latin Link missionaries, it will be nearly impossible for the Latin American missionaries to compete with this budget due to the fact of political, economic and social situation of church members that live on a minimum salary of $250 monthly (£166) or $3,000 annually, compared to £10,400 UK basic salary, and five and a half times more than the average Peruvian income. This economic reality shows one reason why I am suggesting the possibilities of new models of partnership to make new missiological contributions with the new emergent Latin American movement, especially for sending missionaries from the South to the Northern hemisphere. In this way, theology in context is crucial for the new understanding of reciprocal contextual collaboration in mission for Latin Link if they want to increase the number of long-term members and Step and Stride short-term missions. Also their mission policy must become more flexible and contextual. As Hiebert (1999, 100) concludes: "there is room for spiritual maturation and growth in our theologies", which implies a constant

---

66. John Chapman (2008) Questionnaire: questions 1–2.

testing of our theologies and changing to new understandings according to the Scripture. In fact, one of Latin Link's strengths appears to be that they do not fear to try a new mission policy to meet the demand of the twenty-first century. Other strengths are well-structured written material for promotion, good communication and accountability to the government, and between members and donors. According to Chapman, they have very few casualties with missionaries; this is attributable to the careful process for receiving and training candidates for cross-cultural mission.

In assessing if this kind of partnership has been dependent on the power of God or on the power of money, Latin Link states that they recognize God's sovereignty and that their goal is to glorify God.[67] However, internal factors like the affluence of church members to support different projects and external factors like the economic stability of Britain have helped the projects Latin Link have developed to be viable. It is not just prayer and confidence in God's power but also the political, social and economic context that has helped this mission to extend their influence in fourteen countries of Latin America.

My final analysis shows that the process of Latin Link has now set the tone for an alternative model, in trying to become a 'traditional mission network' seeking to reflect the new missiological interpretation to confront the challenges of global missiology. Latin Link, as an oriented mission to Latin America, appears to be fighting to invalidate the traditional model of territorial distribution and mission interpreted as only going to distant lands by expanding its influence especially in Switzerland, Germany, Spain and Portugal. According to this new mission atmosphere, it seems that Latin Link will become a clear 'traditional mission network' model, which means that they will remain a traditional model, but merging with principles of the networking and the emergent models. Therefore, Latin Link needs to reconsider the reality of the non-formal new immigrant missionary forces, the recent infiltration to Western territories and the new *perestroika* mission partnership we mentioned in our previous chapter.

---

67. International Handbook (2006, 18).

COMIBAM case study

Historical origins

The Iberoamerican Missionary Cooperation (COMIBAM) comes to light as a result of a missiological dialogue started in 1984 in Mexico (Nuñez and Taylor 1989, 168,[68] see also What is COMIBAM?,[69] Bertuzzi 2006, 91–92) with the object of being a mission tool for the Latin American church to fulfil the *missio Dei*. Some of the key leaders in this process were Jonathan Dos Santos, Luis Bush, Marcelino Ortiz, Galo Vasquez, Rudy Girón, Federico Bertuzzi, Edison Queiros, Roberto Hatch, and Israel Ortiz.[70] COMIBAM has organized three major congresses: São Paulo 1987 with 3,185 delegates, Acapulco 1997 with 2,200 delegates, and Granada 2006 with 1,958 delegates.[71] Some other key leaders supporting these congresses have been Alex Araujo, Carlos Calderon, Emilio A. Nuñez, Guillermo Taylor, Jonathan Lewis (COMIBAM 87), and for Acapulco 97 and Granada 2006, David Ruiz, Carlos Scott, and Jesus Londoño.[72] It seems that this missionary movement emerges to emphasize transcultural mission and church planting, impacting Latin American countries.[73]

COMIBAM's brief history describes a big change in the Latin American mission between the 1900s and the 1980s.[74] In consequence, the roots

---

68. Taylor mentions that he was a member of the continental COMIBAM committee, because he was executive secretary of the World Evangelical Alliance. At COMIBAM first Congress, he was one of the plenary speakers and gave three seminars on mission (See notes on chapter 4, Spiritual Dimensions of Latin America (Nuñez and Taylor (1989, 181)).

69. COMIBAM Internacional (http://www.comibam.org/queescomi.htm).

70. Federico Bertuzzi, interview in Pattaya, Thailand (3 November 2008). See also the brief history of COMIBAM Primer Congreso Misionero Iberoamericano: Luz para las Naciones, São Paulo, Brazil 23–28 November (1987).

71. David Ruiz interview in Pattaya, Thailand on 1 November 2008. For the statistics of Granada 2006, see COMIBAM, General Report of the III Iberoamerican Mission Congress (13–17 November, 2006 Granada, Spain).

72. COMIBAM Primer Congreso Misionero Iberoamericano: Luz para las Naciones, São Paulo, Brazil 23–28 November 1987. Information for COMIBAM 97 and COMIBAM 2006 emerges from data registered in my participation in those congresses.

73. See also Nuñez and Taylor (1989, 45).

74. COMIBAM's brief history illustrates how since the 1980s this missionary spirit grew, especially with local congregations like Nazaret church in El Salvador, Verbo, Elim y Centro Biblico el Camino in Guatemala, Baptist Church of Santo Andre (São Paulo,

of COMIBAM go back to June 1983, when the Brazilian, Jonathan Dos Santos,[75] founder of the Brazilian Antioquia Mission before the First Brazilian Congress of Evangelization in Belo Horizonte, suggested celebrating a continental Latin American mission congress to Luis Bush who as pastor of the 'Iglesia Nazareth' organized 'MISION 84' that was held in El Salvador, one of the events that confirmed the growing interest in mission by the Latin American Protestant church.[76] Bush was eager for missions; he explains that there were eleven lay leaders with him from the church he pastored in El Salvador, called Iglesia Nazaret, who went to a mission conference at SETECA in late 1970's. They then as local church had a 'Mission 80' inviting other churches. AMEN in Peru came to the gathering of 2,000 leaders from eleven countries for 'Mission 80' that was held at Nazareth church.[77]

On the other side, Theodore Williams,[78] former executive secretary from the Missions Commission of the World Evangelical Alliance, Allen

---

Brazil); denominations like Assemblies of God of Brazil, and Methodists for Chile; theological seminars like SETECA. Compare the contribution of some mission societies like Misión Antioquia from Brazil, AMEE (Ecuador), AME (Guatemala), MIES (El Salvador), Junta de Misiones Mundiales (Brazil), Misiones Mundiales (Argentina), the Federación de agencias misioneras-FEDEMEC (Costa Rica), etc,. But movements like AMEN (Peru), CONELA, CLADE I, II, II and IV are not considered. (See COMIBAM Primer Congreso Misionero Iberoamericano: Luz para las Naciones, São Paulo, Brazil 23–28 November 1987.)

75. An American missionary, Barbara Burns, supported Dos Santos in promoting mission in Brazil before the beginnings of COMIBAM. She points out that Dos Santos, Queiros and Desio Acevedo were key leaders of the Brazilian missionary movement (Personal interview in Pattaya, Thailand 4 November 2008). In his article 'The Latin American Missionary Movement: A New Paradigm in Missions', Rudy Giron confirms that the original process began in 1983. See (http://www.ad2000.org/celebrate/giron.htm).

76. 'MISION 84' in El Salvador had 1,000 delegates (Luis Bush, email sent to the author on 25 November 2009). See further 'A Brief History of COMIBAM in Primer Congreso Iberoamericano', São Paulo, 23–28 November 1987. Also see Ekstrom 'El Espiritu de COMIBAM' (http://www.comibam.org/ponencias/lima/ponencia2.htm).

77. The first night there was an 'apagon' (power-cut). It was during the time of violence in El Salvador (Luis Bush, email sent to the author on 25 November 2009 at 23:44).

78. The Missions Commission was launched in Korea, 1975, under a Korean woman missiologist Chun Chae Ok as its first Executive Secretary and later the Indian, Theodore Williams. As Taylor points out, the MC emerged as a player in the global mission scene with its early focus on 'Two-Thirds World emerging missions'. See WEA, Taylor (http://www.worldevangelicals.org/wea/history.htm). This early focus of the WEA-MC seems to me why Williams was pivotal in supporting COMIBAM's initiative. My finding indicates that the WEA-MC seems to claim that COMIBAM becomes the 'success' story of their

Finley, Fred Simmons, All Lutz from Cristianos Nacionales (CNEC), Larry Keyes and Larry Pate from SEPAL,[79] also had the same aim.[80] Thus, during the Lausanne Committee in Stuttgart, Germany, in June 1984, members of the Latin American regional group of Lausanne were conscious of a continental Congress. Therefore the same year, Marcelino Ortiz and Galo Vasquez, president and secretary, members of the Confraternidad Evangelica Latinoamericana (CONELA[81]), called for a meeting December 1984 in Mexico to reflect on and analyse the possibilities of a Latin American Congress.[82] Representatives of ten Latin American Christian organizations and some internationals were present and all of them agreed to co-participate in the first Iberoamerican Mission Congress, including Spanish and Portuguese speaking people of Europe. Therefore, an organizing committee was appointed with the target of involving churches and

---

effort as MC leadership was directly involved in the organization. See Lewis, 'Regional and National Mission Structures', SA06: WEA Mission Commission, Global Issues Summit, 18–24 June 2006, Goudini Spa, South Africa (http://www.worldevangelicals.org/commissions/mc/mc_ southafrica /resources /Lewis %20-%20Mission%20structures.pdf). Martin Lee agrees that the very few staff of WEA-MC did invest more time in building links with COMIBAM. However, he thinks that COMIBAM developed itself with little external input. None of the other mission networks, even in Europe or North America, have strong regional networks, so Latin America is different from the rest of the world here (personal dialogue by email with Martin Lee, Global Connections Director in the UK on 19 November 2008).

79. SEPAL means Servicio Evangelizador para America Latina (Evangelistic Service for Latin America).

80. According to Jonathan Lewis, it is stated that WEA-MC tried to generate corresponding 'replicable' structures in each region and nation. The goal was to see organized, recognizable 'Regional Missions Movement'; the strategy was to work through REGIONAL missions movements. Therefore, COMIBAM is seen by the western approach, as "the MC 'success' story" due to the fact that from the beginning WEA-MC through Theodore Williams and team supported COMIBAM. See Lewis 2006 Regional and National Mission Structures, SA06: WEA Mission Commission, Global Issues Summit, 18–24 June, Goudini Spa, South Africa, (http://www.worldevangelicals.org/commissions/mc/mc_southafrica/resources/ Lewis%20% 20Mission%20structures.pdf).

81. The conservative movement Latin American Evangelical Fellowship–Confraternidad Evangelica Latinoamericana (CONELA), emerged in 1982 under the influence of Luis Palau as a reaction against the ecumenical Latin American Council of Churches (CLAI). See Stoll (1990, 134–135, 174–175).

82. See further Nuñez and Taylor (1989, 168). Marcelino Ortiz was an associate of Luis Palau and President of CONELA (Stoll 1990, 174). Jesus Londoño mentions that CLADE I and CONELA played a role in the context of missionary awareness in Latin America (Email sent to the author 31 October 2008).

leadership of Latin American countries.[83] The policy for funding was that two-thirds part of the budget had to be the responsibility of COMIBAM and other finances were received from the World Evangelical Fellowship and Cristianos Nacionales. National consultations were held in each country with the aim of providing experiences, data and models of mission. In 1985 a mission Consultation in São Paulo, Brazil, was held to promote 'COMIBAM 87'.[84] In 1986,[85] at the First Iberoamerican Theological Consultation in Guatemala, it was the conclusion that COMIBAM should become not just an event, but a process of a Latin American missionary movement namely the first Iberoamerican Missionary Congress, later changed to Iberoamerican Missionary Cooperation.[86] Therefore, the word 'cooperation' has been a key element in promoting the mission philosophy of this mission network. My finding is that that the Brazilian, Dos Santos, could be defined as the seminal thinker of COMIBAM, Bush as the ideologist and Queiros as the practitioner and promoter at the beginning of the movement. For Bush, COMIBAM started when it became clear that God was calling his people in Latin America into global missions.[87] The year 1984 seems crucial in bringing about the emergence of a structured Latin American missionary network rooted in a decision made by key leaders of the evangelical Latin American arena at that time. A second finding is that the First Brazilian Congress of Evangelization in Belo Horizonte 1983, 'MISION 84' and 'CONELA 84' are the seminal work to promote what was later called COMIBAM.

---

83. Bertuzzi explains that the first COMIBAM committee was formed by Luis Busch, Emilio A. Nuñez, Israel Ortiz, Roberto Hatch, Edisson Queiros, Jonathan Dos Santos and Federico Bertuzzi. This committee was elected for the period 1985 to 1989 (interview of Federico Bertuzzi by the author in Pattaya, Thailand on 3 November 2008). Although this network includes in its vision Spain and Portugal the main focus is on Latin American mission enterprise.
84. History of COMIBAM, Primer Congreso Misionero Iberoamericano, São Paulo 1987. See also Bertil Ekstrom (http://www.comibam.org/ponencias/lima/ponencia2.htm).
85. History of COMIBAM, Primer Congreso Misionero Iberoamericano, São Paulo 1987.
86. Bertil Eckstron clarifies that it started as a congress and developed to co-operation after the event in São Paulo (data provided by email on 21 October 2008). See also Bertuzzi (2006, 92).
87. Luis Bush (information by email sent to author on 25 November 2009).

Preceding COMIBAM 1987 (Busch and Lutz 1990, 119), the research conducted by the Global Mapping Project located at the Center for World Missions (USCCWM) in Pasadena analyzed the state of the church in Latin America, and each country had its own COMIBAM committee to obtain statistical data. It was then processed to produce the first 'Atlas of COMIBAM'[88] and wider mission literature produced with the support of American organizations as never seen before in Latin America, challenging the Latin church to know their own reality and make their mission strategy.[89] The fact that USCWM which helped COMIBAM from the beginning gave the origin of what I call the COMIBAM's black legend, which is related to the managerial influence they received at the beginning of its process, taking for granted the 'unreached people' missiology.[90] By contrast, Taylor's opinion is that "it was not a Ralph Winter importation to Latin America".[91] However, Davies will later confirm my view, which supports the claim that COMIBAM is an indigenous Latin American initiative

---

88. COMIBAM has produced a new missionary atlas for Granada 2006 'Planisferio Misionero' with statistics of principal religions, principal languages, Amerindian groups, missionary growth of the South, mission field of the Iberoamerican missionaries and less concentrated evangelized people. In the same line the Cape Town 2010 Congress has produced a missionary map 'The Third Lausanne Congress on World Evangelization' emphasizing a projection of evangelicals by continent 1960–2010, and has distributed the world in twelve regions: East Asia, South Asia, Southeast Asia, Caribbean, EPSA (English, Portuguese and Spanish-speaking Africa), Eurasia, Europe, Francophone Africa, Latin America, MENA (Middle East and North Africa), North America, South Pacific. It is interesting that both maps have a different missiological contribution but the same evangelical target of accomplishing the great commission, a strong characteristic in evangelicalism. See maps of both congresses.

89. Publishing literature was under the leadership of Emilio A. Nuñez, Carlos Calderon and Alex Araujo. Material like Manuel de Misiones para la Iglesia Local (Eugenio Campos), Manual para el establecimiento de iglesias (Jorge Patterson), Manual Clase (Guillermos Taylor), Reto Iberoamerican, etc., was some of the material distributed for COMIBAM 1987. See further Primer Congreso Misionero Iberoamericano, São Paulo 1987. It is worth saying that PROMIES in Peru produced between 1986–1989 the first statistical data of evangelical churches in Lima with donations from Tearfund UK; Tito Paredes and Steward McIntosh coordinated the effort (telephonic dialogue with McIntosh 27 November 2008).

90. See Escobar 'Managerial Missiology' in the *Dictionary of Mission Theology* (2007, 216–218).

91. William Taylor is the Global Ambassador of the WEA and the Mission Commission; dialogue by email from London (received on 14 October 2008).

but with a mission strategy borrowed in Winter's missiological proposal.[92] Speakers of COMIBAM 1987 were 30 percent Americans, 47 percent Latin Americans and 13 percent from the rest of the world.[93] Also three key leaders empowered the organization: Edison Queiros, Rudy Girón and Federico Bertuzzi who was treasurer from 1985 to 1989.[94]

COMIBAM was formally organized after São Paulo 1987 and presidents have been appointed as follows: Luis Bush[95] (*Argentinean*) 1985 to 1989 (the congress was in 1987 and COMIBAM as a movement started after that, but Bush was the chairman of the conference board); Rudy Girón (*Guatemalan*) 1989 to 1997; Bertil Ekstrom (*Brazilian*) 1997 to 2000; David Ruiz (*Guatemalan*) 2000 to 2006; and Carlos Scott (*Argentinean*), elected president in 2006 before the COMIBAM third congress in Granada (italics mine).[96]

The mission context

Latin America defined by Reid as 'The Forgotten Continent' or by Stoll as 'Is Latin American Turning Protestant?' becomes the political, economic, social, cultural and religious context where COMIBAM develops its mission activity.[97] Works like *Religion and Political Conflict in Latin*

---

92. The reason is that Winter (Stoll 1990, 83–97) left Fuller in 1976 to initiate the USCWM to target the new emergent movement he probably visualized ten years before COMIBAM started, equally as other emergent movements from Asia and Africa, which started to appear in the 1980s. Winter tried to promote at least 300 cross-cultural missionaries at the beginning and then to impact mission agencies from the South through his new movement. For example he visited Peru in 1980 to catched the attention of AMEN, a Peruvian indigenous mission society founded by my father. Later, in 1989, Winter seems to support the establishment of the Third-World Missions Association of mission agencies. (http://www.missionfrontiers.org/1989/0607/jj899.htm).
93. COMIBAM, Primer Congreso Misionero Iberoamericano, São Paulo 1987. (See description of speakers).
94. Federico Bertuzzi, interview in Pattaya, Thailand, 3 November 2008.
95. Bush mentions that this happened through the steering committee in relation to the COMIBAM 87 event (email sent to the author on 25 November 2009).
96. Bertil Ekstrom, former President of COMIBAM (data provided by email on 19 October 2008). Bush who served as senior pastor at the Iglesia Nazaret in El Salvador, coined the term '10/40 window' and served as the international director of the 'AD2000 & Beyond Movement: A Church for Every People and the Gospel for Every Person by AD2000' (See Bush 1999, http://www.ad2000.org/staff/luis.htm).
97. 'The Forgotten Continent' describes the political, social and economic situation of Latin America from the development of a new liberal economy. See Reid (2007). While

America (Levine 1986), and recent research by the Brazilian, Paul Freston, *Evangelical Christianity and Democracy in Latin America* (Freston 2008), identify weaknesses and strengths of the Latin American constituency.[98]

In my understanding, COMIBAM emerges under the context of Latin American internal factors of the 1980s, characterized by: political violence (Shining Path, Sandinistas, Zapatistas, etc.), increasing poverty, military conflicts (i.e. the Malvinas conflict 1982, Sandinistas' civil war in Nicaragua 1979 – Reid 2007, 4, 23, 25, 101, 123, 204), participation of evangelicals in politics (Freston 2008), agrarian reform issues, the Marxist option, diluted economy, unemployment, and Pentecostal growth. Sociologically, the colonial period structured the social classes in Latin America with upper class, mestizos, indians and blacks (Nuñez and Taylor 1989, 87), but in the twentieth century a new upper- and upper-middle class emerged with power in politics, commerce and industrial activities and from the lower classes emerged an upper-lower to lower-middle class of labour workers, many as members of industry and agriculture, and a small white middle class of business, government workers and professionals.

It is reported that in 1900 there were 50,000 evangelicals in Latin America but 'The Panama Congress' reported for 1916 a growth to 126,000 and the Montevideo Congress 1925 reported 252,000 (Nuñez and Taylor, 153–154). In contrast to these figures, in 2005 the rapid numerical growth is estimated to be 80 million evangelicals where second to fourth evangelical generation belong to traditional denominations, but the majority belong to the Pentecostal and charismatic movement mentioned in the first chapter. The fact is that Pentecostal churches practise massification (mega-churches) and atomization (micro-churches), components of the same

---

Reid emphasizes the new political liberal system of some countries in Latin America, Stoll analyses the growth of the evangelical movement from a sociological perspective suggesting the evangelical growth as a challenge for reformation in Latin American politics. See also *Evangelicals and Politics in Asia, Africa and Latin America* (Freston 2001).

98. Daniel H. Levine and contributors from a Catholic perspective bring insights of the influence of religion in politics, especially what Levine (1986, 6) calls popular religion, and poverty seen as the product of 'structural inequalities' that can be changed. Freston tries to address the issues of evangelical growth in politics and how this affects the hegemony of Catholic monopoly through case studies of five countries: Brazil, Peru, Mexico, Guatemala and Nicaragua. He assumes that "the region is becoming pluralist rather than Protestant" (2008, 17). For the case of Peru see Freston (2001, 237–229).

organism (Campos 2008; Freston 2001, 293–302; 2008, 11–15), with strong leadership – mainly hierarchical.[99] In addition, COMIBAM reveals aspects of the impact of Lausanne 1974, The Latin American Theological Fraternity, CONELA, OC ministries through SEPAL, etc. (Stoll 1990, 73, 124, 174).

In the case of Peru, which is our focus, COMIBAM influences the national network CONAMI that has two theological and missiological tendencies under the influence of the CONEP, and UNICEP plus FIPAC. The second, a similar institution to CONEP, belongs to the new charismatic movement which has gathered independent churches since 2003, and FIPAC is the Pentecostal pastors' fraternity. The first unifies the traditional institutions, which mainly represent old denominations, national ministries and mission organizations.[100] This fragmentation in the Peruvian church seems to emerge as a result of inadequate participation of evangelicals in the political arena to support Fujimori's election after the 1990s (Lopez in Freston 2008, 135, 139–145), damaging the roots of Peruvian Protestantism, which has had a degree of unity (Freston 2001, 238). Political democratic waves arrived in Peru in 1978 followed by economic growth from the 1990s as in Mexico, Central America, Chile and Brazil (Reid 2007, 120, 137–138).

---

99. Atomization implies that each small church has to grow numerically and each megachurch practises a massive social attitude with an individualistic view and a pyramidal and vertical leadership. See further Campos' article 'Renovacion del Liderazgo y Hermeneutica del Espiritu', *Cyberjournal for Pentecostal-Charismatic Research* (http://pctii.org/cyberj/cyberj13/bernado.html).

100. The Concilio Nacional Evangelico del Peru (CONEP), started in 1940, and the Union Nacional de Iglesias Cristianas del Peru (UNICEP) was founded 22 April 2003 after a split with CONEP. The FIPAC is a charismatic association of pastors initiated in the 1990s and UNICEP works under the leadership of Humberto Lay and Robert Barriger (Lopez in Freston 2008, 141, 159). See also World Council of Churches (http://www.oikoumene.org/en/member-churches/regions/latin-america/peru/conep.html). CONEP represents the evangelical church before the state and Peruvian society (http://www.concilionacionalevangelico.org/index.php?option=com_content&task=view&id=12&Itemid=27). For FIPAC see (http://www.unicep.org.pe/historia.php). For further study on CONEP see Lopez (unpublished thesis 1997) *The Evangelical Church and Human Rights in Peru: A Critical Evaluation of the Theology of Mission of the National Evangelical Council of Peru from 1980–1992, with Special Reference to its Understanding and Practice of Human Rights*. See also Freston (2001, 238).

Analysis of mission development

Type of mission structure

COMIBAM is a network with an emphasis on mobilizing Latin American people in mission.[101] Therefore, the distribution of power and reciprocal freedom rests on the national movements, which have a right to decision making as autonomous bodies but are linked to the mission spirit of COMIBAM. Financial autonomy avoids dependence and each national movement has its own budget. But how does COMIBAM share the control of power and decision making? Jesus Londoño, former executive Director, clarifies that COMIBAM has designed a government process which includes the eight established regions and the twenty-five national missionary movements. The mission board is formed by eight directors, one for each region; it has the role of presenting requests and needs of national missionary movements with the purpose that decision making and programmes of COMIBAM can focus on supplying their needs. Moreover, the International Assembly includes four members of every country, the national missionary movement coordinator, and coordinator of the three networks that are church and pastors, mission agencies and training centers. This implies that each representative brings the voice of the national movement to the assembly.[102]

---

101. Londoño states that COMIBAM's mission strategy is based on the network concept as a tool to propagate, construct and develop a missionary vision in Iberoamerica. COMIBAM is not an agency because they do not send missionaries directly but it empowers those actors, agencies and training centres that in the mission process churches take its role too. (Data provided by Jesus Londoño to the author from Granada on 31 October 2008).

102. Jesus Londoño Questionnaire answered to the author from Granada Spain (31 October 2008).

Case Studies of Three Models of Partnership   253

The operational mission structure of COMIBAM is organized into three departments,[103] three networks[104] and five programmes.[105] Twenty-five national missionary movements (from Latin America, the Caribbean, Canada, USA, Spain and Portugal) develop a reciprocal network with five targets:[106] strengthening of national missionary movements, focus on unreached people, Iberoamerican missiology, leadership development, and cooperation and global connections. The mission theology of COMIBAM sees the church as a missionary force, seeking to transform the Iberoamerican church as capable of extending the gospel to every nation.[107] Here, I see a similar strategy to Latin Link, in the sense that COMIBAM seems to use the house model approach, trying to involve national movements in making decisions and sharing the control of power.[108] COMIBAM's organization has a mission board, a president, an executive director and eight

---

103. Departments: (1) Department of Information and Research – maintains the dynamic flow of information on the state of world mission between those who produce it and the missionary movement in Latin America; (2) Development Department – assists with the search for means of financial support so that COMIBAM International can fulfil its mission; and (3) Publications Department – promotes and coordinates the production of written and audiovisual materials aimed at spreading the missionary vision.

104. COMIBAM's Networks: (1) *Training Centre Network* – facilitates the ongoing task of ensuring quality missionary training through forums and consultation between professors and training centres. (2) *Sending Structures Network* – builds a network of Latin American sending agencies and structures, which will permit the exchange of experience and information in order to increase their efficiency. And (3) *Churches and Pastors Network* – provides the necessary tools for the development of a missionary vision among pastors and leaders and assists with the laying down of a strategy for the mobilization of national churches.

105. Programmes include: (1) Intercession Programme – builds up a prayer network for the spiritual support of Latin American missionaries and their work on the mission field. (2) Reach One Ethnic Group Programme – this programme (AUE) provides data for the national church and national committees so that they can become mobilized to send missionaries and to reach unreached people groups. (3) Comprehensive Care for Missionaries Programme – establishes a team whose aim is to develop programmes, materials and contacts which promote efficient pastoral care for Latin American missionaries. (4) Strategic Alliances and Missionary Cooperation Programme – provides training and consultancy for the development, formation and operation of strategic alliances at the local level and facilitates their integration into existing ones. (5) Linguistic Training Programme.

106. See Directorio de COMIBAM (http://www.comibam.org/equipo.htm).

107. COMIBAM Internacional: Que es COMIBAM?. See Estructura operacional de COMIBAM (http://www.comibam.org/queescomi.htm).

108. It seems that COMIBAM structure is a circular model that implies decentralized control of power (different from the hierarchical model).

regions, which are as follows:[109] Hispanics of North America, Mexico, Central America, Andean countries, South Cone,[110] Brazil, Caribbean, and Iberian Peninsula.[111]

The Guatemalan, David Ruiz (2003, 52–53), states that networks can be developed through a relational philosophy of networks that engage a world which moves to a new stage of management from a hierarchical to an informational era through respectful relationships.[112] I agree with Ruiz when he states that this model provides strong respectful relationships between national, regional or functional networks, with four characteristics of strategic alliances to facilitate a healthy relationship as follows: (1) discussion not related primarily to money but to objectives and outcomes, (2) the emerging leadership of the South comes to the table with an open mind and explores new ways of cooperation, (3) Third World churches provide a high level of enthusiasm and consciousness of their role in global evangelism, and (4) values and expectations of relationships between regions of the Two-Thirds World. This characteristic seems to be part of COMIBAM's mission philosophy.

---

109. Countries are organized as follows: USA (COMHINA), Canada (unknown), Mexico (COMIMEX), Belize (unknown), Guatemala (CONEM), El Salvador (MIES), Honduras (FEMEH), Nicaragua (MMTN), Costa Rica (FEDEMEC), Panama (unknown), Venezuela (CNM), Colombia (CCMM), Ecuador (COMEC), Peru (CONAMI), Bolivia (unknown), Argentina (Red de Misiones Mundiales), Uruguay (COMIBAM Uruguay), Paraguay (CONAMI), Chile (COMIBAM Chile), Brazil (COMIBAM Brazil), Cuba (COMIBAM Cuba), Dominican Republic (COMIDOM), Puerto Rico (RECOMI), Spain (COMIES), Portugal (Aliança Evangélica Portuguesa). See Directorio de COMIBAM (http://www.comibam.org/equipo.htm) and Bertuzzi (2006:109).

110. South Cone includes: Chile, Paraguay, Argentina and Uruguay. The first meeting of COMIBAM South Cone was held in Argentina on 13 February 2007. See COMIBAM Cono Sur (http://comibamconosur.blogspot.com/).

111. Ibid. See Como se forma COMIBAM?.

112. Ruiz is former COMIBAM president, who provides insights of the Two-Thirds World missiology in relation to the new initiative of the WEA to promote mission networks.

The Network Structure of COMIBAM[113]

International Assembly
President, Executive Director, directors of the eight regions, national coordinators, and networks coordinators of each country
Mission Board
President, Executive Director, directors of the eight regions
Executive Committee
Executive Director, the head of departments, networks and programmes

Department	Networks	Programmes
Department of Information and Research	Training Centre Network	Intercession Programme
Development Department	Sending Structures	Reach One Ethnic Group Programme
Publications Department	Churches and Pastors Network[114]	Comprehensive Care for Missionaries Programme
		Strategic Alliances and Missionary Cooperation Programme
		Linguistic Training Programme

Regions							
Hispanics of North America	Mexico	Central America	Andean Countries	South Cone	Brazil	Caribbean	Iberian Peninsula
USA Canada	Mexico	Belize Guatemala El Salvador Honduras Nicaragua Costa Rica Panama	Venezuela Colombia Ecuador Peru Bolivia	Argentina Uruguay Paraguay Chile	Brazil	Cuba Dominican Republic Puerto Rico	Spain Portugal

---

113. COMIBAM Internacional Comite Ejecutivo, http://www.comibam.org/equipo.htm (Online, accessed on 22 October 2008 at 20:45).

114. COMIBAM has a clear written policy to mobilize pastors and local churches. See (http://www.comibam.org/docs/rmip_plan.pdf).

Main characteristics

COMIBAM defines the principal reason of its existence as being to glorify God by strengthening the national missionary movements through provision of necessary service in order to help the local church accomplish the great commission.[115] In this sense, I agree that COMIBAM has the following characteristics: this movement empowered by the Spirit of God is not a human invention, COMIBAM has grown by the influence of the self-sacrifice of people in mission,[116] and intentional relationships with key leaders have been one of the pivotal elements of its growth. Therefore, I define COMIBAM as one of the Spirit's movement in Latin America; it is a network with a spontaneous reciprocal contextual collaboration, which in Jesus Londoño's view has three major strengths to accomplish the mission: vision, relational capital and high leverage.[117]

More precisely, COMIBAM's mission statement declares its vision is to see the Iberoamerican church as a missionary force, and its mission is to help the Iberoamerican church to be transformed into a missionary people capable of proclaiming the gospel to every nation.[118] In answering, what is COMIBAM?, Londoño points out that COMIBAM is a movement in its philosophical definition. Its mission strategy is based on the network concept which has external difficulties like: the great distance and cultural differences between countries (Iberomaerica is not an homogeneous territory), denominationalism or institutionalism are barriers, a heavy agenda

---

115. Ibid. See Como se forma COMIBAM.

116. Most of the missionaries involved in COMIBAM have risked their lives, families and children by going into mission with no appropriate budget, and no spiritual support of local pastors. In consequence, this mission dichotomy between local churches and missionaries seems to generate a diluted effort that hinders the growing of more Latin American candidates.

117. The three major strengths to accomplish COMIBAM's mission are: (1) Vision. God-breathed, clear, concise and passionately challenging, striving to see the Iberoamerican church as a missionary sending force. (2) Relational capital. COMIBAM is built on a solid base of profound relationships with 400+ churches, agencies, training centres and leaders in the continent. And (3) High leverage. Through these relationships God has allowed their influence, knowledge, experience and resources to be used towards its vision and mission, via networks and partnerships facilitated. (Data provided by Jesus Londoño to the author from Granada, Spain on 31 October 2008).

118. COMIBAM Internacional: Que es COMIBAM? (http://www.comibam.org/queescomi.htm).

that does not allow the fulfilment of the great commission, a lack of resources to promote more encounters and personal relationships (relationship is a core non-negotiable value in Iberoamerica), and doctrinal differences which do not allow cooperation.[119] Within the influence of these external factors COMIBAM empowers its vision through the national missionary movements which have three networks: (1) church and pastors' network, which serves to include all local churches with a missionary plan to support missionaries and to hold missionary conferences; (2) centres of missionary training, which help people to obtain missionary training in cross-cultural mission; and (3) the sending structures' network, which includes denominational and interdenominational mission agencies. Thus, they target finding resources for the 'unreached people'.[120] In analyzing COMIBAM's reciprocal contextual collaboration, Girón states that COMIBAM struggled towards the western dilemma between modalities and sodalities as the sender of missionaries. The conclusion was to promote cooperation between missionaries, local churches, mission agencies and international cooperation, a missiological emphasis of Scott and Londoño.

Now, I outline five phases of COMIBAM's development:

First phase: Dialogue and promotion (1983–1989) under Luis Bush's leadership. A phase of becoming a missionary force uniting missionary efforts – the local church was defined as the one who sends missionaries and the mission agency as the specialized ministry of sending missionaries. In attending COMIBAM 87, I noticed three key characteristics.[121] Latin American enthusiasm, the emergence of a missionary consciousness, and the influence of pragmatic missiology to develop as soon as possible mission structures for sending more missionaries. The impact of this congress has been raising the consciousness of the Latin American church to become a sending church instead of just a receiving church. One of the strengths of this congress was to mobilize 3,000 key leaders of the Latin American church and observers from the rest of the world. A weakness

---

119. Jesus Londoño, Questionnaire answered to the author (31 October 2008).
120. Ibid. COMIBAM Internacional: Que es COMIBAM?
121. I attended COMIBM 1987 as a delegate of Iglesia Misionera Evagelica in Peru.

was the emphasis on pragmatic missiology, leading the movement to promote the urgent formation of new mission agencies and the sending of not well-prepared missionaries. As a result, COMIBAM had its first Mission Consultation Adopt A People (6–10 October 1992), which empowered the promotion phase (Bertuzzi 2006, 151).

COMIBAM appears to be the strongest Latin American regional network to empower mission within the Latin American churches. Similarly regional movements are currently working through the structural, social and political system of the evangelical movement as in the case of the Asian Evangelical Alliance (AEA), member of the World Evangelical Alliance; 'Back to Europe Initiative' (Spain); the India missions association (IMA), which has 40,000 missionaries; the Movement for African National Initiatives (MANI), focused on catalyzing, mobilizing and multiplying the resources of the churches in Africa;[122] the Philippine Mission Association (PMA), etc.[123]

Second phase: Growth and self-identity (1989–1997), under Rodolfo Girón's chairmanship. This is a phase of mobilizing local churches to fulfil the great commission through the 'unreached people' missiology.[124] An international office was established in Guatemala City, several offices were opened; new Latin American authors' books like *Hacia una misionología evangélica Lationamericana* (Nuñez 1997), *Diccionario hispanoamericano de la misión* (Deiros 1997) were produced.[125]

---

122. For MANI, data provided by the Continental Coordinator Reuben Ezemadu (email sent on 10 November 2008). Also see *Models, Issues and Structures of Indigenous Missions in Africa* (Ezemadu 2006), MANI has its own information on the Website. See the Pamphlet of MANI, also see (http://maniafrica.com/WhoWeAre/Brochures/tabid/245/Default.aspx).

123. For IMA, data provided by K. Rajendran, General Secretary of IMA (Pattaya 3 November 2008).

124. In Rodolfo Giron's understanding, one of the most peculiar themes of the COMIBAM has been the local church as the base and the heart of missions. See 'The Latin American Missionary Movement: A New Paradigm in Missions' (http://www.ad2000.org/celebrate/giron.htm).

125. See COMIBAM Bibliografía Misionera (http://www.comibam.org/docs/bibliografia.pdf).

The 'Adopte un Pueblo' (Adopt a People) movement was strongly embraced by many churches in the continent to adopt the 'unreached peoples group', especially in the 10/40 Window. In Miami, Florida, the magazine 'Ellos y Nosotros' (Them and Us) was edited and distributed. COMIBAM 1997, held in Acapulco from 27 to 31 October, gathered 2,200 mission leaders, pastors, missionaries and mission board members to assess the work of missions over the last ten years in Ibero-America, to learn from the many lessons and to project the mission effort into the new millennium with renewed understanding and energy.[126] The main target of COMIBAM 97, in Bush's understanding, was to assess whether Latin America had, in fact, produced a mission force and, if so, how effective it was. In Ruiz's perspective, the target of COMIBAM 1997 was to evaluate the movement and to make projections for the future;[127] Bertuzzi (2006, 173, 190) points out the dangers of western influence and Rudy Girón[128] helped to find COMIBAM's own identity. This is a phase of growth in numbers and in maturity. Evaluation included the following aspects:[129]

1. COMIBAM 87 listed around 60 organizations and 1,600 missionaries, but at COMIBAM 97 there were 4,000 Ibero-American cross-cultural missionaries serving around the world, 40 percent of whom serve in Latin America itself.
2. The need of establishing training centres for missionaries was recognized.

---

126. COMIBAM was held in 1997, two weeks after the hurricane 'Pauline', which provided a setting that allowed for a compassionate mission expression; water was distributed and an offering was raised for people who had suffered in the hurricane. The mayor of Acapulco addressed the conference and thanked the participants for their positive contribution to the city. See Miller report (http://www.christianitytoday.com/outreach/articles/missionmindedlatinos.html). Rudi Girón confirms data of delegates given by Miller in his article 'The Latin American Missionary Movement: A New Paradigm in Mission' (http://www.ad2000.org/celebrate/giron.htm).
127. David Ruiz, personal interview held in Pattaya, Thailand on 1 November 2008.
128. At COMIBM 1997, Girón completed his term as President of COMIBAM International (1989–1997).
129. Rudy Girón, was president of COMIBAM International from 1989 to 1997. In Acapulco he was consecrated to the next phase of their ministry as a missionary to Russia. See Bush (1997) in COMIBAM 97: 'An Assessment of the Latin American Missions Movement' (http://www.ad2000.org/re71216.htm).

3. Many countries of the continent established a national missionary movement.
4. Bertil Ekstrom, elected president at COMIBAM 1997, presented a vision for the future, seeking to be a facilitator and a catalyst, working to strengthen existing mission efforts in Latin America and to start new ones.

It appears that David Ruiz's influence was decisive in strengthening Winter's unreached people missiology eight months before the Acapulco congress 1997, this through the Regional Consultation for Adopt-A People coordinators, San Salvador, 4–6 February 1997. That consultation expressed the intentional effort to provide a mission strategy for the movement in Acapulco 1997, but lacks a critical analysis of what Schreiter (2004) and Bevans (2007) call a local theology.[130]

Third phase: Transitional institution (1997–2000), under Bertil Ekstrom's chairmanship. The principal agenda of this phase was strengthening the national missionary movements; creating and directing resources from Iberoamerica; strengthening partnership communication between players of the movement; and to form a Latin-American financial base for the movement. This phase concluded with the implementation of a more democratic leadership ending with the First International Assembly in Lima,

---

130. San Salvador Consultation 1997 reaffirmed the mission strategy of 'unreached people', a commitment made by COMIBAM at the Adopt a People (AAP) consultation in October 1992 held in San Jose, Costa Rica, to reach 3,000 unreached peoples. On that occasion, Ruiz affirmed that 'Adopt a People' "was major component of COMIBAM's programme to enable Latin churches to effectively participate in reaching the unreached people". This was the mission strategy that COMIBAM Congress 1997 empowered, closely linked to the USCWM. Patricio Paredes, Director International of Adopt a People department, and Federico Bertuzzi, secretary of COMIBAM, were present at that San Salvador consultation with David Ruiz, the executive director at that time. See Phil Bogosian's report, Director of Global Adopt-A-People Campaign, Manila, Mission Frontiers, May–June 1997, 1–8 (http://www.missionfrontiers.org/1997/0506/mj9714.htm). In the same year the GCOWE '97 (Global Consultation on World Evangelization) Pretoria, South Africa, was held from 30 June to 5 July 1997. The conference was to focus on the Joshua Project 2000 unreached people groups. See *Mission Frontiers*, May/June 1997 (http://www.missionfrontiers.org/1997/0506/mj973.htm). These facts confirm the huge influence of Winter's missiology within evangelicalism.

Peru, in 2000; mission architects of this phase are Bertil Ekstrom and David Ruiz.[131] Ruiz was appointed president and Londoño executive director.

Equally, at the First International Assembly 2000 in Lima, Peru, Ekstrom explained what was the spirit of COMIBAM in eight statements: a Latino spirit, a missionary spirit, a humble spirit, a volunteer spirit, a pioneer spirit, an enthusiastic spirit, a spirit of excellence, and a spirit of partnership.[132] The question is whether this contextual spirit of COMIBAM was sometimes road-blocked by external factors of the managerial missiology. Ekstrom cites the issue of improvization as an internal factor of COMIBAM spirit, and the difficulty to evaluate the impact due to dynamic growth.[133]

Fourth phase: Institutional network (2000–2006) under David Ruiz's chairmanship. Fundamental work was addressed to the Summit of Strengthening National Leadership and Regional Leadership, Spain (2002[134]), the II International Assembly, El Salvador (2003),[135] II Summit of leadership, Spain (2005), etc. This phase culminates with the Congress at Granada, COMIBAM 2006, where the elected president, the Argentinian, Carlos Scott (2006, 73), stated that 300 mission organizations and about 4,000 cross-cultural missionaries were registered in 1997 and for 2006,

---

131. The idea was that once those national movements were strong enough, the leadership of the COMIBAM movement would be placed in their hands. Thus far the leadership of COMIBAM had been self-appointed, now the new structure opened a way to a more 'democratic' leadership, although the leadership was supported by the churches and leaders of the continent. See Girón (http://www.ad2000.org/celebrate/giron.htm). This democratization of sharing power expresses a sign of mature reciprocal contextual collaboration between the executive committee and the national missionary movements.

132. For Ekstrom (2000, 11_3), all the 'spirits of COMIBAM' are connected to a spiritual and cultural driven force so that in the case of partnership he states that, "collaboration among the different segments of the movement and formation of strategic partnerships is fundamental to evangelizing unreached people groups". The first 'spirit' implies that COMIBAM was born and has developed within both a Latin American context and a Latin American culture. See further 'The Spirit of COMIBAM', plenary address at the First International Assembly, Lima Peru 2000 (1–3).

133. Ibid., 2.

134. See 'Manual de la Cumbre de Liderazgo', Noviembre 2002 Madrid, España (http://www.comibam.org/ponencias/cumliespa/index.htm).

135. The II Assembly was held from 10 to 14 November 2003. See Gloria Bustamante (http://www.membercare.org/images/regions/comibam_03.pdf).

more than 8,500 missionaries and 400 mission structures, investing $3,000,000 of financial Latin American effort.[136] As a participant observer, I identify four key characteristics:[137] the emphasis on a suffering theology, a self-evaluation of twenty years of mission activity with weaknesses and strengths, a pneumatogical influence for the way to go forward, and a sense of mission maturity by avoiding the triumphalism of 1987.[138]

Regarding COMIBAM's external factors, Scott's analysis of 2005 identifies four weaknesses of the Latin American church:[139] the danger of putting biblical principles at risk; a lack of teaching of the whole gospel; the need for new forms of government and leadership; and few local churches and a lack of pastor's involvement in mission.[140]

At COMIBAM 2006, Scott (73) injected a missiological paradigm that indicates a more inclusive mission theology by pointing out contextualization, multicultural cities, immigrants, refugees and an honest way to find new cooperative models in mission. If this new interpretation permeates COMIBAM missiology, the movement would impact widely, avoiding the exclusiveness of the 'unreached paradigm'. Additionally, as a result of

---

136. It was estimated that more than 8,000 Ibero-American missionaries are working cross culturally and more than three million dollars ($3,000,000) is raised by their supporting churches every month. See WEA-AGORA-News, Mission Commission, September 2006 (http://www.worldevangelicalalliance.com/newsletter/mc_september.htm).

137. I attended Granada 2006 on behalf of Mission for the Third Millennium.

138. See also a summary of COMIBAM 2006 in Federico Bertuzzi's view in Lausanne Connecting, Point 2006, 'Thousands Attend COMIBAM Congress' (http://www.lausanne.org/lausanne-connecting-point/2006-december.html#5). See also the perspective of Alicia Saddock from CAM International (http://www.caminternational.org/SymphonyCore/ resources/ upload /files/ attachments/COMIBAM%20Conference%20 2006.pdf).

139. Scott provides a wide picture of COMIBAM in 'A Sketch on the Mobilization of the Latin American Church: Characteristics, Tendencies, Strengths and Challenges', *Connections,* The Journal of the World Evangelical Mission Commission (2005, 18–20) http://www.worldevangelicalalliance.com/commissions/mc/mc_southafrica/resources/Connections_Oct_2005.pdf. See also Escobar (2003:,166), in *The New Global Mission* who provides some stastistical figures.

140. Ibid. Scott (2005, 18–20). On the same analysis, Scott addresses ten challenges, which I have summarized in the seven points that follow: (1) a deeper understanding of an integral missiology in the foundation of churches, (2) to emphasize the missionary nature of the church, (3) to re-orient a christological mission theology, (4) effectiveness of people in mission, (5) to grow in unity, (6) understanding the Holy Spirit in mission, (7) adequate resources to equip and train mission candidates in collaboration with the local churches. See further Scott (2005, 18–20).

the survey started in 2004 under the supervision of the Brazilian, Levi Carvalho, COMIBAM's general report 2006 highlights the following issues (internal factors) that need urgent attention in relation to missionaries:[141] (1) missiological studies are relegated to a secondary place, (2) studies in languages are rarely practised,[142] (3) there are few churches committed to the total amount of necessary support, (4) a high percentage of missionaries have not been adequately prepared for cross-cultural ministry,[143] (5) missiology is still insufficient or nonexistent in many cases, (6) the majority of missionaries have neither health insurance nor retirement plans, (7) there is a weakness in strategic communication between agency leaders/mission boards and missionaries, and (8) it is necessary to attend to the needs of missionaries through more appropriate member care.[144] In fact, the book *Worth Keeping: Global Perspectives on Best Practice in Missionary Retention* (Hay Lim, Blocher, et al. 2007), gives key alternatives for missionary attrition and four chapters on missionary care. Moreover, the

---

141. This report was sent to the author on 21 December 2006 and posits three phases of research: information of missionaries on the mission field (2004–2006), an analysis of the weaknesses and strengths of mission structures of the movement (2007), and during 2008, the target was to analyze the results of the mission models COMIBAM is promoting. See the introduction and the content of the General Report of the III Iberoamerican Mission Congress (2006).

142. The International Mission Board of The Southern Baptist Convention in 'Planting with Passion's Handbook' (Jerry Rankin for reference) provides a chapter on Cross Cultural Witness, which can be helpful in COMIBAM's analysis of cultural adjustment and communicative language teaching and learning.

143. The Book *Send Me* (Hoke and Taylor 1999) offers an interesting cross-cultural church planter profile, but the question is if this detailed assessment profile can be contextualized to the need of the Latin American mission force.

144. The Member care programme at COMIBAM started in 1994 at the Panama meeting, followed by the United Kingdom 1996 meeting at All Nations Christian College; Acapulco 1997 at the COMIBAM Assembly where Carlos Nasser was appointed the first coordinator, and Marcia Tostes in 1998; a member care meeting was held in Brazil 1999; a continental consultation on missionary member care was held in Lima , Peru 2000; presentations of member care were given in Argentina (2001), Guatemala and Panama (2002), the El Salvador-II COMIBAM Assembly goals for the member care were redefined. See Global Member Care Resources (http://www.membercare.org/mchistoryibero.asp). This process shows that COMIBAM has been aware of the issues in sending missionaries, which denied the myth that they did not care for people in the mission field. The book *Worth Keeping: Global Perspectives on Best Practice in Missionary Retention* (Hay, Lim, Blocher, et.al) has four chapters on missionary care: chapter 13, Personnel Care; chapter 14, Personnel Care in Team Building and Functioning; chapter 15, Personnel Care in Conflict and Teams; and chapter 16, Member Care.

report acknowledges the sacrificial spirit of Latin missionaries who lack financial resources for their ministries.[145] On the other hand, this is the first time that COMIBAM has brought 288 missionaries from the mission field both to participate in the First Iberoamerican Missionary Retreat in Sierra Nevada, Spain, and for the COMIBAM's Congress.[146]

The British, Paul Davies, a former Latin Link missionary and an ex-member of the executive COMIBAM committee, in explaining what has hindered the impact of COMIBAM in the last ten years, says:[147]

> What is I think one of the big things is the fact that we focused on raising mission awareness with missionaries but not so much with pastors and churches. I guess that in some ways that is the result of our para-church roots. But this has meant many missionaries wanted to go but they often announced to their churches that God had called them but didn't involve the church from the beginning.[148]

In connection with what is mentioned above, Davies' analysis mission theology of COMIBAM as follows:[149]

1. Weaknesses: Too much North American missiology. At the beginning the deep involvement of the United States Center for World Mission (USCWM) was detrimental to an indigenous

---

145. The General Report of COMIBAM 2006 in Granada provides a excellent tool for a deeper analysis of the missionary movement, including statistics of spiritual discipline, a biblical and missological training, approval and financing of studies, budget and selection of field and ministry, the church and the field, a field specialist, gender, marital status and leadership, financial issues, relationships among workers, communication between agency leaders and missionaries, adaptation to the field, singles, success and failure, work and rest and preliminary conclusions from different track groups.

146. Of 288 missionaries, 59 were couples, and some of them brough their children. There were 187 married and 101 single missionaries, representing 22 Iberoamerican countries, working in 62 different countries around the world (see the Report of the First Iberoamerican Missionary Retreat, Sierra Nevada, 2006).

147. Davies was asked by David Ruiz and Jesus Londoño, in 2003 in Buenos Aires to be a member of the executive committee of COMIBAM (email from Davies 21 October 2008).

148. Paul Davies Questionnaire, question 2 (Answered 21 October 2008).

149. Ibid., Question 3.

(autochthonous) theology of mission emerging. This is especially true of the 'unreached people group' and 10/40-window theology. When it is combined with a highly pragmatic strategy such as the managerial missiology (S. Escobar) this makes for an untheological approach. Also it tends towards a 'marketing style' missiology rather than an integral mission. Success is judged through numbers, not faithfulness. Also the reductionism does make the theology manageable and easy to communicate.

2. Strengths: The motivational factor. Individuals are motivated to get involved in God's mission.

It appears that an issue with COMIBAM's mission theology is that 'unreached people', coined by Winter in 1974, implies an exclusive missiology for exclusive targets.[150] This missiological influence comes through Fuller Theological Seminary, the US Center for World Mission and the AD2000 movement.[151] Luis Bush who coined the '10/40 window' with a similar methodology of unreached targets to Winter, as one of the key promoters at the beginning of COMIBAM, seems to be engineering transplanting this managerial missiology to COMIBAM from its beginning.[152] This missiology was defined in Granada as part of the 'spirit of COMIBAM', which definitely has to be reoriented with a macro inclusive missiology if they want to increase its roots in a contextual Latin American missiology.[153]

---

150. It is said that, at the Lausanne 1974 Congress, Winter introduced the term 'unreached people groups' with the purpose that cross-cultural evangelization should be the primary task of the church. See 'History and Heritage of Lausanne Movement' (http://www.lausanne.org/sv/about.html).

151. In his article 'AD2000 and Beyond: Towards a Conceptual Model', Bush presents the principles of strategies to reach the unreached people. See *Working Together with God to Shape the New Millennium*, Evangelical Missiological Society, (2000, Number 8). Bush's AD2000 movement came to an end but the fact is that Bush is considered a great mobilizer, leader and promoter of missions (personal dialogue with Federico Bertuzzi on 3 November 2008). His passion led him to organize a mission congress in Jerusalem 2000, which was cancelled a few days before the event due to the fact that the visa workers in Israel went on strike. See press release, 22 December 2000 (http://www.ad2000.org/celebrate/wooding.htm).

152. In Bertuzzi's opinion, Bush was an ideologist of greater vision who invented COMIBAM, AD2000, The Joshua Project (interview by the author in Pataya, Thailand 3 November 2008).

153. Personal data collected at the COMIBAM Congress in Granada 2006.

Two questions that need deeper analysis are:[154] Why COMIBAM is recognized as a Latin American movement? Davies explains that COMIBAM is Latin in its loose structure. It is a network not a directive organization, which David Ruiz was especially concerned to maintain. It is almost counter-cultural at times in its wish to divest (*to take away status or power, free from something,* italics mine) itself of power. But it is very Latin in recognizing that if it tried a top-down approach, it would fail. Has COMIBAM autonomy to decide its mission policy and how is their freedom in reciprocal contextual collaboration with the Western missiology maintained? Davies states that because it is, in theory, a bottom-up organization, then COMIBAM executive responds to the needs of the bases not the other way round. I agree that this has meant a diverse approach and often one that is misunderstood by Western missions, which thinks that by talking with COMIBAM it is speaking with the representative of Latin America intercultural mission, but COMIBAM should in reality only serve not direct.

Fifth phase: Global influence (2006–2009) under Carlos Scott's chairmanship. Scott and Londoño argue that "COMIBAM does not yet see a correlation between the large number of Iberoamerican evangelicals and an increased sending of missionaries to the least reached ethnic groups".[155] They express concern that missionaries are sent without the appropriate training, strong financial support, adequate pastoral care and appropriate planning for the return. However, they have set the goal of doubling the missionary force from 10,000 to 20,000. To that end, they addressed the following objectives: (1) to strength national and regional movements, (2) to strength the regionalization and decentralization of COMIBAM, and (3) to focus on unreached people, which implies recognizing areas of the world that the gospel has not yet reached or where it has not yet grown significantly. My finding is that after COMIBAM 2006, Scott and Londoño seem to be reengineering a new mission theology, overcoming the narrow 10/40 window missiology by including the whole world as the *missio Dei's*

---

154. Ibid., Questions 4–5.
155. Scott and Londoño 'Where is COMIBAM International Heading?: Strategic Focal Points', an article written after COMIBAM 2006, (http://www.comibam.org/docs/whereiscomibamheading.pdf).

plan. This theological approach provides the beginning of a new reciprocal contextual collaboration, which is expressed as follows:

> Among the challenges are the large multicultural cities, the re-evangelization of the West, being a testimony of a world of religious pluralism and among unreached people regardless of where they are (whether they are in large cities or 'closed countries'), linguistic and translation, contextualization, being agents of reconciliation amidst religious persecution and deep suffering in a world of violence, displacement, refugees, immigrants.[156]

In consequence, global reciprocal contextual collaboration in Scott and Londoño's new approach seems,

> to maintain a good understanding of the unity in the community of the believers, an increased participation in global missions, involvement in the global church, sharing global challenges through the active and holistic gospel, a sincere search for partnership models, as well as an understanding of missions as a process rather that a project.[157]

---

156. See Scott and Jesus Londoño 'Where is COMIBAM International Heading?: Strategic Focal Points' (http://www.comibam.org/docs/whereiscomibamheading.pdf).
157. Ibid.

The missionary development of COMIBAM 1987–2006[158]

President	Congress	Mission structures	People in mission
Data before COMIBAM 1987		60	1,600
Luis Bush 1985–1989 Rudy Girón 1989–1997	São Paulo 1987 3,185 delegates	300	4,000
Bertil Ekstrom 1997–2000 David Ruiz 2000–2006	Acapulco 1997 2,200 delegates	400	9,265
Carlos Scott 2006–	Granada 2006 1,958 delegates	Remains to be seen	Remains to be seen
Projection of growth	Next congress 2016?	520	20,000[159]

COMIBAM Peru

The Mission National Cooperation–Peru (CONAMI–PERU)[160] was formed in July 2000 as part of the COMIBAM network. Seven missions joined forces for making the preparations for the First COMIBAM International Assembly, held in Lima, Peru, 13–18 November 2000 (Hockings 2008). Current members are: Segadores Missionary Association,

---

158. COMIBAM, III Congreso Misionero Iberoamericano (2006, 73). For data of presidents, I use Bertil Ekstrom's information (provided on 19 October 2008). Data of delegates comes from unpublished material of COMIBAM 1987, (see also COMIBAM Internacional: Que es COMIBAM? http://www.comibam.org/queescomi.htm), COMIBAM 1997 and data for COMIBAM 2006 is taken of the General Report of the III Iberoamerican Mission Congress (2006, 1). Data for missionaries of 2006, see COMIBAM, Missionaries from Latin America, Spain and Portugal (http://www.comibam.org/transpar/ing/catalog2006/gif/Slide8.gif).
159. A methodology to obtain the projection for new mission structures is based on 30% average growth in the last ten years. 'Global Mission, Results from Recent Years', provides a target to double the 9,265 number of missionaries (http://globalmissionscott.blogspot.com/2008/04/results-from-recent-years-comibam.html).
160. The Cooperación Nacional de Misiones (CONAMI–PERU) Mission National Cooperation.

The Christian and Missionary Alliance Church, Operation Mobilization, MISUR Mission, Latin Link, SIM Mission, Wycliffe Bible Translators, Iglesia Cristo Vive (The Living Christ Church), Iglesia Hasta lo Último de la Tierra (Till the Ends of the Earth Church). Peter Hocking, former president of CONAMI–Peru, explains the nature of this national network:[161]

> CONAMI is a missionary network that seeks to help the churches in Peru become involved in missions, as well as teaching them ways to do missionary work better. It is linked up with COMIBAM International, being its official representative in Peru.

In relation to the policies of CONAMI, especially personnel and finances, Hocking explains that since this is a network, the member organizations join voluntarily (though there are conditions), and they maintain their autonomy.[162] Each member organization is represented in the planning meetings by two official members, chosen by their organization, and presented to the CONAMI Board by means of a letter. A 5-member board is elected by the members every two years. Every member organization is expected to send a representative to the monthly planning meetings, even though they may not be board members. Finances are raised in the following ways: monthly membership dues which can be paid every 3–6 months, income from missionary events such as training seminars and conferences, and special gifts for special needs from member organizations.

CONAMI's mission theology in Hocking's understanding has the following characteristics:
1. The focus of God's redemptive plan (throughout the OT and the NT) is to save people from every tribe and nation in the world, so that every nation might know and serve him.
2. For this reason, the priority in missions should be the evangelization of the unreached nations (or people groups) of the world, until each has healthy churches.

---
161. Peter Hocking, Questionnaire answered from Lima, Peru, 24 March 2008.
162. Ibid.

3. God's agent for this task during OT times was Israel, but at present it is the church through its local congregations. He has raised up para-church organizations and missionary networks to help the church do her job, rather than compete or replace her.
4. Though the mission (task) of the church is broad, she is not doing mission until she evangelizes beyond her local influence (i.e. beyond her 'Jerusalem') according to Acts 1:8.
5. There are four human agents involved in the missionary task: the local churches, missionaries,[163] missionary training centres, and sending agencies.

CONAMI's mission theology looks solid but the reality raises concern about the lack of participation of local churches in sending missionaries clearly illustrated in the no more than 100 Peruvian missionaries abroad.

Missionary movement in Peru involves Peruvian churches and is growing. In Hocking's perspective, the most active denominations are the Christian Missionary Alliance churches, Baptist churches, Independent Brethren churches, IME, and Assembly of God churches. Some tribal churches have begun sending missionaries to other tribes in Peru (especially the Shipibos, Piros, Machigengas, and Cashinahuas are doing this). Two missionary networks exist in Peru: CONAMI and RAP (Peruvian Amazon Network). There are four cross-cultural missionary training programmes: CAMIT (of FAIENAP in Pucallpa), ETAE (of Segadores, in Lima), CILTA (of Wycliffe, in Lima), and FATELA (of the Christian and Missionary Alliance, in Lima). On the other hand, the following foreign mission groups are in the final stages of leaving Peru: Summer Institute of Linguistics, the South American Mission, the Swiss Indian Mission, and Pioneers Mission. However, there are still twenty unreached tribes in Peru. These are mostly small, nomadic, primitive tribes.

Hocking concludes that the present challenges of CONAMI include at least three factors: the unreached tribes of the jungle, the Muslims of Lima and Tacna, and the support of Peruvian missionaries.

---

163. CONAMI seeks to facilitate greater cooperation between candidates for the field and missionaries.

Conclusion with an evaluation of positive and negative tensions

The reality that COMIBAM has become a motivating mission tool provides signs of the emerging mission from Asia, Africa and Latin America impacting the missionary gravity centre South to North, developing a more christological relationship within influential circles.[164] So COMIBAM is a networking model that seems to practise some aspects of the mission theology of reciprocal contextual collaboration, but needs to be more radical in its theological understanding. As a matter of fact, I agree that COMIBAM alone is not the only evidence of the Spirit's missionary movement of Latin America; other networks like the Latin American Theological Fraternity (FTL) have emerged from the same Spirit in the South.

Somehow, COMIBAM fails to develop multidirectional mission traffic[165] and a missiological diaspora[166] – both key elements of an inclusive missiology. However, this model leads me to understand that the 'New Catholicity' (Schreiter 2004) of Christian expansion will include a wider spectrum of a missionary force within a variety of a theological and missiological hermeneutical horizons, including local theologies permeated

---

164. This new relationship of free traffic somehow is expressed through written literature published by the World Evangelical Alliance, Wycliffe International-Americas Articles, Lausanne World Pulse, etc. See Wycliffe International-Americas-Article, 'The Emergent Latin American Bible Translation Force' (http://www.wycliffe.net/home/Americas/Articles/tabid/422/Default.aspx?id=am0803012); the papers of David Ruiz, 'The Ibero-American Church is on its Way to the III Ibero-American Missions Congress' (La Iglesia Ibero Americana de camino al III Congreso Misionero Iberoamericano), in Lausanne World Pulse (http://www.lausanneworldpulse.com/perspectives.php/538/11-2006?pg=1).

165. It seems that COMIBAM has a unidirectional missiology and concentrates efforts in distant lands of unreached people and the 10/40 window. What about Europe as a mission field? And the mission to the six continents? And the new mission force from the West to the South?

166. I apply this term to an emphatic dissemination of theological and missiological thinking to include the immigrant force. Diaspora implies scattering of language, culture, or people: a dispersion of a people, language, or culture that was formerly concentrated in one place. See MSN Encarta Dictionary (http://uk.encarta.msn.com/dictionary_1861702254/diaspora.html); diaspora describes any group that has been dispersed outside its traditional land. It also implies any religious group living as a minority among people of the prevailing religion. See Infoplease Dictionary (http://dictionary.infoplease.com/diaspora).

through the dynamic interaction between gospel, church and culture.[167] Thus, COMIBAM needs to be aware of implementing theologies elaborated out of the context without considering realities where the kerygma has to be proclaimed.[168] In this sense, the work of Sharon E. Heaney (2008), *Contextual Theology for Latin America,* can be helpful for a new theological implementation.[169]

The fact that theological reflection is one of the main issues in COMIBAM's network compels them to include a clear Trinitarian and God's kingdom theology. Equally there is a need for contextual theology with a transformational missiological approach, an inclusive missiology avoiding the managerial missiology's influence. In contrast, perhaps the main strengths include success in motivating people to mission, relational collaboration with mission agencies and networks,[170] organization of resources with volunteers and self-support involvement, the virtue of making network attractive, etc. Moreover, it is imperative to strengthen its *missio ecclesia,* avoiding practising a dichotomised missiology, dividing church's mission from mission societies,[171] lacking reciprocal contextual collaboration between local churches and the sending structures, due to the fact that

---

167. The gospel is translatable to each context, the church announces the same gospel's essence to each culture, and the gospel and the church are incarnated in a specific context, and provide a Christian identity within a variety expressed through different cultures. These are the key elements of an inclusive missiology.

168. For a contextual Latin American mission theology, we suggest going hand in hand with the help of local theologies developed by mission theologians such as Bevans (2007); *Theology of the Cross Roads*, Costas (1976); for the biblical theology of material possession, Blomberg (1999), and for an understanding of faith and practice from an evangelical perspective, the recent work of Heaney (2008) *Contextual Theology for Latin America.*

169. Heaney (2008, 1, 5, 127), maintains that Latin American theology is relatively unknown in the West, provides insights of a theology from a historical and cultural context, systematizing the thoughts of key Latin American evangelical theologians with pivotal theologies such as Christology, ecclesiology and missiology.

170. This kind of reciprocal development is seen in the WEA-MC that from the beginning was directly involved in the organization of COMIBAM, investing time and effort more than any other regional movement MC has promoted. See Lewis 2006 Regional and National Mission Structures, SA06: WEA Mission Commission, Global Issues Summit, 18–24 June, Goudini Spa, South Africa, (http://www.worldevangelicals.org/commissions/mc/mc_southafrica/resources/Lewis%20%20Mission%20structures.pdf).

171. An issue is that 'The majority of missionaries have the responsibility for raising their own support, even though they are in the mission field the majority of the time' (General Report of the III Iberoamerican Missions Congress).

missionaries struggle with financial support;[172] second, COMIBAM needs to build new bridges of contextual collaboration between their national networks and local pastors and COMIBAM's mission theology might perhaps become systematically re-engineered in reciprocal contextual collaboration with the Latin American Theological Fraternity. Additionally, the following aspects need a deeper study:

1. To clarify the difference between 'movement' and 'network'.[173]
2. To analyze elements of the traditional model they would implement.
3. To resolve the gap between local churches and mission structures.
4. To analyze seriously the difficulties with 'unreached people' mission theology.[174]

As for analysis of promoting the participation of local churches in mission, the spontaneity of the Latin spirit to overcome barriers and obstacles of economic affluence confirms that COMIBAM's growth is in the process of missiological maturity. Despite virtues and faults, COMIBAM is a Latin movement due to the identity of its missionaries, percentage of their support, leadership and historical roots, obtaining its own identity and dynamism, using foreign resources without diluting their independent autochthonism. COMIBAM appears as an indigenous Latin American movement due to the fact that Latin leaderships initiated the seminal thinking, decision making, power control and the agenda, but in its implementation has taken up the 'unreached people' of Winter's missiology, going to distant lands and applying the 10/40 window theory from Bush's American pragmatism. The fact is that the unreached people perspective

---

172. See the general report, section for financial arrangements for missionaries: half of the missionaries have no health insurance in the field; more than half of the missionaries have no retirement plan, 18% hope to have one before they die; more that half of the missionaries have no prepared plan for possible emergencies in the field.

173. It is important for COMIBAM to clarify the difference between 'movement' and 'network'; the second, as it was clarified in chapter 3 of this book, provides a tool to unite and share resources for mission between different autonomous bodies with the same missiological target, the first relates to the revival of Protestant Christianity; it is not only a social process or an invented human experiment. A missionary movement has a Spirit's power that empowers and directs the *missio Dei* in dynamic tension within theological, missiological, political, social, cultural, economic, etc., factors of a concrete context.

174. For 'unreached people', see for example the critical analysis of David Stoll (1990, 81–83, 97).

lacks inclusive missiology (the need of the whole world, yet America and Europe need to be defined as unreached peoples, too).[175] However, despite some weaknesses, strengths have promoted COMIBAM's growth, becoming a motivating model with a clear Latin American identity, taking part in God's redemptive plan, empowered by the Spirit, but within tensions of either still promoting imperial paradigms like the Western traditional models or exporting its model as paternalistic intervention hindering the development of more appropriate models.

It seems that COMIBAM exemplifies the new involving phase of globalization, which includes regionalism, which revived and changed dramatically in the 1980s and gained strength in the 1990s, also with a powerful influence in Christianity. COMIBAM, seen in its mission structure, is not an exception to the influence of a regional philosophy, emerging in James Mittelman's thinking as a resistance to "rival forces from above and from below"(2000, 111), sometimes with overlapping regional projects, which have global tendencies like the autocentric, development, neo-liberal, degenerated, and transformative.[176] In applying this to the *missio Dei*: *autocentric* relates to self-growth with no consideration of other regions of mission; *development* includes freedom, context, policy, goals, economy, personnel, seeking the improvement of the economy, etc.; *neo-liberal* implies the free fluency in mission; *degenerated* expresses the painful relations in mission.

COMIBAM's network needs to explore new forms of transnational reciprocity, crossing borders and encapsulating in its characteristics considerations of the multipolar context, protectionist pressures of dying models, regional integration, and disintegrative process in its mission for the twenty-first century (Mittelman 2000, 113–114), within mission tensions

---

175. It seems that COMIBAM have not rethought their 'unreached people' missiology, which needs an urgent theological freedom from Winter's influence. This leads to a danger of pragmatic mission activity, using a borrowed missiology hindering the movement for a lack of contextual Latin American missiology. Therefore, local theologies, as the model of the Latin American Theological Fraternity, which includes the political, social, economic, cultural and spiritual context, will contribute to strengthen the movement. However, the effort made so far must be applauded.

176. See further James Mittelman (2000, 113–114), *The Globalization Syndrome: Transformation and Resistance*.

between traditional and the emergent partnership paradigms.[177] Finally, Carlos Scott, a relational mission-minded leader, and the Colombian, Jesus Londoño, as the former COMIBAM's ideologist, have been key leaders targeting raising 20,000 missionaries[178] in the following years,[179] which remain to be seen within characteristics of the emergent missionary movement that includes a beauty of commitment for the *missio Dei,* compassion for the lost and hope for the church.

St James Church, Muswell Hill, London case study

The historical origin

The Anglican church of St James was established in Muswell Hill, North London, in a building constructed in 1842, which was replaced by a new building in 1902.[180] In 1903, 700 parishioners queued for services in the morning and 400 for evening worship.[181] At present, Muswell Hill[182] belongs to the Borough of Haringey, one of the 32 boroughs of Greater London with a population of 225,000.[183] It appears that St James Church

---

177. Multipolar implies a multifaceted approach that superpowers are not driving the new regionalism from outside and above, it is more spontaneous and emerges from below; protectionist pressures, I refer to the traditional missions trying to survive by merging with one another; regional integration refers to providing a multilateral cooperation to reduce conflicts; disintegrative process marks the dividing of territorial mission into regional blocks. James H. Mittelman (2000) develops an analysis of transformation and resistance of the global perspective.

178. Global Mission, results from recent years (http://globalmissionscott.blogspot.com/2008/04/results-from-recent-years-comibam.html).

179. See Scott 'Praying for COMIBAM' (http://www.comibam.org/docs/prayforcomibam_001.pdf); in 'Cambios Teologicos en la Fuerza Misionera', Londoño, an OC International missionary suggests a constructive and inclusive missiology (http://www.comibam.org/ponencias/IIAsamblea/CTEFM.htm; http://www.onechallenge.org/).

180. The Muswell Hill website (http://www.muswell-hill.com/index2.htm).

181. Ibid. (http://www.muswell-hill.com/index2.htm).

182. The early history of Muswell Hill's origin goes back to the time when the Bishop of London, Lord of the Manor of Hornsey, granted 65 acres of land to an order of nuns in the mid-twelfth century. See The Muswell Hill website (http://www.muswell-hill.com/index2.htm).

183. The Borough of Haringey was formed in 1965 by the joining of Tottenham, Wood Green and Hornsey. See Londononline (http://www.londononline.co.uk/boroughs/).

survived the difficulties of the Second World War with some parts of the building affected.[184] Alex Ross a former St James' vicar states:

> St James began when the church in Hornsey (*actual London Borough of Haringey*) during the middle of the nineteenth century wanted to start a church in Muswell Hill. At that time there was no Church of England in Muswell Hill and so they began with a small building halfway down St James's Lane.[185]

Michael Bunker (1988, 37), a former Vicar of St Matthew's Church, states that during the 1970s, the income at the Anglican churches went down and a decision by the church authorities was made to examine which churches should be closed, which should remain open, and which should be merged. Bunker decided voluntarily to merge St Matthew's Church with another church. Thus, in 1978 he met Bill Allam, the vicar of St James, who agreed to amalgamate both churches. St Matthew was closed and the congregation followed Bunker as the new vicar of St James, a 'low' Anglican evangelical church (52), leading the church from 1978 to 1992[186] (Bunker 1988, 7, 38, 73).

St James Church is a local church made up of middle class professional and managerial people with demanding and responsible jobs; Bunker (1988, 91) points out that one reason why staff have been set up was in order to provide commitment for busy people that had no time for helping the growth of the church. Vicars who have made an impact on St James' life since the 1970s were Michael Bunker (1978–1992), the 'architect' who helped the church to grow in strength, and Alex Ross (1993–2007), the visionary for planting churches and doing mission locally and globally. From February 2008 to 2012, Kim Swithinbank who worked in America has been vicar. His aim was to strengthen the congregational structure in order to provide a new phase for a growing church under the influence of

---

184. The church was partially destroyed by incendiary bombs in 1941 until restored in 1952 (Jimmy Pepiatt, information sent to the author by email on 14 January 2009).
185. Data provided by Alex Ross (16 December 2008). Italics mine.
186. Data provided by Alex Ross. Questionnaire, question 1 (sent to the author on 16 December 2008).

biblical teaching, prayer, strong evangelism through the Alpha course, and being a more relational church.[187] Jimmy Peppiatt, chair of the building committee who came to St James in the late 1940s, mentions additionally three vicars that have contributed to St James' growth: Preb.Dunn (1931–58), Norman Bainbridge (1958–66) and Bill Allam (1966–1977).[188] Chris Green has benn St James' vicar since January 2014.

Moreover, St James develops mission relations with similar Christian churches working in Muswell Hill, such as the Methodist, Reformed, Baptist and recently the Wilton Community Church and Grace Church (which met in a pub at the beginning of the work). Those churches meet together, especially for prayer.

The mission context

St James, which is our third case, develops its reciprocal contextual collaboration in connection with local churches and mission societies both within and outside of Great Britain, which has a population of 60 million people.[189] On this basis, this local church reflects a variety of theological opinion, and its mission activity is developed within a political context that can be described as stable.[190]

---

187. Data provided by Kim Swithinbank at the annual report of St James 2007, held on April 2008.

188. For Jimmy Peppiatt, Preb.Dunn (1931–58) was committed to serving God in the local community (a "low church congregation at this time"); Norman Bainbridge (1958–66) was ahead of his time, but a great theologian, and teacher; Bill Allam (1966–1977), a saintly man, but he was ill; Michael Bunker (1978–1992) helped to joint St Matthews (from Creighton Ave) to St James; Alex Ross, vicar from 1993 to 2007, promoted more bible study groups and prayer meetings, midweek activities, such as CD (Christian Discipleship), and emphasis on personal commitment to our Lord Jesus Christ, and Peppiatt does not mention any specifics of Kim Swithinbank, vicar since 2008 (information sent to the author on 14 January 2009).

189. City Population: Great Britain and Northern Ireland (http://www.citypopulation.de/UK-London.html#Stadt_alpha).

190. It has been pointed out that the gospel probably arrived to Britain in the third century. The first martyr was Alban, executed around 210 (see Cathedral and Abbey Church of St Albans, http://www.stalbanscathedral.org.uk/index1.htm) and three British bishops were present at the Council of Arles in 314 AD. Moreover, since the days of Augustine from Rome, the first Archbishop of Canterbury in 597 (Neill 1958, 8, 11; Howe 1977, 16; Edwards 1998, 4, 6, 17), England was a Catholic country for about a thousand years, and its Catholic community has survived even after the period of the

When it comes to the religious context, during the 1990s issues like the ordination of women, troubles with financial management, and the growing influence of evangelicalism led Anglicans towards disintegration (Hastings 1986, xi–xiii; Jenkins 2002, 121).[191] Ian Murray (2000, 103; Jenkins 2002, 87) states that there are 26 million baptized members of the Church of England, although less than a million attend regularly. In addition, this observation is complemented by what Hastings calls (1986, 665) the 'residual religion'.[192] This internal ecclesiological factor provides evidence that Europe is a 'dying continent', since the spiritual decline expressed in less churchgoers in the British church seems to be a pathological symptom in those European countries which are Protestant by tradition, and also this phenomenon can be seen in the context of Catholic countries like Spain and Ireland.[193] Similarly, Peter Brierley (2004, 20) agrees that Christianity in the First World is in decline at present.[194] In contrast to this critical approach, there is in Britain an evangelical movement that reflects the *missio Dei* in events such as the Keswick Convention (1875), which gathers 12,000 annually;[195] Spring Harvest (1979) 45,000;[196] the Alpha Course (1970s) initiated at Holy Trinity Brompton (HTB), which runs 33,500 courses worldwide in 163 countries and in which two

---

Protestant Reformation. According to Howe (1977, 16) also in 597 the Celtic Christians sent their own missionaries to Germany and Switzerland.

191. For Jenkins (2002, 121), one example is the hostile tension between North and South at the 1998 Lambeth Conference.

192. 'Residual religion' refers to the existence of informal religion, called folk religion – those who have no regular connection or clear beliefs (Hasting 1986, 665).

193. See further the analysis of the Evangelical Alliance 1982–2001 in UK (Warner 2007, 41–66); an overview of the 1990s in *A History of English Christianity 1920–2000* (Hastings (2001, x), and Jenkins (2002, 95–96). In contrast, Burges (2002, 42) provides figures of 5,820,000 Pentecostals and charismatics in Britain.

194. See Peter Brierley's article 'Evangelicals in the World of the 21st Century', 3 May 2004, 1–22 (http://www.lausanne.org/documents/2004forum/LCWEvangelicals.pdf).

195. The Vicar of St John's, Canon Harford-Battersby, began the first Keswick Convention in 1875 in the little town of Keswick in the Northwest of England, situated in the region known as The Lake District. See The Keswick Conference Centre (http://www.keswick.org/estdetails.asp?id=1950615361), and http://www.keswickconvention.ca/2009_pg6.htm).

196. See Spring Harvest (http://www.springharvest.org/main-event-sh/category_index.php?id=6). See also Warner's Spring Harvest case study (2007, 67–86).

million people in Britain and eleven million worldwide have participated;[197] Christianity Explored, founded by Rico Tice from All Souls Church, which runs 4,000 courses once a year across 34 countries, including 500 in Britain;[198] The Proclamation Trust (1984) founded by Dick Lucas, then Rector of St Helen's, Bishopsgate, London, which attracts annually 1,000 delegates interested in expository preaching through the Evangelical Ministry Assembly (EMA).[199] Rob Warner (2007) provides detailed case studies of Alpha and Spring Harvest in *Reinventing English Evangelicalism*.

St James' mission activity is developed within a variety of theological tensions, which have the following basic characteristics:

1. Hastings (1986, 109; Oliver 2008, 41; Day 2008, 130–136), in A *History of English Christianity*, states that the heart of theological Anglicanism lies in the Thirty-nine Articles and the *Book of Common Prayer*, which together inform the church's prayer, and the historic episcopate, which informs the church's government.[200]

2. In the Anglican church (Hastings 1986, xxi; Oliver 2008, 39) there has existed, traditionally, a so called 'high' church (which is very liturgical and mostly Anglo-Catholic) and a 'low' church (which is less liturgical, and mainly evangelical), while four basic theological tendencies can now be noted: the Anglo-Catholic,[201]

---

197. The Alpha Course (http://uk.alpha.org/). For a detailed analysis see 'Alpha: A Second Case Study in Evangelical Exceptionalism' in *Reinventing English Evangelicalism, 1966–2001* (Warner 2007, 115–137).

198. Jenny Cooks, email sent from London to the author on 14 January 2009. See also Christianity Explored (http://www.christianityexplored.org/about-us/rico/). See also Warner (2007, 133).

199. See The Proclamation Trust, 'The History of the Proclamation Trust' (http://www.proctrust.org.uk/about/history.htm).

200. In contrast, the Free Churches took the Bible as the key element of ministry and its authority as supreme doctrine, and for Free churchmen, the Anglican liturgy had no freedom (Hastings 1986, 109). *The Principles of Theology* provides a deep analysis of the Book of Common Prayer. See Griffith Thomas (1978).

201. For Simon Oliver, Catholic Anglicanism has five marks: (1) the authority and Catholic nature of the Church of England vested in the Episcopate and Apostolic succession, (2) the revival of the religious life, (3) the importance of patristic studies, (4) a high sacramental theology and the practice of auricular confession, and (5) a liturgical ritualism. See further 'Catholic Anglicanism: The Development of a Tradition' (Anglicanism: Essays in History, Beliefs and Practice, *Trivium* 38, 2008).

the evangelical, the liberal (Badham 2007, 58–70[202]) and the charismatic, which has been given direction by Michael Harper since 1964 (557).[203]

3. Despite theological variety, the ancient church in England was historically the reformed Church of England, but still claims to be Apostolic, Catholic, Reformed and Protestant.[204]

4. The Church of England is a state church; the Queen (as head of the church) established in 1970 the supreme legislative authority through three houses: bishops, clergy and laity (Hastings, 546).

5. Evangelical Anglicans are theologically reformed, some Calvinist, others Arminians (Yates[205] 2008, 2–3), episcopal in government, and missiologically holistic, as clarified especially by John Stott (Hastings, 617), one of the leading figures among Anglican evangelicals, as well as by Jim Packer and Tom Wright (2008), who in *Anglican Evangelical Identity* define the fundamental content of Anglican Evangelicalism. The second seeks to clarify what it means to be an evangelical today and the first clarifies the fundamental doctrines of evangelicalism.[206]

---

202. For example, liberal Anglicanism adopted an historico-critical approach to the Bible and disbelief in hell was pronounced as legal in 1864, and since the 1960s a more tolerant attitude to homosexuality. For further reading see Badham's essay, 'Liberal Anglicanism: A Rational Approach to Theological Interpretation' (*Trivium* 38, 2008, 57–70).

203. Personal dialogue with Steve Griffin (London, 18 January 18 2009), also interview with Will Hunter-Smart, held in London on 26 January 2008. See also Yates in *Trivium* 38 (2008, 17)

204. See Anglican Church of Australia, 'A History of Anglicanism' (http://australia.anglican.org/index.cfm?SID=2&SSID=5).

205. Nigel Yates provides a historical overview of the Anglican move from Calvinist to Arminian theology. See further 'Historical Anglicanism: Changes in the Concept of a Via Media' (Yates, Trivium 38, 2008, 1–17).

206. Packer characterizes evangelical Christianity as pure, unitive (not sectarian), and rational; in doctrine, it stresses the supremacy of the Holy Scripture, the majesty of Jesus Christ, the lordship of the Holy Spirit, the priority of evangelism, and the importance of fellowship. Wright explains the theological angle of dogmatic exclusivists, the establishment exclusivists and the idealistic constitutionalists (the traditional evangelical side). See further Packer and Wright (2008).

In terms of theological considerations, St James is an Anglican Evangelical Low Church that appears to support GAFCON,[207] and which reflects its allegiance to Anglican tradition through its use of the *Book of Common Prayer* in its 8:00am service.[208]

In the case of Peru, which is our focus, St James has made a mission link with an emergent Peruvian church, the Iglesia Misionera Evangelica, an independent evangelical movement founded in 1985 which has sent missionaries to Europe to promote a Latin-American missional theology, and to establish a church among the Latin-American people in London in 1997. It was in reciprocal contextual collaboration with St James since 1997, a church among the Latin American people in London. From the same missiological perspective, St James has had clearly identified with the emergent church by sending short-term mission teams every two years to Peru since 1999. We will analyze this missiological perspective below.

As a nation, Peru has the challenges of its shanty towns, especially in its capital city Lima. It is estimated that in 1972, 50 percent of the population lived in the city, and by 2000 this figure increased to 71 percent. Likewise, 49 percent of the population are classified as poor, of whom 20 percent live in extreme poverty. Sociologically, 54 percent of the population is indigenous (quechuas), 33 percent *mestizo* (indigenous and Spanish mix), and 12 percent white, including Japanese, Chinese and African minorities.[209] Reid (2007, 213–217, 23) states that *Sendero Luminoso* (Shining Path) devastated the Peruvian economy of the 1980s, while in the 1990s the nation suffered the disease of colera, such that 75 percent of those between 15 to 29 sought to emigrate (mainly to the United States, Chile and Spain).

---

207. See 'The Global Anglican Future Conference' (GAFCON), held at Jerusalem, from 22–29 June 2008. Leaflet distributed at St James Church, Muswell Hill in July (2008: 1–4). See also the comments of GAFCON by Mark Oxbrow 'Anglicans and Reconciling Mission: An Assessment of Two Anglican International Gatherings' (*International Bulletin of Missionary Research,* Vol 33, No 1 January 2009: 9–10), and Titus Presler 'The Impact of the Sexuality Controversy on Mission: The Case of the Episcopal Church in the Anglican Communion' (*International Bulletin of Missionary Research,* Vol 33, No 1 January 2009, 16).

208. St James has five Sunday services: 8:00 am, 9:30 am, 11:15 am, 5:00 pm and 7:00 pm.

209. Global Connections (2004), people, culture and life style (http://www.globalconnections.co.uk/ Resources/Global%20Connections/Mission%20Issues/2006/Peru.pdf). See also Reid (2007, 213–222).

However, an anti-poverty programme appears to have been working well since 2001, resulting in sustained economic growth, although the country lacks adequate public services, such as health, education, transport, etc.[210]

Analysis of mission development

Type of mission structure

Thus far we have seen the traditional model as represented by Latin Link, as well as the networking model of COMIBAM. Here, our third model, which we refer to as the emergent model, includes a church-church mission relationship between St James and the Iglesia Misionera Evangelica (IME) in Peru. This model is represented by St James Church, through its World Mission Group (WMG), and the Iglesia Misionera Evangelica (IME) in Peru. My assumption is that this model has developed an emergent mission policy since these local churches promote mission in and through their own mission structure, as they seek to develop a church-to-church mission relationship, rather than simply a church-to-mission society relationship. However, it is necessary to clarify that the emergent model includes structures of the traditional model and the networking model in addition to the church-to-church structure. In fact, the WMG's policy has involved the support of four St James missionaries; five foreign missionaries; three non-members missionaries and eleven mission organizations within the UK and overseas.[211] Likewise, the WMG supports some special projects, and the sending of short-term mission teams. St James' World Mission Group (WMG), which began before 1993, was initially chaired by T. Moore,[212] later by John Lenton, then Ann Twisleton (1999–2001), Heather Payne

---

210. Somehow the economic stability began with the policy of President Alejandro Toledo during 2001–2006; for example, salaries of teachers were raised to $330 monthly in 2006 but failed to improve the whole educational system with its 300,000 teachers compared to the 1.4 million of Mexico. See further Reid (2007, 13, 244–245).
211. Will Hunter-Smart's interview with the author held on 26 January 2009 at St James' office.
212. Alex Ross, information by email to the author on 29 January 2008.

(2001–2002),[213] Sandie Walker (2003–2004), Greg Prior (2004–2005), and Will Hunter-Smart (2005–2009).[214]

Former WMG chairman Will Hunter-Smart states that this committee's mission policy can be described as 'informal'.[215] This assumption confirms my finding that St James Church's missiology reflects the emergent model, according to which the WMG selects candidates for short- and long-term mission, maintains a flexible budget of financial support, and administers 10 percent of St James' total income, which is estimated at £36,000 each year.[216] This model has similarities to the Swedish Pentecostal model in the sense that both channel their mission effort through the local church's mission committee. Moreover, characteristics of the emergent partnership such as flexibility, less bureaucracy, and the support of emergent missionary movements are part of St James' policy, as they collaborate with the IME church in Peru, the Baptist church in Malawi, the Sierra Leona project, and others. Hunter points out that the WMG has three roles:[217]

1. Distribution of 10 percent of the church's income, which is £36,000.
2. To support the existing St James' missionaries.
3. To keep the profile of the WMG on the agenda of the church by being aware of:
   a. Christians in the world.
   b. the needs of those from St James who are going overseas.

The WMG structure works under the PCC Committee, becoming a sub-committee of the PCC formed by six St James' members plus the minister for mission, who meets six times a year with the main agenda being financial support for missions.[218]

---

213. Ann Twisleton, telephone conversation from London, held on 28 January 2009.
214. Will Hunter-Smart's interview held on 26 January 2009 at St James' offices.
215. Will Hunter-Smart's interview, 2009.
216. Ibid.
217. Ibid.
218. Ibid.

Main characteristics

Ecclesiastically, St James Church, Muswell Hill in North London, belongs to the Diocese of London in the London Borough of Haringey.[219] Key leaders from the 1980s to 2007 have been Jonathan Thorton,[220] Julian Slater and Simon Upcott as church wardens; Jimmy Peppiatt[221] and John Lenton as PCC leaders.[222] Since 2009 an emphatic ecclesiology has included six mission theological foundations at St James:[223]

1. Living in intimate relationship with the Father.
2. Depending totally on the Spirit.
3. Submitting radically to God's will and Word.
4. Passionately seeking the lost.
5. Humbly serving the needy.
6. Living in loving community.

Missiologically speaking, Britain is a multicultural, multilingual and multifaith country. Hastings (1986, xxi) describes late twentieth-century English Christianity as influenced by the growth of non-Christian religions such as Islam, Hinduism, and Buddhism, but also points out the increasing 'humanistic' attack on the surviving Anglican church. Within this context, St James operates the *missio Dei* locally and globally within the following process:

---

219. I use the term ecclesiastically, which refers more to church government, rather than 'ecclesiologically' which is more theological.

220. Thorton was treasurer during 1982–1987, and church warden from 1987 to 2008. (Information provided by email to the author on 8 February 2009).

221. Peppiatt was confirmed by the Bishop of Edmonton and later invited to join the church youth club in 1953; eventually he became leader, a Sunday School teacher and later Superintendent. He has served on the PCC since 1956, and has had various roles such as Bible study leader, leader of the Saturday mornings 9:30 prayer meeting; current roles consist of leading the 9:30 service welcomers, garden team, finance committee, chair of building committee (Information sent to the author on 14 January 2009).

222. The PCC (Parochial Church Council) is the elected body of lay church members who meet periodically to help ordained and other staff members to evaluate their direction and policy.

223. Information received from Catherine Ellerby, sent to the author by email on 16 January 2009. The former motto 'To love Christ and make him known' (pamphlet distributed at St James' services on 13 January 2008), has been replaced by 'To live as Jesus lived, to love as Jesus loved', including the key text: 'Live a life of love, just as Christ loved us and gave himself up for us' Ephesians 5:2.

St James' characteristics under the leadership of three vicars

Minister	Michael Bunker	Alex Ross	Kim Swithinbank
Ministry	1978 to 1992	1993 to 2007	2008 to 2012
Growth	229 to 501	537 to 890	890 to ?
Theology	Evangelical	Evangelical	Evangelical-Charismatic
Missiology	Locally and globally	Locally and globally	Locally and globally

Finances

The fact that the WMG practises an informal financial policy, confirms my finding that St James is part of the emergent missionary movement.[224] Therefore, its financial system has implied collaboration with their main mission links, as is shown below:

---

224. Will Hunter-Smart's interview with the author held on 26 January 2009 at St James' office.

Reciprocal contextual collaboration of St James' World Mission group[225]

St James' Missionaries	Foreign Missionaries	Non-members missionaries	Mission Organizations
Heather Payne	In Soo and Seung Ho	Paul Bendor Samuel	St Ann's Tottenham (London)
Folusho Ajibade	Nam Young	Miriam Mason	Educaid
John Paul and Susan Aranzulla	Samuel Cueva and Noemi Yupanqui	Peter Kennely	ORADEA (Rumania)
Richard and Valery Brueton			IFED (Italy)
			IME (Peru)
			AGAPE (UK)
			Pathway (UK)
			Nflame
			Interserve
			Derby City Mission
			K.C. Centre (London)

At the same time, the financial policy implies not giving money if they are not requested, projects needing a strong and sustainable link with St James, and that there is a priority on supporting individuals who go on STM. Thus, this mission policy, as Hunter states, becomes a more relational partnership; more people are involved directly and there is a potential for more relationships.[226] As part of the mission philosophy, the main elements of the WMG are represented by 'the four p's': pounds (financial support), prayer (for mission partners), publicity (making the church aware of mission), and people (how to support them and sending teams).[227]

Here, I will limit myself to analysing the relationship between St James and the Iglesia Misionera Evangelica in Peru (IME), where reciprocal

---

225. Ibid. For mission organizations see archives of the WMG, 'Main Misisions–2007'.
226. Will Hunter-Smart's interview, 2009.
227. Ibid.

contextual collaboration has been developed mainly in two ways, by collaboration in planting a Spanish congregation in London and by sending short-term mission teams to Peru.[228]

Reciprocal missiology

In tune with the Majority World missionary movement practice, which we have defined previously as the emergent missiology, Peruvian missionaries of the Iglesia Misionera Evangelica (IME) in Huancayo, Peru, were sent in 1997 to work in church planting among the Spanish-speaking people in London, a multicultural city in which 400,000 Latin American people live. The same year, Alex Ross made a verbal agreement with the IME missionaries to develop a reciprocal contextual collaboration to start the Spanish congregation at the premises of St James. This can be defined as spontaneous collaboration, which is less formal but includes honesty, trust, maturity and relational chemistry.[229] The primary focus of this analysis provides that at least six elements of reciprocal contextual collaboration were the pivotal elements to make possible a reciprocal commitment between St James and the IME church in order to send STM to Peru. These are as follows: reciprocal trust, reciprocal interest, reciprocal transparency, reciprocal maturity, reciprocal respect and reciprocal freedom. Thus, pivotal elements were developed within the context of personal relationship between the leadership of the two churches.

In relation to the lack of freedom (autonomy[230]), reciprocal interdependence (economy[231]) and sharing the control of power in decision making (authority[232]), which would affect the possibility of finding new

---

228. As a participant and observer, in reciprocal agreement with Vicar Alex Ross and the WMG, a decision was made to send the first SMT to Peru in August 1999.

229. Theological implications of partnership include: real friendship which takes time, and a need for "chemistry that comes from heaven".

230. I use the word autonomy as self-determination, self-government and self-rule.

231. Economic reciprocal interdependence implies accountability, not that both partners contribute equally.

232. I use the definition of authority as a person or group having the right and power to command, decide, rule, or judge. See thesaurus.com (http://thesaurus.reference.com/browse/authority).

appropriate models of partnership between the Western and the Third World churches, Ross's assumptions are: [233]

> From St James' perspective, I doubt if there is a lack of freedom. I think we are really fairly autonomous and able to feed in what we wanted in mission. I'm not sure what reciprocal interdependence looks like and I'm not sure how well that would work out between churches from two different cultures, who perhaps in many ways don't know each other. And I think that would be the same in terms of sharing the control of power and decision making. I think you can only enter into these things when you know the people and trust them.

The IME movement reflects a Latin American model of mission through the local church that also has a non-denominational mission structure called Misión IME International (International IME Mission). The IME church promotes a faith mission model of support that implies that missionaries have to provide their own financial support. Ten percent of the support comes from the Peruvian sending churches, while the difference is covered by relatives, friends and friend-churches. In this way St James should be included as a friend-church. Mission organizations do not have major participation in their finances.

I note here some practical support which St James Church has provided to the IME church for developing a reciprocal contextual collaboration since 1997. This includes:[234]

1. Free use of the building for the Spanish-speaking church.
2. Spiritual support received from the leadership and the staff.
3. Being part of St James' staff and a monthly small financial support.

---

233. Alex Ross' questionnaire, question 3 (email from London sent to the author on 20 January 2009). Reciprocal authority refers to a christological relationship where both collaborators in the *missio Dei* act as one like the *missio Trinitatis*.

234. Papers presented by Samuel Cueva at the Latin American Forum, Global Connections, on 18 October 2003. See also *Dictionary of Mission Theology* (Corrie 2007, 274–275).

4. Helping with a donation of $15,000 to buy the building of the IME church in Cerro de Pasco, Peru.
5. Making a 'Christmas appeal' for the IME church in Lima, Peru.
6. Providing the logistic work for organizing international mission conferences.
7. Providing legal support for getting visas for speakers.

On the other hand, the IME church has been supporting St James Church in the following way:

1. Motivating the British church in global mission.
2. Sending short-term mission teams (STM) to Peru every two years since 1999.
3. Strengthening the prayer meeting services every Friday at 6 am.
4. Helping to initiate what used to be the 5 pm service at St James.
5. Contributing to the ongoing task of the World Mission Group.
6. Regular participation at St James' services of IME missionaries.
7. Promoting the mission model between St James and the IME church.

Short-term mission teams

It is probably the case that the main contribution from the IME church to St James has been in the task of sending STM teams to Peru. This mission policy started in 1999 by sending St James' members to gain cross-cultural experience. It was carried out every two years, and involved visiting three IME churches in Peru during three weeks in August. Five STM teams have been sent to Peru; in 1999 the team was made up of seven people; in 2001 it was made up of ten; in 2003 of four; in 2005 of five, and in 2007 of six.[235] The fact that most of the STM volunteers managed to be involved in the life of St James after their STM experience testifies to its success. As a consequence, St James decided to empower this mission by sending

---

235. Members of the STM teams are as follows: 1999 – Ann Twisleton, Heather Payne, Isobel Lee, Peter Kluger, Edward Thornton, Richard Brueton, Geoff Tennant; 2001 – Heather Payne, Isobel Lee, Peter Kluger, Luis Appiah, Alex Thornton, Edward Thornton, Neil Tyler, Foluso Ajibade, Alex Appado, Noemi Cueva; 2003 – Jennifer Griggs, Luis Appiah, Dan Dartington, Noemi Cueva; 2005 – Fernando Cuevas, Jennifer Griggs, Margaret Stoves, Ruth Adamson, Noemi Cueva; 2007 – Richard Dominy, Kathy Dominy, Hanly Fourie, Elizabeth Bennett, Ruth Shellard, Noemi Cueva.

new teams to Malawi (2003), Romania and Sierra Leona (2006), and since 2007 triplet teams have been sent in parallel to India, Uganda, and Peru.[236]

Under this missiological process, St James sent STM teams to Romania and to Sierra Leona in 2006 and both have been involved in practical projects and sharing the gospel.[237] For these trips the WMG had a 'World Mission Sunday' consisting of giving feedback on the summer mission.[238] As noted, the summer mission 2007 included sending STM teams to Peru, Uganda and India.[239] In analyzing this mission activity, twenty people were involved and three elements were clearly noticed: (1) from the receiving church, there was an expression of thanks for sending STM, (2) an attitude of service on the part of the STM people, and (3) very well-organized trip and evangelistic events.[240] In contrast, the 2008 STM plan for Romania was cancelled due to both an external reason that an appropriate link was unable to be found, and an internal reason that Alex Ross handed the church over to Kim Swithinbank.[241]

It appears that STM have made the following contribution to St James: first, they have mobilized the local church to participate in mission more directly, and second they have created a consciousness of being more involved with the local church after the STM. Therefore, it seems to be crucial to understand that, first, STM are a tool for providing new committed members to the local church, second, that resources are employed to mobilize potential candidates to serve their local church, and third, STM provides candidates for long-term mission. As a participant observer, STM has also increasingly become a 'tunnel process' to involve lay people in local and global mission. This has been the case with Heather Payne who worked in long-term mission in India; Folusho Ajibade, a former missionary in France; Richard Brueton as a former doctor missionary in Malawi, Isobel

---

236. St James Church, minutes of the WMG, held on Monday 9 October 2006; St. James Church, minutes of the WMG held on Monday 8 October 2007.
237. See minutes of the WMG, held on Monday 9 October 2006.
238. Ibid.
239. See minutes of the World Mission Group held on 23 November 2006. The first STM to India was set up for 26 July to 16 August 2007 (Will Hunter-Smart's email to Heather Payne, archive of WMG 24 April 2007).
240. See minutes of the WMG held on Monday 8 October 2007.
241. See minutes of the WMG held on Monday 19 May 2008.

Lee taking up an active role on the PPC; as well as Richard and Kathy Dormandy, and Dan Dartington, committed to St James' life at that time.

Two approaches were used in determining the selection of the STM candidates. One approach between 1999 and 2005 was to select candidates by personal invitation through the WMG. The second approach started in 2007 by producing more appropriate leaflets to promote STM at all St James' services, which helped to increase interest on STM.

Mission relations

In analysing the STM to Peru, former 1999 STM member, Isobel Lee, considers that some of the weaknesses have been a lack of focus on English teaching and a lack of involvement in social action.[242] As a result of too much activity, perhaps there was a lack of an appropriate relationship with people within evangelism. Strengths, according to Lee, included encouragement to the team before the trip; agreement to get support for raising funds by writing to the church family and learning some Spanish words were helpful; during the trip, suitable hosts by the Peruvian church as well as opportunities to present the gospel in hospitals, children homes, public squares, parks, churches, schools, colleges, restaurants, houses, universities and language schools.[243] Lee points out that, while staying in three different cities (Lima, Huancayo and Cerro de Pasco), the journeys allowed the STM to get to know each other as a team which helped to build relationships.[244] In connection with Lee's perspective, Richard and Kathy Dominy, former 2007 STM, point out that STM is a great way to see another country and to meet Christians in a different culture.[245] Heather Payne, another

---

242. Data provided by Isobel Lee, a short-term mission team member to the author on 14 December 2008.
243. Ibid.
244. Ibid. Also to spend time with the church members of the Peruvian church playing volleyball, football, singing and eating together helped relationships with the receiving church.
245. In terms of preparation the Dominys suggest a better idea of what activities previous teams to Peru had been involved in; feedback and lesson-planning resources are indispensable. After the STM it is suggested encouragement to give more feedback to the church, which would lead to more benefits to St James and also encourage people to get involved in future mission trips (email from Richard Dominy sent to the author on 21 December 2008).

former STM to Peru, suggests that St James' improvements need promotion among young people and some feedback in the main church service.[246] It seems to me that this analysis confirms the seminal work that STM to Peru has brought to St James during 1999 to 2009.

Regarding strengths, Hunter points out that STM, first of all, generates a great deal of support for any missionary they support and, second, gives individuals a missionary perspective with the aim of eventually producing long-term missionaries. Some weaknesses include that sometimes it can be difficult to develop the right programme for the STM. One example is the STM to Uganda, in which they went with a mission plan to run a holiday club, but the church in Uganda wanted to provide experience of Uganda.[247] Comparing the traditional model, such as Latin Link with St James, Hunter explains that for the Western mentality, the first looks safer than the second due to the fact that they have the expertise in sending STM.[248] Thorton, taking the example of Interserve International, argues that the local church needs mission agencies to do mission.[249]

The emergent model does not deny the need of structures such as the traditional model operates, thus, both models provide opportunities for promoting an increasing participation of people. With a spirit of cooperation, characteristics can equally be interchangeable; therefore, traditional and emergent models operate concurrently. While the second tends to emphasize the presence of local churches, the first model provides strong structures for selecting, training and sending long-term missionaries. In this case, St James is distinct from the traditional model in the sense that the church's members have been heavily involved in sending STM, and people have more opportunity to participate as the WMG becomes more flexible for recruiting candidates. Thus, the emergent model provides a contribution to mission, and St James tries to develop this approach by

---

246. Heather Payne, questionnaire answered to the author on 22 December 2008.
247. Will Hunter-Smart's interview with the author held on 26 January 2009.
248. Ibid.
249. Thorton says: "I personally see Interserve International picking up the pieces in the mission field relating to churches that send missionaries direct. Also people like Interserve International do a lot of pastoring and care for such people on an informal basis and this is 'free-loading' on their goodwill" (information sent to the author on 8 February 2009).

sending STM through its WMG mission structure, which concurrently supports different traditional models. Consequently, regarding the local church, this case study shows complementarily the following strengths that STM provides to St. James, characteristics that can be interchangeable with the traditional model: [250]

1. Keeping the church thinking globally.
2. Challenging the membership to mission.
3. People return from STM with a positive attitude to the local church.
4. People grow in their Christian faith.

In connection with our analysis, it seems to me that the greatest missiological element of the 2007 STM to Peru has been the implementation of the social mission plan called Proyecto Alegria (The Joy Project), inaugurated on 4 August 2007 on the premises of the IME church in Huancayo, which initially consisted of providing a weekly breakfast for 50 poor children.[251] The target group which the IME focused on are children in extreme poverty between 5 and 11 years old, all at-risk children as they work in the streets, are victims of child abuse, are academically behind or have dropped out of school, are malnourished and above all come from families with precarious incomes.[252] Initial financial support came from the Buckhurst Hill Baptist Church, London, in providing £1,040 budget for a whole year.[253] For 2008, St James promised to send £1,100 but this

---

250. Will Hunter-Smart's interview, 2009. In the case of the North American model, Robert J. Priest and Joseph Priest (2008, 53–73) point out that 55% of recent students' short-term mission trips were in Spanish-speaking countries. To improve and promote short-term missions, they suggest that: (1) missiologists must place the short-term mission movement at the centre of research, (2) seminaries and colleges should include in mission studies a lecture on short-term mission, (3) our engagement for short-term mission must be positive and constructive, and (4) students involved in a short-term mission must receive academic credit. See further Robert J. Priest and Joseph Priest 'They see everything, and understand nothing' (2008, 53–73, Missiology, Volume XXXVI, Number 1, January).

251. See the first bulletin of the Proyecto Alegria (The Joy Project) edited in September 2007 in Peru.

252. Ibid. Proyecto Alegria's first bulletin. Children come from 4 areas of the Huancayo city (Mercado Modelo, Mercado Mayorista and surrounding areas, Ladrillera de Palián and Cerrito de la Libertad).

253. See archives of St James Church WMG: Support Request Form from the IME Church (2007, 2).

was delayed due to its poor cash flow.[254] In consequence, the IME church struggles to make the 'Proyecto Alegria' survive.[255] However, since 2013, ALEGRIA has provided a weekly breakfast for nearly 100 children.

Our analysis shows that all the STM to Peru before 2007 have been fulfilling one mission mandate but neglecting the second mandate, which is related to social responsibility. Perhaps this was the greatest weakness of the STM between St James and the IME church in Peru. It may have been strengthened under a critical analysis of mission mobility for the task.

While it is well known that the centre of gravity in mission lies in the emergent church, I agree with Priest and Priest when, quoting Robert Wuthnow, they state that demography does not have equal influence and power.[256] This implies that the vast proportion of Christian material resources come from Europe and the American churches. Hence, STM people come from those Christian contexts with greater material resources and collaborate with those who have less, not the other way around. Thus, the nature of STM activity seems missiologically expressed as a form of collaborative participation "in witness and service with Christians who are already present locally".[257]

In many cases, the emergent church has no formal links with any foreign organization. However, the majority church organizes evangelistic outreach by collaborating with STM from the Western church when possible. STM serves as an 'open door' for the receiving churches in their evangelistic, social and evangelical presence. For this reason, the book *Maximum Impact Short Term Mission* (Peterson, Aeschliman and Sneed 2003, 127–149, 151–162) seriously recommends the threefold STM process of pre-field,

---

254. Minutes of WMG held on Monday 19 May 2008.
255. The Alegria Project rests on the IME church's hands with decision made by its leadership to help financially since November 2007 (information given by Maria Nickl to the author 28 January 2009).
256. Robert J. Priest and Joseph Paul Priest "They see everything, and understand nothing": Short-Term Mission and Service Learning (Missiology Volume XXXVI Number 1, January 2008, 66).
257. Ibid.

on-field and post-field, as well as a threefold participant process which includes senders, goers and host receivers.[258]

I also agree with Dawn Lewis-Anderson when she concludes that independent, one-way relationships are culturally inappropriate, since interdependence is the biblical model (as the New Testament speaks of 'one another' 56 times), and this provides a theological basis for allowing others to serve us even as we serve them.[259] This theological ingredient avoids arrogance and self-righteousness from the STM participant.

A critcal mission theology
A critical aspect at St James has been its finances with a gap of £80,000–£150,000 each year. But for former vicar, Alex Ross, this was not an issue due to the fact that he does not believe in reserves to avoid complacency. For Ross, the factor that hinders the generosity of affluent people is the lack of commitment to Christ.[260] Therefore, weaknesses that affect the mission theology at St James in Ross' words are: The leadership of the church was probably not mission minded enough and that was probably reflected in the life of the church. And, as with many people in the UK, we have become rather insular because of the demise of the Empire and Commonwealth. There are feelings of guilt, rejection and tiredness of being involved in the wider world. The strengths are: If there was somebody who was a real mission enthusiast then there was real potential and space for them to enthuse the church and get something going. And they did have some wonderful links with people like the *IME missionaries* (italics mine), which I think these days are essential in world mission. In interpreting Ross' view, it may be concluded that St James' mission theology rests in God's hands and it has been developed for God's glory.

---

258. For a helpful discussion on STM see the chapter of 'A Biblical and Theological Basis' (Peterson, Aeschliman and Sneed 2003); the MA summarized findings of Daniel McDonough and Roger P. Peterson, 'Can Short-Term Mission Really Create Long-Term Career Missionaries?' Results of STEM's Second Major Scientific Study on the Long-Term Effect of Short-Term Mission (Minneapolis, Minnesota, STEMMinistries, 1999), and also Roger Peterson and Timothy D. Peterson, 'Is Short-Term Mission Really Worth the Time and Money?: Advancing God's Kingdom Through Short-Term Mission' (1999).
259. Dawn Lewis-Anderson, 'Maximizing Short-Term Mission Trips Participant Manual' (http://stmt.pbwiki.com/Downloads, 2009, 22).
260. Alex Ross, Questionnaire, question 1–2, sent to the author on 20 January 2009.

In the case of St James and the IME church relationships, Ross points out that,

> The partnership between IME and St James happened basically because *Peruvian missionaries* arrived at St James and I recognized good Christian brothers and we began to build on that. We met many, many times over the years and there was a mutual trust and confidence in each other. I found it a real privilege to be involved with *IME missionaries* and to let our mission teams go and serve with *IME missionaries* in Peru. And I think that is what happened in the New Testament and still happens today. It's God bringing Christians together who can then serve him in mission around the world (italics mine).[261]

Conclusion with an evaluation of positive and negative tensions

It seems to me that over the twenty-first century this emergent model is bound to spread and to bring new mission energy to the global engagement as a result of an increasingly relational missiology. After seventeen years of reciprocal collaboration (1997–2014)[262] between St James and the IME church, this emergent model provides four key elements that can be contextualized in any reciprocal North-South contextual collaboration.

- First, it must be recognized that mission cannot be developed in isolation, as it is vital to find reciprocal collaborators under God's kingdom mission theology.
- Second, the emergent model emphasizes unity in diversity, as joint projects are undertaken with no consideration of denominational boundaries, but rather within the unity of Christ's body. In this sense, the present case can become a spontaneous

---

261. Ibid., question 4.
262. St James decided to support the IME church to plant a Spanish-speaking congregation since November 1997 at the time Alex Ross was the vicar of St James.

theological 'laboratory' for 'evangelism, reconciliation and combating poverty'.²⁶³
- Third, mission of the twenty-first century should be a mission of reciprocal interdependence, which includes the ingredients of respect, reciprocal participation, and unconditional and intentional support for the other's missionary initiatives.²⁶⁴
- Finally, the idealistic and unrealistic assumption that a biblical reciprocal contextual collaboration will provide easy reciprocal agreements under God's kingdom mission theology must be avoided. In any collaboration there will be a dynamic and creative tension of strengths and weaknesses, but not an intentional 'higher' against 'lower' mission relationship; God's church is responsible for this missionary dynamism.

When it comes to the STM mission relationship, therefore, a critical analysis of mission mobility for STM to Peru seems necessary in order to highlight the need to find ways to involve more St James' people in STM. In this regard, we recommend that at least 10 percent of the congregation be intentionally encouraged to take part in global engagement²⁶⁵ and to organize a mission plan for their holidays, including more financial help.²⁶⁶ One of the challenges relates to the English conversation classes programme, developed by the STM since 2005, since there was no appropriate continuity of regular classes when the STM team finished its work in Peru. It

---

263. See further 'The Church of Scotland World Mission Council, 2006 General Assembly Report, Proposed Deliverance', (http://www.churchofscotland.org.uk/extranet/xga/downloads/gareports06worldmission.doc).

264. A missionary theology of harmonious freedom overcomes theological, cultural, social and economic roadblocks when both sides work in humility and *christological freedom*.

265. I agree with former STM Richard and Kathy Dominy's perspective that given the size of St James there are relatively few people that get involved in the mission trips, so perhaps there could be more publicity and encouragement for specific groups to get involved, for example 'The Source' 20s to 30s group (information sent to the author 21 December 2008).

266. St James has provided partial financial support for STM candidates as a result of requesting help, which differs from offering scholarships in the STM promotion. In *The Essential Guide to Short Term Mission Trip*, David Forward (1998, 67) identifies three common approaches to STM finances: (1) each individual pays for himself or herself, (2) the church mission budget pays for the entire team, (3) scholarships are awarded based on need. For further discussion see *The Essential Guide to the Short Term Mission Trip* (Forward 1998).

was necessary to find alternatives to provide long-term support for English teaching as a foreign language. Thus, a more committed and holistic mission enterprise from the side of the WMG would be achievable.[267] An issue that has not been addressed has to do with the possibility of maintaining regular information for those who went to Peru with the STM programme. Perhaps this is one of the difficulties that hinders success in attracting more candidates to the STM to Peru and elsewhere.

Missiologically, it is important to clarify that St James is not an emergent church, although it practises an emergent model which is characterized by a more relational form of participation on the part of the donors, a flexible mission policy, the inclusion of non- traditional missionaries, and an apparent desire to trust in God's provision for the fulfilment of the Great Commission. Since the source of this model lies on the periphery of a marginal economy, as well as social and political instability, its form of spirituality is marked accordingly. Indeed it was the IME church and its missional theology which entered into contact with St James church, not vice-versa.[268] One positive side of this model, and essential for emergent partnership, is the commitment to relationships rather than to hierarchical submission and administration. As Ross points out, it is the personal contact that matters because it provides a relational approach.[269] As we mentioned in chapter 3, the emergent model has been shaped by grassroots churches which are independent of traditional mission structures and denominations. This is the case that IME's mission reciprocity has developed with St James' in planting churches, mobilizing STMs, and promoting mission in Europe intentionally.

Some internal factors that I want to stress in the process of the reciprocal contextual collaboration between any emergent mission model (such as the local-to-local church or an indigenous mission agency model) are theological freedom (reciprocal autonomy), power-sharing (reciprocal authority)

---

267. See 'Teaching English for Foreign Language', paper presented at Global Connections on 28 March 2001 (http://www.globalconnections.co.uk/resources/missionissues/topic/strategies/TEFL.htm).
268. Alex Ross, Questionnaire, question 4, sent to the author 20 January 2009.
269. Ibid., question 3.

and generous sharing (reciprocal giving).[270] These threefold missiological factors are rooted in reciprocal interdependence within a christological relationship. These factors are integrated components and translatable. The first involves reciprocity of truth, confidence and respect for cultural, theological and ecclesiological distinctives. The second refers to the reciprocal effort to maintain an appropriate distribution of the control of power in making decisions. Neither collaborator has more power that the other, since both have the same authority in decision making. The third implies appropriate financial support, time, gifts, abilities, etc.

Despite the fact that British missions such as SAMS, Latin Link and SIM International are currently working in Peru,[271] my finding is that St James has broken new ground given that this British local Anglican church has chosen to work with a non-denominational Peruvian church, even though there is an Anglican diocese in Peru. The question emerges: why this particular missiological approach? I am guided by three theological assumptions. The first is an emphasis on God's kingdom theology. The second is the christological *missio* relationship, between Alex Ross as a missional-minded leader[272] and Peruvian missionaries. The third is the reality of answered prayer, since this missional intention of reciprocal contextual collaboration with St James was preceded by many years of prayer on the part of the IME church in Peru.

In addition, to all that has been analyzed before, lines of reciprocal accountability are indispensable in mission structures. Missiologist Alex Araujo defines accountability, in its broadest sense, as the condition whereby the motives and actions of one person or entity are subject to review, examination and judgment by another person or by an authority structure.[273]

---

270. Generous sharing implies money, time, gifts, abilities, etc.; it must be a reciprocal given, which does not relate to quantity but to generosity. It is a harmonious 'give and take'.
271. Global Connections (2004) Latin American Forum, Focus on Peru, Missionary Activity (http://www.globalconnections.co.uk/Resources/Global%20Connections/Mission%20Issues/2006/Peru.pdf)
272. Alex Ross' questionnaire, question 4 (email from London sent to the author on January 20 2009).
273. Information sent by Alex Araujo of Partners International to the author on 21 February 2011

This implies that people have to be accountable to others; thus, a suitable view of accountability in Christian mission must be biblically and theologically informed. Araujo states that missions with internal accountability, well informed, involved and responsible provide stability, direction and credibility to the mission structure, for this mutual trust and clear goals help them to be accountable (Taylor 1994, 121, 126);[274] thus, "accountability and evaluation accompany responsibility" (Wright 2000, 168).[275] In practice, accountability within the emergent model seems to be more subjective, while the traditional model tends to be more objective; however, each view has its own values and they can complement each other. Objective accountability within the traditional model provides more techniques and management orientation, as can be seen in the case of accountability for finances and personal action; accordingly, those factors help to hold each one accountable. In the case of the Latin American experience, accountability tends to be more relational, looks more subjective (but not in all cases) often based on nuance, indirect signals, and can be inclined in favour of some and against others, explains Araujo.[276] We conclude that mission collaboration requires structures of reciprocal accountability, both objective and subjective, which must be both vertical and horizontal working at the same time; the second, being accountable to the person you work with as a co-worker, and the first, being accountable to those in a higher organizational level (Whitehead 1991, 54–55, 175). In this sense, *Worth Keeping* (Hay et al. 2007) provides serious analysis for understanding the complexity of accountability, evaluation and auditing[277] for mission activity, which can be helpful for the traditional, emergent and networking models.

---

274. See also 'Managing Accountability' in *Building Strategic Relationships* (Rickett 2008, 53–61).

275. Walter Wright (2000, 12, 92, 188) provides lines of basic accountability such as accountability to God, to the organization, reviewing and evaluation of the plan, performance standards, and accountability for ourselves.

276. Information sent by Alex Araujo of Partners International to the author on 21 February 2011.

277. See further 'the organizational audit' (Wright 2000, 89).

Summary of the three case studies

In chapter 2 it was mentioned that the church is by nature missionary. On this basis, the local church is the primary agent of mission, just as the church is itself an object of the *missio Dei* (Bosch 1991, 387). However, mission history shows that all Protestant mission structure models have been developed according to a western pattern of doing mission through mission societies. This type of missiology, which tends to perpetuate the artificial split between church on the one hand and mission on the other, set the pattern for evangelical mission throughout the nineteenth and twentieth centuries. However, as the scale of the local-to-local church and the non-formal mission model increases, it appears to threaten the traditional mission structures of the western mentality.[278] In anti-reciprocal attitude, this missiological fear would serve to dilute the biblical view of a Trinitarian mission theology and the christological mandate of unity in diversity. Therefore, by promoting more emphasis on flexibility and bottom-up structures within the traditional models, this attitude will benefit the important task of facilitating merged or combined mission models for the accomplishment of the *missio Dei*. We acknowledge however that traditional missions are in a period of adjusting their attitude towards indigenous movements and encouraging wider reciprocal participation. As such, changes are evident in mission structures, which reflect a combination of mission models, to the extent that some are becoming an amalgam of different models in response to the increasing demands of the twenty-first-century mission. This is the case with SIM[279] working now in Latin America; with the European Christian Mission (ECM), which is now developing a Spanish and Latin American sending section with offices in

---

278. See also the discussion during the 1990s in Butler (Taylor 1994, 8).
279. Sudan Interior Mission (SIM) began in 1893, with a vision to preach the gospel the 60 million people of the Sudan area in sub-Saharan Africa. In 2000, they adopted the trade name for 'Serving in Mission' (SIM), and now they are also working in Asia and in Latin-American in Bolivia, Chile, Ecuador, Paraguay, Peru and Uruguay. In relation to collaboration they see churches to which SIM relates empowered to fulfil their missionary potential with SIM as a catalyst, assisting them through creative, interdependent partnerships. See further SIM, Serving in Mission (http://www.sim.co.uk/where_we_work/south_america, Online, accessed on 5th October 2011 at 10.28).

Brazil and Portugal (together but not mixed);[280] with Interserve, with its largely long-term recruitment; and recently, a short-term placement can also be arranged. In the case of Wycliffe, the following changes are evident: within a process started in 2009, the name of 'Wycliffe International' has been replaced with 'The Wycliffe Global Alliance'. This is due to the fact that 'The Wycliffe Global Alliance' is the group which now connects all partners and member organizations that are involved in Bible translation around the world. Each of these entities is autonomous with its own board. In the past, only member organizations were part of Wycliffe. Now, they have many diverse partners and member organizations working together. When Wycliffe began many years ago, the organizational culture and the process were very 'US' in nature. Now, a global leadership is in place, which, with its extremely diverse team, serves the new mission structure and is making changes to honour the uniqueness and diversity in the global body of Christ.[281] One example is that they are changing a 'hierarchical partnership structure' for a 'participatory partnership structure'.[282]

---

280. Francisco Gross, director of ECM for Spain and Latin America, explains that ECM has had a strong link with Latin American and other non-Western churches as well as sending bodies for nearly 20 years (but that structural change is as recent as 2003 and 2005), and that non-Western missionaries have been received into their field, with all the blessings and challenges that that entails. One of the strongest non-Western areas has been Latin America. He clarifies that the 'Sending Section' is marked because ECM International works as 'an alliance of sending bodies' or sending sections from the more mature and traditional missional sending countries in the world (e.g. Britain, USA, Australia, Ireland and others) and that the vision is to promote something at the same level as these non-Western countries. Contacts have also been made in Korea and in South Africa; he also indicates that ECM is widening its network, but that the intention is to make these non-Western (or non-traditional) bodies as functional and efficient as the traditional ones. The aim is that all work together, empowering and promoting missions and their European mission agenda at the same level (each one on its own place with 'covenant-based' relationships, but also allowing their own identity, cultural input and own challenges as well). ECM is also trying to find local partnerships with indigenous sending bodies. In the case of the Latin American and Spanish section, ECM have worked (and are working) with SEPAL, Seteca, COMIBAM (and their inner networks of churches and indigenous promoting bodies), various local churches and denominations, etc., (information by email sent to the author by Francisco Gross on 10 October 2011).

281. Each of the partner and member organizations is deeply committed to seeing all people have access to God's word in their language. Often there are MOUs (Memorandums of Understanding) which guide how a partnership will work in a specific area (information by email, sent to the author by Mary Lederleitner on 4 October 2011).

282. See further Wycliffe Global Alliance (http://www.wycliffe.net/AboutUs/ANewName/tabid/99/language/en/ Default.aspx, accessed on 4 October 2011).

This case attests to the fact that some traditional missions are becoming an amalgam of different models in response to the increasing demands of the twenty-first-century mission. Thus, a movement towards combined models seems to be the way forward for the twenty-first-century mission. I maintain that the networking and emergent models offer an exciting and appropriate way forward for the twenty-first century,[283] and that traditional models will evolve through interaction with these two models towards a movement of different and interconnected mission models. It is clear that at present a missional reality of models appears to be either of one kind or another, and is changing in becoming a movement towards a synthesis of different kinds. Therefore, in conformity with the report 5, 'Forms of Missionary Engagement' of Edinburgh 2010 (Balia and Kim 2010, 121), I argue that the local church and mission societies are the two basic mission structures that are necessary and influential to all mission models. These two structures work in dynamic tension to better understand the nature of this shared mission, which has its own vulnerability.

To conclude our critical analysis, as Escobar (2009, 196) states, "mission of the twenty-first century requires well-established and durable institutions". On this basis, we acknowledge that well-established and durable institutions are two weaknesses of the emergent model, whose practitioners continue to learn as they form appropriate mission structures to face the global mission scenario. In this light, 'well-established and durable missions' are strengths of the traditional model, due to its long-lasting durability within nineteenth- and twentieth-century mission history.

There is no turning back to a provincial interpretation, which implies that the first and second mission models are better than the third model or vice-versa. Mission models, to a great extent, are appropriate depending on the context in which they are used; some are untranslatable. As Costas points out (1976, 328), mission is specifically the fulfilment of the great news of reconciliation in Christ, which includes freedom, community and

---

283. See further "The Church of Scotland World Mission Council, 2006 General Assembly Report, Proposed Deliverance", which provides a view of the participation of the local church under the New Testament model with efforts made by these churches to share with one another their human, material and spiritual resources (http://www.churchofscotland.org.uk/extranet/xga/downloads/gareports06worldmission.doc).

hope. This is why mission structures are tools for this missionary theology, not an end in themselves.

Part IV

Towards a New Form of Mission Collaboration for the 21st Century

CHAPTER 6

A Novel Innovative Model Related to Reciprocal Contextual Collaboration in Creative Tension

Introduction

At this point, an examination of new perspectives of mission in the light of reciprocal contextual collaboration will be helpful. As we saw in earlier chapters of this study, the nature and use of reciprocal contextual collaboration in Christian mission will be central to the evangelical movement. In chapter 1 it was established that reciprocal contextual collaboration involves a constructive, dynamic and renewed relationship in creative tension which is undertaken between two or more of Christ's disciples in order to accomplish the *missio Dei* through the christological double mandate which affects the universe and the human being for the glory and benefit of God's kingdom. The christological mandate implies a historical, theological, political, economic, social and cultural dimension to the redemptive mission. Therefore, the nature of reciprocal contextual collaboration is rooted in the relational character of biblically guided relationships.

Here, in chapter 6, we outline, first, a missionary theology and, second, a biblical approach to the foundation and nature of any mission theology which is based on reciprocal contextual collaboration. Third, we shall provide a basic foundation for reciprocal contextual collaboration. Fourth, we shall clarify the importance of God's glory in mission. Fifth, we shall propose a spiral mission theology with reference to its key components, organic values, biblical assumptions, and key motives. Sixth, we will provide three mission tensions that are at work in any reciprocal contextual collaboration. Finally, we shall describe four models: the synergy, spontaneous, integrated and the contextual, which reflect the mission philosophy of reciprocal contextual collaboration and involve the decisive and conscious participation of the Majority World in the mission enterprise of the twenty-first century.

Mission theology of reciprocal contextual collaboration

A reciprocal contextual collaboration mission theology reflects Alister L. McFadyen's point (1990, 27; Moltmann 1981, 174; Barrett 1978, 512)[1] in *The Call to Personhood*, that personal identity within the Trinity identifies not just unique individuals but the form of relationship peculiar to them; the three divine Persons are united by sharing uniquely in a common nature (substance). Therefore, the Father, Son and Spirit are Persons in relation and Persons only through relations.[2] In this sense, we understand reciprocal contextual collaboration as a missionary theology of teamwork in which the members are not strictly divided into separate entities.[3] While they may function differently, the members work united as one body through a strong relationship and with the same goal to improve

---

1. McFadyen gives a similar understanding to that of Moltmann (*The Trinity and the Kingdom* 1981, 174) and Barrett (*The Gospel According to St John* 1978, 512) provides a complementary view of John's gospel theology to explain the unity between the Father and the Son and yet they remain distinct.

2. The unity and fellowship of the Persons of the Trinity provide the intellectual means to harmonize *personality* and *sociality* in mission relations of the church without denying the one to the other. But in the western approach it seems that individuality has sacrificed the social aspect of the Trinity, which offers a model of community mission. Therefore, "the disappearance of the social doctrine of the Trinity has made room for the development of possessive individualism in the Western World". See Moltmann *The Trinity and the Kingdom of God* (1981, 199).

3. "The unity of the church is strictly analogous to the unity of the Father and the Son. The Father is in the Son and the Son is eternally with the father in the unity of the Godhead, active alike in creation and redemption" (Barrett 1978, 512). Therefore, "the Father and the Son are one and yet remain distinct" (512).

contextual approaches to the *missio Dei*, God's kingdom and God's church. However, the doctrines of the fall and original sin explain the way in which humanity has distorted appropriate relations with God and with one another, but which can be overcome through appropriate practice of a model based on the relationship between Father, Son and Holy Spirit, according to which the individuality of each Person is achieved through a Trinitarian process of existing in and for others (McFadyen, 29, 42). In the case of the church, this is seen in the biblical affirmation of Christ's body, according to which there are different members but one body.[4] So the church's witness naturally overflows with a practical form of fellowship rooted in an internal focus of the Trinity (Flett 2009, 9); reciprocal fellowship is the missionary nature of the church too.[5] As we can see below, mission models must obey God's mission plan for redemption of the whole creation.

---

[4] The expression of unity is shown in the case of the *missio Dei*, where there is no dichotomy between God's being and God's action; both work reciprocally and interdependently. For further reading see 'Missio Dei: A Trinitarians Envisioning of a Non-Trinitarian Theme', John Flett (*Missiology*, Number 1, January 2009, 5–17). Similarly, Moltmann (1993, 54), in *The Church in the Power of the Spirit*, states that the *missio ad extra* reveals the *missio ad intra*, but the second is the foundation. Thus, procession (movements) of the sending of Jesus from the Father and the sending of the Spirit by the Son and the Father relate to God himself. Put in another way, the procession of the Spirit of Christ is eternally the Spirit who proceeds not only from the Father, but also from the Son.

[5] As the missionary nature of the church is to proclaim the gospel, or to have compassion for the poor, it is also by nature to have fellowship within local churches, mission structures, and ministries of God's church.

Mission models obeying God's plan for restoring creation

Mission theology	Perfect creation	Fallen world	New mission
God's eternal will: creation of good things and perfection of harmonious relationship	In God's image (Gen 1:26–27) Perfect relationship: freedom to serve God and one another	With Adam's fall (Rom 5:12–21) Relationship: broken with roadblocks	Christ's kingdom glory (1 Cor 15:20–28). Relationship: restored freedom and reciprocity
God's missionary plan: redemption of everything due to the presence of the fallen world	Reciprocal Trinitarian freedom In love, harmony peace and justice	Disunity and sinful nature with personal and social sin effects	New creation (Rom 7:14–25, Gal 3:28, Eph 2:11–22)
God's church: collaboration of God's redemptive will through reciprocal contextual collaboration by different models of mission.	No barriers, peace, reciprocal sharing	Disharmony, discrimination, war, conflicts, injustice	Perfect freedom and harmony for God's glory
God's message: reconciliation through Christ	Man is authorized to co-participate in harmony	Man is alienated by sin	Man is liberated from sin through Christ

The dimensional *perichoresis* of the Trinity (eternal communion that is a Trinitarian unity),[6] the political tension of the church (ecclesiology), the

---

6. The Greek word *Perichoresis* means 'permeation without confusion'. It refers to the mutual inter-penetration and indwelling within the threefold nature of the Trinity – Father, Son and Spirit. Thus, each person of the Trinity shares completely in the life of the other two in perfect harmony but the distinctions between the persons are preserved. Perichoresis relates to the 'divine dance', the eternal communion of the Father, Son and Holy Spirit. See further Seng-Kong Tan, 'A Trinitarian Ontology of Mission', *International*

dynamic tension of the kingdom, and the relational tension of collaborators (through models of mission), which together bring imaginative and creative tensions to reciprocal contextual collaboration, emphasize the fact that collaboration in mission is mainly a reciprocal relationship in freedom of sharing, reciprocal trust, truth in the gospel, unity in diversity, respect for dignity, and common goals for God's glory.[7] These characteristics relate also to asymmetrical mission reciprocity due to their qualitative nature, contrary to the quantitative approach. So asymmetrical reciprocity is not identical on both sides; for example, while one might give money, the other might provide loyalty. Reciprocal mission theology is asymmetrical in the added sense that quality defines the relationship between two or more autonomous bodies. This asymmetrical aspect overcomes the misunderstanding regarding equality. Asymmetrical reciprocity implies that one participant brings personnel or buildings and the other provides trust, or technology/opportunity, etc. Consequently, a missional understanding of mission labourers working together, as we belong and work for the same kingdom, therefore grounds a reciprocal contextual collaboration mission theology that will help us to find new appropriate models of mission through autonomy (of individuals without individualism), freedom (to be shared, not imposed), interdependence (in harmony, without domination) of mission co-participants. This mission theology promotes dialogue and reciprocity within a non-manipulative[8] but truthful interdependent communication, as it is the fundamental character of the Trinity.[9]

The Trinitarian life, and on that basis a Trinitarian reciprocal contextual collaboration, is to be expressed in the daily life of the church. This Trinitarian ecclesial life is rooted in love (God's eternal nature of love); it

---

Review of Mission Volume 93 (2004, 279–296); Grenz (2004, 81); Boff (1988, 134–135). In the evangelical arena mainly, the fellowship model of the church is emphasized through Christ's relationship.

7. Truth is propositional; it is a property, a characteristic or attribute only of propositions. For a wider concept of biblical truth, see John W. Robbins' article 'The Biblical View of Truth', 240–241, February and March 2005 (http://www.trinityfoundation.org/PDF/240-241-BiblicalViewofTruth.pdf).

8. McFadyen (1990, 32) speaks of communicative autonomy for independent communication.

9. See further Alister L. McFadyen (1990, 113–150), *The Call to Personhood*.

is communal (there is a functional relationship, not a hierarchical one); it is transparent (absolute confidence and truth); rooted in humility (there is recognition of cultural identity by accepting differences), in submission (respect, first to God, then to our fellow mission worker) and happiness (no one is happier than God, who gives joy to the church through reciprocal co-participation in the *missio Dei)*. Reciprocal contextual collaboration is a kingdom mission with a mission theology led by the Spirit, through the Son, to the Father. This understanding gives the church a theological view that speaks to the human need for relationships, communication and unity within diversity. This implies that there is a reciprocal contextual collaboration, which appears manifested in different responses to the mission mandate by the people of God. Therefore, reciprocity in mission theology can be understood as follows:

1. Reciprocal contextual collaboration as partnership.
2. Reciprocal contextual collaboration as strategic alliances.
3. Reciprocal contextual collaboration as cooperation.
4. Reciprocal contextual collaboration as business in mission.
5. Reciprocal contextual collaboration as evangelism.
6. Reciprocal contextual collaboration as social responsibility
7. Reciprocal contextual collaboration as mobilization.
8. Reciprocal contextual collaboration as liberation.
9. Reciprocal contextual collaboration as celebration.
10. Reciprocal contextual collaboration as building two-way bridges

Within a theology of mission reciprocity we mean by 'reciprocal' equivalent, relating to complementary functions between two or more persons or institutions, and to giving or doing something in return for something else. Synonyms are retributive, complementary, shared, joint and correlative. The Quechua words *ayni* and *minka* relate to reciprocity, which in the Peruvian Quechua context means a community work focus on social participation to benefit a society by sharing a work of common goals.[10] It has a relationship in community with the emphasis in working together

---

10. For Chapman, reciprocity as *Ayni* and *Minka* implies maintaining equilibrium. See Chapman (2006, 252).

in harmony,[11] with different purposes, such as to help an individual or a family to participate in the harvest of products, or constructing houses or public buildings, but always with a retribution for those who helps. *Minka* has characteristics of celebration, solidarity, a collaborative spirit and team working philosophy.[12] Esteban Both (Padilla and Yamamori 2001, 117–119), in 'The biblical basis for integral mission in the context of poverty' (in which he elucidates the social relational model theory given by Alan Fiske), points out that one principle to overcome poverty relates to justice and reciprocity.[13] While for many 'reciprocal' is synonymous with 'mutual', since both involve a two-way relationship,[14] here we would like to clarify a difference. While the term 'reciprocal' (from the Latin word *reciprocus*) involves a complementary action on the part of two or more people or institutions, 'mutual' (from the Latin *mutuus*) involves an emphasis on parties united by interchange in the same act performed at the same time, such as a mutual covenant, mutual love, etc.[15] However, reciprocal, a two-way relationship concentrated in making a response, is distinct in the sense that one party acts by way of return or response to something previously done by the other party, as in reciprocal compassion, reciprocal vision, or reciprocal trust, where for example, one gives finances and the other responds with thanksgiving (asymmetrical reciprocity). Furthermore, reciprocity integrates a theological meaning of sharing (either partake or participate), which affirms participation with others. It implies 'contribution

---

11. Reciprocity as *Ayni* and *Minka*, implies equilibrium. See Chapman (2006, 252).

12. *Minka* is practiced in Peru, Ecuador, Bolivia and Chile. See 'La Minga en Movimiento', published on 3 October 2008, http://lamingaenmovimiento.wordpress.com/la-minga/ (accessed on 30 July 2010 at 9:31)

13. Alan Fiske is one of the pioneering thinkers of the relational model theory. See Marco Verweij's article 'Towards a Theory of Constrained Relativism: Comparing and Combining the Work of Pierre Bourdieu, Mary Douglas and Michael Thompson, and Alan Fiske' in *Sociological Research Online* (http://www.socresonline.org.uk/12/6/7.html).

14. See Encyclo Online Encyclopedia, http://www.encyclo.co.uk/define/reciprocal (Accessed on 7 August 2010 at 22:20). The University of Notre Dame defines reciprocal as interchanged, mutually, reciprocal and reciprocity, and also implies the idea of borrow and lend; see University of Notre Dame, Latin Dictionary and Grammar Aid, http://www.archives.nd.edu/cgi-bin/lookit.pl?latin=mutuus (Accessed on 5 August 2010 at 17:50).

15. Mutuality means 'shared in common', but some language critics have objected to this usage because it does not include the notion of reciprocity (The Free Dictionary, http://www.thefreedictionary.com/mutuality).

with' (Rom 12:13) or 'distribution of' (Rom 12:8), such as sharing possessions (Luke 6:38, Heb 13:16, 1 John 3:17–18); sharing power (sharing of authority for decision making on priorities, allocating personnel and financial resources); and sharing spiritual gifts. It is within this reciprocal understanding of biblical collaboration that sharing in mission becomes both natural and possible.[16] Sharing is the organizing principle of the *oikonomia* and social justice (Hong-Jung 2002, 581), and for Craig Blomberg (1999) sharing material possessions becomes pivotal in biblical theology.[17] Later we will see the tensions of the reciprocal sharing spirit.

Reciprocal co-participation in mission means, therefore, that a kingdom action on the part of one member (or institution) receives a positive answer from the other member (or institution). At that point the members arrive at reciprocity in goals, relationships, purpose, motives, strategies, etc. Accordingly, it seems to me that the emphasis on mutuality in mission (having something in common or shared), developed especially in the missiological thought of the WCC during the 1950s to the 1980s has lacked a clear explanation of mutual missiology and what we refer to as mission reciprocity, which stresses the emphasis of quality of relationship by making a positive response to help one another as Christ's body.[18]

For reciprocal mission theology, we suggest that one of God's kingdom co-laborers has to start the dialogue or to provide a mission proposal and then others have to make a response. That response would have two different answers within a positive or negative attitude: negative answer (no-reply,

---

16. See more on 'biblical sharing' in *Dictionary of Mission Theology* (Corrie 2007, 274). For Lee Hong-Jung, sharing would indicate more than reciprocity of giving and receiving, but also more than mutual recognition of needs (*International Review of Mission*, Vol. XCI No. 363, October 2002). See also Kirk (1999).

17. Blomberg's conclusion of a biblical theology for material possessions is as follows: material possessions are a good gift from God; are simultaneously one of the primary means of turning people away from God; it is necessarily a redeeming process of transformation in the area of stewardship; extremes of wealth and poverty are intolerable; and finally, we must not elevate material possessions in the Bible to a central role as salvation. See further Blomberg *Neither Poverty nor Riches*, (1999, 243–246).

18. Despite that some dictionaries provide that 'mutual' and 'reciprocal' are synonymous words, we prefer to make a distinction because of the emphasis on Christ's body theology, where all the participants have something to share with joy. Mutual seems to be more 'quantity', seeking equality, while reciprocal seems to be more relational, allowing asymmetrical participation in mission.

let me think, or I do not think so) or a positive answer (I like your project, let's work together, let's make a decision, or let's join efforts).[19] The term reciprocal (adjective) is interchangeable with the following concepts: complementary (to improve each other), correlation (relationship depends on one another and vice versa), interchange (exchange things with each other), interdependence (dependence on each other), reciprocate (verb transitive, to give and take) and reciprocity (a noun that denotes interchanging for the benefit of both collaborators).[20] Therefore, we will use these terms in an interchangeable approach in order to avoid a reductionist view of reciprocal mission theology, as defined in our chapter 2.

An appropriate mission theology of reciprocity implies that churches belong to one another (1 Cor 12:12–27; Eph 4:1) as they confess Christ as the only Saviour (Eph 4:5), as they are led by the same Trinitarian God (2 Cor 13:14), and by Holy Scripture (2 Tim 3:16) and as they are empowered by the same Holy Spirit (1 Cor 12:13; Eph 1:13, 4:4). Under this theological foundation, mission collaboration therefore sees the church as an indivisible unity (Eph 4:16), called to proclaim the good news in accordance with the *missio Dei*, God's kingdom and Trinitarian mission theology that we have discussed in chapter 2. Consequently, traditional, networking, emergent, and indigenous movements of local churches, mission societies and mission networks in a variety of national, regional or international groups, are not allowed to compete (Eph 4:1). Rather, they are all mission structures allowed under God's will, called to contribute to the extension of God's redemptive missionary plan, which includes both the restoration of creation and the human being. Thus, reciprocal contextual collaboration's mission theology is foundational to accomplish the christological *missio* mandate (that implies the double mandate, evangelism and social responsibility), which is developed within an organic church rather than only to a structural church. Relevant for this theological context is Alan Hirsch's

---

19. For Boff (1988, 129), reciprocity supposes at least two presences relating to each other and so reciprocity between two presences. Thus, reciprocation and con-natural beings feel a certain attraction to one another; as the attraction is greater, communion becomes more perfect but there will never be fusion as each retains its identity with a desire of fusion as one.

20. See Oxford English Dictionary (2005, 198, 219, 528, and 855).

(2006) exploration, *The Forgotten Ways,* of organic systems and the pros and cons of institutions in mission.[21] In relation to the church as the body of Christ, Addicott (2005, 3), in his chapter 'Body Matters – Why?', suggests that three new paradigms have come to light for twenty-first-century mission: partnering, relationships and synergy, and these are in contrast to the three old paradigms: pioneering, resources and strategy. Below, I limit myself to providing a summary of the mission theology of reciprocal contextual collaboration.

---

21. For the organic church and institutional organizations see further Alan Hirsch (2006, 185–187).

Mission theology of reciprocal contextual collaboration

Elements	*Missio Dei*	*Missio Ecclesiae*	*Missio Context*
Reciprocal	Trinitarian theology	Biblical freedom	Interdependence mission theology
Contextual	Supra-cultural principles of freedom theology	Reciprocal christological relationship	Consider both internal and external factors
Collaboration	Under God's kingdom mission theology	Mission theology of compassion and generosity,	Prophetic *missio imagination*
Physical	Freedom, generosity and reciprocity	Multicultural teams and simple lifestyle	Non-territorial Non-denominational
Social	Freedom from personal and social sin	Practising a unity theology	Empowering the new emergent church
Cultural	Developing a theology of cultural identity	Holistic mission relationship	African, Asian and Latin American
Economic	Sharing the control of power and decision making	Overcoming disparities in economy	Recognition of the immigrant, bi-vocational missionary force
Spiritual	Trinitarian	Diversity submitted to unity	Local and global
Missional	Fulfilment of the double mission mandate	*Metanoia* relationship	Development of local theologies

Biblical approach to reciprocal contextual collaboration

At this point we approach the biblical text in order to study those interchangeable words which are applicable within reciprocal contextual collaboration for the mission activity of the church: labourer as worker (*ergatēs*); joint-worker, a worker together with (*sunergos*); and fellow-worker, as in holding with (*metochē*). These words are applicable within reciprocal contextual collaboration for the mission activity of the church.

First, **labourer**, which means a mission worker (*ergatēs*),[22] who in God's kingdom is called to serve in his vineyard. A labourer in mission implies a joint-worker, a 'fellow worker' (see Phil 4:3, 1 Thess 3:2, Phlm 1:24). Hence, the biblical notion of labourer avoids an intrusive missiology. Jesus uses labourer in different contexts: labourer for the harvest (Matt 9:37; Luke 10:2), labourer for God's kingdom (Matt 20:1), and labourer who is worthy of his wages (i.e. financial support, Luke 10:7). The apostle Paul echoes this third teaching when writing to Timothy (1 Tim 5:18), as does James, who also uses labourer in the context of prevention of any injustice in financial matters of salaries (Jas 5:4).

Second, the noun **co-labourer,** from the original Latin *collaborare*, refers to the one who labours with another, an associate in labour.[23] This concept is interchangeable with 'fellow worker' (*metochē*),[24] the original old English concept of partner, which means an associate,[25] or 'joint-worker' (*sunergos*),[26] a person who joins with others in some activity or endeavour, or a 'labourer' (*ergatēs*), a worker. The mission theological meaning of co-labourer and fellow worker is indicated by the apostle Paul when he addresses his associates in mission such as Epaphroditus (Phil 2:25), Clement (Phil 4:3), and Philemon, "our fellow worker" (Phlm 1:1). These words

---

22. Analytical Concordance to the Holy Bible (1977, 581).
23. Oxford English Dictionary (2005,188).
24. Analytical Concordance to the Holy Bible (1977, 341).
25. Oxford English Dictionary (2005, 188).
26. Analytical Concordance to the Holy Bible (1977, 581). The role of *sunergos* means responsible action by the worker and knowledge of the relevant techniques (Tippet 1987,17).

convey the idea of submission to someone who has been given permission to work for a given purpose. In fact, it is God's kingdom for which one works, and it is the *missio Dei* with which one works, all through Christ's invitation. 'Labourer', 'co-labourer' and 'fellow worker' draw attention to the mission theology gravity centre of the *missio Dei*, God's kingdom and a Trinitarian missiological approach, which must be developed in fellowship (*koinōnia*) with the Trinity, reflecting this understanding within relationships of the church.

Therefore, the church is not the owner of the mission enterprise; mission is not based on the initiative of denominations, movements, mission societies, networks or local churches. Thus, when you decide voluntarily to enter into a mission relationship with others, you become a labourer, co-labourer or fellow worker with someone else or from someone else. It is a mission relation of two-way traffic where individuality and autonomy do not end but rather work within the freedom of reciprocal agreement. There is a double tension of privilege and responsibility when one is chosen by Christ to take on active co-participation in his redemptive mission.

Third, there is a biblical aspect linked to reciprocal contextual collaboration. This is the collaborative core value of skills distribution described in 1 Corinthians 3:7–17. The apostle Paul defines the whole church as God's fellow workers and, then in a *crescendo* missionary theological reflection, Paul states that he has been chosen by the grace of God to lay a foundation as an expert builder, and that someone else is building on it, "using gold, silver, costly stones, wood, hay or straw". So Paul concludes that, "neither he who plants nor he who waters is anything, but only God, who makes things grow". Within the vast diversity of mission projects in the global mission engagement, this mission theology insight must be recovered emphatically. The assumption is that every fellow mission worker has been chosen by God to do something for God's kingdom and must submit his or her plan to God's provision, design and skills. Otherwise there is a danger of competition, duplication or distraction from the right mission model for working together. Therefore, acknowledgement of skills and undistorted communication, which is genuine and truly responsible, are fundamental values in reciprocal contextual collaboration.[27]

Fourth, a biblical aspect relates to spiritual gifts which are given to the saints,[28] and helps us to overcome the myth that mission activity is only for mission professionals or members of the clergy. Biblically speaking, as part of the Christian body, each member has at least one spiritual gift (Rom 12:4–8, 1 Cor 12:11), which is given to equip him or her for collaboration in God's kingdom purposes. In Paul's theology it is seen that the manifestation of the Spirit is given to each believer, and the same Spirit distributes to each one individually as he wills (1 Cor 12:7–11). In a complementary way, Paul adds that the body is in fact made up of not one member but of many, that there are indeed many members, yet, one body. In this way, there should be no schism in the body; rather, the members should have the same care for one another (1 Cor 12:14–26). In a complementary biblical understanding, Addicott (2005, 7) uses the Pauline metaphor of the body to point out that despite the church's mission diversity, there is only one body.[29] However, as Addicott (2005, 119–137) warns, the reality is that there are at least five missiological differences which must be addressed carefully. These are as follows: first, cultural differences, which include the way decisions are made, the way time is regarded, the way status is viewed, attitudes to shame, and attitudes to accountability; second, differences in gifting and contribution; third, differences with regards to preferred roles; fourth, differences in style of relating to one another; and fifth, differences in theology.

---

27. For Alister I. McFadyen (1990, 119), God's communication is its creative appeal to personal autonomy, which is capable of interpersonal relationships through responsible dialogue led by Christ's presence.

28. Rooted in this biblical foundation, every redeemed Christian should have an active and specific role in the *missio Dei* as they are the elect people of God to proclaim the good news of the gospel (1 Pet 2:9).

29. For Addicott (2005, 6), the concept of 'body-work' is God's idea that derives from a Trinitarian doctrine of community in harmony.

Foundational reciprocal contextual collaboration

For reciprocal contextual collaboration there are three foundational quests: the mission quest, the church's quest, and the quest of the mission strategy. The first refers to the *missio Dei*, God's kingdom, Trinitarian mission theology, God's church and christological mission; the second quest refers both to the missionary nature of the church and to the church's mission activity, which is developed under the guidance of a Trinitarian mission theology with a christological emphasis;[30] and the third quest refers to the ways, models and structures the church uses as tools to accomplish the *missio Dei*. In relation to these three foundational quests, Andrew Kirk, in *What is Mission?* (Kirk 1999), tries to clarify mission quest through theological exploration. In *Models of the Church*, the Roman Catholic, Avery Dulles (Dulles 1974), offers five models of comparative ecclesiology that shed light on the church's quest.[31] An evangelical approach consisting of twelve biblical images of what the church is, and what the church ought to be, is provided by John Driver in *Images of the Church in Mission* (Driver 1997). Works like The New Catholicity (Schreiter 2004), and Models of Contextual Theology (Bevans 2007), offer insights into our understanding of the quest for a mission strategy. [32]

The mission philosophy assumptions regarding reciprocal contextual collaboration can be defined in the following characteristics: (1) Encouragement and reciprocal support for the development of a reciprocal mission theology which is Trinitarian. (2) Accessibility of a theological approach to contextual reciprocity for all God's people, whether in positions of leadership or not. (3) A worldview which is intentional in its desire to develop mission relationships. (4) The intention to promote autonomous decision making of new mission models under christological freedom. (5) Economic support from those who have more to those who have less – this

---

30. The starting point of all discussion for church's mission is what Jesus said and did about God's missionary plan of salvation. See Kirk (1999, 42).

31. Comparative ecclesiology relates to a systematic reflection on the points of similarities and differences in the ecclesiology of different denominations (Dulles 1974, 1).

32. For the quest of the mission strategy see also *Biblical Foundations and Contemporary Strategies: Missions* (Rheenen 1996); *Customs, Culture and Christianity* (Nida 1954), and *Body Matters* (Addicott 2005).

in reciprocal recognition of the biblical understanding of Christ's body. Accordingly, I provide the key elements of foundational reciprocal contextual collaboration, which are as follows:

First, 'reciprocal' implies that we are the body of Christ with diverse and multiple ministries with gifts and resources to help one another reciprocally. Therefore, it is taken for granted that mission reciprocity is developed through trust, truth, time and togetherness. This fourfold 'T' basis needs to be carried out naturally among people joined within traditional, networking or emergent mission models.[33]

By the concept of 'trust', I mean trusting God and one another absolutely, which becomes pivotal in all mission theological teaching; trust refers to reciprocal confidence. Second, a biblical and theological understanding of truth affirms that the Holy Spirit leads the church into the truth (John 16:13), that was Jesus' promise to the church (John 14:16–19).[34] Therefore, truth refers to honesty, transparency and integrity – speaking the truth – as the Apostle Paul says: "letting one's 'yes' be 'yes' and one's 'no' be 'no'" (Eph 4:25), and thus this implies christological truth from which derives the truth for all missions on earth; truth refers to the reciprocal commitment of doing mission according to biblical principles.[35] The 'time' concept is rooted in God's time; it is God's *kairos*, which should influence the church's mission activity; thus, time refer to God's *kairos* when both entities in collaboration are in conditions of working reciprocally and at least one of them has reached more maturity. And finally the fourth 'T', togetherness, has a strong foundation in biblical theology as a community of interest in God's kingdom; togetherness is understood as the association of working together in relation to mission; Jesus calls people to love one another (John 13:34–35); the apostle Paul develops a theology of 'one another', and 'Christ's body'. All ministries and gifts are for the same purpose, to equip the church (Eph 4:11–12), and to fulfil God's mission (Matt

---

33. Trust in love remains for the shape, the content and the claim of the biblical gospel itself (Wright 2006, 41).

34. See further Paul Hiebert in *Anthropological Reflections on Missiological Issues* (1994, 232).

35. Truth is something factual; the things that correspond to fact or reality (See msn. Encarta Dictionary, http://uk.encarta.msn.com/dictionary_1861799034/truth.html).

28:19–20), as a community mission with a unique purpose: to proclaim the gospel in word and in deed for God's glory.[36]

The dispute over the concept of truth has a significant dimension in the study of philosophy and epistemology; the Greek word for truth, *aletheia*, means correspondence or coherence, and implies factuality or reality.[37] The literal meaning of *aletheia* is the state of being evident, not hidden.[38] Truth in classical understanding indicates that the direct opposite of truth is falsehood; therefore, truth means the state of being in accord with a particular fact or reality.[39] Theories of truth are studied in different disciplines such as theology, science and morality (Kirk and Vanhoozer 1999, 33).[40] In theology, truth is a quality of God, thus, God's communication of truth is in complete harmony with his nature, revealed ultimately in Christ; he himself is the embodiment of truth – truth that is personal and absolute, eternal and relational, objective and experiential (Scott in Moreau 2000, 972; Weston in Corrie 2007, 403).[41] Therefore, it is important at least

---

36. On the same note, a reciprocal mission theology for the mission activity of God's church is rooted in the fact that God's church works under the affirmation of christological truth.

37. See further *Diccionario Teologico del Nuevo Testamento* Vol. IV (Coenen, Beyreuther and Bietenhard 1980, 332–343), and *Dictionary of Mission Theology* (Corrie 2007, 403). The traditional concept of truth goes back at least to some of the classical Greek philosophers such as Plato, Socrates, and Aristotle. Aquinas accepted that both reality and truth are objective and that both depend upon God for their existence. See further *Evangelicals and Truth* (Hicks 1998, 10, 18–20, 22, 40).

38. In contrast, for Heidegger, *aletheia* means unconcealedness or unconcealedment, a clear departure from the traditional concept of truth. See further Gorner (2000, 112).

39. In *Mission Under Scrutiny*, Kirk (2006, 102) explains that the Christian interpretation of reality corresponds precisely to the way human beings experience it; this reality gives the most satisfying and most coherent answers to the permanent questions about existence that humans persistently pose.

40. A brief summary of the main features of the traditional theories of truth are provided in *To Stake a Claim* (Kirk and Vanhoozer 1999b, 30–33), three of them are: the central insight of the correspondence theory is that a belief (or statement) is true if it corresponds to reality, the world and the facts, or how things are;. for the coherence theory, a belief is true (or false) if it coheres (or fails to cohere) with a particular system or set of beliefs; and the pragmatic theory of truth states that truth is what the community of inquirers would ultimately agree, but experience and scientific inquiry are still the most effective guides to achieve it.

41. In relation to theological truth claims, Kevin Vanhoozer (1999b, 124) states that this is a statement about the meaning of the whole and, as such, will matter to everyone, and must involve proposition (objectivity) and passion (subjectivity). Truth is ultimately about the Word of God and the difference it makes to human beings.

to distinguish between definitions of (the meaning of) truth and criteria for determining or recognizing whether particular beliefs (propositions or sentences) in a certain context are true; hence, the nature of truth consists essentially in a kind of correspondence, whereas coherence is the criterion of truth (Kirk and Vanhoozer 1999b, 29).[42]

Within theological thinking, the classical approach to truth relates to the so-called 'revealed truth', which is regarded as absolute and unchanging; it is God's divine revelation through Scripture (John 17:7).[43] For this reason, the following theological characteristics can be suggested (West 1999, 8–11): (1) Truth is the quality of a living relationship, grounded in Christ as the self-revelation of the triune God. (2) Truth becomes falsehood when it is no longer true to the relationship with God; it lies in continual witness to God who judges, corrects and transforms all human claims. (3) Truth is historical; it comes to us in events in which God is at work, it is found inside history, in the concrete ways God deals with us in its particular events. Accordingly, christological truth has a crucial role, as it is pivotal in providing objectivity in harmony with knowledge for a mission theology that can share the truth of the gospel.

For example, in *The Age of the Network,* Jessica Lipnack and Jeffrey Stamps suggest that reciprocity as a form of future-oriented and cooperative behaviour becomes the most productive type of horizontal network since it enables economic development (1994, 187). We infer that the new 'social capital' of mission is trust, truth, time, togetherness, reciprocity, and

---

42. Hicks (1998, 10) states that the classical understanding or the traditional concept of truth has four components: (1) objectivity – truth is outside of us and independent of us, (2) universality – truth is the same the world over and for all people; cultural differences do not affect it, (3) eternity – truths last for ever, 'backwards' in time as well as 'forwards', and (4) intelligibility – we as human beings are able to discover, comprehend and know the truth.

43. See further Robert Priddy 1999 'Understanding and Truth', chapter 7 of the book *Beyond Science* (http://robertpriddy.com/bey/7.html). Since the church believes in God, it believes that ultimately the only truth which will remain is that of God therefore it is the truth, not the fact, which becomes influential. We are dealing with the biblical and theological understanding of truth. For the philosophical understanding of truth see *Stanford Encyclopedia of Philosophy,* first published 13 June 2006 (http://plato.stanford.edu/entries/truth/).

appropriate mission models.[44] The fact is that God's people have to trust God and one another reciprocally; we have to develop a form of communication which is based on reciprocal truth; there must be a time to reciprocate appropriately; and togetherness provides for a joyful mission because people work as one body, as Christ's body.[45]

Therefore, reciprocity, as seen from above, clarifies that the church's reciprocal mission belongs to and is empowered by a Trinitarian God, while reciprocity from below affirms that the church's reciprocal mission belongs to Christ's body, which is called to sustain with joy and transparency a reciprocal mission theology of unity in diversity within all varieties of mission models of the church's mission activity. Moreover, reciprocal mission from above stresses emphatically that God is the owner of the mission, and that he has made a covenantal plan to include his church within his redemptive mission. Hence, the church is a steward, with the responsibility which goes along with this privilege.[46] At the same time, reciprocal mission from below affirms that the church is chosen, equipped and empowered to fulfil God's mission in a covenantal response of humble obedience.

Second, 'contextual' implies the incarnational attitude of the Christian mission that includes conscious acknowledgement of the reality of the social, political, religious, cultural and economical context. This relates to René Padilla's (1986, 81) remark that "the great difficulty that Christians have in relating theology to social, economic, and political issues is closely connected with their lack of an adequate christological foundation". In the

---

44. Lipnack and Stamp (1994, 177) suggest that the new wealth of social capital is based on trust, reciprocity, and network. For a wider explanation of truth in the context of dimensions of church renewal see Stott (1992 261–262) in *The Contemporary Christian*.

45. All Christian mission under the *missio Dei*, God's kingdom theology, and Trinitarian theology are reciprocal by nature. Negatively, this implies a continual battle against anti-reciprocity. Positively, it implies a mission theology of a reciprocal harmony, which is transparent in trust, truth, time and togetherness. Therefore, a reciprocal mission activity of the church lies in the power of a redeeming God who operates as the Father, Son and the Holy Spirit.

46. Calvin B. DeWitt suggests that God's creation is a creation of symphony, where human beings are stewards of this symphonic gift, which has a divine appointment to safeguard the integrity of creation. DeWitt points out that biblical principles of stewardship yield an increase in knowledge, understanding and wisdom, which produce a robust stewardship. See further 'To strive to safeguard the integrity of creation and sustain and renew the life of the earth' (Walls and Ross 2008, 85–93).

context of mission reciprocity, incarnational Christology becomes foundational for all models of mission. Therefore, contextual is in line with what we have seen in chapter 4, that one of our five theological presuppositions for mission reciprocity is that there is no appropriate Christian reciprocal contextual collaboration without consideration of contextual theologies.

In chapter 4 above, Bevans' (2002) six models of contextual theology were noted. In this regard, the 'translation model' is considered the most common for its original flexibility to accommodate to a particular culture, which has to be done under the key presupposition that the gospel is supra-cultural and supra-contextual.[47] This means that gospel values must be preserved rather than the values or practice of the culture. Under this approach, the gospel is the judge of all contexts not vice-versa (Bevans 2007, 44). Thus, divine revelation is presuppositional and context becomes secondary, but it must be a presupposition considering God's manifestation in human life and society. The difficulty with this model is that the gospel always needs a context, which clearly relates to a specific culture, and we need to discern how to make contextual the gospel we preach. From a similar understanding, all appropriate models for mission must take seriously a mission reciprocity theology, including supra-cultural and supra-contextual values, but giving at the same time, high consideration to the context in which it has to be implemented, transformed, adapted or even replaced. For example, this is the case with the missionary work in 'restricted areas' of the world, where missions operate in a different way, like the traditional mission does in sending tentmakers (Lai 2005).[48] Hence,

---

47. Supra-cultural means that the principles or values can be applied to every culture, and supra-contextual means that the gospel can be applied to every context, but both work together not separately. The gospel always comes in a determined context, never isolated from the context. "The gospel is always inculturated" (Bevans 2007, 43). This is why it is possible to speak of and to discover contextual models of mission.

48. Patrick Lai (2005, 22–27) develops a mission theology for training, sending and allocating tent-makers; he defines five types: T-1 tentmakers are Christians who are employed abroad in the course of their careers without any initial commitment to cross-cultural evangelism; T-2 tentmakers have a calling from the Lord for a specific country, so they receive training knowing the reality of the country and they apply for work in that direction; T-3 tentmakers differ in that for part of their income, they receive support from others – they are owners of a business and have flexible time for ministry; T-4 tentmakers do not work for a company, they are not regular missionaries in the eyes of society and most of them work in NGOs (Non-Government Organizations) with non-missionary

mission structures have to be more contextual in time and in strategy, in policy and in critical analysis under the scrutiny of a reciprocal contextual mission theology.

Regarding the anthropological model, called the indigenous, ethnographical or inculturation model, Bevans (2007, 54–53, 56, 58–59) suggests that this model deals primarily with the preservation of the cultural identity of Christians, almost the opposite of the translation model, in which the primary concern is the preservation of Christian identity.[49] Thus, the fundamental approach of this contextual theology is culture, the authentic cultural identity, seeking God's revelation and self-manifestation within the values, patterns and concerns of a particular context. For this model, context is unique, so the message is an encounter with God's love and power within people's lives; it is not an imported foreign message. But a danger is that this model becomes a cultural romantic view, where critical analysis becomes necessary to deny the pros and cons of each context. In the same way, a contextual approach for mission models needs to consider the interdependent and global context of the present reality of the mission enterprise. This implies that neither local nor regional, nor global models have to work in isolation, rather they should be joining together to help in providing more appropriate models for the mission enterprise by one accepting the context of the other in reciprocal freedom and harmonious relationship. As every effort of contextual theology is an effort of translation

---

identity. This category includes social and health workers, medical personnel, teachers, agronomists, engineers, etc.; and finally, a T-5 tentmaker is really a regular missionary, not a tentmaker, but because of the visa they are registered as business people but they raise financial support as regular missionaries.

49. An alternative model to the translation and the anthropological model is the praxis model, which is identified with the theology of liberation and practical theology for Bevans (2007, 70), which refers to a particular context and is understood in terms of social change (mission as transformation), using the historical-critical method, which implies right thinking with right acting; it has a relevant theology, but is committed to Christian action (72). However, it usually involves action first and then reflection on the action, hence, this model has a circular movement (76). Theologically, this model sees God's presence as an invitation to people to cooperate with God in his mission plan of "healing, reconciling and liberating" (75). Missiologically, this model takes the context more seriously than any other model; it looks like a radical model for contextual theology. See further Bevans (2007, 70–79).

(Bevans, 61), it is the same effort for reciprocal contextual collaboration in finding new appropriate contextual models of mission.[50]

A contextual missiology, therefore, must consider the context of poverty, suffering, climate change, homelessness, joblessness, uncertainty, wealth, economic affluence, etc., where the mission activity is taking place, otherwise there is a danger of practising an implementation of foreign models of mission that are strange to the context and risk being obsolete, potentially out of the context. Hence, there is no appropriate mission reciprocity if mission models do not consider the contextual realities of the mission context. To put it another way, contextual means common boundaries with the context; it is an interaction of the mission and the context, which works together, influencing each other and connecting reciprocally.[51] The most common issues of contextual reciprocity seem to be (Butler 1994, 10–11): cultural differences, lack of effective communication, finance issues, personality conflicts and lack of clear objectives. For these reasons we have to consider that Jesus' ministry was contextual in its message, contextual to his time and contextual in his model.

Third, 'collaboration' implies that the *missio Dei* belongs to God and we are just collaborators in the christological freedom of God's kingdom; we are stewards, ambassadors to cooperate with God, thus all we do in mission is for God's glory. Given this foundation we do not want to provide a reductionist approach for the participation of the church in mission.[52] What we want to radically clarify is that the owner of the mission is God. Hence, God's ownership, in his sovereign love, has given an invitation to the church to be part of his redemptive missionary plan that has an emphatic Christology, which, as Christopher Wright (2006, 57) points out, is clear that it is in Jesus that we meet God. Theological images of

---

50. For Bevans (2007, 61), translation includes present experience such as culture, social location and social change but also experience of the past such as Scripture and tradition.

51. Van Engen (1996, 31) states that, "contextual interfaces appropriately with the context". 'Interfaces' suggests a point of interaction, two things or people acting together. (*MSN Encarta Dictionary*, http://uk.encarta.msn.com/dictionary_1861723633/interface.html).

52. In *The Mission of God*, Christopher Wright clarifies the distorted understanding of the *missio Dei* theology in some circles, where *missio Dei* is understood as God's involvement with no consideration of the church. See further Wright (2006, 63).

collaboration include those of the ambassador and the steward. The second refers to a person who holds an administrative role and the first refers to a person who represents someone. Newbigin (1995, 188) associates 'stewardship'[53] as a common metaphor that describes the church's relation to the gospel, and Padilla (Yamamori 2003, 301) relates human vocation in creation with a God-given identity to cooperate with God's missionary plan.[54] For Barth (1949, 146–147) the life of the church is determined in her service as ambassador and by its commission to deliver the message as a herald (*la compagnie de Dieu*).[55] Bosch (1979, 42–43) complements Barth's suggestion in *A Spirituality of the Road* by stating that 2 Corinthians 5:20 expresses so clearly the personal involvement of Christians as Christ's ambassadors.[56] Moreover, collaboration incorporates multiple interdependent participants in mission, rather than constructing a unique authoritative position. Thus, collaboration as seen from above depends on the gifts and the power of the Spirit, while collaboration from below involves human and material resources.

As we clarified in chapter 1, reciprocal collaboration does not primarily have to do with quantity, but quality, because reciprocity is strongly related to the pneumatogical work of the Spirit who empowers the work of each co-participant in mission with a relational character. In fact, a relationship that increases trust and reciprocity provides the missional atmosphere or context for new appropriate models of mission. When it comes to the term collaboration, Ernie Addiccott (2005, 93–94), in *Body Matters*, points out that the old concept of partnership differs from the term network in that the second does not achieve a reciprocal agreement, but rather cooperation to help each other to achieve what each has already planned to do.

---

53. In *The Open Secret*, for Newbigin (1995, 188), "the church and those called to any kind of leadership in the church are servants entrusted with that which is not their property but is the property of their Lord"; it is the mysteries of God which are entrusted to the church (2 Cor 4:7; 1 Cor 4:1; Eph 1:9–10, 6:19).

54. See further Padilla in *On Kingdom Business* (Yamamori 2003: 300–304). See also the concept of stewardship in 'Funding for Evangelism and Mission', Lausanne Occasional Paper No. 56 (David Claydon Editor, Vol 3 2005, 144–145).

55. See further Barth (1949, 141–148), *Dogmatics in Outline*. Paul defines himself as an ambassador of Christ (Eph 6:20).

56. For Bosch (1979, 42), Christ's ambassador means a personal representative with the message as it is related to the metaphor of branches of John chapter 15.

Collaboration, on the other hand, refers to the desire to develop together a common plan, vision and resources. This form of collaboration between the people of God does not have the aim to glorify themselves, but God. Theologically, collaboration emphasizes the work of God in reciprocity with his church (the God who invites the church and the church who responds to God), and consequently the work of the church in response to God for the glory of God. This is the reason why a mature or healthy spirit of collaboration becomes foundational in mission. This collaborative spirit challenges us to strengthen and promote a relational leadership (Wright 2000), as well as a transformational collaborative type of leadership (Stagich 2001), which involves a quest for a clear understanding of synergy, spontaneous, integrated and contextual models of mission that we will discuss later on.[57]

Reciprocity is rooted in the spiritual, moral and supra-cultural biblical values of unity, truth, trust, humility, patience, harmony, flexibility, accountability, local decision making, respect of personal identity, interdependence, etc., which expresses quality not quantity, characteristics of a reciprocal mission theology. Reciprocal contextual collaboration implies the rejection of any sense of guiltiness of either superiority or inferiority like paternalism, colonialism, imperialism, individualism and independentism. Our theological assumption is that we have been created in the image of a relational God, who challenges us to prioritize collaboration in mission according to biblical relationships, which are linked to the intentional action to reciprocate with others. Thus, the joy of true relational collaboration life has a pivotal link with the glory of God the Father, Son and Holy Spirit.

The glory of God in reciprocal contextual collaboration

In the Old Testament, the glory of God is shown to God's people, reminding them that the mission of God belongs to him and that in his sovereign

---

[57]. See the works of Walter C. Wright (2000), *Relational Leadership: A Biblical Model for Leadership Service,* and Timothy Stagich (2001), *Collaborative Leadership and Global Transformation.*

love he has decided to share his mission with his chosen people. We can see this through Abraham's calling (Gen 12), Moses' experience at the burning bush (Exod 3), Jacob's encounter with God (Gen 28, 32), and the consecration of the temple. It is also seen in the prophetic ministry of Isaiah, Jeremiah, Habakkuk. Thus, David's prayer of 1 Chronicles 29:11 must become foundational for new appropriate models of mission: "Yours, O Lord, is the greatness and the power and the glory".

In the New Testament, John's gospel develops a theology of God's glory (dóxa), which implies dignity, honour, and majesty – qualities that belong only to God and which human beings can only recognize.[58] To apply this term to human relationships is impossible.[59] Thus, God's glory has two components: essential glory and declarative glory. The first refers to God's own self-glory and the second to the contribution of exalting God's name and its attributes (Frost 2006, 279).[60] Indeed, Milne (1993, 185) defines God's glory as the divine manifestation of his divine majesty (Exod 16:7–10) revealed in Jesus' ministry (John 1:14).[61] The Johannine Gospel tells us that Jesus obeys, renounces himself and has an attitude of self-determination to accomplish God's mission for the glory of God. From this theological assumption, chapter 17 is the climax of John's narrative of God's glory in relation to the radical obedience of the Son to the Father, totally expressed in the crucifixion.[62] A suggestion similar to Barrett's (1978, 513) is offered by Milne (1993, 239),[63] and by Balthasar (2004, 187).[64] Balthasar's *The Glory of the Lord* tends to consider the most significant theological

---

58. For Moltmann (1993, 58) *doxa* means, both in the Old and in the New Testament, the divine power and glory, the divine unfolding of splendour and beauty. This term is used for both the Father and the Son (Isa 6:3, 40:5; Rom 6:4; 1 Cor 2:8; 2 Cor 4:6; 1 Tim 3:16).

59. *Diccionario Teologico Del Nuevo Testamento* vol. II (1980, 227–233)

60. The Westminster Catechism states four primary ways to glorify God: appreciation (admiration), adoration (worship), affection (delight) and subjection (service). See further Frost (2006, 280), *Exiles.*

61. See further Milne, *The Message of John* (1993, 185–189).

62. See further Charles K. Barrett (1978, 513–514), *The Gospel According to St John: An Introduction with Commentary and Notes on the Greek.*

63. For Milne, this radical obedience is shown in that "the Son seeks the Father's glory; the Father seeks the Son". See Milne (1993, 239).

64. The work of the German Catholic Hans Urs von Balthasar is well analyzed by Stanley J Grenz (2004).

aesthetics in relation to the transcendent God's glory.[65] By complementing previous contributions, Moltmann (1981, 126–128; 1993, 59) adds the concept of Trinitarian glorification, and states that the Spirit glorifies the Father and the Son by freeing men for fellowship with them, accompanied with joy and thanksgiving.[66]

The glory of God is shown in every aspect of Jesus' ministry, when he submits all his life and mission in obedience to the Father. In fact, Jesus' model mission under God's glory, which the Father shares with the Son, is seen in the narrative of transfiguration (which means both a glorifying and a transformation),[67] an event reported by the Synoptic Gospels (Matt 17:1–9; Mark 9:2–8;l and Luke 9:28–36). Therefore, a mission theology of reciprocity must be developed under God's plan, as he is the owner of the universe, so he must be glorified and honoured by the church's mission activity. However, to glorify God is to have compassion on people and God cannot be glorified at the expense of man (Bosch 1979, 14).[68]

---

65. See 'Trascendental Trinitarianism' in *Rediscovering the Triune God* (Grenz 2004, 184). In Grenz's view (186–187), Hans Urs von Balthasar has written a trilogy of books as a composite work: *The Glory of the Lord*, *The Theo-Drama*, and *The Theo Logic*, which relate to glory, goodness and truth-aesthetics, drama and logic. Balthasar makes a connection between the philosophical concept of beauty and the theological idea of glory, thus, he affirms that it becomes the divine splendour as manifested in Jesus Christ, who pours the divine goodness on humankind, which takes the form of a drama; as Grenz (188–189) comments, this is the dramatic flow of God's history with humankind to reconcile the world in Christ. But controversies of these works rely on the suggestion that he was not really a theologian, because he pursued doctoral studies in the German language, not in theology, and he went further than the feminist theologian Elizabeth Johnson (Grenz 2004, 182).

66. For Moltmann, "the Spirit is the glorifying God and the unifying God; the Spirit is not an energy proceeding from the Father or from the Son; it is a subject (a Person) from whose activity the Son and the Father receive their glory and their union, as well as their glorification through the whole creation". In glorification through the Spirit, this proceeds from the Spirit, through the Son to the Father. See Moltmann *The Trinity and the Kingdom of God* (1981, 126–127). See also *The Church in the Power of the Spirit* (Moltmann 1993, 57–60). For the theme of the glory, see also Boff (1988) *Trinity and Society*, chapters VIII–XI.

67. Moltmann, *The Trinity* (1981, 123).

68. For Bosch (1979, 14–15), many denominations have discovered their tragic failure in love. So to glorify God is not one of balance but rather of tension between the church called out of the world and sent into the world and so avoiding a pietistic interpretation of mission.

Theologically, we clearly understand that the church has been designed to work for God's glory, which is nurtured under a Trinitarian mission theology as the perfect model for relationships within the community's mission. It is also nurtured by God's kingdom theology as the ruler of everything. Thus, Paul's missionary theology of Ephesians 3:21 must become a tool for new appropriate models of mission: "to him be glory in the church and in Christ Jesus throughout all generations". Under the same theological insight, Bruce Milne (1993, 185) states that Jesus gives the final glory to the Father through his supreme act of obedience unto death, and that in return the "Father will reciprocally crown and glorify the Son". Missiologically, in my view, to honour God implies both missionary obedience and the practice of reciprocal mission co-participation, which amalgamated becomes the attitude of reciprocal truthful relationships of new appropriate models of mission bringing about a normal and natural mission activity.

The spiral mission theology

For reciprocal contextual collaboration, what we may refer to as a spiral mission theology is also foundational. Such a theology implies participation towards an evangelical catholicity, a theology that permeates God's church, by developing appropriate models of doing mission, impacting positively the traditional, networking, and the emergent models as well as the new mission model (reciprocal multipolar contextual engagement) we will propose later on. It also implies the use of historical, theological or missiological circles around a central point that constantly increases or decreases according to the *missio ecclesiae's* activity. This central point is God's missionary plan. Hence, a positive spiral mission theology is rooted within the content of the *missio Dei*, God's kingdom (which includes eschatology), Trinitarian mission theology, christological *missio ecclesiae*, mission models and the world mission circles; the first five are treated in chapter 2, which nurture the missionary dimension and the missionary intention of the church.

Spiral missiology is foundational in fulfilling the *missio Dei*, which has a centripetal (to gather to worship God and be a witness locally) and centrifugal (to send out the church to proclaim the gospel globally) force given by the Spirit.[69] Above all, the spiral mission theology states that the gospel, as John Stott (1992, 68) clarifies, is not human speculation but divine revelation; it is developed not by the pressures of advertisement or personality but by the Holy Spirit. Thus, in a conclusive way, Stott (69) adds that "the gospel comes from God, focuses on Christ and is authenticated by the Holy Spirit". This theological understanding implies that the spiral mission theology is based on the Trinitarian evangelism of the New Testament.

By theological spiral mission we do not mean the spiral of Archimedes, which suggests a spiral curve formed by a point which moves at a constant speed to or from a fixed point and along a line which also rotates at constant speed about the point.[70] Spiral missiology has different speeds, as it depends on an understanding of and obedience to the mission mandate on the part of the church throughout the world. For the church, the fixed point is the missionary God, the Trinitarian God who is revealed in Christ, the pivotal centre of mission. In consequence, a spiral missiology of reciprocal contextual collaboration includes the people of God who share a common mission theology, interest, model, activity, strategy, goals, motives, etc., in order to be a viable fulfilment of the mission mandate. As seen from above, the spiral begins with God who as Father, Son and Holy Spirit sends the church into the world. As seen from below, the spiral begins with an understanding of the church's obedience to the *missio Dei*. Therefore, there is a dynamic tension between the spiral as viewed from above and the spiral as viewed from below within reciprocal contextual collaboration in mission activity.

The *missio Dei* has an intentional activity of redemption, which is transcendent and immanent from above, and the church develops its mission

---

69. For Stott (1992, 335), the authentic Christianity of the Bible is an explosive centrifugal force, which pulls us out from our narrow-centeredness.

70. See further Pappus iv 21–25 on Archimedes' spiral, translated by Henry Mendell (http://www.calstatela.edu/faculty/hmendel/Ancient%20Mathematics/Pappus/Bookiv/Pappus.iv.21-25/ Pappus.iv.21_25.html) and also Wolfram MathWorld, Archimedes' Spiral (http://mathworld.wolfram.com/ArchimedesSpiral.html).

activity empowered by the Spirit and contextual collaboration from below. Hence, the target of the spiral mission theology is to contribute to a faithful and effective mission (the total activity the church is sent into the world to do) and evangelism (the total activity the church does to proclaim the gospel with a living testimony in action), based on radical submission to the authority of the Scripture.[71] As the *missio Dei* has an intentional activity of extension, the spiral mission theology has an intentional mission influence to permeate the whole mission activity of the church. So we assume that through spiral mission theology it would be possible to find new appropriate model of mission.

We can summarize spiral mission theology as follows:

1. The central point of the theological spiral is the *missio Dei* within a christological emphasis, which has its source in God the creator, redeemer and owner of everything.[72]
2. The presence of the incarnated Jesus Christ is the pivotal centre of the *missio Dei*, God's kingdom, God's church and Trinitarian theology for missiological thinking. Christ is the pivotal centre and the Spirit is the agent of the *missio Dei* and from this theology the principles of reciprocal contextual collaboration have emerged.
3. Spiral mission theology is rooted within the interconnected content of the *missio Dei*, God's kingdom, Trinitarian, christological, *missio ecclesiae* and eschatological mission circle, which nurture a reciprocal contextual collaboration of the church under an intentional influence.
4. Spiral mission theology has interconnection to the *missio trinitatis*, which has a transcendent and immanent mission activity producing reciprocal relationships.

---

71. In his chapter 'Responding to the World', Stott provides five central roles of the church: mature discipleship, intellectual integrity, ecumenical progress, effective evangelism, and personal humility. See further *The Contemporary Christian* (Stott 1992, 173–185). Kirk (1999, 56–57) clarifies the difference between mission and evangelism.
72. Christology emphasizes the historical event of Christ as the eternal king of God's kingdom.

5. Spiral mission theology has a centripetal (the local church) and centrifugal (the *missio ecclesiae* in the world) force empowered by the Holy Spirit.
6. Spiral mission theology of reciprocal contextual collaboration includes the *ecclesia* which is the instrument of blessing to the nations, who share a common mission theology, interest, creed, activity, strategy, goals, motives, etc., in order to be a viable fulfilment of the mission mandate through appropriate mission models.
7. As seen from above, the spiral begins with God who as Father, Son and Holy Spirit sends the church into the world.
8. As seen from below, the spiral begins with an understanding of the church's obedience to the *missio Dei*. Therefore, there is a dynamic tension between the spiral as viewed from above and the spiral as viewed from below within reciprocal contextual collaboration in its mission activity.
9. Spiral mission theology has an intentional mission influence to permeate the whole mission activity of the *missio ecclesiae*. The *missio Dei* has an intentional activity of extension, which is Trinitarian, transcendent and immanent from above, and the church empowered by the Spirit develops its mission activity within contextual collaboration from below.
10. The target of spiral mission theology is to contribute to a faithful and effective, conscious, compassionate, shared and reciprocal integral mission by the *ecclesia* going out into the world, proclaiming and doing both evangelism and social responsibility, based on radical submission to the authority of the Scripture.
11. Spiral mission theology states that the gospel is not a human speculation but a divine revelation developed not by the pressures of advertisement or personality but by the Holy Spirit (Stott 1992, 68). This implies the Trinitarian evangelism of the New Testament.
12. Spiral mission theology does not move at a constant speed to or from a fixed point. Spiral missiology has different speeds, as it depends on an understanding of and obedience to the mission

mandate on the part of the *ecclesia* throughout the world. For the church, the fixed point is the missionary God, the Trinitarian God who is revealed in Christ who is the owner of God's kingdom.

We should say, therefore, that the source of mission is the *missio Dei*, the incarnation is revealed in Jesus Christ, the power of mission is the Holy Spirit, and relationships are developed under the *missio trinitatis*' influence, the instrument of mission is the church, models are shaped under reciprocal contextual collaboration and the context of mission is the world.

The spiral mission theology

Mission theology	The centre	Nature
Missio Dei	God revealed in Christ	God is the owner, the redemptory mission belongs only to him, and Christ is the pivotal centre of mission.
God's kingdom	Kingdom's rules	God rules everything
Missio Trinitatis	Trinity God the Father, Son and Holy Spirit	God's transcendence and immanence, the economic and immanent Trinity.
Missio Ecclesiae	The church	Co-participants of God's mission plan for God's glory, based on radical submission to the authority of the Scripture.
Mission models	Operational and structural systems	God's tools with a mission theology with understanding of unity, freedom, autonomy and reciprocity.
World	Redemption of people and creation	Mission of the church with a centripetal and centrifugal mission.
Reciprocal contextual collaboration	New appropriate mission models under reciprocal multipolar contextual engagement	A new approach to interpret the church's participation in the *missio Dei* and God's kingdom

The following diagram portrays spiral mission theology:

SPIRAL MISSION THEOLOGY

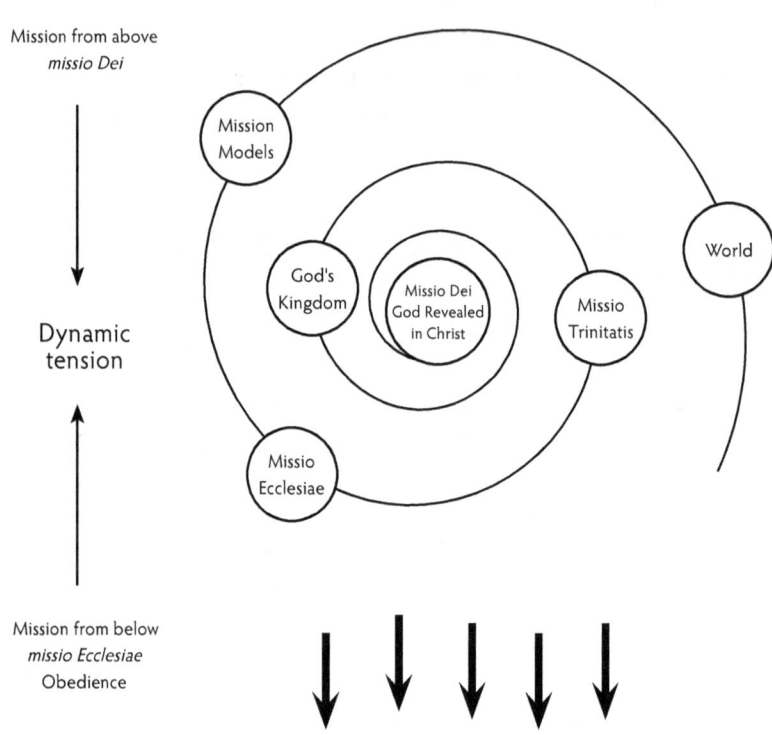

Reciprocal multipolar contextual engagement

Circles: The spiral has an interconnected mission theology

Spiral: It has an expansive influence, which does not involve strictly linear logic.

It has different speeds depending on the understanding of and obedience to the mission mandate.

It has a Trinitarian emphasis producing reciprocal relationships.

It has an intentional mission influence to permeate the whole mission activity of the church.

It has a centripetal and centrifugal force empowered by the Holy Spirit.

Arrows: Reciprocal contextual collaboration originates in spiral mission theology.

Spiral mission theology drives and empowers reciprocal contextual collaboration.

There is a dynamic missionary tension from above (*missio Dei*) and from below (*missio Ecclesia*).

Reciprocal contextual collaboration feeds models for reciprocal multipolar contextual engagement.

Here, I limit myself to providing four key foundational factors that reciprocal contextual collaboration mission theology proposes for new appropriate models of mission. This includes the components, organic values, biblical assumptions and principal motives, all of which are vital within the mission activity.

Key components of reciprocal contextual collaboration

Following Walter Wright (2000, 8), who describes a centred relationship with God as one which involves five components – solitude, study, worship, community and ministry[73] – here we provide five key components of an appropriate reciprocal contextual collaboration as follows:

---

73. Wright (2000, 8) states that 'solitude' implies time for listening to God without distraction; 'study' is reflection on the Bible; 'worship' focuses on personal devotion in the presence of Christ; 'community' regards time to celebrate shared relationships, and finally, 'ministry' regards time to make a contribution for God's kingdom.

1. Reciprocal participation. This implies reciprocal selection on the part of two autonomous mission collaborators to accomplish a common task. Its duration can be short- or long-term.
2. Contextual approach. It relates to an incarnational Christology, which shapes common goals within a relational approach and considers seriously the political, economic, social, cultural and religious context of mission.
3. Collaborative thinking. This is rooted in Trinitarian theology, God's kingdom, *missio Dei*, *missio ecclesiae* and christological mission theology to empower mission reciprocity within an integral mission for both the glory of God and the benefit of the church and its mission activity.
4. Flexible missiology. Reciprocity relates more to personal relationships, which provide a more flexible policy of mission relations, than to structural missiology.
5. Relational theology. Reciprocity is strongly related to the pneumatological work of the Spirit who empowers the work of each co-labourer in mission with a relational character, so mission relations are empowered by a relational theology.

Key organic values for healthy reciprocal contextual collaboration

Organic values imply that the church is not only institutional but also organic, spiritual, and communal in nature (Costas 1974, 33). Organic values relate to the internal development within the church's mission activity. Therefore a church in mission needs the depth of quality and the life of an organic mission theology as the church is a living organism by nature. Here, we provide five organic values:

1. Dependence on the Holy Spirit. All the strategies must submit to the guidance of the Spirit if new colonialist or new paternalistic views are to be avoided.
2. Prayerful approach. Like Jesus, who prayed fluently and regularly during his ministry, reciprocal contextual collaboration requires prayerful collaborators for God's kingdom in order better to discern the right course of action.

3. Reciprocal affinity. This includes relational proximity and harmonious thinking within committed co-participants in mission. In this way, strong and stable mission relationships will be nurtured. 'Missiological chemistry' is pivotal to affinity, which generates compatibility between fellow mission-workers.
4. Intentional relationships. Reciprocity is rooted in the spiritual, moral and supra-cultural biblical values of unity, truth, trust, humility, patience, harmony, thankfulness, commitment to relationships, flexible policy of relationships, co-responsibility, accountability, local decision making, respect for personal identity, interdependence, appropriate questions and answers, etc. Intentional relationships include a double vision, a vision for co-participation with others and a vision for finding, maintaining and improving healthy relationships
5. Contextual structures. It is conceivable that traditional, networking and emergent models might be combined, merged or mixed in innovative ways. What matters is an understanding and practice of a biblical relationship nurtured by God's kingdom.

Key biblical assumptions regarding reciprocal contextual collaboration

Here we summarize the biblical basis of reciprocal collaboration as follows:
1. A radical recognition that all benefits and missionary work are for God's glory.
2. An ethical attitude within reciprocal mission theology of trust, confidence, humility, friendship, honesty, etc., that leads to reciprocity of mission between mission co-labourers.
3. A radical understanding of reciprocal renunciation of personal benefit on the part of the autonomous mission bodies.
4. An integral commitment to the idea that every traditional, networking or emergent reciprocal model rests on a theology of the Body of Christ (unity within diversity), on biblical principles of kingdom collaboration (belonging within freedom), and on a christological mandate (purpose within strategy).

5. A radical determination to safeguard the true gospel within an evangelical catholicity in order to accomplish the mission mandate of the *redemptoris* mission.

Key motives of reciprocal contextual collaboration

If a motive is something which gives rise to an action or is a goal to be achieved, we might ask: what are the motives for an appropriate reciprocal contextual collaboration? We want to summarize these as follows:

1. To glorify God becomes the 'supreme motivation' (John 17:1).[74]
2. To contribute to the mission enterprise with more appropriate models of mission (John 17:4).[75]
3. To help the church to make a positive, active and radical response to the mission mandate by practising a 'reciprocal ownership' (John 17:10).[76]
4. To permeate the whole church with a *missio Dei*, Trinitarian and God's kingdom theology. This is the way to promote a unified missionary theology (John 17:22).[77]
5. To interchange resources in different ways under a reciprocal mission theology (John 17:24).[78]

---

74. See Milne (1993, 241).

75. Based in John 17:4, Milne (1993, 241) claims that if the motive in mission is God's honour, then promoting mission through human organizations, or to practise human egos, must be condemned. He emphatically states that we do mission for God's glory.

76. It is indicated that ownership of the mission is reciprocal between the Father and Son (Milne (243).

77. For Milne (247), the unity Jesus affirms is characterized not by the effort of human ingenuity but by the glory Jesus has given the church, which is the glory the Father has given to him.

78. As Jesus wanted his disciples to see his glory (death and resurrection), he also wants to allow the church to see his glory by helping the church to accomplish their missionary task. This should become a glory model for mission that can help the church to be concentrated in God's power not in human strength nor in human power but in Jesus' paradigm of finishing the work the Father has given him to do. See further Milne (251).

Mission tensions in reciprocal contextual collaboration

Within reciprocal contextual collaboration there are both positive and negative tensions, given that the tendency towards excessive autonomy in mission organizations tends either to cancel or postpone the quest for more appropriate models of mission on the one hand, or to face them on the other. While we acknowledge the tensions of theological understanding, duplication, culture identity, imposed models of mission, financial matters, control of power, etc., which influence the mission activity, as mentioned above, here I limit myself to three basic tensions: competition, the role of the leadership, and the 'reciprocal sharing spirit'.

Competition: One of these tensions has to do with competition, which is the spirit of post-war and post-modern society. In this sense the theology of 'one another', which implies a communitarian theology, is essential to reconstruct a redistribution of resources for the mission enterprise. Disunity is an evil spirit that divides the church into many radically autonomous entities which lack a sense of biblical and evangelical catholicity. This is due to a certain 'hermeneutical interference', which results in a disregard for the biblical doctrine of the Body of Christ, of the gifts which he has given, and of the reason for those gifts.

The role of leadership: A second tension relates to the role of leadership.[79] Those motives for an appropriate reciprocal contextual collaboration mentioned before offer the possibility of a missiology of reciprocal understanding within a christological leadership (Christ–like leadership) with the following characteristics: (1) a determination to live in holiness, (2) a determination of humble service, (3) a determination to simple lifestyle, (4) a determination to live with compassion for the poor, and (5) a determination to practise contextual flexibility. All of these determinations work with five ingredients such as vision, hard labour, perseverance,

---

79. For further reference to the theme of leadership, see the three types which Max Weber calls the legal-rational, traditional and charismatic in *Economy and Society: An Outline of Interpretative Sociology* (Weber 1968); Stott (1992, 172–177, 184) suggests that a good leader should be a worship leader, with faith and obedience to God and hope in God, with harmony, which expresses intellectual integrity, and humility that contrasts arrogance; Lai (2005, 186–190) speaks in connection with the tent-making movement.

service, and discipline (Stott 1984, 486–498).[80] By complementing these five determinations, the Hungarian Támas Czövek (2006, 229–230; Ford 2000, 212–226), in *Three Seasons of Charismatic Leadership*, develops what he calls the neglected area of charismatic leadership.[81] He provides basic principles when he argues that transitional leadership is necessary, that the required leadership is the precondition for resolving a crisis, that transition in leadership should be prepared and implemented with great care, that independence and determination are two requirements for the emerging charismatic leader, that careful examination is necessary to recognize potential leadership skills, and that charisma is always granted for the benefit of God's plan. Accordingly, Patrick Lai (2005, 187), in his book *Tentmaking,* notes that mission team leaders are decision-makers whose three most desirable qualities are humility, honesty and sacrifice. Lai (175), in the context of recruiting a team for business as mission, explains that it is essential to consider the maturity and experience of a candidate: those who do not meet these standards should be eliminated. While Czövek gives an account of principles of leadership, Lai states the three key qualities.[82]

As the five 'determinations' mentioned above are based on a christological model, this very brief profile offers basic clues to strengthening the vision, qualities and character of mission leaders. The fact is that appropriate mission models require a collaborative leadership with a double

---

80. In *Issues Facing Christian Today* Stott (1984, 485–498) develops the marks of a Christian leadership perspective. For the tensional aspect of leadership see Lingenfelter and Mayers (1986).

81. By charismatic leadership, Czövek refers to a leader chosen by divine intervention. He uses three types of models: the Saul type, the David type and the Solomon type. See further Czövek (2006). Leighton Ford states that there has been a cycle of four generations: the GI generation (veterans of World War II), the Silent Generation (those who become adults in the 1950s), the Baby Boomers (those who become adults in the 1960s) and the Generation X (those born in the 1970s). See Ford 'Challenging, Nurturing and Forming Leaders for 2010' in *Working Together with God to Shape the New Millennium: Opportunities and Limitations* (Corwin and Mulholland 2000, 212–226).

82. From the same evangelical perspective Wright (2000), in *Relational Leadership,* provides seventeen key values of leadership, relating to people, work and relationship, while from a secular view, Stagich (2001), in *Collaborative Leadership,* underlines the importance of global interdependence and synergy. Some of the key leadership values are: people (intrinsic worth, commitment to mission, etc.), work (participation produces ownership of results, fun and joy in the work, etc.), relationships (within truth, friendship). See further Wright (2000, 134–137). See also Tiplady (2003b, 129–132), and Lingenfelter (2008).

determination to discover new appropriate mission models and to live under those basic characteristics mentioned before. These determinations will provide a positive mission atmosphere within a global leadership mission where most of the negative and positive tensions usually emerge.

Reciprocal sharing spirit: A third tension comes in the light of what we call the reciprocal sharing spirit within the church. This leads to adopting initiatives that connect and expand the mission theological spiral through reciprocal sharing of concerns among key mission leaders, such as the polarities (oppositions) and the multipolarities (appropriated and alternative ways of working together) for the benefit of the mission enterprise.[83] The reciprocal sharing spirit includes the recognition of weaknesses and strengths in mission projects, mission structures, mission theology, etc. Above all, a reciprocal sharing spirit becomes fundamental in sharing power, sharing possessions and sharing resources between mission co-labourers for the sake of the *missio Dei*.

This reciprocal sharing spirit, described by Bosch (1995, 36, 38) as 'indivisible solidarity', should allows us to look at the world with compassion, together fighting every form of injustice, oppression, fatalism, and alienation. Thus, we suggest that a reciprocal sharing spirit is indivisible from the spiral missionary theology that will help to overcome economic and social disparity and the illusion of superiority in mission collaboration (Bonk 1991, 50–52).[84] Temptations of behaviour without a missionary theology of sharing, increase negative missionary tensions that we must have to face, and which Patrick Lai (2005, 187 190) insightfully refers to as the characteristics for a christological leadership under humility, honesty, sacrifice, passion, entrepreneurial spirit, vulnerability, and responsibility. However, as Padilla (2003, 302) points out, "the synergy of being, doing and saying[85]

---

83. Denton Lotz claims that it is difficult to develop partnership in endeavours when one person has nothing and the other everything. He emphasizes that true partnership implies biblical *koinonia* and sharing of resources. See further Lotz in 'Paradigm Shifts in Mission' (*Evangelical Review of Theology*, Vol 32 No 1 January 2008, 16–17).

84. Bonk (1991, 49) claims that it is difficult to deny that economic disparity, which is not simply a cultural difference, becomes a roadblock to fraternal social reciprocity.

85. Richard Niebuhr describes five approaches of the exclusive or paradigmatic model such as Christ against culture, the Christ of culture, Christ above culture, Christ in paradox with culture, transforming culture. See further Niebuhr, *Christ and Culture* (Harper and Row Publisher, 1951).

brings the evangelistic and cultural mandate together", similarly, a reciprocal sharing spirit goes beyond that of leadership, it is grounded under the stewardship exercise of God's creation. We have been created to cooperate with God, thus, sharing the gospel is co-participation with God's purposes in Jesus Christ to transform the totality of human life (302).

Innovative models relating to reciprocal contextual collaboration

Dulles's thesis in *Models of the Church* (1974) points out that each model has its strengths and limitations, so the models we propose here are not meant to supersede the others in the sense of displacing them, but to complement them. Thus, the value of the new model I propose is that it draws attention to 'blind spots' in the other models. We clarify that we want to avoid the use of isolated biblical texts for our models and accept that there is no uniform view of mission (Bosch, in Phillips and Coote 1993, 188).[86] Instead of using the term 'paradigm', which refers to concrete puzzles/solutions of different models (Kuhn in Dulles 1974, 21)[87] or worldview, we have chosen the term 'model' for three reasons.[88] First, model refers to a form of mission activity; second, model gives a theological understanding of doing mission; and third, model connects missiologically with the reality of how to practise mission. As the term model, which is synonymous of representation, pattern, example, prototype, archetype, and design, has been used in physical and social science, a model brings theoretical

---

86. In 'Reflections on Biblical Models of Mission', Bosch provides four cardinal missionary motifs for constructing models in biblical perspective: compassion, *martyria*, God's mission and history. See further Phillips and Coote, *Toward the 21ʳᵗ Century in Christian Mission* (1993, 180–187).

87. Dulles states that each paradigm brings its own favourite set of images, its own rhetoric, its own values, certitudes, commitments and priorities. It is also rooted within a particular set of preferred problems but he concludes that we have to recognize that our favourite excellent paradigm does not resolve all questions. See further Dulle*s, Models of the Church* (1974, 23–24).

88. Bevans (2007, 30) defines paradigm as a worldview, which involves a set of commitments or positions that cannot easily be related to others; it represents a very distinct way of understanding reality and gives rise to a particular set of questions that are only possible within that understanding.

understanding of a reality that can provide conceptual tools, vocabulary and facts that may be verified by experiment (Dulles 1974, 15).[89] Although they cannot provide the whole picture, they can give angles of vision. Hence, model in the same way as images and symbols provides knowledge of reality, neither false nor subjective (30), thus, an image employed reflectively and critically can become a model (Dulles 1974, 15). Models (Dulls 1974, 17) may be approached as explanatory (serve to synthesize what we already know) or as exploratory (leading to new theological insights). Also they can be exclusive or paradigmatic (involve a set of commitments or positions) and inclusive or descriptive or complementary, which provides experience from one to another model (Bevans 2007, 30–31).[90] The four models we provide will help us to deal with complex, differentiated realities (Bevans 2007, 30) under an inclusive methodology in order to avoid distortions of the reality. These are models of operation that take seriously the context, which start with a different point of view of mission theology, but all models emerge to operate under an inclusive and integral mission that recognizes that proclamation and social involvement are necessary components of the mission and task of the church (Chester 2002, 3).[91]

As we have developed traditional, networking and the emergent mission models in chapter 3, here we will see how these relate to reciprocal contextual collaboration and how they have to consider the new mission theology that reciprocal contextual collaboration provides under an inclusive and integral mission, which involves four models of reciprocal multipolar contextual engagement: synergy, spontaneous (the novel element), integrated and contextual mission models. See the following diagram.

---

89. Bevans (2007, 31) defines models in the sense that when "it is often used in theology it is referred to a theoretical model, it is a 'case' that is useful in simplifying a complex reality, and although such a simplification does not fully capture that reality, it does yield true knowledge of it".

90. Bevans (2007, 30) suggests that an exclusive model refers, for example, to Christology and ecclesiology when we accept that there is no other way to think of Christianity's salvation through Christ.

91. A history, mission theology and some case studies of 'integral mission' can be seen in *Justice, Mercy and Humility: Integral Mission and the Poor* (Tim Chester, editor, 2002).

Reciprocal multipolar contextual engagement

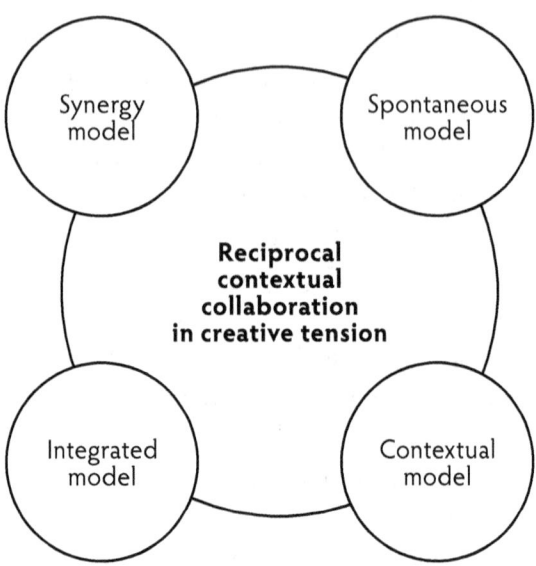

The synergy model recognizes the importance of effectiveness, and it is mission- mandate centred, while the spontaneous model puts much emphasis on the Spirit-intention, diversity and less formal structure without denying the need for appropriate structures. The most radical of the four models is the contextual model, which emphasizes freedom, cultural identity and the context. In the integrated model, collaboration between two or more autonomous bodies rests on interdependence. Thus, each body works by sharing resources or personnel for the same purpose, target or plan. In some cases, one body becomes merged with the other through the purpose or the vision. As planning becomes essential, perhaps sometimes a weaknesses of the synergy model relates to an 'over-optimistic' view, which means that it is expected that nothing has to fail in planning to achieve greater results; a joint-effort will not produce automatic results. For a synergetic effectiveness, it is necessary to evaluate, change and make necessary adjustments in the process of implementation of a synergy model. The spontaneous model has problems of credibility and with regards to the formation of appropriate structures, as does the contextual model, while the integrated model runs the risk of lacking appropriate distribution of power and decision making. Since every model must maintain reciprocity within its mission activity, so unity in diversity between components of Christ's body is a key element. As all the models bear in mind the mission plan under God's creation and redemptive mission, their strengths are based on reciprocal mission theology and interdependence in relationships.

Speaking of structures, a synergy model tends to merge and to concentrate mission activities but not structures (structures do not lose their autonomy; they work as separate autonomous bodies). In contrast the integrated model tends to work as autonomous structural entities networking or it can become merged (two bodies are merged to become one autonomy body and we call this a radical merging, or one body depending on the other in reciprocal collaboration as strategic alliance or amalgamated collaboration). The spontaneous model has non-restricted structures with more freedom theology, while the contextual models cry out for the local view, freedom, cultural identity and interdependence. All the mission structures tend to become autonomous but interdependent to one or the other model.

The four models we propose strike, as we noted in chapter 2, an intentional and conscious missionary theology of the *missio Dei,* God's kingdom, Trinitarian and christological approach. The *missio Dei* manifests God's mission ownership and has chosen his church to collaborate in his mission plan; the *basileia* theology implies reciprocity in freedom, truth, and harmony, a unique and unrepeatable event of the lordship of Christ for the glory of God;[92] a Trinitarian theology helps to understand that relationship in mission is reciprocal and the fact that the Trinitarian God relates to the created universe as Father, Son and Holy Spirit; God our Creator, Redeemer and Sanctifier becomes foundational in each model; finally, christological mission refers to the incarnated model of mission, which offers a model of the public ministry of Jesus as the one who is acknowledged as the Son of God, and is anointed by the Spirit of God to make the whole creation free of personal and structural sin. In these

---

92. Moltmann (1965, 224) in *Theology of Hope* points out that, for God's kingdom, "the *pro-missio* of the kingdom is the ground of the *missio* of love to the world".

models, Christ is the vital pivotal centre, and the Spirit, the vitally important focal agent of the *missio Dei*. Consequently, the church as part of God's kingdom has been chosen as the instrument to accomplish the mission of God. Illustrative diagrams below portray the basic procedure of the four models along with its basic presuppositions and then we provide a map of the four models.

Synergy Model
Concentrating efforts
to produce effectiveness

Spontaneous Model
Spirit intention
producing diversity and flexibility

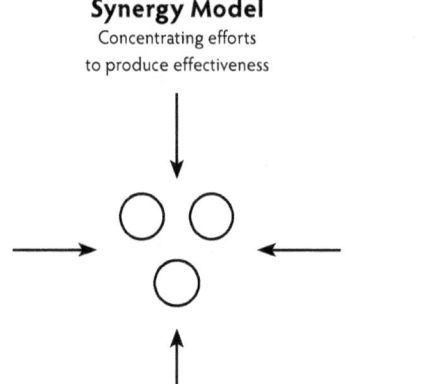
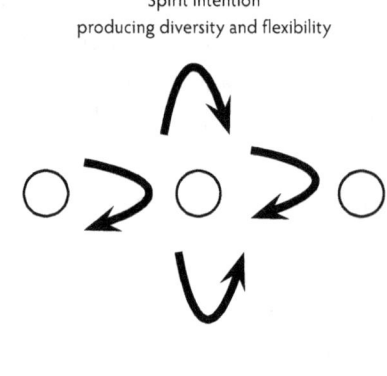

Integrated Model
Reciprocal components
producing unity and merging

Contextual Model
Freedom, cultural identity and context
producing interdependence

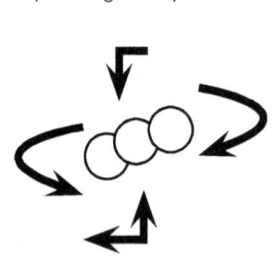

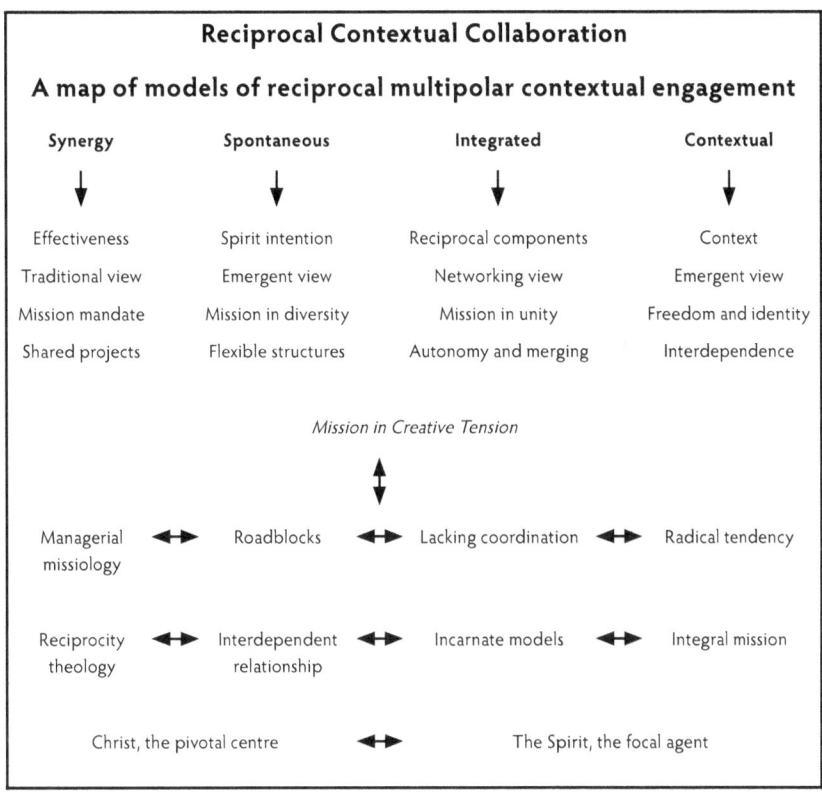

Models (see appendices) that have made an impact in the mission activity of the evangelical movement, which we have not considered either in chapter 3 or in this chapter, and which will need further study, are the monastic model, the Bible distribution model, the immigrant model, the mainline Protestant churches model, the faith mission model, and the Pentecostal model. Diachronically and synchronically, the evangelical mission in Latin America has adopted at least ten models that have been developed in this order: beginning of Protestant missions (1790), Bible distribution (1820), mission to distant lands and immigrant mission (1850), mainline Protestant churches (1900), faith missions (1916), Pentecostal movement (1950), networking model (1980), the emergent model (1990), global mission (2000) and the implementation of the reciprocal multipolar contextual engagement (2010).[93]

The Synergy Model

The synergy model allows mission co-operators to work more effectively together and achieve more than they would individually. Synergy means combined force or cooperative action.[94] For Timothy Stagich (2001, 12), synergy is the event in collaborative groups whereby both the group and the individual benefit by the same act at the same time.[95] Its philosophy includes the interaction of two or more agents or forces, which produces a greater effect than the sum of the individual effects. It is a cooperative interaction between groups to create combined effects.[96] An understanding that the *missio Dei*, God's kingdom, and Trinitarian theology, have a synergetic relationship produces a positive impact on the models of mission. The fact is that reciprocal missiology stimulates a more sustained analysis of how best to realize these synergies. However, the possibility that a reciprocal theology of unity will create the synergy needed to provide the best appropriate models of reciprocal collaboration in mission brings an expectation of new global mission engagement. Addicott (2005, 13–14) points out that synergy is combined energy, united action and parts working together as a whole which helps to overcome an individualistic approach on the part of each mission organization, which, without denying their own identity, find a strong common interest.

The synergy model relates to participatory work of God's people within a reciprocal exchange of spiritual and material gifts. From a theological

---

93. Roger Greenway using as sources Paul Pretiz and David Stoll identifies seven waves of 'Protestant Mission Activity in Latin America' in *Coming of Age: Protestantism in Contemporary Latin America* (Miller 1994, 175–195). See also David Martin *Tongues of Fire* (1990, chapter 1–7; Escobar 'Latin America' in *Towards the 21st Century in Christian Mission* (Phillips and Coote 1993, 125–135).
94. *Oxford English Dictionary* (2005, 1050).
95. Stagich states that the fundamental values essential for effective collaboration include reciprocal benefit, mutual respect, appreciation of diverse contributions and shared understanding (2001, 29). At the same time he points out that the sharing of experience collaboratively facilitates a powerful synergist force (32).
96. *Oxford English Dictionary*. See interactive (2005, 528), cooperative (215), and effect (317).

perspective, a synergetic model has the goal of joining efforts to make an impact and contribution for God's kingdom. In consequence, this model is rooted basically in six values: humility, self-renunciation, a kingdom collaboration approach, shared projects, effectiveness and avoiding duplication. These six values allow mission labourers to collaborate in a wider sense within different initiatives. The synergy model provides benefits for avoiding duplication and is constantly dynamic so as to provide a synergetic effect in mission. Therefore, new appropriate models for mission would exploit the obvious synergies between the traditional, networking and emergent models. However, considerable synergy in merging these models remains to be seen, as there are clear distances between them. There are hidden and distorted models from the inherited synergy already on board. But the positive side is that there are some emergent models that are in progress and which anticipate the new synergy mission models. This is the case with short-term mission, business as mission, the NGO model, and mission for street children. For example, the 'Viva Network' includes more than 70 mission associations which pursue goals that transcend organizational boundaries, and aims to network all Christian missions interested in working with children at risk around the world.[97]

The risk of the synergy model would be the practice of romantic dreams or actions where there is no greater result despite the effort of summing up the contribution of two bodies as one synergetic endeavour. Some of the enemies of the synergy model are disunity, suspicion and lack of trust within a foundational mission theology, which is expressed in a variety of efforts, which intend the same purpose but which dilute the effect on the results. Therefore, we regard effectiveness as a key component of the synergy model, since a synergistic church, as Bruce K. Camp points out (Bonk 2003, 239), has a tendency to joint action by agents, that when taken together increase the effectiveness of both. Shiva Ramu (1997), in his book *Strategic Alliances,* suggests that expected synergy is the justification

---

97. See further (Viva Network (http://www.viva.org/?page_id=53).

for most business mergers, so its philosophy implies increasing the value of combined or merged institutions.[98]

The *minka* model becomes an alternative approach to the synergy model. Anything that is accomplished through joint effort by the community in the Peruvian Quechua culture is called *ayni*, which means co-operative labour. *Minka* means voluntary work on a communal project – it is a reciprocal arrangement (Chapman 2006, 43).[99] The Peruvian missiologist, Fernando Quicaña (1997, 130), confirms that the Quechua term *ayni* means co-operative labour. Hence, an *ayni* community has a foundational threefold law to maintain trusting relationships, which are *ama suaw* (do not steal), *ama llulla* (do not lie) and *ama quella* (do not be lazy).[100] Under this view, reciprocity is a reciprocal arrangement according to which there is no relationship without the 'reciprocal' element, and therefore no community, because the equilibrium is destroyed since (a) things have value only if they can be exchanged reciprocally, and (b) true equality can be experienced only reciprocally.[101] The alternative model *minka* can be seen within the Minka Fair Trade, founded in 1976 to combat poverty in Peru, in which over 3,000 democratic organizing producers are associated in order to facilitate development in marginalized areas of Peru. *Minka* is a Quechua term that means 'co-operative'. They define their mission philosophy as one which,

> reflects a system of values that champion education and *training* by defending quality, responsibility, opportunity, fulfilment, perseverance, creativity, solidarity and reciprocity[102] (italics mine).

---

98. Ramu cites Hans Hinterhuber's categories networks (1997, 27–28), which include four types of networking that may be helpful to find appropriate synergy: vertical (franchizing and subcontracting), horizontal (alliances), internal networks (profit centres), and diagonal network (interdisciplinary).

99. Debora Chapman (2006, 41) speaks of *ayni* in the context of communal reciprocity in the Peruvian Quechua culture.

100. See Quicañas' article 'La Realidad de las Sociedades Indigenas' in *Las Misiones Latinas Para el Siglo XXI* (COMIBAM 1997, 130–131).

101. See further Chapman (2006, 43).

102. The aim of Minka was to partner with producer communities to promote commercialization of production oriented towards foreign markets, which has enabled

The synergy model describes five characteristics of participative dimensions of a relational approach to mission: participation of the individual mission body, participation in decision making, participation in a common goal, participation in resource availability, and participation in reciprocal care. Accordingly, the synergy model provides reciprocal collaboration between different mission organizations, networks or local churches in order to make a greater impact according to their vision and goals by providing expertise, information, joint projects, a united strategy, social impact, etc.

One example is the Micah Network, an evangelical mission enterprise initiated in Kuala Lumpur in 1999, under the leadership of René Padilla, to support projects in poorer countries.[103] In May 2007, the Micah Network had 300 member organizations and around 160 associate members, the majority of which come from low-income countries. In May 2005, representatives from the Micah Network met in Melbourne, Australia, to discuss issues of partnership. They recognized that this term can imply a level of mutuality in organization to organization relationships – a sharing of goals, aspirations, and power – that is extraordinarily difficult to achieve and sustain. Because of this, for the Micah Network, this kind of partnership relationship honours God, and provides an outstanding vehicle for integral mission. As a result, two documents were produced: the Micah Network Partnership Guidelines and the Micah Network Values.[104]

A similar synergetic model is reflected in the Micah Challenge (Edwards 2008, 1, 2), that was launched on 15 October 2004 at the United Nations Millennium Campaign under two founding bodies, the Micah Network and the World Evangelical Alliance. It was initiated as a global evangelical response to the poor and involved a double response both to God and to governments. In Joel Edwards' words, this is a 'redemptive movement' not as a hostile anti-government protest, but as a critical partner with the government (2008, 2). The Micah Challenge works in thirty-four countries

---

producers' direct contact with the international markets, and to obtain a better income of their products. See further Fair Trade Organization ((http://www.minkafairtrade.com/home.html).

103. History of Micah Network (http://en.micahnetwork.org/about_micah_network/history).

104. Ibid.

with a mission policy of being a movement and not to become an exclusively evangelical club (11).[105] The Micah Network and Micah Challenge experienced a missional metamorphosis that led them to form the new 'joint WEA/Micah Council' for a mission campaign against poverty, and the Micah Challenge became the official name of this new synergetic network, involving both national supporting and voices of decision makers from the South (7).[106] The Micah Network and Micah Challenge, however, remain as autonomous mission networks. The following diagram portrays the synergy models.

The Synergy Model

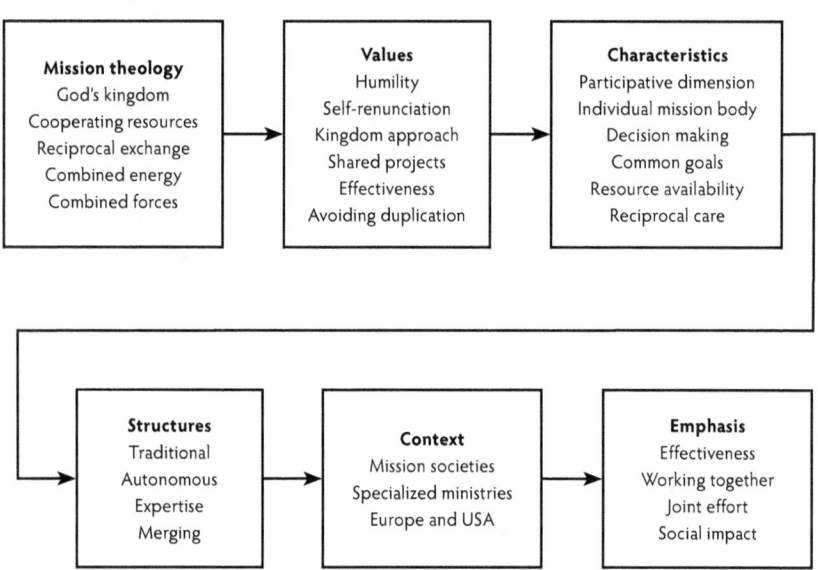

---

105. For further reading see the chapter "Micah Challenge: The Story So Far" in *Micah's Challenge* (Hoek and Thacker 2008)

106. Before joining in a synergy model, the Micah Network and Micah Challenge were concerned that issues of trade and justice were lacking in the campaign (Hoek and Thacker 2008, 7)

> **The Synergy Model**
>
> **Alternative title:** working together model; cooperating model.
>
> **Mission theology:** God's kingdom, cooperative resources, reciprocal exchange, combined energy, combined forces.
>
> **Values:** Humility, self-renunciation, kingdom approach, shared projects, effectiveness, avoiding duplication.
>
> **Characteristics:** participative dimension of relational approach as individual mission body, decision making, common goals, resource availability, reciprocal care.
>
> **Structure:** tends to be traditional, autonomous, expertise, merging activities, top-down.
>
> **Context:** mainly used by mission societies and specialized ministries, especially Europe and USA.
>
> **Emphasis:** effectiveness, working together, joint effort, social impact.
>
> **Positives:** emphasizes mission mandate theology and develops good mission policies.
>
> **Negatives:** emphasizes rigid mission structures, false claim of universality, tendency to practise managerial missiology.
>
> **Tensions:** creating roadblocks by managerial missiology, rationalistic and rigid tendency.
>
> **Examples:** traditional models, networking model, Minka model, Micah Network, The Micah Challenge, the ONG, The Viva Network, synergetic participation of Paul, Barnabas, James, apostles, elders and church at the council of Jerusalem (Acts 15).

The Spontaneous Model

This model comes to mind in the light of three perspectives: First, the biblical perspective given in John's Gospel (3:8), "the wind blows wherever it pleases; so it is with everyone born of the Spirit". Second, the theological perspective, under the architectural unity of Luke and Acts (Penny 1997, 16–18), which also implies four aspects: it does not depend on foreign initiatives, does not depend on foreign financial support, does depends on the

Spirit initiative, (Roland Allen 1962, 146, says that "the Spirit of Christ is the spirit of initiative"), and does operate under the whole gospel, through the church and to the world.[107] The basic force of the spontaneous model becomes quite literally spontaneity, not academic discussion, spiritual experience, or systematic argumentation (Moltmann 1996, viii; Allen 1927; 6–7).[108] In this line it will be necessary to find the fundamental differences from other models and perhaps the many common factors they have. This model provides new spaces to accomplish God's mission; experimenting between the times, models that one never could imagine. This is the theological context of the flow of the Spirit for the spontaneous model.[109] And the third is the missiological perspective, given by the reality of new forms undertaken by the church in mission since the 1980s, especially within what we call the non-conventional models (different from the traditional model), as a result of external factors (political, economic, etc.) which include the migration model, the volunteer model, self-support model and the local church model but also the exponential growth of the Pentecostal movement.[110] This implies that the spontaneous model always has a mission structure; as such, spontaneous mission does not deny the validity of structures, but does not give them first priority.

---

107. We relate the whole gospel and church to the internal factor, and the external factor relates to the world, which includes dynamic changes such as political, social, economic or cultural change.

108. See Roland Allen (1927–2006 new edition) *The Spontaneous Expansion of the Church*. Allen defines spontaneous expansion as the irresistible attraction of the Christian church by others and the addition of new churches, which has an exhorted and unorganized spontaneous expansion beyond that of highly modern organized missions that appeal for funds and methods to make proselytes (7–8).

109. The spontaneous model is in line with what Newbigin (1994, 30–31) in *A Word in Season* says: "*The Holy Spirit* is able to create under totally different conditions the forms of the church in such a way that they belong to that place and people, instead of being mere pale reproductions of the form of the church with which we have been familiar so that they have their own authentic roots within the life and experience of the people themselves" (Italics mine).

110. Steven J. Land (1993, 21–22) gives Barrett's statistical data of Pentecostal growth (including traditional Pentecostals, charismatics and 'third wave') as 327 million affiliate church members in 1988, growing 19 million a year and 5,400 per day, 29 percent white and 71 percent non-white. The majority come from Asia, Africa and Latin America. Each year, 14 percent of mainline charismatic churches have become independents since 1970, forming more that 100,000 white-led charismatic independent churches across the world, organized into forty or so major networks.

There are two factors that help to shape the mission structure of the spontaneous model: external factors, which seem to be mainly those of the state (the movement of peoples through immigration laws such as the European community law, the asylum seekers law, etc.), government work (in which Christians are sent by their government), professional work (people moving through their profession), and above all economic factors (people moving because of economic disparities). The internal factors mobilize people through business as mission, and independent indigenous mission structures like Pentecostal models or independent churches, etc.[111] The spontaneous model provides new flexibility and the more relational emphasis of non-conventional structures (non-restricted) in reciprocal collaboration according to a 'new permission' empowered by the Spirit. For this reason, this model might also be defined as the 'pneumatical model' (non-conventional model). The foundational value of this model rests on the basis of a non-traditional mission model, using more of a non-formal networking structure in most cases.

Put in another way, the spontaneous model relates to what Walls (1996, 10) stated in the 1990s that, "theology in the Third World will be, as theology at all creative times has always been, about doing things, about things that deeply affect the lives of numbers of people". Walls' prophetic imagination implies the work of God's will, Scripture and context, always doing something different but for the same purpose, which is to fulfil the redemptive missionary plan. Spontaneous models appear as in William Carey's time, when the church needed a new concept of mission and a new instrument for mission. The appropriate instruments chosen were mission societies and the concept, distant lands (Walls 1996, 243). The instrumental society, as the voluntary association of Christians, was a pragmatic answer to a needy church, taking the analogy of commerce as a model, subverting all the classical forms of church government and initial societies originated out of the establishment (Walls, 246–247, 249).

In its mission structure the spontaneous model can be described as bottom-up rather than top-down, since there is no hierarchical approach.

---

111. It was estimated in the 1990s that one in four of all full-time missionaries in the world were Pentecostal/charismatic, developing effective conscientization of *contextual proclamation* (Land 1993, 22, italics mine).

Rather, this model envisions more of a 'round table' when it comes to power and decision making. This can be seen in local-to-local church models, mission networks, ministry organizations and independent missions such as Church Grace and Wilton Community Church in Muswell Hill, London, or Gospel Printing Mission, London.[112] All of these examples work under the horizontal relational model.[113] It is also evident in the migration model, according to which Christians from Latin America arrive in Spain and then after a few months start a congregation in their homes and then rent a building in which to meet. Under the spontaneous model there are 70 Latin American churches in Barcelona, founded between 2000 and 2008 by the migrant movement with no support from either the traditional structures or the formal burgeoning networking. It is the emergent model which is behind these new churches.[114]

This model has the following characteristics: it tends to be spontaneous, free for sharing, free from the status quo; it is less bureaucratic, simpler, less rationalistic, and more flexible in decision making. It has written policies and oral policies.[115] This novel model is guided by the felt need to reconstruct a new theology of mission reciprocity. In fact, one of the clear factors of the spontaneous model is migration, where the gospel has been transported by Christian immigrants in different periods of time, and especially since the 1980s, within a mission diaspora from poor to rich countries due

---

112. For example, a church plant initiative of St James Church in Muswell Hill is Grace Church. The work was initiated in 2004 under the leadership of Phillip Sudell, a former St James associated vicar. On its fourth anniversary it showed a stable church with 50 regular adult attendants and 50 children. Their commitment to Bible study is one of the key elements for its growth, where 70% of its membership attends this mission activity. They still collaborate with St James in fellowship and prayer meetings but not financially (Data provided by Geoff Broadhurst at Grace Church, during its fourth anniversary 5 October 2008).

113. Wilton Community Church was re-started after a simple, honest and frank dialogue between the leadership of St James Church, Muswell Hill, and the leadership of the former church. Grace Church started as a result of a 'round table' dialogue between Alex Ross and Phillip Sudell in 2004.

114. Data from my dialogue with Miguel Juez (Barcelona 22 January 2009).

115. Oral policies are related to what we call a 'corporative culture' (what the majority usually does).

to different external (political, economic and social) factors. Tippet refers to migration as mission mobility (1987, 90).[116]

A vivid expression of the impact of the spontaneous model is given by the Filipino leader, Robert Lopez. He explains that they are raising 200,000 Filipino tentmakers all over the world. There are some nine million Filipinos in 197 countries, with nearly 2.2 million in the Middle East and Arabian Peninsula. They have been educating, encouraging, equipping and enlisting the brethren from within and without the Philippines to be witnesses to all nations, especially the least reached. Currently, they estimate that there are about 50,000 brethren witnessing cross-culturally. There are already thousands of Filipino churches outside the Philippines.[117]

In the article 'Argentina towards maturity', Daniel Bianchi suggests for missionary retention that finances of Argentinian missionaries seem to be problematic as it is difficult to receive sustained and adequate financial support, but in spite of this limitation they use resources effectively.[118] Yet the missionary combustion in that country works through the spontaneous model, like Miguel Juez working among the immigrants in Barcelona or Federico Bertuzzi, who has worked mobilizing people to mission in Granada, both Argentinian missionaries with no fixed budgets. Similarly is the case of the Peruvian, Juan Zuñiga, planting churches in Madrid with a very stretched budget, supported by his sending church, the Christian and Missionary Alliance of Lima, Peru, only for 4 years.[119]

Moreover, the spontaneous model has a more relational emphasis, empowered by the Spirit, which most of the time overcomes the conventional formalities and bureaucratic and expensive administration that are found in most traditional models. However, it is fundamental to clarify that the Holy Spirit is not separated from the work of the Son and the Father (Hiebert 1994, 232). Hiebert (232) points out that they are the work of

---

116. For Tippet, Christian community in Rome emerged through migration growth; the New Testament churches in Rome produced a spontaneous expansion in the imperial capital. See Alan Tippet, *Introduction to Missiology* (William Carey Library 1987, 56, 91, 205).

117. Robert Lopez, information provided to the author by email from Manila, on 29 March 2009.

118. See Daniel Bianchi (2008, 3) 'Argentina towards maturity', article send to the author on June 2008.

119. JuanZuñiga, personal dialogue with the author in Madrid on December 2006.

one God. The Spirit's action is God at work in the church, leading them to obey and glorify Christ as Lord.[120] That is a Trinitarian mission theology.

The Holy Spirit becomes the fundamental 'capital' power of any reciprocal collaboration initiative, and he empowers co-participants with the spontaneous combustion required to achieve what the *missio Dei* requires for its purposes. This action, however, is a contextual activity; it is not developed in a vacuum or in a naked context[121]

Now we want to present a missiological discussion of the spontaneous model addressed by Roger Parrot by using a metaphor of the sailboat and the powerboat that can be helpful to understand the internal and external tensions of the mission activity of the church. Parrott,[122] chair of the 2004 Forum for World Evangelization of the Lausanne movement, develops a missiological metaphor of the powerboat and the sailboat, related to reciprocal contextual collaboration that we link to the spontaneous model. Parrott states:

> As the ways of the church have become influenced by our culture, too many Christian ministries have constructed powerboats that charge ahead, essentially ignoring the wind of God – at least until the wind becomes too strong, threatening to capsize them. Instead, God wants us to prepare to catch his wind by using our God-given gifts to build a sailboat that will go only where the Lord leads us.

Parrott suggests six benchmarks for personal ministry to encourage looking at conflicting characteristics of powerboats and sailboats as good measures of reciprocal mission. This was analyzed through the Issue Group called

---

120. Hiebert (1994, 231–232) insists that the Holy Spirit has four fundamental actions: the power of the Spirit is at work to convict people of sin (Rom 8:16), the Spirit leads the church into truth (John 16:13), the Spirit transforms our lives (2 Cor 3:18), and the power of the Spirit is manifest in the preaching of the gospel (Luke 4:18–19).

121. By vacuum I refer to isolation and by naked context to lacking incarnational presence. Hence, the Spirit's action works in symmetrical harmony within the *missio Dei* as a Trinitarian Person, that is contextual activity.

122. See Roger Parrott's article '2004 Forum for World Evangelization Opening Address', Lausanne Thailand information sent by Alex Araujo to the author on January 21 2009 (http://www.lausanne.org/2004-forum/opening-address.html).

'Boat Building for Evangelism: Scuttle our Powerboats, and Learn to Sail'. It seems that the focus of that group was to encourage the church to sink the powerboats of ministry they had built, and learn again, to sail only on the wind of God. These six benchmarks are as follows:

- First, choosing to build either a sailboat or a powerboat begins with the core decision of where we place our trust. A sailboat is designed to trust completely in the pattern of the wind, while a powerboat trusts in the motor.
- Second, sailing requires concentration and outward vision, while a powerboat encourages a downward gaze. A sailboat listens to the wind and finds ways for the boat to respond, while in contrast a powerboat's motor is all that you hear.
- Third, sailing requires constant preparation, while a powerboat is a gas-and-go operation. It is clear that the preparation of a sailboat is complex and demands meticulous maintenance, while a powerboat gives immediate gratification.
- Fourth, the direction and speed of the wind determine the course of a sailboat, while a hand on the motor turns a powerboat. A powerboat's speed may impress others, but God's wind helps the mission to arrive on time even if the wind is slower than we might like it to be.
- Fifth, a sailboat is admired in all waters, while a powerboat is often unwelcome. The same thing happens in ministry when relationships, programmes, competition, cultural insensitivity, big ideas and plans, or even the arrogance of egos and logos become like powerboats – rough, self-centred, power-based, and polluting. In fact, the ministry motors generate pollution, noise, and disruption that can create a dead zone that scares away all the fish and the other fishermen. In contrast, a sailboat does not disrupt anything around it and the beauty of its nature makes both the people and the mission relax.
- Lastly, sailing demands our complete effort on the water, while a powerboat offers a comfortable way to look like a sailor. Sailing looks so relaxing, but nothing could be further from the truth. It is a challenging and constant work, which demands that you stay

attentive, are always thinking, and use the best gifts. By contrast, a powerboat is fairly predictable, offering a relatively secure day on the water.

In conclusion, Parrott states that the mission agendas must catch God's wind, and reminds us that the wind of God is always present – most often it is a guiding gentle breeze, which helps the church into a great mission service.

With a similar understanding, the Brazilian Alex Araujo has developed an idea of 'Catching the Wind' in article by that title presented at the North-South dialogue at the World Evangelical Alliance–Mission Commission held in Pattaya in November 2008.[123] He points out that the wind of the Spirit must become the leading power tool in contemporary mission, allowing mission boards to give more appropriate space to Spirit-guidance. From an African perspective, Duncan Olumbe provides insights into mission collaboration in his article 'Dancing a Different Dance'.[124] Olumbe warns global South leaders "not to copy the dance of the North" by adopting the northern methodologies through three models of mission: Power Dance (related to global secular power), Imitation Dance (related to inappropriate partnership) and Position Dance (related to inappropriate special status and positions of power in mission). In a complementary missiological approach, the British Mark Oxbrow, former International Director of CMS, makes a response to Araujo and Parrott by pointing out that the power boat paradigm does not only belong to the North, since there are some power boats as well as sailboats cruising in the mission contexts of Asia, Africa and Latin America.[125] He suggests that a critical issue for the South and the North relates to the 'alternative energy' for mission collaboration, seeking the wind and learning how to accept God's power.[126] This implies a missional attitude of 'working with' the wind of God rather than being simply 'blown along by' it. Second, relationships are key, since

---

123. Alex Araujo 'Catching the Wind' paper presented during the dialogue 'North South' at the World Evangelical Alliance–Mission Commission held in Pattaya in November 2008, unpublished material.
124. See the whole article 'Dancing a Different Dance'. Data provided by Reuben Ezemadu, sent to the author the 31 October 2008, unpublished material.
125. See the article of Mark Oxbrow 'Sailing Close to the Wind: A Response to Roger Parrot and Alex Araujo' (article sent to the author on 3 March 2009, unpublished material).
126. Ibid., 2.

it takes time to relate cross-culturally in the 'school of mistakes'. Third, to use the word 'poor' for a financial condition threatens to distort the biblical understanding of wealth sharing. Fourth, contextual issues address the reality of 'informal' or non-intentional missionaries. Fifth, there is a challenge of misconception and misunderstanding the meaning of communication across cultural mission which distorts mission relationships.[127]

Araujo suggests that a primary intent of his metaphor is to illustrate our relationship with the power that moves the church forward as follows:[128]

1. The church moves by the power and guidance of the Spirit.
2. The Spirit moves when and where he wishes and we have no control over him.
3. Powerboat thinking is incompatible with that reality; we cannot store Holy Spirit power in tanks to be used according to our plans and strategies.
4. The way for us to move forward in Christ is to learn how to respond to the Spirit's moving, to his timing, direction and intensity. Sailing helps to make that specific point clear; though it may serve many other illustrative purposes, I would not want secondary applications to distract us from this primary intent.

It seems to me that Parrott employs a strong argument for dependence on the *missio Dei*, that Araujo provides an alternative model for collaboration in mission, that Olumbe warns us not to photocopy the 'Northern' model, while Oxbrow criticizes the need for an 'alternative energy' for mission. Here, I would like to propose a fifth alternative. In all of these missiological analyses, it appears that there is a lack of reflection on the *missio Dei* and a Trinitarian mission theology. The tendency may come as a result of a pragmatic mission activity, which is understandable from the perspective of mission leaders. But what is needed is an influx of a spiral mission theology in order to avoid mission polarization. Therefore I propose that within a spiral mission theology boats can be fixed, since it provides tools for fixing both powerboats and

---

127. Ibid., 3–6.
128. Linked to Parrott's powerboat and sailing metaphor, Araujo finally concludes that it is possible to push a metaphor too far from its initial intent. For him, sailing is a wonderful figure of speech to illustrate a lot of spiritual realities. But we can confuse the key message by stretching the metaphor. Alex Araujo in response to Mark Oxbrow (email sent to the author on 6 February 2009).

sailboats, and allows the spontaneous combustion of the Spirit to provide alternative models of mission. In fact an additional model for the spontaneous model can be the volunteer model, rooted in the experience of the student volunteer movement of the nineteenth-century mission (Wallstrom 1980).[129] As we know, the greatest impact of the volunteer movement culminated in Edinburgh 1910, under the leadership of John Mott. In contemporary perspective, volunteers want a return for the investment of their time, which for Wright (2000, 156) is a foundational principle. But Christian volunteers are at present crossing political, economic, social, racial, and cultural borders with no idea in most cases what is going on with them in relation to formal mission activity. It is essential for the mission establishment, therefore, to be open to working the spontaneous model. The following diagram portrays the spontaneous model.

The Spontaneous Model

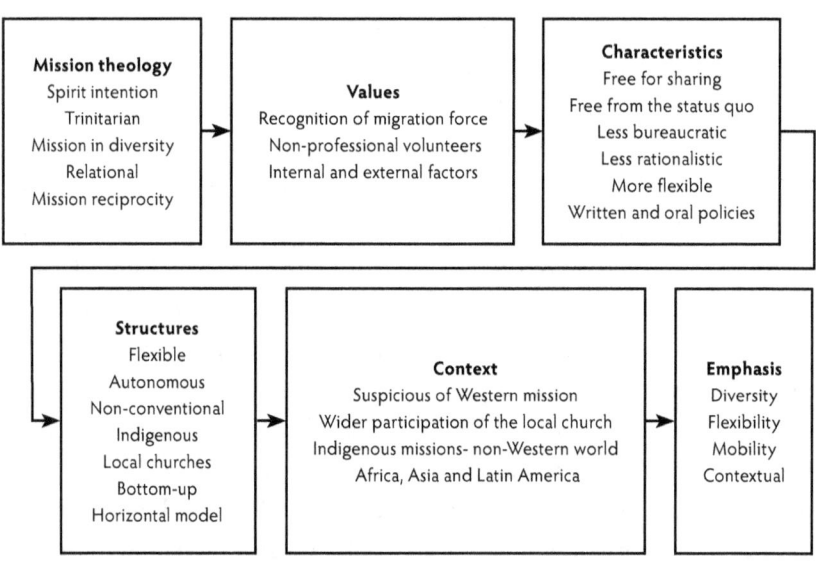

---

129. We would compare the volunteer model with the Student Volunteer Movement (SVM) created in 1886 with students in USA and Canada. See further Timothy C. Wallstrom, *The Creation of a Student Movement to Evangelize the World* (William Carey International Press 1980).

> **The Spontaneous Model**
>
> **Alternative title:** 'the pneumatic model'.
>
> **Mission theology:** Spirit intention, Trinitarian, mission in diversity, relational, mission reciprocity.
>
> **Values:** recognition of migration mission force and non-professional mission volunteers, external and internal factors of mission.
>
> **Characteristics:** free for sharing, free from the status quo, less bureaucratic, less rationalistic, more flexible, has both written and oral policies.
>
> **Structure:** flexible, autonomous, non-conventional, indigenous, local churches, bottom-up, horizontal model.
>
> **Context:** basically suspicious of Western mission, wider participation of the local church and indigenous missions of the non-Western world in Africa, Asia and Latin America.
>
> **Emphasis:** diversity, flexibility, mobility and contextualized.
>
> **Positives:** takes flexibility seriously, can be used by conventional and non-conventional missionaries.
>
> **Negatives:** indigenous mission societies are in danger of copying western models, weak structures.
>
> **Tensions:** weakness to overcome roadblocks of economy and reciprocal power.
>
> **Examples:** emergent models, independent churches, indigenous missions, Philippine example, Argentinian example, Peruvian example, sailboat and the powerboat metaphor, the Spirit spontaneous movement in the Antioch church (Acts 13:1–12).

The Integrated Model

In his book, *Integrity*, Jonathan Lamb (2006) provides a model of life for people who want to practise the integrated model. Lamb points out a spiritual call to work in community mission, confronting the challenges under the scrutiny of an integrity-life in whole aspects of Christian mission. Hence, the integrated model includes an appropriate form of Christian life with openness to a trans-local mission that allows practitioners to become integrated to a ministry but in relation to a global mission understanding.

From this perspective we provide a corollary: the greater the integrity-life with an integrated global vision, the greater is the integration as participation with others in mission. This implies that the strengths of a mission structure will depend on appropriate mission components. Therefore, the integrated model is rooted in the variety of components (autonomous parts) of the model, keeping reciprocity within its mission activity as components of Christ's body, so interdependence is the key element. In fact, this model would be related to the 'global model' or 'glocal-structure model', where the structure rests on team leadership and structural abilities, which involve the hard work of consulting, research, and planning, all of those abilities, which are in any case the ingredients for an appropriate integrated model.

The integrated model can be connected to a *circle integration* model where the principles of traditional structures are integrated to the foundations of either or both the networking and the emergent model. There is no central power but a sharing power where each component has a reciprocal function and the model does work if they function together as Christ's body. To put it another way, all ministries are indispensable as they work for the same purpose and the same kingdom. The concept of the Universal church and God's kingdom is behind of this model. This model can be called 'the amalgamated model' as all missions work for the 'same body' as one body and that provides a mission model where none are better than the other.

The integrated model includes the using of all resources in an integrated agreement where both mission co-labourers work for the same purpose and goal, which is related to the kingdom of God, becoming united in spirit and in deed. This includes affection, common interest, and economic interdependence.

Missions with this model are Operation Mobilization (OM) founded by George Verwer in 1957, which has 3,000 missionaries working in 85 countries;[130] and YWAM, founded by Loren Cunningham and mobilizing

---

130. The role of OM in the body of Christ is to motivate, develop and equip people for world evangelization, and to strengthen and help plant churches in the Middle East, Europe, South and Central Asia. Currently, OM includes a mission with one ocean-going mission ship. OM emphasizes personal evangelism, literature distribution, street outreach, relief and development and other creative means. Ministry Watch.com (http://www.ministrywatch.com/profile/Operation-Mobilization.aspx).

people from over 149 nations.[131] These are clear examples of integrated models; all the teams and ministries in each country are integrated to a network of its mission structure, but mobilizing the church in a non-denominational way.

Another example of the integrated model is the 'Faith2share' network, which has the purpose of strengthening indigenous movements for the mission of God.[132] It is international, multicultural, evangelical and committed to partnership with local and national churches of many different backgrounds. Mark Oxbrow, the International Director, states that the Faith2Share has nineteen members.[133] It began by building a network within Africa, Asia, Europe and North America of Anglican missions, but more recently has expanded to a more interdenominational network. There is a commitment to work more closely with the emergent movements.[134] With this in mind, Faith2Share operates with three fundamental proposes: to provide a supportive fellowship to the senior leadership of member agencies, to strengthen the mission of each member movement by the effective sharing of resources in mission, and to encourage the establishment of, and then to partner with and support, new and emerging mission movements, especially in the global South.[135] In all of this, Faith2Share operates through the fellowship of the General Secretaries and other leaders of the movement and has an annual (or several regional) Leadership Consultation(s), tele-conferencing, and ongoing bilateral relationships; resources can be

---

131. YWAM International (http://www.ywam.org/Default.asp?bhcp=1). Loren Cunningham, student of the Assemblies of God College in Springfield, USA, spent a part of his summer break in Nassau, Bahamas, as a participant in a gospel quartet in 1956. While there, Loren had a vision to work with youth and then in 1960 he founded YWAM. (http://www.ywam.org/contents/abo_his_1960.htm at 22:10)

132. Fath2Share has an evangelistic target with the following characteristics: Christ-centred, Bible-based, committed to conversion, and expecting transformation. See further Faith2Share, 'A Short Introduction to the Faith2Share Network' (2009).

133. Faith2Share network, information sent to the author by Mark Oxbrow on 20 February 2009. Also see (Faith2Share (http://www.faith2share.net/AboutUs/tabid/132/Default.aspx)

134. See Faith2Share (2009), 'A Short Introduction'.

135. Ibid.

shared through their private website, conferences for mission personnel and shared funding programmes.[136]

Tim Chester (2002, 2) clarifies the notion of integral mission by stating that the words *misión integral* come from Latin America, and closely echo the idea of holistic mission. For Michael Smitheram, in his article 'Consensus-Driven Christians', integral mission is similar to 'pan-integral' (wholemeal bread), but the importance is not that separate ingredients have been brought together (integrated), but rather that nothing has been taken out.[137] Therefore, the integrated model comes with the same intentional understanding and determination that nothing of the biblical values, nor of good human and material resources, has been taken out. These values are considered key ingredients in developing appropriate models of mission; thus, all the mission components become an integral part of the model; nothing has more value than the integration of all components as a whole.

Regarding the integrated model, there seems to be a tendency to develop strategic alliances in the market world, especially incremented after the Second World War period, initiating first of all alliances in mineral and metals, and then developing alliances with the new emerging industries, such as automobiles, airlines, biotechnologies and information technology (Ramu 1997, 98–99). There are key elements of functional reciprocal contextual collaboration, such as vision-fusion, field-fusion, gifts-fusion, corporation-fusion, reciprocal-fusion, substantial-fusion and knowledge-fusion.

For example, General Motors integrated (purchased) Electronic Data Systems in 1984 with the expectation that considerable synergy would result. The two British missions CMS and SAMS merged in 2010, and were called recently a truly global mission society.[138] Vivid examples of

---

136. See further (Faith2Share (http://www.faith2share.net/AboutUs/tabid/132/Default.aspx).

137. Tim Chester (2002, 2) clarifies the difference between integral mission, transformation and development. Integral means that all (evangelism and social responsibility) are necessary to be complete as a whole. See Michael Smitheram's article 'Consensus-Driven Christians' (http://www. Micahchallenge .org/ uploaded_docs/ BTHW/Consensus-driven%20Christians.doc).

138. Bishop Pat Harris, SAMS' President states that on 29 November 2008, SAMS Great Britain General Council took the significant and strategic decision (84% voting in favour) "to approve in principle a merger of the Society and CMS". This decision was made to provide better engagement with the new indigenous missionary movement. This does not

the integrated model are developed by Chris and Foluso Enweren, pastoring a church in Shurdington Village, Gloucestershire, UK, in collaboration between ECM, St James Church and other supporters;[139] Habitat for Humanity International (HFHI), founded by Millar Fuller in 1976, has integrated social responsibility with evangelism, and working in 100 countries has built more than 300,000 houses as a non-profit, non-denominational Christian charity, helping low-income families to get decent and affordable housing.[140]

An addition to the integrated model would be the multicultural (multidiverse) model. For this Orlando Costas (Padilla 1976, 143–161), in *The New Face of Evangelicalism*, provides tools for "churches in evangelistic partnership" by answering three fundamental questions: Why an evangelistic partnership? On what basis? In which direction? For the third he offers three principles: (1) multiple strategies of varying situations, which include goals, manpower, material and tactical approaches (155); (2) multiple ministries for a multidimensional task, with a pluralistic approach to the Christian ministry which implies the fulfilment of church witnessing vocation (157); and (3) multiple forms of evangelistic partnership, providing a wider view of the narrow interpretation that mission can be expressed only organizationally by both local and regional councils like the World Council of Churches or the International Missionary Council (158). He argues that we need a pluri-form ministry and pluri-structural expressions of the church. I agree with Costas, given that the church is diverse in gifts/composition, pluri-fom, and that the church on the other hand is diverse in organization/structure, so pluri-structural. In the same line of thought, reciprocal contextual collaboration provides tools for a more appropriate

---

mean that the name of SAMS will disappear but that the structure will work as regional partner of CMS to work in Africa, Asia and Europe (SAMS, http://www.samsgb.org/news.html#newsitem8). John Martin, CMS head of communication, announced the approval to merge with SAMS in Oxford on 20 January 2009. The process was fully completed in February 2010 (http://www.cms-uk.org/Whoweare/CMSandSAMS/tabid/485/language/en-GB/Default.aspx).

139. Newsletter from Chris and Foluso Enweren sent by email to the author on 2 April 2009.

140. See Habitat for Humanity (http://www.habitat.org/eca/how/about_us.aspx). Habitat tries to help (http://www.habitat.org/intl/eca/81.aspx). Habitat does not work in Peru.

gift composition for mission reciprocity because of its Trinitarian mission theology and its biblical emphasis of christological freedom.

In the context of a globalized economy, the business as mission model (kingdom entrepreneurship) has become an integrated mission model between business and ministry, although this model was developed by the Moravians in 1732.[141] Tetsunao Yamamory and Kenneth Eldred (2003) in *On Kingdom Business* provide case studies, essays and conclusions clarifying that the traditional Western missionary movement has failed to mobilize Christian business professionals in mission and recently this has increased as a novelty tool.[142] 'The Lausanne Occasional Papers' (Clayton 2005) bring insights between business as mission, tentmakers and marketplace.[143] They are full-time business owners rather than business employees. Kingdom entrepreneurs can be either mono-cultural or cross-cultural business owners, called by God to do ministry through business.[144] This model can be called the 'caterpillar model', which is symbiotic because

---

141. Tentmaking came naturally to the Moravians by forming companies for profit, especially plantations, agriculture, all the trades and industries, organizing the so called 'general economy'; Count Zinzendorf placed his entire economy at the service of the Unitas Fratrum, known as the Moravians who should earn their own living first as a fundamental teaching of work for others. Moravians really integrated mission with economic activity and this enabled them to support a much higher proportion of missionaries than the average denomination (Danker 2002, 25, 28, 30, 32–33, 57). See further William J. Danker, *Profit for the Lord: Economic Activities in Moravian Missions and the Basel Mission Trading Company* (1971–republished 2002, 16).

142. For Yamamori (2003, 7–8) there are two types of tentmaker: workers in a secular job but acting as a missionary (job takers) especially for the so called 10/40 window, and second what he emphasizes in his mission theology by referring to those called *kingdom entrepreneurs* (job makers), people who start small to large business for profit, working not as front line to get into closed countries but as real enterprises to cover real human needs, which can be carried out in either a mono-cultural or a cross-cultural setting.

143. The 'Lausanne Occasional Paper' (2005, 285–286) defines theologically business as mission, "as a renewed call where God has established the institution and practice of business as a means of fulfilling his creation mandate to steward and care for all of creation; God is realizing the power of business to aid in the task of fulfilling the great commission, making disciples of all nations; God longs to be glorified through our business activities". See the whole study and bibliography of the theme (Clayton 2005, 285–362).

144. For the cross-cultural kingdom business, Yamamori (2003, 9) defines as cross-cultural business owners, called by God, to do ministry through business in restricted-access countries. He has identified three types of kingdom entrepreneurship: cases of strong business and weak ministry, cases of strong ministry and weak business, and cases of strong business and strong ministry.

of its entrepreneurial mission philosophy.[145] It has interchangeable characteristics of the integrated (business and ministry) and the contextual model (sometimes working in countries of restricted access).[146] 'Pura Vida Caffe', located in Seattle, Washington, helps street children in San Jose, Costa Rica; Global Engineering and Management Solutions, and Gateway Telecommunications Service, are vivid examples of integrated kingdom business (Rundle and Steffen 2003, 21, 145, 163, 181).[147] Before the synthesis of the integrated models, there follows a diagram portraying the integrated model.

---

145. The 'caterpillar models' is symbiotic (any interdependent benefit of two things), due to the fact that it seeks the benefit of both ministry and business, it becomes accessible to restricted areas of mission and avoids dichotomy of work and ministry.

146. For a discussion on the multifaceted nature of kingdom business or business as mission see David Befus 'Kingdom Business: A New Frontier in Missions' (*Evangelical Mission Quarterly*, April 2002 Vol 38, No 2, 204–209); Befus is former president of the Latin America Mission; Steve Rundle and Tom Steffen *Great Commission Companies: The Emerging Role of Business in Mission* (Downers Grove, Illinois, InterVarsity Press, 2003); Tom Steffen and Mike Barnett (eds) *Business as Mission: From Impoverished to Empowered* (William Carey Library 2006). This book is a collection of resulting essays on the subject of kingdom business organized in 2005 by the Evangelical Missiological Society, which devoted their regional and annual conferences to the subject of Business as Mission; Michael R. Baer, *Business as Mission: The Power of Business in the Kingdom of God* (YWAM Publishing, 2006). See also the Business as Mission Resource Centre *YWAM Connect*, Papers and Articles (https://www.ywamconnect.com/ubasicpage.jsp?siteid=29315&pageid= 349942).

147. Rundle and Steffen claim against the spiritual vocational hierarchy such as missionaries, pastors, social workers, etc., and challenge business Christians to become more active in mission. Also they provide three case studies of kingdom business. See further Rundle and Steffen, *Great Commission Companies* (2003, 145–191).

The Integrated Model

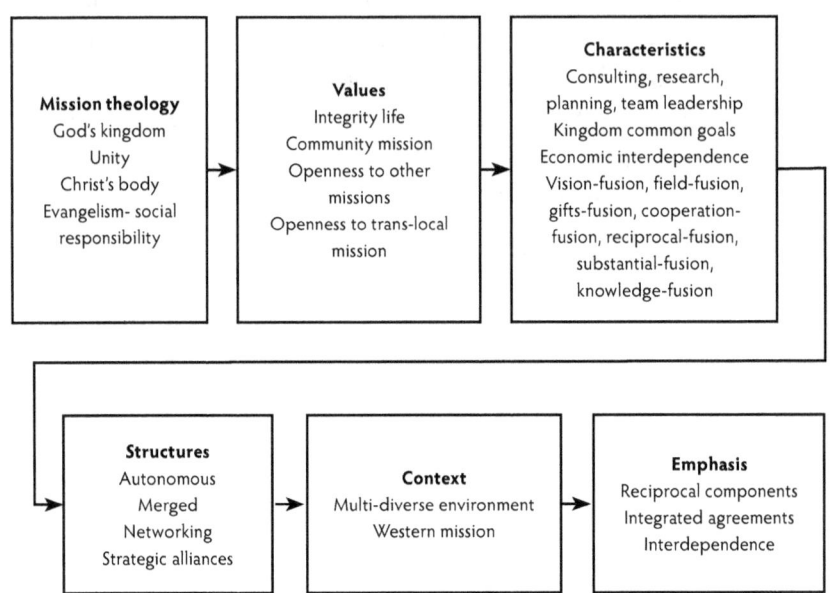

> **The Integrated Model**
>
> **Alternative title:** the amalgamated model, global model, global structure model, circle integration model.
>
> **Mission theology:** God's kingdom, unity, Christ's body, evangelism and social responsibility.
>
> **Values:** Community mission, integrity life, openness to other missions, openness to trans-local mission.
>
> **Characteristics:** consulting, research, planning, team leadership, kingdom common goals, economic interdependence, vision-fusion, field-fusion, gifts-fusion, cooperation-fusion, reciprocal-fusion, substantial-fusion, knowledge-fusion.
>
> **Structure:** autonomous, merged, networking, strategic alliances.
>
> **Context:** fundamentally for the western mentality but has a multidiverse environment.
>
> **Emphasis:** reciprocal components, integrated agreements.
>
> **Positives:** Practice of multiple strategies, multiple ministries and multiple forms of evangelism.
>
> **Negatives:** weak composition of pluri-form ministry and pluri-structural missions lacking strong Trinitarian mission theology and reciprocal theology.
>
> **Tensions:** strengths of mission structures depend on appropriate mission components; primary focus must be the mission not the mission structures.
>
> **Examples:** networking model, business as mission, OM, YWAM, CMS, SAMS, HFHI, the integrated mission movement from Jewish to Gentiles' mission (Acts 10 and 11).

The Contextual Model

We should start by saying that this model relates to a *kenotic* model, based on Jesus' total renunciation of kingship since, being in very nature of God, he took the nature of a servant (Phil 2:6–8).[148] This model is centred in local theologies and in what I refer to as the prophetic imagination.[149] This is a model of mission collaboration which includes principles of local theologies and a missiological understanding, which emphasizes christological freedom, cultural identity and the context. Political, economic and social concern is pivotal in this model. Reciprocal contextual collaboration overcomes a reductionist perspective based on a narrow interpretation of the *missio Dei*, God's kingdom and God's church. The contextual model deals with a theology of freedom, justice, mercy and compassion in all contexts (especially of poverty and lacking economic affluence). This novel model relates basically to:

1. The dynamic tension of the kingdom (compassion for the poor). In a global reality of competition compassion for those in need becomes forgettable. Poverty is not an issue of simply those who have less; it is a reality of the whole economic system. Thus, if a mission model has to be competitive, the only reason must be innovative compassion to reverse and combat poverty in its different forms. The kingdom of God has included and will include people in need of spiritual, physical and economic support.

2. The relational tension of the Trinity (is a relational mission tension possible?). Relationships between the persons of the Trinity could in theory disintegrate, but this is of course impossible because of the love, beauty and perfect harmony the Bible affirms they provide according to their own nature. Thanks to this ontological impossibility, there is hope of practising positive tensions within the relationships of all participants of God's mission. Therefore, mission calls for humility and christological freedom to confront negative tensions and in turn produce mature and responsible relationships.

3. The political tension of the church (what could the role of new structures of mission be?). The contextual model seeks not to overcome all the undesirable models, but to reverse and to develop a critical analysis

---

148. See further Ed Mathews, 'Christ and Kenosis: A Model for Mission', *Journal of Applied Missiology*, Vol 2, Number 12001 (http://www.ovc.edu/missions/jam/kenosis.htm).

149. Samuel Cueva, unpublished material, papers presented in Lima, Peru, May 2006, for the Christian and Missionary Alliance's mission conference.

of different models to find incarnational models that fit the context more appropriately. This relates to the practice of justice.

4. The missiological tension of collaboration in mission (how can Westerners support the new forces of mission for the Latin American church?). The contextual model cries out to help contexts in desperate need of economic aid in food, child protection, agriculture, ecology, health care, sanitation, etc. This has a strong connection with mercy.

The *missio* reciprocity, *missio* context and *missio* collaboration are included in the reciprocal contextual collaboration of the contextual model, which emphasizes gospel, culture and church, under the 'biblical oil' of truth, reciprocity, respect, maturity, friendship, honesty, accountability and freedom. Contextual models also relate to the view of developing mission projects or programmes specified in time, context and purpose such as Compassion International, which works in Peru to help children in need;[150] the London City Mission to evangelize the city, especially the poor;[151] Tearfund, a Christian relief and development agency building a global network of local churches to help eradicate poverty;[152] or STM that has become a massive expanding impact of a contextual model in comparison to the decreasing traditional long-term mission candidates.

An addition to the contextual model would be the 'missiological imagination' model. This model is centred in my understanding of the prophetic

---

150. Compassion was founded by the Rev Everett Swanson in 1952 to provide Korean War orphans with food, shelter, education and health care, as well as Christian training. Today, Compassion International exists as a Christian child ministry that releases children from spiritual, economic, social and physical poverty and enables them to become responsible, fulfilled Christian adults, helping more than 1 million children in 25 countries. In the case of Peru, 48,700 children participate in more than 220 child development centres. See further (http://www.compassion.com/about/aboutus.htm).

151. London City Mission was founded by the Scot, David Nasmith, in May 1835, to extend the gospel in London, especially to the poor without any reference to denominational distinctions; missionaries are employed and paid by the institution. See *Streets Paved with Gold: The Story of the London City Mission* (Howat and Nicholls 2003, 21, 23, 25).

152. Tearfund has a ten-year vision to see 50 million people released from material and spiritual poverty through a worldwide network of 100,000 local churches. They connect people to this global network of local churches to transform lives materially and spiritually. Its motto is: "Be part of a miracle", which means they work with the whole person, through the local church, as part of the global church. See Tearfund (http://www.tearfund.org/About+us/default.htm).

imagination.[153] By prophetic imagination I mean the innovative ways to develop the mission task for the fulfilment of the *missio Dei*. It tries to overcome the absence of mission creativity. In this sense, the prophetic imagination model is related to the new ways of non-Western traditional views of doing mission. It implies mission creativity from the context of the Third Church of emergent partnership movements to promote new models for mission. Hence, prophetic missiological imagination relates to systematic thinking to promote ideas and alternatives to accomplish the mission mandate. It is prophetic by including a contextualized understanding and the role of participants in mission.[154] Albert Einstein[155] said that the imagination is more powerful than knowledge because, where there are needs, the imagination becomes active as we try to solve our problems. The imagination drives us to think about new things, new alternatives etc. The book *The Prophetic Imagination* by Walter Brueggemann (2001) suggests living an authentic life by building a more perfect society.[156] In the 2 Corinthians 8, the apostle Paul tells us about the poor churches in Macedonia taking part in mission. Their attitude was one of motivation, challenge and empathy, which invites us to imagine what the situation was like in the churches

---

153. Samuel Cueva, unpublished material, papers presented in Lima, Peru, May 2006 for the Christian and Missionary Alliance's Missions Conference.

154. The following explanation can help us to understand a wider sense of prophetic imagination in terms of action: "Prophetic action has three different functions: to criticize and denounce, in speaking truth to power; to energize and encourage people struggling under unjust conditions in depressed societies; and to mediate or serve as intercessor, bringing the word of God before the community, and the concerns of the community before God. This threefold witness of biblical prophecy may provide inspiration for our churches in situations of injustice and oppression. Prophecy is a missionary task, and our understanding of the prophetic function in mission requires further elaboration in our particular situations". See further CWM's Network of Theological Enquiry, 'The People of God Among All God's Peoples', http://www.cwmnote.org/round.php (Accessed on 16 August 2010 at 10:20).

155. See further Moments in Life, 'Ten Amazing Lessons You Can Learn From Albert Einstein' (http://walli.dk/?p=297).

156. Brueggemann (2001, 40) suggests that imagination must come before the implementation; it is the vocation of the prophet to keep alive the ministry of imagination. For the practice of ministry, he understands that Jeremiah practises radical criticism against the royal consciousness and Isaiah practises radical energizing against the royal consciousness (115). Therefore, he concludes that prophetic ministry has the task to evoke an alternative community, the practice of the acts of ministry, and also seeks the public sharing of pain, affirming a future joy of God's kingdom (116–118).

in Macedonia (2 Cor 8:1–15). Therefore, prophetic imagination helps us to discover appropriate solutions for new mission models for the challenges of the twenty-first-century mission.[157]

Made up of poor people, the churches in Macedonia were churches with very little possibility of being able to make the necessary financial commitment which corresponded to the needs of the church's dynamic mission of the first century. But their imagination went beyond human effort. They did not think about their circumstances in their social context as a political and religious denomination. It was the proclamation of the gospel which set them on fire and they lived by imagining themselves saturating every place in the Roman Empire with the gospel. They knew that this was the solution for the problems of poverty and social inequality amongst the rich and poor of that time. In his letter to the Romans, the apostle Paul mentions again the presence of poor churches co-participating with the church in Jerusalem, "For Macedonia and Achaia were pleased to make a contribution for the poor among the saints in Jerusalem" (Rom 15:26). What were Paul's plans for mission? They were to motivate the church in Rome to raise funds for a missionary plan in Spain, which was based on a missiological imagination.

In fact, the church needs to live an incarnational faith in order to see a prophetic imagination of the gospel and a world transformed by Christ's powerful message. Without a doubt, it is possible to co-participate in mission in the context of poverty where the church's prophetic imagination is something real. Indeed this is something which Christ has planned, since he included the poor in the mission of salvation and peace to the captives.[158] Here we provide at least one existing model of prophetic missiological imagination,[159] in the sense that this model tries to overcome the absence of mission creativity by the church in order to accomplish the mission of God.

---

157. See for example the imaginative model of the African Zimbabwean church-to-church relations with a transformational approach (Marcia Sheffler, *Transformation*, Vol 25 No 4, October 2008, 255–270), or the Peruvian model of Segadores mission working in church planting, training and mobilization for missions (http://segadoresperu.com/index.php?page=home).

158. Cueva, 'Misiones Desde un Contexto de Pobreza' (2007, 7).

159. Ibid.

Prophetic contextual imagination: two-way co-participation, poor churches to rich churches, poor churches to even poorer churches, and poor and very poor churches to rich churches. This model practises 'prophetic imagination' through sharing economic contributions, regular prayers, evangelistic presence in society, and the sending of native missionaries within and outside of their local boundaries. Accordingly, sharing becomes the key element. For example, the Latin American mission PMI is sending missionaries from poor Latin American countries to very poor countries in restricted zones of mission;[160] the Baptist church 'Vida Nueva' in Peru supports missionaries to India, Ecuador, Argentina;,[161] and the Peruvian Christian and Missionary Alliance 'Lince' in Lima has sent missionaries to USA, the UK, France, Spain, Norway, Japan, and India, in some cases with full support and in other cases with partial support.[162]

Based on 2 Corinthians 8, some characteristics of contextual prophetical imagination among the churches in Macedonia can help us find new mission models. Some of these are: co-participation with love, joy, generosity, will, honour, equality, imagination, without complexes, selfishness, and sadness, undemanding and without excuses. For the sake of brevity, I will discuss only four of these:

1. Co-participation with love. Participating in mission depends on our missionary heart: "Tell me how much you give to mission and I will tell you how much you love mission." The church can participate within its abilities, or even beyond its abilities (2 Cor

---

160. Also some North American missions cooperate with PMI within specific projects, but not to support missionaries. Information provided by Federico Bertuzzi from Granada, Spain, to the author on 9 February 2011.

161. The church 'Vida Nueva' in Lima has 19 missionaries. In Ecuador and Argentina they work with deaf people, and in Panama they work with the Jewish community, and they are planning to send a couple to China. Regarding the Peru itself, they have three on the coast, seven in the jungle and two in the Peruvian Sierra and all of them are church planters, as this is their goal, and their mission committee develops the sending process, which includes pastoral care, financial support (with a monthly budget of $6,000) and accountability matters. The church prays regularly for missionaries as they send regularly their request for prayers as a kind of accountability to them (electronic information sent by Tomas Pace, Senior Pastor of 'Nueva Vida' church to the author from Lima, Peru, on 11 February 2011).

162. See further Cueva (2007b, 10–12) 'Como Promover Misiones en la Iglesia Local', unpublished material, papers presented in Lima, Peru, 29 May to 3rd June 2007 for the Christian and Missionary Alliance's Missionary Conference.

8:3) as the churches in Macedonia did. Participation is defined by love and not context. A mission in the context of poverty is qualitative, of the heart, and not quantitative. This enables us to give beyond our abilities (8:3). We give for love of God (1 Cor 13:3).
2. Co-participation with joy. The joy of salvation generates security in God, trust, and joy to participate in the mission plan. This joy is not temporary, nor circumstantial. Therefore, even when the church is limited in what it can give, the church serves with joy in mission, while the spiritual joy, which transcends the temporary, gives joy to participate not with sadness or out of need (2 Cor 9:7).
3. Co-participation with generosity. Liberality (2 Cor 9:13) refers to the generosity which makes God's people free to give. Missionary theology teaches that those who distribute their resources should do so generously (Rom 12:8). In Exodus 35:5–9 we can see the attitude of a generous heart. Deuteronomy should be interpreted in the context of obedience to mission. The point of reference to support mission concertedly is that God's provision is sufficient (2 Cor 9:8). The only Biblical reasons for material prosperity is to be generous in God's mission (2 Cor 9:11–13).
4. Co-participation with will. Giving voluntarily is an attitude of disposition – a mentality which is marked by a willingness to work together. The church in Corinth gave gratefully (2 Cor 8:3), and this attitude of gratitude enables us to give voluntarily. The will has a disposition to give (8:12) which moves one to be spontaneous (8:17); it is expressed practically (8:19), and it is what your heart suggests (9:7).

The economic phenomenon of the industrial revolution generated an integrated international economy and since the fall of the socialist bloc there has emerged what we know as a global economy.[163] This economic process

---

[163]. In 1837 the United Kingdom reached an annual average income of $200 dollars per inhabitant, France did this in 1852, Germany in 1886 and Italy in 1909. In 1900 Latin America reached a per capita income of $100 dollars, but in 1960 the difference with Europe grew to the point where the rich countries went up to $1,500 annual income

has made Latin America a poor continent, on par with Asia and Africa – even though the Asians from the 'tiger zone' have improved, along with India. It is in this context that the Latin American church is participating in the *missio Dei*, and that the challenge of poverty has brought us to consider a model of contextual prophetic imagination which propels the migratory, innovative, and bi-vocational models – three models in which poor churches become the focal point for missionary co-participation. The following diagram portrays the contextual model.

The Contextual Model

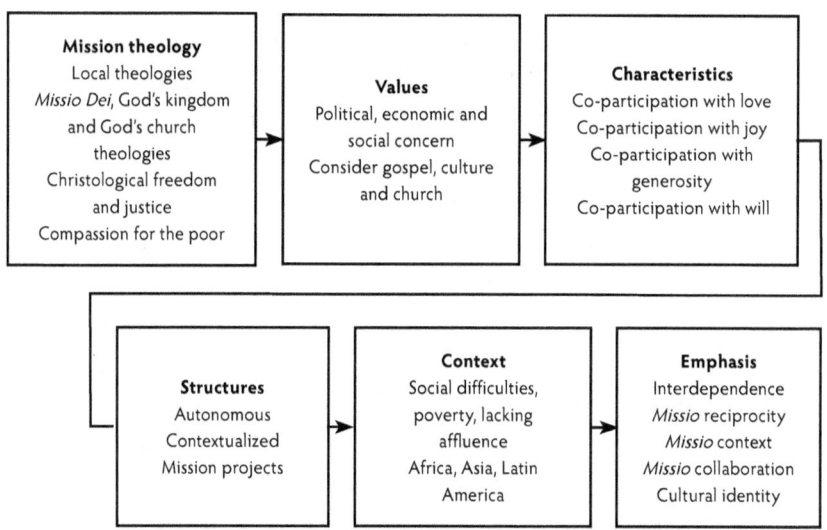

---

while Latin America went up to between $200–$300. The explanation for this sudden change is the industrial revolution which began in the 18th and 19th century in Western Europe, America, part of Oceania and the old Soviet Union and Japan (Padilla and Yamamori 2001, 22). See further René Padilla and Tetsunao Yamamori (2001, 22), *Misión Integral y Pobreza*, CLADE IV, Consulta, Buenos Aires, Kairos Ediciones.

> **The Contextual Model**
>
> **Alternative title:** the kenotic model, the servant model, the prophetic imagination model.
>
> **Mission theology:** local theologies, *missio Dei*, God's kingdom and God's church theologies, christological freedom and justice, compassion for the poor.
>
> **Values:** political, economic and social concern, consider gospel, culture and church.
>
> **Characteristics:** co-participation with love, co-participation with joy, co-participation with generosity, co-participation with will.
>
> **Structure:** autonomous, contextualized, promoting mission projects.
>
> **Context:** especially applied to contexts of political, economic and social difficulties, poverty and lacking affluence.
>
> **Emphasis:** interdependence, *missio* reciprocity, *missio* context, *missio* collaboration, cultural identity.
>
> **Positives:** helps to encourage participation of the new missionary movement emerging from growing churches in Asia, Africa and Latin America, practice of integral mission.
>
> **Negatives:** lacking promotion of prophetic imagination for avoiding dependence on western power.
>
> **Tensions:** radical tendency to consider context above biblical principles.
>
> **Examples:** networking and emergent models, Compassion International, London City Mission, Tearfund, Short Term Mission, the contextual imagination of churches in Macedonia (1 Cor 8), Paul's contextual imagination mission to Rome and Spain (Rom 15).

Between those models previously mentioned, an additional mission model, which is also a contextual model that needs urgent attention, is the 'diaspora model',[164] which describes any Christian group that has been 'dispersed' from its traditional land. This model practises a missiological diaspora,

---

164. See the example provided by Andrew Walls in 'The Scottish Missionary Diaspora', where he points out that the Scottish missionary diaspora cannot be confined to the missions of Scottish churches; they formed part of the English personnel and sometimes

which we mentioned in chapter 5.[165] This can also be called the 'marginal model' of doing mission outside the burgeoning mission models. The diaspora and the exile model are sociological models, which emphasize no connection with traditional models, but a challenging decision to accomplish the *missio mandate* by moving through migration of studies, work, regrouping families, etc., where non-conventional missionaries practise a collaborative mission.[166] This diaspora model must be seen as a complement to the 'remnant model' which implies that everywhere the church is, God is doing something with and through his church, and both models must try to be a more spontaneous and integrated model with a simple life-style to develop the mission task.

Conclusion

This chapter has attempted to bring together a missionary and biblical theology of reciprocal contextual collaboration, its foundations, some mission tensions, the proposal to practise the spiral mission theology and four mission models under a *reciprocal multipolar contextual engagement,* which demand a cross-mission pollination before mission fertilization of this process can be taken seriously.

To conclude this chapter, the new configuration of twenty-first-century mission shows that traditional, networking and emergent models are revolutionizing themselves by combining their strengths. As we understand it, traditional models of mission societies serve local churches and individuals

---

American mission societies. See further Andrew Walls in *The Cross Cultural Process in Christian History* (2002, 259–272).

165. The diaspora model or the migration model has the advantage of living in countries where they went mainly for economic improvement but later gained the residence permit. The disadvantage of this model is that many of these groups have become a kind of ghetto and do not try to integrate in the country of adoption. This will require a major study, but the model has produced a great impact in church planting among minority groups like the Peruvians in Spain, Colombians in London, or Mexicans in USA.

166. The diaspora model implies an emphatic dissemination of theological and missiological thinking to include the immigrant force, which has links with the exile model, that refers to those who are outside of their land; they are 'there', mainly because of financial need. It suggests the idea that the mission force has been sent by external factors such as political or economic.

who voluntarily join the missionary vision of the mission society.[167] This is the case of Latin Link in Peru, for example, working in a more relational attitude with the Peruvian church. In addition, mission within intentional missionary activity from non-Western countries provides evidence that mission is now from everywhere to everyone.[168] As we mentioned in chapter 3, the traditional model can in some cases be hierarchical, more bureaucratic and top-down in its approach to the mission activity, but with its expertise in training and sending long-term missionaries,[169] whereas the emergent model with its own limitations such as economy and well-trained missionaries, appears to be structured more around grassroots movements from churches of the periphery, flexible policies to include conventional and non-conventional missionaries, faith mission influence and bottom-up leadership. These differences provide evidence that there is room for a more appropriate model for mission in the twenty-first century. In this sense, Escobar's analysis indicates at least three factors to create an appropriate mission atmosphere in the future within the new relations to the Majority World (2002, 105–106):[170] (1) these churches would not like to lose the missionary vigour expressed in the total mobilization that characterizes their missionary patterns, (2) these churches need assistance in training of missionaries, but it has to be contextual, and (3) structures are indispensable, however, they have to be contextual. With regard to contextuality, Escobar (Ortiz and Baker 2002, 106, 107) states:

---

167. Traditional models of mission have their origin in the monastic movement (González 1984, 137–150), and in modern Protestant mission under the influence of William Carey. For its time, Carey's model was reactive, as it arose on account of the churches' failure to evangelize the world at the start of the 18th century. Accordingly, all mission societies belong to the model of mission corporations like secular companies, but with the added element of spirituality for the mission enterprise. Thus, cooperation rests on the moral interpretation of the word society.

168. See the whole contribution of Escobar in 'Mission from Everywhere to Everyone: The Home Base in a New Century', *Edinburgh 2010: Mission then and Now* (Kerr and Ross 2009, 185–198).

169. Michael Frost and Alan Hirsch (2003, 21), in *The Shaping of Things to Come*, provide characteristics of the traditional church, with reference to its hierarchical, bureaucratic, and top-down leadership; similar characteristics are developed in the traditional mission model, which still influences current models.

170. Escobar provides a synthetic view of the process of the 'Latin American Mission Boards and Societies'. See further *Evangelical Dictionary of World Missions* (Moreau 2000, 559–560).

This contextuality is very important, considering the framework of disparity that we observe. Support structures that reflect the needs and demands of an affluent society require drastic revision. With an adequate ecclesiological basis we may be able to enter into partnership in which Western and non-Western churches enter into partnerships characterized by reciprocity and mutuality. After all, that is what characterized the practice and the teaching of the Apostle Paul.

The new appropriate models we have presented here can be regarded as new tools, never before considered systematically, that will bring a new mission atmosphere in which we might reciprocally re-engineer models as Christ's body, eager to deliver the gospel in innovative ways, understanding that the global mission belongs to the global church. Perhaps a mixture of the traditional model with its expertise and experience in recruiting, training and sending long-term missionaries, and the new presence of the emergent model with its own limitations, as we considered before, will innovate mission in the twenty-first century by becoming a more networking structure, while the synergetic, spontaneous, integrated and contextual model can offer global Christianity its flexibility, and pneumatical view.

Our thesis is that the evangelical movement of the twenty-first century must take part in a new reciprocal contextual collaboration, taking seriously both the spontaneous model and simultaneous synergy, amalgamated by the integrated and contextual models in an evangelical catholicity, all rooted under synchronic and harmonic movements of a spiral mission theology. It must be a *doxa* mission, a *basileia* kingdom for God's glory under those models of **reciprocal multipolar contextual engagement.**

Part IV

Towards a New Mission Reciprocity for the 21st Century

CHAPTER 7

Conclusion and Challenges for Reciprocal Contextual Collaboration in the Evangelical Movement for the 21st Century

Introduction

This final chapter presents conclusions of the study by pointing out the relevance of reciprocal contextual collaboration for appropriate mission models. We will consider seriously the Latin American sense of mission reciprocity, the political and social context of mission reciprocity for the twenty-first century, and the need to implement a reciprocal contextual collaboration mission theology as the way forward for strengthening the mission enterprise in order to find new appropriate models of mission. This chapter will also provide some challenges related to reciprocal contextual collaboration, its practice and its mission theology. This missionary theology leads us to some challenges like the need for missiological change, a new mature relationship, new goals within relationships, new structures of mission, and a new global mission theology for twenty-first-century mission. Some assumptions have been made in order to highlight the relevance and influence of mission reciprocity throughout these last two decades.

In this conclusion I provide an overview of the work in order to bring into perspective the implications and relevance of each chapter for an evangelical reciprocal contextual collaboration. Then, I will offer some challenges regarding the reciprocal contextual collaboration examined here.

Reciprocal contextual collaboration as the new definition of partnership

From the beginning of this study we began to use the word 'partnership', but slowly in the process of the research we opted for *reciprocal contextual collaboration*, a concept that was defined in chapter 1, in which the historical perspective of partnership was explored. In fact, it has been clarified that our personal perspective influences our understanding of partnership in Christian mission, just as our perspectives bring practices that need to be evaluated continually in order to find new ways of understanding different perspectives to accomplish the *missio Dei*. This is why we consider it indispensable to understand the different approaches of partnership that have been developed by the Christian mission enterprise through different models. This implication has been discussed through the historical, theological and missiological roots of the evangelical movement within three understandings: the ecumenical (Edinburgh 1910 to Whitby 1947), the evangelical (Lausanne 1974 to Amsterdam 2000), and the Latin American (CLADE I 1970-VI 2000) understanding of partnership. This analytical historical process helped to define a new concept of partnership called reciprocal contextual collaboration understood as reciprocal relationship of harmonious freedom in creative tension, which exists between two or more of Christ's disciples as they seek to accomplish the *missio Dei* through the christological double mandate, which includes commitment to the cosmos and people for the glory and benefits of God's kingdom. The christological mandate implies a historical, theological, political, economic, social and cultural dimension of the redemptive mission. As described in chapter 1, for the purpose of clarity, we have used three aspects for our definition: reciprocal, contextual, and collaboration. At the same time we have approached our definition from three perspectives: historical, theological and missiological.

- 'Reciprocal' implies that we are the body of Christ with diverse and multiple ministries, with gifts and resources to help one another reciprocally.
- 'Contextual' implies the incarnational attitude of Christian mission that includes conscious acknowledgement of the reality of the social, political, religious, cultural and economic context.
- 'Collaboration' implies that we acknowledge that the *missio Dei* belongs to God and that we are just collaborators in God's kingdom in freedom of a prophetic imagination.

The recovery of a mission theology of reciprocal contextual collaboration

In our study we have discovered some principal elements of reciprocal mission and its theology that can help any model of mission to critique its content and results, as well as to offer new alternatives for more appropriate models of mission. Thus, six key theological elements were set up in chapter 2, which are as follows: partnership and the *missio Dei* concept, partnership and God's kingdom, partnership and God's church, a Trinitarian theology of partnership, a christological theology of partnership, and a missiological understanding of partnership in Paul's theology. It has been demonstrated that these six theological aspects of mission theology are fundamental to any model for the mission activity. The *missio Dei* and the Trinitarian theology in particular are urgent elements that need to be recovered in the evangelical mission theology as vital components of a contextual missiological reflection.

The *missio Dei* is grounded in a Trinitarian theology which derives from the very nature of God himself, and from this assumption emerges the nature of co-participation in mission with the purpose of doing everything for his glory. This is also the purpose of reciprocal contextual collaboration in mission, wherever, whenever and by whomever Christian collaboration is developed. The church's aim is to serve God's reign, seeking first his kingdom – *basileia* – and his righteousness. In this line, the evidence is that there is no appropriate reciprocal contextual collaboration mission theology without the presence of the incarnated Jesus Christ; he is the pivotal centre of the *missio Dei*, God's kingdom, God's church and missiological thinking. The Spirit is the agent. We conclude that Christology is pivotal to produce appropriate mission models for the twenty-first century. The new landscape – or 'new global order' – according to Peruvian missiologist Samuel Escobar, in *The New Global Mission*, will demand the massive accumulated experience of evangelical missionary activity (23) to recover a healthy reciprocal contextual collaboration mission theology.

Reciprocal contextual collaboration within current models

It has been found constructive in chapter 3 to approach three current models of partnership in mission by analyzing the main characteristics, policies and impact on the evangelical movement. To avoid distraction we made reference to three models that are influencing the mission evangelical enterprise: Traditional Partnership (***traditional reciprocal mission***) between mission societies and churches, Innovative Networking Partnership (***networking reciprocal mission***) between mission societies in a non-territorial way, and Emergent Partnership (***emergent reciprocal mission***) between local churches and indigenous mission societies. The focus of chapter 3, therefore, was to distinguish pros and cons of each model.

We arrived at the conclusion that traditional partnership has been influenced by traditional Protestant countries like Great Britain, Germany, the Netherlands, Switzerland, the Scandinavian countries and the United States. It has tended to be a rigid, unidirectional, and absorbent model. Latin Link, OMF and CMS are examples of the traditional partnership, which are in a process of re-engineering themselves such as including the support of non-Western initiatives.[1] These missions have tended to develop

---

1. To see the new mission configuration process in the case of CMS, see for example, CMS pamphlet, 'SHARE: Global mission with a Latin Heart', Issue 3, 2010, 1–15; CMS pamphlet 'Mid-Africa News', Issue 1, 2011, 1–8, and CMS pamphlet, 'Were you there?: Remembering 2009–2010' (the summary 2009–2010, Financial Summary), and the new poster entitled 'CMS working in Latin America'.

a rigid policy for recruiting candidates, which became the focal point for long-term missionaries (none of them have worked with non-conventional missionaries thus far); this is unidirectional because all the decisions are made by the mission board; it is hierarchical, more top-down; it is absorbent in trying to maintain the status quo of its mission activity. However, we acknowledge that the rigidity of these traditional missions is changing for more flexible trends than was the case twenty years ago. New waves of traditional models are in the process of redesigning their mission structure by implementing a more integrated missiology, which implies flexible, multidirectional and participatory views, as they seek more opportunities for working together with non-Western missions; this is the new configuration of the twenty-first-century mission. Such is the case of the Micah Network, working to combat poverty and injustice among suffering people in the world (Chester 2002, 14); Interserve working in central Asia and recently operating in Brazil; or Pioneers and Frontiers working in church planting (Pocock, Van Rheenen and McConnell 2005, 213). Interserve is an example of an older mission that is changing for a new model, which they call 'Interserve Reloaded', which includes an evaluation to identify the strengths and weaknesses of the current status of its mission activity (Hay et al. 2007, 225). These examples are signs that traditional models are moving to provide space for new initiatives in a variety of ways. In the case of Latin Link, rigidity is shown when they work with conventional missionaries and do not provide alternatives for non-conventional missionaries.[2] However, they are trying to re-invent themselves by becoming a more networking structure or what Escobar has called international structures, which relate to the challenges of global missiology. In contrast, the networking model is formed by independent institutions that share the same (or a similar) purpose to accomplish one mission task. They seek each other out in order to share resources and skills, but they do not lose their individual identity as mission structures, local churches or mission networks, since what is stressed is a relationship between autonomous bodies.

---

2. A well-structured organization is a sign of this rigidity in relation to finances and recruiting missionaries. One of the reasons is the careful selection of the candidate and also covering of insurance and salaries is compulsory for going overseas.

The third, the emergent partnership (emergent reciprocal mission), has four characteristics as mission from below: (1) they do not come from people in positions of power or privilege; (2) they are those who have little material, financial or technical support; (3) they are open to the power of the Spirit; and (4) churches of ethnic minorities, as well as immigrant churches, are the main ones involved. Emergent partnership (emergent reciprocal mission) is influenced by southern Christianity, with grassroots churches, popular Protestantism, mission from the periphery, or indigenous (or independent) churches. Emergent partnership was defined as the missionary movement of the 'Third Church', which includes that of Africa, Asia and Latin America, and which emerges from the new missiological context for a new reciprocal contextual collaboration. The emergent model is more flexible, bipolar and autonomous.

Each of these three models – traditional reciprocal mission, the networking reciprocal mission and the emergent reciprocal mission – must be taken into consideration as we seek to find a new appropriate model of mission in the twenty-first century. These models can be defined as the basic mission models of the new global missiology. They are not liminal models, in the same sense that liminal spaces of airports or hotels are considered to be.

In spite of the fact that each model's basic patterns are clearly defined and delineated, they might be mixed, combined or amalgamated in order to find more appropriate models of mission for 'the multicentric Christian church' (Walls and Ross 2008, 202), or the new multipolar mission engagement.

The global context of reciprocal contextual collaboration for the 21st century

Political, economic, social and cultural processes since the 1990s have been affected by different kinds of global technology, violence, war and threats, such as the Gulf War (1991), the wars of Afghanistan (2001) and Iraq (2003), and since 2009 the increasing nuclear tensions of North Korea and Iran, to say nothing of the Middle East conflict. Above all, the world lives in a time of global terror after the fatal consequences of 11 September 2001 (New York), 11 March 2004 (Madrid) and 7 July 2005 (London). This new reality challenges the church's mission such that static models of mission are no longer valid within a dynamic mission tension which is developed in a context of global economic crisis, terror, violence, disaster, injustice, uncertainty and a migratory move as never seen before. Appropriate mission models must take into account this new global order very seriously. As we recall what we studied in chapter 4, the reality of rapid global change in the last two decades has shown that these facts provide signs of opportunities for a new theological interpretation of freedom, power, justice, etc., in dialogue with contemporary global issues and reciprocal mission collaboration.

Thus, I limited myself to giving a brief discussion by focusing on five theological presuppositions for Christian mission collaboration, which will lead us seriously to consider the need for more appropriate models of mission:

1. There is no appropriate Christian reciprocal contextual collaboration without biblical freedom.
2. There is no appropriate Christian reciprocal contextual collaboration without a consideration of contextual theologies.
3. There is no appropriate Christian reciprocal contextual collaboration without a consciousness of the influence of external factors in mission (which I dealt with under missiological issues).
4. There is no appropriate Christian relationship without sharing the control of power and decision making (addressed under economic issues).
5. There is no appropriate Christian reciprocal contextual collaboration without a reciprocal christological relationship (which was dealt with under relational issues on partnership).

It was noticed that the geographical myth that mission has only to do with distant countries, and the like, produced a peripheral missiology, which becomes problematic when it comes to the need to find a creative form of mission collaboration between co-workers in mission.

My assumption is that the *perestroika* reciprocal mission collaboration of the twenty-first century will not improve appropriately if political, economic, cultural and social reciprocal mission collaboration issues are not addressed radically under a Trinitarian mission theology and christological *missio freedom*. A great concern was noticed regarding economic disparity and relational issues in mission collaboration, which compels us to accept that there is no appropriate Christian co-participation in mission without a reciprocal christological relationship, which produces a *metanoia* relationship under a kingdom *missio* relationship, a christological *missio* relationship, and a holistic *missio* relationship, which contrasts with superficial or culturally-conditioned relationships.

Despite the effort the church has made throughout mission history, the development of mission reciprocity reveals needs that require serious consideration if we want to find appropriate models for the twenty-first-century mission. In this sense, seven things which are lacking and five characteristics of weaknesses for the development of mission collaboration between the 'old mission' and the 'new emergent mission' during these last twenty years were identified in chapter 4. These findings will contribute to a penetrating analysis for a biblical dimension of christological *missio* relationships.

Reciprocal contextual collaboration within the Latin American church

At the beginning of our research we formulated the hypothesis that the instability and dependence of the Latin American reciprocal contextual collaboration in mission can be overcome through a more holistic biblical teaching that can lead to a more mature participative church in mission. Our research has clearly revealed that despite political, sociological and economical limitations, the church in Latin America is growing numerically and its mission expansion is putting to use different models of a reciprocal missiology, with varying strengths and weaknesses. However, an intentional use of the spiral mission theology in their mission endeavour will be required.

Three different case studies of models for reciprocal contextual collaboration helped to analyse the impact, mission policy characteristics, as well as strengths and weaknesses. These cases were different in their origins and theological influence. Therefore, the aim of chapter 5 was to clarify differences between the traditional model, the innovative networking, and the emergent models.

In relation to thinking and practice on mission, it appears that mission societies are trying to reinvent themselves by approaching a wider mission participation to confront the new challenges of twenty-first-century mission. In the case of Latin Link it was renamed in 1991 to renew itself by focusing on Latin America within a wider perspective of global mission, investing effort in extending its work to Spain, Germany, Switzerland and Portugal. They also started to develop a more relational missiology by seeking to work with people instead of only mission structures. In the case of COMIBAM this movement started with Latin American thinkers, but they received the impact of 'unreached missiology', because they endorsed this philosophy by forming mission agencies without considering the principles of indigenous missiology. However, a trend towards contextualization and indigenous missions seems to appear with more emphasis after the 1990s.[3] Thus, faith missions appear as new mission structures in the non-Western world that are independent and have no connection with historic Protestant churches.[4] The mission development shows that more mission agencies are becoming more networking because of the influence and impact of a global missiology and this reaction is because mission is never static, it is always dynamic.

Accordingly, it seems that Latin Link will come to reflect a clear 'traditional mission network' model, which means that they will retain patterns of the traditional model, but merge them with principles of the networking and the emergent models. Therefore, Latin Link, together with the

---

3. It is important to recognize that a few indigenous missions have been working in some countries, such as Asociación Misionera Evangélica Nacional (AMEN) founded in Peru in 1946 by Juan C. Cueva (Bulletin AMEN 1959) or the Methodist Pentecostal Church founded by Willis Hoover in Chile (Anderson 1999, 25).

4. Mission societies began in the euphoria for cross-cultural mission engendered under the influence of Carey in the 1790s. The voluntarism model was another kind of mission development in evangelicalism producing a great impact. Ralph Winter was one of great defenders of mission societies trying to reinforce this model through his 'sodality missiology', and 'unreached missiology', which has made a great impact on the evangelical movement after Lausanne 1974.

new atmosphere of reciprocal missiology, needs to reconsider the missionary presence of the non-formal new immigrant mission forces, the recent infiltration of western lands, and the new *perestroika* mission collaboration. A critical aspect has been noticed regarding the budget of £24,850 per couple for Latin Link missionaries, which will make it difficult for the Latin American missionaries to catch up with this budget due to the political, economic and social situation of church members that live on a minimum salary of $250 monthly (£166) or $3,000 annually, compared to $16,600 (£10,400) UK basic salary, and eight times more than the average Peruvian income. The mission development shows that the Latin American church is sending thousands of missionaries with a minimum salary to different continents, especially to Africa, Asia and Muslim countries.[5] It is the spontaneous reciprocal mission combustion of the grassroots churches of Africa, Asia and Latin America that sustains this new missionary movement. It is "what seemed to be the margins" but "Christianity is now a predominantly non-Western religion" (Walls and Ross 2008, 199).

The development of COMIBAM as a mission network for mobilizing Latin American people in mission has shown the following process: regarding distribution of power and reciprocal freedom it rests on national movements, which have a right to make decisions as autonomous bodies but are linked to the mission spirit of COMIBAM. Financial autonomy avoids dependence and each national movement has its own budget. The major concern that is hindering the movements becomes its theological reflection. This is one of the main issues in COMIBAM's network that compels them to adopt a clear Trinitarian basis and theology of God's kingdom. Equally there is a need for contextual theology with a transformational missiological approach, an inclusive missiology avoiding the influence of what Samuel Escobar (2003, 167) calls a managerial missiology. As Sharon Heaney (2008) suggests in *Contextual Theology for Latin America*, Latin American mission theology must be systematized if a greater contribution to the bourgeoning Western missiology is to be made. COMIBAM has a

---

5. There is no financial limitation to cross all kinds of borders by these missionaries; it is a call from the Spirit who empowers their models of mission, paying a double sacrificial effort of weak and inexperienced mission structures. Most of the time, they get by with less than basic salaries, with no consideration as to holidays, pensions or life insurance.

positive achievement during the last twenty years by empowering its vision through national missionary movements which have three networks: (1) church and pastors' network, (2) centres of missionary training, and (3) the sending structures' network. In the process of implementing a conscious missionary vision in Latin America, we have found five key phases of COMIBAM's network. First phase – dialogue and promotion (1983–1989), second phase – growth and self-identity (1989–1997), third phase – transitional institution (1997–2000), fourth phase – institutional network (2000–2006), and fifth phase – global influence (2006–2016?). The fact that COMIBAM has become a motivating mission tool provides signs of a networking model that seems to practise some aspects of the mission theology of reciprocal contextual collaboration; a radical view in its theological understanding will strengthen their mission activity.[6] Somehow, COMIBAM will need to develop multidirectional mission traffic and a missiological diaspora, which are key elements of an inclusive missiology. Additional facts that need deeper study are: the precise difference between 'movement' and network needs clarification; elements of the traditional model that might be implemented properly need to be analysed; the gap between local churches and mission structures needs to be bridged; the difficulties with the 'unreached people' mission theology requires analysis.[7] The positive side is that COMIBAM has made an impact through its significant effort from a context of poverty, while its networking model of mission in 25 countries has helped to mobilize more than 8,000 missionaries from a Latin American context. Undoubtedly it is a pneumatological movement with appropriate discernment for healthy relationships; its Latin American identity, and its maturity to go forward within a context of poverty and sociopolitical instability, have made COMIBAM an impacting networking model that has something to share in a very short period of time; that indeed deserves acknowledgment.

---

6. As a matter of fact, I agree that COMIBAM's work and other networks like the Latin American Theological Fraternity (FTL) have emerged from the same Spirit in the 'South'.
7. Paul Davies (2006, 178) is more radical in his approach to COMIBAM when he argues that such movements "reject higher biblical criticism; are theologically and politically conservative, anti-liberal with a narrow definition of mission, restricted to verbal proclamation and Church planting".

The development of St James as an emergent model has shown the following process: St James has an intentional approach to strengthening mission through the participation of local church to local church mission relations. Reciprocal contextual collaboration of the St James World Mission Group includes the support of St James' missionaries, foreign missionaries, non-member missionaries and mission organizations. The primary focus of this analysis indicated that at least six elements of reciprocal contextual collaboration were pivotal elements in facilitating a reciprocal agreement between St James and the IME church with a view to initiating a Spanish-speaking congregation and to sending an STM to Peru. These are as follows: reciprocal trust, reciprocal interest, reciprocal transparency, reciprocal maturity, reciprocal respect, and reciprocal freedom. One of the missiological achievements between St James and the IME church in Peru has been the sending of an STM team to Peru every two years, thereby making the following contribution to St James: they have mobilized the local church to participate in mission more directly, and they have created a consciousness of being more involved with the local church after the STM. These results indicate, first, that STMs are a tool for providing new committed members to the local church; second, that resources are employed to mobilize potential candidates to serve their local church; and third, STM provides candidates for long-term mission. STM has also increasingly become a 'tunnel process' to involve lay people in local and global mission. It was found that in many cases the emergent church has no formal links with any foreign organization, so in the case of St James, it was the Peruvian church who initiated a mission relationship, which can be defined as a 'providential mission encounter' for appropriate reciprocal mission collaboration.

Among the internal factors which we stressed in the process of the reciprocal contextual collaboration between any emergent mission model (such as the local-to-local church or an indigenous mission agency model) were: theological freedom (reciprocal autonomy), power sharing (reciprocal authority) and generous sharing (reciprocal giving). This threefold missiological principle is rooted in reciprocal interdependence within a christological relationship. These factors are integrated components and translatable.

I conclude that the emergent model will bring new mission energy to the global engagement as a result of an increasingly relational missiology, and four key elements that can be contextualized in any reciprocal 'North-South' contextual collaboration: first, it must be recognized that mission cannot be developed in isolation; second, the emergent model emphasizes unity in diversity, as joint projects are undertaken with no consideration of denominational boundaries, but rather within the unity of Christ's body; third, mission of the twenty-first century should be a mission of reciprocal interdependence, which includes the ingredient of respect, reciprocal love, and unconditional support for the other's missionary plans – ingredients which traditional missions, networks or emergent models have yet to consider intentionally in their mission agendas; finally, in any collaboration there will be a dynamic and creative tension of strengths and weaknesses, but not an intentional 'higher' versus 'lower' mission relationship. As we mentioned before, there is no turning back to a provincial interpretation, whereby the first and second mission models are better than the third model or vice-versa. Mission models, to a great extent, are appropriate depending on the context in which they are used; however, some are untranslatable.

Obstacles in relation to the Latin American church in mission such as denominationalism, lack of missiological unity, imperial motives (impure motives), paternalistic mission, guilt for the past, anti-christological relationship, a narrow mission hermeneutic, individualism, confusion between unity and diversity, diluted Trinitarian theology, spirit of competence and duplication, economic disparity, misuse of autonomy, and global suspicion of Western missiology are not incidental factors and irreversible. They correspond to missiological thinking and world issues that cannot be separated from it. These issues have fostered mission in Latin America's twenty-four countries in one way or another. Therefore, a *missio* collaboration from the Latin American perspective includes an awareness throughout the development of the evangelical mission of a fragmented political, economic, social and cultural society which has taken many forms due to the lack of a stable democracy, economic affluence, increasing poverty and lack of employment, which makes Latin America a vulnerable continent that struggles to overcome unemployment, terrorism, violence, drugs production, street children, and state corruption. From this political, sociological, economic and cultural context emerges the divine miracle of a growing evangelical church that lives within this dialectic and dynamic mission tension, which either consciously or unconsciously affects its co-participation in the mission enterprise.

Our research has also revealed that the development and characteristics of partnership in mission caused a lack of freedom in the relationship, dependence and sharing the control of power. These are some factors that have affected the possibility of finding new appropriate models for mission. Within the three main models such as the traditional, networking and the emergent mission model, we found in our research a need for reciprocal distribution of power, freedom in the relationships, and a decreased dependency on Western missions – needs which must be addressed radically through a mission policy of reciprocal missiology, in spite of the efforts which have been made during the last twenty years by many of their mission leaders. As evidence we note that the weak depend on the strong, and that the strong direct and set up the agenda for the weak. However, the Latin American church has become conscious of the need for setting up a more contextual mission agenda, but above all the Spirit is intervening to mobilize the emergent church according to a new reciprocal mission collaboration theology.

The relevance of mission models in reciprocal multipolar contextual engagement

A major aspect of reciprocal contextual collaboration has to do with the fact that we are the body of Christ with diverse and multiple ministries, with gifts and resources to help one another reciprocally; the contextual reality implies the incarnational attitude of Christian mission that includes conscious acknowledgement of the reality of the social, political, religious, cultural and economical context, while the concept of collaboration implies that we acknowledge that the *missio Dei* belongs to God and that we are collaborators in God's kingdom in the freedom of a prophetic imagination. We have concentrated on the particularity of the evangelical movement in order to arrive at a global understanding of what mission collaboration is all about. Therefore, this implies that the present study will require additional research on Protestant and ecumenical missiologies respectively, which then will provide the basis for a comparative analysis of evangelical and Catholic reciprocal contextual collaboration.

At the very heart of this study lies the notion of reciprocal contextual collaboration as a central locus of the church's mission reciprocity. This implies a missionary tension developed by the church to sustain a true unity within diversity, which has a diverse theological, sociological, cultural and economical background. This diversity is the subject of Veli-Matti Karkkainen's (2002) *An Introduction to Ecclesiology,* which offers an overview of different perspectives that can help us to understand how God is working with his church through different contexts and understandings of mission. However, Karkkainen will need an additional study to rank among theologians, due to the fact that he proposes a 'destandardized' church (i.e. one which is focused on the local community in its worship of God and service to one another) within an industrial captivity (2002, 217). For Karkkainen (2002, 214), industrialization was built on the ideas of specialization, effectiveness and calculation, and the church came to be dominated by the same ethic. In consequence, the church needs to be destandardized if it wants to find appropriate models for mission.

This influence has been developed by the Western mission enterprise, which has moved from a structured effort to represent local churches or denominations to representing mission societies whose headquarters emerge in autonomous and independent mission activities, mainly far removed from a reciprocal mission collaboration – and this extends to what they are doing on behalf of local congregations. This attitude has produced a mission of individual participation by those who want to contribute financially rather than operate by involving the participation of local congregations. This reality must take an imperative change if we want to see the relevance of appropriate models of mission within the twenty-first century global mission.

At the beginning of the research a main question was formulated with a view to discovering what are the possibilities for bringing about appropriate partnership models for the evangelical movement during the twenty-first century. The research has clearly confirmed that, in fact, there are great possibilities for models of appropriate mission collaboration. This has been worked out under the heading of new forms of mission collaboration, presented in chapter 6, with the following outcome:

First, it has been demonstrated that there are in fact new possibilities for new forms of mission collaboration through the provision of four mission models: the synergy model, the spontaneous model, the integrated model, and the contextual model. Thus, it is imperative to search within the evangelical constituency for new forms of kingdom collaboration in order to discover the rich variety of new models for missions that are operating within the conventional and non-conventional mission enterprise, without denying the effort made by traditional, networking or emergent models such as the British mission, Latin Link, which operates in fourteen countries of Latin America; the networking model, as in the case of COMIBAM; or the local-to-local church model of St James Church, London, and the IME church in Peru.[8]

Second, a spontaneous mission model has been proposed as a novel innovative model related to reciprocal contextual collaboration. This model has been developed gradually with the aid of external factors such as political, economic and global migration, and above all the Spirit moving the southern church within a new global mission engagement, which has an environmental influence of both 'unification and uniformity' (Davies 2006, 174), and characteristics of multipolar and bipolar directions. Under internal factors we have seen those of people being mobilized to mission through business as mission, and through independent indigenous mission structures, including those of the Pentecostal, independent movement, and local church models. This mission model is characterized by flexibility, mobility and the more relational emphasis, which is characteristic of non-conventional structures. As seen in our research, this 'pneumatical model' (non-conventional model) rests on the basis of a non-traditional mission model, using more of a non-formal networking structure in most cases. The spontaneous model, the synergy model, the integrated model and the contextual model have together been proposed as an appropriate mission model for the twenty-first mission century, all under the heading

---

8. For the conventional and non-conventional missiology, see Samuel Cueva, 'Missions, Missionaries and the Evangelization of Europe: Toward an Integrated Missiology' (unpublished material 2009).

of a *reciprocal multipolar contextual engagement*. The relevance and implications of these models can be summarized in the following way: the synergy model is marked by a concentrated effort to produce effectiveness, the spontaneous model by the Spirit's desire to produce diversity and flexibility, the integrated model by its reciprocal components producing unity and merging, while the contextual model is marked by freedom, cultural identity and interdependence which recognizes a diversity of contexts. All of these models are relevant due to their capacity to implement and complement one another reciprocally.

Third, the way forward we have proposed for discovering and strengthening new appropriate models of mission involves the spiral mission theology that will provide tools for a new hermeneutical mission theology, and will help us to find more appropriate contextual mission models within evangelical movement. Spiral mission theology implies the use of historical, theological and missiological circles around a central point, which is God's missionary plan that constantly increases or decreases according to the *missio ecclesiae's* activity. It was noticed that a positive spiral mission theology is rooted within the content of the *missio Dei*, God's kingdom (which includes eschatology), Trinitarian mission theology, christological *missio ecclesiae*, mission models and the world mission circles. As was explained, as seen from above, the spiral mission theology begins with God who as Father, Son and Holy Spirit sends the church into the world. As seen from below, the spiral mission theology begins with an understanding of the church's obedience to the *missio Dei*. Therefore, conscious missiological recognition that there is a dynamic tension between the spiral mission theology as viewed from above and the spiral mission theology as viewed from below is necessary. In mission activity there will always be both negative and positive tensions within reciprocal contextual collaboration which will produce new appropriate contextual models for mission.

Fourth, a clear understanding of the context for the development of the spiral mission theology will help the church to provide more appropriate models for mission under continual tension from above (the *missio Dei* leading the church), and from below (the *missio ecclesiae* influencing the world). This missiological tension includes the need for appropriate models that make a contribution and offer a clear response to global climate change, to the resurgence of nationalistic identity (Castells 1997, 27), to the era of technological industry, to the increasing number of abandoned street children, to the reality of more desperate poor people in need of food, to the lack of houses for lower income families, to diseases such as depression, HIV/AIDS and cancer, to interreligious dialogue in multicultural contexts, etc. It seems that the new models for mission must include an integrated missiology which confronts the realities of suffering and of a rapidly changing world. At the same time, the spiral mission theology will help to strengthen the unity of the church by overcoming a narrow interpretation of isolated projects as the result of westernized individualism that has infiltrated the mission activity of the church. Disunity, duplication and isolation must be replaced and rejected, as it is a wave that comes from time to time to alter and destroy our pure motives for mission. In contrast, a humble spirit of working together without denying our own identity, but rather taking for granted that we are just fellow labourers, stewards, and ambassadors of God's kingdom, is necessary for appropriate models of mission for the twenty-first-century mission.

All models for mission in the twenty-first century are relevant if they are rooted in three biblical tasks: first, to proclaim the gospel, which includes social responsibility in order to accomplish the *missio Dei*; second, to sustain the unity of the church by accepting that all appropriate models are varieties of the permissive diversity God gives to the church; and third, to work for the glory of God as the main central purpose of doing mission for God's kingdom. To glorify God is the supreme goal for mission; it is the objective of mission.[9] The goal of Christian mission is in fact the glorification of God, which is seen in the death and resurrection of Jesus through a continual renunciation and sacrificial life. This is the way forward for all Christian models for the mission of the twenty-first century if they want to remain appropriate models of reciprocal mission.

---

9. See further Martin Erdmann (1998, 213).

Reciprocal contextual collaboration and the global church mission in context

The fact that Latin American reciprocal contextual collaboration in mission has become a tool in the development of the evangelical movement, despite its limitations in the political, economic and sociological context, compels us to say that context is crucial if the church wants to discover new appropriate models for mission. Mission history shows that mission practitioners diluted the context because of their cultural identity or because of their mission structure. In the 1970s, Orlando Costas (1974, 165) warned that it was important not only to be aware of alternative structures but also to develop a relevant mission theology, thereby helping both mission societies and church to find their own contextual models. During the 1990s, Butler (Taylor 1994, 9) suggested that what the church needed was not to discover new models of mission but to make them more effective – that was the key point. And in 2006, Paul Davies (2006, 39, 74–75) proposed, under the concept of mission-seeking effectiveness, that the church engage in concrete political action.[10] However, the proposals of both Butler and Davies are incomplete if we do not add the need for contextual models for mission, all in tune with the socio-political reality of each context. In this sense, to establish universal generalizations without serious consideration of the mission context is inappropriate.[11] Thus, context and models are two sides of the same coin; they are integrated elements which must work in harmonious reciprocity. As an indigenous church is defined as such by its own context, similarly a contextual model of mission is defined by its own context.[12] This does not deny the historical and universal reality of the church. Rather, the dynamic mission tension challenges us to find ways to put into practice a contextual model without denying the historical universal character of the church. A reciprocal mission theology is a key element to that answer; this in connection with one of the five theological

---

10. This is what Miguez Bonino calls 'historical projects', a limited measurable attempt model of political and economic organization in obedience to God (Davies 2006, 74).
11. See further Costas (1974, 168–171) *The Church and its Mission: A Shattering Critique from the Third World*.
12. Indigenous relates to a specific cultural and historical situation (Costas 1974, 171).

presuppositions for mission reciprocity we have seen in chapter 4, namely that there is no appropriate Christian reciprocal contextual collaboration where there is no consideration of contextual theologies.

As has been recognized by Walls (1996, 10) in *The Missionary Movement in Christian History*, by Jenkins (2002) in *The Next Christendom,* and by the vast majority of mission theologians and practitioners of the 1990s, the Latin American evangelical minority of the nineteenth century has now become part of the Majority World of evangelicalism. This change must take into account the new mission activity of the twenty-first mission century. This missionary movement of the 'Third Church' should include the study of mission models from the wide spectrum of historical, evangelical, Pentecostal and charismatic churches that have been taking part in global mission. It will be a failure for evangelical catholicity if inadequate attention is drawn to those models developed by the Pentecostal and charismatic movements – the fastest growing churches in the world. In the light of this, Allan Anderson (2004) provides relevant tools in *An Introduction to Pentecostalism*.[13] As was mentioned before, we predict that reciprocal multipolar contextual engagement will play an important role in challenging the global church to engage with appropriate models for mission.

Reciprocal contextual collaboration mission and cross-mission pollination

We are in a critical moment in which reciprocal contextual collaboration in mission cries out for a cross-mission pollination (to transfer the seed to others) in order to bring new mission fertilization (giving birth) according to a reciprocal multipolar contextual engagement during the twenty-first-century mission of the church. Therefore, we must remind the church that mission is not a synonym for church; neither is mission a synonym for

---

13. See also the work of Steve J. Land, *Pentecostal Spirituality: A Passion for the Kingdom* (1993); Jürgen Moltmann, *Pentecostal Movements as an Ecumenical Challenge* (1996); John Michael Penney, *The Missionary Emphasis of Lukan Pneumatology* (1997); Allan Anderson and Walter Hollenweger, *Pentecostals After a Century: Global Perspectives on a Movement in Transition* (1999).

missions. The existence of this distinction leads us to the epistemological understanding that there must be an intrinsic relationship between church and mission, which emerges from the very missionary nature of the church and from the missionary nature of the *missio Dei*. This theological assumption draws attention to the reality of what I call the 'hypostatic mission' relation between church and mission, as it is the relation between mission and evangelism, or evangelism and social responsibility, referred to traditionally as the double mandate, or contextually as the *misión integral*. God has given a call and the church has been chosen, equipped and empowered by the Spirit to fulfil its mission. But it is the church's responsibility to find appropriate models for the sake of the twenty-first century global mission.

Due to the factors mentioned above, the church has spiritual authority to develop different forms of models to make possible its mission. This spiritual power, which comes from the triune God, enables the people of God to cooperate in God's redemptive mission of all creation until the kingdom of God will be visible to every creature. In this sense, all models of mission become tools to provide appropriate manifestations of the body of Christ by fulfilling the mission of God through the mission of the church. The fact is that some models will become more useful than others and other models will become obsolete in some contexts, but all models will create mission tensions due to the dynamic work of the church and the Spirit. It is also right to say that appropriate models are not governed solely by internal factors, such as a good training or sending policy; they depend also on external factors, such as politics, economy, culture and especially on the power of the Spirit, blowing wherever he wills, and changing whatever is necessary for the sake of God's kingdom.

The following suggestion offers models for further study within reciprocal contextual collaboration. While it is not definitive or authoritative, its purpose is to foster wider missiological reflection and dialogue so that these models can become mission tools for the discovery of new appropriate models for reciprocal mission. We also indicate that these models somehow are operating within the global mission scenario, and can be mixed, joined or developed in isolation:

1. Multipractical model (oriented to multiple tasks). This would be the case of missions with a variety of ministries, working

simultaneously, such as church planting, mission aids and short-term mission.

2. Radical model (oriented to combat poverty). Integral mission is associated with the radical model to fight against injustice and poverty.[14]
3. Immersed model (concentrated on specific projects). A vivid example would be Compassion International and the Viva Network working with poor children.
4. Submerged model (for restricted zones of mission). NGOs and business as mission follow the pattern of the submerged model.
5. Solidarity model (emphasis on sharing resources). This model helps to avoid the 'banking model', where mission is developed from one side without the contribution of the other side. Kingdom collaborations theology lies behind this model.
6. Identification model (helps to discover new needs in mission). This would be done through evaluations, audits or statistical data; specialized missions are dedicated to research in different fields such as religion, poverty or mission.
7. Servanthood model (emphasis on the christological view). A simple lifestyle, compassion and humility characterize this model.
8. Cybernetic model (helps in providing resources for mission through the Internet). More missions are using the advantages of the Internet and web pages, and Facebook.
9. Family model[15] (emphasizes the membership component). The business model views people as stockholders, while the family model sees them as members.
10. Diaspora model (emphasis on the migration reality). Global issues such as political, economic, social and cultural questions are addressed here; the Lausanne Diaspora Network is an example.

The development and characteristics of mission collaboration have brought to light issues that require revitalized and appropriate reciprocal mission

---

14. The book *Justice, Mercy and Humility* (Chester 2002) provides insights for the radical model.

15. For the business model and familiar model see Robert Brynjolfson's 'From Synthesis to Synergy: The Iguassu Think Tank' (Taylor 2000, 482–483).

models for the twenty-first century. Competition, duplication and a lack of missional pastors are some of the key issues, but above all there is a need for conscious and intentional recognition that mission belongs to God and that we are just collaborators of God's kingdom. The vast and immense financial resources of the West, where millions are spent to promote its own projects, allows it to maintain the status quo of obtaining financial resources and to sustain bourgeoning mission models that in some contexts are no longer acceptable. This would be the case with the new network *'Ethne to Ethne'*, which tries to continue with the AD2000 movement initiative and duplicates the effort of traditional missions which have the same aim. These models encourage mission structures to persist in promoting American projects of the 10/40 window strategy, with the target of winning souls, but failing to integrate social responsibility within the projects. Thus, the target implies originating more funding for what Guthrie (2000, 69)[16] calls a 'marketing approach' or what Escobar calls 'managerial missiology'. As we mentioned earlier, 'unreached people missiology' tends to develop a managerial missiology, elaborate techniques outside of the context of mission-seeking quantified results. The fact is that after 11 September, the Americans-sending missions are less and less welcome in the Muslim world; this is mainly due to political or ideological factors within the new mission scenario. At the same time, it is widely recognized that there is a socio-political change with more cons than pros to traditional ways of sending missionaries to restricted areas of mission. In this way, contextualization will help to develop more suitable models for one or another context. It is evident that the model of the NGOs is increasing,[17] and that the cases of missions working in restricted zones with conventional missionaries are changing for a more business as mission model.[18] In this re-

---

16. See further the whole analysis of 'unreached people missiology' (Guthrie 2000, 67–82).

17. The theological concept of this new network is problematic because of its emphasis on 'unreached peoples' missiology. They state that *Eth-nê* is the Greek word Jesus used for 'nation' – a word which means tribe, ethnic group or people. Our world today has 6.4 billion individuals living in 234 geo-political nations but over 16,000 *ethnê*, or people groups, by country. Of those *ethnê*, more than 6,900 groups remain least reached .See further Ethne to Ethne (http://www.ethne.net/de/about/why-ethne).

18. See the work of Tetsunao Yamamori and Kenneth A. Eldred (editors) 2003 *On Kingdom Business: Transforming Missions Through Entrepreneurial Strategies*.

gard, a fundamental question is this: Will there be any possibility that those missions with control of economic and technological power might develop a new reciprocal mission with small missions from the rest of the world to support them in making their own appeals by using the Western mission network as a mission structure? This is a fundamental utopia question that remains open during the next decades of a proclaimed global missiology.

Challenges for reciprocal contextual collaboration in the 21ˢᵗ century mission

We must not fail to mention that the development and characteristics of reciprocal contextual collaboration in mission to and from Latin America have brought about issues and results, which indicate the need for more appropriate mission models for the twenty-first century. In consequence, there are missiological challenges that will need to be faced by the evangelical movement. As the American dream seeks targets for reaching new transactions and levels in the entertainment industry (McDaniel 2007, 7[19]), equally it is extremely important and necessary to understand that the moral sustainability of capitalism is no longer valid.[20] Corruption and a hedonistic, sensual and sensationalistic cultural approach are some of the marks of the market global economy; God's church has to face this inevitable reality. Rose Dowsett (Tiplady 2003, 149) explains that one of the tragedies of western domination (through wealth) becomes the mass media and technology, the great export of western values and materialism to the poor countries. This is an anti-reciprocal attitude of compassion to the suffering and less-privileged people that must be denounced.

When it comes to Europe, the continent does suffer with the same characteristics found in the American lifestyle, in addition to an individualistic tendency towards self-protection and a productivist-consumerist spirit of

---

19. Charles McDaniel analyses theology and economics in *God and Money: the Moral Challenge of Capitalism*. See further (2007).
20. See also René Padilla and Chris Sugden (editors) 1985 *Text on Evangelical Social Ethics 1974–1993*, Grove Booklet on Ethics No. 58, Bramcote, Nottingham, Grove Books Limited.

Western society. We clarified that Europe has become a 'dying' continent due to the fact that spiritual and moral values are no longer indispensable as they were in the past. This is not to deny the mission activity of God's church in Europe, however, for there are great mission initiatives, too. It is also necessary to observe that this continent will need to accept the new missionary force of the emergent church and the challenges of new creative mission tension, which will require the constant reinvention of innovative models of reciprocal contextual collaboration in mission within a postmodern, post-Christian and post-global mission scenario.[21] In this context, some challenges that I want to pose for further critical reflection and for a deeper study of reciprocal mission theology within the evangelical church are as follows:

1. A matter which commands our attention has to do with 'two-way mission collaboration bridges', a missiological proposal for radical improvement between mission co-participants within the global mission engagement. Two-way mission traffic is continually engaged with critical analysis and its development is encouraged through the Latin American movement 'Mission for the Third Millennium', aimed at mobilizing missionaries to all continents, promoting action and reflection about missionary practice, and making a contribution to global missiology with three aims: theological, missiological, and ecclesiological.[22]

2. Issues in personal relationships become an unresolved challenge for a new mature relationship between mission participants, which have to take the 'oil' of freedom, trust and humility, mission relations as we have proposed under a christological *missio* relationship. Two facts must be taken into account for any appropriate mission relations: first, it is certain that we live in a time in which personal relationships are shaped enormously by cultural diversity and a wide variety of worldviews, and second, the mature relationship which develops must be rooted in biblical

---

21. There is a tendency to provide the need of a new order in the West. See for example William Rees 2009, 'How China's Millions can save the West', newspaper *The Mail on Sunday* March 8, 7.

22. See further, misiontercermilenio.org

models that can be contextualized without denying the intrinsic values of a Trinitarian mission theology and a christological mission reciprocity within relationships. A *metanoia* relationship for mission relations becomes an essential reinforcement in the church's mission.

3. Given the prospect that reciprocal contextual collaboration will provide a mission theology of freedom, reciprocity, trust, shared decision making, and shared control of power, we face the urgent task of helping local churches to enable them to play a major role in the context of the new global missiology. This might be done through critical reflection on the mission enterprise and practising more communal and liminal churches.[23] One example of participatory mission is the missional churches that have the aim to preach a more contextual message for the audience and to be a missionary church.[24] The planting of churches through organic movements would help churches play a major role in mission.[25] Bruce K. Camp (2003, 238) is right when he argues that churches look to mission agencies to set the mission agenda.[26]

---

23. 'Liminality' describes the transition process accompanying a fundamental change of state or social position, and 'community' means that people are driven to find each other through a common experience or ordeal, humbling, transition and marginalization. It involves intense feelings of social togetherness. Both liminality and communities provide the dynamics of the Christian community to form themselves around a common mission (Hirsch 2003, 220–221).

24. Frost and Hirsch suggest the theological approach that a missionary God sends the church, thus this 'sending' is embodied and lived out in the missional impulse; it is God's mission that compels the church to reach a lost world (2003, 129). See further *The Shaping of Things to Come* (Michael Frost and Alan Hirsch 2003). In *Exiles: Living Missionally in a Post-Christian Culture,* Frost suggests five types of practice for a missional church: hospitality, generosity, justice, environmental stewardship and the practice of mission. See further Michael Frost (2006, 69–70). For further studies see also *The Shaping of the Things to Come: Innovation and Mission for the 21st Century Church* (Michael Frost & Alan Hirsch 2003), and *Untamed: Reactivating a Missional Form of Discipleship* (Alan Hirsch and Debra Hirsch 2010). For a wider definition and implications of a missional church, see further Claydon (2005, 568–579).

25. Alan Hirsch argues that consumerism is detrimental to discipleship, so we need a model of a cell-base church, which is related to organic churches (not a cell church). See further Hirsch (2006, 31–34; 42–48).

26. For further study, see Bruce K. Camp 'A Survey of the Local Church's Involvement in Global/Local Outreach' in *Between Past and Future: Evangelical Mission Entering the Twenty-First Century* (Bonk 2003, 203–243)

This is what happens in cases when churches tend to be very passive by relying entirely on the work of mission organizations, therefore, as mission agencies have a crucial role to play in setting the mission agenda, this needs to be in a close relationship and harmony with churches. As we understand, mission is not only to give money to the mission society, it belongs to the church's missionary nature and strengthening missional churches would perhaps make them more active in this regard. In this sense reciprocal multipolar contextual engagement will play a pivotal role in modelling a new reciprocal missiology.

4. Regarding economic affluence, supporting the emergent missionary churches becomes a challenge for wealthy churches as they are demanded increasingly to share with more participation to support the less privileged. There is a calling to the people of God to overcome a narrow understanding of generous participation in mission, this vis-à-vis reciprocal mission relationships. For the flow of healthy mission relations, accountability is a matter of fact that both sides of mission co-participants are called to develop reciprocally (Rowe 2009, 149–159).[27] The weight of tradition and traditional models must not stand in the way of the search for new alternatives of material provision to fulfil the *missio Dei*, despite the fact that the risk of dependence will be a danger (Harriers 2008, 261).[28]

5. At the leadership level within new global mission educational institutions, in which there is a vision for multicultural teams within a reciprocal mission theology under God's kingdom mission collaboration, new academic curricula will be urgent, including modules such as global missiology, contextual models of mission, spontaneous and migration missiology. It seems that western

---

27. See further Jonathan Y. Rowe 'Dancing with Elephants: Accountability in Cross-Cultural Christian Partnership', *Missiology: An International Review* (Vol XXXVII, No. 2, April 2009, 149–159).

28. See further Jim Harriers 'Material Provision or Preaching the Gospel: Reconsidering Holistic [Integral] Mission', *Evangelical Review of Theology*, (Vol 32 No. 3 July 2008, 257–270).

practitioners promoted a kingdom leadership with a narrow view to the task of acknowledging and understanding the future role of non-Western missiology. Thus, dynamic and innovative models of mission place a question mark over traditional missions that have maintained the status quo, in some cases becoming obsolete, out of touch with the context. A global reciprocal mission will involve taking into account the speed, time and location for changing models according to the rapidly changing global mission where leadership will have a pivotal role. Perhaps this will be the case of the WEA-Leadership Institute, trying to promote leadership development, healthy, viable and influential.[29]

6. The urgency of promoting a simple life style has been a forgotten area within the Western evangelical world, despite the fact that this issue has been addressed by the Lausanne movement, and in particular by René Padilla (1985, 136) since the 1980s.[30] This is a great challenge for a global mission theology of reciprocal contextual collaboration in mission, where ostentation on the part of the Western church, over and against the biblical simple life style, has to be re-oriented, encouraged and evaluated continually. The increasing poverty of the less privileged of the world call on the global church for a reciprocal compassion between those who suffer for lack of material possessions, and for those who suffer desperately with emotional illnesses such as despair, depression and anxiety. The aim to support the global church not only in terms of helping the poor church, under the rubric of 'the option for the poor', but also according to a biblical notion of unity in the church, will require a new mission reorientation in local churches, starting with a new biblical instruction with local pastors and mission minded leaders. One might seek ways to build a

---

29. See the new project of the WEA-Leadership Institute (2007), launched at the WEA-General Assembly 2008 in Pattaya, Thailand, with the aim to address the leadership needs of national evangelical alliances (http://weali.org/tiki-index.php?page=about+wea-li). Personal conversation with Robert Brynjolfson, appointed academic director (2 November 2008, Pattaya, Thailand).

30. See also Padilla's insight in 'Taking Hold of the Life that is Truly Life', in *On Kingdom Business,* Yamamori and Eldred, Editors (2003, 310–314).

communal missiology through such means as the *Minka* model, which we mentioned in our study of some models of mission, or through the participatory development model known as transformational development, which has influenced the NGOs model, particularly in the African context (Scheffler 2008, 261).[31]

7. The dimensional tension of the Trinity, which leads us to the new possibility of relational mission creativity and a sustainable relationship between mission co-participants, comes to be of critical importance as we seek to propose appropriate mission models that would reflect the fullness of mission. Trinitarian theology challenges the church to understand clearly that, as the doctrine of the Trinity speaks of a mystery of three persons in one God; reciprocal contextual collaboration speaks of a kind of mystery of two or more co-participants in doing mission, working in harmony and expressing different phases, characteristics and policies of the same missionary nature. As Trinitarian theology expresses the fact that God the Father is Creator (as seen in the *Apostles Creed*), so too reciprocal mission collaboration in creative tension affirms that creativity expresses the image of the creator-Pantocrator. This means that God has sovereign power, and is able to sustain his church in reciprocal relational unity.

An individualistic approach to reciprocal mission theology gives a distorted idea of the unity in the Godhead, as if God were three 'dislocated' persons lacking substantial ontological relationship. This can be the negative influence of Western culture in the understanding of the *missio Dei*, and must be removed from any healthy reciprocal missiology. God is one God in three persons. The word person is meant to express not only three ways God is, or 'three modes of being', as it is stated by the modalistic view (Lash 1992, 33). Person and relation are interdependent moments of reciprocal relationships, therefore, persons exists as they exist for others; the three divine Persons are united by

---

31. See further Marcia Scheffler 'Partnership and Participation in a Northern Church–Southern Church Relationship', *Transformation* (Vol No. 4, October 2008, 255–270).

sharing uniquely in a common nature (McFadyen 1990, 27). The Trinity consists of a plurality of persons with individual identity or consciousness, therefore the Godhead constitutes also a social Trinitarian community.

The orthodox teaching of the Trinitarian doctrine is that God is one God in three eternal coexistent persons: the Father, the Son, and the Holy Spirit.[32] This Trinitarian clarification becomes a missionary theological challenge the church needs to face urgently in order to understand what a reciprocal unity within the body of Christ means. The horizontal and vertical dimension of reciprocal relationship implies responsibility before God and others; therefore the tension of an orthodox Trinitarian doctrine yields a definition of harmonious individuality, a self-identity (not individualism), providing a formative relation with God and mission co-participants. The individuality of the Trinitarian Persons is achieved thorough a reciprocal relational process between the three Persons of the Trinity. Thus, the church is challenged to develop this Trinitarian model of relationship. As William J. Larkings Jr (1998, 175) states:

> The triune God is the sending one par excellence, enabling *the church* and guiding faithful witness through adversity, the crossing of cultural thresholds, and any other impediment to the progress of the gospel to the end of the earth (italics mine).

8. The political tension of the church, which relates to ecclesiology, challenges twenty-first-century mission regarding the role of Western mission structures, as compared with those of new models of mission that are emerging within the African, Asian and Latin American churches. The dynamic tension of the kingdom compels us to be aware that socio-political concern has become basic to a missionary theology.

---

[32]. As a denial of the Trinity, modalism teaches that God is a single person who has revealed himself in three modes or forms. A different danger is that of Tritheism, which teaches that in the one Trinity there are three gods.

9. Considering the missiological tension of the co-participants in reciprocal mission, it remains to be considered how the Latin American church can be supported as one of the new forces of mission under a christological relationship of reciprocal freedom.
10. The scrutiny and implementation of the spiral mission theology becomes a fundamental, central and essential challenge to evangelical movement within the new global mission engagement.

Challenges for a dynamic missiology of North-South mission collaboration

As we have observed in our missiological discussion, there is a different and changing mission context in the Northern and Southern hemispheres. There is at the same time a new global economy spreading through all kinds of global systems, whether political, sociological, economic, cultural, or religious. It appears that critical horizons of new mission systems are on the way, based on global religious orders, global macro economies, and global economic production. This implies that in a globalized world there will be less territorial emphasis in defining reciprocal contextual collaboration in mission between co-participants. Categories of 'North' and 'South' will tend to be no longer valid for strengthening collaboration in mission as globalization tends to absorb local missiology. Economic, political and religious systems of the European Union, China, India, the Tiger zone, G7, G8, G20, etc., will have more influence than the territorial one. To respond to this reality, it will be essential to accept and to work with a conscious reciprocal missiological thinking, approaching seriously the reality that the composition of ethnic Christianity has changed, and that this change includes, fundamentally, the social and economic distinction whereby "the average Christian in the world is poor and very poor under the standards of the American and European believers" (Jenkins 2006, 68). Within this approach I find three challenges that will provide a framework for further discussion within the twenty-first *missio* collaboration enterprise of a global church:

1. The southern church leading the new reciprocal mission collaboration with the North.
2. The church in China and India leading the new reciprocal contextual forms of collaboration in the mission of the twenty-first century.
3. Mission societies working under the leadership of local missional pastors with a sense of both the church's local reality and the global.

At the same time, it is necessary to bear in mind that dialogue between North and South has implicit missiological tensions, due to the fact that they have differences of cultural identity and context. In this sense, it seems to me that a negative side of the dialogue on mission collaboration which was held at the WEA Mission Commissions in Pattaya 2008 has to do with a systemic tendency to promote the traditional model of mission, due to the fact that there was no evidence of inclusive missiological thinking by taking account of the non-traditional missionaries. The positive side relates to the recognition and conscious analysis of what was referred to as "the dynamics of the changing mission landscape", that are influencing the dynamic changes of the global mission by reshaping the traditional church and mission in the twenty-first century. These include the following aspects: [33]

- Mission fields becoming *mission forces.*
- Daughter churches becoming *Mother* churches.
- Drivers of the mission enterprise becoming *fellow-passengers* in the mission movement.
- Key-players expected to become *team-players.*
- Spectators becoming key-players and *active participants* in the mission arena.
- Those on the receiving end now agitating for space to make their *own contributions*, set their *own agenda*, and take their *own initiatives.*
- Emerging missions now *fully emerged.*

---

33. See the 'North and South Dialogue', The Task Force of WEA MC Global Missions Dialogue (email sent by Reuben Ezemadu to the author, 14 November 2008).

Conclusion and Challenges for Reciprocal Contextual Collaboration 421

In the newspaper *The Mail on Sunday* (8 March 2009, 8) there appeared an article entitled 'How China's Millions can Save the West', written by the British columnist, William Rees Mogg.[34] This article explains Joseph Schumpeter's thesis related to *Business Cycles* (1939), which argued that recessions are a necessary part of the process of growth. He claims that 'creative destruction' releases resources and clears the way for innovation in connection with the leadership of a 'new man'. The example provided is China, which has shown that recession, which causes strong economic difficulties, has in fact for them become an opportunity for growth. Mission for the twenty-first century must be aware that we are living in the context of a global recession which started in September 2008 with the bankruptcy of key banking industries – a difficult time after the Cold War in 1990. The United States has become stronger than the Soviet Union and China, but since 1980, China's economic growth has been 8 percent each year, in contrast with the declining Western economy, and even Japan. What happened with China? It is claimed by Rees Mogg (2009, 8) that China was set free in 1980 by the economic reform of Deng Xiaoping.[35] By comparing this political and economic situation it seems to me that the mission enterprise has experienced in the 1980s a huge 'creative collapsing' in its mission policy and mission structures, and there have emerged new mission spaces to accept that there are other ways to do mission, through the non-conventional model, kingdom business, or the migratory models, to mention just some of them. The challenge is not to pull down the traditional

---

34. The same article by William Rees Mogg appeared on the Mail Online, 'How China's Millions can Save the West', on 7 March 2009 (http://www.dailymail.co.uk/debate/article-1160180/WILLIAM-REES-MOGG-How-Chinas-millions-save-West.html?ITO=1490). For 'creative destruction', see also McDaniel (2007, 6).

35. Under Hu Jintao's presidency, China is expanding its economic influence to Africa. At present, some 800 Chinese companies operate in Africa, not from Beijing, but from Hong Kong as a base. See Daniel Howden's article 'Money and Mandarin Lessons Fuel China's Move into Africa' (*The Independent*, 15 October 2009; 22, 2009). In an article in the same newspaper, 'China in Africa – a growing presence', Ian Birrell remarks that since the fall of the Berlin Wall in 1996, China has turned to Africa (e.g. Chad, Sudan, Guinea, Liberia, Congo, Ethiopia, etc.); in 2008, £66 billion in trade was achieved by focusing on natural resources of the African soil, on infrastructure, including roads, railways, schools, stadiums, and on the selling of Chinese goods (*The Independent*, 15 October 2009; 23, 2009).

model, but rather to create new spaces for experiencing new forms of mission, overcoming the impact of the burgeoning evangelical missiology.

It seems that the way forward to produce an influx of new missiological reflection for appropriate models for mission will include the disappearance of the 'North-South' concept based on the following: (1) There is an increasing tendency towards a new order in the global world, based on religion, economy, and industrial production, not on the geographical one. (2) Static states based on geographical policy will tend to remain isolated as the global economy tends to link countries in a set of networks or integrated economic models like the European Union, the Mercosur in Latin America,[36] the Tiger zone in Asia,[37] the Asia-Pacific Economic Corporation (APEC),[38] etc. (3) The internationalization of mission will increase as it is the tendency of the global order, which can be seen through different models of networking; even the traditional models of mission are merging, amalgamating or combining the use of networks, as can be seen from the same tendency within the emergent models. How will the evangelical movement respond to these new global political and economic challenges? Will it be by finding contextual models of reciprocal mission? Just as the economist Castells (1966, 98) maintains that it is right to understand that market penetration is not reciprocal, so reciprocal missiology will demand the humility to recognize that the Western mission activity has been failing in its practice of a *reciprocal multipolar contextual engagement*, for it

---

36. Mercosur aims to create a continent of free trade area. Members are Brazil, Argentina, Paraguay, Uruguay; associated members includes Peru, Chile, Bolivia, Colombia and Ecuador. See NEWS BBC 'Channel, Profile: Mercosur-Common Market of the South' (http://news.bbc.co.uk/1/hi/world/americas/5195834.stm).

37. The Tiger zone includes South Korea, Taiwan, Singapore and Hong Kong, with a new global economy structured in rules of assimilation, and enhanced new information technologies both in products and in process and the strategic capacity to use new technologies. Therefore the development process includes relationships between technology, economy, state and society. See further Castells, *End of Millennium*, Vol III (1998, 244)

38. APEC is a forum for facilitating economic growth, cooperation, trade and investment in the Asia-Pacific region. APEC was established in 1989. See further (http://www.apec.org/apec/about_apec.html). Peru, as one of the 21 APEC members hosted the last meeting on 22–23 November 2008 in the capital city of Lima. See further (http://www.livinginperu.com/news/7873). See *The Globalization Syndrome* (Mittelman 2000, 9, 115, 142). John Ravenhill (2001) provides a brilliant and insightful analysis of APEC since its formation in 1989.

lacks contextualized models which do not deny the essence of the gospel. The same anti-reciprocal missiology will remain a danger for the emergent church as they may fail in mission by seeking market penetration, as they still receive the impact of European and the American missiological influence. A triumphalistic approach represents the kind of arrogance that produces the invalidation of any appropriate reciprocal missiology.

Historical and new perspectives on reciprocal contextual collaboration for the 21st century mission

Origin	Model	Structure	Characteristics	Impact
1790s Carey's influence	Traditional	Mission societies	Mission stations; channel the effort of local churches.	Mobilizing the church to distant lands
1980s Global philosophy's influence	Networking	Mission agencies, movements, denominations, local churches and individual ministries	Informal and formal relationships; direct and indirect collaboration	Mobilizing the church in sharing resources
1990s Context of suffering and the impact of poverty	Emergent	Local churches, Indigenous missions Migration movement	Less bureaucratic Peripheral of marginal economy Short-term mission Tentmakers Business as mission	Mobilizing the church in innovative ways
2010s 21st century mission challenges' influence	Synergy Spontaneous Integrated Contextual	Conventional and non-conventional	Effectiveness Spirit emphasis Amalgamated Incarnational	To be seen as reciprocal multipolar contextual engagement

This research has clearly revealed possibilities for finding new appropriate models of reciprocal cooperation for the twenty-first century, as long as radical changes are made to the missiological interpretations in the theology of mission collaboration, to decision making, to the control of power, in favour of a more contextual reciprocal collaboration with the Majority World – which is the new emerging mission movement. We used a historical, theological and missiological approach on the assumption that there can be new models of co-participation if we change the theological interpretation of cooperation and develop new understandings of biblical relationships related to the theology of the poor that is described, narrated, and exemplified through the Old and the New Testaments. A theology of the kingdom and a new clarification of the purpose of the church need to be included in the new theology of reciprocal contextual collaboration, which thus far has been understood only as producing mission collaboration for extending God's kingdom through raising more money for missions, which represents the narrow and reductionist theological and missiological interpretation which has generated a very territorial mission enterprise. I proposed the urgency of recovering the truth that neither the church nor mission societies are the owner of the mission. Mission starts with God and belongs to him, as he invites the church to cooperate with him in his redemptive plan, which includes the recovery of social concern regarding injustice and suffering, and cultivating a caring attitude to the poor. *Texts on Evangelical Social Ethics* (Padilla and Sugden 1985) describe clearly the process of theological concern for world evangelism that must include an imperative concern for the suffering world, as poor nations are dominated economically by the multinational corporations mainly of the West. This is the increasing reality whereby models of mission must provide a contextual and urgent response not by condemning evangelical liberation movements, but by recognizing them as new tools for creating justice and a mission of integral solidarity. There are at least three goals that can help us to find more appropriate models for the twenty-first evangelical mission.

First, the goal of understanding the church as a tool. While the *missio Dei* may be explained by parables that all members of the church will understand, a kingdom of God theology will require a clear popular theology that can be passed on to the post-modern evangelical person, while the political theology which is related to the new ecclesiology will need to be altered radically, in my view, in favour of an understanding of the church on earth as a transitional body called to accomplish the *missio Dei*, which is implicitly and explicitly designed for the glory of God who is the creator of everything. Christian reciprocal mission collaboration, then, becomes a tool that helps to establish the *basileia* – which is God's kingdom as it is explained through the whole Bible. In this way it is necessary to find more models of reciprocal mission that can work in a creative mission tension, and one of them should be the theological, missiological, and ecclesiological practice of spontaneous mission collaboration, which involves more flexibility in our mission models, which includes accountability, evaluation and audits.

Second, the goal of fostering intentional relational mission reciprocity. As the Latin American churches are growing very fast, and becoming part of the Majority World, a new missiological approach to the Asian, African and Latin American churches will require an understanding that the Latin American churches have at least sixty million evangelicals at present. This reality shows us that there is a real need for clear understanding of new policies aimed at a more relational integrated co-participation, and that a new theology of interdependence in freedom will need to be analysed critically through the traditional, networking and the emergent collaborative mission models that have been operating during this last twenty years.

Third, the goal of establishing common ground. The sharing of control of power and decision making, and the fomenting of more participative critical reflection on the part of Latin American evangelical leaders would strengthen reciprocal mission collaboration. This will tend to be more spontaneous, creating more flexible missiological models within a creative tension of spiritual, economic and cultural issues for both Western and Latin American mission co-workers. This approach will help to create more space for practitioners and theorists as they reflect on the new mission theology of reciprocal contextual collaboration. This approach can provide models of reciprocal mission according to a more appropriate relational missiology. Sharing power and decision making should be linked to a threefold insight rooted in a *metanoia* relationship: these are kingdom *missio* relationship, christological *missio* relationship, and holistic *missio* relationship, each of which is to be distinguished from a merely personal relationship, which at times seems polite, superficial or conditioned by the cultural context.

In *Mission in the 21st Century* (2008), Andrew Walls and Cathy Ross explore five marks of global mission (as developed by the Anglican Consultative Council between 1984 and 1990), as follows: (1) to proclaim the good news of the kingdom, (2) to teach, baptize and nurture new believers, (3) to respond to human need by loving service, (4) to seek to transform unjust structures of society, and (5) to strive to safeguard the integrity of creation and sustain and renew the life of the earth. As these marks come to be shaped by non-Western reflective practitioners, what will emerge will be missiological space for increasing reciprocal freedom, sharing of gifts, resources and dialogue, aimed at mission-fermentation of new appropriate models for mission. Within a similar concern, *Global Missiology for the 21st Century* (2000) contains the 'Iguassu Dialogue', a missiological consultation, which provides insights of forty-one topics for wider critical analysis of the evangelical movement's concerns for the mission of the twenty-first century. In this sense, I totally agree with Walls (2008, 202) when he states:

> Lands that were once at its heart are now on the margins, others that were on the margins are now at its heart. It has no single centre; above all, the idea of a 'home base' in Europe and North America, such as the Edinburgh fathers took for granted in 1910, is long past. The church now has not one but many centres; new Christian impulses and initiatives may now be expected from any quarter of the globe. Christian mission may start from any point, and be directed to any point. *This is* the new multicentric Christian church (italics mine).

This study has made it clear that the new multicentric Christian church (Walls 2008, 202), or what we have defined as the multipolar mission of the twenty-first century, will develop mission models within a reciprocal multipolar contextual engagement of increasing 'speed' mission changes as never imagined before; it will be a challenging time for the Latin American church and the global mission scenario.

Bibliography

Primary Sources

Mission archives, letters, bulletins, CDs, conversations and electronic information

Araujo, Alex. 2009. Brief comments for clarity in response to Mark Oxbrow, email sent to the author on 6 February 2009.

———. 2011. "Accountability for Faithfulness in Mission Partnership", information sent by Alex Araujo of Partners International to the author on 21 February 2011.

Barker, Charlotte. 2008a. Latin Link Statistics. Information provided by email to the author 11 September 2008.

———. 2008b. Latin Link Mission, current long-term members. Data provided to the author on 19 September 2008.

———. 2008c. Latin Link Mission. Data provided to the author on 14 October 2008.

Bazán, Ana. 2008. ABS Latin Promotions, Felíz día del Inmigrante Peruano, Happy Peruvian Immigrant Day, email from Peru on 18 October 2008.

Bertuzzi, Federico. 2011. PMI Information provided from Granada, Spain, to the author on 9 February 2011

Broadhurst, Geoff. 2008. Data provided to the author at Grace Church, during its fourth anniversary 5 October 2008.

Brynjolfson, Robert. 2008. World Evangelical-Leadership Institute (WEA-LI), data provided to the author at the WEA-Missions Commissions consultation, Pattaya, Thailand, personal conversation on 2 November 2008.

Bush, Luis. 2009. Information by email sent to author on 25 November 2009.

Ekstrom, Bertil. 2008. Presidents of COMIBAM, data provided from São Paulo, Brazil, on 19 October 2008.

———. 2008. Personal conversation in relation to COMIBAM with the author in Pattaya, Thailand, at the beginning of the World Evangelical Alliance-Mission Commission held on 30 October 2008.

Ellerby, Catherine. 2009. Information sent from St James to the author by email on 16 January 2009.

Enweren, Chris and Foluso Enweren. 2009. Newsletter from Shurdington Village, Gloucestershire UK, sent to the author by email on 2 April 2009.

Escobar, Samuel. 2011. Electronic Information provided to the author, in relation to the origins of the Fraternidad Teológica Latinoamericana on 3 February 2011.

Espinoza, Rosa. 2007. Alianza Cristiana y Misionera de Lince, Lima, Peru, telephone information from Lima to the author on 17 to 22 May 2007.

Gross, Francisco. 2011. Information sent by email to the author on 10 October 2011.

Han, Heewoo. 2009. "How to be gifted and godly" (2), 1 Corinthians 12:12–31, All Souls Church, Langham Place, London, C149/01-CD.

Hunter, Will. 2007. First short-term mission to India, email to Heather Payne, Archive of WMG 24 April 2007.

Juez, Miguel. 2009. Migrant Latin-American churches in Barcelona, data provided to the author of my dialogue in Barcelona on 22 January 2009.

Kirk, Andrew. 2007. Personal dialogue by email, relating to the Missio Dei concept and Trinitarian theology, London, October 25 2007.

Lee, Isobel. 2008. Data provided to the author on 14 December 2008.

Lee, Martin. 2008. Global Connections Director, personal dialogue with the author by email in the UK, 19 November 2008.

Lesson, Jonathan. 2008. Data provided at the Christ Church Latin Link event, London, 7 September 2008.

Lederleitner, Mary. 2011. Information by email, sent to the author on 4 October 2011.

Lunt, Robert. 2008. *Significant Dates relating to SAMS,* "SAMS Mission Education" med@samsgb.org, (Data provided by email received on 13 April 2008 at 1:10pm).

———. 2008. *Missionaries from SAMS* (Data provided by email received on 2 April 2008 at 3:41pm).

McIntosh, Steward. 2008. *Electronic dialogue* (Information provided on 20 March 2008).

Morales, Evo. 2008. "Carta del presidente boliviano contra las nuevas medidas anti-inmigratorias que la UE busca aprobar", email from "MINKA NEWS" minkanews@btconnect.com, (received on 16 June 2008 at 10:23am).

Nickl, Maria. 2009. Proyecto Alegria, Information telephonically given to the author on 20 January 2009.

Olsson, Carlos. 2011. Founder of the Church 'Casa de Oracion' in Chulucanas, Peru. Information sent to the author on 3 October 2011, from Lund, Sweden.

Oxbrow, Mark. 2009. Information of Faith2Share, sent to the author on 20 February 2009.

Pace, Tomas. 2011. Electronic information sent by the Senior Pastor of 'Nueva Vida' church from Lima, Peru to the author on 11 February 2011.

Padilla, René. 2006. Personal data written at the Latin American Forum, Global Connections, London, 24 September 2006.

———. 2007. Data provided at the mission conference organized by the London Institute of Contemporary Christianity at the Club House, London, September 2007.

Palmer, Hugh. 2009. "How to be gifted and godly" (1), 1 Corinthians 12:1–11, All Souls Church, Langham Place, London, C149/01.

———. 2009. "How to be gifted and godly" (3), 1 Corinthians 13:1–13, All Souls Church, Langham Place, London, C149/02.

———. 2009. "How to be gifted and godly" (4), 1 Corinthians 14:1–25, All Souls Church, Langham Place, London, C149/02.

Parrott, Roger. "2004 Forum for World Evangelization Opening Address", Lausanne Thailand information sent by Alex Araujo to the author on 21 January 2009 http://www.lausanne.org/2004-forum/opening-address.html (Online, accessed on 26 January 2009 at 7:40).

Proyecto, Alegria. 2007. First bulletin of the Proyecto Alegria (The Joy Project) edited in September 2007 in Huancayo, Peru.

September11.com, Complete International Achives of September 11, 2001 http://www.september11news.com/ (Accessed 17 June 2008 at 5:45 pm).

Slater, Julian. 2009. Data provided to the author on 9 January 2009 by email from London.

Swithinbank, Kim. 2008. "The need of a skeleton at St James' church", data provided at the annual report of St James 2007, held in April 2007.

———. 2008. Personal dialogue related to short-term missions with the vicar of St James Church, Muswell Hill, London (2 July 2008 at 5:30 pm).

Taylor, William. 2008. *World Evangelical Alliance*, Electronic information provided on 18 April 2008.

———. 2008. *World Evangelical Alliance*, Historical document sent from USA to Samuel Cueva, by email on 19 April 2008.

The Twenty-Fifth Milestone. 1936. A record of those who serve, *Bulletin of the Evangelical Union of South America*, London, United Kingdom Vol. XV, no. 4, July-August.

Twisleton, Ann. 2009. Telephone information from London, held on 28 January 2009.

Venning, Mark. 2008. Harrison & Harrison of Durham, email sent to the author on 17 December 2008.

Zuñiga, Juan. 2007. Electronic information sent to the author on 17 May 2007 at 10:29 pm.

Interviews and questionnaires

Araujo, Alex. 2002. Eight personal interviews with the author held in Pattaya, Thailand on 31 November 2008.

Baker, Simon. 2008. Questionnaire answered to the author on 6 October 2008.

Bertuzzi, Federico. 2008. Personal interview with the author held in Pattaya, Thailand on 3 November 2008.

Burns, Barbara. 2008. Personal interview with the author in Pattaya, Thailand on 4 November 2008.

Chapman, John. 2008. Questionnaire answered from London to the author on 13 September 2008.

Chavez, Wilson. 2007. Personal questionnaire answered in April 2007.

Davies, Paul. 2008. Questionnaire answered from Easneye, Ware, Hertfordshire, All Nations Christian College to the author on 21 October 2008.

Dominy, Richard and Kathy 2008. Questionnaire about short-term mission, information sent to the author on 21 December 2008.

Durst, Marcel. 2008. Questionnaire answered from Switzerland to the author on 9 September 2008.

Ford, Donald. 2008. Questionnaire answered from London to the author on 6 October 2008.

Harrison, Stuart. 2009. Personal interview by the author held in Edinburgh on 5 March 2009.

———. 2009a. Interview held in Edinburgh on 5 March 2009.

———. 2009b. Interview held in Edinburgh on 6 March 2009.

Hocking, Pedro. 2008. Questionnaire answered to the author, from Lima Peru on 24 March 2008 at 12:43pm (pjbirder06@yahoo.es.).

Hunter, Will. 2009. Interview with the author held on 26 January 2009 at St James' office in London.

Lee, Martin. 2008. Global Connection, questionnaire answered on 13 March 2008, 9:22am.

Londoño, Jesus. 2008. Questionnaire answered from Granada, Spain to the author on 31 October 2008.

McIntosh, Stewart. 2008. Telephone Interview from London by the author on 30 September 2008.

Morales, Abel. 2008. Questionnaire, information provided by email to the author from Dallas, USA on 27 October 2008.

Nickl, Enrique. 2009. Personal interview held in Huancayo, Peru on 9 August 2009.

Peppiatt, Jimmy. 2009. Questionnaire, information sent by email from London to the author on 14 January 2008.

Ruiz, David. 2008. Personal interview with the author held in Pattaya, Thailand on 1 November 2008.

Ross, Alex. 2008. Questionnaire answered from London to the author on 16 December 2008.

———. 2009. Questionnaire, question 3, email from London to the author on 20 January 2009.

Shepherd, Claudio. 2009. Telephone interview held in London on 1 December 2009.

Taylor, William. 2008. Dialogue by email from United States of America to the author on 14 October 2008.

Thorton, Jonathan. 2009. Questionnaire, Information provided by email to the author on 8 February 2009.

Tower, Alan. 2008. Questionnaire answered from Reading-UK to the author on 8 September 2008.

Vazquez, Tony. 2008. Personal interview held in Madrid on 6 May 2008.

Unpublished material, manuscripts and documents

Araujo, Alex. 2008. "Catching the Wind" paper presented during the dialogue "North South" at the World Evangelical Alliance-Mission Commission held in Pattaya, 30 October – 3 November 2008, unpublished material.

Anglican Church of Australia. "A History of Anglicanism", http://australia.anglican.org/index.cfm?SID=2&SSID=5 (Online, accessed on 13 January 2009 at 5:20 pm).

BBC NEWS Channel, Profile: G8, 17 September 2008 http://news.bbc.co.uk/1/hi/world/americas/country_profiles/3777557.stm (Online, accessed on 19 January 2009 at 12:20).

BBC NEWS Channel, 7 July Bombings, Overview, http://news.bbc.co.uk/1/shared/spl/hi/uk/05/london_blasts/what_happened/html/default.stm (Accessed 17 June 2008 at 10:05 pm)

Bush, Luis. 1997. COMIBAM 97: "An Assessment of the Latin American Missions Movement", 15th December, 1–4, http://www.ad2000.org/re71216.htm (Online, accessed on 20 October 2008 at 3:55 pm).

Bush, George. 2001. "We Are a Country Awakened to Danger and Called to Defend Freedom". The text of President George W. Bush's address to the USA Congress on the evening of September 20, 2001. See the whole papers at http://www.september11news.com/PresidentBushSpeech.htm (Accessed 17 June 2008 at 9:45 pm).

Bustamante, Gloria. 2008. Report of the II International Assembly, http://www.membercare.org/images/regions/comibam_03.pdf (Online, accessed at 4:20 pm on 21 November 2008).

Cathedral and Abbey Church of St Albans, http://www.stalbanscathedral.org.uk/index1.htm (Online, accessed on 16 January 2009 at 11:20 am).

Chapman, Deborah. 2006. *Florencio Segura: Communicating Quechua Evangelical Theology Via Hymnody in Southern Peru*, doctoral thesis, University of Edinburgh, unpublished material, http://www.era.lib.ed.ac.uk/bitstream/1842/1565/2/Chapman +D+07+thesis.pdf (Online accessed on 25 February 2009 at 11:10 pm).

CLADE IV. 2000. Congreso Latinoamericano de Evangelización: Documento de Trabajo CLADE IV, Quito Ecuador, September 2000.

Christianity Explore, http://www.christianityexplored.org/about-us/rico/ (Online, accessed on 13 January 2009 at 7:58 pm).

Church, M. et al. 2002. "Participation, Relationships and Dynamic Change." University of London, Working Paper no. 121, (http://www.ucl.ac.uk/DPU/publications/working%20papers%20pdf/WP121%20final.pdf (Online accessed on 15 March 2009 at 8:20 pm).

City Population: Great Britain and Northern Ireland, http://www.citypopulation.de/UK-London.html#Stadt_alpha (Online, accessed on 16 December 2008 at 3:35 pm).

CMS pamphlet "Mid-Africa News", Issue 1, 2011:1–8.
CMS pamphlet, "SHARE: Global mission with a Latin Heart", Issue 3, 2010:1–15.
CMS pamphlet, "Were you there?: Remembering 2009–2010" (includes the summary 2009–2010, Financial Summary).
CMS Poster entitled "CMS working in Latin America: evangelistic, resourcing leaders and transforming communities, making disciples".
COMIBAM Bibliografia misionera, http://www.comibam.org/docs/bibliografia.pdf (Online, accessed 5 December 2008 at 9:10 am).
COMIBAM. 1987. Primer Congreso Misionero Iberoamericano: Luz para las Naciones, São Paulo, Brazil 23 to 28 November.
COMIBAM. 1997. Segundo Congreso Misionero Iberoamericano: Las Misiones Latinas para el Siglo XXI, Acapulco, Mexico 27 to 31 October 1997, Miami, UNILIT.
COMIBAM. 2001. Departamento de Desarrollo, Plan de Trabajo by Hugo Morales, coordinator of Programa de Cooperación de Alianzas, http://www.comibam.org/depart/desarrollo/desarrolo.htm (Online, accessed on 21 October 2008 at 8:45 pm).
COMIBAM. 2002. "Manual de la Cumbre de Liderazgo" Noviembre, Madrid, España, http://www.comibam.org/ponencias/cumliespa/index.htm (Online, accessed 21 November 2008 at 5:15 pm).
COMIBAM Internacional. 2005. "Programa de Mobilizacion de Pastores e Iglesias", 1–8, http://www.comibam.org/docs/rmip_plan.pdf (Accessed 19 October 2008 at 7:45 pm).
COMIBAM Internacional. Programa de Movilización de Pastores e Iglesias, http://www.comibam.org/docs/rmip_plan.pdf (Online, accessed on 12 November 2008 at 10:45 am).
COMIBAM. 2006. El Movimiento Misionero Iberoamericano, Catalogo 2006 http://www.comibam.org/transpar/ing/catalog2006/gif/Slide8.gif (Online, accessed on 21 October 2008 at 8:55 pm).
COMIBAM. 2006. Missionaries from Latin America, Spain and Portugal, http://www.comibam.org/transpar/_menus/ing/01web-ib.htm (Online, accessed on 21 October 2008 at 9:10 pm).
COMIBAM Report. General Report of the III Iberoamerican Mission Congress, November 13–17 2006 Granada, Spain, http://comibam.org/docs/report_comibamIII_en.pdf (Online, accessed 20 October 2008 at 8:50 am).
COMIBAM Internacional: Que es COMIBAM? http://www.comibam.org/queescomi.htm (Accessed on 21 October 2008 at 9:20 pm).

COMIBAM Internacional Comite Ejecutico, http://www.comibam.org/equipo. htm (Online, accessed on 22 October 2008 at 8:45 pm).

COMIBAM. 2006. Tercer Congreso Misionero Iberoamericano: Resultados y desafios entre los no alcanzados, Granada, España, 13–17 November 2006.

COMIBAM. 2006. General Report of the III Iberoamerican Mission Congress, 13–17 November 2006, Granada, Spain.

Cooks, Jenny. 2009. Christianity Explorer's origins, email sent from London to the author on 14 January 2009.

Concilio Nacional Evangelico del Peru, Quienes Somos? http://www. concilionacionalevangelico.org/index.php?option=com_content&task=view &id=12&Itemid=27 (Online, accessed on 27 October 2008 at 12:15).

CrossGlobal Link, *Membership,* online at http://www.crossgloballink.org/Our_ Story, (Accessed 18 April 2008 at 4:50 pm).

Cueva, Samuel. 2003. Papers presented at the Latin American Forum-Global Connections on 18 October.

———. 2003. Personal data from the first meeting to form the first team for the St James' 5 pm service, held in London.

———. 2005. *Spanish Speaking Churches in London: A Survey of the evangelical churches in London,* researched 27/09/05 – Actualized 04/03/08, unpublished material.

———. 2006. Personal data collected at the COMIBAM Congress in Granada 2006.

———. 2007. "Misiones Desde un Contexto de Pobreza", unpublished material, papers presented in Lima Peru, 29 May to 3 June 2007 for the Christian and Missionary Alliance's Mission Conference.

———. 2007b. "Como Promover Misiones en la Iglesia Local", unpublished material, papers presented in Lima, Peru, 29 May to 3 June 2007 for the Christian and Missionary Alliance's Missionary Conference.

———. 2009. "Misión, Misioneros y la Evangelización of Europa: Hacia una Misiología Integradora", Paper presented at the Mission Consultation "Back to Europe", Torremolinos, Spain, 13–16 May 2009, unpublished material.

Duncan, Graham A. 2007. Partnership in Mission: A critical, historical evaluation of the relationship between 'older' and 'younger' churches with special reference to the World Mission Council policy of the Church of Scotland, Faculty of Theology, University of Pretoria, in the subject, Church History, online at http://upetd.up.ac.za/thesis/available/etd-10172007-122745/unrestricted/00front.pdf.

Ekstrom, Bertil. 2000. The Spirit of COMIBAM, plenary addressed at the First International Assembly, Lima Peru 2000 (1–3), unpublished material.

Ekstrom, Bertil and William D. Taylor. *Mission Commission Structure: An Open Architecture of Relating, Connecting and Docking.* Online at http://www.worldevangelicals.org/commissions/mc/mission_structure.htm (Accessed on 17 April 2008).

Escobar, Samuel. 1995. "Faith and Hope for the Future: Toward a Vital Evangelical Theology for the 21st Century" presented first at the WEF 1995 p. 1–31, appeared in the *Evangelical Review of Theology* (October 1996).

Ezemadu, Reuben. 2008. "North and South Dialogue", The Task Force of WEA MC Global Missions Dialogue, article sent by email to the author, 14 November 2008.

G8 Summits, Hokkaido, Japan, Official Documents, 9 July 2008, http://www.g8.utoronto.ca/summit/2008hokkaido/2008-summary.html (accessed 10 July 2008 at 7:40 pm).

Global Connections 2004 Focus on Peru, People, culture and life style, http://www.globalconnections.Co.uk/Resources/Global%20Connections/Mission%20Issues/2006/Peru.pdf (Online, accessed 20 January 2009 at 6:10 pm).

Global Mission, Results from Recent Years, http://globalmissionscott.blogspot.com/2008/04/results-from-recent-years-comibam.html (Online, accessed 16 November 2008 at 10:40 pm).

Global Connections, http://www.globalconnections.co.uk/aboutus/history.htm (accessed 17 February 2008 at 10:20 pm).

Great Commission Roundtable, http://www.icta.net/gcr/html/networks.html (Online, accessed 17 April 2008 at 9:15 pm).

Global Member Care Resources, MemCa, The Missionary Member Care Program of COMIBAM International, http://www.membercare.org/mchistoryibero.asp, (Online, accessed on 12 November 2008 at 10:01 am).

Instituto Nacional de Estadistica, http://www1.inei.gob.pe/inicio.htm; (Online, accessed on 3 September 2008).

Kirton, John. What is the G20? Department of Political Science, Centre for International Studies, University of Toronto, http://www.g8.utoronto.ca/g20/g20whatisit.html (Accessed 10 July 2008 at 6:30 pm).

Latin Link Banner History sent by Marcel Durst to the author from Switzerland, 8 September 2008.

Latin Link International Handbook. Edited 1998. International Executive June 1994.

Latin Link International Handbook. Second Edition 2006, second version agreed at the International Assembly in Cochabamba, Bolivia.

Latin Link. 2008. Prayer Calendar.

Latin Link. Support Levels 2008–2009, information provided by Charlotte Barker on 10 September 2008.

Latin Link. Stride and Step Costs, information provided by Charlotte Barker on 19 September 2008.

Latin Link. Step Teams, http://www.stepteams.org/apply.php#01 (Online, accessed on 19 March 2009 at 4:30 pm).

Latin Link. Stride, http://www.latinlink.org/stride.asp (Online, accessed on 19 March 2009 at 4:50 pm).

Lausanne Movement about Lausanne History and Heritage of Lausanne Movement, http://www.lausanne.org/sv/about.html (Online, accessed 7 November 2008 at 9:05 pm).

Lewis, P. Jonathan. 2006. Regional and National Mission Structures, SA06: WEA Mission Commission, Global Issues Summit, June 18–24, Goudini Spa, South Africa, http://www.worldevangelicals.org/commissions/mc/mc_southafrica/resources/Lewis%20-%20Mission%20structures.pdf (Online, accessed on 18 November 2008 at 12:50).

Londoño, Jesus. 2003. "Cambios Teologicos en la Fuerza Misionera", II Asamblea Internacional de COMIBAM, San Salvador, El Salvador, 10–14 November, http://www.comibam.org/ponencias/IIAsamblea/CTEFM.htm (Online, accessed 21 November 2008 at 4:45 pm).

Lopez, Dario. 1997. *The Evangelical Church and Human Rights in Peru: A critical Evaluation of the Theology of Mission of the National Evangelical Council of Peru-from 1980–1992, with Special Reference to its Understanding and Practice of Human Rights.* Oxford Center for Mission Studies (unpublished thesis).

Motessi, Alberto. 1988. "Los Angeles 88" *Congreso Internacional para la Evangelización del Mundo Latino,* 25–29 July 1988, Los Angeles, USA.

Mundus: Gateway to missionary collections in the United Kingdom, History of SAMS http://www.mundus.ac.uk/cats/61/1054.htm, (Accessed 5 March 2008, at 1:35 pm).

New Delhi Speaks: The Message of the Third Assembly New Delhi, with the Reports of the Assembly's Section on Christian Witness, Service and Unity and an Appeal to All Governments and Peoples 1962, London: SCM Press Ltd.

Newell, Marv. *Our Story,* http://www.crossgloballink.org/Our_Story (Accessed 18 April 2008 at 4:20 pm).

———. http://www.highbeam.com/doc/1G1-173923117.html (Accessed 18 April 2008 at 2:05 pm).

Niebuhr, Helmut Richard. Harvard Divinity School, Andover-Harvard Theological Library, bMS 630, *Papers 1919–1962* http://www.hds.harvard.edu/library/bms/bms00630.html (Accessed 21 June 2008 at 6:12 pm).

Olumbe, Duncan. "Dancing a Different Dance", data provided by Reuben Ezemadu, sent to the author on 31 October 2008, unpublished material.

Ostry, Sylvia. Globalization and the G8: Could Kananaskis Set a New Direction? Centre for International Studies of Toronto, unpublished material, http://www.utoronto.ca/cis/skeltonlecture_ostry2002.doc (Accessed 10 July 2008 at 5:50 pm).

Overseas Missionary Fellowship (OMF) History: http://www.omf.org/omf/uk/about_omf/omf_cim_history (Accessed 28 February 2008, at 12.05 pm).

Oxbrow, Mark. 2009. "Sailing Close to the Wind: A response to Roger Parrot and Alex Araujo", (Article produced in February, sent to the author on 3 March 2009, unpublished material).

Partnership for world Mission (PWM) 2008 mission http://www.pwm-web.org.uk/partners.shtml (accessed 13 April 2008, at 3.02 pm).

Padilla, René. 2008. "The Global Challenges that the Church Faces Today", Global Connections Consultation, held at the Church Mission Society (CMS) office, Oxford on 8 October 2008.

Palomino, Miguel Angel. 1999. "The Latin Church in Mission." Latin Link Conference, The Hayes Conference Centre, Swanwick, Derbyshire, 22 May 1999.

Rankin, Jerry. 2001. "Planting with Passion: Field Personnel Orientation: Seven Dimensions of the IMB Field Personnel." Rockville, Virginia, unpublished material.

Report of the First Iberoamerican Missionary Retreat, Sierra Nevada, 11–13 November 2006.

Ruiz, David. 2003. "The Two Third World Mission Movement takes advantages of new models of networking: A Report on the Emerging WEA/MC Network", *Connections,* The Journal of the World Evangelical Alliance, June, 52–53. http://www.worldevangelicalalliance.com/commissions/mc/mc_southafrica/resources/Connections_June_2003.pdf (Online, accessed 18 October 2008 at 10:15 pm).

Saddock, Alicia. 2007. *COMIBAM Conference 2006: Celebrating the Advances of Spanish-Speakers in Mission Outreach*, Communications Coordinator CAM International, http://www.caminternational.org/ SymphonyCore/ resources/

upload /files/ attachments/COMIBAM%20Conference%202006.pdf (Online, accessed 20 October 2008 at 9:05 pm).

Scott, Carlos. 2005. "A Sketch on the Mobilization of the Latin American Church: Characteristics, Tendencies, Strengths and Challenges", *Connections,* The Journal of the World Evangelical Mission Commission, 18–20, http://www.worldevangelicalalliance.com/commissions/mc/mc_ southafrica/resources/Connections_Oct_2005.pdf (Online, accessed on 17 October 2008 at 3:20 pm).

Scott, Carlos and Jesus Londoño. "Where is COMIBAM International Heading?: Strategic Focal Points." http://www.comibam.org/docs/ whereiscomibamheading.pdf (Online, accessed on 22 October 2008 at 10:05 pm).

Scott, Carlos. 2006a. "New Chapter of the Acts of the Holy Spirit." COMIBAM 2006 Tercer Congreso Misionero Iberoamericano: Resultados y desafios entre los no alcanzados, Granada, España, 13–17 November 2006.

Scott, Carlos and Jesus Londoño. 2006b. Reporte General del III Congreso Misionero Iberoamericano, Noviembre, 13 al 17 del 2006, Granada, España. Unpublished document sent to the author on 21 December from COMIBAM International.

St James Church. 2006. Minutes of the WMG held on Monday 9 October 2006.

———. 2006. Minutes of the WMG held on 23 November 2006.

———. 2007. Archives World Mission Group: Support Request Form from the IME Church, 2 February 2007.

———. 2007. Minutes of the WMG held on Monday 8 October 2007.

———. 2007. "Main Missions 2007", archives of the WMG, Muswell Hill London, United Kingdom.

———. 2008. Minutes of the WMG held on Monday 19 May 2008.

SAMS History http://www.samsusa.org/about_history.html (Accessed 5 March 2008 at 1:15 am).

Saracco, Norberto. 1989. *Argentine Pentecostalism: Its History and Theology,* Unpublished Ph.D. Thesis, University of Birmingham, United Kingdom.

Shared Reading Comments: A tentative definition of social facts, http://www.csudh.edu/dearhabermas/read09.htm#samantha01 (accessed 2 July 2008 at 10:10).

Shock Tactics Force a UN Showdown on Mugabe, *The Times,* Wednesday, 9 July 2008, pp32–33.

Taylor, William World Evangelical Alliance, History, http://www.worldevangelicals.org/wea/history.htm (Online, accessed on 18 November 2008 at 3:35 pm).

"The Church of Scotland World Mission Council, 2006 General Assembly Report, Proposed Deliverance", http://www.churchofscotland.org.uk/extranet/xga/downloads/gareports06worldmission.doc (Online, accessed on 9 February 2009 at 2:20 pm).

The Church of England Year Book. 2004. 120th Edition, Church House Publishing.

Thomas, Chacko. 2006. "Latin America Blessing the World-Personal Reflections on COMIBAM", Lausanne Connecting, Point December, http://www.lausanne.org/lausanne-connecting-point/2006-december.html#5 (Online, accessed 12 November 2008 at 8:29 am).

What is the G8? What does the G8 Stand for? University of Toronto, Munk Centre, International Studies at Trinity College, http://www.g7.utoronto.ca/ (Accessed 10 July 2008 at 6:15).

World Council of Churches, National Evangelical Council of Peru, http://www.oikoumene.org/en/member-churches/regions/latin-america/peru/conep.html, (Online, accessed on 27 October 2008 at 12:02 pm).

World Evangelical Alliance. http://www.worldevangelicals.org/wea/. Accessed 17 April 2008 at 12:48 pm).

Wycliffe International. "The Emergent Latin American Bible Translation Force", 1–2, http://www.wycliffe.net/home/Americas/Articles/tabid/422/Default.aspx?id=am-0803012 (Online, accessed 19 October 2008 at 7:58 am).

Pamphlets and newspapers

Birrell, Ian. 2009. "China in Africa a growing presence." *The Independent*, Thursday 15 October 23, 2009.

Fatih2Share, "We believe faith needs to be shared", www.faith2share.net

"Faith in the Local Church", conference entitled "For Joy", London Thursday 5–Saturday 7 June 2008.

GAFCON 2008. "The Global Anglican Future Conference", held at Jerusalem, from 22–29 June, leaflet distributed at St James Church-Muswell Hill on 1–4 July 2008.

Howden, Daniel. 2009. "Money and Mandarin lessons fuel China's move into Africa." *The Independent*, October 15, 22 2009.

Mapa Planisferio Misionero distributed at COMIBAM 2006, Granada, 13–17 November 2006.

Map of the The Cape Town 2010 Congress. "The Third Lausanne Congress on World Evangelization", distributed at the General Assembly of the World Evangelical Alliance, Pattaya, Thailand, 25–29 October 2008.

Movement for African national Initiatives (MANI), Africa's Time Has Come, Website: www.MANIafrica.com (Online, accessed 18 January 2009 at 8:20 pm).

Rees Mogg, William. 2009. "How China's Millions can save the West", Newspaper *The Mail on Sunday 7,* 8 March 2009.

St James Church. 2008. Holy Communion, pamphlet distributed at St. James' services on 13 January.

Secondary Sources

Books

Abraham, K. C., ed. 1990. *Third World Theologies: Commonalities and Divergences,* Maryknoll. New York: Orbis Books.

Addicott, Ernie. 2005. *Body Matters: A Guide to Partnership in Christian Mission.* Washington: Interdev Partnership Associates.

Alves, Ruben A. 1970. *Protestantism and Repression.* London: SCM Press Ltd.

Allen, Roland. 1927. (2006 New edition) *The Spontaneous Expansion of the Church and the causes which hinder it.* Cambridge: The Lutherworth Press.

———. 1962. *Missionary Methods: St Paul's or Ours?* Grand Rapids, Michigan: Eerdmans Publishing Co.

Anderson, H. Allan and Walter J. Hollenweger, eds. 1999. *Pentecostals, After a Century: Global Perspectives on a Movement in Transition.* Sheffield: Academic Press Ltd.

Anderson, Allan. 2004. *An Introduction to Pentecostalism.* Cambridge: Cambridge University Press.

Anderson, Gerald and Thomas F. Stransky, eds. 1976. *Mission Trends No 3: Third World Theologies.* New York: Paulist Press/ Eerdmans Publishing Co.

Anderson, Gerald H. et al., ed. 1994. *Mission Legacies: Biographical Studies of Leaders of the Modern Missionary Movement.* Maryknoll, New York: Orbis Books.

Anderson, Sheldon, Jeanne A. K. Hey, Mark Allen Petersen, Stanley W. Toops, and Charles Stevens, eds. 2008. *International Studies an Interdisciplinary Approach to Global Issues.* Colorado: Westview Press.

Austin, E. James. 2000. *The Collaboration Challenge: How non-profits and business succeed through strategic alliances.* San Francisco: Jossey-Bass Publishers.

Baer, Michael R. 2006. *Business as Mission: The Power of Business in the Kingdom of God.* Seattle, Washington: YWAM Publishing.

Balia, Daryl and Kirsteen Kim, eds. 2010. *Edinburgh 2010 Volume II: Witnessing to Christ Today.* Oxford: Regnum.

Barrett, Charles K. 1978. (Second edition) *The Gospel According to St John: An Introduction with Commentary and Notes on the Greek Text.* London: SPCK.

Barth, Karl. 1949. *Dogmatics in Outline.* London: SCM Press.

———. 1962. *The Epistle to the Philippians.* London: SCM Press.

Bauerochse, Lothar. 1996. *Learning to Live Together.* Geneva: WCC Publications.

Bebbington, David W. 2005. *The Dominance of Evangelicalism: The age of Spurgeon and Moody.* Downers Grove, Illinois: InterVarsity Press.

Bediako, Kwame. 1992. *Theology and Identity: The Impact of Culture upon Christian Thought in the Second Century and in Modern Africa.* Carlisle, Cumbria: Regnum.

Beckford, Robert. 2000. *Dread and Pentecostal: Political theology of black church in Britain.* London: Society for Promoting Christian Knowledge.

Berg, Clayton L. and Paul E. Pretiz. 1996. *Spontaneous Combustion: Grass-Roots Christianity, Latin American Style.* Pasadena, California: William Carey Library.

Berryman, Phillip. 1987. *Liberation Theology: The Essential Facts About the Revolutionary Movement in Latin America and Beyond.* London: I. B. Tauris and Co Ltd.

Bertuzzi, Federico. 2006. *El Despertar de las Misiones.* Barcelona: Editorial CLIE.

Bevans, B. Stephen. 1992. (Seventh Edition 2007) *Models of Contextual Theology: Faith and Culture.* Maryknoll, New York: Orbis Books.

Bevans, Stephen B. and Roger P. Schroeder. 2004. *Constants in Context: A Theology of Mission for Today.* Maryknoll, New York: Orbis Books.

Blomberg, Craig L. 1999. *Neither Poverty nor Riches: A Biblical Theology of Material Possessions.* Grand Rapids, Michigan: Eerdmans Publishing Co.

Boff, Leonardo. 1987. *Introducing Liberation Theology.* London: Burns and Oates.

———. 1988. *Trinity and Society.* London: Burns and Oates.

Bonino, Jose Miguez. 1997. *Faces of Latin American Protestantism.* Grand Rapids, Michigan: Eerdmans Publishing Co.

Bonk, Jonathan J. 1991. *Mission and Money: Affluence as a Western Missionary Problem.* Maryknoll, New York: Orbis Books.

———, ed. 2003. *Between Past and Future: Evangelical Mission Entering the Twenty-first Century.* Pasadena, California: William Carey Library.

Bosch, David. 1979. *A Spirituality of the Road.* Eugene, Oregon: Wipf and Stock Publishers.

———. 1991. *Transforming Mission; Paradigm Shifts in Theology of Mission.* Maryknoll, New York: Orbis Books.

———. 1995. *Believing in the Future: Towards a Missiology of Western Culture.* Valley Forge, Pennsylvania: Trinity Press International.

Brownson, James V. 1998. *Speaking the Truth in Love: New Testament Resources for a Missional Hermeneutic.* Harrisburg, Pennsylvania: Trinity Press International.

Bruce, Frederick Fyvie. 1989. *New International Biblical Commentary, Philippians.* Peabody, Massachusetts: Hendrickson Publishers.

Brueggemann, Walter. 2001. *The Prophetic Imagination.* Minneapolis, Minnesota: Fortress Press.

Buhlmann, Walbert. 1976. *The coming of the Third Church.* Maryknoll, New York: Orbis Books.

Bunker, Michael. 1988. *The Church on the Hill: The remarkable rebirth of a local church.* Eastbourne, Sussex: MARC.

Bush, Luis and Lorry Lutz. 1990. *Partnering in Ministry: The Direction of World Evangelism.* Downers Grove, Illinois: Intervarsity Press.

Bush, Luis. 2000. *Working Together with God to Shape the New Millennium.* Evangelical Missiological Society Series Number 8. Pasadena, California: William Carey Library.

Butler, Phill. 2006. *Well Connected: Realizing power, restoring hope through kingdom partnership.* Milton Keynes: Authentic Media.

Campbell, William S. 2006. *Paul and the Creation of Christian Identity.* London: T&T Clark International.

Castells, Manuel. 1997. *The Power of Identity*, Volume II. Malden, Massachusetts: Blackwell Publishers.

———. 1998. *End of Millennium, The Information Age: Economy, society and culture,* Volume III. Malden, Massachusetts: Blackwell Publishers.

Chester, Tim, ed. 2002. *Justice, Mercy and Humility: Integral Mission and the Poor.* Milton Keynes: Paternoster.

Christian Aid. 1988. *Banking on the Poor: The Ethics of Third World Debt.* Oxford: Christian Aid.

Claydon, David, ed. 2005. *A New Vision a New Heart a New Call,* Volume I and II, Lausanne Occasional Papers from the 2004 Forum for

World Evangelization, hosted by the Lausanne Committee for World Evangelization in Pattaya, Thailand. Pasadena, California: William Carey Library.

———, ed. 2005. *A New Vision A New Heart of Renewed Call*, Volume III "Funding for Evangelism and Mission", Lausanne Occasional Paper no. 56.

Consejo Evangélico de Madrid 2003 *Las Iglesias y la Migración: Contenido integro de las conferencias y trabajos presentados en las jornadas celebradas el 25 y 26 de Abril de 2003 en el Seminario Teológico UEBE de Madrid.* Madrid: CEM.

Corrie, John, ed. 2007. *Dictionary of Mission Theology: Evangelical Foundations.* Nottingham: IVP.

Corwin, Gary and Kenneth B. Mulholland, eds. 2000. *Working Together with God to Shape the New Millennium: Opportunities & Limitations*, Evangelical Missiological Society, no. 8. Pasadena, California: William Carey Library.

Cosden, Darrell. 2004. *A Theology of Work: Work and the New Creation.* Carlisle, Cumbria: Paternoster.

Costas, Orlando. 1974. *The Church and its Mission: A Shattering Critique from the Third World.* Wheaton, Illinois: Tyndale House Publishers.

———. 1976. *Theology of the Crossroads in Contemporary Latin America, Missiology in Mainline Protestantism: 1969–1974.* Amsterdam: Rodopi.

———. 1979. *The Integrity of Mission: The Inner Life and Outreach of the Church.* San Francisco: Harper & Row Publishers.

Cox, Harvey. 1995. *Fire from Heaven: The Rise of Pentecostal Spirituality and the Reshaping of religion in the Twenty First Century.* New York: Addison-Wesley Publishing Company.

Cueva, Samuel. 1991. *La Iglesia Local en Misión Transcultural.* Terrasa, Barcelona: Editorial Clie.

———. 2004. *Misión para el Tercer Milenio, Construyendo Puentes Misioneros de Doble Vía.* Terrasa, Barcelona: Editorial Clie.

Czövek, Támas. 2006. *Three Seasons of Charismatic Leadership: A Literary-Critical and Theological Interpretation of the Narrative of Saul, David and Solomon.* Milton Keynes: Regnum.

Davies, Paul. 2006. *Faith Seeking Effectiveness: The Missionary Theology of José Míguez Bonino.* Zoetermeer: Boekencentrum.

Deiros, Pablo. 1997. *Diccionario Hispanoamericano de la Misión.* Miami: UNILIT.

Dorr, Donal. 2000. *Mission in Today's World.* Maryknoll, New York: Orbis Books.

Driver, John. 1997. *Images of the Church in Mission.* Pennsylvania: Herald Press.

Dulles, Avery. 1974. *Models of the Church.* New York: An Image Book.

Edwards, David L. 1998. *English Christianity: From Roman Britain to the Present Day.* London: Harper Collins Publishers.

Engelsviken, Tormod et al. eds. 2008. *Mission to the World: Communicating the Gospel in the 21st Century*, Essays in Honour of Knud Jorgensen. Carlisle, Cumbria: Regnum.

Escobar, Samuel. 2002. *Changing Tides: Latin America and World Mission Today.* Maryknoll, New York: Orbis Books.

———. 2003a. *The New Global Mission: The Gospel from Everywhere to Everywhere.* Downers Grove, Illinois: Intervarsity Press.

———. 2003b. *A Time for Mission: The Challenge for Global Christianity.* Leicester: IVP.

Evangelical Alliance. 1993. *Money for God's Sake.* London: the Evangelical Alliance.

Ezemadu, Reuben, ed. 2006. *Models, Issues and Structures of Indigenous Missions in Africa: A compendium of the Consultation on Indigenous Missions in Africa.* Ibadan, Nigeria: ACCLAIM.

Fee, Gordon. 1999. *Philippians.* Downers Grove, Illinois: Intervarsity Press.

Ferguson, Sinclair B. 1996. *The Holy Spirit:* Contours of Christian Theology. Downers Grove, Illinois: Intervarsity Press.

Fiedler, Klaus. 1994. *The Story of Faith Missions.* Oxford: Regnum Books International.

Freston, Paulo. 2001. *Evangelicals and Politics in Asia, Africa and Latin America.* Cambridge: Cambridge University Press.

Freston, Paul, ed. 2007. *Evangelical Christianity and Democracy in Latin America.* New York: Oxford University Press.

Forward, David C. 1998. *The Essential Guide to the Short Term Mission Trip.* Chicago: Moody Press.

Frost Michael and Alan Hirsch. 2003. *The Shaping of the Things to Come: Innovation and Mission for the 21st Century Church.* Peabody, Massachusetts: Hendrickson Publishers.

Frost, Michael. 2006. *Exiles: Living Missionally in a Post-Christian Culture.* Peabody, Massachusetts: Hendrickson Publisher.

Gadamer, Hans G. 1982. *Truth and Method.* Crossroad Publishing Company, New York.

Graham, Billy. Evangelistic Association 2001. *"Amsterdam 2000" The Mission of the Evangelist: A Conference of Preaching Evangelist.* Minneapolis, Minnesota: World Wide Publications.

Green, Michael. 1988. *The Message of Matthew.* Leicester: InterVarsity Press.

Grenz, Stanley J. 2004. *Rediscovering the Triune God: The Trinity in Contemporary Theology.* Minneapolis: Fortress Press.

González, Justo. 1984. *The Story of Christianity Volume I: The Early Church to the Dawn of the Reformation.* New York: Harpers San Francisco.

———. 1985. *The Story of Christianity, Volume 2: The Reformation to the Present day.* New York: Harper Collins Publishers Ltd.

———. 1986. (10th edition) *A History of Christian Thought, Volume 2: From Augustine to the Eve of the Reformation.* Nashville: Abingdon Press.

———. 1987. *A History of Christian Thought, Volume 3: From the Protestant Reformation to the Twentieth Century.* Nashville: Abingdon Press.

———. 1993. (New edition) *A History of Christian Thought, Volume I: From the Beginning of the Council of Chalcedon.* Nashville: Abingdon Press.

———. 1996. *Church History: An Essential Guide.* Nashville: Abingdon Press.

Groody, Daniel G. and Gioacchino Campese, eds. 2008. *A Promise Land, A Perilous Journey: Theological Perspectives on Migration.* Notre Dame, Indiana: University of Notre Dame Press.

Gunton, E. Colin. 1993. *The One, The Three and The Many, God, Creation and the Culture of Modernity.* New York: Cambridge University Press.

Gutierrez, Gustavo. 1973. *A Theology of Liberation.* Maryknoll, New York: Orbis Books.

———. 1983. *The Power of the Poor in History.* New York: Orbis Books.

Guthrie, Stan. 2000. *Missions in the Third Millennium: 21 Key Trends for the 21st Century.* Milton Keynes: Paternoster.

Hastings, Adrian. 1986. *A History of English Christianity 1920–2000.* London: SCM Press.

Hay, Rob, Valery Lim, Detlef Blocher, Jaap Ketelar and Sara Hay. 2007. *Worth Keeping: Global Perspectives on Best Practice in Missionary Retention.* Pasadena, California: William Carey Library.

Heaney, Sharon E. 2008. *Contextual Theology for Latin America: Liberation Themes in Evangelical Perspective.* Milton Keynes: Paternoster.

Hicks, Peter. 1998. *Evangelicals and Truth: A Creative Proposal for a Postmodern Age.* Leicester: Apollos.

Hirsch, Alan. 2006. *The Forgotten Ways.* Grand Rapids, Michigan: Strand Publishing.

Hiebert, Paul G. 1994. *Anthropological Reflections on Missiological Issues.* Grand Rapids, Michigan: Baker Books.

———. 1999. *Missiological Implications of Epistemological Shifts: Affirming Truth in a Modern/Postmodern World.* Harrisburg, Pennsylvania: Trinity Press International.

Henry, Carl F. H. and W. Stanley Mooneyham. 1967. *One Race, One Gospel, One Task: World Congress on Evangelism, Official Reference: Papers and Reports,* Volume II. Minneapolis, Minnesota: World Wide Publications.

Hesleam, S. Peter. 2002. *Globalization: Unravelling the New Capitalism.* Cambridge: Grove Books Limited.

Hoekendijk, Johannes C. 1966. *The Church Inside Out.* London: SCM Press.

Hoek, Marijke and Justin Thacker. 2008. *Micah's Challenge: The Church's Responsibility to the Global Poor.* Milton Keynes: Paternoster.

Hoke, Steve and William Taylor. 1999. *Send Me: Your Journey to the Nations.* Pasadena, California: World Evangelical Fellowship.

Howat, Irene and John Nicholl. 2003. *Streets Paved with Gold: The Story of the London City Mission.* Scotland: Christian Focus Publication Ltd.

Howe, John. 1977. *Our Anglican Heritage.* Fullerton, California: David C. Cook Publishing Co.

Hollenweger, Walter J. 1972. *The Pentecostals.* London: SCM Press.

Jenkins, Philip. 2002. *The Next Christendom: The Coming of Global Christianity.* New York: Oxford University Press.

———. 2006. *The New Faces of Christianity: Believing the Bible in the Global South.* New York: Oxford University Press.

Jewett, Paul K. 1991. *God, Creation and Revelation: A Neo-Evangelical Theology.* Grand Rapids, Michigan: Eerdmans Publishing Co.

Johnstone, Patrick and David Barret. 2002. *Operation World.* Korea: Joy Press.

Karkkainen, Veli Matti. 2002. *An Introduction to Ecclesiology.* Downers Grove, Illinois: Intervarsity Press.

Kerr, David and Kenneth Ross, eds. 2009. *Edinburgh 2010: Mission Then and Now.* Oxford: Regnum.

Kessler Jr., John. 1967. *A Study of the Older Protestant Missions and Churches in Peru and Chile,* With Special Reference to the Problems of Division, Nationalism and Native Ministry, Goes, Oosterbaan and Le Cointre.

Kimball, Don. 1987. *Power & Presence: A Theology of Relationships.* San Francisco: Harper & Row Publishers.

Kirk, Andrew. 1979. *Liberation Theology: An Evangelical View from the Third World.* London: Marshall, Morgan and Scott.

———. 1980. *Theology encounters revolution.* Leicester: InterVarsity Press.

———. 1983. *Theology and the Third World Church.* Downers Grove, Illinois: Intervarsity Press.

———. 1998. *The Meaning of Freedom: A Study of Secular, Muslim and Christian Views.* Carlisle, Cumbria: Paternoster Press.

———. 1999. *What is Mission?: Theological explorations.* London: Darton, Longman and Todd Ltd.

Kirk, Andrew and Kevin Vanhoozer, eds. 1999b. *To Stake a Claim: Mission and the Western Crisis of Knowledge: Mission and the Western Crisis of Knowledge.* Maryknoll, New York: Orbis Books.

Kirk, Andrew. 2006. *Mission under Scrutiny: Confronting Contemporary Challenges.* Minneapolis: Fortress Press.

Kraakevik, H. James and Dotsey Welliver. 1991. *Partners in the Gospel: The strategic role of partnership in world evangelization.* Wheaton, Illinois: Billy Graham Canter.

Krallmann, Gunter. 1992. *Mentoring for Mission: A Handbook on Leadership Principles Exemplified by Jesus Christ.* Hong Kong: Jensco Ltd.

Ladd, George E. 1959. *The Gospel of the Kingdom: Scriptural Studies in the Kingdom of God.* Grand Rapids, Michigan: Eerdmans Publishing Co.

———. 1974. A *Theology of the New Testament.* Grand Rapids, Michigan: Eerdmans Publishing Co.

———. 1966. *Jesus and the Kingdom: The Eschatology of Biblical Realism.* London: SPCK.

Lai, Patrick. 2005. *Tentmaking: The Life and Work of Business as Mission.* Colorado Springs: Authentic.

Lalive D'Epinay, Christian. 1977. *Haven to the Masses,* A Study of the Pentecostal Movement in Chile. London: Lutterworth.

Land, Steve J. 1993. *Pentecostal Spirituality: A Passion for the Kingdom.* Sheffield: Sheffield Academic Press.

Larkin Jr, William J. and Joel F. Williams, eds. 1998. *Mission in the New Testament: An Evangelical Approach.* Maryknoll, New York: Orbis Books.

Lash, Nicholas. 1992. *Believing Three Ways in One God: A Reading of the Apostles' Creed.* London: SCM Press.

Levine, Daniel H. ed. 1986. *Religion and Political Conflict in Latin America.* Chapel Hill, North Carolina: The University of North Carolina Press.

Lingenfelter, Sherwood G and Marvin K. Mayers. 1986. *Ministering Cross-Culturally: An Incarnational Model for Personal Relationships.* Grand Rapids, Michigan: Baker Academic.

Lingenfelter, Sherwood G. 2008. *Leading Cross-Culturally: Covenant Relationships for Effective Christian Leadership.* Grand Rapids, Michigan: Baker Academic.

Mackay, John. 2001. *The Other Spanish Christ: A Study in the Spiritual History of Spain and South America.* Eugene, Oregon: Wipf and Stock Publishers.

Marsden, George M. 1980. *Fundamentalism and American Culture: The Shaping of Twentieth-Century Evangelicalism 1879–1925.* New York: Oxford University Press.

———. 1991. *Understanding Fundamentalism and Evangelicalism.* Grand Rapids, Michigan: Eerdmans Publishing Co.

Martin, David. 1990. *Tongues of Fire: The Explosion of the Protestantism in Latin America.* Oxford: Blackwell.

McDonough, Daniel and Roger P. Peterson. 1999. *Can Short-Term Mission Really Create Long-Term Career Missionaries?: Results of STEM's Second Major Scientific Study on the Long-Term Effect of Short-Term Mission.* Minneapolis, Minnesota: STEMMinistires.

McDaniel, Charles. 2007. *God and Money: The Moral Challenges of Capitalism.* Lanham, Maryland: Rowman & Littlefield Publishers, Inc.

McFadyen, Alistair I. 1990. *The Call to Personhood: A Christian Theory of the Individual in Social Relationships.* Cambridge: Cambridge University Press.

McGrath, Alister and J. I Packer. 1993. *Matthew: The Crossway Classic Commentaries.* Wheaton, Illinois: Crossway Books.

McGrath, Alister. 1995. *Evangelicalism and the Future of Christianity.* Downers Grove, Illinois: Intervarsity Press.

———. 1999. *Christian Spirituality.* Oxford: Blackwell Publishing.

McIntosh, Stewart. 1986. *Una Introducción a la Misiología Latinoamericana.* Lima: Pucema.

———. 1993 *Siete Ensayos de la Realidad Misiológica.* Lima: Pucema.

Milne, Bruce. 1993. *The Message of John.* Leicester: IVP.

Migliore, L. Daniel. 1991. *Faith Seeking Understanding: An Introduction to Christian Theology.* Grand Rapids, Michigan: Eerdmans Publishing Co.

Miller, R. Daniel, ed. 1994. *Coming of Age: Protestantism in Contemporary Latin America.* London: University Press of America.

Mittelman, James H. 2000. *The Globalization Syndrome: Transformation and Resistance.* New Jersey: Princeton University Press.

Moltmann, Jurgen. 1965. *Theology of Hope.* London: SCM Press.

———. 1981. *The Trinity and the Kingdom of God.* London: SCM Press.

———. 1988. *The Trinity and the Kingdom of God.* London: SCM Press.

———. 1993. *The Church in the Power of the Spirit.* Minneapolis: Fortress Press.

Moltmann, Jurgen and Karl Josef Kuschel, eds. 1996. *Pentecostal Movements as an Ecumenical Challenge.* London: SCM Press.

Moreau, Scott and Mike O'Rear. 2002. "Missions Fund Raising", *Evangelical Mission Quarterly*, Vol. 38, (2): 236–240, April. Morton, Scott. 2007 Funding your Ministry. Colorado Springs: NavPress.

Motyer, Alec. 1984. *The Message of Philippians.* Nottingham: InterVarsity Press.

Murray, Ian H. 2000. *Evangelicalism Divided: A Record of Crucial Change in the Years 1950–2000.* Edinburgh: The Banner of Truth Trust.

Muskus, Eddy J. 2002. *The Origins and Early Development of Liberation Theology in Latin America.* Carlisle, Cumbria: Paternoster Press.

Neill, Stephen. 1952. *Christian Partnership.* London: SCM Press.

———. 1958. *Anglicanism.* Middlesex, England: Penguin Books.

Newbigin, Leslie. 1958. *One Body, One Gospel, One World.* London and New York: International Missionary Council.

———. 1986. *Foolishness to the Greeks: The Gospel and Western Cultures.* Geneva: World Council of Churches Publication.

———. 1988. *The Relevance of the Trinitarian Doctrine for Today's Mission.* London: Edinburgh House Press.

———. 1994. *A Word in Season: Perspectives on Christian Missions.* Grand Rapids, Michigan: Eerdmans Publishing Co.

———. 1995. *The Open Secret, An Introduction to the Theology of Mission.* London: SPCK.

Nida, Eugene. 1954. *Customs, Culture and Christianity.* London: The Tyndale Press.

———. 1968. *Religion Across Cultures: A Study in the Communication of Christian Faith.* New York: Harper and Row Publishers.

Niebuhr, Helmut Richard. 1928. *The Social Sources of denominationalism.* Cleveland, Ohio: The World Publishing Company.

———. 1951. *Christ and Culture.* New York: Harper & Row Publishers.

Niebuhr, Reinhold. 1947. (Edition 2005) *Moral Man and Immoral Society.* London: Continuum Impacts.

Nuñez, A. Emilio and William Taylor. 1989. *Crisis in Latin America, An Evangelical Perspective.* Chicago: Moody Press.

———. 1997. *Hacia una misiología evangélica Lationamericana.* Miami: UNILIT.

Ortiz, Manuel and Susan Baker, eds. 2002. *The Urban Face of Mission: Ministering the Gospel in a diverse and changing world.* Phillipsburg, New Jersey: P&R Publishing.

Packer, Jim and Tom Wright. 2008. *Anglican Evangelical Identity: Yesterday and Today*. London: The Latimer Trust.

Padilla, René, ed. 1976. *The New Face of Evangelicalism: An International Symposium on the Lausanne Covenant*. Downers Grove, Illinois: Intervarsity Press.

———. 1985. *Mission Between The Times: Essays on the Kingdom*. Grand Rapids, Michigan: Eerdmans Publishing Co.

Padilla, René and Chris Sugden, eds. 1985b. *How Evangelicals Endorsed Social Responsibility: Text on Evangelical Social Ethics 1975–83*. Nottingham: Grove Books Limited.

Padilla, René and Tetsunao Yamamori, eds. 2001. *Misión Integral y Pobreza*, CLADE IV, Congreso Latinoamericano de Evangelización, Consulta. Buenos Aires: Kairos Ediciones.

Paredes, Tito. 2000. *El Evangelio: Un Tesoro en Vasijas de Barro*, Perspectivas Antropológicas y Misiológicas de la relación entre el evangelio y la cultura. Buenos Aires: Kairos Ediciones.

Penney, John Michael. 1997. *The Missionary Emphasis of Lukan Pneumatology*. Sheffield: Sheffield Academic Press.

Peters, George W. 1972. *A Biblical Theology of Missions*. Chicago: Moody Press.

Peterson, Roger and Timothy D. Peterson. 1991. *Is Short-Term Mission Really Worth the Time and Money?: Advancing God's Kingdom Through Short-Term Mission*. Minneapolis, Minnesota: STEMMinistires.

Peterson, Roger; Gordon Aeschliman and R. Wayne Sneed. 2003. *Maximum Impact Short-Term Mission*. Minneapolis, Minnesota: STEMPress.

Phillips James M. and Robert T. Coote, eds. 1993. *Toward the 21st Century in Christian Mission*. Grand Rapids, Michigan: Eerdmans Publishing Co.

Prien, Jurgen Hans. 1978. *Die Geschichte des Christentums in Lateinamerika* (The History of Christendom in Latin America). Germany: Vandenhoeck and Ruprecht in Gottingen.

Pike, B. Fredrick. 1973. *Spanish America 1900–1970. Traditional and Social Innovation*. London: Thames and Hudson Ltd.

Phillips, James M. and Robert T. Coote, eds. 1993. *Toward the 21st Century in Christian Mission*. Grand Rapids, Michigan: Eerdmans Publishing Co.

Pocock, Michael, Gailyn Van Rheenen and Douglas McConnell, eds. 2005. *The Changing Face of World Missions: Engaging Contemporary Issues and Trends*. Grand Rapids, Michigan: Baker Academic.

Ramu, Shiva. 1997. *Strategic Alliances: Building Network Relationships for Mutual Gain*. New Dehi: Response Books.

Ravenhill, John. 2001. *APEC and the Construction of Pacific Rim Regionalism*. Cambridge: Cambridge University Press.

Reid, Michael. 2007. *Forgotten Continent: The Batle for Latin America's Soul*. London: Yale University Press.

Rickett, Daniel and Dotsey Welliver, eds. 1997. *Supporting of Indigenous Ministries*. Wheaton, Illinois: Billy Graham Center.

Rickett, Daniel and Omar Gava. 2005. *Alianzas Estratégicas*. Buenos Aires: Kairos.

Rundle, Steve and Tom Steffen. 2003. *Great Commission Companies: The Emerging Role of Business in Mission*. Downers Grove, Illinois: Intervarsity Press.

Russell, Letty M. 1979. *The Future of Partnership*. Philadelphia: The Westminster Press.

Sampson, Philip; Vinay Samuel and Chris Sugden. 1994. *Faith and Modernity*. Oxford: Regnum Books International.

Saracco, Norberto. 1992. *La Nueva Religiosidad Evangélica: La Comunidad en que Vivo*. Avila Mariano Editor. Miami: FLET.

Schirrmacher, Thomas. 2000. *Hope for Europe: 66 Theses*. Kothen, Germany: VTR.

Schreiter, Robert J. 1985. *Constructing Local Theologies*. Maryknoll, New York: Orbis Books.

———. 2004. *The New Catholicity: Theology between the Global and the Local*. Maryknoll, New York: Orbis Books.

Schumpeter, Joseph. 1939. *Business Cycles: A Theoretical, Historical and Statistical Analysis of Capitalist Process*. New York: Mc Graw-Hill.

Segundo, Juan L. 1976. *The Liberation of Theology*. Dublin: Gill and Macmillan.

Stagich, Timothy. 2001. *Collaborative Leadership and Global Transformation*. Miami Beach, Florida: Global Leadership Resources.

Stanley, Brian. 1990. *The Bible and the Flag: Protestant Missions and British Imperialism in the Nineteenth and Twentieth Century*. Leicester: Apollos.

Steffen, Tom and Mike Barnett, eds. 2006. *Business as Mission: From Impoverished to Empowered*. Pasadena, California: William Carey Library.

Stoll, David. 1990. *Is Latin America Turning Protestant? The Politics of Evangelical Growth*. Oakland, California: University of California Press.

Stott, John. 1992. *The Contemporary Christian*. Leicester: IVP.

———. 1994. *Issues Facing Christians Today*. Grand Rapids, Michigan: Zondervan.

———, ed. 1996. *Making Christ Known: Historic Mission Documents from the Lausanne Movement 1974–1989*. Carlisle, Cumbria: Paternoster Press.

Taber, Charles. 2003. *The World is too much with us: 'Culture' in Modern Protestant Mission*. Macon, Georgia: Mercer University Press.

Taylor, William, ed. 1994. *Kingdom Partnerships for Synergy in Missions*. Pasadena, California: William Carey Library.

———, ed. 2000. *Global Missiology for the 21ˢᵗ Century: The Iguassu Dialogue*. Grand Rapids, Michigan: Baker Academic.

Tjorhom, Ola. 2004. *Visible Church-Visible Unity: Ecumenical Ecclesiology and "The Great Tradition of the Church"*. Collegeville, Minnesota: Liturgical Press.

Thomas, Norman, ed. 1995. *Reading in World Mission*. London: SPCK.

Thomas, Griffith W.H. 1978. *The Principles of Theology*. London: Vine Books Ltd.

Tippet, Alan. 1987. *Introduction to Missiology*. Pasadena, California: William Carey Library.

Tiplady, Richard, ed. 2003a. *One World or Many?: The Impact of Globalization on Mission*. Pasadena, California: William Carey Library.

———. 2003b. *World of Difference: Global Mission at the Pic 'N' Mix Counter*. Carlisle, Cumbria: Paternoster Press.

Tizon, Al. 2008. *Transformation after Lausanne: Radical Evangelical Mission in Global Local Perspective*. Oxford: Regnum.

Van Engen, Charles. 1996. *Mission on the Way: Issues in Mission Theology*, Grand Rapids, Michigan: Baker Books.

Van Engen, Charles, Dean S. Gilliland and Paul Pierson, eds. 1999. *The Good News of the Kingdom: Mission Theology for the Third Millennium*. Eugene, Oregon: Wipf and Stock Publishers.

Vinay, Samuel and Chris Sugden, eds. 2009. *Mission as Transformation: A Theology of the Whole Gospel*. Eugene, Oregon: Wipf and Stock.

Visser 't Hooft, Willen A. ed. 1962. *The New Delhi Report: The Third Assembly of the World Council of Churches 1961*. London: SCM Press.

Volf, Miroslav. 1998. *After Our Likeness: The Church as the Image of the Trinity*. Grand Rapids, Michigan: Eerdmans Publishing Co.

Walls, Andrew. 1996. *The Missionary Movement in Christian History: Studies in the Transmission of the Faith*. New York: Orbis Books.

———. 2002. *The Cross-Cultural Process in Christian History*. London: T&T Clark International.

Walls, Andrew and Cathy Ross. 2008. *Mission In The 21ˢᵗ Century: Exploring the Five Marks of Global Mission*. Maryknoll, New York: Orbis Books.

Wallstrom, Timothy C. 1980. *The Creation of a Student Movement to Evangelize the Wold*. Pasadena, California: William Carey International Press.
Warner, Rob. 2007. *Reinventing English Evangelicalism, 1966–2001*. Milton Keynes: Paternoster.
Warren, Max. 1956. *The Study of an Idea*. London: SCM Press.
———. 1964. *Perspective in Mission*. London: Hodder and Stoughton.
———. 1967. *Social History and Christian Mission*. London: SCM Press.
West, Charles C. 1999. *Power, Truth and Community in Modern Culture*. Harrisburg, Pennsylvania: Trinity Press International.
Wink, Walter. 1984. *Naming the Powers: Language of Power in the New Testament*. Philadelphia: Fortress Press.
———., 1986. *Unmasking the Powers: The Invisible Forces That Determine Human Existence*. Philadelphia: Fortress Press.
———. 1992. *Engaging the Powers: Discernment and Resistance in a World of Domination*. Philadelphia: Fortress Press.
Whitehead, D. James and Whitehead, Evelyn. 1991. *The Promise of Partnership, A Model for Collaborative Ministry*. New York: Harper San Francisco.
Winter, Ralph and Steven C. Hawthorne, ed. 1981 Perspectives on the World Christian Movement. Pasadena, California: William Carey Library.
Winters, L. Alan. 1985. *International Economics*, Third Edition. London: George Allen and Unwin Publlishers Ltd.
Wright, Christopher J. H. 2006. *The Mission of God: Unlocking the Bible's Grand Narrative*. Downers Grove, Illinois: IVP Academic.
Wright, Walter C. 2000. *Relational Leadership: A Biblical Model for Leadership Service*. Carlisle, Cumbria: Paternoster.
Wong, James; Peter Larson and Edward Pentecost. 1973. *Mission from the Third World*. Singapore: Church Grow Study Center.
Yamamori, Tetsunao and Kenneth A. Eldred, eds. 2003. *On Kingdom Business: Transforming Missions Through Entrepreneurial Strategies*. Wheaton, Illinois: Crossway Books.
Yates, Timothy. 1978. *Venn and Victorian Bishops Abroad: The Missionary Policies of Henry Venn and their Repercussions upon the Anglican Episcopate of the Colonial Period 1841–1872*. London: SPCK.
———. 1994. *Christian Mission in the Twentieth Century*. Cambridge: Cambridge University.
Young, Amos and Peter Heltzel, eds. 2004. *Theology in Global Context, Essays in Honor of Robert Cummings Neville*. New York: T&T Clark International.

Zizioulas, John D. 1985. *Being as Communion: Studies in Personhood and the Church*. Yonkers, New York: SVS Press.

Zysman, John and Schwartz. 1998. *Enlarging Europe: The Industrial Foundations of a New Political Reality*. California: International and Area Studies IAS.

Journals, articles, bulletins and magazines

Badham, Paul. 2008. "Liberal Anglicanism: A Rational Approach to Theological Interpretation." Anglicanism: Essays in History, Beliefs and Practice, *Trivium* 38, Journal of the University of Wales, Lampeter, Trivium Publications, 57–70.

Befus, David. 2002. "Kingdom Business: A New Frontier in Missions." *Evangelical Mission Quarterly* 38 (2): 204–209, April.

Bertuzzi, Federico. 2006. "Thousands Attend COMIBAM Congress." Lausanne Connecting, Point, December, http://www.lausanne.org/lausanne-connecting-point/2006-december.html#5 (Online, accessed 12 November 2008 at 8:22 am).

Brierley, Peter. 2004. "Evangelicals in the World of the 21st Century." Article for 2004 Forum on World Evangelization (3 May): 1–22, http://www.lausanne.org/documents/2004forum/LCWEvangelicals.pdf (Online, accessed 20 January 2009 at 11:20 pm).

Bogosian, Phil. 1997. "The Regional Consultation for Adopt-A People Coordinators San Salvador, February 4–6, 1997 Lays the Foundation for Thousands of New Adoptions by Latin Churches." *Mission Frontiers*, May/June 1997, http://www.missionfrontiers.org/1997/0506/mj9714.htm (Online, accessed on 20 October 2008 at 10:10 pm).

Bradford, Tolly. 2007. "Networking: Global Perspective on Nineteenth Century British Mission." *Missiology* XXXV (4): 375–380, October.

Bush, Luis. 1999. A Church for Every People and the Gospel for Every Person by AD 2000, Luis Bush, Bibliographical Information Sheet, http://www.ad2000.org/staff/luis.htm (Online, accessed on 20 October 2008 at 3:25 pm).

Campos, Bernardo. 2008. "Renovacion del Liderazgo y Hermeneutica del Espiritu." *Cyberjournal for Pentecostal-Charismatic research*, http://pctii.org/cyberj/cyberj13/bernado.html (online, accessed on 18 October 2008 at 4:35 pm).

Campbell, William S. 2008. "Unity and Diversity in the Church: Transformed Identities and the Peace of Christ in Ephesians." *Transformation, An International Journal of Holistic Mission Studies* 25 (1): 15–25, January.

Cartledge, Mark J. 2008. "Pentecostal Theological Method and Intercultural Theology." *Transformation, An International Journal of Holistic Mission Studies* 25 (2–3): 92–100, April/July.

Crew, Willie. 1997. "GCOWE '97 (Global Consultation on World Evangelization) Pretoria, South Africa, June 30–5 July, 1997." *Mission Frontiers*, May/June, http://www.missionfrontiers.org/1997/0506/mj973.htm (Online, accessed on 12 November 2008 at 7:10 pm).

Danaher, James. 2008. "Our Journey into the Truth, Beauty and Holiness of the Gospel." *Evangelical Review of Theology* 32 (1): 56–64, January.

Davies, Paul. 2004. "Preparing and Supporting Latin Americans in Mission", papers presented at Global Connections Latin American Forum, London, November, 1–7, http://www.globalconnections.co.uk/OneStopCMS/Core/CrawlerResourceServer.aspx?resource=617dcc5024e444f5b8484cec6fb0edf8&mode=link&guid=f1ea183341bc40f39f09db80fb5dceb7 (Online, accessed on 17 October 2008 at 2:35 pm).

Daugherty, Kevin. 2007. "Missio Dei: The Trinity and Christian Missions." *Evangelical Review of Theology* 31 (2): 151–168, April.

Day, Juliette. 2008. "Liturgical Anglicanism: Contemporary Worship in an Historical Context." Anglicanism: Essays in History, Beliefs and Practice, *Trivium* 38, Journal of the University of Wales, Lampeter, Trivium Publications, 130–136.

"El Parlamento Europeo aprueba la nueva directiva de inmigración", email from MINKA NEWS intermediatv@btconnect.com, (Received on 18 June 2008 at 1:26 pm).

Engelsviken, Tormod. 2003. "Missio Dei: The understanding and misunderstanding of a theological concept in European churches and missiology." *International Review of Mission* XCII (367): 481–497.

Flett, John. 2009. "Missio Dei: A Trinitarian Envisioning of a Non-Trinitarians Theme." *Missiology*, no. 1, (January): 5–17.

Fretz, Glenn. 2002. "Towards interdependence ministry Partnership." *Missiology* 38 (2): 212–218, April.

Girón, Rodolfo. 2000. "The Latin American Missionary Movement: A New Paradigm in Missions", http://www.ad2000.org/celebrate/giron.htm (Online, accessed on 13 November 2008 at 12:05 pm).

Global Connections. 2001. Teaching English for foreign language, current issues in TEFL and global mission's paper given on 28 March, http://www.globalconnections.co.uk/resources/missionissues/topic/strategies/TEFL.htm (Online, accessed on 20 January 2009 at 12:45 pm).

Guder, Darell. 2009. "Missio Dei: Integrating Theological Formulation for Apostolic Vocation." *Missiology* XXXVII (1): 63–73, January.

Hein, Martin. 2003. "That the World might be saved through Him: Opening worship and meditation on John 3:17." *International Review of Mission* XCII (367): 478–480, October.

Heller, Karin. 2009 "Missio Dei: Envisioning an Apostolic Practical Theology." *Missiology* XXXVII (1): 47–60, January.

Henzel, Jan. 2008. "From Discord to Concord." *European Journal of Theology* XVII (1): 13–17.

Hemphill, Kenneth. 2007. "Nurturing Biblical Fellowship", Baptist Press, News with a Christian Perspective, Posted on May 15 2007, http://www.bpnews.net/BPFirstPerson.asp?ID=25657 (Accessed on 15 February 2008).

Hoedemaker, Ber. 1995. "The Legacy of J. C. Hoekendijk." *International Bulletin of Missionary Research* 19 (4): 166–170, October.

Hong-Jung, Lee. 2002. "Beyond Partnership, Towards Networking: A Korean Reflection on Partnership in the Web of God's Mission." *International Review of Mission* XCI (363): 580–581, October.

Kay, William K. 2008. "Apostolic Networks in Britain: An Analytic Overview." *Transformation, An International Journal of Holistic Mission Studies* 25 (1): 32–41, January.

Kiefer, James E. Biographical sketches of memorable Christian of the past: "Alban, first martyr of Britain", http://www.justus.anglican.org/resources/bio/189.html (Online, accessed on 16 January 2009 at 11:10 am).

Knell, Bryan. 2001. *Structure and Strategy*, Global Connections, UK, http://www.globalconnections.co.uk/findresources/missionissues/topic/UKchurch/churchmission.htm.

———. 2001. "How to Encourage World Mission", London, Administry Guide.

Laing, Mark. 2009. "Missio Dei: Some Implications for the Church", *Missiology* XXXVII (1): 89–98, January.

Matthey, Jacques. 2002. *Grenzenlos – Boundless, 50th anniversary of the World Mission Conference, Mission Festival and Congress, August 16–21, 2002 Willingen, Congress 'Missio Dei' God's Mission Today: Summary and Conclusion, Reflectors' report*, pp 1–8, online at http://www.wcc-coe.org/wcc/what/mission/willingen.html (accessed 19 October 2007).

Miller, David L. 1997. *Christianity Today.com Outreach and Evangelism Today*, 7 December, http://www.christianitytoday.com/outreach/articles/missionmindedlatinos.html (Online, accessed 20 October 2008 at 1:55 pm).

Minor, Okuyama. 2002. "The Answer is Mt. 10:23" (173–175). The Fifth Asia Church Leaders Conference on Evangelism, ALCOE V 2002 Partnership in the Gospel: The Lausanne Movement in the 21ˢᵗ Century Asia, 26–29 August 2002, Seoul Presbyterian Church, Seoul, Korea.

Niles, Preman. 2002. *Toward the fullness of life*: *Intercontextual relationships in mission: Report from a missiology consultation.* London, 14–19 April, 2002 (Online, accessed 19 October 2007).

Oliver, Simon. 2008. "Catholic Anglicanism: The Development of a Tradition." Anglicanism: Essays in History, Beliefs and Practice, *Trivium* 38, Journal of the University of Wales, Lampeter, Trivium Publications, 39–56.

Oxbrow, Mark. 2008. Article *What do the Mission Agencies do?* http://www.pwm-web.org.uk/features/article1.shtml (accessed 19 April 2008 at 3:50 pm).

———. 2009. "Anglicans and Reconciling Mission: An Assessment of Two Anglican International Gatherings." *International Bulletin of Missionary Research* 33 (1): 9–10, January.

Padilla, René and Chris Sugden, eds. 1985. *Text on Evangelical Social Ethics 1974–1993,* Grove Booklet on Ethics no. 58, Bramcote, Nottingham: Grove Books Limited.

"Partners in Mission: The Practice and the Promise" *Council for World Mission, Live the Good News*, Monday 7 January 2008, http://server.cwmission.org/statements/partners-in-mission-the-practice-and-the promise.html (Accessed 11 July 2008 at 12:30 pm).

PM International 2006 *Catalogo de Oportunidandes*, Revista anual.

Presler, Titus. 2009. "The Impact of the Sexuality Controversy on Mission: The case of the Episcopal Church in the Anglican Communion." *International Bulletin of Missionary Research* 33 (1): 16, January.

Priest, Robert J. and Joseph Paul Priest. 2008. "They see everything, and understand nothing": Short Term Mission and Service Learning. *Missiology* XXXVI (1): 53–73, January.

Quicaña, Fernando. 1997. "La Realidad de las Sociedades Indigenas" in *Las Misiones Latinas Para el Siglo XXI*, COMIBAM, 130–131.

"Revista Digital INTEGRALIDAD del CEMAA", integralidad@cemaa.org, 4º Edición (Electronic Magazine received on 2 August 2008).

Rosendal, Østergaard Lise and Joel Nielsen. "To Network or not to Network: NGO Experiences with Technical Networks" http://www.intrac.org/docs/To%20network%20or%20not%20to%20network.doc (Accessed 14 June 2008 at 8:20 am).

Rowe, Jonathan Y. 2009. "Dancing with Elephants: Accountability in Cross-Cultural Christian Partnership." *Missiology: An International Review* XXXVII (2): 149–159, April.

Saracco, Norberto. 1988. Charismatic Renewal and Social Change: A Historical Analysis from a Third World Perspective. *Transformation: An International Journal of Holistic Mission Studies* 5 (4): 14.

Scopes, Barrie. 2008. "A Journey Towards Partnership." *Council for World Mission,* 30 January, http://server.cwmission.org/academic-papers/a-journey-towards-partnership-3.html, (Accessed 11 July 2008 at 12:15 pm).

Scheffler, Marcia. 2008. "Partnership and Participation in a Northern Church–Southern Church Relationship." *Transformation, An International Journal of Holistic Mission Studies* 25 (4): 255–270, October.

Seng-Kong, Tan. 2004. "A Trinitarian Ontology of Missions." *International Review of Mission* 93 (369): 279–296.

Santoso, Iman. 2002. "Networks and the Great Commission" (169–172). The Fifth Asia Church Leaders Conference on Evangelism, ALCOE V 2002 Partnership in the Gospel: The Lausanne Movement in the 21st Century Asia, 26–29 August 2002, Seoul Presbyterian Church, Seoul, Korea.

Share: The magazine of the South American Society, 10, Issue 1, winter 2008. http://www.samsgb.org/eventsandresources/documents/share08is1.pdf (Accessed 27 February 2008 at 10:35 pm).

Steuernagel, Valdir. 1995. "Social Concern and Evangelization: The Journey of the Lausanne Movement." *International Bulletin of Missionary Research 1991* 15 (2): 53–56, April.

Stott, John. 1995. "Twenty Years After Lausanne: Some Personal Reflections." *International Bulletin of Missionary Research* 19 (2): 50–55, April.

Sunqist, Scott. 2009. "Missio Dei: Christian History Envisioned as Cruciform Apostolicity." *Missiology* XXXVII (1): 33–45, January.

Taylor, R. Barry. 2007. "Culture since 1985." *Missiology* XXXV (2): 145–156, April.

Turner, Max. 2007. "Human Reconciliation in the New Testament with Special Reference to Philemon, Colossians and Ephesians." *European Journal of Theology* XV (1): 37–45.

Wagner, Ross. 2009. "Missio Dei: Envisioning an Apostolic Reading of Scripture." *Missiology* XXXVII (1): 19–30, January.

Walls, Andrew. *Papers from Towards 2010, Carrying the Gospel to all the non-Christian World, The Great Commission* 1910–2010, online at http://www.

towards2010.org.uk/downloads/t2010paper01walls.pdf (Accessed 17 April 2008 at 11:00 pm).
Wickeri, L. Philip. 2004. "Mission from the Margins." *International Review of Mission* 93 (369): 182–198.
Windrem, Robert. 2005. "No Evidence al-Qaida knew of Madrid plot." *NBC News*, msnbc, http://www.msnbc.msn.com/id/7158191/ (accessed 17 May 2008 at 7:20 pm).
Winter, Ralph. 1998. Report from Brazil: COMIBAM'87 The Meeting of the Century, *Mission Frontiers, The Bulletin of the U.S. Center for World Mission*, 1–4 http://www.missionfrontiers.org/1988/01/j883.htm (Accessed 20 October 2008 at 9:10 am).
Yates, Nigel. 2008. "Historical Anglicanism: Changes in the Concept of a Via Media." Anglicanism: Essays in History, Beliefs and Practice *Trivium* 38, Journal of the University of Wales, Lampeter, Trivium Publications, 1.

General information on internet

Asia-Pacific Economic Cooperation (APEC), (http://www.apec.org/apec/about_apec.html (Accessed on 11 September 2009 at 9:52 pm).
Asia-Pacific Economic Cooperation (APEC), "20th APEC Ministerial Meeting began today in Lima." Living in Peru.com, http://www.livinginperu.com/news/7873 (Accessed on 11 September 2009 at 10:05 pm).
Adam Matthew Publications: Imaginative publishers of research collections http://www.adam-matthewpublications.co.uk/collections_az/RBMU4/description.aspx_
http://www.adam-matthew-publications.co.uk/aboutus/index.aspx_(Online, accessed on 24 September 2008 at 12:55 pm).
Brown, Caroline. 2001. Adam Matthew Publications, Imaginative Publishers of Research Collections. http://www.adam-matthew-publications.co.uk/digital_guides/regions_beyond_missionary_union_parts_1_to_5/rbmu-archival-history.aspx?h=Caroline%20Brown (Accessed on 12 August 2008 at 1:30 pm).
Business as Mission Resource Centre *YWAM Connect*, Papers and Articles, https://www.ywamconnect.com/ubasicpage.jsp?siteid=29315&pageid=349942 (Online, accessed on 7 April 2009 at 11:49 pm).
Compassion International, http://www.compassion.com/about/aboutus.htm (Online, accessed on 14 April 2009 at 10:10 pm).

Dorward, David, http://www.adam-matthew-publications.co.uk/collections_az/rbmu-2/description.aspx?h=RBMU (online, accessed on 3 October 2008 at 2:45 pm).

Ekstrom, Bertil 2000 "El Espiritu De COMIBAM", Ponenecias de la Asamblea Internacional de COMIBAM: Lima, Peru, Noviembre, http://www.comibam.org/ponencias/lima/ponencia2.htm (Online, accessed 21 November 2008 at 3:20 pm).

Fair Trade Organization, http://www.minkafairtrade.com/home.html (Online, accessed on 27 February 2009 at 11:25 pm).

Faith2Share, http://www.faith2share.net/AboutUs/tabid/132/Default.aspx (Online, accessed on 26 March 2009 at 11:10 pm).

Global Connections 2004 Latin American "Forum, Focus on Peru", Missionary Activity http://www.globalconnections.co.uk/Resources/Global%20Connections/Mission%20Issues/2006/Peru.pdf (Online, accessed 20 January2009 at 3:05 pm).

Harris, Pat. 2008. SAMS' President declaration to merge CMS and SAMS, 29 November 2008, SAMS Great Britain General Council, http://www.samsgb.org/news.html#newsitem8 (Accessed on 30 March 2009 at 5:30 pm).

Habitat for Humanity International, http://www.habitat.org/eca/how/about_us.aspx (Online, accessed on 7 April 2009 at 11:10 am).

Habitat for Humanity International (HFHI), http://www.habitat.org/intl/eca/81.aspx (Online, accessed on 7 April 2009 at 11:25 am)

History of the Micah Network. http://en.micahnetwork.org/about_micah_network/history (online, accessed on 25 February 2009 at 8:10 pm).

Hyperdictionary. http://www.hyperdictionary.com/dictionary/reciprocity (Online, accessed on 2 March 2009 at 2:10 pm).

INTR 532. http://www.wheaton.edu/intr/Moreau/courses/532/biblio/theolatam.htm. Information relevant themes.

Keswick Convention. http://www.keswickconvention.ca/2009_pg6.htm (Online, accessed on 30 January 2009 at 11:05 pm).

K12 Academics. http://www.k12academics.com/england_name_origin.htm (Online, accessed on 29 January 2009 at 10:30 am).

Londononline. http://www.londononline.co.uk/boroughs/ (Online, accessed on 16 December 2008 at 1:51 pm).

Martin, John. 2009. CMS Head of Communication, announced Trustees of CMS voted to integrate CMS with SAMS, special general meeting held in Oxford on 20 January. http://www.cmsuk.org/Default.aspx?tabid=151&articleId=1277&articleType=ArticleView&SkinSrc=%5bG%5dSkin

s%2f_default%2fNo+Skin&ContainerSrc=%5bG%5dContainers%2f_default%2fNo+Container (Online, accessed on 30 March 2009 at 3:46 pm).

Mendell, Henry. Papus iv 21–25 on Archimedes' spiral, http://www.calstatela.edu/faculty/hmendel/Ancient%20Mathematics/Pappus/Bookiv/Pappus.iv.21-25/ Pappus.iv.21_25.html (Online accessed on 25 February 2009 at 11:20 am).

Ministry Watch.com. http://www.ministrywatch.com/profile/Operation-Mobilization.aspx (Online, accessed on 26 March 2009 at 10:45 pm).

Moments in Life 2011. "Ten Amazing Lessons You Can Learn From Albert Einstein", http://walli.dk/?p=297 (Online, accessed on 7 May 2007 at 10:45 am).

MSN Encarta. United Kingdom http://uk.encarta.msn.com/encyclopedia_761553483/United_Kingdom.html (Online, accessed on 13 January 2009 at 10:10 am).

Mission for the Third Millennium. misiontercermilenio.org (Accessed on 15 June 2009 at 5:45 am).

Mundus, Gateway to Missionary Collections in the UK, http://www.mundus.ac.uk/cats/3/1229.htm (Online, accessed on 10 August 2008 at 12:40 pm).

NEWS BBC. "Channel, Profile: Mercosur-Common Market of the South", http://news.bbc.co.uk/1/hi/world/americas/5195834.stm (Accessed on 16 June 2009 at 10:55 am)

OC International. http://www.onechallenge.org/ (Online, accessed on 3 December 2008 at 8:40 pm).

OMF History. http://www.omf.org/omf/uk/about_omf/omf_cim_history (Accessed on 29 November 2009 at 10:28 am).

Rees Mogg, William. 2009. Mail Online, "How China's millions can save the West", on 7 March 2009, http://www.dailymail.co.uk/debate/article-1160180/WILLIAM-REES-MOGG-How-Chinas-millions-save-West.html?ITO=1490 (Accessed on 17 June 2009 at 11:40 pm).

Robbins, W. John. "The Biblical View of Truth", 240–241, February and March 2005, http://www.trinityfoundation.org/PDF/240-241-BiblicalViewofTruth.pdf (online, accessed on 9 March 2009 at 8:10 am).

Scott, Carlos. "Praying for COMIBAM", http://www.comibam.org/docs/prayforcomibam_001.pdf (Online, accessed on 12 November 2008 at 10:30 am).

Spring Harvest, http://www.springharvest.org/main-event-sh/category_index.php?id=6 (Online, accessed on 13 January 2009 at 7:10 pm).

Segadores Mission. "Alcanzando a los no Alcanzados", http://segadoresperu.com/index.php?page=home (Accessed on 6 April 2009 at 10:31 pm).

SIM, Serving in Mission. http://www.sim.co.uk/where_we_work/south_america (Online, accessed on 5 October 2011 at 10:28 am).

Smitheram, Michael. "Consensus-Driven Christians: The G8, the World Summit and How Understanding Integral Mission is Inspiring Evangelical Christians to Advocate with the Poor." This article first appeared in '*The Lausanne World Pulse*' magazine, Sept 2005, http://www.micahchallenge.org/uploaded_docs/BTHW/Consensus-driven%20 Christians .doc (Online, accessed 12 March 2009 at 10:20 am).

Tearfund. http://www.tearfund.org/About+us/default.htm (Online, accessed on 15 April 2009 at 2:50 pm).

The Alpha Course. http://uk.alpha.org/ (Online, accessed on 13 January 2009 at 7:35 pm).

The Commonwealth@60, "United Kingdom History", http://www.thecommonwealth.org/YearbookInternal/145192/history/ (Online, accessed 19 January 2009 at 2:20 pm).

The Commonwealth, Directgov, Public services all in one, http://www.direct.gov.uk/en/Governmentcitizensandrights/UKgovernment/TheUKandtheworld/DG_073421?cids=Google_PPC&cre=Government_Citizens_Rights (Online, accessed 19 January 2009 at 2:48 pm).

The Keswick Conference Centre. http://www.keswick.org/estdetails.asp?id=1950615361 (Online accessed on 13 January 2009 at 5:14 pm).

The Muswell Hill Website. http://www.muswell-hill.com/index2.htm (Online, accessed on 16 December 2008 at 1:45 pm).

The Proclamation Trust, "The History of the Proclamation Trust", http://www.proctrust.org.uk/about/history.htm (Accessed on13 January 2009 at 8:10 pm).

Thesaurus.com http://thesaurus.reference.com/browse/authority (Online, accessed on 5 February 2009 at 1:45 pm).

University of Notre Dame, Latin Dictionary and Grammar Aid. http://www.archives.nd.edu/cgi-bin/lookit.pl?latin=mutuus (Accessed on 2 August 2010 at 11:20 am).

Verweij, Marco "Towards a Theory of Constrained Relativism: Comparing and Combining the Work of Pierre Bourdieu, Mary Douglas and Michael Thompson, and Alan Fiske." *Sociological Research online,* http://www.socresonline.org.uk/12/6/7.html (online, accessed on 2 March 2009 at 3:20 pm).

Unión de Iglesias Cristianas Evangélicas del Perú (UNICEP), http://www.unicep.org.pe/historia.php, (Online, accessed on 27 October 2008 at 12:45 pm).

Viva Network. http://www.viva.org/?page_id=53 (Accessed on 3 March 2009 at 12:20 pm).

Wolfram MathWorld, Archimedes' spiral http://mathworld.wolfram.com/ArchimedesSpiral.html (Online, accessed on 25 February 2009 at 11:40 am).

World Evangelical Alliance-Leadership Institute (WEA-LI), http://weali.org/tiki-index.php?page=about+wea-li (Accessed on 30 June 2009 at 6:10 pm).

Wycliffe Global Alliance. http://www.wycliffe.net/AboutUs/ANewName/tabid/99/language/en/Default.aspx (Online, accessed on 4 October 2011 at 10:30 pm).

YWAM History. http://www.ywam.org/contents/abo_his_1960.htm (Online, accessed on 26 March 2009 at 10:20 pm)

YWAM International. http://www.ywam.org/Default.asp?bhcp=1 (Online, accessed on 26 March 2009 at 10:01 pm).

Dictionaries

Anderson, H. Gerald et al. 1994. *Mission Legacies.* Maryknoll, New York: Orbis Book.

Anderson, Gerald H., ed. 1998. *Biographical Dictionary of Christian Mission.* Grand Rapids, Michigan: Eerdmans Publishing Co.

Burges, Stanley M., ed. 2002. *The New International Dictionary of Pentecostal and Charismatic Movements.* Grand Rapids, Michigan: Zondervan.

Coenen, Lothar; Erich Beyreuther and Hans Bietenhard. 1980. *Diccionario Teológico Del Nuevo Testamento* vol. II. Salamanca: Sigueme.

———. 1980. *Diccionario Teológico del Nuevo Testamento* vol. IV. Salamanca: Sigueme.

Corrie, John, ed. 2007. *Dictionary of Mission Theology: Evangelical Foundations.* Nottingham: IVP.

Moreau, A. Scott, ed. 2000. *Evangelical Dictionary of World Missions.* Grand Rapids, Michigan: Baker Books.

MSN encarta Dictionary, http://uk.encarta.msn.com/dictionary_1861723633/interface.html (Online, accessed on 31 March 2009 at 6:15 pm).

Soanes, Catherine and Sara Hawker. 2005. *Oxford English Dictionary.* Oxford: Oxford University Press.

The Free Dictionary: http://encyclopedia.thefreedictionary.com/Godhead+(Christianity (Accessed 07 December 2007, at 10:15 am).

Young, Robert. 1977. (Eight edition) *Analytical Concordance to the Bible.* Guilford and London: United Society for Christian Literature, Lutherworth Press.

Web Dictionary.Co.uk, http://www.webdictionary.co.uk/definition.php?query=network (Accessed 14 February 2008).

Bible

New International Version. 1960. Nashville, Tennessee: Broadman and Holman Publishers.

APPENDIX 1

Three Basic Models of Mission

The Traditional Model

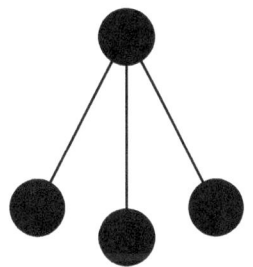

Structured, uni-directional, specialized

The Networking Model

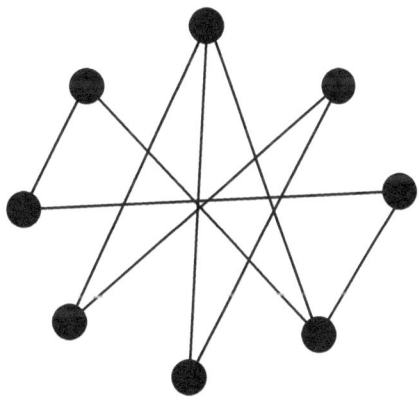

Orientational multidirectional, relational

The Emergent Model

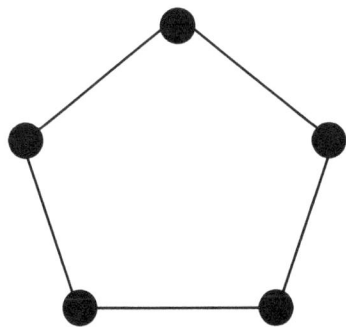

Flexible, bipolar, autonomous

APPENDIX 2

Latin Link Roots and History[1]

1855	Dr. Robert Reid Kalley, known as the 'wolf from Scotland' by Catholics, arrives with his wife Sarah in Rio de Janeiro, Brazil, and they become the first Protestant missionaries, starting a mission in the city of Petropolis in 1856.
1873	Henry Grattan Guiness founds the 'East London Training Institute for Home and Foreign Missions', in Stepney Green, Clapham, London.
1892	Formation of the 'Help for Brazil Mission' by Sara Kelley with Hudson Taylor of CIM as advisor to the new mission.
1895	The Canadian 'South American Evangelical Mission' was founded as a result of a book written by Lucy Guiness. They sent missionaries to Argentina and Brazil.
1899	The East London Training Institute, changed its name to Regions Beyond Missionary Union, and continues as Halcr Colleges to train missionaries.
1901	RMBU starts work in India.
1903	The Colleges of Union trained 1168 people, working in different places: Australia and New Zealand, 26; North and Central America, 170; Europe, 233 (177 in the UK); Asia, 182 (103 in China), Africa, 215 (96 in Congo); and Further Training 61.[2]

---

1. Data from the Latin Link Banner History sent to the author by Marcel Durst from Switzerland 8 September 2008.
2. Data from Adam Matthew Publications (Online 24 September 2008).

1907	The Bolivian Indian Mission, later known as 'Andes Evangelical Mission' was founded by the New Zealander George Allan in Bolivia to minister the Quechuas.
1908	RMBU has registered 91 missionaries in the mission field.
1910	The Edinburgh World Mission Conference decided that Latin America does not need missionaries, by interpreting that it is an evangelized continent. In response to the Edinburgh 1910, RMBU passes responsibilities for all its South American work over to the newly founded mission EUSA.
1911	The Evangelical Union of South America (EUSA) was founded on 9 May with 13 RBMU missionaries from Argentina and 18 from the South American Evangelical Mission (SAEM). A little later 19 missionaries from the RBUM-Peru also join EUSA. Harry and Susan Strachan, both recruits of Harley Colleges working at that time in Argentina, became charter members of the new mission EUSA.
1913	The mission 'The Help for Brazil Mission' joined EUSA.
1916	Ann Soper (and Rhod Gould), graduate of women's Training Center of Harley Colleges, leaves for Peru as an independent missionary to set up a mission base in the area of Lamas.
1920	Stuart McNairn became the first EUSA executive secretary, and Dr Campell Morgan its first president.
1921	On 24 July, Harry and Susan Strachan founded the 'Latin American Evangelization Campaign' (LAEC), which later became the 'Latin American Mission' (LAM).
1932	Ann Soper founded the Peru Inland Mission.
1939	British pastor Ebenezer Vine joins the RBMU.
1940	RBMU starts work in Irian Jaya.
1947	UK board founds RBMU North America and Canada.
1948	Peru Inland Mission becomes part of RMBU. Through this decision, RBMU was back in South America as a separate mission to EUSA.
1950	RMBU starts missions in Nepal.

1976	Colin Grant was EUSA-UK Secretary. From 1976 to 1990, Dennis Smith is EUSA-UK secretary. Geoff Larcombe is RMBU-UK Executive Secretary (1976–1991).
1977	The North American RMBU becomes independent from the British RMBU, over control and charismatic issues and matters of principles and practice. In 1995 on 3 June, the North American RBMU merges with World Team and ceases to exist as RMBU International.
1979	Donald Ford became General Secretary of EUSA from 1 April 1976 until February 1991.[3]
1982	Andes Evangelical Mission joins EUSA.
1988	On July of this year discussion began between EUSA and RBMU-UK to develop a new mission organization to and from Latin America. Key leaders were Donald Ford and Dennis Smith form EUSA, and David Craig, Geoff Larcombe and Brian Chilver form RBMU.
1985	Donald Ford is General Secretary of EUSA until 1990.
1991	On 5 June the two UK missions EUSA and RMBU (Peru) both works in Peru merge to form Latin Link, a new mission structure starting with 61 members working in five different countries. The Scottish John Chapman becomes the first International Director from February 1991 to 2002.
1992	Samuel Escobar is appointed International Consultant until 1998.
1994	The First International Assembly (January-February), in Cochabamba, Bolivia, attended by 41 delegates.
1998	The second International Assembly in Kaway-Peru.
1999	A core group is set up to help and advise John Chapman.
2002	The third International Assembly held at Caraguatatuba, Brazil. The first Latin Link International Council formed from RBMU and EUSA leaders. The formal and bigger Core Team starts working on the basis of the 'House Model' with Marcel Durst who takes over as International Team Leader.

---

3. Data provided by Donald Ford, EUSA General Secretary (2008).

2006	The fourth International Assembly in Cochabamba, Bolivia. (February). Approval to implement Marcel Durst's new ideas related to the Strategy Commitment model.
2009	The appointing of the new International Team Leader from 2010 (March).

APPENDIX 3

The Place of COMIBAM in the Protestant Historical Global Mission

Year	Event	Key leaders	Impact
1846	Formation of the Evangelical Alliance UK		Formation of the World Evangelical Alliance in 1912
1910	Edinburgh Congress	John R. Mott and Joseph H. Oldham	Postponing Latin America as a mission field
1916	Panama Congress		Developing of denominations in Latin America
1946	AMEN, first indigenous mission society founded in Peru	Juan Cueva	Roots for indigenous Latin American missiology
1966	Berlin Congress	Billy Graham	Beginning of interest in world evangelization in the evangelical movement on saving souls

1969	Foundation of the Latin American Theological Fraternity (FTL): CLADE I (Bogota 1969), CLADE II (Lima 1979), CLADE III (Quito 1992) and CLADE IV (Quito 2000).	Samuel Escobar, René Padilla, Pedro Arana, Orlando Costas	Roots of an evangelical Latin American mission theology with an emphasis on social responsibility.
1974	Lausanne Congress	Billy Graham	World evangelism saving souls and weaknesses on social responsibility
1975	Formation of the WEA-Mission Comission in Korea	Chun Chae Ok and Theodore Williams	Emphasis on Third World Emerging Missions
1983	Suggestion for a Latin American continental mission Congress	Jonathan Dos Santos to Luis Bush	Roots of COMIBAM. Seminal thinking for COMIBAM
1984	'Mision 84' Guatemala (April 84) Lausanne Mission Consultation-Stuttgart-Germany (June 84) Call for a consultation (December 84-Mexico)	Organized by SETECA. Organized by Lausanne Committee for World Evangelisation CONELA-Marcelino Ortiz and Galo Vazques	Mission fertilization of COMIBAM Decision made to organize a Continental Congress; people from WEA-MC support intentionally this project
1985	São Paulo Declaration COMIBAM Committee (June 85)	Luis Bush, Jonathan Dos Santos,	Decision made to organize COMIBAM 87 in São Paulo

1986	First Iberoamerican mission Consultation	Luis Bush	Afirmacion de Guatemala (Guatemala Affirmation-June 1986) 'More than a congress, COMIBAM will become a process.
1987	First COMIBAM São Paulo-Brazil	Luis Bush, Rudy Giron, Jonathan Dos Santos, Edison Queiros, Federico Bertuzzi	3,000 Latin American leaders declare that Latin America is no longer a missionary field but a sending field. 300 new mission organizations and 4,000 formal missionaries.
1997	Second COMIBAM Acapulco, Mexico, 27–31 October. Purpose: Evaluation of the Iberoamerican missionary movement, projection, training, and inspiration for missions	Rudy Giron, Bertil Ekstrom, David Ruiz,, Federico Bertuzzi	400 mission organizations and 9,265 Iberoamerican formal missionaries
2006	Third COMIBAM Congress, Granada, Spain, 13–17 November.	David Ruiz, Carlos Scott, Jesus Londoño	Production of a new atlas for mission. Gather 288 missionaries from the mission field in Granada. Mission Statistics conducted by the Brazilian Levi Decarvalho. To hold the congress in Europe. Minor presence of American influence and participation as main speakers. A contribution of a theology of suffering.

APPENDIX 4

Analysis of the Short Term Mission Trips to Peru

Before - During - After
Senders-Goers-Receivers

Weaknesses	Evaluation	Recommendations
Insufficient planning before the trip by the sending church.	To have a better idea of what activities previous teams have done.	Promotion should start 6 months before the STM.
Lack of adequate feedback to the sending church after the STM.	Five minutes of feedback is not good enough for reports of the goers after the STM	Encouragement to do more feedback to the church after the STM
Few translators on the team	Too much work for one translator	Sending two translators with the STM
Lack of focus on English teaching and of involvement in social action	STM lead people to want to understand the global economic order.	To have wise and loving concern for the receiving church.
Lack of experience in street evangelism by the participants.	Strong sense of identity as ambassador of the sending STM church	To receive training of how to enter in a different culture to evangelize.
Receivers expect more than the team can do	Clarify between sender and receiver the target of evangelism, social work and social presence.	Prepare a manual of STM from the local church perspective.

Strengths		
Agreement to get support for raising funds by writing to the church family	Senders provide a grant to every STM goers.	Clarify before the STM that financial help for potential candidates is available.
Learning some Spanish words provided before the trip.	More awareness of learning key words by the STM.	Facilitate a list of key words and music in Spanish.
Encouragement to join the trip before the STM	Promotion and challenge the church needs more advertisement targeting promotion among young peoples.	Prepare suitable information for each STM to each different country.
Experience of some travellers to Latin America	To find for each trip people interested in Latin America culture and the church.	To be part of Global Connections' Latin American Forum and similar institutions.
Blessed by fellowship with team and with the receiving church	Need a strategy to maintain mission relationship initiated between the goers and the receivers.	To promote an annual celebration of the goers and to send an annual gift through a Christmas' appeal.
STM is a great way to see another country and to meet Christians in a different culture	Gives a wider sense of the worldwide church	Encourage people to get involved in future mission trips.

Good planning by the receiving church of a range of activities. opportunities to present the gospel in hospitals, children's homes, public squares, parks, churches, schools, colleges, restaurants, houses, universities and language schools.	To coordinate participation of both evangelism and social work.	To inform needs by the receiving church before starting the promotion of the STM.
Good hospitality by the receiving church	Good attitude of the goers in bringing gifts for the receivers	Established a pattern of small gifts for the goers

APPENDIX 5

Ten Influential Models of Mission in Latin America

Diachronic mission		**Synchronic mission**
1790	Traditional mission models (diachronic contextual impact of monopolar models)	
1800	Bible distribution (James Thompson)	
1850	Mission to distant lands (traditional mission model influence-Allen Francis Gardiner)	
	Immigrant mission (mostly British Anglicans and Presbyterians)	
1900	Mainline Protestant churches (Anglicans, Methodist, Presbyterians and Baptists).	
1916	Faith missions (Western and indigenous models, RBMU, CAM, AMEN, etc).	
1950	Pentecostal movement (Assemblies of God)	
1980	Networking mission models (seminal models)	
1990	Emerging models (the Majority World seminal models)	
2000	Global mission (multidirectional)	
2010	Reciprocal multipolar contextual engagement (spiral mission theology)	
Historical mission models		**Current mission models**

Positive and negative mission tensions

**New mission cross-pollination and cross-fertilization
under
reciprocal contextual collaboration mission theology**

**Building two-way bridges of appropriate models for the 21st century mission
through**
reciprocal multipolar contextual engagement

Langham Literature and its imprints are a ministry of Langham Partnership.

Langham Partnership is a global fellowship working in pursuit of the vision God entrusted to its founder John Stott –

> *to facilitate the growth of the church in maturity and Christ-likeness through raising the standards of biblical preaching and teaching.*

Our vision is to see churches in the majority world equipped for mission and growing to maturity in Christ through the ministry of pastors and leaders who believe, teach and live by the Word of God.

Our mission is to strengthen the ministry of the Word of God through:
- nurturing national movements for biblical preaching
- fostering the creation and distribution of evangelical literature
- enhancing evangelical theological education

especially in countries where churches are under-resourced.

Our ministry

Langham Preaching partners with national leaders to nurture indigenous biblical preaching movements for pastors and lay preachers all around the world. With the support of a team of trainers from many countries, a multi-level programme of seminars provides practical training, and is followed by a programme for training local facilitators. Local preachers' groups and national and regional networks ensure continuity and ongoing development, seeking to build vigorous movements committed to Bible exposition.

Langham Literature provides majority world pastors, scholars and seminary libraries with evangelical books and electronic resources through grants, discounts and distribution. The programme also fosters the creation of indigenous evangelical books for pastors in many languages, through training workshops for writers and editors, sponsored writing, translation, strengthening local evangelical publishing houses, and investment in major regional literature projects, such as one volume Bible commentaries like *The Africa Bible Commentary*.

Langham Scholars provides financial support for evangelical doctoral students from the majority world so that, when they return home, they may train pastors and other Christian leaders with sound, biblical and theological teaching. This programme equips those who equip others. Langham Scholars also works in partnership with majority world seminaries in strengthening evangelical theological education. A growing number of Langham Scholars study in high quality doctoral programmes in the majority world itself. As well as teaching the next generation of pastors, graduated Langham Scholars exercise significant influence through their writing and leadership.

To learn more about Langham Partnership and the work we do visit **langham.org**

www.ingramcontent.com/pod-product-compliance
Lightning Source LLC
Chambersburg PA
CBHW050300010526
44108CB00040B/1908